THE ADA IN PRACTICE

Revised Edition of
"The New ADA: Compliance and Costs"

Deborah S. Kearney, PhD

RSMeans.

THE ADA IN PRACTICE

Revised Edition of
"The New ADA: Compliance and Costs"

Now Includes:

- *ADA Enforcement — with Legal Precedents from Settled Cases*

- *Illustrated Compliance Product Selection Guide*

- *25 Low-Cost Compliance Solutions*

- *OSHA, Workers' Compensation and the ADA*

Deborah S. Kearney, PhD

RS Means.

Copyright 1995

R.S. Means Company, Inc.

Construction Publishers & Consultants

100 Construction Plaza

P.O. Box 800

Kingston, MA 02364-0800

(781) 585-7880

*A **Construction Market Data Group** Company*

The editors for this book were Mary Greene and Phil Waier. The production manager was Helen Marcella; the production coordinator was Marion Schofield. Composition was supervised by Karen O'Brien. The book and jacket were designed by Norman R. Forgit.

Printed in the United States of America

10 9 8 7 6 5 4 3

Library of Congress Cataloging in Publication Data

ISBN 0-87629-384-4

"The historic pattern of excluding persons with disabilities from the mainstream of society served to create and perpetuate certain myths or misconceptions about people with disabilities. The residue of such misperceptions remains with us today. Yet in the later stages of the twentieth century, these notions really have no place..."

Charles D. Goldman, Esq.
Author of the 1991 *Disability Rights Guide*
Media Publishing; Lincoln, Nebraska

TABLE OF CONTENTS

PREFACE

The first edition of this book, titled *The New ADA: Compliance and Costs*, was published in 1992, to coincide with the enactment of the ADA. Both the original edition and the second edition are devoted to understanding and implementing Titles I-IV of the Act. It remains essential that design modifications not only meet the requirements of the law, but also enhance the comfort and productivity of people with disabilities.

It was difficult to predict in 1992 how quickly and to what extent various entities would comply with the law, how many and what kinds of complaints would be addressed to the enforcing authorities, and what kinds of settlements (and at what cost) would be reached in court. After the more than four years since the enactment of ADA, facility managers, business owners and state and local governments have begun to address the ADA's requirements. Many are still in the planning stages, some are waiting to see how reasonable accommodation is being reached in actual practice. How are conflicts, ambiguities and budget restrictions being resolved? Have there been changes in any of the ADA's requirements as a result of what has been learned in implementing them? Are there creative, acceptable alternatives in some cases to the more obvious and more costly solutions? This revised second edition answers these questions and provides this information. It shows how the Americans with Disabilities Act is being interpreted, complied with and enforced in actual practice. The book has been updated to reflect the latest rulings from the governing authorities, the number and kinds of complaints that are being filed, and the outcomes. Many cases are cited in both Chapter 3, an update on ADA Enforcement, and in Part IV, "The ADA Modification Factors."

Chapter 4 is new information on managing the essential job functions of employees across ADA, OSHA, and Workers' Compensation requirements. This chapter points out some of the ways in which one can reduce the legal complexities of these sometimes overlapping requirements, while increasing productivity, efficiency and quality in an organization.

Also new to this edition is the "ADA Compliance Product Selection Guide," an illustrated compendium of products for ADA compliance and for the enhancement of both lifestyle and productivity for disabled people. These are products from leading manufacturers for a wide variety of applications that solve compliance problems, often in creative, cost-effective ways. This section begins with professional guidance for qualifying both a compliance product and a sales representative.

Chapter 31, "25 Low-Cost Compliance Solutions," is particularly significant among the new features of this edition. It is a collection of cost-effective, creative solutions to compliance requirements based on the author's extensive experience as a designer of barrier-free accommodations.

The latest resolutions on detectable warnings and automated teller machines have been added at the end of Appendix A. The costs have been consolidated in Appendix M and have also been updated.

INTRODUCTION

After two decades of effort by disability rights activists to increase public awareness and develop a congressional response, the Americans with Disabilities Act was passed. This legislation affirms the goals of equal opportunity and independence for Americans with physical and mental disabilities by banning discrimination in employment. One of the most beneficial effects of the Title I of the ADA is the expected increase in employment of people with disabling conditions. This will result in their enjoying the right to work at jobs suited to their skills and training. They will enjoy a higher standard of living and full integration into society as consumers, citizens, and patrons. Being an employee with the benefits of employment also means access to health insurance benefits, and more preventive health care. Such preventive health care can reduce the likelihood of secondary conditions of disability, such as the chronic depression that commonly results from discrimination. Employment helps people to develop lifestyles and workstyles that maintain their well being.

100 million Americans—four of every ten people—have physical or mental impairments that interfere with their daily life activities (National Center for Health Statistics, 1989). The functional limitations of these potential and actual employees makes disability one of the largest issues facing employers today.

As modern medicine has progressed in prolonging life, the survival for people of working age (18 to 64 years) after traumatic injury or disease has increased by 22%. In addition, many exciting advances have occurred that reduce the severity of functional limitations. One of the most significant is the administration of the steroid methylprednisone within eight hours of the occurrence of a spinal cord injury. Where once a person would have been fully paralyzed, he or she might now retain sufficient function to walk with the aid of crutches and braces. These advances are even more significant when they enable a person to avoid a lowered quality of life resulting from severely limited work opportunities.

The bar graph, on the following page, illustrates disabilities in connection with lifetime costs of injury by cause. The important fact to understand about this table is that 60% of the cost is attributed to reduced or lost productivity—the market value of lost work due to temporary or permanent disability. It is estimated that 44 billion dollars are lost each year in productivity for people injured in the age group 18-44 who do not return to work.

How do medical advances and disability affect employers? At this time, medical advances are directly related to increasing life expectancy. During the current 75-year life expectancy, a newborn can be expected to experience an average of 13 years with a functional limitation. The impact of this on employers is to expect to "reasonably accommodate for physical limitations" for all employees at some time in their work history.

Medical advances are not only increasing life span, but also our quality of life. In the 1990s disabilities are being identified and reduced as science advances in the following areas:

1. ***An increase in knowledge of risk factors***—biological, environmental and social, as well as physical and lifestyle characteristics that are causally associated with health-related conditions. For example, our understanding of the risk associated with heart disease and diet has lowered the incidence of the disease. As the practice of prenatal care has increased, we have decreased mental retardation due to fetal alcohol syndrome.

2. ***An increase in our understanding of quality of life issues,*** or one's sense of personal independence and dignity, as clear determinants of how well people respond to the challenges of disability. For example, a person with cancer who has a support system lives an average of 18 months longer than those who do not. A person with chronic depression can maintain employment successfully with the help of prescription medications, thereby reducing the chance of worsening depression due to unemployment, and the potential risks of substance abuse and even fatality.

   NOTE: Accommodation for people with psychological difficulties is an average of 4.3 years during a work life that spans 18-65 years. Reasonable psychological accommodation is an issue in most employment situations.

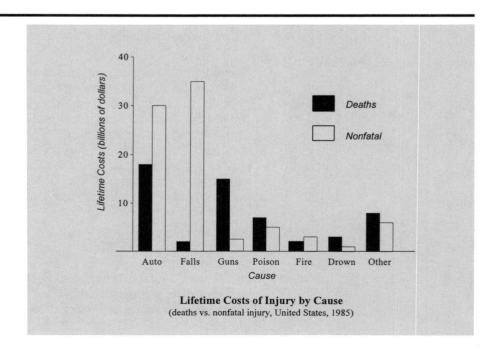

Lifetime Costs of Injury by Cause
(deaths vs. nonfatal injury, United States, 1985)

3. ***An increased understanding of the disabling process*** is allowing more interventions to prevent worsening of primary and secondary conditions. For example, if a person with a stroke can, through the use of assistive devices, regain competencies, then the primary condition of muscle atrophy and the secondary condition of depression may be avoided.

4. ***An increased understanding of injury-related disabilities*** is decreasing with the use of safety belts in motor vehicles, the use of designated drivers in groups of people using alcohol, and emergency medical teams' ability to save not only lives, but more functional capacities.

5. ***A broadening knowledge of the aging process*** is allowing the use of more interventions to increase stamina and reduce disease. For example, it is known that proper exercise and diet can reduce decline in bone densities, thereby reducing the likelihood of injury during falls.

Employment of people with functional limitations resulting from disability, aging, disease or injury is more likely to succeed because of medical advances and the Americans with Disabilities Act. The significance of the Americans with Disabilities Act, for both individuals and employers, cannot be overstated. Whether measured in terms of its societal or economic consequences, the positive impacts of the Act are clear. What is more important is that for the first time, it is now an American policy to address the prevention of disability and the alleviation of its consequence through an approach that contributes to the gross national product, instead of draining it.

Part One

OVERVIEW OF THE AMERICANS WITH DISABILITIES ACT

Part One

INTRODUCTION

Part I is an introduction to the Americans with Disabilities Act intended to put the Act into context with other codes, as well as the agencies that regulate and enforce it. Key terms and provisions are highlighted, and Titles I – IV are outlined. This section, which also addresses the spirit and intent behind the Act, establishes a framework for the reader — a starting point for identifying, planning and budgeting for modifications.

New in this edition are Chapters 3 and 4 in Part I. Chapter 3, "Enforcing the ADA," is a review of the number and kinds of cases that have been brought to the Department of Justice and the Equal Employment Opportunity Commission since the ADA went into effect. Several examples of settled cases are cited to illustrate the problems that are most often being raised, and the solutions that have been deemed legally acceptable.

Chapter 4 addresses the issue of defining job functions, and using organized job descriptions to efficiently manage the requirements of the ADA, OSHA, and Workers' Compensation.

Chapter One

THE ADA
DEFINED

The Americans with Disabilities Act (ADA) gives civil rights protection from discrimination to individuals with disabilities, just as the Civil Rights Act of 1964 protects individuals on the basis of race, sex, national origin, and religion. It guarantees equal opportunity for individuals with disabilities in employment, public accommodations, transportation, state and local government services, and telecommunications.

No longer can lack of access to a building be the point of denial for employment. Disabled people who are qualified are now guaranteed the opportunity to be able to apply for jobs. No longer can public buildings (hotels, restaurants, shops, lawyers' offices, theaters, supermarkets or museums) be inaccessible to disabled customers. This affects an estimated 3.8 million businesses. Public transportation must also be available on a regular basis to serve the needs of the disabled.

All state and local government services must be accessible, and communication services available to people with disabilities. For example, TDD's (telecommunication devices for deaf persons) or similar devices must be available to the deaf.

Who is *disabled?* According to the Equal Employment Opportunity Commission (EEOC), a disabled person is one who has a physical or mental condition that substantially impairs a major life activity such as walking, breathing, seeing, or the ability to work, or one who has a history of impairment such as a chronic condition that has lasted more than six months, or is regarded by others as having such an impairment. (See Figure 1.1.)

Civil Rights Statutes

The Americans with Disabilities Act provides protection for people with disabilities, parallel to laws established by the federal government to protect women and minorities from discrimination. The ADA is an amalgam of two civil rights statutes: the Civil Rights Act of 1964 and Title V of the Rehabilitation Act of 1973.

Public Access

Public access is defined in a very expansive manner to include all public and private entities that affect commerce. Access to, and the ability to, safely maneuver within an environment to conduct one's objective is essential. The ADA also requires that public accommodation include *reasonable modifications* to policies, procedures, and practices based on the obstacles to the physically-challenged person inherent in the site. The expectation of retrofitting for reasonable accommodation is what is "readily achievable," that is, what can be accomplished without much difficulty or expense (such as ramping steps or adding grab bars).

Further, the bill requires the provision of auxiliary aids, those devices necessary to enable persons who have visual, hearing, or sensory impairments to have access to goods, services, privileges, or facilities. The auxiliary aid requirement is flexible, allowing public accommodation to take the form of one of several alternatives, as long as the result is an effective solution without "undue burden," as determined on a case-by-case basis.

Employment

The ADA requires employers to make *reasonable accommodations* to the known physical or mental limitations of a qualified applicant or employee, unless such accommodations would cause undue hardship to the employer. (See the Glossary at the back of the book for a definition of "undue burden"

DISABILITY

The term disability means with respect to an individual: (A) a physical or mental impairment that substantially limits one or more major life activities; (B) a record of such an impairment; (C) being regarded as having such an impairment.

Physical or Mental Impairment		Major Life Activities	Record of Impairment	Regard as Impaired
Physiological disorder, contagious disease, cosmetic disfigurement or anatomical loss in one or more system:	Mental or psychological disorder including:	Major life activities include:	The individual has:	The individual has:
• Neurological • Musculoskeletal • Respiratory • Cardiovascular • Reproductive • Digestive • Genito-urinary • Hemic • Lymphatic • Skin • Endocrine	• Mental retardation • Organic brain syndrome • Emotional or mental illness • Specific learning disabilities	• Self-care • Manual tasks • Walking • Seeing • Hearing • Speaking • Breathing • Learning • Working	• A history of impairment or • A record of having been misclassified as having an impairment	• An impairment not limiting a major life activity, but treated as disabled by the covered entity. or • No impairment, but treated as disabled by the covered entity
• Substance abuse*				

* Does not include a current , illegal abuser

Reprinted with permission from the ADA Compliance Guide, Thompson Publishing

Figure 1.1

and other terms of ADA law.) Reasonable accommodation includes a wide variety of actions, including: making work sites accessible, modifying existing equipment, providing new devices, modifying work schedules, restructuring jobs, reassigning an employee to a vacant position, and providing readers or interpreters.

Enforcement and Remedies

With respect to public accommodation, the bill limits relief available in private suits to injunctive relief, attorneys' fees, and court costs. Individual plaintiffs may file meritorious suits.

With respect to employment, the ADA provides remedies under Title VII of the Civil Rights Act of 1964, including administrative enforcement by the EEOC. After those remedies are exhausted, there is the right to sue in federal court for injunctive relief and monetary relief in the form of back pay. There are 43 million Americans with disabilities who are potential candidates for employment opportunities and see barrier-free design as a necessary link between employers and themselves. Their hope is that cost effective *barrier-free design and technology* will create their opportunity. The need for barrier-free design and technology that is both cost effective and easily available to the disabled is well documented. If the Americans with Disabilities Act is to be successful and made useful to individuals, barrier-free design and technology must be:

- consumer responsive so that hidden capabilities of talented individuals can be used and new skills developed,
- modified in such a way as to allow a physically challenged person to compete on an equal basis with any person when seeking compensated employment,
- introduced so as to allow person(s) involved to have control over their lives and be able to more fully interact with the non-disabled,
- delivered by personnel who have both the expertise and sensibility to use the technology to provide training and services in a practical and applied manner, and
- supported by reimbursement systems and private sector incentives.

The problem is fitting jobs to people, and providing people with the right technologies is the focus of the Americans with Disabilities Act Audit, presented in Parts III and IV of this book.

Chapter Two

INTRODUCTION TO TITLES I-IV

Title I: Employment

The regulatory body for Title I of the Americans with Disabilities Act is the Equal Employment Opportunity Commission. The Act requires employers to ensure equal opportunity for disabled applicants applying for jobs, and for current employees seeking transfers and promotions. Discrimination is prohibited in all aspects of employment practices and policies, including social activities.

The most important definitions to consider in Title I are: **Essential Job Functions**, defined by EEOC as the fundamental duties of the employment position desired or held by the individual with a disability. Three issues may be considered:

1. whether a current job exists to perform a function (e.g., a welder),
2. how many other employees perform that function (e.g., data entry), and
3. what degree of skill and expertise is required (experience, education, and interpersonal relations).

Reasonable Accommodations, defined by EEOC as any change in the work environment or in the way things are customarily done that enables an individual with a disability to enjoy employment opportunities. Examples are the structure of time on the job and the provision of supports in the form of personnel or equipment.

Direct Threat To Self Or Other, considered by the EEOC to apply to those employees who pose a substantial risk to themselves and others which cannot be eliminated or reduced. Employers are expected to weigh the duration of the risk, the nature and severity of the potential harm, and the likelihood and imminence of harm occurring. Threats considered by the EEOC are those which currently exist as occupational hazards and that would be exacerbated by a disability.

Undue Burden is an action or remedy that would cause significant difficulty or expense. Financial hardship depends on the financial resources of a company. EEOC rejected a percent of salary calculation which attempted to say that an investment of more than 10% of a disabled person's salary would be an undue hardship on the employer. EEOC offers no quantitative rules at this time.

The significance of Title I from a design perspective is that buildings and technology must now compensate for disabling conditions. What is difficult is that "reasonable physical and psychological accommodations" are required, but not defined. Additionally, the terms "readily achievable" and "not creating undue burden or hardship on employers" are not quantitatively defined by the ADA.

The case-by-case rule makes it difficult to meet the codes and needs of people with disabilities. For example, the Department of Justice has now ruled that alterations to make passages accessible to primary function areas (bathrooms, telephones, and water fountains) are to be made as long as the cost for alterations does not exceed 20% of the overall price of a planned renovation.

Provisions must be made for access to apply for employment. Important to the application process is the fact that work areas must allow people to be able to demonstrate their skills. For example, if a person has low vision, and a lack of appropriate signage prevents them from guiding themselves to the personnel office, then the building is not in compliance. If, when the person is offered the job, the work station cannot support the weight of additional equipment required to enable performance of job functions, then "reasonable accommodation" should be made. Reasonable accommodation, in this case, would be a work station that can support the weight of the required equipment.

The following paragraphs summarize the provisions of Title I.

- Employers with 15 or more employees may not discriminate against qualified individuals with disabilities. For the first two years after July 26, 1992, the date when the employment provisions of the ADA go into effect, only employers with 25 or more employees are required to comply (and are subject to fines for failure to comply). Employers with 15 to 24 employees must comply after July 26, 1994. Employers with 0 to 14 employees are not covered entities.
- Employers must reasonably accommodate the disabilities of qualified applicants or employees, unless an undue hardship would result.
- Employers may reject applicants or fire employees who pose a direct threat to the health or safety of other individuals in the workplace.
- Applicants and employees are not protected from personnel actions based on their current illegal use of drugs. Drug testing is not affected.
- Employers may not discriminate against a qualified applicant or employee because of the known disability of an individual with whom the applicant or employee is known to have a relationship or association.
- Religious organizations may give preference in employment to their own members and may require applicants and employees to conform to their religious tenets.
- Complaints may be filed with the Equal Employment Opportunity Commission. Available remedies include back pay and court orders to stop discrimination.

Contacts at EEOC for interpretation of regulations:

To obtain ADA documents:
800-514-0301 (Voice)
800-514-0383 (TDD)

For answers to ADA questions:
800-669-4000 (Voice)
800-669-6820 (TDD)

President's Committee on Employment of People with Disabilities provides information on all titles of the ADA and funds the *Job Accommodation Network (JAN)*, which provides information on the ADA and reasonable accommodation in the workplace.

ADA information:
202-276-6200 (Voice)
202-376-6205 (TDD)

Job Accommodation Network:
800-526-7234 (Voice & TDD)
800-232-9675 (Voice & TDD)

Title II: Public Services and Transportation

Public services accommodations may not discriminate on the basis of disabilities with regard to access to public services and transportation. The regulatory body for Title II is the Department of Transportation. The implementation of Title II requires that all state and local governments, agencies, and departments, regardless of size, refrain from discriminating based on disability. The Act strengthens section 504 of the Rehabilitation Act of 1973 to include all state and local governments, regardless of whether they receive federal funds. Compliance guidelines are the same as Title I based on size of employment. Figure 2.1 lists key information on effective dates, size of agency or department, and appropriate rules to follow.

Title II requires bus and rail transportation to be accessible to disabled persons. Air transportation is not covered by ADA. The law requires new public buses and new train cars in commuter, subway, intercity (Amtrak), and light rail systems to be accessible to disabled riders. All new stations and facilities, and key subway and light rail stations, must be made accessible. Where fixed-route bus service is offered, a public transit agency must also offer paratransit services.

EMPLOYMENT AND STATE/LOCAL GOVERNMENTS		
Size	**Compliance dates**	**Which rules to follow?**
25 or more employees	Jan. 26, 1992	ADA Title I (EEOC)
15-24 employees	Jan. 26, 1994	Section 504 until Jan. 26, 1994 (then ADA title I)
Fewer than 15 employees	Not a covered entity	Section 504

Figure 2.1

From a design perspective, the significance of Title II on public service accommodations is that the physical access to services and transportation must be guaranteed, and procedures and policies must allow disabled people to fully participate in services offered. For example, if a Registry of Motor Vehicles does not have the eye screening test set up to accommodate people with disabling conditions (e.g., at wheelchair height), then they are in violation of Title II of the Americans with Disabilities Act. If the registry's licensing officers cannot test a driver using adaptive hand controls in a handicap-equipped van, then they have not complied with the training necessary for employees to fulfill their job duties relative to the disabled.

In essence, Title II requires that government agencies and departments evaluate equipment and redesign it if necessary, locate services in accessible buildings, and provide the necessary aids for people to find and use services. Provisions for access to use the services in state and local buildings and the right to receive services in a dignified manner are expected under the Americans with Disabilities Act. All required structural changes must be completed by January 26, 1995.

The following items are summarized Title II provisions.

Public Bus Systems

- New buses ordered on or after August 26, 1990 must be accessible to individuals with disabilities.
- Transit authorities must provide comparable paratransit or other special transportation services to individuals with disabilities who cannot use fixed route bus services, unless an undue burden would result.
- New bus stations must be accessible. Alterations to existing stations must be accessible. When alterations to primary function areas are made, an accessible path of travel to the altered area (and the bathrooms, telephones, and drinking fountains serving that area) must be provided to the extent that the added accessibility costs are not disproportionate to the overall cost of the alterations.
- Individuals may file complaints with the Department of Transportation or bring private lawsuits.

Public Rail Systems

- New rail vehicles ordered on or after August 26, 1990, must be accessible.
- Existing rail systems must have one accessible car per train by July 26, 1995.
- New rail stations must be accessible. As with new bus stations, alterations to existing rail stations must be made in an accessible manner.
- Existing "key stations" in rapid rail, commuter rail, and light rail systems must be made accessible by July 26, 1993, unless an extension up to 20 years is granted (30 years, in some cases, for rapid and light rail).
- Existing intercity rail stations (Amtrak) must be made accessible by July 26, 2010.
- Individuals may file complaints with the Department of Transportation or bring private lawsuits.

Privately Operated Bus and Van Companies

- New over-the-road buses ordered on or after July 26, 1996 (July 26, 1997, for small companies) must be accessible. After completion of a study, the President may extend the deadline by one year, if appropriate.
- Other new vehicles, such as vans, must be accessible, unless the transportation company provides service to individuals with disabilities that is equivalent to that operated for the general public.

Additional Information

- Other public transportation operations, including station facilities, must meet the requirements for public accommodations.
- Air Transportation. Air carriers are not covered under the ADA. They are covered by the Air Carrier Access Act (49 U.S.C. 1374 (c)).
- State or local governments may not discriminate against qualified individuals with disabilities. All government facilities, services, and communications must be accessible consistent with the requirements of section 504 of the Rehabilitation Act of 1973.

Contacts at the Department of Justice for Interpretation of Public Services Regulations:

Department of Justice (public services) July 26, 1991, Federal Register, pages 35694-35723.

Contacts for Transportation Regulations:

Architectural and Transportation Barriers Compliance Board (ADA Accessibility Guidelines) July 26, 1991, Federal Register, Pages 35408-35543.

The U.S. Department of Transportation offers technical assistance concerning the public transportation provisions of Title II and Title III of the ADA.

ADA documents and general questions:
202-366-1656 (Voice)
202-366-4567 (TDD)

ADA legal questions:
202-366-1936 (Voice)
202-366-0748 (TDD)

Complaints and enforcement:
202-366-2285 (Voice)
202-366-0153 (TDD)

Electronic bulletin board:
202-366-3764

National Easter Seal Society "Project Action":
202-347-3066 (Voice)
202-347-7385 (TDD)

"Rural Transportation Assistance Program":
800-527-8279 (Voice & TDD)

The U.S. Department of Transportation provides technical assistance concerning the accessibility standards that apply to **air transportation** under the Air Carrier Act (ACAA).

ACAA technical assistance:
202-366-4859 (Voice)
TDD: use relay service

ACAA complaints and enforcement:
202-267-5794 (Voice)
202-267-9730 (TDD)

Title III: Public Accommodations

Title III is regulated by the Department of Justice. The regulations are intended to prevent discrimination against disabled people in places of public accommodation. The ADA prohibits privately owned and operated businesses from denying goods, programs, and services to people who are disabled. Patrons must be accommodated with physical accessibility, auxiliary aids, and policies and procedures that promote the use of places like restaurants, hotels, museums, theaters, libraries, doctors' offices (to include those in private homes), and professional buildings. The regulations apply to entities under ownership and lease agreements. The terms of the lease determine who is responsible for complying.

The significance of Title III, from a design perspective, is that the act provides for the full and equal opportunity for disabled individuals to participate in programs, services, and the acquisition of goods in any public business. Integration is particularly key here. Access should be through the same door as all patrons; availability of goods should be from the same displays; and services should be provided from the same equipment (such as an ATM machine at the bank).

The key design question for each facility is what is *readily achievable*, does not cause *undue burden*, and is *safe*? At a minimum, the Department of Justice expects businesses to remove architectural and communication barriers. Easily accomplished and carried out without much difficulty are actions that do not result in a significant loss of selling or service space or excessive physical changes.

The following are examples of what can be considered readily achievable, arranged according to key factors (defined in detail in Part IV of this book).

Accessibility:	Installing curb cuts, ramps
Adaptability:	Making door knob adaptions
Air Quality:	Removing CO_2
Comfort:	Arranging displays for visual scan
Communication:	TDD's (Telecommunication devices for the deaf)
Density:	Rearranging equipment to accommodate a wheelchair
Division of Space:	Rearranging tables, chairs, vending machines
Equipment:	Using display racks that are accessible by turning
Finishes:	Adding color coding to floors for passage
Image:	Installing full-length mirrors in the bathroom
Lighting:	Adding task lights
Maintenance:	Creating maintenance strategies that allow independence
Noise:	Lowering the decibel levels in offices (e.g., with insulation, barriers)
Passages:	Widening doors
Safety:	Installing flashing alarm systems
Signage:	Installing braille signs in the elevators
Storage:	Adding accessible storage
Temperature:	Zoning rooms appropriately
Windows:	Adding lever handles for opening and closing

The following paragraphs summarize the Title III provisions.

- Public accommodations such as restaurants, hotels, theaters, doctors' offices, pharmacies, retail stores, museums, libraries, parks, private schools, and day care centers, may not discriminate on the basis of disability, effective January 26, 1992. Private clubs and religious organizations are exempt.
- Reasonable changes in policies, practices, and procedures must be made to avoid discrimination.
- Auxiliary aids and services must be provided to individuals with vision or hearing impairments or other disabilities so that they can have an equal opportunity to participate or benefit, unless an undue burden would result.
- Physical barriers in existing facilities must be removed if removal is *readily achievable* (i.e., easily accomplishable and able to be carried out without much difficulty or expense). If not, alternative methods of providing the services must be offered, if those methods are readily achievable.
- All new construction in public accommodations, as well as in "commercial facilities" such as office buildings, must be accessible. Elevators are generally not required in buildings under three stories with fewer than 3,000 square feet per floor, unless the building is a shopping center, mall, or a professional office of a health care provider.
- Alterations must be accessible. When alterations to primary function areas are made, an accessible path of travel to the altered area (and the bathrooms, telephones, and drinking fountains serving that area) must be provided to the extent that the added accessibility costs are not disproportionate to the overall cost of the alterations. Elevators are required as described above.
- Entities such as hotels that also offer transportation generally must provide equivalent transportation service to individuals with disabilities. New fixed-route vehicles ordered on or after August 26, 1992, and capable of carrying more than 16 passengers, must be accessible.
- Public accommodations may not discriminate against an individual or entity because of the known disability of an individual with whom the individual or entity is known to have a relationship or association.
- Individuals may bring private lawsuits to obtain court orders to stop discrimination, but cash damages cannot be awarded.
- Individuals can also file complaints with the Attorney General, who may file lawsuits to stop discrimination and obtain cash damages and penalties.
- Individuals may file complaints with the Attorney General or bring private lawsuits under the public accommodations procedures.

Contacts for information regarding regulations:
Department of Justice, Title III (Public Accommodations) July 26, 1991, Federal Register, pages 35544-35691.

The Department of Justice offers technical assistance to the public concerning Title II and Title III of the ADA.

For ADA documents and questions:
800-514-0301 (Voice)
800-514-0383 (TDD)

Within Washington D.C.:
202-514-0301 (Voice)
202-514-0383 (TDD)

Electronic bulletin board:
202-514-6193

The U.S. Architectural and Transportation Barriers Compliance Board or Access Board offers technical assistance on the ADA Accessibility Guidelines.

For ADA documents and questions:
800-872-2253 (Voice)
800-993-2822 (TDD)

Within Washington D.C.:
202-272-5434 (Voice)
202-272-5449 (TDD)

Electronic bulletin board:
202-272-5448

The National Institute on Disability and Rehabilitation Research has funded centers throughout the country to provide technical assistance concerning Title I, Title II and Title III of the ADA.

ADA technical assistance nationwide:
800-949-4232 (Voice & TDD)

Title IV: Telecommunications

Title IV of the ADA is aimed at the federally regulated telecommunications, such as telephone companies and federally funded public service television. The ADA requires telephone companies to provide continuous voice transmission, relay services that allow hearing- and speech-impaired people to communicate over the phone through TDD's (telecommunications devices for the deaf). In addition, close-captioned messages for hearing-impaired viewers must be available for public service messages.

The significance of Title IV, from a design perspective, is anticipating the needs of the disabled in situations where telecommunications or television may be a part of a person's work or leisure life. If employment involves essential job functions that include television, then provisions for access must be made. If theaters are showing films, closed-captioned options should be considered.

The following items summarize Title IV provisions.

- Companies offering telephone service to the general public must offer telephone relay services to individuals who use telecommunications devices for the deaf (TDD's) or similar devices.
- Individuals may file complaints with the Federal Communications Commission.

Contacts for information on regulations:
FCC, Title IV, TELECOMMUNICATIONS: August 1, 1991, Federal Register, pages 36729-36733.

The Federal Communications Commission provides technical assistance concerning the accessibility standards that apply to **telephones** under the Hearing Aid Compatibility Act.

Hearing Aid Compatibility Act:
202-634-1808 (Voice)
202-632-0484 (TDD)

The Federal Communications Commission also offers technical assistance concerning Title IV of the ADA.

ADA documents and general questions:
202-418-0190 (Voice)
202-418-2555 (TDD)

ADA legal questions:
202-634-1808 (Voice)
202-632-0484 (TDD)

Complaints and enforcement:
202-632-7553 (Voice)
202-632-0485 (TDD)

Other ADA Contacts

The Disability Rights Education and Defense Fund provides technical assistance on all titles of the ADA.

ADA technical assistance:
800-466-4232 (Voice & TDD)

The Foundation on Employment and Disability provides assistance in Spanish, Korean, Cambodian, Vietnamese, Mandarin and Cantonese Chinese, Tagalog, Hindi, Arabic, Armenian, Russian, and Dine.

ADA specialized technical assistance:
800-232-4955 (Voice)
800-232-4957 (TDD)

The U.S. Department of Housing and Urban Development provides technical assistance concerning the accessibility standards that apply to **residential facilities** under the Fair Housing Act Amendments.

Fair Housing Act Amendments:
800-795-7915 (Voice)
800-927-9275 (TDD)

The U.S. Department of Labor, Office of Federal Contract Compliance Programs provides technical assistance concerning the accessibility standards that apply to **federal contractors.**

Section 503 of the Rehabilitation Act:
202-219-9428 (Voice)
800-326-2577 (TDD)

Chapter Three

ENFORCING THE ADA

It was difficult to predict, three years ago when the ADA first became effective, how quickly and to what extent organizations would respond to its requirements, and how the government offices of enforcement would respond to and resolve complaints. This chapter reviews the history of ADA enforcement, with illustrations of cases that have been settled under Titles I-III through April 4, 1994. At the end of the chapter are status report updates from the Department of Justice covering April through December of 1994.

The Americans with Disabilities Act was signed into law July, 1990, and went into effect July 26, 1992. ADA is a landmark, comprehensive civil rights law that protects disabled people with the same rights and access as other Americans. The Department of Justice enforces the ADA's requirements in three areas, defined in Titles I, II, and III.

Title I: Employment Practices

Complaints about violations of Title I (employment) by units of state and local government or by private employers are filed with:

Equal Employment Opportunity Commission (EEOC)
Program Development and Technical Assistance Division
Office of Program Operations
1801 "L" Street, N.W.
Washington, D.C. 20507

As of March, 1995, the Department has had over 39,000 complaints and has hundreds of investigations under way under Title I against public employers. (See Figure 3.1.) In New England 300 cases are currently under investigation.

Title II: Public Services and Transportation

Complaints about violations of Title II by units of state and local government are filed with:

U.S. Department of Justice
Civil Rights Division
Coordination and Review Section
Post Office Box 66118
Washington, D.C. 20035-6118

The Department is currently investigating nearly 800 complaints against units of state and local government under Title II. Seven other federal agencies also investigate Title II complaints and may refer cases to the Department of Justice for litigation.

Title III: Public Accommodations and Commercial Facilities

Complaints about violations of Title III by public accommodations and commercial facilities are filed with:

U.S. Department of Justice
Civil Rights Division
Public Access Section
Post Office Box 66738
Washington, D.C. 20035-6738

EQUAL EMPLOYMENT OPPORTUNITY COMMISSION
AMERICANS WITH DISABILITIES ACT OF 1990 – STATISTICS
FY 1992–FY 1995

ADA Charges	FY 1992[1]	FY 1993[2]	FY 1994	1st Quarter FY 1995[3]	Cumulative Total 7/26/92–12/31/94	
Receipts	999	15,093	18,827	5,008	39,927	
Resolutions	28	4,339	12,673	3,344	20,384	(100%)
Resolutions by Type						
Settlements	6	421	748	186	1,361	(7%)
Withdrawals w/benefits	7	587	1,129	288	2,011	(10%)
Administrative Closures	13	1,832	5,741	1,672	9,258	(45%)
No Reasonable Cause	1	1,398	4,696	1,085	7,180	(35%)
Reasonable Cause	1	101	359	113	574	(3%)
Successful Conciliations	*(0)*	*(33)*	*(121)*	*(34)*	*(188*	*−1%)*
Unsuccessful Conciliations	*(1)*	*(68)*	*(238)*	*(79)*	*(386*	*−2%)*
Merit Resolutions	14	1,109	2,236	587	3,946	
Monetary Benefits	$18,448	$1,006,030	$29,838,040	$9,456,084	$40,318,602	
People Benefited Monetarily	1	60	1,438	397	1,896	
People Benefited Non-monetarily	0	51	584	246	881	
Average Charge Processing Days	25	154	279	297	255	

Data compiled by the Office of Program Operations from EEOC's Charge Data Systems National Data Base.

EEOC's computerized Charge Data System (CDS) is continually updated as data are submitted to EEOC headquarters by EEOC field offices around the country; therefore, statistics may change slightly over time (report run on 1/14/95).

[1] EEOC began enforcing Title I of the ADA on July 26, 1992.

[2] FY 1993 represents the first full year EEOC enforced Title I of the ADA.

[3] FY 1995 statistics include charge receipts from October 1, 1994 through December 31, 1994.

Figure 3.1

The Department is currently investigating over 900 complaints against public accommodations and commercial facilities under Title III.

Legally, What Is a Disability?

Sharon Rennert, ADA technical assistance advisor for the EEOC, takes a decidedly legal stance. "We still have people who have a very limited view of what disability is and forget that the ADA has a specific legal definition." That definition is "a physical or mental impairment that substantially limits one or more of the major life activities; a record of such an impairment; or being regarded as having such an impairment." Major life activities include performing manual tasks, standing, lifting and working, according to the EEOC Title I Technical Assistance Manual.

Part of the problem is the assumption that "disabled" equates with wheelchairs, walkers, crutches, canes, guide dogs, hearing aids and sign language—obvious disabilities. Indeed, advocacy groups for such disabilities were the driving force behind the ADA because people with those disabilities have difficulty getting employment and using public services. However, the ADA clearly mandates accommodation for the blind, the deaf, the learning disabled, the mentally ill and retarded, as well as for people with chronic occupational injuries. How this disabled community sees their need for reasonable accommodation is most clearly illustrated by the impairments most often cited and listed in Figure 3.2.

CUMULATIVE ADA CHARGE DATA FOR JULY 26, 1992–DECEMBER 31, 1994 REPORTING PERIOD		
Total ADA charges received during reporting period: 39,927		
Impairments Most Often Cited	**Number**	**% of Total**
Back Impairments	7,799	19.5%
Neurological Impairments	4,824	12.1%
Emotional/Psychiatric Impairments	4,569	11.4%
Extremities	2,934	7.3%
Heart Impairments	1,833	4.6%
Diabetes	1,473	3.6%
Substance Abuse	1,416	3.6%
Hearing Impairments	1,231	3.1%
Vision Impairments	1,148	2.9%
Blood Disorders	1,054	2.6%
HIV (Sub-category of Blood Disorders)	729	1.8%
Cancer	970	2.4%
Asthma	714	1.8%
(This is not a complete list; therefore, percentages do not add up to 100%. Percentages are rounded off.)		

Figure 3.2

Title I: What's Happened with Enforcement?

When President George Bush signed the Americans with Disabilities Act into law in 1990, organizations worried, while advocates rejoiced. Though embracing its objective to give people with disabilities equal employment and accessibility rights, business leaders predicted the ADA would be a costly burden for companies forced to hire paraplegic, quadriplegic, blind or deaf individuals and refit their plants. Most adopted a "wait and see" attitude on accommodation. Advocates thought that more people with disabilities would be encouraged to seek employment without prejudice.

Now after the four-year anniversary of the ADA's signing on July 26, 1990—the day Title I, the law's chapter on employment practices, expanded to include firms with 15 or more employees—the fallout has not been what anyone, opponent and proponent alike, expected. ADA is a case by case law requiring knowledge of the functional strengths of individuals specific to their unique condition.

Federal Statistics

Compliance hasn't been as costly as feared. An ongoing survey by the Job Accommodation Network (JAN), a resource service of the President's Committee on Employment of People with Disabilities, shows that more than three-fourths of accommodations cost less than $1,000, and more than half cost less than $500. Meanwhile, almost half of the surveyed firms making accommodations valued the benefits at more than $10,000, both in increased productivity and money saved in recruiting, retraining, health insurance and Workers' Compensation costs.

This leads to the other surprising ADA statistic from the Equal Employment Opportunity Commission, the agency enforcing Title I. From the title's implementation on July 26, 1992, through December, half of the commission's 20,171 ADA cases involved charges of improper discharge. This was twice the number of accommodation cases, and four times the number of cases involving hiring practices. (See Figure 3.3.)

Title I was well-intended, but has created difficulties with its case-by-case language: The ADA states that if a person with a disability is qualified for a job by the employer's stated standards of education, experience and skills, the employer must provide "reasonable accommodations" so that the person can do the "essential functions" of the job. Congress left vague both "reasonable accommodation" and "essential functions," to apply on a case-by-case basis: no two disabilities are alike, no two jobs are alike.

"Reasonable accommodation" allows the employer to judge the type of accommodation needed, given the cost, effectiveness and other factors that could create an "undue burden" on the company's operation. "Essential functions" are the end result of the job in question, not how it is done or any additional duties that could be handled by other employees.

In addition, this has often left the burden of "accommodation" inappropriately on either the disabled person or inexperienced human resources personnel and prospective supervisors. The top three complaints since the law's passage involve people with hidden disabilities. These are conditions that cannot be seen by looking, such as chronic pain or speech impairment. The disability is no less real, however, physically, legally or in terms of defining an accommodation.

Some Cases of Note: Formally Settled

Following are some examples from an April, 1994 Department of Justice Status Report. (See the end of this chapter for additional cases from April to December 1994.)

Title I: Employment Settlements

- *A Tennessee county agreed to separate its medical and personnel records, as required by the ADA.*
- *A city in Illinois agreed to reinstate an individual with epilepsy to his position as custodian.*
- *A Pennsylvania county court agreed to provide accommodations for an individual with a learning disability, including daily transcripts and extra time to ask questions during court proceedings.*
- *U.S. v. State of Illinois – The Department of Justice sued the State of Illinois, the City of Aurora, and its police and fire pension funds for excluding police officers and firefighters from its pension funds on the basis of disability. Under the challenged system, police officers and firefighters are required to undergo separate physical examinations, after they are hired, to determine eligibility for retirement and disability benefits. The investigation resulted from the complaint of an Aurora police officer who was ruled ineligible for pension benefits because he has diabetes.*

Title II: Public Services – Settlements

Through lawsuits and both formal and informal settlement agreement, the Department of Justice has achieved greater access to public facilities for individuals with disabilities in over 200 cases. Under general rules governing lawsuits brought by the Federal Government, the Department of Justice

CUMULATIVE ADA CHARGE DATA FOR JULY 26,1992–DECEMBER 31, 1994 REPORTING PERIOD		
ADA Violations Most Often Cited	**Number**	**% of Total**
Discharge	20,171	50.5%
Failure to Provide Reasonable Accommodation	10,264	25.7%
Hiring	4,364	10.9%
Harassment	4,294	10.8%
Discipline	2,947	7.4%
Layoff	2,069	5.2%
Benefits	1,576	3.9%
Promotion	1,495	3.7%
Rehire	1,472	3.7%
Wages	1,385	3.5%
Suspension	910	2.3%

(This list adds up to more than 100% because individuals can allege multiple violations. Percentages are rounded off.)

REMEMBER, THE FILING OF A CHARGE DOES NOT INDICATE WHETHER THE CHARGE HAS MERIT.

Data compiled by the Office of Program Operations from EEOC's Charge Data System's National Data Base.

NOTE: EEOC's computerized Charge Data System is continually updated as data are submitted to EEOC headquarters by the field offices around the country; therefore, statistics may change slightly over time. (This report is based on data as of 1/14/95.)

Figure 3.3

may not file a lawsuit unless it has first unsuccessfully attempted to settle the dispute through negotiations. As a result, most complaints filed with the Department will be resolved before a lawsuit becomes necessary. Many cases are settled after an on-site investigation. .

- *Philadelphia, Pennsylvania—The City of Philadelphia entered an agreement to resolve a complaint involving emergency medical technicians (EMT's) of the Philadelphia Fire Department who had allegedly refused to assist an individual when they learned that he was HIV-positive. The City agreed to conduct mandatory training of the Department's 2,300 EMT's and firefighters regarding universal precautions to prevent the transmission of HIV/AIDS, as well as to provide HIV/AIDS sensitivity training. The city also agreed to develop and publicize a written policy stating that individuals with disabilities shall be given the opportunity to benefit fully from its emergency medical services. The policy is to include disciplinary measures for any individual who fails to follow the city's guidelines. In addition, the city will provide $10,000 in compensatory damages and a written apology to the individual denied services.*

- *Hickman County, Kentucky—Hickman County agreed to develop a compliance plan to provide access to the services, programs, and activities conducted in its courthouse, thus resolving a complaint alleging that a man using a wheelchair was unable to enter the circuit clerk's office to renew his driver's license because the doors were too narrow.*

- *Van Buren County, Arkansas—Van Buren County agreed to relocate county court activities to an accessible site upon request; develop a self-evaluation and a transition plan; adopt a grievance procedure; and place public notices of its nondiscrimination policy and responsibilities under the ADA on county bulletin boards and in local newspapers.*

- *Harris County (Houston), Texas—Harris County agreed to make all of the programs offered in each of its 106 courtrooms and jury assembly rooms accessible, to furnish the auxiliary aids necessary to achieve effective communication in all of the county's programs, and to provide staff training.*

- *Scott County, Arkansas—Scott County agreed to renovate the county courthouse in order to make it readily accessible to individuals with disabilities. Specifically, the county agreed to renovate the courthouse's entrances, rest rooms, door hardware, and drinking fountains.*

- *A Missouri county agreed to install an elevator and make other structural modifications to make its courthouse accessible. In the interim, it will provide alternative means for enabling individuals with disabilities to obtain services.*

- *A Tennessee city agreed to move all city meetings from the inaccessible second floor of the town hall to the city's accessible library. It also built ramps at two entrances to the town hall and remodeled rest rooms in the town hall and library.*

- *Many cities and towns in the East and Midwest have agreed to install elevators in their city halls/courthouses and to undertake other structural changes, such as adding ramps and remodeling rest rooms and entrances, or to make these buildings accessible by moving their programs (e.g., town meetings and services) to alternative accessible locations.*

- *A county in the state of Washington installed an intercom on the first floor of its courthouse annex so that persons can contact offices located on the second floor when they need to have the services provided on the first floor.*
- *A New England town agreed to build a roof over the ramp leading to its 150-year-old town hall to ensure that the ramp does not become blocked by snow.*
- *A small town in Oklahoma agreed to formulate and enforce a written policy prohibiting the misuse of accessible parking spaces at its town hall by nondisabled town officials.*
- *In Iowa, a board of elections agreed to move a polling place to an accessible location.*

Title III: Public Accommodation and Commercial Facilities Settlements

The Department of Justice may file lawsuits in federal courts to enforce the ADA and may obtain court orders including compensatory damages to remedy discrimination. Under Title III the Department may also obtain civil penalties of up to $50,000 for the first violation and $100,000 for any subsequent violation. Following are some examples of litigation on Title III issues, and the outcome. (Refer to the end of this chapter for additional cited cases.)

- *Sardi's Restaurant, New York, New York — Sardi's Restaurant in New York City agreed to resolve a complaint that the restaurant's rest rooms were inaccessible for persons who use wheelchairs or their mobility devices. Sardi's agreed to install an accessible unisex rest room and signage indicating the location of the rest room.*
- *Quality Hotel Downtown, Washington, D.C. — Staff of the Quality Hotel Downtown in Washington, D.C. had not permitted a guest to use a motorized scooter as a mobility device to get to his room. The hotel agreed to pay the complainant $10,000 in damages and to train all employees on the requirements of the ADA.*
- *Intercontinental Hotel, New York, New York — The Department of Justice entered a wide-ranging formal settlement agreement with the Inter-Continental Hotel in midtown New York, a member of a chain of prestigious hotels in major cities. The hotel will make numerous changes to its 691-room facility and procedures over the next five years, including removing physical barriers in public areas such as the front entrance, lobby and ballroom, as well as in 21 guest rooms; providing television decoders, telephone handset amplifiers, visual smoke alarms, and visual door knock and telephone indicators in 35 guest rooms; making elevator modifications to provide access for persons with vision impairments; and modifying reservation and room assignment policies to ensure that accessible rooms are made available to those who request them.*
- *Municipal Credit Union, New York, New York — A branch office of the Municipal Credit Union in New York City was inaccessible to people with mobility impairments. The Credit Union agreed to install a ramp at the entrance, to notify its customers of the ramp, to post appropriate signs, and to instruct the staff to provide assistance when requested by an individual with a disability.*
- *A Utah bank, an Illinois bowling center, an office building, and a Maryland cable television company have all agreed to install*

ramps to make their entrances accessible for people who use mobility devices. The bowling center, office building and cable TV company also agreed to provide accessible parking in their parking lots.

- *An Illinois bank agreed to install automatic doors at its front entrance to make it easier for people with visual, manual, and mobility impairments to gain access.*
- *A national retail chain agreed to provide accessible parking at its stores nationwide.*
- *A major rental car company agreed to provide accessible parking at a major metropolitan airport and to institute valet parking service when needed by customers with disabilities.*
- *A Louisiana fast food restaurant, a Texas grocery store, a health care facility, a shopping mall, an Oregon shopping center and retirement community have all agreed to provide accessible parking in their parking lots. The grocery store and shopping center also agreed to install the curb ramps that a person who uses a wheelchair needs to get from the parking lot to the front door. Two other fast food restaurants agreed to relocate their accessible parking spaces to make them closer to the front door.*
- *A California convenience store of a well-known franchise agreed to make three of its checkout aisles, including one express lane, accessible for people who use mobility devices.*
- *A credit union agreed to lower an ATM machine to make it accessible for persons who use wheelchairs.*
- *A health club agreed to install a lift to enable a wheelchair user to participate in an arthritis rehabilitation program in the club's swimming pool.*
- *A 12-theater complex in Colorado agreed to provide additional seating areas throughout its theaters for people who use wheelchairs.*
- *A California department store agreed to make its rest rooms and fitting rooms accessible for people with manual or mobility impairments, to lower the height of its public telephones and drinking fountains to make them accessible for people who use wheelchairs, and to upgrade its elevators and install signage to make the store accessible for people who have vision impairments.*

Meeting the Needs of People and State and Local Codes

Certification of State and Local Building Codes: The ADA authorizes the Department of Justice to certify state or local laws or building codes that meet or exceed the ADA's accessibility requirements. This is a voluntary program in which states and localities can choose to participate. In a jurisdiction whose law or code has been certified, when a new public accommodation or other commercial facility is built, or an existing facility is altered or expanded, compliance with the local regulations will give the building owner and other responsible parties evidence of compliance with the ADA if the building's accessibility is later challenged under the ADA.

On May 20, 1993, the Department of Justice issued its first response to a request for certification of a state accessibility code. The letter to the state of Washington provided a side-by-side analysis of its standards and the ADA standards as a means of providing technical assistance to offices of the state in identifying minor areas of discrepancy. It was not a formal preliminary determination of equivalency or nonequivalency with the federal accessibility standards.

Other requests for certification have been received from the city of New York, the state of New Mexico, the state of Utah, and the state of Florida. The Department has also responded to a request for technical assistance from the state of New Hampshire and is reviewing requests for technical assistance from the Council of American Building Officials (CABO) on behalf of the American National Standards Institute (ANSI) A117.1 committee, the Building Officials and Code Administrators International (BOCA), and the National Parking Association.

Technical Assistance

The ADA requires the Department of Justice to provide technical assistance to entities and individuals with rights and responsibilities under the ADA. The Department encourages voluntary compliance by providing education and technical assistance to business, industry, government, and members of the general public through a variety of means.

ADA Telephone Information Line: The Department of Justice now provides toll-free "800" service for both voice and TDD callers who have questions about Title II and Title III of the ADA, including the Standards for Accessible Design. Under its expanded hours of operations, operators may be reached from 11:00 a.m. to 5:00 p.m. (EDT) Monday through Friday (except Thursdays, 1:00 p.m. to 5:00 p.m.). The system has been upgraded to accommodate a larger number of callers simultaneously and to provide Spanish language service. Callers may hear recorded information and order materials at any time, day or night. The information line numbers are:

Nationwide
1-800-514-0301 (voice)
1-800-514-0383 (TDD)

Washington, D.C., area
202-514-0301 (voice)
202-514-0383 (TDD)

Summary

Universal Design: One result of the ADA, besides benefiting the population as it ages, becomes injured, disabled or in disease, is the hastening of "universal design," a concept whereby all environments are designed to suit the widest range of people possible. Not everybody has the same intellect, vision, or grip. Not everybody has the same health or genetics. Now architects, designers, and ergonomists who used to base their designs on anthropometric data culled from military recruits of the 1940s and 1950s have changed to human factors as design criteria. Universal design removes the notion of "average" and replaces it with "unique." Now we design doorways for all persons, workplaces for their unique workers, and restaurants for the blind, among others. The ADA requires that the environments fit the individual, not the other way around. The law's underlying intent is to remove presumptions about people with disabilities: what they can and can't do and what is and is not a disability, and whether or not disabilities are observable. People with disabilities oftentimes can use any facility. It might take some reorganizing and up-front money to accommodate the person, but it's ultimately an investment in a longer-term employee, customer, citizen or patron and his or her colleagues, friends and family for years to come.

The following pages cite examples of ADA activities from the Department of Justice—from April–December, 1994. These examples of litigation throughout the country, and the outcome of lawsuits, are useful indicators of acceptable solutions to accessibility issues.

U.S. Department of Justice
Civil Rights Division
Public Access Section

Enforcing the ADA

A Status Report Update from the Department of Justice

(April-June 1994)

This Status Report Update covers the ADA activities of the Department of Justice during the second quarter (April-June) of 1994. Copies of the earlier April 4, 1994, Status Report, which summarizes all activities up to that date, are available through our ADA Telephone Information Line (see page 10).

INSIDE...

The Americans with Disabilities Act (ADA) is a comprehensive civil rights law for people with disabilities. The Department of Justice enforces the ADA's requirements in three areas -

Title I: Employment practices by units of State and local government

Title II: Programs, services, and activities of State and local government

Title III: Public accommodations and commercial facilities

I. Enforcement

Through lawsuits and both formal and informal settlement agreements, the Department has achieved greater access for individuals with disabilities in approximately 250 cases. Under general rules governing lawsuits brought by the Federal Government, the Department of Justice may not file a lawsuit unless it has first unsuccessfully attempted to settle the dispute through negotiations.

A. Litigation

The Department may file lawsuits in Federal court to enforce the ADA and may obtain court orders including compensatory damages and back pay to remedy discrimination. Under title III the Department may also obtain civil penalties of up to $50,000 for the first violation and $100,000 for any subsequent violation.

1. New lawsuits

The Department initiated, or intervened in, the following lawsuits.

Title II

Gorman v. Guitars and Cadillacs, L.P. - The Department intervened in this suit to defend the constitutionality of title II. The Department has

also filed an amicus brief arguing that title II covers police arrest porcedures. (See "amicus briefs," below.)

Title III

United States v. Lira Limited Liability Co. - The Department filed its first lawsuit for violations of the alterations provisions of title III against the owners of the Barolo Grill, a restaurant in Denver, Colorado. The Barolo's owners altered the restaurant in November 1992 without complying with the ADA when they constructed a raised dining area with no ramp or lift for persons who use wheelchairs. The owners also failed to make any path of travel modifications, leaving the restaurant's entrance inaccessible, and failed to remove existing barriers to access where readily achievable.

United States v. Pleasant Travel Service, Inc. and Hawaiian Hotels and Resorts, Inc. - The Department filed its first title III action against a hotel, the Royal Lahaina Resort, in Lahaina, Hawaii (on the Island of Maui). The suit alleges that the owner and operator of the hotel failed to remove architectural barriers to access and made alterations to the hotel that did not comply with the ADA's architectural standards. The hotel has approximately 540 guest rooms, suites and cottages, none of which is accessible to individuals with disabilities. In addition, none of the restrooms in the common area of the hotel is accessible; and there are barriers to access in the hotel's restaurants, tennis courts and swimming pools. In undertaking alterations to the hotel's luau grounds, gift shop, and swimming pool area, the owner and operator failed to provide accessible paths of travel to the altered areas.

2. Consent decrees

Some litigation is resolved at the time that the suit is filed or afterwards by means of a negotiated consent decree. Consent decrees are monitored and enforced by the Federal court in which they are entered.

Title III

United States v. Becker C.P.A. Review - In a consent decree resolving the first case filed by the Department of Justice under the ADA, Becker C.P.A. Review, which prepares over 10,000 students annually to take the national certified public accountant exam, agreed to amend its auxiliary aids policy. Becker will no longer limit its offered auxiliary aids to audiotape transcripts prepared for the instructors' use, and will provide appropriate auxiliary aids and services, including qualified sign language interpreters and assistive listening devices, to students who are deaf or hard of hearing. The company may require a student to attend a consultation meeting, at which time the student would explain his or her individual needs and means of communication. Becker would explain the nature of the class and the proposed auxiliary aid or service. However, Becker may request that the student try its proposed aid or service at a Becker class prior to the session that the student wishes to attend. If the student can articulate, based on experience or skills, why the proposed aid or service will not provide effective communication,

the student will not be required to try out the proposed auxiliary aid or service. Becker also agreed to appoint a national ADA coordinator and to train its staff regarding the policy revision; pay $20,000 to the Department of Justice to be distributed to seven individuals who are deaf or hard of hearing, former Becker students; and establish a $25,000 scholarship fund for accounting students who are deaf or hard of hearing at California State University.

United States v. Harcourt Brace Legal and Professional Publications, Inc. - A consent decree resolved this suit against the auxiliary aids policies of Harcourt Brace Legal and Professional Publications regarding Bar/Bri, the nation's largest preparatory course for individuals studying for bar examinations. The Department's complaint alleged that the Bar/Bri course failed to provide appropriate auxiliary aids to students with vision and hearing impairments. Under the consent decree, filed simultaneously with the complaint, Harcourt Brace agreed to establish a detailed set of procedures for identifying and providing appropriate auxiliary aids and services, including qualified sign language interpreters, assistive listening devices, and Brailled materials, to students with disabilities. In addition, Harcourt Brace has agreed to pay $28,000 in compensatory relief. This award is divided among two students; the California Department of Rehabilitation, which provided the interpreter for one of the students; and the individual who converted the course materials into Braille for the other student. Harcourt Brace also agreed to pay $25,000 in civil penalties, adopt and implement a formal written policy ensuring that auxiliary aids and services are promptly and properly provided, educate Bar/Bri staff regarding students with disabilities, and include information regarding the availability of auxiliary aids and services for students with disabilities in its advertising materials.

Consent Decrees

3. Amicus briefs

The Department files briefs in selected ADA cases in which it is not a party in order to guide courts in interpreting the ADA.

Title II

Crowder v. Kitigawa - The Department filed an amicus brief in the United States Court of Appeals for the Ninth Circuit supporting a challenge to Hawaii's 120-day animal quarantine program for all dogs, cats, and other carnivores, including guide dogs, entering the State. The brief argues that title II prohibits discrimination against individuals with disabilities in all actions of State and local governments, including the quarantine requirements, not just in the "services" or "benefits" they provide, and that there are nondiscriminatory alternatives to the quarantine system which could both protect against rabies and allow individuals with guide dogs to travel freely to Hawaii. Hawaii maintains that the quarantine is necessary to protect against the introduction of rabies into Hawaii. The private plaintiffs, however, allege that the quarantine discriminates against individuals with disabilities who use guide dogs by making it virtually impossible for them to travel to or from Hawaii. The Federal district court ruled against plaintiffs who appealed to the United States Court of Appeals for the Ninth Circuit.

Gorman v. Guitars and Cadillacs, L.P. - The Department filed an amicus brief in this case arguing that police arrest procedures are covered by title II. The Department also intervened as a party to defend against allegations that title II is unconstitionally vague. The plaintiff has paraplegia and uses a wheelchair. His lawsuit alleges that the owner and operators of Guitars & Cadillacs, a country western bar in Kansas City, Missouri, violated his rights under title III of the ADA by refusing to allow him access to the bar where the dance floor is located, and by subsequently having him arrested for trespass when he asserted his right to remain there. The plaintiff also alleged that members of the Kansas City Police Department, the department's chief of police, and members of the department's board of commissioners discriminated against him under title II of the ADA by a failure to make the reasonable modifications in its policies, practices, and procedures necessary to ensure safety during arrest and transportation to the police station. This failure resulted in personal injuries and damage to the plaintiff's wheelchair while he was in custody.

Livingston v. Guice - The U.S. District Court for the Western District of North Carolina dismissed this case in which the Department had filed an amicus brief arguing that States may be sued for damages under title II. This private suit alleges that the State of North Carolina and a State court judge violated title II of the ADA by preventing the plaintiff from entering a courtroom through the only accessible entrance known to her. In dismissing the case, the court held that because of the doctrine of judicial immunity, the judge, and therefore, the State could not be held liable.

Ellen S. v. Florida Board of Bar Examiners - The Department filed an amicus brief supporting a challenge to mental health inquiries made by the Florida State Board of Law Examiners in certifying candidates for admission to the Florida Bar. Florida asks candidates whether they have ever sought treatment for or been diagnosed as having a nervous, mental, or emotional condition, or have ever taken any psychotropic medication. Bar applicants who answer affirmatively must sign a consent form authorizing the release of any and all mental health records. The amicus brief argues that the inquiries are unnecessary and that the Board's procedures unnecessarily impose burdens on people with disabilities in violation of title II.

Amicus Briefs

B. Formal Settlement Agreements

The Department has resolved a number of cases without filing a lawsuit, by means of formal written settlement agreements.

Title II

Fulton, Missouri - The Department settled a complaint filed against the Municipal Court for the City of Fulton and the Office of the Clerk of the Municipal Court. The complaint alleged that the city did not ensure effective communication with persons who are deaf or hard of hearing. The city has agreed to provide appropriate auxiliary aids and services; provide training for personnel; publish a policy that provides reasonable modifications in policies, practices, and procedures for people with disabilities; incorporate instructions for obtaining reasonable modifications in policies, practices, and procedures into the existing language on its traffic citations; and work with the county government to ensure that the municipal courtroom in the county courthouse is accessible.

Waukesha, Wisconsin - Resolving a complaint by a Waukesha city alderman who uses a wheelchair alleging that the city hall was inaccessible, the city agreed to hold its closed deliberations in the accessible room in which it holds general meetings, renovate the first floor men's and women's bathrooms to comply with ADA standards, install two automatic door openers at the building's front entrance, and renovate a van accessible parking space.

Berkeley, California - Agreement was reached with the City of Berkeley, California, to ensure direct access to its 9-1-1 emergency services. Berkeley will modify its current practices to ensure that the services provided to individuals who use TDD's are as effective as those provided to others. The city will also install one TDD at each of its answering stations, provide training of emergency service call takers in the proper operation of TDD's, and develop and implement a public education program to promote the use of 9-1-1 by individuals who use TDD's.

Wadsworth, Ohio - Resolving a complaint alleging that the city hall and city court were inaccessible to individuals with mobility impairments, the City of Wadsworth agreed to make alternative arrangements for program accessibility until a new city hall is completed in the spring of 1995, upgrade its parking facilities and entryway to ensure access to individuals with disabilities, inform and train all city managers and employees on its policies and procedures for providing accessibility to individuals with disabilities, and adopt and publish grievance procedures for prompt and equitable resolution of complaints alleging actions prohibited by title II.

Alexandria, Louisiana - In response to a complaint alleging that a person who is deaf was denied effective communication during a court proceeding because a sign language interpreter was not provided, the Alexandria City Court agreed to provide auxiliary aids when necessary for effective communication and adopted a policy for the provision of sign language interpreters. A TDD was also purchased.

Atlanta, Georgia - The Georgia World Congress Center Authority has agreed to make significant alterations to the Georgia World Congress Center, a large convention facility, and one of the proposed venues for the 1996 Olympic Games. The alterations include widening doors to the auditorium; providing accessible seating for people who use wheelchairs; providing alternatives to turnstile entrances to food service areas; altering specific features in designated food service areas; and altering telephones, restrooms, door hardware, and water fountains.

> *Formal Settlement Agreements*

Genesee County, Michigan - The County Board of Commissioners agreed to make restroom facilities in the probate court house accessible to individuals with mobility impairments.

Title III

Anthony's Pier 4 Restaurant, Boston, Massachusetts - Settlement agreements were reached with the owners and operators of Anthony's Pier 4 restaurant in Boston, Massachusetts, and three other restaurants in the Boston area. Anthony's Pier 4 is one of the five largest restaurants in the United States. The agreements call for a variety of changes to the facilities, including provision of accessible parking spaces, accessible entrances, accessible dining areas, and accessible restrooms. In particular, the agreement with Anthony's Pier 4 calls for reconstructing the front of the restaurant to provide an accessible entrance and accessible restrooms, construction of a ramp to provide access to an outdoor patio, and installation of a mechanical wheelchair lift to provide access to the banquet and meeting rooms on the second floor of the facility. The other three restaurants covered by the agreements are in Swampscott and Yarmouthport, Massachusetts. At each of those, there will be accessible parking, an accessible main entrance, accessible seating areas, and accessible restrooms. Finally, all of the restaurants have adopted policies for serving customers with disabilities.

Arlington, Virginia - Exxon Gas Station in Arlington, Virginia agreed to provide gas dispensing services to persons with disabilities and implement a procedure that would ensure that persons with disabilities could bypass the electronic card reader devices when dispensing their own gasoline. Furthermore, Exxon agreed to install detailed signage describing this procedure.

Hickory, North Carolina - The Department settled a complaint against the owners of the Life Enhancement Center health club regarding allegations that the health club had excluded an individual who uses a wheelchair from the pool and jacuzzi. The health club owners later allowed him to use the pool, jacuzzi, and other equipment, but only if he wore a protective helmet at any time he was out of his wheelchair. Several aspects of the newly constructed facility failed to meet the ADA new construction standards. Under the settlement agreement, the owners agreed to change their previous policies and to allow persons who use wheelchairs to use the pool and jacuzzi, eliminate the protective helmet requirements, and make all changes necessary to bring the facility into compliance with the new construction standards.

Formal Settlement Agreements

C. Other settlements

The Department resolves numerous cases without litigation or a formal settlement agreement. In some instances, the public accommodation, commercial facility, or State or local government promptly agrees to take the necessary actions to achieve compliance. In others, extensive negotiations are required. Following are some examples of what has been accomplished through informal settlements.

Title II

Access to facilities

• The entrance to the building housing a New England State law library was renovated along with the restrooms servicing the library to make the facility accessible to persons with mobility impairments. The library also revised its policy to ensure that appropriate auxiliary aids and services will be provided when necessary.

- A western State department of corrections retrofitted a prison van with a wheelchair lift, developed procedures for providing physical therapy, constructed a ramp to provide access to a prison library, and leveled the entrance to a shower in a cellblock.

- A Colorado county with an inaccessible elevator and restroom in its court house agreed to make structural changes to the restroom, alter the elevator to carry a greater maximum weight, and install a call button in the elevator so persons with disabilities can call for assistance.

Other Settlements

Effective communication

- A western State department of prisons agreed to reschedule a parole hearing so that it could provide a sign language interpreter for an inmate, and agreed to provide a TDD for the facility where the inmate was housed.

Title III

Access to facilities

- A national rental car company is now offering a wide variety of rental cars equipped with hand controls to customers with disabilities at all corporately-owned locations across the country. Additionally, the company is now installing steering knobs free of charge to customers who request them. Hand controls and steering knobs enable persons who have limited use of their lower extremities to drive.

- A Denver restaurant, accessible only by a steep flight of stairs or by narrow winding corridors, agreed, as a readily achievable alternative to barrier removal, to prepare and deliver meals to persons with disabilities who live within three miles of the restaurant and to advertise the availability of this service.

- A Louisiana motel, part of a national franchise, agreed to provide accessible parking spaces, provide an accessible entrance to the front lobby, lower a portion of the front desk, and modify six guest rooms to make them accessible (including two rooms with roll-in showers). The complaint alleged that an individual who uses a wheelchair called the company's 800 reservations number and requested an accessible room in the Baton Rouge area. He was informed that none of the motels associated with the national franchise in that area had accessible rooms.

- A luxury hotel in a large Virginia city agreed to provide two accessible restrooms in the lobby area, accessible signage throughout the building, and six accessible guest rooms.

- A retail, fabric store in a small California city has modified one of the store's entrances so that it is accessible to persons with disabilities. Wider doors and an opening device were installed to enable persons with disabilities to enter the store unassisted. Appropriate directional signage was also installed.

- Small town gas stations in Utah and Wyoming agreed to provide dispensing services for persons with disabilities and not to charge prices above ordinary self-serve prices for such services.

- An exercise training facility operating on two floors in a large California city agreed, as a readily achievable alternative to barrier removal, to open a space on the first floor, which was ordinarily reserved for personalized training, to persons unable to gain access to the second floor. The facility also agreed not to charge additional fees, unless personalized training was requested.

35

- An Atlanta, Georgia, location of a national chain restaurant acquired a portable ramp and installed a doorbell for use by those persons who need access to the ramp. Because of the restaurant's location, installation of a permanent ramp was not readily achievable.

Other Settlements

- The owners of a shopping center in Lexington, South Carolina, built a curb ramp and established accessible parking.

- A Denver restaurant installed a curb ramp to make the front entrance accessible.

Effective communication

- A large, independent California bookstore agreed to provide sign language interpreters upon request for poetry readings that it sponsors and holds at the bookstore. The store will also specify that the service is available in its advertising for the poetry readings.

- Four New York performing arts theaters have installed assistive listening systems, purchased receivers equal in number to at least four percent of available seats, and posted signs indicating the availability of these devices.

- An intercity bus company purchased and installed TDD units at banks of public phones in a large east coast city bus terminal and agreed to ensure that the TDD's are properly maintained.

Policies and procedures

- The Department resolved a complaint against a Jacksonville, Florida, chain restaurant alleging that the manager of the restaurant refused to allow a person with a hearing impairment who was accompanied by a service animal into the restaurant. The restaurant agreed to educate its employees as to the need to make reasonable modifications in policies, practices, and procedures for all people with disabilities, including individuals with hearing impairments who use service animals.

D. Investigations

The Department is currently investigating over 1000 complaints against public accommodations and commercial facilities under title III. The Department also, on its own initiative, is reviewing plans for new construction and alterations of various types of facilities in locations around the country.

In addition, the Department is currently investigating nearly 900 complaints against units of State and local government under title II. Seven other Federal agencies are also investigating title II complaints and may refer cases to the Department of Justice for litigation.

The Department also has a number of investigations under way under title I against public employers. (Enforcement of title I against private employers is handled by the Equal Employment Opportunity Commission.)

36

II. Certification of State and Local Building Codes

The ADA authorizes the Department to certify State or local laws or building codes that meet or exceed the ADA's accessibility requirements. This is a voluntary program in which States and localities can choose to participate. In a jurisdiction whose law or code has been certified, when a new public accommodation or other commercial facility is built, or an existing facility is altered or expanded, compliance with the local regulations will give the building owner and other responsible parties rebuttable evidence of compliance with the ADA if the building's accessibility is later challenged under the ADA. The Department is reviewing requests for certification from the State of Washington, the City of New York, the State of New Mexico, the State of Utah, and the State of Florida.

The Department is also reviewing requests for technical assistance from the Council of American Building Officials (CABO) on behalf of the American National Standards Institute (ANSI) A117.1 committee, the Building Officials and Code Administrators International (BOCA), and the National Parking Association.

Title II Proposed Rule

The Department of Justice has published in the Federal Register a proposed rule to amend the regulations implementing title II and titles III of the ADA. The Department is currently seeking public comment on the proposed amendments. Comments must be received in writing on or before August 19, 1994. The proposal would adopt the ADA Accessibility Guidelines as the ADA Standards for Accessible Design for new construction and alterations covered by title II of the ADA. Under the proposed amendment, title II entities would no longer have the option to apply the Uniform Federal Accessibility Standards.

The proposed rule would also amend the ADA Standards in several ways and add sections 11 through 14, dealing with judicial, legislative, and regulatory facilities, detention and correctional facilities, residential housing, and public rights-of-way. Finally, the proposal would publish the amended ADA Standards for Accessible Design as part 37 of 28 C.F.R., deleting them from Appendix A of part 36 of 28 C.F.R., and would amend title III to refer to part 37.

III. Technical Assistance

The ADA requires the Department of Justice to provide technical assistance to entities and individuals with rights and responsibilities under the ADA. The Department encourages voluntary compliance by providing education and technical assistance to business, industry, government, and members of the general public through a variety of means.

ADA Telephone Information Line

The Department of Justice now provides toll-free "800" service for both voice and TDD callers who have questions about title II and title III of the ADA, including the Standards for Accessible Design. Under its expanded hours of operations, operators may be reached from 10:00 a.m. to 6:00 p.m. (EDT), Monday through Friday (except Thursdays, 1:00 p.m. to 6:00 p.m.). The system has been upgraded to accommodate a larger number of callers simultaneously and to provide Spanish language service. Callers may hear recorded information and order materials at any time day or night. The information line numbers are:

Nationwide
1-800-514-0301 (voice)
1-800-514-0383 (TDD)

Washington, D.C., area
202-514-0301 (voice)
202-514-0383 (TDD)

Grants

Section 506 of the ADA requires the Department to provide technical assistance to entities and individuals affected by title II and title III of the ADA. This section also authorizes the Department to award grants for the purpose of supplementing the Department's technical assistance efforts.

The Department of Justice's solicitation for applications for its fiscal year 1994 Americans with Disabilities Act (ADA) Technical Assistance Grant Program was published in the Federal Register on June 3, 1994. The ADA Technical Assistance Grant Program is designed to develop and implement strategies to disseminate information to entities and individuals with rights and responsibilities under titles II and III of the ADA. The goal of the program is to increase understanding of, and facilitate voluntary compliance with, the ADA nationwide. Applications will be accepted until August 2, 1994.

Publications

Copies of the Department of Justice's regulations for titles II and III of the ADA, the ADA Questions and Answers booklet, the ADA Handbook (limited quantities available), and information about the Department's technical assistance grant program can be obtained by calling the Department's toll-free ADA Telephone Information Line at the number listed above or writing to the address listed below. These materials are available in standard print, large print, Braille, audiotape, and computer disk.

U.S. Department of Justice
Civil Rights Division
Public Access Section
Post Office Box 66738
Washington, D.C. 20035-6738

These materials are also available through the Department of Justice's ADA electronic bulletin board at 202-514-6193.

Copies of the Department of Justice's Technical Assistance Manuals for titles II and III and yearly updates can be obtained by subscription from the Government Printing Office. The subscription for the Title II Manual, which includes annual supplements through 1996. costs $24. The subscription for the Title III Manual with supplements through 1996 costs $25. Call the ADA Telephone Information Line to obtain an order form.

Copies of legal documents and settlement agreements mentioned in this publication can be obtained by writing to:

Freedom of Information/Privacy Act Branch
Room 7337
Civil Rights Division
U.S. Department of Justice
Washington, D.C. 20530

IV. Other Sources of ADA Information

The *U.S. Department of Transportation* offers technical assistance to the public concerning the public transportation provisions of title II and title III of the ADA.

ADA documents and general questions
202-366-1656 (voice)
202-366-2979 (TDD)

ADA legal questions
202-366-9306 (voice)
202-755-7687 (TDD)

Nat'l Easter Seal Society
"Project Action" grant
202-347-3066 (voice)
202-347-7385 (TDD)

Air Carrier Access Act questions
202-376-6406 (voice)

The *Equal Employment Opportunity Commission* offers technical assistance to the public concerning title I of the ADA.

For ordering documents
1-800-669-3362 (voice)
1-800-800-3302 (TDD)

For questions
1-800-669-4000 (voice)
TDD: use relay service

The *Federal Communications Commission* offers technical assistance to the public concerning title IV.

ADA documents and general questions
202-632-7260 (voice)
202-632-6999 (TDD)

ADA legal questions
202-634-1808 (voice)
202-632-0484 (TDD)

Complaints and Enforcement
202-632-7553 (voice)
202-632-0485 (TDD)

The *U.S. Architectural and Transportation Barriers Compliance Board,* or *"Access Board,"* offers technical assistance to the public on the ADA Accessibility Guidelines.

ADA documents and questions
800-872-2253 (voice & TDD)
202-272-5434 (voice)
202-272-5449 (TDD)

The *National Institute on Disability and Rehabilitation Research (NIDRR)* of the *U.S. Department of Education* has funded centers in ten regions of the country to provide technical assistance to the public concerning title I, title II, and title III of the ADA.

ADA technical assistance nationwide
(800) 949-4232 (voice & TDD)

V. How to File Complaints

Title I

Complaints about violations of title I (employment) by units of State and local government or by private employers should be filed with the Equal Employment Opportunity Commission. Call 1-800-669-4000 for the field office in your area.

Title II

Complaints about violations of title II by units of State and local government should be filed with -

U.S. Department of Justice
Civil Rights Division
Coordination and Review Section
Post Office Box 66118
Washington, D.C. 20035-6118
(202) 307-2222 (Voice)
(202) 307-2678 (TDD)

Title III

Complaints about violations of title III by public accommodations and commercial facilities should be filed with -

U.S. Department of Justice
Civil Rights Division
Public Access Section
Post Office Box 66738
Washington, D.C. 20035-6738

40

U.S. Department of Justice
Civil Rights Division
Public Access Section

Enforcing the ADA

A Status Report Update from the Department of Justice

(July-September 1994)

This Status Report Update covers the ADA activities of the Department of Justice during the third quarter (July-September) of 1994. Copies of the April 4, 1994, Status Report (which summarizes all activities up to that date) and the April-June 1994 Update are available through our ADA Telephone Information Line (see page 9).

The Americans with Disabilities Act (ADA) is a comprehensive civil rights law for people with disabilities. The Department of Justice enforces the ADA's requirements in three areas -

Title I: Employment practices by units of State and local government

Title II: Programs, services, and activities of State and local government

Title III: Public accommodations and commercial facilities

I. Enforcement

Through lawsuits and both formal and informal settlement agreements, the Department has achieved greater access for individuals with disabilities in nearly 300 cases. Under general rules governing lawsuits brought by the Federal Government, the Department of Justice may not file a lawsuit unless it has first unsuccessfully attempted to settle the dispute through negotiations.

A. Litigation

1. Consent decrees

Some litigation is resolved at the time that the suit is filed or afterwards by means of a negotiated consent decree. Consent decrees are monitored and enforced by the Federal court in which they are entered.

Title III

United States v. Jack H. Castle, D.D.S., Inc. d/b/a Castle Dental Center - In the first AIDS-related settlement with a dental service under the ADA, a Houston dental office will pay $100,000 in damages and penalties for refusing to treat a patient who revealed that he was HIV-positive. Under the proposed consent order defendant Castle Dental Center, a large chain of dental offices in the Houston area, will pay $80,000 in compensatory damages to a person who was denied dental services because of HIV status, the largest amount of damages obtained to date by the Department on behalf of a complainant. The owner of the Center and its management company will each pay a $10,000 civil penalty to the Federal Government. The defendants will also provide full and equal services to persons with HIV or AIDS, train their staff in nondiscriminatory treatment of persons with HIV or AIDS, and send periodic reports to the Department so that compliance with the order can be monitored.

2. Amicus briefs

The Department files briefs in selected ADA cases in which it is not a party in order to guide courts in interpreting the ADA.

Title II

Helen L. v. Didario - The Department filed an amicus brief in the U.S. Court of Appeals for the Third Circuit challenging the Pennsylvania Department of Public Welfare's (DPW) refusal to provide attendant care services to an individual with a mobility impairment who needs such services in order to live at home with her two children. In order to obtain the assistance that she needs, she was required to enter a DPW-maintained nursing home even though she does not need nursing care. Pennsylvania agrees that the most appropriate setting for the plaintiff is in the attendant care program. The State also agrees that attendant care for the plaintiff in her home would cost Pennsylvania $9,300 less per year than nursing home care. However, the State asserts that the attendant care program is underfunded and that the plaintiff must continue on the waiting list. The Department's brief argues that the title II regulation, which requires public entities to provide services in the most integrated setting appropriate to the needs of the individual with a disability, mandates, in this particular situation, that the plaintiff be permitted to enter the attendant care program.

Clark v. Virginia Board of Bar Examiners -- The Department filed an amicus brief supporting a challenge to inquiries into past treatment for mental illness made by the Virginia Board of Bar Examiners in certifying candidates for admission to the Virginia Bar. The court had earlier ruled that it lacked jurisdiction to consider a challenge to the State's bar admission procedures. It also held that the plaintiff had not presented enough evidence as to her mental health condition to establish that she was an individual with a disability who would be entitled to bring an ADA lawsuit on this issue. After the Department filed its amicus brief in support of plaintiff's motion for the court to reconsider its decision, the court reversed its earlier ruling. It agreed with the Department's position that it did indeed have jurisdiction over the plaintiff's claims and that she had "standing" to bring the lawsuit. The case will now proceed to trial.

Amicus Briefs

Ellen S. v. Florida Board of Bar Examiners -- In another bar examiner case challenging mental health inquiries, the U.S. District Court for the Southern District of Florida rejected the Florida Board of Bar Examiners motion to dismiss, as urged by the Department in its June 29, 1994, amicus brief.

Livingston v. Guice -- The Department filed an amicus brief with the U.S. Court of Appeals for the Fourth Circuit in support of plaintiff's appeal in a title II suit against the State of North Carolina and a State court judge. The suit, brought by a person who uses a wheelchair, charges that the State of North Carolina and a State court judge violated title II of the ADA by preventing the plaintiff from entering a courtroom through the only accessible entrance known to her. The U.S. District Court for the Western District of North Carolina had dismissed the case on the grounds of judicial immunity. The Department's brief in the Fourth Circuit argues that, under Supreme Court judicial immunity cases and the ADA, the State judge is not immune from the claim for injunctive relief made in this case and that the State is not immune from the claim for monetary damages.

LRCAB v. Laconia, New Hampshire -- This case involved a challenge to a city zoning board's decision to deny a special use permit that would have allowed the operation of a center providing services for homeless persons with mental illness. The Department filed an amicus brief arguing that zoning actions can be challenged under title II of the ADA and that the court should not abstain pending a state court review of the zoning decision. The court then issued an order declining to abstain but deferred ruling on the issue of whether zoning decisions are covered by title II.

Title III

Fiedler v. American Multi-Cinema, Inc. -- The Department filed an amicus brief with the U.S. District Court for the District of Columbia arguing that existing motion picture theaters with more than 300 seats must disperse wheelchair seating locations to the extent it is readily achievable to do so. The plaintiff, a person with a mobility impairment who uses a wheelchair, sued American Multi-Cinema, Inc., claiming that its practice of providing only two wheelchair seating locations in the last row of a 374-seat motion picture theater in Union Station in Washington, D.C., violated the ADA. The Department's brief also argues that the privately operated movie theater at issue is a covered place of public accommodation under title III even though it is housed in leased space in a facility owned by the Federal Government. In addition, the brief challenges the defendant's assertion that wheelchair users seated somewhere other than in the last row of an existing theater would always constitute a "direct threat" to the health and safety of other patrons in the event of an emergency.

Posner **Dismissed without Ruling on Religious Exemption** -- The Department intervened in *Posner v. Central Synagogue* to defend the constitutionality of title III's religious exemption in a case alleging violations of the ADA by a synagogue nursery school. The U.S. District Court for the Southern District of New York granted summary judgment for the defendant without deciding the constitutional issue.

IHOP Case Moot Because of Restaurant Fire -- The Department intervened in *Pinnock v. International House of Pancakes*, a suit alleging that a San Diego restaurant failed to engage in readily achievable barrier removal, in order to defend the constitutionality of title III of the ADA. In October 1993, the district court ruled in the Department's favor and granted summary judgment to the United States on the constitutional issues. Because the restaurant was destroyed by fire, the U.S. Court of Appeals for the Ninth Circuit dismissed the defendant's appeal as moot.

B. Formal Settlement Agreements

The Department sometimes resolves cases without filing a lawsuit, by means of formal written settlement agreements.

Title II

Los Angeles, California -- The City of Los Angeles has agreed to take major steps to improve the accessibility of its 9-1-1 emergency telephone services to persons who use telecommunication devices for the deaf (TDD's). The formal agreement resolves a complaint alleging that the City failed to respond to a 9-1-1 call made by a mother who is deaf. After her two-year-old son suffered a head injury, the mother called 9-1-1 on a TDD. After three tries to reach the 9-1-1 center by TDD, she gave up and took her son to the hospital herself. In the settlement agreement, the City agreed to install TDD-compatible equipment at approximately 30 answering stations; properly maintain this equipment and provide emergency backup equipment; provide training for emergency services call-takers in the proper operation of TDD's; and undertake a public education program to promote the use of 9-1-1 by individuals who use TDD's.

> Assistant Attorney General Deval L. Patrick has sent a letter to 250 mayors informing them of the Los Angeles / 9-1-1 agreement and reminding them of their obligation to provide direct access for TDD users to their 9-1-1 systems.

Pinellas County, Florida -- The Pinellas County Sheriff's Office entered a formal agreement involving auxiliary aids issues. The agreement resolves a complaint alleging that the Sheriff's Office did not secure the services of a qualified interpreter for an inmate who was deaf and failed to provide him with a TDD so that he could make outgoing calls. The Sheriff's Office agreed to maintain the additional TDD's that it purchased, to permit inmates and visitors to have access to 800 numbers for the purpose of making calls through telephone relay services, and to establish procedures for securing the services of qualified interpreters whenever necessary to ensure effective communication with individuals who are deaf or hard-of-hearing.

Minnehaha County, South Dakota -- In the first settlement agreement involving public fairs, Minnehaha County has agreed to a wide range of measures to ensure accessibility at the Sioux Empire Fair. The County has agreed to renovate several bathrooms, install two TDD's at pay phones, create an accessible path of travel through the livestock barns and other areas at the fairgrounds, install and upgrade accessible parking, make the vending and ticketing counters and booths accessible, provide materials to Fair

volunteers and patrons regarding the accommodations available for disabled patrons, and adopt a policy that equalizes the number of companion tickets to Fair concerts that patrons with mobility impairments can buy as compared to other patrons.

Title III

Avis Inc., Garden City, New York -- Through a negotiated settlement agreement, the Department resolved its investigation of Avis, Inc., the country's second largest car rental establishment. Under the agreement, Avis has committed to providing rental vehicles equipped with hand controls to persons with disabilities at all corporately-owned locations. Hand controls will be available on eight hours' notice in all major airport locations and on 24 or 48 hours' notice at other facilities, depending on certain factors. Avis agreed to provide training at all corporate locations. Avis will urge all existing licensees to adopt the same measures, and will require all new franchisees and those renewing their contracts to follow the agreement. The agreement also references two previously-resolved investigations, where Avis has made substantial changes to its rental policies to accommodate persons with disabilities. When renting to persons who do not use credit cards, Avis will allow persons who are unemployed due to a disability to substitute verifiable disability-related income in lieu of a verifiable employment history. Also, persons who cannot drive due to a disability will now be able to rent cars in their own name and maintain financial responsibility for a car rental when they are accompanied by a licensed driver.

Formal Settlement Agreements

C. Other settlements

The Department resolves numerous cases without litigation or a formal settlement agreement. In some instances, the public accommodation, commercial facility, or State or local government promptly agrees to take the necessary actions to achieve compliance. In others, extensive negotiations are required. Following are some examples of what has been accomplished through informal settlements.

Title II

Access to facilities

- A Kentucky county court agreed to adopt and publicize a policy requiring court proceedings to be relocated to an accessible location upon reasonable notice from a person with a mobility impairment.

- A small New York town agreed to provide accessible paths from parking to viewing positions at its public baseball fields and install power-assisted doors and accessible water fountains and restrooms in its town hall.

- A Colorado county agreed to provide for accessibility at its courthouse by making changes to its elevator and restrooms.

Policies and procedures

- A west coast State committee of bar examiners agreed to provide an additional testing day for the July 1994 bar exam for an individual with a learning disability.

Title III

Access to facilities

- A Manchester, New Hampshire, pub installed a ramp at its front entrance.

- The owners of a Denver fast food establishment regraded an area of the parking lot to make it level with the restaurant's entrance and installed two accessible parking spaces.

- A Pensacola, Florida, restaurant located on the second floor of a two-story building agreed to make all menu selections from the second floor restaurant available at an accessible location on the first floor of the facility at no additional charge.

- A gift shop in a small town in Minnesota agreed to install a ramp to the front entrance.

- A California museum built a new accessible unisex restroom and modified another set of restrooms to have an accessible stall, lavatory, and other elements.

- A Colorado inn built a ramp at one of the inn's entrances.

- A small town Louisiana fast food chain restaurant relocated its accessible parking spaces so that they are directly in front of the entrance.

- The owners of a medical office building in a small town in Louisiana provided three accessible parking spaces and ramps to a walkway that had formerly impeded access.

- An auto supply store in a small Indiana town removed posts that were barriers to its check-out aisle.

Other Settlements

46

- An upstate New York athletic club agreed to install a ramp to its indoor running track area and to make its weightlifting equipment accessible.

- A Colorado-based rental car company purchased universal hand controls for its rental car fleet and made cars equipped with these controls available on two days' or less notice under most circumstances. The company also modified its policies so that persons with disabilities no longer have to "test drive" hand control equipped rental cars.

- A Wyoming outlet of a national chain of discount department stores restriped its parking lot to provide accessible spaces, installed automatic entrance doors, and agreed to modify its lunch counter to be accessible.

- The owners of two motels in Branson, Missouri, restriped the motels' parking lots to have accessible parking spaces on the shortest accessible route to rooms and amenities, and installed curb ramps.

- A restaurant in a small town in North Carolina, part of a national family restaurant chain, restriped the parking lot to have accessible spaces on the shortest accessible route to the building entrance.

- The Des Moines, Iowa, affiliate of a nationwide rental car company will provide hand controls for persons with disabilities.

Effective communication

- The operators of a multiplex motion picture theater in New York City acquired a permanently installed assistive listening system for each of its six auditoriums and purchased receivers for these systems equal in number to at least four percent of the available seats.

Other Settlements

- An Idaho ski resort lodge acquired equipment necessary to make seven of its rooms accessible to persons with hearing impairments, acquired a TDD for its front desk so that customers who use TDDs will have access to in-room services available to other customers, and agreed to provide training to its staff in the proper use of the equipment.

- A Missouri hotel is now providing TDD's and other devices to hotel guests who have hearing impairments.

Policies and procedures

- Seven gas stations in western States agreed to pump gasoline at no extra charge for persons with disabilities (when there is more than one attendant on duty) and to post signs at the pumps notifying customers of this service.

D. Investigations

The Department is currently investigating nearly 1100 complaints against public accommodations and commercial facilities under title III. The Department also, on its own initiative, is reviewing plans for new construction and alterations of various types of facilities in locations around the country.

In addition, the Department is currently investigating nearly 1400 complaints against units of State and local government under title II. Seven other Federal agencies are also investigating title II complaints and may refer cases to the Department of Justice for litigation.

The Department also has a number of investigations under way under title I against public employers. (Enforcement of title I against private employers is handled by the Equal Employment Opportunity Commission.)

II. Certification of State and Local Building Codes

The ADA authorizes the Department of Justice to certify State or local laws or building codes that meet or exceed the ADA's accessibility requirements. This is a voluntary program in which States and localities can choose to participate. In a jurisdiction whose law or code has been certified, when a new public accommodation or other commercial facility is built or an existing facility is altered or expanded, compliance with the local regulations will give the building owner and other responsible parties rebuttable evidence of compliance with the ADA if the building's accessibility is later challenged under the ADA.

In July 1994, the Department notified the State of Washington that its review has revealed a few remaining areas in which the Washington code is not fully equivalent to the ADA and indicated that, upon correction of those problems, a preliminary certification of the code could be issued. The Washington request was the first request for certification received by the Department. The Department's initial review revealed that the Washington accessibility code, although very progressive, was not fully equivalent to the ADA. Therefore, the Department provided substantial technical assistance to assist the State to make its code equivalent. The State of Washington is now proposing to amend its code to correct the problems identified by the Department. This process is expected to be completed by mid-November.

Requests for certification have also been received from New Mexico, Utah, Florida, and the City of New York. Technical assistance has been requested by the Council of American Building Officials (CABO) on behalf of the American National Standards Institute (ANSI) A117.1 committee, the Building Officials and Code Administrators International (BOCA), and the National Parking Association.

Title II Proposed Rule

The Department of Justice is now reviewing the comments on its proposed rule to amend title II's accessibility standards for new construction and alterations. The public comment period closed on August 19, 1994. The proposed rule would adopt the ADA Accessibility Guidelines as the ADA Standards for Accessible Design for new construction and alterations covered by title II. Under the proposed amendment, title II entities would no longer have the option to apply the Uniform Federal Accessibility Standards.

The proposed rule would also amend the ADA Standards in several ways and add sections 11 through 14 dealing with judicial, legislative, and regulatory facilities, detention and correctional facilities, residential housing, and public rights-of-way. Finally, the proposal would publish the amended ADA Standards for Accessible Design as part 38 of 28 C.F.R., deleting them from Appendix A of part 36 of 28 C.F.R., and would amend title III to refer to part 38.

III. Technical Assistance

The ADA requires the Department of Justice to provide technical assistance to entities and individuals with rights and responsibilities under the ADA. The Department encourages voluntary compliance by providing education and technical assistance to business, industry, government, and members of the general public through a variety of means.

ADA Telephone Information Line

The Department of Justice now provides toll-free "800" service for both voice and TDD callers who have questions about title II and title III of the ADA, including the Standards for Accessible Design. Under its expanded hours of operations, operators may be reached from 10:00 a.m. to 6:00 p.m. (EDT), Monday through Friday (except Thursdays, 1:00 p.m. to 6:00 p.m.). The system has been upgraded to accommodate a larger number of callers simultaneously and to provide Spanish language service. Callers may hear recorded information and order materials at any time day or night. **The information line numbers are:**

> **Nationwide**
> **1-800-514-0301 (voice)**
> **1-800-514-0383 (TDD)**
>
> **Washington, D.C., area**
> **202-514-0301 (voice)**
> **202-514-0383 (TDD)**

Grants

Section 506 of the ADA requires the Department to provide technical assistance to entities and individuals affected by title II and title III of the ADA. This section also authorizes the Department to award grants for the purpose of supplementing the Department's technical assistance efforts.

Under the 1994 Technical Assistance Grant Program, the Department awarded ten grants to the following organizations:

Access Video Fund -- to develop, produce, and distribute a 30-minute documentary, to be aired nationally, to educate the public on the ADA, dispel myths and stereotypes about people with disabilities, and illustrate the positive impact of the ADA on the lives of people with disabilities.

The Arc -- to produce educational materials for police departments and courts about the rights of persons with mental retardation in law enforcement and judicial proceedings; and to continue to reach out to small businesses across the country, to conduct ADA training sessions, and to operate a toll-free ADA technical assistance line that provides information to Spanish-speaking entities and individuals.

Home Builders Institute -- to distribute ADA educational materials produced by the Department of Justice to 190,000 local building contractors, construction tradespeople, and individuals in construction training programs throughout the country.

Key Bridge Foundation -- to train 90 professional mediators in Dallas-Fort Worth, Detroit, Los Angeles, New York, and Orlando-Tampa on the ADA, develop a consumer and mediator guide, and mediate up to 600 ADA complaints.

The National Trust for Historic Preservation -- to develop and distribute an ADA self-study course for the 1,863 local historic preservation commissions and boards throughout the country to assist in identifying accessibility issues and practical solutions for providing access without destroying a building's historic character.

Adaptive Environments -- to continue a project incorporating universal design concepts and specific ADA "how-to" materials into the curricula of architecture, interior design, industrial design, and landscape architecture schools and programs across the country.

Chief Officers of State Library Agencies (COSLA) -- to expand upon a project that placed ADA materials in 15,000 libraries throughout the country, with an emphasis on ADA videotapes, Spanish translations of ADA material, and additional documents developed by the Department's prior grantees.

Disability Rights Education and Defense Fund (DREDF) -- to continue to operate a toll-free ADA information line (1-800-466-4232 (voice & TDD)) to assist persons with disabilities and covered entities with inquiries about the requirements of the ADA, increasing the availability of technical assistance throughout the country, especially for citizens living in the Mountain and Pacific time zones.

Police Executive Research Forum (PERF) -- to expand educational materials for police officers about persons who are deaf, persons with epilepsy, and persons with mental illness.

Publications

Copies of the Department of Justice's regulations for titles II and III of the ADA, the ADA Questions and Answers booklet, the ADA Handbook (limited quantities available), and information about the Department's technical assistance grant program can be obtained by calling the Department's toll-free ADA Telephone Information Line at the number listed above or writing to the address listed below. These materials are available in standard print, large print, Braille, audiotape, and computer disk.

> U.S. Department of Justice
> Civil Rights Division
> Public Access Section
> Post Office Box 66738
> Washington, D.C. 20035-6738

These materials are also available through the Department of Justice's ADA electronic bulletin board at 202-514-6193.

Copies of the Department of Justice's Technical Assistance Manuals for titles II and III and yearly updates can be obtained by subscription from the Government Printing Office. The subscription for the Title II Manual, which includes annual supplements through 1996, costs $24. The subscription for the Title III Manual with supplements through 1996 costs $25. Call the ADA Telephone Information Line to obtain an order form.

Copies of legal documents and settlement agreements mentioned in this publication can be obtained by writing to:

> Freedom of Information/Privacy Act Branch
> Civil Rights Division
> Administrative Management Section
> P.O. Box 65310
> Washington, D.C. 20035-5310

Attorney General Launches National Public Education Campaign

As part of its continuing effort to educate Americans about the ADA, the Justice Department has launched a major national public education campaign. The campaign, which seeks to increase awareness of the landmark law and encourage voluntary compliance, includes distributing public service announcements to media markets and informational kits to libraries across the country.

The public service announcements, which include both radio and television spots, feature Attorney General Janet Reno stressing the importance of the law. The following 60-second radio spot, entitled "Getting In the Door," will be distributed to over 1,000 radio stations:

BACKGROUND:
- Martin Luther King saying, "I have a dream."

ATTORNEY GENERAL JANET RENO:
- "Talk about "civil rights" and people think about a lot of things ... Martin Luther King, the March on Washington, the women's fight for equality.
- But for *one out of seven* Americans, equality means just being able to get in the door, make a phone call, hear a movie, or get a job.
- Now, thanks to the Americans with Disabilities Act, the simplest things in life are no longer barriers to America's 49 million people with disabilities.
- I'm Janet Reno, U.S. Attorney General. If you're not sure what's required under the Americans with Disabilities Act, please call 1-800-514-0301 or visit your local library.
- Again, that's 1-800-514-0301.
- Because the ADA isn't just the way things *should* be -- now it's the *law*."

Two other television spots, which run for 30 and 15 seconds, will be distributed to over 1,800 television stations.

Additionally, the Justice Department is providing 15,000 public libraries with an "ADA Information File." The file was developed and distributed with the help of the Chief Officers of State Library Agencies.

In announcing this educational effort at Washington's Martin Luther King Library, Reno stated that "the library is the center of community life where people from all walks of life go to get the information they need." The file includes over 30 documents offering general information on the ADA's requirements as well as specific information on how various entities can comply with the law. The documents were developed by the Department of Justice and its grantees and other Federal agencies.

To ensure the success of the campaign, the Justice Department will ask citizens to encourage television and radio stations in their communities to air the public service announcements. If a station has not already received the announcements, please contact Lee Douglass, Department of Justice Office of Public Affairs at (202) 616-2765.

51

IV. Other Sources of ADA Information

The *Equal Employment Opportunity Commission* offers technical assistance to the public concerning title I of the ADA.

For ordering documents
1-800-669-3362 (voice)
1-800-800-3302 (TDD)

For questions
1-800-669-4000 (voice)
TDD: use relay service

*   *   *

The *U.S. Department of Transportation* offers technical assistance to the public concerning the public transportation provisions of title II and title III of the ADA.

ADA documents and general questions
202-366-1656 (voice)
202-366-4567 (TDD)

ADA legal questions
202-366-1936 (voice)
202-366-0748 (TDD)

Complaints and enforcement
202-366-2285 (voice)
202-366-0153 (TDD)

National Easter Seal Society
"Project Action" grant
202-347-3066 (voice)
202-347-7385 (TDD)

*   *   *

The *Federal Communications Commission* offers technical assistance to the public concerning title IV of the ADA.

ADA documents and general questions
202-418-0500 (voice)
202-632-6999 (TDD)

ADA legal questions
202-634-1808 (voice)
202-632-0484 (TDD)

Complaints and enforcement
202-632-7553 (voice)
202-632-0485 (TDD)

*   *   *

The *U.S. Architectural and Transportation Barriers Compliance Board, or "Access Board,"* offers technical assistance to the public on the ADA Accessibility Guidelines.

ADA documents and questions
1-800-872-2253 (voice)
1-800-993-2822 (TDD)
202-272-5434 (voice)
202-272-5449 (TDD)

*   *   *

The *National Institute on Disability and Rehabilitation Research (NIDRR)* of the U.S. Department of Education has funded centers in ten regions of the country to provide technical assistance to the public concerning title I, title II, and title III of the ADA.

ADA technical assistance nationwide
1-800-949-4232 (voice & TDD)

*   *   *

The *Job Accommodation Network (JAN)* is a free telephone consulting service funded by the President's Committee on Employment of People with Disabilities. It provides information and advice to employers and people with disabilities on reasonable accommodation in the workplace.

Information on workplace accommodation
1-800-526-7234 (voice & TDD)

52

V. How to File Complaints

Title I

Complaints about violations of title I (employment) by units of State and local government or by private employers should be filed with the Equal Employment Opportunity Commission. Call 1-800-669-4000 for the field office in your area.

Title II

Complaints about violations of title II by units of State and local government should be filed with -

U.S. Department of Justice
Civil Rights Division
Coordination and Review Section
Post Office Box 66118
Washington, D.C. 20035-6118
202-307-2222 (Voice)
202-307-2678 (TDD)

Title III

Complaints about violations of title III by public accommodations and commercial facilities should be filed with -

U.S. Department of Justice
Civil Rights Division
Public Access Section
Post Office Box 66738
Washington, D.C. 20035-6738

53

U.S. Department of Justice
Civil Rights Division
Disability Rights Section

Enforcing the ADA

A Status Report Update from the Department of Justice

(October - December 1994)

      This Status Report Update covers the ADA activities of the Department of Justice during the fourth quarter (October-December) of 1994. Copies of the April 4, 1994, Status Report (which summarizes all activities up to that date), and the updates for the second and third quarters of 1994 are available through our ADA Telephone Information Line (see page 9.)

INSIDE...

The Americans with Disabilities Act (ADA) is a comprehensive civil rights law for people with disabilities. The Department of Justice enforces the ADA's requirements in three areas -

Title I: Employment practices by units of State and local government

Title II: Programs, services, and activities of State and local government

Title III: Public accommodations and commercial facilities

I. Enforcement

Through lawsuits and both formal and informal settlement agreements, the Department has achieved greater access for individuals with disabilities in over 300 cases. Under general rules governing lawsuits brought by the Federal Government, the Department of Justice may not file a lawsuit unless it has first unsuccessfully attempted to settle the dispute through negotiations.

A. Litigation

The Department may file lawsuits in Federal court to enforce the ADA and may obtain court orders including compensatory damages and back pay to remedy discrimination. Under title III the Department may also obtain civil penalties of up to $50,000 for the first violation and $100,000 for any subsequent violation.

1. New lawsuits

The Department initiated, or intervened in, the following lawsuits.

Title I

United States v. City of Pontiac, Michigan -- The Department sued the City of Pontiac for failing to hire Dennis Henderson as a firefighter because of his disability. Mr. Henderson, who lost the sight of his right eye and is medically classified as having monocular vision, has extensive firefighter experience, training, and certifications. His scores on the pre-hire examinations placed him seventh out of approximately 107 applicants on the firefighter new hire civil service list. Pontiac, however, refused to hire Henderson because of his disability. This case stems from a referral of a charge filed by Mr. Henderson with the Equal Employment Opportunity Commission.

Title III

U.S. v. James O. Moyes (d.b.a. Bear Lake Tavern) -- The Department filed a lawsuit against the owner of the Bear Lake Tavern, a restaurant and local landmark in northern Michigan, alleging that he has violated title III of the ADA by failing to take readily achievable steps to remove barriers to the restrooms and other interior elements.

2. Consent decrees

Some litigation is resolved at the time the suit is filed or afterwards by means of a negotiated consent decree. Consent decrees are monitored and enforced by the Federal court in which they are entered.

Title III

United States v. Lira Limited -- The Department settled by consent decree its lawsuit against the Barolo Grill, a restaurant in Denver, Colorado. In November 1992, the Barolo's owners altered the restaurant without complying with the ADA when they constructed a raised dining area with no ramp or lift for persons who use wheelchairs. In the consent order, the defendants admit that they made alterations that were not accessible, did not take any steps to improve the path of travel and took no steps to remove barriers where removal was readily achievable. The order requires the defendants to correct access problems throughout the restaurant, including the installation of a ramp to the new raised dining area. The order also requires defendants to pay $10,000 in civil penalties and $6,000 in damages to four individuals. Defendants have also agreed to host an ADA information seminar to inform other restaurants in Colorado about their responsibilities under the law.

United States v. Reunion Hotel/Tower Joint Venture, et al. -- The Department filed, and resolved by consent decree, a lawsuit involving accessibility problems at the Hyatt Regency Dallas Hotel. Under the consent decree, the Hyatt Corporation and the owners and asset managers of the Hyatt Regency Dallas Hotel agreed to provide 28 fully accessible guest rooms; to modify three sets of restrooms on the first, second, and third floors of the hotel to make them accessible; and to construct ramps providing access to the hotel's swimming pool and hot tub areas. The defendants will also offer 24 individuals with disabilities

compensation in the form of either a return visit to the hotel at the defendants' expense or $1,500 in cash. The consent decree resolved a lawsuit filed on the same day as the consent decree by the Department of Justice in the United States District Court for the Northern District of Texas. The suit alleged that the Hyatt Corporation, which operates the facility, violated title III of the ADA by failing to remove architectural barriers to access where it is readily achievable to do so. Also named as a defendant was the partnership that owns the facility, and its asset manager, the Woodbine Development Corporation. The lawsuit arose from a complaint filed with the Department by several children and adults who attended a conference of the Spina Bifida Association of America at the landmark hotel in June 1992.

3. Amicus Briefs

The Department files briefs in selected ADA cases in which it is not a party in order to guide courts in interpreting the ADA.

Title II

Clark v. Virginia Board of Bar Examiners -- The Department of Justice has filed a number of amicus briefs in this case in the U.S. District Court for the Eastern District of Virginia which challenge inquiries made of Virginia bar applicants about their past mental health treatment history. The Department successfully urged the court to deny defendant's motion for summary judgment. Most recently, the government filed a brief addressing the merits of the case, urging the court to rule that defendant violated title II of the ADA by unnecessarily inquiring broadly into applicants' mental health treatment history. Trial in the case is scheduled for January 1995.

Title III

Neff v. American Dairy Queen -- The Department of Justice filed an amicus brief in the U.S. Court of Appeals for the Fifth Circuit arguing that American Dairy Queen, the national franchisor of Dairy Queen stores, is covered by the ADA as a public accommodation under title III. The plaintiff, a person with a mobility impairment who uses a wheelchair, alleges that American Dairy Queen failed to remove barriers to access in two franchisee-run stores in San Antonio, Texas. The United States District Court for the Western District of Texas granted summary judgment on behalf of the defendant on the ground that, as franchisor, American Dairy Queen does not own, operate, or lease the two stores and therefore could not be held liable as a public accommodation under the ADA. The Department's brief on appeal argues that American Dairy Queen retains enough control in its franchise agreement over the two stores that it can be said to be operating the stores within the meaning of title III and therefore is subject to the ADA's barrier removal requirements.

Chipkevich v. University of Scranton -- The Department participated in this case on appeal in the U.S. Court of Appeals for the Third Circuit to defend the constitutionality of the exemption for religious organizations. The plaintiff sued the University under title III of the ADA and section 504 of the Rehabilitation Act alleging that the school had failed to provide appropriate accommodations for his learning disability. The district court ruled in plaintiff's favor under section 504 but dismissed the ADA claim, finding that the University is an exempt religious organization under title III. On appeal, plaintiff conceded that the University is a religious organization but challenged the breadth of the exemption, arguing that it would be unconstitutional under the First Amendment as an establishment of religion to exempt all activities of the University. The Department argued that the broad exemption does not violate the First Amendment.

Amicus Briefs

Ruling Supports Integrated Seating in Union Station Case

The U.S. District Court for the District of Columbia denied defendant's motion for summary judgment in *Fiedler v. American Multi-Cinema, Inc.*, a case in which the Department filed a brief supporting plaintiff's demand for integrated movie theater seating. The court agreed with the Department that (1) the ADA applies to public accommodations located in space leased from the Executive branch of the Federal government, (2) existing motion picture theaters having more than 300 seats must disperse wheelchair seating locations if it is readily achievable for them to do so, and (3) plaintiff was entitled to a trial on the merits of defendant's assertion that, in an emergency, plaintiff and other individuals who use wheelchairs would constitute a "direct threat" to the health and safety of others if they were allowed to sit in wheelchair seating locations other than at the back of the theater.

B. Formal Settlement Agreements

The Department sometimes resolves cases without filing a lawsuit, by means of formal written settlement agreements.

Title II

Bell Gardens, California -- The Bell Gardens Police Department agreed to provide effective communication with members of the public who are deaf or hard of hearing, including arrestees. This agreement resolved a complaint alleging that the police department failed to provide a sign language interpreter as requested by an individual who was arrested. The police department adopted a policy of providing auxiliary aids and services, including sign language interpreters, in situations where necessary to afford effective communication, and will notify the public and provide training for court personnel about its policies on effective communication.

Manhattan, Montana -- This small Montana town agreed to make its town programs accessible through a combination of town hall renovations and alternative nonstructural measures. The town agreed to install a ramp at one entrance, make the route to this entrance accessible, create one van-accessible parking space, and make the water fountain and bathroom on the first floor accessible. In addition, town council meetings will be moved to the first floor when necessary.

Pickens County, South Carolina -- The Pickens County Court agreed to provide effective communication with individuals who are deaf or hard of hearing. This agreement resolved a complaint that the court denied the request of a woman who is hard of hearing that her daughter be permitted to assist her while she testified by repeating questions so that the complainant could understand them. The court adopted a policy to provide auxiliary aids and services when necessary to afford effective communication, and to give primary consideration to the request of an individual with a disability for a specific aid or service. The court will notify the public and train court personnel about these policies.

Saginaw Township, Michigan -- The Saginaw Township Police Department agreed to provide effective communication with members of the public who are deaf or hard of hearing, resolving a complaint that the police department had failed to provide a sign language interpreter for an arrestee.

Title III

Volume Services, San Francisco, California -- Volume Services, which operates concessions and souvenir facilities at Candlestick Park in San Francisco, has agreed to modify all of its service counters in order to make them accessible to individuals who use wheelchairs, and to make other structural changes, such as adding skirting to protruding objects that would otherwise present a hazard to some individuals with visual impairments. Volume Services has further agreed to implement policies ensuring full and equal access to individuals with disabilities and to implement an employee training program for providing nondiscriminatory service. Under the settlement agreement, Volume Services will also pay $60,000 to a group of complainants and $20,000 to the Disability Rights Education and Defense Fund for attorney's and expert fees. In addition, Volume Services will pay $15,000 to the United States.

Smith Barney, Inc., Washington, D.C. -- The Department reached a formal settlement with Smith Barney, a nationwide financial planning services company, as a result of which Smith Barney will provide financial statements and correspondence in large print to its customers

Formal Settlement Agreements

with vision impairments. (Smith Barney already provides documents in Braille.) The enlarged print documents will be provided free of charge, upon request. Smith Barney will also pay a person who filed a complaint with the Department $1,500. Notice of the service will be sent to 55,000 new customers, and over 40,000 potential customers, each month.

Atrium Mall, Chestnut Hill, Massachusetts -- Atrium Mall provides free shuttle bus service between the Mall and surrounding neighborhoods. The bus provided for this service was not accessible to wheelchair users. As a result of a formal settlement agreement with the Department, the Mall has agreed to lease a wheelchair accessible bus and has paid the complainant $500. This is the first settlement agreement concerning the responsibilities of places of public accommodation to provide accessible transportation.

Formal Settlement Agreements

Bel-Loc Diner, Baltimore, Maryland -- The Department entered into a settlement agreement with the owners and operators of the Bel-Loc Diner, a popular restaurant in Baltimore. Under the terms of the agreement, the owners and operators of the Diner will provide accessible parking spaces, construct a ramp to the Diner's main entrance, and widen the doors in the main entry vestibule. The agreement also requires the Diner to police the use of the accessible parking spaces, make sure they are available for use by individuals with disabilities, and maintain the parking spaces and ramp in good condition, including prompt removal of snow.

Blue Parrot Inn, Key West, Florida -- The Blue Parrot Inn in Key West, Florida, agreed to modify its policy that required a person with a disability

accompanied by a service animal to pay a non-refundable fee for the cost of fumigating the room to exterminate fleas. The Inn agreed to no longer impose the fee, to modify its advertising and brochures accordingly, to educate its staff about the new policy, and to pay the complainant $250 in damages.

C. Other settlements

The Department resolves numerous cases without litigation or a formal settlement agreement. In some instances, the public accommodation, commercial facility, or State or local government promptly agrees to take the necessary actions to achieve compliance. In others, extensive negotiations are required. Following are some examples of what has been accomplished through informal settlements in the fourth quarter of 1994.

Title II

Access to facilities

A city in Iowa agreed to relocate one of its polling places to a facility with an accessible ground floor entrance.

A New Hampshire town agreed to make its programs accessible by renovating the town hall, and relocating or using alternative methods for delivery of certain public library services.

A Florida city agreed to make a polling place accessible by improving an entrance ramp that was too steep for use by individuals who use wheelchairs.

A Missouri city with an old city hall agreed to deliver its services and programs through alternative methods, including sidewalk and mail service, and to move public meetings to accessible locations.

Policies and procedures

A large county in Nevada agreed to address the immediate medical needs of a jailed quadriplegic suspect.

A western State Supreme Court agreed to eliminate questions on its bar application that asked about histories of mental, emotional, and nervous disorders or treatment for use of alcohol and drugs.

Other Settlements

Effective Communication

A small New York community agreed to purchase a public address system in response to a complaint from a hard of hearing citizen who wanted to listen to town board meetings.

A major midwestern State Department of Corrections added a warning light to a forklift to protect inmate workers who are deaf.

A western State court agreed to provide an individual who is hard of hearing with a wireless FM assistive listening system so that he could effectively participate in juvenile proceedings involving his son.

An Ohio court agreed to purchase computerized real-time transcription services for an individual who is hard-of-hearing and cannot effectively use an assistive listening system.

Title III

Access to facilities

A well-known hotel in Ohio agreed to provide ramps to its front lobby and other public areas, additional accessible parking spaces with adequate access aisles, improved accessibility in ten of its guest rooms, and devices for persons with hearing impairments, including TDD's, visual smoke and fire alarms, phone notification devices, and visual door knocks.

Policies and procedures

A dog racing track in Idaho modified it policies to enable persons with mobility impairments to reserve accessible tables and seats, regardless of when they planned to arrive at the track. Its prior reservations policy held tables only until the start of the first race. The track owners also changed the smoking and non-smoking sections to provide accessible tables and seating in each, and removed some barriers to access.

A midwest branch of a national car rental chain agreed to provide hand controls for rental vehicles on 24-hours notice, free of charge, for the entire range of vehicles in its fleet. The company also changed its policy to allow rentals by persons with disabilities who are not licensed drivers. Additionally, the corporate national reservation center dedicated a toll-free telephone line for customers who use TDD's.

D. Investigations

The Department is currently investigating nearly 1100 complaints against public accommodations and commercial facilities under title III. The Department also, on its own initiative, is reviewing plans for new construction and alterations of various types of facilities in locations around the country.

In addition, the Department is currently investigating nearly 1200 complaints against units of State and local government under title II. Seven other Federal agencies are also investigating title II complaints and may refer cases to the Department of Justice for litigation.

The Department also has a number of investigations under way under title I against public employers. (Enforcement of title I against private employers is handled by the Equal Employment Opportunity Commission.)

II. Certification of State and Local Building Codes

The ADA authorizes the Department of Justice to certify State or local laws or building codes that meet or exceed the ADA's accessibility requirements. This is a voluntary program in which States and localities can choose to participate. In a jurisdiction whose law or code has been certified, when a new public accommodation or other commercial facility is built or an existing facility is altered or expanded, compliance with the local regulations will give the building owner and other responsible parties rebuttable evidence of compliance with the ADA, if the building's accessibility is later challenged under the ADA. Certification thus allows local building officials to play a role in ensuring that buildings are constructed to be accessible. It also allows accessibility to be assessed early in the construction process as part of the State or local building permit and inspection processes. Finally, by promoting the incorporation of ADA-equivalent accessibility requirements into local codes, certification makes those requirements more familiar and readily available to local architects and builders, and eliminates possible conflicts with Federal law.

State of Washington -- On December 6, 1994, the Department issued a preliminary determination that the Washington State Regulations for Barrier Free Design meet or exceed the new construction and alterations requirements of the Americans with Disabilities Act. This is the Department's first preliminary determination of the equivalency of a State code. The Department is now beginning the process toward final certification of the Washington code. The remaining steps before a final determination in the certification process will include public notice, a sixty-day public comment period, and informal public hearings in the State of Washington and in Washington, D.C.

The Washington State request for certification was the first received by the Department. The Department's initial review showed that the Washington code was highly progressive regarding accessibility issues and was nearly equivalent to the ADA requirements. The Department provided extensive technical assistance to the Washington Building Code Council to assist in the development of a fully equivalent code. In August 1994, in response to comments by the Department, the Building Code Council proposed amendments to the Washington code to address the remaining areas of nonequivalency. Those amendments received final approval in November.

New York City -- In October 1994, the Department denied a request for certification of New York City's code, which had not been amended since the ADA Standards were issued. The Department's response to the City included a detailed comparison of the submitted code and the ADA Standards for Accessible Design. In addition, the Department provided technical assistance with respect to proposed code amendments.

State of Texas -- On December 1, 1994, the State of Texas became the sixth jurisdiction to make a formal request for certification of its standards.

Requests for certification have also been received from New Mexico, Utah, and Florida. Technical assistance has been requested by the City of New York, the Council of American Building Officials (CABO) on behalf of the

American National Standards Institute (ANSI) A117.1 committee, the Building Officials and Code Administrators International (BOCA), and the National Parking Association.

III. Technical Assistance

The ADA requires the Department of Justice to provide technical assistance to entities and individuals with rights and responsibilities under the ADA. The Department encourages voluntary compliance by providing education and technical assistance to business, industry, government, and members of the general public through a variety of means. Our activities include providing direct technical assistance and guidance to the public through our ADA Information Line and other activities, developing and reviewing technical assistance materials, disseminating technical assistance materials to the public and undertaking outreach initiatives, operating an ADA technical assistance grant program, and coordinating ADA technical assistance government-wide.

The Department sent technical assistance materials to the mayors of 1,053 medium and large-size cities across the United States to help them meet their obligations under title II of the ADA. Assistant Attorney General Deval L. Patrick also urged mayors to contact the Department's toll-free ADA Information Line to obtain further information and assistance.

ADA Telephone Information Line

The Department of Justice now provides toll-free "800" service for both voice and TDD callers who have questions about title II and title III of the ADA, including the Standards for Accessible Design. Under its expanded hours of operations, operators may be reached from 10:00 a.m. to 6:00 p.m. (EDT), Monday through Friday (except Thursdays, 1:00 p.m. to 6:00 p.m.). The system has been upgraded to accommodate a larger number of callers simultaneously and to provide Spanish language service. Callers may hear recorded information and order materials at any time day or night. **The information line numbers are:**

> **Nationwide**
> **1-800-514-0301 (voice)**
> **1-800-514-0383 (TDD)**

Publications

Copies of the Department of Justice's regulations for titles II and III of the ADA, the ADA Questions and Answers booklet, the ADA Handbook (limited quantities available), and information about the Departments technical assistance grant program can be obtained by calling the Department's toll-free ADA Telephone Information Line at the number listed above or writing to the address listed below. These materials are available in standard print, large print, Braille, audiotape, and computer disk.

> U.S. Department of Justice
> Civil Rights Division
> Disability Rights Section
> Post Office Box 66738
> Washington, D.C. 20035-6738

Copies of the Department of Justice's Technical Assistance Manuals for titles II and III and yearly updates can be obtained by subscription from the Government Printing Office. The subscription fee for the Title II Manual, which includes annual supplements through 1996, is $24. The subscription fee for the Title III Manual with supplements through 1996 is $25. Call the ADA Telephone Information Line to obtain an order form.

Copies of legal documents and settlement agreements mentioned in this publication can be obtained by writing to:

> Freedom of Information/Privacy Act Branch
> Room 7337
> Civil Rights Division
> U.S. Department of Justice
> Washington, D.C. 20530

Electronic Access to ADA Documents

The Department of Justice operates an electronic bulletin board system (BBS) that contains its ADA regulations and technical assistance materials as well as some materials from other Federal agencies. These can be downloaded by computer modem by dialing 202-514-6193. The BBS can also be accessed through the Internet. The access codes are telnet fedworld.gov Gateway D, choice D #9.

The Department also has placed a variety of its ADA materials directly on the Internet, including press releases on ADA cases and ADA regulations and technical assistance materials. These materials can be accessed with gopher client software (gopher.usdoj.gov), through other gopher servers (choose 9 for North America, 4 for USA, 1 for All, and look for DOJ, which currently is option 342), with World Wide Web software (http://www.usdoj.gov), or through the White House WWW server (http://www.whitehouse.gov). The Department's press releases are located under the Office of Public Affairs. Other ADA materials are located under Litigating Organizations, Civil Rights Division.

IV. Other Sources of ADA Information

The *Equal Employment Opportunity Commission* offers technical assistance to the public concerning title I of the ADA.

For ordering documents
1-800-669-3362 (voice)
1-800-800-3302 (TDD)

For questions
1-800-669-4000 (voice)
TDD: use relay service

*   *   *

The *U.S. Department of Transportation* offers technical assistance to the public concerning the public transportation provisions of title II and title III of the ADA.

ADA documents and general questions
202-366-1656 (voice)
202-366-4567 (TDD)

ADA legal questions
202-366-1936 (voice)
202-366-0748 (TDD)

Complaints and enforcement
202-366-2285 (voice)
202-366-0153 (TDD)

National Easter Seal Society
Project Action grant
202-347-3066 (voice)
202-347-7385 (TDD)

*   *   *

The *Federal Communications Commission* offers technical assistance to the public concerning title IV of the ADA.

ADA documents and general questions
202-418-0500 (voice)
202-632-6999 (TDD)

ADA legal questions
202-634-1808 (voice)
202-632-0484 (TDD)

Complaints and enforcement
202-632-7553 (voice)
202-632-0485 (TDD)

*   *   *

The *U.S. Architectural and Transportation Barriers Compliance Board, or "Access Board,"* offers technical assistance to the public on the ADA Accessibility Guidelines.

ADA documents and questions
1-800-872-2253 (voice)
1-800-993-2822 (TDD)
202-272-5434 (voice)
202-272-5449 (TDD)

*   *   *

The *National Institute on Disability and Rehabilitation Research (NIDRR)* of the U.S. Department of Education has funded centers in ten regions of the country to provide technical assistance to the public concerning title I, title II, and title III of the ADA.

ADA technical assistance nationwide
1-800-949-4232 (voice & TDD)

*   *   *

The *Job Accommodation Network (JAN)* is a free telephone consulting service funded by the President's Committee on Employment of People with Disabilities. It provides information and advice to employers and people with disabilities on reasonable accommodation in the workplace.

Information on workplace accommodation
1-800-526-7234 (voice & TDD)

Learn About the ADA in Your Local Library

To make access to ADA information as easy as a trip to your local library, the Department of Justice, through a grant to the Kansas State Library and the Chief Officers of State Libraries Agencies (COSLA), has sent an ADA Information File containing 35 technical assistance documents to 15,000 libraries across the country. Most libraries have placed the File at the reference desk. The Information File contains the following materials:

LAW AND REGULATIONS

Public Law 101-336
The Americans with Disabilities Act of 1990 as enacted by Congress.

Title II Regulation
The final rule implementing subtitle A of title II of the Americans with Disabilities Act which prohibits discrimination on the basis of disability by public entities.

Title III Regulation
The final rule implementing title III of the Americans with Disabilities Act which prohibits discrimination on the basis of disability by public accommodations and commercial facilities.

Title III Regulation; Transportation Facilities and Accessible Automated Teller Machines (ATMs) (1/18/94)
The final rule that amends Appendix A to the Department of Justice regulation implementing title III of the Americans with Disabilities Act by incorporating accessibility guidelines for transportation facilities and by adopting amendments to the reach range requirement for accessible automated teller machines and fare vending machines.

Title III Regulation; Detectable Warnings; Joint (4/12/94)
The joint final rule that temporarily suspends until July 26, 1996, the requirements in the ADA Standards for Accessible Design for detectable warnings at curb ramps, hazardous vehicular areas, and reflecting pools.

continued...

66

DOCUMENTS PRODUCED BY FEDERAL AGENCIES

Technical Assistance Manuals

Title I Technical Assistance Manual and Resource Directory
A manual developed by the U.S. Equal Employment Opportunity Commission that provides technical information on the employment provisions of the ADA and includes an extensive resource directory of related programs and organizations.

Title II Technical Assistance Manual (1993 edition)
A manual developed by the U. S. Department of Justice, updated annually, that provides technical information on the title II requirements covering State and local government programs and services.

Title III Technical Assistance Manual (1993 edition)
A manual developed by the U.S. Department of Justice, updated annually, that provides technical information on the title III requirements covering public accommodations and commercial facilities.

Status Report

Enforcing the ADA - A Status Report from the U. S. Department of Justice
A 17-page report that provides the current status of DOJ's enforcement efforts, including information on litigation, and formal and informal settlement agreements under titles II and III.

Questions and Answers

ADA Questions and Answers
A pamphlet developed jointly by the U.S. Equal Employment Opportunity Commission and the U. S. Department of Justice that contains the most frequently asked questions about titles I, II, and III.

BUSINESSES

Food Industry

ADA Answers for Foodservice Operators
A 48-page guide developed under a DOJ grant by the National Restaurant Association and the National Center for Access Unlimited that provides an overview of the title III requirements that affect the food industry.

continued...

Facilities Survey & Budget Book (Supermarkets)
A 22-page survey and budget document developed under a DOJ grant by the Food Marketing Institute that focuses on removal of barriers in supermarkets.

Grocery Stores: Access Equals Opportunity
A 30-page booklet developed under a DOJ grant by the Council of Better Business Bureaus Foundation that addresses compliance issues under title III for grocery stores.

Restaurants & Bars: Access Equals Opportunity
A 30-page booklet developed under a DOJ grant by the Council of Better Business Bureaus Foundation that addresses compliance issues under title III for restaurants and bars.

Ten Step Action Plan (Supermarkets)
A brochure developed under a DOJ grant by the Food Marketing Institute that outlines an action plan to be used by supermarkets in achieving compliance with the ADA.

Health Care Facilities

ADA: Answers to Questions Most Commonly Asked by Hospitals and Health Care Providers
A 12-page brochure developed under a DOJ grant by the National Rehabilitation Hospital that answers the questions most frequently asked by health care providers about their obligations under the ADA.

Information for Persons with Disabilities: Access to Public and Private Health Care
A brochure developed under a DOJ grant by the National Rehabilitation Hospital that explains the obligations of health care providers under titles II and III.

Medical Offices: Access Equals Opportunity
A 30-page booklet developed under a DOJ grant by the Council of Better Business Bureaus Foundation that addresses compliance issues under title III for medical and health care facilities.

Self-Evaluation Checklist for Health Care Facilities
A 44-page checklist developed under a DOJ grant by the American Foundation for the Blind that provides guidance for health care providers in making their services and facilities accessible for persons who are blind, deaf-blind, or visually impaired.

Hotels and Motels

Accommodating All Guests; The ADA and the Lodging Industry
A 70-page guide developed under a DOJ grant by the American Hotel & Motel Association that provides information on the requirements of the ADA as they apply to the lodging industry.

continued...

Self-Evaluation Checklist for Hotels and Motels
A 36-page checklist developed under a DOJ grant by the American Foundation for the Blind that provides guidance for hotels and motels in making their services and facilities accessible for persons who are blind, deaf-blind, or visually impaired.

Child Care

Child Care Settings and the ADA
A two-page fact sheet developed under a DOJ grant by The Arc that provides information on the ADA requirements that apply to child care centers and family day care homes.

Other

Car Sales & Service: Access Equals Opportunity
A 30-page booklet developed under a DOJ grant by the Council of Better Business Bureaus Foundation that addresses compliance issues under title III for automobile dealers, rental establishments, and service stations

Fun & Fitness Centers: Access Equals Opportunity
A 30-page booklet developed under a DOJ grant by the Council of Better Business Bureaus Foundation that addresses compliance issues under title III for recreation facilities and fitness centers.

Retail Stores: Access Equals Opportunity
A 30-page booklet developed under a DOJ grant by the Council of Better Business Bureaus Foundation that addresses compliance issues under title III for retail stores.

COMMUNICATION ACCESS

Communication and the ADA
A four-page fact sheet developed under a DOJ grant by the American Speech-Language-Hearing Association that provides guidance on complying with the ADA requirements for communicating effectively with persons who have hearing or speech impairments.

Communication Fact Sheet
A two-page fact sheet developed under a DOJ grant by the American Speech-Language-Hearing Association that provides an overview of various communication disabilities and methods that can be used to achieve effective communication.

continued...

Of Consuming Interest: A Guide to Titles II and III of the ADA for People with Vision Loss

A 49-page guide developed under a DOJ grant by the American Foundation for the Blind presented in a questions and answers format that contains information about the ADA for individuals who are blind, deaf-blind, or visually impaired.

Testing Accommodations for Persons with Disabilities: A Guide for Licensure, Certification and Credentialing

A 20-page manual developed under a DOJ grant by The Association on Higher Education and Disability that is aimed at agencies that administer or utilize tests for licensure, certification, or credentialing.

Toward Equal Access: Providing Information Access Services to Blind and Visually Impaired Persons Under the ADA

An eight-page booklet developed under a DOJ grant by the National Federation of the Blind that provides information on the ADA requirements for providing written material in formats accessible to persons with vision impairments.

STATE AND LOCAL GOVERNMENTS

Take Another Look: Police Response to Seizures and Epilepsy

A 98-page document developed under a DOJ grant by the Police Executive Research Forum that provides law enforcement personnel with information on how to recognize and respond effectively to a person who has a seizure disorder.

Title II Action Guide

A guide developed by Adaptive Environments Center, Inc., under a grant from the National Institute on Disability and Rehabilitative Research, U. S. Department of Education, that explains compliance obligations for State and local government programs and services.

RESOURCE LISTS

ADA Nationwide Resources

A 43-page document developed under a DOJ grant by the Food Marketing Institute that contains a list of Federal resources, regional centers for technical assistance, State councils that provide information and referral services, private organizations, and a list of publications on disability.

Telephone Numbers for ADA Information (U.S. Department of Justice)

A list that contains telephone numbers of Federal agencies responsible for providing information about the ADA and organizations funded by the Federal Government to provide ADA information.

V. How to File Complaints

Title I

Complaints about violations of title I (employment) by units of State and local government or by private employers should be filed with the Equal Employment Opportunity Commission. Call 1-800-669-4000 for the field office in your area.

Titles II and III

Complaints about violations of title II by units of State and local government or violations of title III by public accommodations and commercial facilities should be filed with -

U.S. Department of Justice
Civil Rights Division
Disability Rights Section
Post Office Box 66738
Washington, D.C. 20035-6738

71

Chapter Four

MANAGING ADA, OSHA & WORKERS' COMPENSATION

Correct use of job descriptions as a unified management team initiative is a key factor in ensuring cost effective compliance with ADA, OSHA, and Workers' Compensation. In fact, it provides a unique opportunity to reduce the legal complexities of all three of these legal requirements. The Americans with Disabilities Act is a new statute that is not working at cross purposes with your goals for productivity, safety, and quality. Reasonable accommodation, when related to "essential functions," will actually work to *increase* productivity, efficiency, quality, and safety. The outcome is profit.

Key Elements of the Management Program

A Management System that integrates ADA, OSHA, and Workers' Compensation is based on defining essential functions and reasonable accommodation. ADA requires a management strategy to respond systematically to the standards in the law, and productivity requirements that match each essential job function with the unique needs of disabled individuals. The following six program elements meet the mandates of the Americans with Disabilities Act, OSHA (worker safety and reduced injuries), and Workers' Compensation initiatives (injury prevention, loss control and returning people to work after injury).

Planning
Organizations must have a corporate plan to recruit, maintain, return to work, and promote people with disabilities. It is important to plan for disabilities, whether they arise from disease, physical and or mental impairments, injury or aging (loss of stamina or vision, arthritis).

Administrative Controls
Organizations must put into place policies and procedures that guide employees and supervisors in the application of rules and regulations of the workplace. The goal is to improve safety and prevent injury. Examples in offices include ergonomic safety practices such as adjustable seating and taking breaks.

Work Site Assessment
The analysis of high, medium, and low risk jobs will help organizations to maintain safety standards by applying improved job methods in specific environments.

Hazard Engineering

Organizations that have developed a corporate plan will use hazard engineering controls to prevent injury and support productivity. For example, having tools that can be used by both the left and right hand provides "reasonable accommodation" for amputees (ADA). Offering appropriate seating to a person returning to work following surgery (back, carpal tunnel, etc.) is another type of hazard engineering control.

Medical Management

Organizations need medical management strategies that review trends in occupational illnesses and injuries to create safe work environments for all employees, regardless of their functional strengths and limitations. For example, if there is a frequency of cuts to hands and fingers, this indicates a need to make a change. Change could be as simple as increased lighting (task lighting) or providing work gloves.

Training

Organizations should have training for managers, supervisors and employees to maintain productivity and efficiency, while reducing stress and fatigue. Meeting this goal will have a positive outcome for all individuals by empowering employees to have more knowledge and responsibility for their individual safety—both in the workplace and in their lifestyle outside the workplace.

Reasons for a Management Strategy

This management strategy is equally appropriate for all industries, whether service or manufacturing, health care, or schools and universities. The intent is to support employers and employees through what really happens in their lives (aging, injury, disease, and disability). People get injured at work, at home and at play. People have disease. The second most frequent disease in America is Arthritis. With the advent of "high-tech" medicine and new medications, more people in disease are returning to work than ever before.

A management strategy is essential for *three key reasons*. First, there is a productivity goal of cooperation and incentive for improvement between employees and employers built into the Americans with Disabilities Act. Second, there is a positive relationship between the Americans with Disabilities Act, OSHA, and Workers' Compensation. Third, Reasonable Accommodation is intended to address both physical and psychological impairments.

Reason 1: Employers Working with Employees

The goal of Title I of the Americans with Disabilities Act is to prohibit discrimination against a qualified individual with a disability. The spirit of the act for Title I employment is to promote employee/employer involvement. By July 26, 1994, all employers who employ 15 or more workers had to be in compliance. As of April 30, 1993—8,505 ADA charges had been filed with EEOC. This actually represents only 1 of every 1,000 employers. Early on, the trend has been for people with disabilities to work with employers, not against them.

Reason 2: A Positive Relationship

There is a positive relationship between the Americans with Disabilities Act, OSHA, and Workers' Compensation. The Americans with Disabilities Act should be viewed in the context of legal compliance with other acts, in particular the Occupational Safety and Health Act of 1972 and state laws that apply to Workers' Compensation.

It simplifies your legal complexities when you "cross reference" your ADA strategies with all relevant regulatory bodies. This will maintain the highest level of compliance, while minimizing the legal exposure of your organization. A worst case example:

When the ADA was first enacted, a safety manager concluded that, due to his height, a wheelchair user would not be able to use the eye wash in a chemical splash emergency. Consequently, the disabled employee was denied a promotion. The result was an ADA citation on behalf of the employee. The ruling stated that the employer could make "reasonable accommodation" by lowering the eye washer. Further, the disabled employee did not create an eminent threat of risk to himself or others.

Unifying your ADA and OSHA strategies to comply with the Occupational Safety and Health Act limits legal exposure to erroneous assumptions.

OSHA is endeavoring to assure safe and healthy working conditions for working men and women by authorizing enforcement of the standards developed under the Act, by assisting and encouraging states in their efforts to assure safe and healthy working conditions, and by providing for research, information, education, and training in the field of occupational safety and health.

Section 5A of the General Duty Clause states that each employer—(1) shall furnish to each employee employment and a place of employment which are free from recognized hazards that are causing or are likely to cause direct or serious harm to employees; (2) shall comply with occupational safety and health standards promulgated under this Act.

Complying with ADA and OSHA at the same time will save time and money as well as the risk of citation. For example, OSHA has numerous standards (see list) supported by state laws that include notification and record keeping requirements as well as a written program that states the means and methods that employers are taking to ensure compliance and prevention of occupational illness, injury, and fatalities. The written plan is site-specified, and applicable standards are expected to be followed depending on the location of the workplace (confined space standard), the materials and equipment (handling of hazardous materials), equipment (lock out/tag out), substances that are present (air quality), processes used, job methods, and type of services, or product provided (ergonomics).

Standard OSHA training programs include:

- Complete Safety Policy Manual
- Accident Prevention Program
- Lock-out/Tag-out Program
- Respiratory Protection Program
- Hearing Conservation Program
- Employee or Supervisory Safety Training
- Chemical Hygiene Plan
- Hazard Communication Program
- Confined Space Program
- Emergency Action Plan
- Safety and Health Program
- Prevention Maintenance Program
- Assured Equipment Grounding Conductor Program
- Housekeeping Plan
- Crane & Derrick Safety Manual
- Medical Surveillance Program
- Ergonomics Program
- Infection Control Program

- Written Operation Plan for Emergency Situations
- Bio-Safety Manual
- Work Practices Program
- Programs to comply with all substance-specific OSHA standards
- Programs for any other OSHA rule or state law that requires employers to adopt a written program

Integration of ADA and OSHA should pay particular attention to the safety policies and procedures that reduce risk. For example, many people who are mobility impaired are excellent candidates for data entry positions. However, these positions are at risk for the repetitive motion syndrome "Carpal Tunnel Syndrome." Therefore, it is important to access the safety issues of a wheelchair user for the proper "fit" to their work surface, equipment, and materials. Compliance in this case would be to ADA for matching the person's skills to the essential job function, with safety issues reviewed (number of breaks, job task variety, correct placement, and access to equipment), and seeing that the person is trained, not only in job functions, but in safety issues (OSHA). OSHA is currently working on a proposal that would require businesses to identify five "signal risk factors", such as repetitive motions and forceful hand exertions, that might present an ergonomic hazard in the workplace.

ADA and Workers' Compensation laws have to work together because both are written for workers with limitations. The ADA covers people with chronic conditions (permanent, over six months) which is often the case for people who have been injured and desire a "return-to-work status" of full, modified, or temporary adjusted duty. The essence of both laws is the integration of people with disabilities. Both ADA and Workers' Compensation are also interested in the safety of individuals. Six basic objectives underlie Workers' Compensation laws.

1. Provide sure, prompt, and reasonable income and medical benefits to their dependents regardless of fault.
2. Provide a single remedy and reduce court delays, costs, and workloads arising out of personal injury litigation.
3. Relieve public and private charities of financial drains from uncompensated industrial accidents.
4. Eliminate payment of fees to lawyers and witnesses as well as time consuming trials and appeals.
5. Encourage maximum employer interest in safety and rehabilitation through appropriate experience rating mechanisms.
6. Promote frank study of causes of accidents (rather than concealing fault), and reducing preventable accidents and human suffering.

The Americans with Disabilities Act, OSHA, and Workers' Compensation laws overlap significantly on points of accessibility and safety. Therefore, reasonable accommodation strategies can work very well for employers who have available job descriptions that clearly state "essential job functions." With essential job functions defined, an employer can accommodate jobs for disabling conditions while maintaining a safe and productive environment.

See Figure 4.1, a chart that shows how the ADA can affect the outcome of a Workers' Compensation claim.

ADA and Workers Compensation Present a Number of Potential Scenarios

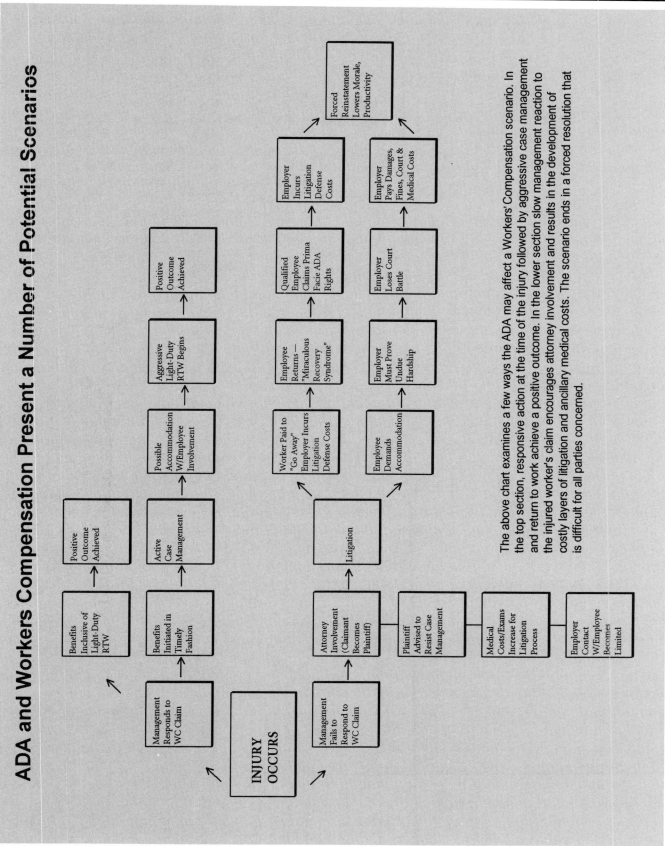

The above chart examines a few ways the ADA may affect a Workers' Compensation scenario. In the top section, responsive action at the time of the injury followed by aggressive case management and return to work achieve a positive outcome. In the lower section slow management reaction to the injured worker's claim encourages attorney involvement and results in the development of costly layers of litigation and ancillary medical costs. The scenario ends in a forced resolution that is difficult for all parties concerned.

Figure 4.1

Reason 3: Physical and Psychological Disability

Under ADA and Workers' Compensation, reasonable accommodation refers to both physical and mental impairments. Stress is becoming compensable under Workers' Compensation and, if chronic, is covered under ADA. (See Figure 4.2, a chart showing the incidence of various types of Workers' Compensation claims.)

Criteria for Reasonable Accommodation

Employee challenges and opportunities are the essence of the Americans with Disabilities Act for the creative employer. People with disabilities usually have more strengths than limitations. They are an active and talented group, as well as an important asset to the labor pool. They should be part of the team who develops strategies for reasonable accommodation according to ADA requirements. Often, both physical and psychological accommodation to environments is necessary to support work activities.

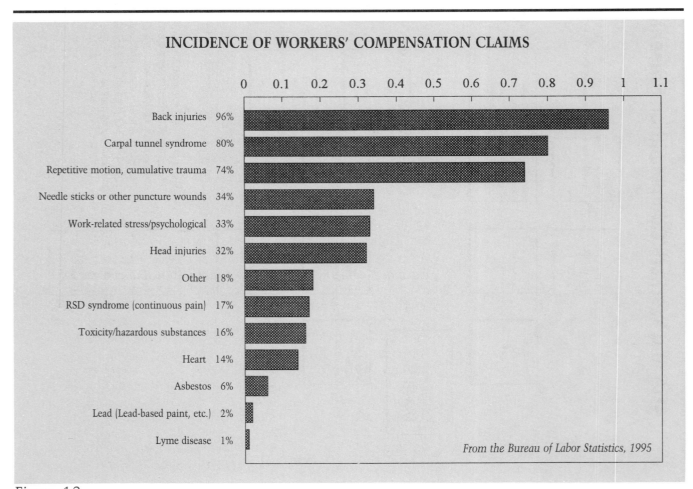

Figure 4.2

The following criteria allow for a creative approach in dealing with both the complex and the simple solutions to reasonable physical and psychological accommodation. The objective of this approach is employer and employee satisfaction.

The most important criteria for Reasonable Accommodation:

1. Job categories should fit the "standard occupational categories" used by the Department of Labor.
2. Employees should have equal access to the resources and materials necessary to the job, such as test equipment, co-worker meeting areas, or parts for assembly.
3. Skills should be added to a job description only if they are considered standard in terms of accepted Department of Labor occupational categories.
4. Use of equipment should be considered as part of reasonable accommodation and universal design. For example, the hearing impaired person uses a telephone by typing the message to be sent and receives a typed response on a small screen which is part of the phone/TDD.
5. Fifty percent of the ADA is devoted to people who are mentally impaired. Do not ignore their importance. For example, people with dyslexia are considered to be mentally impaired by virtue of their brain physiology. A person with dyslexia will accomplish a job function to the desired productivity standard, but may not perform the function in a typical way or time frame.

Accommodating for people with mental impairments is not as simple as not putting a claustrophobic in a confined space, but it is not as difficult as some managers might expect. The most difficult part of accommodating someone with mental difficulties is understanding and accepting the disease from the employee's perspective. With acceptance, strategies for maintaining an employee who is battling mental illness are possible. Additionally, employers must understand that people recover from mental illness; however, it may take as long as ten years and as many as fifty trials with medications. The chances for recovery seem to be increasing with the current medical advances in understanding the "organic" nature of mental illness, e.g., the brain's chemistry.

In general, successful psychological accommodations begin with finding ways to reduce stress. Here are some examples of successful psychological accommodations for employees with a variety of mental disabilities:

- *A person with severe depression was accommodated with an expanded "window" of work opportunity—one that allowed him to work within a productivity standard of one week, instead of daily expectations. Additionally, he was allowed to work at home. This accommodation allowed the person to do his work without fear of penalty for absenteeism during depressive episodes.*
- *A person with Post-Traumatic Stress Syndrome was accommodated by being allowed to avoid all meetings that required that she speak. All of her work summaries were delivered to supervisors and peers by voice mail and memo.*
- *A person with obsessive-compulsive behavior of handwashing was given hand wipes (hundreds per day) by her doctor to use at her desk. The employer accommodated this behavior since it reduced her constant need to take breaks to wash her hands.*

- *Persons with Mental Retardation are often accommodated with job routines that require a minimum of decision making in the form of repetitive tasks.*
- *A person experiencing anxiety attacks was paired with a peer professional for a short period of time who would "fill in" to answer questions when necessary.*

There are many neurotic disorders such as anxiety, personality disorders (such as obsessive-compulsive behaviors), and affective disorders (such as depression) that can be accommodated in the workplace. However, there are disorders that must be treated and accommodated outside the workplace (such as sexual deviations, alcohol and drug dependence). The first rule of accommodation for people with mental disabilities is to develop accommodations that maintain independence and dignity without compromising therapeutic gains. The second rule is the health and safety of all workers. In all cases of accommodation for mental disabilities, it is important when medication is being used for the physician in charge to understand the essential job functions and advise the employee as to any safety risks.

In summary, a management strategy for the integration of ADA, OSHA, and Workers' Compensation is best accomplished with the right team of professionals. Reasonable accommodation through essential job functions is the key to minimizing legal risk. The application of this strategy will help an organization to achieve its goals of productivity, safety, quality, and profitability.

Part Two

ACHIEVING REASONABLE ACCOMMODATION

Part Two

INTRODUCTION

Meeting the needs and meeting the codes of the Americans with Disabilities Act is achieved by implementing "reasonable accommodation." The Act is written to cover two distinct areas of reasonable accommodations: for people with physical disabilities and for people with mental disabilities. The disabilities or "impairments" are defined as those which substantially limit activities such as walking, talking, seeing, hearing or caring for oneself. The goal of the ADA is to design environments that support the strengths that people have, and to "reasonably accommodate" for their limitations.

In order to meet both code requirements and the needs of people with disabilities, three issues must be understood. The first involves addressing the requirements of each title of the ADA.

Title I: Employment

Title II: Public Service and Transportation

Title III: Public Accommodations

Title IV: Telecommunications

The goal of meeting the needs of the disabled is consistent throughout all four titles. Reasonable accommodation has to do with designing environments and policies that allow people to compensate for limitations with environmental and policy supports, such as ramps with handrails and doorways of sufficient width to access a wheelchair.

The second issue, meeting the codes, is determined by understanding which codes apply under which title and applying the codes to a specific site for specific disabilities. For example, a museum must reasonably accommodate both employees (Title 1) and patrons (Title III). While signage is clearly outlined in the ADA guidelines, the lighting for signage may be standardized using American National Standards Institute guidelines. Meeting the codes is also complicated by some state and city standards that are more stringent than the ADA. For example, the state of New York, Massachusetts and Florida Architectural Barrier Guidelines are perceived to be stronger than the ADA.

The third issue is the "case by case" rule within the ADA, which raises a new and high standard for architects and interior designers. In essence, the ADA challenges them to meet the codes and the needs of people with disabilities with environments that are flexible, adaptable, safe, and that will not obsolesce. Designs have to encompass the needs of people with the functional limitations that may be part of being disabled.

Chapter Five

REASONABLE PHYSICAL ACCOMMODATION

The Americans With Disabilities Act, 1990, was written to reduce barriers that limit the opportunity for disabled people to fully participate as potential and permanent employees and consumers. The most frequent question asked regarding the Americans with Disabilities Act, 1990, is "What is reasonable physical accommodation?" The answers to date have been nebulous for two reasons. First, the act was written in a spirit to promote voluntary cooperation. The act is therefore dependent on ethics and makes compliance more complicated by failing to clearly define how one does business in a socially responsible manner. The Equal Employment Opportunity Commission (EEOC) defines reasonable accommodation as "any change in the work environment or in the way things are customarily done that enables an individual with a disability to enjoy equal employment opportunities." The second reason for vague definitions of reasonable accommodation is the bias people have based on the limits of their expertise and experience. The lawyers have one answer, the interior designers another, the architects a third answer, and people with disabilities a fourth, fifth and sixth. Their answers do not necessarily conflict, but they are not cohesive, conclusive, or easily translated into actions. This makes it particularly difficult for facilities managers who wish to provide reasonable physical accommodations that meet the codes, standards, and the statutes of the act, as well as the needs of valued employees and customers.

To define reasonable accommodations for people with physical disabilities, it is important to first define physical disabilities. The act defines physical disabilities as those which substantially limit one or more of life's major activities, including self care, manual tasks, walking, seeing, hearing, speaking, breathing, learning, and importantly, working. The incidence in the population of these disabilities is listed below.

Statistics of Note	
Disability	**Population in Millions**
Blind	1.7
Visually Impaired	13
Communication Difficulty	2.5
Hard of Hearing	7.7
Mobility Impaired	19.2
Wheelchair Users	8

Defining reasonable accommodation for people with physical challenges is complicated by *four critical elements*. These are:

1. the environment in which the person will act as an employee or consumer
2. the standards, codes and statutes which define ADA
3. the number of functional limitations that coincide with each disabling condition
4. the objective of each person interacting in the environment.

Therefore, for facilities managers to design reasonable accommodations to meet Title I requirements, they must systematically follow this six-step audit strategy. (See Parts III and IV for guidance for performing the audit, and evaluation factors.)

First, audit the facility's environments using factors that define and zone the environment into manageable facets. Second, define which standards, codes, and statutes must be applied to each factor. Third, plan solutions based on the range of disabling conditions for which "reasonable accommodations" are being designed. Fourth, at this juncture, to the extent possible, it is important to ask the people for whom you are designing "reasonable accommodations" what they need. Fifth, audit data must be used to design and develop "reasonable accommodations" in a cost effective manner. Sixth, modifications must be carried out. (Criteria must be in place for evaluating the extent to which cost effective strategies were implemented that meet the codes and the needs.) **These six steps represent a valid analytical approach that results in site-specific definitions of "reasonable accommodation," and legally demonstrate that a commitment to the spirit and the statutes of the ADA have been met.**

Step I: Auditing the Environment with Factors

The following 20 factors (explained and tied to specific ADA provisions in Part IV) have been found to be most useful in auditing facilities and structuring designs to meet both the code and the need. The factors cover all issues identified by people with disabilities as critical to their successful use of environments as employees, guests, patrons, and citizens. The factors are used to guide design or modifications by focusing on each area as it relates to a disability. The factors should be reviewed both by each functional limitation, and to assess the overall success of the design.

If a person is in a wheelchair, access is an issue in many parts of a building. Access can be accomplished with ease, or there may be an impediment to mobility, depending on the design. For example, a ramp that is not heated in winter can cause accidents due to the accumulation of ice or snow. Parking lot lights that are not kept in repair can create an extra hazard for people with disabilities. Finishes such as rugs that are a busy pattern of dots can cause people with visual acuity problems to become disoriented. Handrails that have sharp edges can be a safety issue. Furniture that is too densely arranged can be an impediment to mobility. Seating that is uncomfortable can cause lowered productivity.

The 20 Key Factors

- Accessibility
- Adaptability
- Air Quality
- Comfort
- Communication
- Density
- Division of Space
- Equipment
- Finishes
- Furniture
- Image
- Lighting
- Maintenence
- Noise
- Passages
- Safety
- Signage
- Storage
- Temperature
- Windows

Accessibility
Mobility within a space; manipulation of objects and equipment within a space; and ease of participation in activities throughout should be ensured.

Adaptability
Flexible furnishings, equipment and fixtures should allow reasonable accommodation, no matter what the disability.

Air Quality
Ongoing, responsible management of contaminant/odor sources, HVAC systems operations, and the needs of building occupants.

Comfort
Design should fit equipment to people, not people to equipment.

Communication
Communication should be enhanced with quiet rooms and modes of communication that fit the strengths of the person.

Density
A feeling of spaciousness and high visibility are important.

Division of Space
Space should be divided to integrate people around the use of shared equipment. The status of a location for a disabled person is the degree to which access is enhanced.

Equipment
Technology should be provided to enhance capability without compromising disability [controls on computer hardware (keyboards) and software.] Adaptive and assistive devices increase the opportunity to be independent.

Finishes
All surfaces should be easily maintained, with either smooth wall coverings and/or laminated surfaces. Reflectance should be 40 to 60%.

Furniture
Furniture should be adaptable and flexible, designed to enhance the person's strengths and increase their capacity.

Image
Coordination of color and furnishings with existing furnishings enhances image and comfort.

Lighting
Individual task lighting should be provided as needed to prevent fatigue. Full spectrum total room lighting is easiest on one's eyes. Glare control is essential.

Maintenance

Minimum maintenance should be required, thereby reducing attention to the needs of the disabled.

Noise

Noise should be minimized, as it is a fatigue factor that lowers everyone's resistance to stress.

Passages

Mapping a building properly is essential for ease of access.

Safety

Safety is a primary concern for everyone, disabled or not.

Signage

Signage should clearly guide the newest person to any area of the building. Luminescence and lettering are critical.

Storage

Storage areas should be accessible and uncluttered to allow independent access to supplies.

Temperature

If possible, it is preferable to zone to individual needs.

Windows

Natural light is the best, psychologically.

Step II: Defining Applicable Standards
Step III: Planning Solutions

The standards, codes, and statutes which most clearly apply to ADA by factor are shown in Figures 5.1 and 5.2.

Ergonomics

"The science of ergonomics seeks to adapt the job and workplace to the worker by designing tasks and tools that are within the worker's capabilities and limitations."

— OSHA

Ergonomics is one aspect of a proactive approach to improving safety, productivity, and quality in the workplace. These principles can be applied to prevent both overt and cumulative traumas. A macro-ergonomics approach is starting, based on socio-technical system design principles. Technical sub-systems include: equipment, tools, environment/work site design, and software. Social sub-systems are job training and design. Safety professionals should be the key to prevention and control, thus leading to decreased injuries, illnesses and lower associated expenses.

Engineering departments should use ergonomics in setting up manageable and safe work sites. Designers and manufacturers should work together to create manufacturing processes that are safe for humans, while being technically effective. They should also take into account in their designs the wide spectrum of employee ages and abilities. Personnel managers should recognize the relationship between the satisfaction of all workers and increased productivity and quality.

STATE STANDARDS, CODES, AND STATUTES					
	Local Building Code	Natl. Electrical Code	Archi-techural Barriers	NEMA	U.L. F.M.	NFPA
Accessibility	✔		✔		✔	✔
Adaptability	✔	✔			✔	
Comfort					✔	
Communication					✔	✔
Density	✔					✔
Division of Space	✔	✔				✔
Equipment		✔		✔	✔	✔
Finishes					✔	✔
Furniture						✔
Image	✔		✔			
Lighting				✔	✔	
Maintenance		✔			✔	✔
Noise	✔					
Passages	✔		✔			
Safety		✔		✔		✔
Signage	✔	✔				✔
Storage	✔		✔			✔
Temperature						
Air Quality						
Windows						

Figure 5.1

FEDERAL/NATIONAL STANDARDS						
	ADA 1990	OSHA H&S	ANSI	Architect Barr. 1968	Intl. Standards	Veterans Administration	EPA
Accessibility	✔			✔		✔	
Adaptability	✔						
Comfort			✔		✔		✔
Communication	✔						
Density		✔					✔
Division of Space		✔					
Equipment		✔			✔		
Finishes					✔		
Furniture			✔				
Image	✔						
Lighting					✔		
Maintenance		✔					
Noise		✔					
Passages				✔		✔	
Safety		✔					
Signage	✔						
Storage	✔			✔			
Temperature			✔				✔
Air Quality			✔				✔
Windows			✔				

Figure 5.2

To design for reasonable accomodation, it is important to understand that disabilities represent a range of functional limitations, for which accommodations are to be made. See Figure 5.3 from the 1990 National Census, which shows the functional limitations of the population in thousands.

Step IV: Asking for Input from Physically Challenged Employees

Employers must take the time to tour their facility with physically challenged employees and discuss the elements the employee feels should be modified or changed to allow her/him to achieve complete and proper job performance. The following question should be asked, and the checklist (Figure 5.4) used in the evaluation process.

How can we accommodate your needs in the following areas in order for you to be more productive on the job?

	1990 CENSUS DATA (In Thousands)								
Functional Limitation	**Total** (includes 85+ years old)	**Males**				**Females**			
		Under 18	18-44	45-69	70-84	Under 18	18-44	45-69	70-84
Difficulty Interpreting Information	2,722	492	283	363	311	241	220	311	340
Limitation of Sight	4,509	146	532	833	342	118	403	1,148	731
Total Blindness	396	14	45	72	53	4	27	43	78
Limitation of Hearing	1,077	223	184	131	66	153	124	117	66
Total Deafness	1,700	80	80	452	307	80	80	205	243
Limitation of Speech	4,442	563	325	909	640	365	284	584	570
Susceptibility to Fainting, Dizziness or Seizures	13,288	262	821	3,510	1,232	210	1,079	4,057	1,780
Incoordination	6,513	648	1,430	1,108	450	374	827	921	617
Limitation of Stamina	19,176	853	1,404	4,766	1,766	627	1,853	5,299	2,150
Limitation of Head Movement	12,680	150	1,690	2,312	569	179	1,342	3,376	1,619
Limitation of Sensation	4,887	60	859	1,193	221	37	616	1,367	459
Difficulty in Lifting and Reaching with Arms	12,281	192	1,803	2,544	714	159	1,595	4,001	1,771
Difficulty in Handling and Fingering	10,278	598	1,295	1,952	632	315	1,066	3,281	1,661
Inability to use Upper Extremities	328	4	84	105	26	9	26	46	20
Difficulty in Sitting	13,146	168	1,815	2,440	574	192	1,420	3,480	1,632
Difficulty in using Lower Extremities	18,031	317	2,358	3,446	1,134	324	2,181	5,203	2,628
Poor Balance	11,211	248	1,313	1,921	681	218	1,208	3,374	1,879

Figure 5.3

	Essential to Accommodate	Manageable	No Accommodation Needed
Accessibility			
parking			
curbing			
ramps			
entrances			
elevators			
doors			
platforms			
water fountains			
public telephones			
Bathrooms			
toilet			
stalls			
sizes			
grab bars			
sink bars			
stall access			
turning radius			
Adaptability			
psych. control			
enhancements			
grip & reach			
controls			
Comfort			
seat position			
seating			
Communication			
desk telephones			

Figure 5.4

	Essential to Accommodate	Manageable	No Accommodation Needed
Density			
assembly area			
Division of Space			
office design/layout			
Finishes			
Floors			
Walls			
Ceilings			
Furnishings			
desks			
furniture			
library areas			
Image			
Lighting			
task			
Maintenance			
Noise			
hearing			
sound			
noise			
Passages			
doors/doorways			
tactile cues			
walkways			
stairways			
corridors			
Safety			
designing			

Figure 5.4 (cont.)

	Essential to Accommodate	Manageable	No Accommodation Needed
Signage			
labeling			
entrances			
composition			
mapping a room			
mapping a building			
exterior			
interior			
identification			
overhead			
Temperature/Air Quality			
Windows			

Figure 5.4 (cont.)

Figure 5.5 is a Job Description Analysis, which can be used to evaluate employee needs based on their particular disabilities, while updating job descriptions.

When designing environments to accommodate disabling conditions, it is important to remember that the observable part of a person's disability does not necessarily define their most critical need for accommodation. For example, a person with multiple sclerosis who may be mobility-impaired and therefore using a scooter, may actually need more aids for limitations of grip and grasp than for mobility. It is crucial to ask for input from the people for whom you are developing "reasonable accommodations." It is worth noting that more often than not, the challenged person cannot provide you with solutions. Because they are disabled does not mean they are designers or engineers on their own behalf. Some have the training or innate ability to devise solutions, but most do not.

Figure 5.6 is a chart showing the strengths that are likely to be retained by physically challenged people who have certain disabilities. These are important considerations in designing disability-specific solutions. The check marks indicate strengths they possess.

Figure 5.7 is an audit checklist used to assess a facility and develop reasonable accommodations to meet the needs of an employee under Title I.

Step V: Using Audit Data to Design Reasonable Accommodation

Data should now be used to design and develop reasonable accommodation to allow each employee or consumer independence and dignity in the environment(s).

The following summarized case study shows the process of assessing a facility and developing reasonable accommodations to meet a particular employee's needs under Title I.

Work Site Factor Overview and Recommendations

Accessibility

Access into the building is accomplished from the ground-level doors or an underground parking lot. The worker, a 34-year-old public relations specialist for a non-profit organization, has paraplegia, a condition of paralysis that involves two extremities. He uses a wheelchair, and has decreased grip and grasp functions and speech limitations. His work requires some travel. He has a personal care attendant to aid and assist him with accessibility.

Recommendations

Changes made to accommodate accessibilities, thereby increasing independence and dignity would include: power wheelchair, doors that swing two ways, mirrored corners to guide turns and clearance in passages.

Adaptability

The work site area was designed with "donated" modular furniture that has been configured in an "L" shape to accommodate a straight line from the worker's office door to position him at his desk. Once at his desk, the access and organization of the worker's work is difficult for him to manage with one hand. Currently, his work is organized in piles in the center of his desk by "most recent correspondence."

An analysis of the data yielded the following results:

Competency-Based Job Description

Description of Functions Note the activities that pertain to the employee's job. Rate the frequency. 1 = Least frequent task 2 = Most frequent task	Rate Functions #1-10 1 = Least frequent 10 = Most frequent	Where is Physical Stress Most Prevalent? W = Weight (Shifting) R = Reach (Overextended) P = Posture (Incorrect) F = Force (Excessive) R1 = Repetition (Constant) R2 = Rest (Inadequate)
Assembles		
Carries		
Calculates		
Cleans		
Climbs		
Collates		
Dials		
Drives		
Files		
Holds		
Indexes		
Inserts		
Lifts		
Maintains		
Opens		
Pulls		
Pushes		
Removes		
Schedules		
Sits		

Figure 5.5

Description of Functions Note the activities that pertain to the employee's job. Rate the frequency.	Rate Functions #1-10 1 = Least frequent 10 = Most frequent	Where is Physical Stress Most Prevalent? W = Weight (Shifting) R = Reach (Overextended) P = Posture (Incorrect) F = Force (Excessive) R1 = Repetition (Constant) R2 = Rest (Inadequate)
Speaks		
Stamps		
Stands		
Staples		
Threads		
Turns		
Types		
Unfolds		
Uses Keyboard		
Walks		
Weighs		
Writes		
Other		
Other		
Other		

Please check (if any apply to employee)

____	01	Post Polio	____	11	Deaf
____	02	Muscular Dystrophy	____	12	Blind
____	03	Heart Problem	____	13	Paraplegic
____	04	Cerebral Palsy	____	14	Quadriplegic
____	05	Spina Bifida	____	15	Incontinence
____	06	Head, Spinal Cord Injury	____	16	Arthritis
____	07	Lungs	____	17	Back Problem
____	08	Multiple Sclerosis	____	18	Diabetes
____	09	Amputee	____	19	Nerve, Muscle Disorder
____	10	Epilepsy	____	20	Stroke

Figure 5.5 (cont.)

Check the time units, and indicate the amount of time expected for an employee to complete a piece, task, or project.

Expected Productivity Rates:	Piece	Task	Project
[ ] Minutes			
[ ] Hours			
[ ] Days			
[ ] Weeks			

Check any known or observed difficulties (e.g., anger over family/financial problems and an ulcer).

Factors of Stress and Fatigue

[ ] Anger
[ ] Anxiety
[ ] Children
[ ] Commuting
[ ] Depression
[ ] Extra Job
[ ] Financial Difficulties
[ ] Headaches
[ ] Hypertension
[ ] Interruptions

[ ] Lack of supervision
[ ] Need of supervision
[ ] No independence
[ ] Respiratory illness
[ ] Sleep disorders
[ ] Smoker
[ ] Time constraints
[ ] Ulcers or gastro disorder
[ ] Other _____

_____

Figure 5.5 (cont.)

STRENGTHS AND DISABILITIES

Capability Enhancements: Motivation, Commitment, Technology   ✔ = Strengths

Note: This chart illustrates that most disabilities have more strengths than limitations.

	Mobility	Speech	Vision	Smell	Psych	Hear	Reach
Arthritis	(✔)	✔	✔	✔	✔	✔	(✔)
Asthma		✔	✔	✔	✔	✔	✔
Cerebral Palsy			✔	✔	✔		
Cancer	✔	✔	✔	✔	✔	✔	✔
Disk (back) Injury		✔	✔	✔	✔	✔	
Head Injury	(✔)	(✔)	(✔)	(✔)	(✔)	(✔)	
Learning Disability	✔		✔	✔		✔	✔
Parkinson's Disease		✔	✔	✔	✔	✔	
Polio		✔	✔	✔	✔	✔	
Spinal Cord Injury		✔	✔	✔	✔	✔	
Stroke		(✔)	(✔)	✔	✔	✔	

Figure 5.6

AMERICANS WITH DISABILITIES ACT CHECKLIST								
	Intellect	Hearing	Sight	Speech	Mobility	Reach Grip & Grasp	Stamina	Coordi-nation
Accessibility								
Mobility								
Parking								
Curbing								
Ramps								
Entrances								
Elevators								
Doors								
Platforms								
Water Fountains								
Public Telephones								
Bathrooms								
Toilet								
Stalls								
Sizes								
Grab Bars								
Sink Bars								
Stall Access								
Turning Radius								
Adaptability								
Psych. & Disability								
Psych. Control								
Enhancements								
Grip & Reach								
Controls								
Comfort								
Seat Position								

Figure 5.7

AMERICANS WITH DISABILITIES ACT CHECKLIST (cont.)								
	Intellect	Hearing	Sight	Speech	Mobility	Reach Grip & Grasp	Stamina	Coordi-nation
Seating								
Communication								
Desk Telephones								
Density								
Assembly Areas								
Division of Space								
Office Design/Layout								
Finishes								
Floors								
Walls								
Ceilings								
Furnishings								
Desks								
Furniture								
Library Areas								
Image								
Lighting								
Task Lighting								
Maintenance								
Noise								
Hearing								
Sound								
Passages								
Doors/Doorways								
Tactile Cues								
Walkways								
Stairways								

Figure 5.7 (cont.)

AMERICANS WITH DISABILITIES ACT CHECKLIST (cont.)								
	Intellect	Hearing	Sight	Speech	Mobility	Reach Grip & Grasp	Stamina	Coordi-nation
Corridors								
Safety								
Designing								
Signage								
Labeling								
Entrances								
Composition								
Mapping a Room								
Mapping a Building								
Exterior								
Interior								
Identification								
Overhead								
Temperature								
Air Quality								
Windows								

Figure 5.7 (cont.)

Recommendations

The worker's work surface has to accommodate a computer display and keyboard that will allow him to be positioned appropriately for visual and keying access. The work surface supports should include:

- A tilt board to mount papers for ease of reading.
- A copyholder to ease visual access to computer screen.
- Pen with adapted circumference for writing.
- Page-turning support.

Comfort

The reach requirements and the limitations of posture and positioning are critical factors in accommodating the worker at his desk. Currently, all designs to accommodate his comfort have to capitalize on his right orientation to his work. Work needs to be within accessible and flexible reach. Desktop modifications can support his work from papers to computers.

Recommendations

Reorganize the work area to allow the worker to access materials and organize them with meaningful objectives.

Communication

Communication is currently managed internally with close proximate interaction between the worker and his secretary and co-workers. It appears that telephone communication is limited.

Recommendations

Rearrange the space to accommodate staff access, while maintaining staff and visitor access to the worker.

Density

The worker's office is dense with furniture that is inaccessible to him. For example, the VCR requires that he ask for assistance in loading and operating the machine. There is no maneuverability in the office.

Division of Space

The office environment is designed in a linear fashion to accommodate work areas by function and access to resources, co-workers, and equipment. The layout of the work environment appears to accommodate staff by status. The best feature of this space is the access to natural light with all the offices having windows. The exception spaces are the conference room and work areas that are considered "reception areas."

Recommendations

A re-design of the layout to enhance productivity for all staff would involve creating a resource area for all shared equipment (copier, postage meter, mail station) to save steps in the preparation and processing of paperwork. In addition, an office layout map, which the front receptionist can use to direct visitors, would allow the worker's area to be rearranged to facilitate his work without compromising his access to visitors.

Furniture

The worker's current work surfaces and wheelchair do not integrate well for accomplishing the job tasks. The desk and office area need to be reorganized to support job tasks and increased productivity.

Recommendations

The worker's current work surface should be redesigned to accommodate his height and reach requirements, while supporting a vocational strategy to increase his work life opportunities.

Image

The worker should be positioned in his office to increase his options at visibility from his desk. His office should be arranged to increase visual access to the exterior of his office and his secretary. Since visual access is one of the worker's strengths, he may wish to fully view what goes on inside his office and outside of his office as people pass by his door. If visual access is too distracting, then his secretary and he should alter their positions in a way that facilitates his full visual access. This would result in a more professional image.

Recommendations

The attributes of image to be considered are:

- An organized presentation for both the professional and visitors.
- Being able to greet visitors with one's eyes, not one's ears.
- Being able to greet visitors face first, not being disadvantaged by having one's back to them.
- Capacity-building technologies to increase productivity, while reducing stress and fatigue, such as mechanical supports, computer technologies and communication systems.

Lighting

Current lighting is fluorescent in ceiling mounts that are baffled to diffuse light and cause less glare. No task lighting is individually positioned for staff. The available lighting adds lux intensity which keeps the room consistently bright (approximate lux between 60,000 and 80,000) with a minimum of shadowing.

Recommendations

To compensate for the effect of fluorescent lighting, which is limited spectrum (reduces the eyes' ability to see full spectrum of primary colors), the computer that the worker uses should be contrasted for brightness and glare-coded to increase visual acuity. This can be accomplished with adjustments to each software program.

Maintenance

Maintenance of safer passages was identified.

Recommendations

Clear hallways.

Noise

The office operates as a technology-based environment with computers, printers, and normal conversation as the background noise (40 to 55 decibels). Noise sensitivity does not appear to be a problem for the worker.

Recommendations

None.

Passages

The office is accessible down one main passage from the elevator to the office lobby and into each office. However, the access to the ladies' and men's rooms is difficult due to the narrow hallway and the clutter in the aisle. Accessibility is very difficult in the toileting facilities.

Recommendations

The corridor should be aligned so that at any one time, two people in wheelchairs could be passing through the office.

The worker's toileting facilities should include: A fully accessible toilet and sink, both of which must meet accessibility criteria and allow for a 5' turning radius. Top of toilet should be between 17–19″. Grab bars should also be installed on either side of the toilet (at a height of 24″, ANSI 4.16.4 and .6). Door frames/entrances should be wide enough to accommodate wheelchair access. Vanities should include access of minimum dimensions of 2′-3″ high, 2-1/2′ wide, and 1′-7″ deep. Hot water pipes should be insulated to prevent scalding. Tops of basins should be a maximum height of 2′-10″ and a maximum depth of 6-1/2″ (ANSI 4.19). Faucets should operate with lever handles or single lever controls (ANSI 4.19). Infrared automatic faucets are another option. Emergency switches/pulls should be installed in case the worker has any difficulties.

Safety

The office is a safety-oriented environment for office workers as exemplified by their desire to meet all of the standards and guidelines necessary to accommodate for everyone's capabilities. One point of question is how the evacuation procedure would be carried out in the event of a fire.

Recommendations

- Corridors need to be cleared.
- Protective equipment needs to be provided.
- Evacuation procedures need to be clearly defined and at least one fire drill performed to train staff.
- A safe smoking area and safety procedures should be established.

Signage

The office is departmentalized with access only to employees (who appear to circulate through the same areas each day) and invited guests.

Recommendations

Signage should be installed in order for visitors to easily map the office.

Storage

Resources are stored in file cabinets which require a secretary's help to access. The ergonomic concern is the worker's lack of independent access to material and resources. The weight of the files and file drawers requires too much grip and grasp since they do not roll easily.

Recommendations

Files should be made accessible by organized frequency of use. A bookshelf area deep enough for files that can be accessed by the worker independently is necessary (see examples in Part IV, "Accessibility").

Temperature/Air Quality

Temperature is not zoned, but is on a building system. Temperature and air quality difficulties were not noted.

Windows

An expanded view to the outside is not accessible to the worker because of the mini-blinds, which are operated with a hand motion that the worker cannot make due to limitations of reach and grip.

Recommendations

A new office configuration that allows access to the natural light would be helpful. The worker could operate the spindle on the mini-blinds if he could get alongside the window.

Step VI: Evaluation Criteria

The three main goals of an Americans with Disabilities Act Audit are:

1. To provide information from which to design reasonable accommodations for functional limitations.
2. To encourage reasonable accommodations that foster an increase or maintenance of capability in mobility, strength, stamina, visual acuity, hearing, tactile and thermal sensitivity, and psychology.
3. To provide recommendations that are flexible, accommodating, adaptive, and not easily obsolesced.

Recommendations should cover the following key issues for facilities managers. Reasonable accommodation designs should make the best use of:

- function and fitness to meet productivity standards
- integration with all work environments
- ease of maintenance operations
- aesthetics and image
- lowered first costs and life cycle costs
- bulk purchase agreements of existing inventory
- appropriateness of modification within hierarchal management guidelines

Chapter Six

REASONABLE PSYCHOLOGICAL ACCOMMODATION

Employers seeking to address the requirements of the Americans with Disabilities Act are increasingly developing the misperception that the easiest response is to remove architectural barriers to employment, i.e., add a ramp and grab bar. This point is reinforced by the numbers of ADA consultants who focus on the parts of the Act that involve physical alterations and related tax credits. However, equally important to implementation of the ADA is **"Reasonable Psychological Accommodation"** for persons with mental difficulties. The Act specifically reads "mental impairments" (mental retardation, organic brain syndrome, emotional or mental stress, and specific learning disabilities) that substantially limit one or more life activities, e.g., working. Yet, on this aspect of the Act, there is a notable lack of expertise and information from which employers can determine a strategy. In response to the need for clarity and simplicity, Work Stations, Inc. conducted research, using actual employees at their work sites, to define the multiple facets of "reasonable psychological accommodation." The Equal Employment Opportunity Commission (EEOC) states, "An accommodation removes or alleviates barriers to equal employment opportunities, enabling disabled people to apply for a job, perform essential job functions, and enjoy benefits and privileges equal to their non-disabled co-workers."

Psychological/mental difficulties in the workplace are limitations that directly affect productivity due to the "functional" nature of the psychological disorders. For example, a person who is depressed may not be able to maintain speed or concentration to perform a task. A person who has anxiety attacks may not be able to hold tools steady due to excessive sweating. A person with a phobia to closed rooms may not be able to work in a confined warehouse space. The functional nature of disorders can act to limit a person's productivity in several different ways. As an employer, one may have to work with people who have difficulty with interpersonal relations which may make written and verbal communication unclear. A person may concurrently have difficulty handling tension, an inability to relax, a limited sense of humor, and a myopic view of the job's importance, and may become overwhelmed by normal pressures. They may also not be adaptable or flexible, see only one way to handle a situation, and focus on problems rather than solutions. These functional limitations may lower productivity by increasing stress-related distraction from tasks and illnesses, and may result in tardiness or absenteeism.

These functional limitations are exhibited by all employees at one time or another, but may be exacerbated by a person's psychological state. Therefore, *reasonable psychological accommodations* are those which serve to lessen stress and fatigue, while promoting productivity and efficiency. Critical interventions by employers are necessary to implement reasonable psychological accommodations. Five variables make the difference. They are: work structure, work plans, acceptance of employees' life pressures, setting an employee standard, and clarity in supervision.

Work Structure

Helping someone with psychological problems to fit well into the organization requires a systematic process linking job descriptions to individual work plans and the performance appraisal into one personnel management system. The person should be aware of the mission of the company and its annual goals. For the individual, a statement of the job objectives is essential. The objectives should clearly relate to job tasks. Do not underestimate the importance of understanding one's job tasks in relation to overall goals and objectives.

Work Plans

Work plans should define the organizational mission, goals and objectives, with resources assigned and time lines for completion of tasks. These items should be included:

Organization:

Mission: This is the statement of the grand plan.

Goals: Statement of annual expectations as part of the grand plan.

Objectives: A precise specification of a goal.

Tasks: Who will do what, with whom, with what resources, in what time frame.

Job Descriptions

The development of a clear competency-based job description is a necessity for setting priorities, achieving acceptable productivity levels, and training. The job description should include:

Position Title:

Description of Functions: Defines the broad categories of the job. Words to describe function here would be: "responsible for," "develops, plans and reviews."

General Competency: This section provides actual interview questions that could be used. An example might be: "How would you monitor inventory?"

Training: Defines expected education and/or training requirements.

Performance Appraisal

The final step in work structure is to be able to give clear and concise feedback on job performance. By using the work plan as the accepted standard, all subjectivity is removed from the process.

People succeed with structures that are adaptable and flexible. Specific accommodations to each job should allow the person to work efficiently on a schedule that prioritizes the essential tasks, with necessary resources in a manageable time line. Work plans should outline goals and objectives, and tasks. A clear productivity standard should allow the person to use their time to complete essential functions.

Work Changes

To the extent possible, career opportunities and changes in job routines, supervision, work locations, equipment or conditions should be introduced with clear communication and time lines, allowing the individual to prepare and adapt.

Contributors To Stress

Alleviate work site environmental difficulties by eliminating environments that are depressing, uncomfortable, or hazardous. Provide the necessary resources (equipment, information and supervision). Allow input to decision making. Reward a good job. Resolve conflicts (ethical and professional).

Personal Life Pressures

Understand that in addition to the person's mental difficulties, they also experience the same stress that the typical employee feels when faced with the pressures of their personal life. All employers must deal with an employee who experiences a decrease in productivity due to changes. These changes may be of residence, death of a family member or friend, crisis of significance (job loss, drug problem), separations and divorce, the start of a new relationship, long term illness, new family member, financial crisis, legal difficulties, or victimization (crime or abuse). Such difficulties are faced by all employees at some point during their adult life. In addition, daily life includes money pressures, conflicts with mates and children and the limitations on time for family, friends, and oneself.

Setting an Employee Standard

It is particularly important for people with mental difficulties to maintain a standard of presentation. When essential to the job, make it clear what the dress code is for your facility. A change in adherence to the dress code is sometimes an early warning that the difficulties are becoming overwhelming. A clear smoking and alcohol policy is essential for all employees.

Clarity in the Supervision Strategy

Clearly define the job expectations and as the job necessitates, provide peer support on projects, maintain information support, and define the conflict resolution strategy. Be accommodating to behaviors that are normative to the person (idiosyncratic), the need the person may have for support from their doctor or counselor, as well as the right not to talk about difficulties. Limit distractions and interruptions. Understand that changes in medications may result in changes in behaviors.

Survey to Determine Necessary Accommodations

Figure 6.1 is a survey that can be used to interview employees to help them define the reasonable psychological accommodations they require to maintain productivity in the workplace.

REASONABLE PSYCHOLOGICAL ACCOMMODATION

This survey is designed to help your employees define the reasonable psychological accomodations required to maintain productivity in the workplace.

This is a three-part survey:

  I. Functional job strengths and limitations
  II. Work stressors
  III. Recommendations of reasonable accommodations

Ia. FUNCTIONAL JOB STRENGTHS AND LIMITATIONS

(Please circle "S" for Strength and "L" for Limitation)

Strengths	Limitations	
S	L	Awareness of ability and limitations
S	L	Condition is stable
S	L	Full range of skills to perform the job
S	L	Can read and write
S	L	Can be trained to perform the job
S	L	Can do the job with peer support
S	L	Can do the job with technology support
S	L	Can do the job with organization support
S	L	Understands work schedules
S	L	Understands dress codes
S	L	Interpersonal skills
S	L	Can take direction
S	L	Can finish work or tasks on time
S	L	Appropriate supervision requirements
S	L	Deals with change appropriately
S	L	Deals with conflict appropriately
S	L	Anticipates difficulty
S	L	Adaptability
S	L	Flexibility
S	L	Consistency
S	L	Caution
S	L	Safety orientation
S	L	Assertiveness
S	L	Can plan ahead
S	L	Can say no
S	L	Can negotiate
S	L	Can plan time
S	L	Can concentrate
S	L	Can ask for supervision
S	L	Can seek information
S	L	Is patient
S	L	Works with satisfaction and pride
S	L	Faces problems
S	L	Has a sense of humor

Figure 6.1

Ib. SENSORY COORDINATION STRENGTHS AND LIMITATIONS

(Please circle "S" for Strength and "L" for Limitation)

Strengths	**Limitations**	
S	L	Memory
S	L	Perception
S	L	Vision
S	L	Hearing
S	L	Speech
S	L	Olfactory
S	L	Use of upper body
S	L	Grip and grasp
S	L	Mobility
S	L	Strength
S	L	Stamina
S	L	Self care and personal hygiene

II. WORK STRESSORS

Please check stressors that affect work performance and/or job functioning so that accommodations can be made. (Check all that apply)

IIa. Work Structure

Work Site Environment

[ ] Poor accessibility

[ ] Unadaptable

[ ] Uncomfortable

[ ] Poor communication

[ ] Dense/crowded

[ ] Disorganized

[ ] Poorly divided

[ ] Lack of equipment

[ ] Inadequate furniture

[ ] Inappropriate finishes

[ ] Inadequate lighting

[ ] Difficult to maintain

[ ] Noise

[ ] Inaccessible passages

[ ] Unsafe

[ ] Inadequate signage

[ ] Inaccessible storage

[ ] Unhealthy temperature/air quality

[ ] Window problems

Please explain any work site modification needs.

_____

_____

_____

Figure 6.1 (cont.)

IIb. The Job

[ ] Too many tasks
[ ] Not enough tasks
[ ] Routines boring
[ ] Conflicting priorities
[ ] Conflicting timelines

[ ] No job description
[ ] No work plan
[ ] No standard of production
[ ] Not enough resources
[ ] Not enough personnel

IIc. Interpersonnel Interactions

[ ] Confusing communication
[ ] No direct supervision
[ ] Input not valued
[ ] No rewards
[ ] No recognition
[ ] No promotion opportunities
[ ] No feedback from supervisor

[ ] Conflict with co-workers
[ ] Isolated
[ ] Discrimination
[ ] Pressured
[ ] Too much responsibility for other staff
[ ] Harassment

IId. Feelings About The Job

[ ] I dislike my boss
[ ] I like my boss
[ ] I do not like my job
[ ] I like my job
[ ] I do not get enough pay
[ ] I like my pay
[ ] I do not like the ethics
[ ] I like what we do
[ ] I do not feel committed
[ ] I am respected
[ ] I do not use my skills
[ ] I make a difference
[ ] I participate in decisions
[ ] I need _____ for supervision.
[ ] I need environmental changes which are _____ .

[ ] I need to be able to leave work for
_____ .
[ ] I need to interact with people
How? _____ .
[ ] I do best when _____ .
[ ] I work in one location
[ ] I work close to home
[ ] I work at home
[ ] I require increase in technology to support job
[ ] I require tasks broken down into support job
[ ] I require more flexible hours
[ ] I require time off for doctors visits
[ ] I require increased supervision
[ ] I need shorter work week
[ ] I require minimal job tasks and functions
[ ] I require schedule of work

[ ] Other_____ .

Figure 6.1 (cont.)

IIe. Current Life Difficulties

[ ] Moving to a new place
[ ] Difficulties in current living situation
[ ] Death in the family or of a friend
[ ] Family conflict
[ ] Separation or divorce
[ ] Home is not safe

[ ] Illness
[ ] New family member
[ ] Not enough money
[ ] Legal difficulties
[ ] Crime victim
[ ] No friend or support system

IIf. Support Systems

[ ] People to talk to
[ ] People to help me
[ ] People who understand me

[ ] People spend time with me
[ ] I have hobbies and leisure time

IIg. Caring About Self

[ ] Eats nutritionally
[ ] Takes medications regularly
[ ] Maintains weight (not over or under)
[ ] Maintains an exercise program
[ ] Likes body image

[ ] Takes care of personal hygiene (bathing, teeth)
[ ] Sees a physician regularly
[ ] Relaxes
[ ] Avoids smoking
[ ] Avoids alcohol

III. JOB ACCOMMODATIONS

Check all that apply:

[ ] Job description
[ ] Work plan
[ ] Supervision
[ ] Performance appraisal
[ ] Appreciation of illness
[ ] Appreciation of life stressors

[ ] Hours of work should be

_____ .

[ ] The resources I need are

_____ .

[ ] My job tasks should be

_____ .

Figure 6.1 (cont.)

A Final Word On Reasonable Psychological Accommodation

If employees do well, the organization does well. That is the real incentive for *reasonable psychological accommodation.* Organizational analysts have been supporting reasonable accommodations for years by defining organizational effectiveness with words like: *growth, productivity, profit, efficiency, goal attainment, and low turnover.* The Americans with Disabilities Act provides an opportunity to focus on organizational effectiveness. It asks employers to support people with physical and mental challenges in satisfying jobs with a clear organizational structure, using the resources of 1990s technological equipment and knowledge, to be adaptable and flexible in the pursuit of meaningful work and careers.

The best outcome of reasonable psychological accommodations for persons with mental difficulties is to be able to achieve a productive and effective work life. Therefore, reasonable psychological accommodation becomes successful when the person can succeed with adaptable work structures.

Chapter Seven

REASONABLE ACCOMMODATION FOR THE WHOLE PERSON

Reasonable accommodation for disabled people and their spectrum of limitations (due to age, injury and/or disease) is complicated because the physically challenged population depends on specific designs to compensate for limitations. No other population depends as heavily on design. Their needs are dynamic across many settings, and they rely on the creativity of designers, as well as their commitment to doing socially responsible work. Designers are in the best position to reduce the stigma of being physically challenged from one of dependence on people to one of independence through ADA, barrier-free design and technology. Since the 1970s, attitudes have changed on the "worth of the person" with disabilities. Keeping the momentum going is the ADA initiative. The role of facilities managers and designers in meeting the needs of the disabled is to create environments that:

- Serve the capabilities of the whole person (e.g., mobility, vision, speech, grip and grasp, hearing, intellect, psychology, strength and stamina), and to creatively compensate for the increases and decreases in capability.
- Plan for adaptations, not obsolescence. Designs are needed that increase productivity and efficiency, maintain health and safety, and reduce stress and fatigue.

Serving the capabilities of the whole person involves consideration of many ADA factors that can compensate for increased limitations. Disease and injury can affect the body and the mind in many complex ways; therefore, orientation and ease in one's environment is essential.

The most noticeable and overall diminishment in capability usually involves mobility. With most physically challenged people, their difficulty with ambulation in either walking or in using a wheelchair results in slower reactions, excessive use of energy to move and reposition for movement, and loss of equilibrium and visual perspectives from being fixed for forward movement. An outcome of limits in mobility is the increased stress and fatigue that the physically challenged experience in trying to manage in their environments. Repositioning for reach requires stamina, strength and coordination that is often beyond the flexation and extension possible for either injured or diseased joints. Design must therefore create environments that work well in circumferences, as opposed to linearly angled areas that require extra effort in which to move or reach. Figures 7.1a and 7.1b are examples of modified office environments.

Office with Specialized Adaptive Furnishings

Figure 7.1a

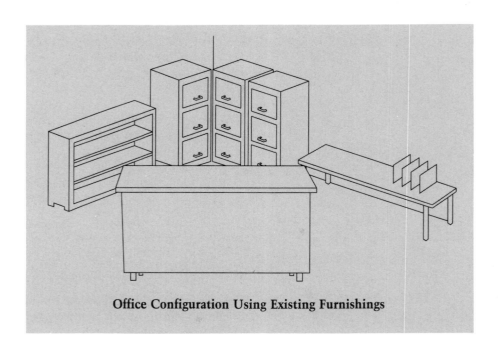

Office Configuration Using Existing Furnishings

Figure 7.1b

Factors of fatigue and stress are part of employment and everyday living. An important aspect of barrier-free design is to identify the causes of stress and fatigue by analyzing data on environments. This data can be used to calculate a full range of innovations to compensate for limitations and meet the requirements of reasonable accommodation.

A 1986 Work Stations, Inc. study of wheelchair users found the most **frequent causes of fatigue** to be:

- Balancing forward and on each side of the wheelchair.
- The need to shift positions to move off of pressure points.
- Gaining lumbar support.
- Muscle tension in the neck and upper back.
- Skin abrasions from powering or manually operating a wheelchair.
- Inclining and reclining difficulties at the backrest, seat surface, posterior thigh and ischial muscle.
- Positioning and remaining poised for reaching.

Frequent Causes of Stress:

- Limitations in visual scanning, both forward and peripheral.
- Intensity of concentration required during mobility.
- Limitations of reach.
- Dependence on others for help.
- The frequency of inaccessibility in environments.
- Impacting environmental barriers.
- Misjudging passageways.
- Feeling of difference.
- Perception of others' impatience and lack of understanding.

Even though stress and fatigue are lessened by barrier-free design and technology, they may still be a factor of low productivity that require work schedule modifications.

Interviewing Employees/ Applicants

Questions That Can Be Asked

It is important that both employers and employees realize that it is necessary to go through an interviewing process. The process should reveal the needed information in terms of the person's ability to complete a job. Pre-employment medical inquiries are generally prohibited. Employers should take care to avoid asking questions unrelated to the essential duties of the job, including inquiries related to health and disabilities unless absolutely job-related and consistent with business necessity.

It must be noted that an employer has the right and duty to inquire about the person's ability to do a job. Given that, the employer *should* ask certain questions. Prospective and current employees should answer all appropriate questions truthfully. Deliberate untruthfulness may be the basis of an employer refusing to hire or taking disciplinary action against a current employee.

Here are some commonly asked key questions.

1. What is your attendance record at school or at your present job?
2. Do you have a license to _____ ? (Fill in the blank with license necessary for the job, e.g., driver or chauffeur's license).
3. Where did you go to school and why?
4. What organization are you affiliated with now, or have you been affiliated with in the past, as a volunteer which shows your

experience or qualifications for the position for which you have applied?

5. Who referred you here?
6. What are your personal and professional goals?
7. State the names, addresses and telephone numbers of your previous employers and why you accepted and left each job.
8. Do you have the ability to perform the job functions?
9. On what basis do you believe you are qualified for the position(s) for which you applied or wish consideration?
10. What work experience(s) have you had that make you qualified for the position(s) for which you have applied or wish consideration?
11. What are your employment strengths and weaknesses as related to this job?
12. Are you willing to accept employment on condition that you pass a job-related physical examination?

These questions are not trick questions used to obtain information about a person's disability. Rather, each goes to a legitimate purpose regarding the performance of duties and the employer's personnel practices.

A Few No-Nos

While there are definitely questions that can and should be asked, there are also questions which most definitely should not be asked. Here are some questions not to be asked *unless the question relates to a bona fide occupational qualification consistent with business necessity. In rare circumstances in which an employer believes it is necessary to ask one of these taboo questions, they are advised to consult legal counsel and to have detailed documentation justifying the question before the interview.*

1. Do you have a physical or mental handicap or disability?
2. How did you become disabled?
3. Would you need special or expensive accommodations to do the job for which you have applied?
4. Do you have epilepsy, multiple sclerosis, etc.?
5. What medication, if any do you take on a regular basis?
6. Are there any restrictions on your driver's license?
7. Do you commonly become tired at work in the afternoon?
8. Are you often too tired to get to work on time in the morning?
9. Can you travel independently?
10. Do any of your children, your spouse, or others in your family have physical or mental handicaps?
11. Have you ever had a seizure, heart attack, etc.?
12. Is your diet restricted for any reason?

Part Three

PERFORMING THE AUDIT

Part Three

INTRODUCTION

Part III focuses on the audit process—from setting goals for the audit, to establishing a team of in-house participants, and selecting qualified consultants. The actual audit will begin with an evaluation of existing conditions as they compare with both ADA-required provisions, state and city codes, and other modifications that might be made to enhance the comfort or productivity of disabled people.

Chapter Eight

GOALS OF THE AUDIT

The primary goal of the audit should be to provide information from which to design reasonable accommodations for functional limitations. Those accommodations should foster increased capability in mobility, strength, stamina, visual acuity, hearing, tactile and thermal sensitivity, and psychology, incorporating the following recommendations:

   a.   flexible—furniture/equipment easily moved.
   b.   accommodating—for all physical disabilities.
   c.   adaptive—for all customers and employees.

Recommendations should be consistent with the goals and objectives of: facilities managers, employees, and customers, and should address the organization's goals for its environment.

1. From the facilities manager's point of view, the designs should make the best use of:

   a.   aesthetics and image
   b.   ease of maintenance and operations
   c.   function and fitness
   d.   lowered first costs and life cycle costs
   e.   responsiveness of a status marking system
   f.   bulk purchase agreements of existing inventory
   g.   integration with other work places

2. The goal for employees is a design that will meet their expectations and needs in the following areas:

   a.   Accessibility: ability to access with ease.
   b.   Adaptability: use adaptations with success while remaining inconspicuous.
   c.   Comfort: feel comfortable in all areas of a site.
   d.   Density: can negotiate spaces without a barrier due to density or division of space.
   e.   Division of Space: can negotiate spaces without a barrier due to density or division of space.
   f.   Finishes: enhance visual acuity, mobility, and image.
   g.   Furnishings: fit the body with ease.
   h.   Image: is appropriate to the person's position as employee, guest, patron, or citizen.

    i. Lighting: illuminates without glare.

    j. Maintenance: supports the person's tasks or objective.

    k. Noise: is not a fatigue factor.

    l. Passages: support mobility.

   m. Safety: is not a concern.

    n. Signage: is a guide.

    o. Storage: is accessible.

    p. Temperature and air quality: are acceptable to EPA standards.

    q. Windows: are an access to the larger environment.

3. For organizations that have on-site customer contact, other design factors must be considered. They must be able to independently use environmental supports and accomplish objectives through:

    a. redundant cuing

    b. landmarks: water, decorating, dramatic spatial changes

    c. personalized areas

    d. accessibility

    e. illumination levels

    f. sounds

    g. olfactory enhancements

    h. signage

4. Environmental recommendations will:

    a. increase opportunities for individual choice

    b. encourage independence

    c. compensate for changes in employee/customer perception and sensory acuity

    d. decrease unnecessary mobility

    e. encourage social interaction

    f. stimulate participation in activities offered

    g. reduce conflict and distraction

    h. provide a safe environment

    i. make activities accessible

    j. improve client, staff, and facility image

    k. plan for growth and change in individuals

A focus on safety and work injury prevention should become a continuous part of your audit team focus.

Figure 8.1 is an audit form used to evaluate an existing facility to determine modifications required to comply with ADA Title III, Public Accommodation. The form can also be used on an individual basis with a specific employee to meet Title I.

Title I and Title III Accommodations. Title I audits should include the input of the physically challenged employee. Title III audits can be performed by facility management or other knowledgeable personnel.

Date:_____

Audit Performed by:_____

Area Audited:_____

	ADA Code Reference	No Accommodation Needed	Manageable	Essential to Accommodate	Action Required
Accessibility					
parking					
curbing					
ramps					
entrances					
elevators					
doors					
platforms					
water fountains					
public telephone					
stairs					
Bathrooms					
toilet					
stalls					
sizes					
grab bars					
sink bars					
stall access					
turning radius					
Adaptability					
psych. control					
enhancements					
grip & reach					
controls					

Figure 8.1

	ADA Code Reference	No Accommodation Needed	Manageable	Essential to Accommodate	Action Required
Comfort					
seat position					
seating					
Communication					
desk telephones					
Density					
assembly area					
Division of Space					
office design					
layout					
Finishes					
Floors					
Walls					
Ceilings					
Furnishings					
desks					
furnishings					
library areas					
Image					
Lighting					
task					
Maintenance					
Noise					
hearing					
sound					
noise					
Passages					
doors					

Figure 8.1 (cont.)

	ADA Code Reference	No Accommodation Needed	Manageable	Essential to Accommodate	Action Required
doorways					
tactile cues					
walkways					
stairways					
corridors					
Safety					
designing					
Signage					
labeling					
entrances					
composition					
mapping a room					
mapping a building					
exterior					
interior					
identification					
overhead					
storage					
Temperature					
Air Quality					
Windows					

Figure 8.1 (cont.)

Management of Compliance Disputes

Avoiding disputes is certainly the best solution. The best way to avoid disputes is to foster strong communication between designers and those who will be using the "reasonable accommodations." The users are frequently overlooked because those who need are frequently not the same as those who buy. Disputes on reasonable accommodation develop from three perspectives, potentially, and at three distinct project phases.

The project starts with defining the scope relative to meeting the code and agreeing on costs. There is potential for further problems in the middle of a project if designs are changed or time lines are not being met. At the end of a project, the problems arise if users are not satisfied with the outcomes. It is, therefore, beneficial to have the right people agree on the project in scope and cost to meet the codes and the needs at the beginning of a project. The appropriate people include:

- designers
- legal representation
- architects
- highest level decision makers, e.g., employer/business owner
- superintendent of buildings
- town board of selectmen
- building inspector
- citizen lobbies/user representatives

Avoid media coverage if possible, as it tends to inflame issues. Disputes should be settled by whomever is able to certify a plan. Whenever there is a question of legal compliance, contact the appropriate federal agency and ask for a legal opinion in writing.

Chapter Nine

SETTING UP THE AUDIT TEAM

The Americans with Disabilities Act is a wide-ranging civil rights statute that was written to prohibit discrimination against people with disabilities. Protected under the act are an estimated 43 to 100 million Americans with physical and mental impairments that substantially limit activities such as walking, talking, seeing, hearing, or caring for oneself.

Under Title I, the law bars discrimination in employment, requiring most employers to make reasonable accommodations for qualified employees. Title II is devoted to public services, prohibiting discrimination in services, programs, or activities of a public entity. Title III prohibits discrimination in public accommodations such as hotels, restaurants, stores, theaters and museums. In essence, a person with a disability has the right to fully participate in society as an employee, guest, citizen or patron of any facility in America.

This chapter is intended to help you evaluate who should be on your team when you audit facilities. The most productive ADA audit is usually the result of a team approach. The team should be comprised of people with expertise and experience. The team should, ideally, have a balance of knowledge that relates to the Americans with Disabilities Act. Recommended team members include:

Human resource professionals with a minimum of five years experience in the recruitment and maintenance of valued employees.
Contribution to the team: Knowledge of writing job descriptions, interviewing skills, and human relations, as well as providing an interface with unions and public relations.

Ergonomics specialist or human factors engineer with a minimum of five years experience, with a particular emphasis on safety and a full understanding of the functional limitations that profile disabilities. A design background is essential, as is the ability and willingness to be an expert witness.
Contribution to the team: Knowledge of the relative impact of single site analyses of individual jobs and the radius of effect to all workers, patrons, guests, or citizens who may use a facility. The ability to design and develop cost effective solutions to reasonable accommodation plans.

People with disabilities who have knowledge of reasonable accommodation, from both their own experience and the experiences of their peers, but who are not biased toward accommodation of their particular disability.

Contribution to the team: Experience with cost effective accommodations that really make a difference, and the attitudinal issues for people with disabilities.

Safety engineering expert with a minimum of five years experience in facilities management within whatever standards, codes or statutes now impact on the facility.
Contribution to the team: Knowledge of safe practice and the how-to's of any modifications that may be proposed to meet "reasonable accommodation."

Occupational health nurses with experience in the accident and safety issues on a site and knowledge of disabilities, functional limitations, and the relationship of the Americans with Disabilities Act, and the state rules on Workers' Compensation.
Contribution to the team: Advisor on "reasonable accommodation" proposals, interface to potential employees who may be recruited or return to work after disease, injury, or disability. Advisor on what the effects of aging may have on a functional limitation. Data analyst on current injury and risk factors.

Supervisors selected to represent specific sites who have experience in how jobs are performed, safety issues, regulations, and the use of a facility by outside people who may be guests, patrons, or citizens.
Contribution to the team: Real knowledge of how people with functional limitations can be accommodated so that they may use a facility in whatever capacity is intended.

On-site or off-site architect(s) should have knowledge of functional limitations and how a facility can make environmental changes to accommodate current and future needs with designs that are adaptable, flexible, and will not obsolesce. Should have five years of experience in designing facilities for people with limitations and understand the issues of aging. Should be able to work as a team member with data from all members. Should fully understand the ADA. Also, the ability and willingness to be an expert witness.
Contribution to the team: Cost effective designs to maintain productivity and safety, while reducing fatigue in environments.

Facilities managers who are responsible for the full facility changes that relate to both the immediate and long range goals.
Contribution to the team: Planning for the capital necessary to effect change within a reasonable time line. Management of the environmental changes with internal staff or external vendors.

The audit should be conducted using the 20 factors for the total site, with particular emphasis on safety and essential job functions. The audit plan should then be put into place, representing each factor's compliance to codes and a strategy to come into compliance.

The audit plan is a facility's legal documentation that they are making changes to reasonably accommodate their sites. Cost analysis of accommodations must be included to document "undue burden." A sample compliance plan is shown in Figure 9.1.

SAMPLE COMPLIANCE PLAN				
Factor	**Action Plan**	**Responsible Staff**	**Cost**	**Time Line**
Access	Add canopy to front ramp	physical plant	$4,000	July 93
Adaptability	Listening aid	audio staff	$95 each	July 92
Comfort	Bench seats in lobby	facilities manager	$220 each	July 93
Density	Remove partitions	physical plant	overhead	July 92
Division of space	Relocate data input operators to first floor	physical plant	overhead	July 92
Finishes	Repaint hallways	physical plant	$4,000	Jan 93
Furnishings	Redesign work stations	ergonomist	overhead	Jan 93
Image	Reconfigure reception desk	physical plant	overhead	July 93
Lighting	Add glare screens	facilities	$29 each	July 93
Maintenance	Remove storage from bathroom	physical plant	overhead	July 92
Noise	Add acoustical panels	facilities	$39 each	Jan 93
Passages	Change hinges	facilities	overhead	Jan 93
Safety	Add handrails to ramp	physical plant	overhead	July 92
Signage	Put in braille signage	facilities	$29 each	July 93
Storage	Add low racks	facilities	$1,000	July 93
Temp./Air Quality	Add fans	facilities	$20 each	July 93
Windows	Change hardware	facilities	$10 each	Jan 93

Figure 9.1

Chapter Ten

HOW TO FIND AND GET THE BEST OF CONSULTANT SERVICES

How often has this happened in your organization? A problem or crisis arises and your organization does not appear to have a good handle on the problem or a sense of the best solution. In addition, there seems to be a core of related problems.

At this point, when both management and staff are overwhelmed, someone suggests bringing in a consultant. Often someone else suggests a consultant they've heard about or have heard speak at a conference. With urgency, that consultant is immediately called; ostensibly hired on good faith. Then, the one and only review meeting takes place with the consultant and the perceived key people (the supervisor of the person who identified the problem, one upper management person, and the person who recommended the consultant). The expectation is a "quick" solution, often based on the assumption that the consultant has the expertise and experience from which to build a response.

What you get is either the "best advice" you've ever gotten or a solution so unrelated to the problem that it makes everyone involved frustrated or embarrassed. In addition, the advice may be delivered orally as "words of wisdom" available for review only by the best of "note-takers," or worse, written up by the consultant in length and language which may further disguise the problem and solutions.

Upon being billed, organizations informally try to assess the success of the consultant. What is often expressed is that the consultant was either excellent or useless. There is no in-between. The consensus is that one of every five consultants is worth "whatever the cost." That one in five success rate is what keeps organizations hooked and hopeful. Because every once in a while, an organization gets a brilliant insight that moves them in a direction that they wanted to go. How do the "excellent consultants" succeed? In two ways: they solve problems in a timely fashion with available resources. Second, and at least as important, the staff agree and understand the proposed solutions. Why? Because their "excellent consultant" succeeded by using their input and solutions that their staff can implement. On the other hand, consultants are seen as useless when the advice has been inappropriate as well as somehow offensive to staff. Staff seem to be most offended when they have been excluded from the process, but expected to be part of the solution.

Defining What (and Whom) You Need

First, you have to clearly define the problem. That means document the history, talk to the involved staff, and define the implications of the problem. Second, clearly define the expected solutions. Solutions should consider both the ideal and the practical, given the resources available. Using your problem definition and expected solutions will help you define the expertise of the consultant you need, but there is more to succeeding. You also need to know the kind of consultant that will fit with the staff in your organization. First, you need an expert. An expert is someone who knows more about an area than anyone else from a practical as well as innovative perspective.

Second, you need an objective and unbiased opinion. And third, you need a total commitment to agreed solutions.

In spite of time pressures, it is prudent to scrutinize a consultant as closely as a potential employee. Do not rush into hiring based on a perceived aura of "expertise." The importance of "organizational fit," experience, and education are critical to a consultant's success. Define the kind of consultant you need with these credibility criteria in mind.

Locating the Right Consultant

Know where to look for a consultant. First, don't rule out internal people. Often the expertise lies within your own organization, but it takes a redefinition of staff time and status to use internal personnel. Second, use several approaches to find your consultant, thus expanding your ability to review a number of consultants' approaches without costing you too much time.

Second, call your local library and ask the reference person in charge of your area of need whom they know to be experts. Third, the Small Business Administration is often an excellent resource. Academic institutions may also have a myriad of consultants within each department. Call professional associations in the area. Talk to other consultants with whom you've had success. In sum, use as many available resources as possible to build a selection pool.

Selecting the Right Consultant

Use an interview process to assess the consultant's ability to solve your problem. Review their resume and check all references. Ask for a copy of other contract reports. Be assured of both competence and credibility. If you have time, ask for an outline of their approach to solving your problem.

Getting the Most Out of Your Consultant

Review your problem with the consultant, but ground the problem by providing the consultant with a total picture of what your organization is about. Give the consultant an organizational chart, a tour, and a brochure. Allow the consultant to define the key people to be involved. Allow time for a secondary assessment of the problem. Do not constrain the information. Make the consulting a priority. Set aside adequate time for communication. Review progress daily. Make all available documentation available. Set time lines realistically. Include all of these points in your contract. Make sure that the consultant has agreed to your expected outcomes for success. Insist on a final report and define the form of the report. Then have the consultant do a presentation of the recommendations to those who are expected to implement any changes. At this point, ask questions. It is important to know from what database the consultant is making recommendations, e.g., experience, literature, interviews, observations, and that he or she has used a methodologically sound data collection and analytical procedure. Or, are the recommendations based on an actual trial or integration of several of the above methods?

Post-implementation, have the consultant agree to a follow-up consultation to assess the success of the recommendations. This assessment should include corrective strategies where failures have occurred. The importance of follow-up is critical to succeeding with consultants. With the "excellent" consultant, the assessment may give you even more ideas. Even with the "useless" consultant, it at least provides you and the consultant with an opportunity to get the job done right. The follow-up also allows continuity on a project to a clear and successful end.

Qualifying Your ADA Consultant

The consultant should possess skill and dedication. They must be able to focus on capability—not disability, and be able to create an image oriented to the individual (including independence and dignity). A good understanding of the disability and aging realities is also important. The consultant should be committed to research and should be quality and detail-oriented.

In summary, the right choice should have a balance of personal experience, professional experience, education, good fit, skill, and creative ability. Consultants should also have a knowledge of: accessibility, adaptability, air quality, comfort, communication, density, division of space, equipment, finishes, furniture, image, lighting, maintenance, noise, passages, safety, signage, storage, temperature, and windows. Your consultant should not have a bias toward any disability, nor limited resources, and should have significant practical experience in the field.

Qualifying manufacturers of the ADA-compliant products you purchase is also important. See the introduction to the Compliance Product Selection Guide at the back of this book for guidance.

Part Four

ADA MODIFICATION FACTORS

Part Four

INTRODUCTION

Part IV contains 20 chapters that address the key factors to consider in planning modifications that will meet ADA standards and support independent, dignified use of a facility. New to this edition are separate, expanded chapters on Temperature and Air Quality. Updates are included for many of the factors, such as the "Green Lights" program, new guidelines for energy efficient lighting in Chapter 22. Settled ADA case examples are cited in many instances to illustrate legally acceptable solutions to compliance problems. These cases have been settled with the participation of the Department of Justice, and have been published in DOJ "Report Updates."

The last chapter in this part of the book, "25 Low-Cost Compliance Solutions," presents creative, less costly alternatives to standard modifications for ADA compliance.

Design Factors

"Good design costs no more than bad design." — Yvonne Clearwater, Ph.D., designer of habitats in space for NASA.

Bad design under the Americans with Disabilities Act is done to meet the codes as legally required, but not the needs of people. The ADA design factors presented in Part IV are intended to be a practical guide for designers seeking to meet *both* the needs and the codes of the Americans with Disabilities Act. Meeting the need means accounting for the full range of functional limitations, while meeting the codes means fulfilling the requirements of the ADA, and accounting for the full range of federal and state codes, statutes, and standards. The ADA design factors covered in Part IV are the result of a four-year study of people with disabilities, interacting in settings across America as employees, residents, guests and patrons, and citizens. Factor data was collected as part of a design process developed to evaluate, design, and deliver "reasonable accommodation." Environments were designed to maximize the participation of people with disabilities. Sites were evaluated pre- and post-design intervention to determine which factors were most important to enhancing productivity and efficiency, while reducing stress and fatigue. The twenty design factors are:

- Accessibility
- Adaptability
- Air Quality
- Comfort
- Communication
- Density
- Division of Space
- Equipment
- Finishes
- Furniture

- Image
- Lighting
- Maintenance
- Noise
- Passages

- Safety
- Signage
- Storage
- Temperature
- Windows

Meeting both the codes and the needs is crucial to designs that intend to provide reasonable accommodation for people with disabling conditions. A structured, researched, proven design approach to the Americans with Disabilities Act is of enormous importance.

Good design that provides reasonable accommodation by meeting the needs and the codes promotes one's right to independence and dignity to live, to work, and participate in social/leisure activities with equality.

The twenty factors promote three basic elements of good design.

1. Designs that meet the code and the needs are flexible, adaptable and accommodating to all functional limitations and aging.

2. Designs that meet the code and the need increase people's capabilities in a safe manner, with primary safety being focused on the prevention of falling and injuries to hands and fingers.

3. Designs that meet the codes and the needs do not obsolesce. To develop designs that achieve reasonable accommodation, the factors must be integrated into a framework that allows design to be interactive in three ways. Each factor must be accounted for within a code, statute, or standard for each functional limitation. Reasonable accommodation is a complicated design process because it requires interactive design. Figure IV.1 summarizes a framework checklist for evaluating the code and the need by each factor for each disabling condition

Bad design, relative to the Americans with Disabilities Act, is driven by codes, standards and statutes, without accommodating for needs. The consequence of designs which only meet the codes is that over time, it will wind up costing more than good design in money spent to redo work, and in lost revenues, lawsuits, and loss due to lowered productivity, increased injury, and lost dignity. However, the worst consequence of bad design is that people are compromised unnecessarily. The following examples by factor illustrate these points:

Accessibility

If a ramp meets the code on slope, but is not canopied to meet the needs of people who are mobility-impaired, then a restaurant may be avoided and revenues lost.

Adaptability

If a door meets the code for access to entrances, but swings only in one direction, it does not meet the need for maneuverability for people with mobility impairments.

Air Quality

If a building is meeting the American Society of Heating, Refrigeration and Air Conditioning Engineers (ASHRAE) standard for fresh air in an office building, yet the building is still trapping humidity, airborne fibers, etc., then people who have respiratory disease will suffer.

Comfort

There is no comfort code in the Americans with Disabilities Act, yet to meet the needs of people with disabilities, proper seating is important to maintain comfort and productivity.

Communication

Communication strategies are code-focused (in the Americans with Disabilities Act) on hearing and speech impairments, yet if one has Multiple Sclerosis, a speaker phone adaptation is essential to maintaining communication when one has limited hand use and coordination.

Density

Meeting the codes regarding the density of patrons in a restaurant is usually determined by a certain square footage per person. To meet the needs, designs must now account for a minimum of 5% of capacity set aside for disabled individuals. Meeting the needs of people with disabilities means not being segregated for any reason.

Division of Space

Meeting the code on layout may mean having the required number of handicapped bathrooms per public building. However, meeting the need means considering the placement of the bathrooms with attention to travel patterns.

	ADA 1990	OSHA H&S	ANSI	Architect Barr. 1968	International Standards	Vet. Adm.
Accessibility	✔			✔		✔
Adaptability	✔					
Comfort			✔		✔	
Communication	✔					
Density		✔				
Division of space		✔				
Equipment		✔			✔	
Finishes					✔	
Furniture			✔			
Image	✔					
Lighting					✔	
Maintenance		✔				
Noise		✔				
Passages				✔		✔
Safety		✔				
Signage	✔					
Storage	✔			✔		
Temperature				✔		
Air quality			✔			
Windows			✔			

Figure IV.1

Equipment

Meeting the code on equipment may mean having a TDD available for the deaf on site. Meeting equipment needs for people with disabling conditions means buying equipment that can be adapted for special needs, e.g., voice recognition software, material handling carts.

Finishes

There is no code requirement for wall finishes, yet meeting the need for increasing visual acuity clearly involves finishes. For example, contrasting the color of a handrail against a painted surface can add to the utility of handrails by helping to maintain one's orientation in hallways with corners.

Furnishings

There is no specific code governing furnishings, yet meeting the need clearly requires consideration of counter heights and locations when designing for public accommodation.

Image

There is no code to address image, yet how one "fits" in an environment has a clear impact on one's status. One's location and furnishings have always been a clear indication of status. What people with disabilities report most is that their image should not be eroded by conspicuous modifications that call attention to their disabilities.

Lighting

Meeting the codes on lighting usually is concerned most with achieving illumination for the least cost and with the least labor intensity for maintenance. Meeting the needs of the disabled means providing them with the ability to use lighting independently to enhance visual acuity and maintain productivity.

Maintenance

Maintenance is not addressed by a specific ADA code, yet to meet the needs of the disabled, maintenance is critical. Flickering fluorescent lights can cause epileptics to have seizures. Slippery floors can cause accidents for the sight- and mobility-impaired. Clutter in hallways can be an impassable obstacle for those in wheelchairs.

Noise

The codes that mostly apply to noise are the OSHA codes on excessive decibel levels in factories (85 decibels and above), yet noise is a critical need factor for people in general to maintain productivity. Noise fatigues most people over a period of time, and can be distracting to people with visual impairments who rely on audible cues.

Passages

There are many codes that address passages, including the Architectural Barriers codes, as well as state and federal codes. Meeting the need means consideration in the design of passages, not just in terms of width and turning radius, but also travel distances through passages to essential services.

Safety and Security

Meeting the codes on safety has to do primarily with OSHA regulations. Meeting the need for safety and security involves designing lighting that illuminates walkways, and security systems that protect the disabled from crimes of violence.

Signage

Signage is clearly written into the codes of ADA to allow the blind to manage mobility with the aid of braille. Yet, meeting the needs of many disabled (and non-disabled) individuals has to do with the importance of signs being visible under many lighting conditions, and making sure they are useful independent of assistance.

Storage

The codes use examples of storage to illustrate reach and access to resources. Meeting the needs of people with disabilities has to do with more than just reach and height requirements. It also has to do with how and where designers incorporate storage as a factor that allows access to resources in the immediate area, such as one's work area, as well as where shared resources are stored.

Temperature

Meeting the needs often requires additional consideration for people who may have temperature sensitivity due to disease or medications. Zoned areas for temperature control as well as small air-circulating devices meet the need.

Windows

There is no specific code concerning windows other than on hardware to operate the windows. However, meeting the need means creating environments that allow people a feeling of expanse to the outside world. This could be accomplished with appropriate lighting or the opportunity to take breaks in an area with windows.

Chapters in this section are devoted to each of the modification factors just listed. Each chapter reviews building components related to that particular factor, and outlines both Title III ADA requirements (with numbered references) and Title I recommendations. Other relevant codes are listed as well. Sections entitled "Meeting the Need" provide guidance for meeting the needs of disabled people, sometimes by exceeding the requirements of the ADA. These are considerations worth making when planning modifications to a facility, as they may improve operations and productivity of the residing business or its commercial success.

In summary, the Americans with Disabilities Act is perhaps the most complicated statute ever written because it expects designers to be able to choose which legal guidelines are most important (state versus federal and state versus city), and to know how to design in situations where all three titles of the act apply. For example, in the hospitality industry, a hotel must accommodate guests (Title III), employees (Title I), and vehicles that transport guests (Title IV). Designers must also accommodate within each site by meeting the needs and prioritizing. Should accommodation begin with the current disabled employees or those who may be applying for positions? To reduce the complication of the Americans with Disabilities Act, the 20 factors provide a structure with which to evaluate, design, develop and deliver "reasonable accommodation" that meets the codes and the needs. This researched, proven design approach is provided as a way of achieving good design that costs no more than bad design.

Chapter Eleven

ACCESSIBILITY

Accessibility is achieved by meeting specific requirements of the ADA, and also by addressing, as effectively as possible, the needs of people with disabilities. Like the other "Factors" chapters that follow, this chapter will examine accessibility from both points of view—the standards set by the ADA and other codes, and what can be done to enhance and sometimes exceed those requirements to better meet the need. Here and in several of the next 19 chapters, examples have been added of cases that have been settled, with the participation of the Department of Justice. These cases are examples of what states, townships, facilities and businesses have done to meet the law, the code, and the need.

In assessing the code requirements, there are often creative, alternative ways of complying. Chapter 31 provides some low-cost solutions to consider. The Compliance Product Selection Guide at the back of the book offers sources for many related products.

Key Definitions of Accessibility

1. The ability to move into, out of, and throughout a facility.
2. The ability to manipulate objects and equipment within a space.
3. Ease of participation in activities throughout the space, including social activities.

Meeting the Code

[Architectural and Transportation Barriers Compliance Board, 1982 (36 CFR 1190)], [Uniform Federal Accessibility Standard (UFAS)], (ADA Titles I, II, and III, ANSI 4.3/4.6.) Meeting the codes means addressing the requirements of ADA and other applicable national codes, as well as state and local regulations. To make a facility accessible to the physically challenged, one must evaluate, and most likely modify, parking, entrances, elevators, ramps, water fountains and coolers, and bathrooms. The following paragraphs include recommendations for each of these categories.

Parking

(ATBCB 1190.60, UFAS 4.6) Parking spaces should be located near an access door or elevator that is marked "Handicapped Accessible." All parking lots must set aside and identify at least one handicap parking space. Handicap parking spaces should be wider than normal to allow a car or van door to open fully. There should be a minimum of five feet of clearance on at least one side of the vehicle and a four foot wide passageway in front of or behind the vehicle. The total length of any enclosed space (such as a garage), should be not less than 20 feet. (See Figure 11.1.) This length is specified to allow a wheelchair to be mobile around any vehicle for entry and transfer. All lighting should either be constant or be on for no less than 15 minutes to provide adequate time for transfer. See ADA, "Act Guidelines" (ADA-AG) in Appendix A Sections 4.1.2 and 4.6.

Curbing (ATBCB 1190.70, UFAS 4.7) For all walkways, a curb ramp must be provided at any intersection. (See Figure 11.2.) The curb ramp must be at least four feet wide and have a slope no greater than one inch of rise for every foot. Transitions between two surfaces must be smooth. Curb ramps must be of a non-slip surface. Figure 11.2 also shows examples of two different approaches to curb ramps. See ADA-AG Sections 4.1.6, 4.7, 4.8 and 4.29.2.

Cases Initiated or Intervened in by the Department of Justice (D.O.J.)

Title II:

- *An Arizona police department agreed to allow an individual with a mobility impairment to use his motorscooter on roads and sidewalks within city limits anywhere that conventional wheelchairs are allowed.*
- *Kinney v. Yerusalim, Pennsylvania — In agreement with an amicus brief filed by the Department of Justice, the U.S. Court of Appeals for the Third Circuit ruled that the ADA requires cities to install curb ramps when they resurface streets. This Title II lawsuit was brought against the city of Philadelphia by a group of people with mobility impairments.*

Title III:

- *Organizers of the Mississippi Delta Blues Festival, which draws some 10,000 to 20,000 spectators each year, took a number of steps to make its parking, seating, rest rooms, and festival grounds accessible for people with disabilities.*

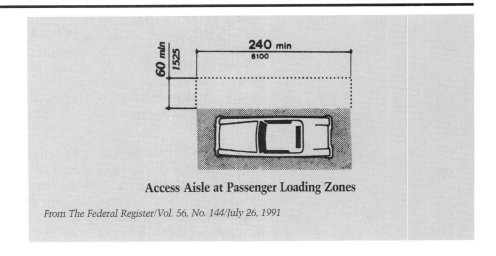

Access Aisle at Passenger Loading Zones

From The Federal Register/Vol. 56, No. 144/July 26, 1991

Figure 11.1

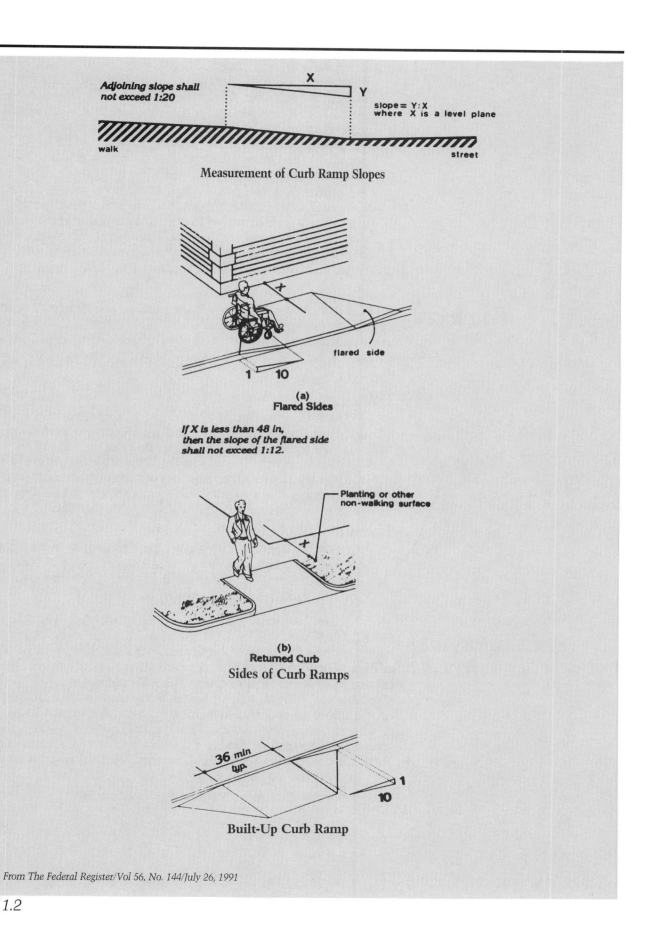

Measurement of Curb Ramp Slopes

**(a)
Flared Sides**

*If X is less than 48 in,
then the slope of the flared side
shall not exceed 1:12.*

**(b)
Returned Curb**

Sides of Curb Ramps

Built-Up Curb Ramp

From The Federal Register/Vol 56, No. 144/July 26, 1991

Figure 11.2

- *U.S. vs. Allright Colorado, Inc., Colorado—The Department entered into a consent decree resolving its lawsuit against Allright Colorado, a company that owns or operates over 100 parking lot facilities in Denver. Under the agreement, Allright will add well over 400 accessible parking spaces to its facilities and will instruct parking attendants to monitor the slots and ticket cars that are improperly parked in accessible space. Allright paid a $20,000 civil penalty to the United States because of the alleged delay in moving toward compliance.*
- *A Louisiana fast food restaurant, a Texas grocery store, a health care facility, an Oregon shopping center, and a retirement community have all agreed to provide accessible parking in their parking lots. The grocery store and shopping center also agreed to install the curb ramps that a person who uses a wheelchair needs to get from the parking lot to the front door.*

Entrances

(ATBCB 1190.120, UFAS 4.14) There must be at least one (1) primary entrance accessible for persons in wheelchairs. Figure 11.3 shows minimum access clearances and maximum doorway depth. See ADA-AG Sections 4.1.2, 4.1.3, 4.1.6, 4.1.7, 4.14.1, and 4.30 for detailed entrance requirements.

Settled Cases

Title II:

- *Madison County, Florida—The Board of Commissioners of Madison County agreed to install an elevator, **widen doors,** renovate toilet facilities and water fountains, and install appropriate signage to make its programs at the Madison County Courthouse accessible for persons with mobility impairments. The County also will submit an interim plan for making its programs accessible until the renovations are completed.*

Title III:

- *A Louisiana steamboat company agreed to improve accessibility for passengers with mobility impairments on two of its boats. It eliminated access barriers in its dining and entertainment areas and made its rest rooms accessible.*

Elevators and Platform Lifts

(ATBCB 1190.100, UFAS 4.10) (ANSI/ASME A117.1-1991) Provide handrails on all three sides of the elevator, 32 inches above the floor. Minimum cab size should be 67 inches to accommodate a wheelchair's forward and circular movement. Elevator controls should conform to ANSI A117.1 standards with controls that are visual, tactile, and audible. Timing of signals on the automatic door should be at least six seconds to allow positioning of wheelchairs for ease of entrance and exit. Figures 11.4—11.6 show acceptable elevator dimensions for controls, access, and maneuverability. For details on elevators, see ADA-AG Sections 4.1.3, 4.1.6, 4.5, 4.10, and 4.30. For platform lifts, see Sections 4.1.3, 4.1.6, 4.2.4, 4.5.1, 4.11, and 4.27.

(See previous case example, Madison County, Florida)

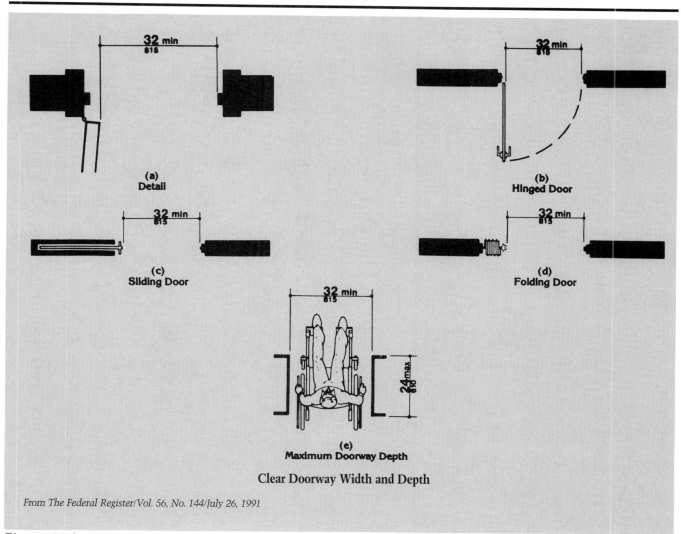

(a)
Detail

(b)
Hinged Door

(c)
Sliding Door

(d)
Folding Door

(e)
Maximum Doorway Depth

Clear Doorway Width and Depth

From *The Federal Register*/Vol. 56, No. 144/July 26, 1991

Figure 11.3

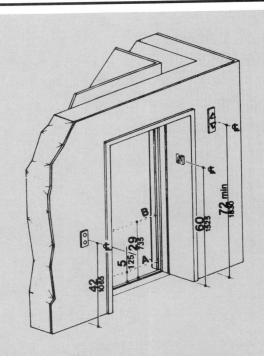

NOTE: The automatic door reopening device is activated if an object passes through either line A or line B. Line A and line B represent the vertical locations of the door reopening device not requiring contact.

Hoistway and Elevator Entrances

From *The Federal Register/Vol. 56, No. 144/July 26, 1991*

Figure 11.4

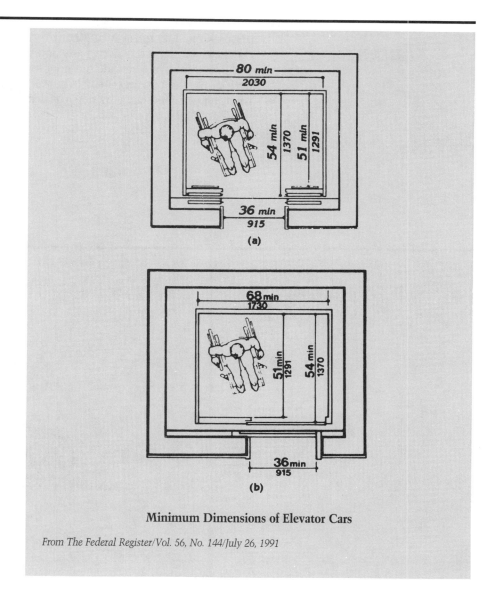

Minimum Dimensions of Elevator Cars

From The Federal Register/Vol. 56, No. 144/July 26, 1991

Figure 11.5

Platforms at Entrances/Exits

(ATBCB 1190.110, UFAS 4.11) Platforms must be designed to accommodate door swing. The minimum platform must extend at least one foot beyond the strike jamb on the side of any doorway. The platform must be at least five feet deep and five feet wide if a door swings toward the walk. If there is no door or the door swings away from the platform, the minimum platform area must be three feet deep by five feet wide. Refer to the ADA-AG Sections 4.8.4 and 4.13.6 for details.

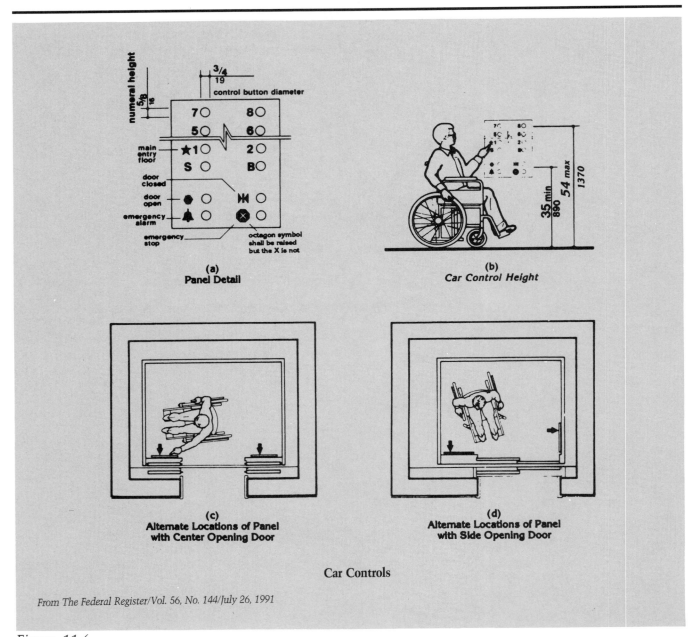

(a) Panel Detail

(b) Car Control Height

(c) Alternate Locations of Panel with Center Opening Door

(d) Alternate Locations of Panel with Side Opening Door

Car Controls

From The Federal Register/Vol. 56, No. 144/July 26, 1991

Figure 11.6

Settled Cases

Title II:

• *A Missouri county agreed to install an elevator and make other structural modifications to make its courthouse accessible. In the interim, it will provide alternative means for providing services to individuals with disabilities.*

Ramps

(ATBCB 1190.70, UFAS 4.8) Ramps should have a maximum slope of one inch for every foot. The surface should be non-slip. There must be a level platform at the top and bottom. Platforms must be located at not more than 30 foot intervals and at every turn. Ramps must have at least one handrail at the 32 inch height that extends one foot beyond the top and bottom of the ramp. (See Figure 11.7.) The minimum platform on any ramp is three feet deep by five feet wide when door swings away from the ramp. The minimum platform requirement if a door swings onto the ramp is five feet wide by five feet deep. A platform must extend at least one foot beyond the strike jamb side of any doorway. See ADA-AG Section 4.1.6, 4.1.7, 4.5, 4.8, and 4.26 for details.

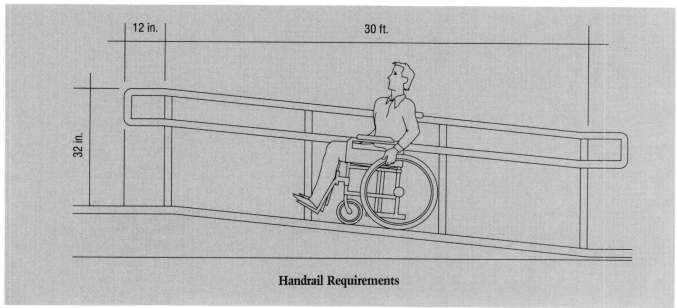

Handrail Requirements

Figure 11.7

Settled Cases
Title II:

- *A Tennessee city agreed to move all city meetings from the inaccessible second floor of the town hall to the city's accessible library. It also built ramps at two entrances to the town hall and remodeled rest rooms in the town hall and library.*

Title III:

- *Emerald Lanes, Greenwood, South Carolina—The owners of Emerald Lanes, a bowling center, agreed to construct a ramp and a new door at the front entrance; build a new, accessible unisex rest room and vestibule leading to it; and add accessible parking. The agreement resolved a complaint from an individual who uses a wheelchair for mobility who could not watch his children participate in a bowling league and banquet because the facility was inaccessible.*
- *A Utah bank, an Illinois bowling center, an office building, and a Maryland cable television company have all agreed to install ramps to make their entrances accessible for people who use mobility devices. The bowling center, office building, and cable TV company also agreed to provide accessible parking in their parking lots.*

Water Fountains and Coolers

(ATBCB 1190.160, UFAS 4.15) Drinking water should be accessible with up-front spouts and controls that can be hand or floor-operated. Drinking cups may also be provided to promote accessibility. Accessible height should be no more than 36 inches. The recess into an alcove should not be less than 30 inches wide for accessibility. (See Figure 11.8.) Refer to sections 4.1.3 (10), 4.15, and 4.27.4 of the ADA-AG.

Settled Cases
Title II:

- *Scott County, Arkansas—Scott County agreed to renovate the county courthouse in order to make it readily accessible to individuals with disabilities. Specifically, the county agreed to renovate the courthouse's entrances, rest rooms, door hardware, and* **drinking fountains.**

Public Telephones

(ATBCB 1190.210, UFAS 4.31) Telephones must be placed so that they can be reached by person(s) in a wheelchair or those with disabilities such as short stature, amputees, and quadriplegics. Coin slots must not be more than 48 inches from the floor. (See Figure 11.9.) Refer to Sections 4.1.3 (17), 4.1.6 (1.e), 4.4.1, and 4.31 in the ADA-AG. See Chapter 15, "Communication," for requirements including TDD's, large numbers for the visually-impaired, etc.

Settled Cases
Title III:

- *Empire State Building, New York, New York—The owners and operators of the Empire State Building agreed to take wide-ranging measures to ensure access to public areas of the building. The agreement mandates changes to the lobby, entrance, observations decks, rest rooms and* **telephones.**

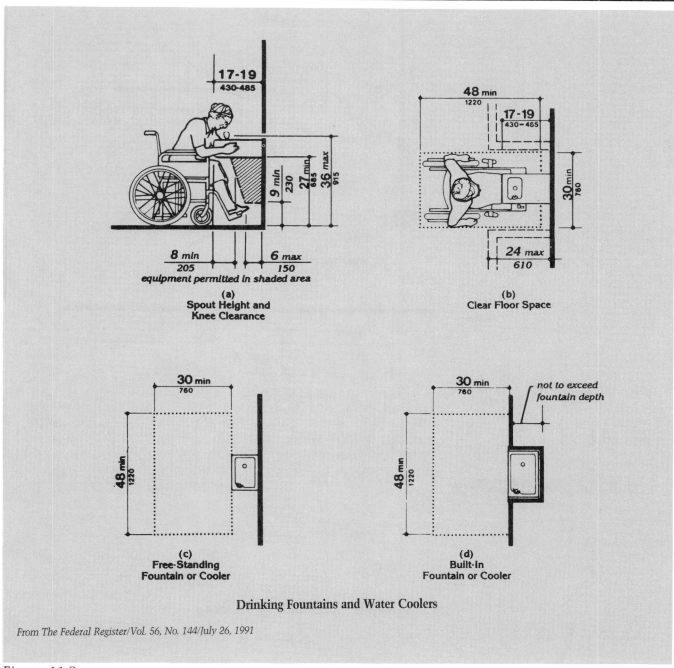

(a)
Spout Height and
Knee Clearance

17-19
430-485

9 min
230

27 min
685

36 max
915

8 min
205

6 max
150

equipment permitted in shaded area

(b)
Clear Floor Space

48 min
1220

17-19
430-485

30 min
760

24 max
610

(c)
Free-Standing
Fountain or Cooler

30 min
760

48 min
1220

(d)
Built-In
Fountain or Cooler

30 min
760

not to exceed
fountain depth

48 min
1220

Drinking Fountains and Water Coolers

From The Federal Register/Vol. 56, No. 144/July 26, 1991

Figure 11.8

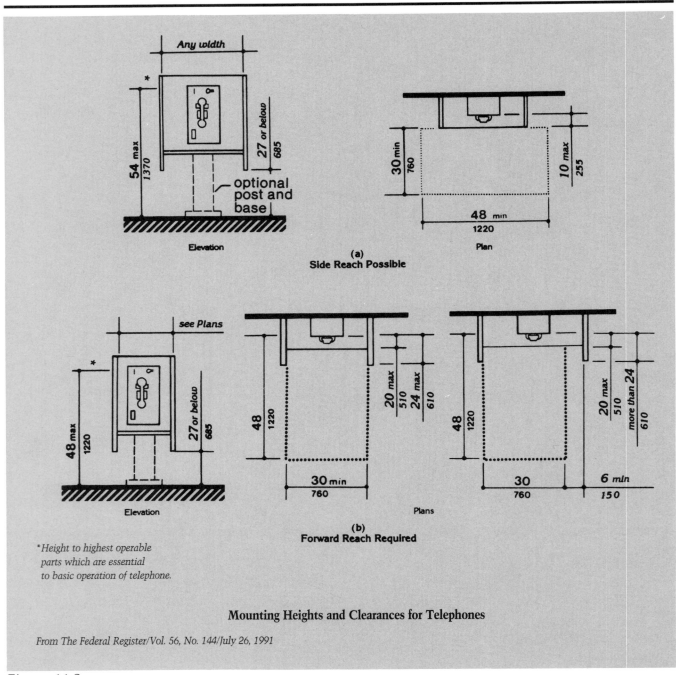

*Height to highest operable
parts which are essential
to basic operation of telephone.

Mounting Heights and Clearances for Telephones

From The Federal Register/Vol. 56, No. 144/July 26, 1991

Figure 11.9

Bathrooms

(ATBCB 1190.150, UFAS 4.23) To increase accessibility and usability, bathrooms should be designed to accommodate the maximum amount of maneuvering possible for the physically challenged person, their wheelchair, and the possibility of a second person either assisting or using the bathroom separately. If there is a stall toilet, the area must be at least 36 inches wide and 56 inches deep, and have a clear door opening of 32 inches. The door must swing out. Stalls must have handrails on each side which are 33 inches high and parallel to the floor. These should be 1-1/2 inches in diameter, with 1-1/2 inches of clearance between the rail and the wall, and fastened securely at the ends and center. The lavatory seat must have narrow, shallow aprons, and any drain or hot water pipes should be covered or insulated to protect the person from burns or abrasions. Toilet rooms for men must have wall-mounted urinals with the opening of the basin no more than 17" from the finished floor. A mirror or shelf above the lavatory must be no higher than 40 inches above the floor and should ideally be tilted for reflectance. If medicine cabinets are provided, one or more usable shelves must be available at a height no greater than 44 inches above the floor. Towel racks and dispensers must be mounted no higher than 40 inches from the floor. The bathroom floor should be non-slip. Commercial rubber tile with a raised pattern is recommended to reduce the risk of slipping and falling on a wet surface. All bathroom fixtures must conform to ANSI standard A112.19.2. (See Figures 11.10 – 11.13). See Sections 4.1.2 (6), 4.1.6 (3e), 4.1.7 (3c), 4.16, 4.17, 4.18, 4.19, 4.20, 4.21, 4.22, 4.23, 4.24, 4.26 and 4.27.4 for requirement details, including for bathtubs and showers.

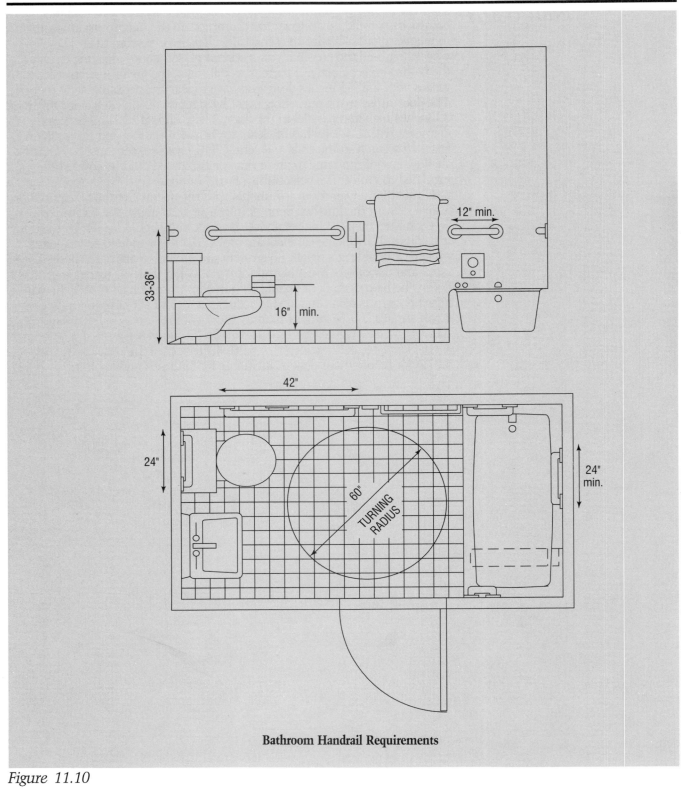

Bathroom Handrail Requirements

Figure 11.10

158

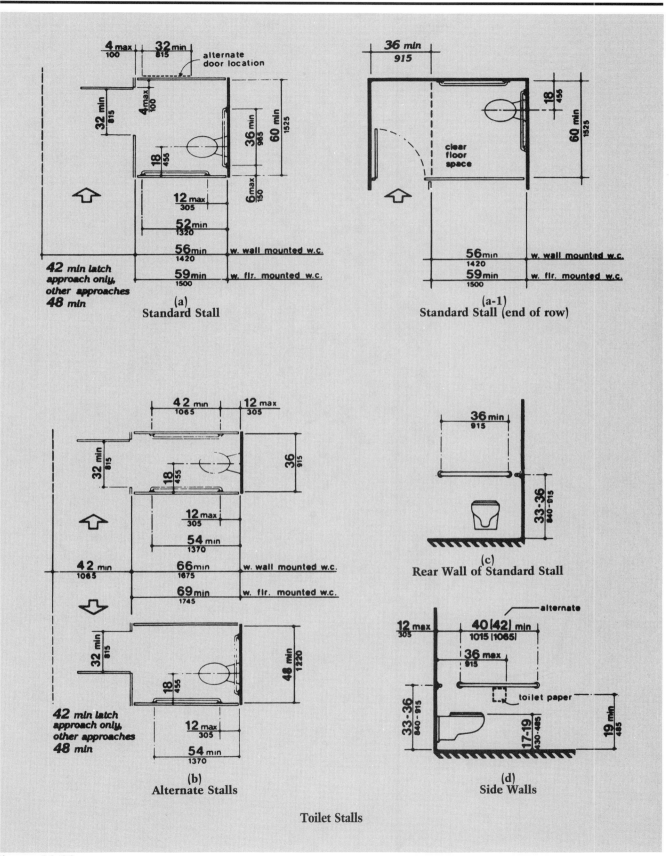

(a)
Standard Stall

(a-1)
Standard Stall (end of row)

(b)
Alternate Stalls

(c)
Rear Wall of Standard Stall

(d)
Side Walls

Toilet Stalls

Figure 11.11

159

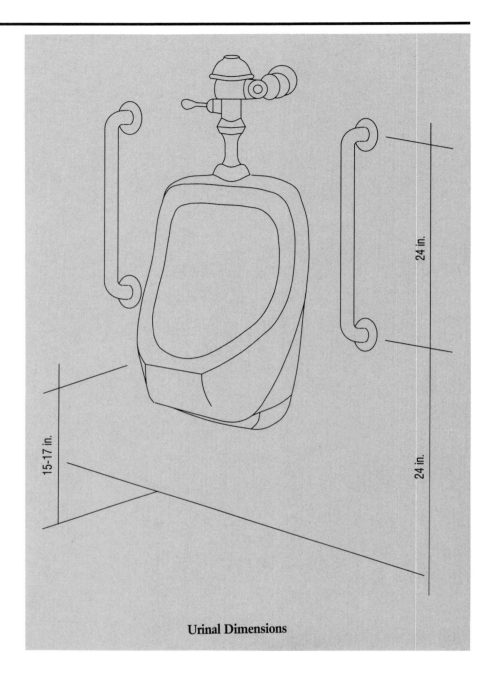

Urinal Dimensions

Figure 11.12

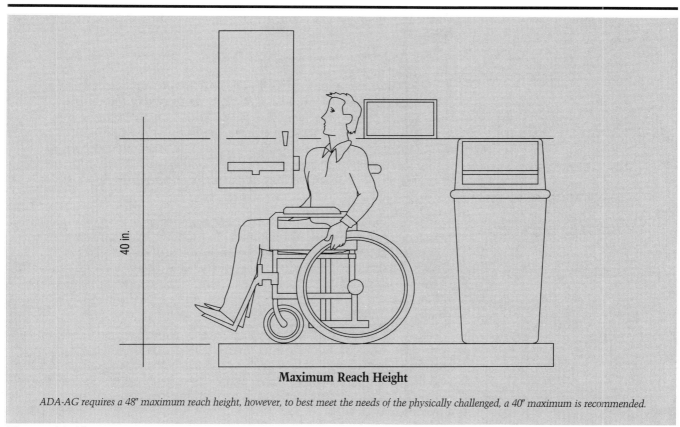

Maximum Reach Height

ADA-AG requires a 48″ maximum reach height, however, to best meet the needs of the physically challenged, a 40″ maximum is recommended.

Figure 11.13

Settled Cases
Title III:

- *A motel in Louisiana agreed to provide accessible parking, to make its front desk and lobby rest rooms accessible, and to* **make six guest rooms accessible for guests with mobility impairments, including converting to roll-in showers in two of the rooms.**
- *Sardi's Restaurant, New York, New York—Sardi's Restaurant in New York agreed to resolve a complaint that the restaurant's rest rooms were inaccessible for persons who use wheelchairs or other mobility devices. Sardi's will install an accessible unisex rest room and signage indicating the location of the rest room.*

Meeting the Need

Spinal cord injury, stroke, disease (e.g., multiple sclerosis), or neurological impairments often result in limitations in mobility. Therefore, designs must accommodate wheelchairs, walkers, canes, and scooters in site-specific areas. All usable areas/facilities must be accessible (beginning with the outside of the building)—from the parking lot to the entrance, elevators, platforms, ramps, water coolers, telephones and bathrooms—for the physically challenged person.

Meeting the need means designing access that allows a person to be mobile with safety and comfort. Meeting the mobility needs means having doors, corridors, and passages wide enough for maneuverability, and ramps, elevators and lifts as an alternative to stairs. Some examples of access that meets people's needs are ramps with canopies, parking lots with daytime luminescence at night, heated handrails, ramps and walks and signage that can be seen from 4 sides from 30 feet away.

Chapter Twelve

ADAPTABILITY

Adaptability is an important consideration in the ADA, and in meeting the needs of people with disabilities. While building codes and the ADA-AG address adaptations through certain modification requirements, still more can be done in this area to support the independence and productivity of disabled individuals. Truly effective adaptations to environments must include policies and procedures to guide organizational actions toward access for people with disabilities.

This chapter reviews code and ADA standards, and recommends further measures. Some cases that have been settled with the participation of the Department of Justice are listed to show the kinds of solutions that have been reached since the ADA was enacted.

Key Definitions of Adaptability

1. Flexible furnishings, equipment and fixtures that allow safe productivity without stress and fatigue, no matter what the range of human capabilities and needed equipment (e.g., wheelchairs, walkers, removable seating).
2. Adaptive and assistive devices that support slower reaction times, decreases in stamina and strength, loss of balance, and low vision and hearing (e.g., remote controls for lighting and equipment).
3. Policies and procedures to enhance the integration of people with disabilities.

Meeting the Code

Meeting the codes for adaptability involves making modifications to existing spaces to accommodate physically challenged individuals by meeting ADA and code requirements such as those noted in "Grasp and Reach Enhancements" in this chapter. There are many available options for furnishings, hardware, and devices to promote accessibility and better viewing/reading—many of which are discussed in this chapter and shown in the **Compliance Product Selection Guide** at the back of this book.

Following are some examples of adaptations made in response to challenges based on the ADA.

Title II:

- A Pennsylvania county court agreed to provide accommodations for an individual with a learning disability, including daily transcriptions and extra time to ask questions, during court proceedings.
- A State board of law examiners agreed to allow an individual extra time (time and one-half over two days) to take the State bar examination as an accommodation for his learning disability.

Title III:

- A Texas movie theater that had prevented a woman from bringing a box of cookies into the theater for her diabetic child agreed to modify its policy against outside food and beverages by making an exception in the case of medical necessity.
- A bar in Illinois agreed to modify its policy of refusing to serve alcohol to customers who appear to be drunk based on the way they walk. A customer who has Parkinson's disease had been refused service because staff assumed he was drunk due to the unsteady gait associated with his disability.
- A famous restaurant in New York City that had turned away a customer who was wearing sneakers due to a mobility impairment agreed to modify its dress code by making an exception when necessary to provide service to a person with a disability.
- A Nevada hotel agreed to offer its barrier-free rooms at the same rate as its other rooms, including at those times when promotional or special rates are offered.

Panels and Furniture

(ATBCB 1190.170, UFAS 4.27, U.L, ADA Titles I, II, III & IV) The work sites should be designed with modular furniture that has been reconfigured to accommodate a straight line from the office door to the person's position at their desk. If the work surface has to accommodate a computer display and keyboard, these should be positioned to adapt for visual and keying access. Figure 12.1 shows a space configuration where furnishings and partitions create zones of passage through lobby areas.

Grasp and Reach Enhancements

Adaptability in all Design Hardware (ANSI A117.1) ANSI A117.1 is the standard for building elements such as kitchen counters, sinks and grab bars to be added to, raised, lowered or otherwise located or altered so as to accommodate the needs of persons with different types or degrees of disability. Examples of cost effective design considerations for disabled people are lever handles on all doors. (See Figure 12.2). All hardware on doors and cabinets and windows should be operable with one hand, taking into consideration the grip and grasp strength of the individual. A tight grip for twisting and turning is not acceptable. All doors, cabinets and windows should be operable with one hand and not require excessive strength. See Sections 4.16.4, 4.17.6, 4.20.4, and 4.26 of the ADA-AG in Appendix A for more detail on grab bar requirements. Refer to Section 4.13 for hardware requirements. See Sections 4.2.5 and 4.2.6 for reach limitation requirements.

Controls

(ATBCB 1190.170, UFAS 4.17, U.L) Controls should accommodate visibility and reach. All switches and controls for lights, heat, windows, fire alarms or any other controls involved in frequent and/or essential use should be set no higher than 48 inches above the floor nor lower than 15″. The use of remote controls to control the light system and equipment can be a

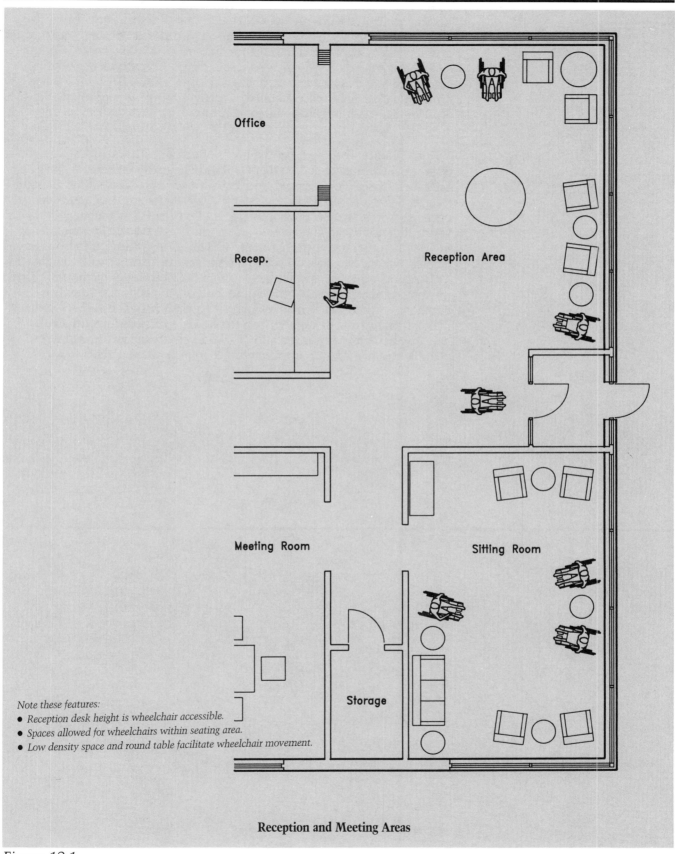

Office

Recep.

Reception Area

Meeting Room

Sitting Room

Storage

Note these features:
- *Reception desk height is wheelchair accessible.*
- *Spaces allowed for wheelchairs within seating area.*
- *Low density space and round table facilitate wheelchair movement.*

Reception and Meeting Areas

Figure 12.1

productivity asset and can also be critical to safety, convenience and security. Remote control systems are operable either from a transmitter or manually and transmit signals to appliance modules. Modules are plugged into outlets and appliances are plugged into the modules ready to be activated. Controls should accommodate visibility and reach. Figure 12.3 shows work space configured to enhance reach capabilities. Figures 12.4 and 12.5 show reach limits and clear floor space required to access controls. See ADA-AG Section 4.27 for details on requirements for controls.

Vision Enhancements

Vision enhancements to meet the needs of people with vision impairments begin with the understanding that environments must enhance the use of the other senses. For example, people with low vision depend on auditory feedback as cues to location and safety. Typical cues are automatic door openers. Arrival at new environments is often sensed by a change in temperature or background sounds. Cues such as a change in a handrail to indicate a corner are also important. Variations in lighting are also used to differentiate between areas. Tactile patterns at ramps may be used to indicate a change in slope on a walkway. Meeting the need for the vision-impaired means organizing routes of travel into systems to encourage cognitive mapping. Furthermore, it requires keeping passages free of obstacles. Contrasts in color and texture of surfaces help to provide spatial orientation. Grab bars and handrails provide balance. Noise levels should be lowered where possible to allow visually impaired people to pick up on auditory cues.

Lever-type Door Handles

Figure 12.2

Computer Screens

(International Standards Organization VDT Color Standards, 1988) The increase and excessive use of inappropriate colors on computer display images has necessitated the development of standards for their color specifications. Image interpretation depends on the design of an image and how closely it represents an object or how easily its representation or function can be learned. When correctly used, color enhances perception and cognition and improves user performance.

Special Viewing Conditions

Detection of a color and its identification and appearance are all affected by the peripheral angle and distance at which it is viewed. Where rapid color detection is required, red and green should be avoided beyond a viewing angle of 40 degrees, yellow—50 degrees, and blue—60 degrees. For viewing distances beyond 60 cm, high saturations and large luminance contrasts should be used, and saturated colors on dark backgrounds avoided.

Continuous Reading

For continuous reading tasks, desaturated spectrally close colors (cyan, green and yellow) should be used for the main screen content to avoid accommodation problems and disruptive after-images.

Color Coding

Hues should match common cultural stereotypes and conventional associations with conditions or actions being represented. The meanings of colors should be obvious or clearly indicated (as well as displayed on screen). Red should be used only to display critical conditions or error messages, and yellow for warning.

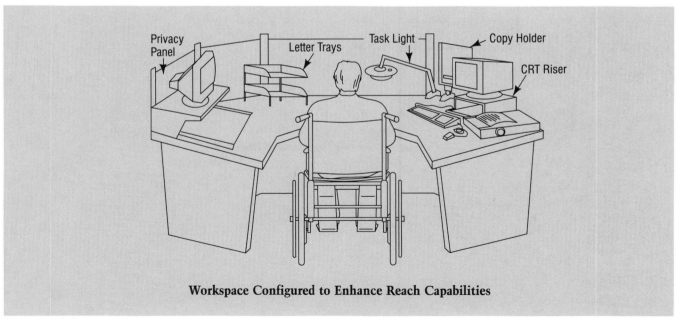

Workspace Configured to Enhance Reach Capabilities

Figure 12.3

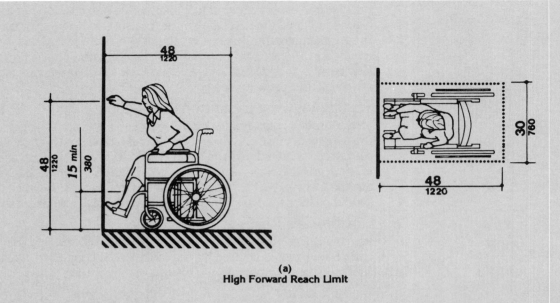

(a)
High Forward Reach Limit

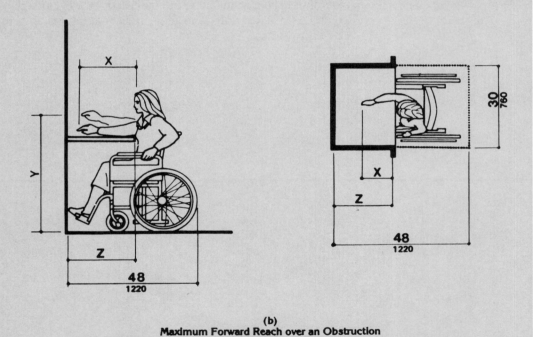

(b)
Maximum Forward Reach over an Obstruction

NOTE: x shall be ≤ 25 in. (635 mm); z shall be ≥ x.
When x < 20 in. (510 mm), then y shall be 48 in. (1220 mm) maximum.
When x is 20 to 25 in. (510 to 635 mm), then y shall be 44 in. (1120 mm) maximum.

Reach Limitations

From The Federal Register/Vol. 56, No. 144/July 26, 1991

Figure 12.4

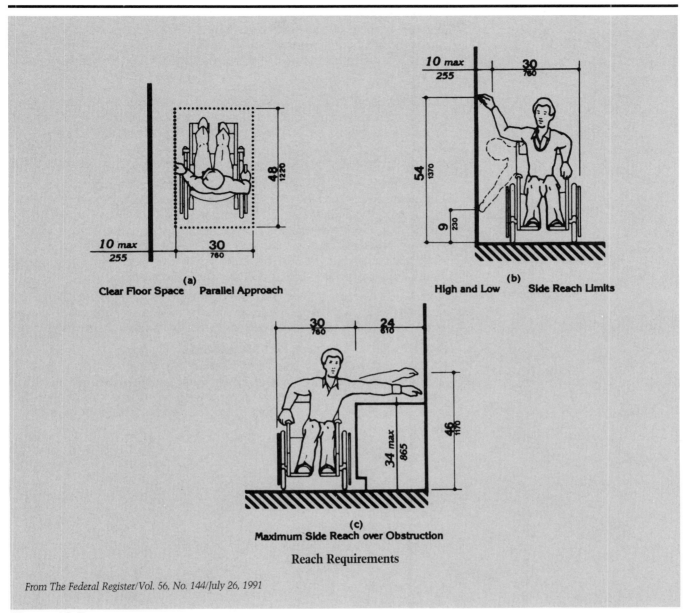

(a)
Clear Floor Space   Parallel Approach

(b)
High and Low   Side Reach Limits

(c)
Maximum Side Reach over Obstruction

Reach Requirements

From The Federal Register/Vol. 56, No. 144/July 26, 1991

Figure 12.5

Number and Legend

Only the number of colors appropriate for an application should be used and, if the meaning of a color must be recalled, no more than 4 to 5 colors should be used. Where more colors are required, a legend should be provided.

Meeting the Need: Social Integration

All public rooms must be equally accessible for both the challenged and the fully functioning person. Physical challenges do not necessarily reduce one's need for social interaction. In fact, facilitating the opportunity for social interaction is an extremely important aspect of the design of environments for disabled people. The ADA states: *equal opportunity at social interaction.*

Meeting the need means designing adaptations that allow a person to be integrated socially into the seating areas comprised of chairs and couches. Some examples of adaptations that promote social integration are removable seating that allows wheelchairs to be integrated with group seating at stadiums and auditoriums, providing straws as part of a table place setting for people with spasms to use for drinking, or ergonomic hand controls on vending machines that allow for self-service with independence.

Meeting the need for the control of equipment is providing controls that have convenient vertical and horizontal reach, and having automated systems that do not require rapid movement or agility on the part of users.

Psychological Control Enhancements

To avoid any negative psychological effects due to the environment, it is essential to give the individuals using the space as much control over it as possible. For example, if it is possible to zone controls for room temperature for disabled people, do so. Another example is having a call button in the bathroom.

Chapter Thirteen

AIR QUALITY

While the ADA does not focus on specific air quality requirements, it is important to address this issue—to prevent illness in a healthy population of building users, and to enhance the health, productivity and comfort of disabled people. The key facilities challenge regarding ADA and indoor air quality is maintaining a comfortable and healthy work environment. This is a complex subject because so many factors contribute to, or detract from, healthy indoor air. This chapter will review problem sources and code standards, and, finally, will offer nine steps toward better air quality.

Factors Affecting Indoor Air Quality

Indoor air quality is not a simple, easily defined concept. It is a constantly changing interaction of a complex set of factors. Four of the most important elements involved in the development of indoor air quality problems are: a source of odors or contaminants; a problem with the design or operation of the HVAC system; a pathway between the source and the location of the complaint; and the building occupants.

The EPA has estimated that we are exposed to two to five times more pollution indoors than outdoors. Since the majority of us spend 80% to 90% of our time indoors, air pollutants in sealed environments have been proven to have a significant effect on the health of people. Why?

New building interiors, common office supplies and equipment, furnishings, detergents, paints, and even humans contribute to a toxic blend of gases, organic compounds, irritants and microbial contamination inside a typical building. This problem is compounded by several factors: "tighter" buildings in response to energy consumption concerns, inadequate HVAC system maintenance and operation procedures, and increased use of synthetic materials and misapplication of those materials.

Airborne toxins can cause a variety of physical symptoms, including headaches, skin irritations, respiratory ailments, and fatigue. Labeled "sick building syndrome" (SBS), these symptoms worsen with prolonged exposure and subside when the employee leaves the building. SBS may lead to the more dangerous "building-related illness" (BRI), in which symptoms may be traced to bioaerosols. BRI was the cause of the deadly Legionnaire's Disease outbreak.

Meeting the Code (Indoor Air Quality Act of 1991 – S.455)

Litigation is increasing as workers become more aware of SBS and BRI. Both are generally defined as 20 percent or more of the occupants being affected by poor indoor air quality. Symptoms, which may include irritation of the eyes, nose or throat; headaches; lethargy and difficulty concentrating, are typically relieved shortly after leaving the affected building.

Recent court actions have included a $900,000 damage award after an insecticide used on an office carpet made employees ill; $16 million in damages to a Missouri family that claimed the building materials used in their home caused chronic formaldehyde poisoning; 400 of 700 employees at the DuPage County Courthouse in Illinois filed suit against architects and contractors who designed and built their $53 million facility; and a $37 million Florida county administration building built in 1987 that required $26 million in alterations to offset IAQ (indoor air quality) problems, with the contractor held responsible for $7 million.

In order of frequency, these factors have been identified as contributors to sick building syndrome:

1. Operating faults and poor maintenance
2. Basic design errors
3. Changed function/changed heat load
4. Inadequate ventilation
5. Poor air distribution
6. Inefficient filtration
7. Contaminated ductwork

The following is a breakdown of problems (survey by NIOSH):

- Lack of outside air
- Poor air distribution

Indoor contaminants

- Tobacco smoke
- Adhesives
- Liquid photocopier
- Boiler additives

Outdoor contaminants

- Car exhaust

Biological contaminants

- Bacteria
- Fungi
- Unknown

Building fabric

- Volatile furniture emissions
- Adhesive vapors

Air Quality Definitions

These are the characteristics of good indoor air quality:

- Temperature 72°F to 78°F
- Humidity 40% RH to 60% RH
- Air velocity 20 fpm to 35 fpm in ducts
- Dilution ventilation 20 cfm per person

Meeting the Code

[ANSI/ARI (Air Conditioning/Refrigeration Institute) 210/240-89] The Indoor Air Quality Act of 1991 (S.455) states that any new building or renovation must maintain/operate an HVAC system that provides a minimum of 20 cubic feet/minute of outdoor air per occupant. Ductwork in these buildings must keep leakage to less than 3% and provide for not less than 0.75 air changes/hour at 25 pascals. VAV boxes incorporate dampers that adjust the volume of air to the zone or room. The air supply is modulated by electric or pneumatic motors that control the dampers. As a general rule, the dampers should always be left open at least 25 or 30 percent of their capacity. The use of synthetic materials which release volatile organic compounds as off-gasing should be reduced.

The following are examples of emission rates on materials or products that may be introduced into the environment. Rates should be thought of as milligrams of a specific chemical being released (off-gassed) from each square meter of surface per hour. This information should be used in conjunction with other criteria to design a flush-out program.

Low Emitting Materials and Products (Indoor Air, July/August)	
Material/Products	**Maximum Emissions**
Flooring Materials	.6 mg/h per m^2
Floor Coatings	.6 mg/h per m^2
Wall Materials	.4 mg/h per m^2
Wall Coatings	.4 mg/h per m^2
Movable Partitions	.4 mg/h per m^2
Office Furniture	2.5 mg/h per workstation

One key tool for controlling indoor air quality is a well-designed and maintained HVAC system. Particularly important are the system's filtration components, because they must be relied upon to remove very small, breathable particulates before they reach human lungs. Filters should always be high quality, and well fitted to eliminate gaps that may allow unfiltered air flow, and should be regularly maintained.

IAQ problems are complex, often with many causes. However, researchers suspect that SBS and BRI may be caused by airborne formaldehyde, volatile organic compounds, asbestos, tobacco smoke, fungi, microbes, and a number of other toxins and irritants.

Chemical and Dust Allergies/Reactions

Formaldehyde: This is the most common chemical irritant in modern buildings. It is difficult to build without formaldehyde; the chemical is in plywood, particleboard, stain-resistant carpets, insulation, and adhesives used for flooring. Exposure to formaldehyde can bring on a sore throat and a tingling nose in sensitive individuals. The good news is that the amount of formaldehyde emitted by these products decreases over time.

Pesticides: Usually, pesticide irritation leads to problems with skin, eyes or respiratory tract. Pesticides can also affect the digestive tract (nausea, diarrhea) and nervous system (headache, dizziness). Read labels and use correctly!

Carbon Monoxide: Gas appliances, including furnaces and stoves, emit this deadly byproduct. At low doses, carbon monoxide causes dizziness and flu-like symptoms; at higher doses, the gas is lethal. Using ventilation fans around gas appliances and keeping burners properly adjusted can help reduce the problem.

Solvent: Benzene, found in paints, varnishes and solvents, can cause respiratory problems. The key to avoiding problems is to read the label and use the products only as directed.

Dust: Because dust settles from the air very quickly, furniture and carpets are the most affected. Vacuuming furniture and carpets weekly cuts down substantially on dust. Getting the dust out of the air is easier, but less effective. Air filters trap only the dust in the air, so any dust that has already fallen to the ground stays put. Combining regular cleaning with air filters is more effective, since the filter will trap the air that cleaning stirs up.

Mold: These simple organisms thrive in areas of high humidity. Even if your climate is not naturally humid, using a humidifier can encourage the growth of molds. Keep humidity to a minimum by running air conditioning or a dehumidifier during humid seasons.

Common Symptoms Groups	Interventions
Headache, lethargy, nausea, drowsiness, dizziness	• If onset was acute (sudden and/or severe), arrange for medical evaluation, as the problem may be carbon monoxide poisoning. • Check combustion sources for uncontrolled emissions or spillage. • Check outdoor air intakes for nearby sources of combustion fumes. • Consider evacuation/medical evaluation if problem isn't corrected quickly. • Consider other pollutant sources. • Check overall ventilation; see if areas of poor ventilation coincide with complaints.
Congestion; swelling, itching or irritation of eyes, nose, or throat; dry throat; may be accompanied by non-specific symptoms (e.g., headache, fatigue, nausea)	• May be allergic, if only small number affected; more likely to be irritational response if large number are affected. • Urge medical attention for allergies. • Check for dust or gross microbial contamination due to sanitation problems, water damage, or contaminated ventilation system. • Check outdoor allergen levels (e.g., pollen counts). • Check closely for sources of irritating chemicals such as formaldehyde or those found in some solvents.
Cough; shortness of breath; fever, chills and/or fatigue after return to the building	• May be hypersensitivity pneumonitis or humidifier fever. A medical evaluation can help identify possible causes. • Check for gross microbial contamination due to sanitation problems, water damage, or contaminated HVAC system.

Common Symptoms Groups	Interventions
Diagnosed infection	• May be Legionnaire's Disease or histoplasmosis, related to bacteria or fungi found in the environment. • Contact your local or State Health Department for guidance.
Suspected cluster of rare or serious health problems such as cancer, miscarriages	• Contact your local or State Health Department for guidance.
Other stressors; discomfort and/or health complaints that cannot be readily ascribed to air contaminants or thermal conditions	• Check for problems with environmental, ergonomic, and job-related psychosocial stressors.

Meeting the Need

As regards the ADA, facility managers are charged with maintaining a comfortable, healthy work environment. This is a significant responsibility regarding IAQ. The proactive approach to maintaining healthy indoor air quality begins with collecting and evaluating data on it. Steps should then be taken by building engineers to eliminate any potential trouble spots in HVAC systems. Problems can be prevented before they result if the following 9 steps are taken:

1. Survey employee air quality complaints.
2. Set the outside air ventilation rate to meet the ASHRAE level of 20 cfm/person.
3. If necessary, modify air distribution to agree with furniture layout to increase distribution efficiency.
4. Check airtight integrity of the HVAC unit and filter holding frames.
5. Ensure that the filter efficiency is in accordance with ASHRAE standards.
6. Review the location of outside air intakes to ensure that they are not near pollutant sources, or downwind of such sources.
7. Have the HVAC system inspected on a semi-annual basis, and cleaned as determined by the inspection report.
8. It is also suggested that the use of indoor houseplants may be an inexpensive way to aid in improving indoor air quality, due to their oxygen/carbon dioxide exchange properties.
9. Select building materials and products with low emissions of toxic substances. As a starting point, consult the Environmental Protection Agency or the American Institute of Architects for guidance in selecting environmentally acceptable building products.

Although it remains difficult to differentiate between the perception of health risks and their actual cause, a proactive approach to healthy indoor air is clearly better than having to later neutralize the harmful effects of high emissions. While the effects of exposure to such chemicals is still controversial, it seems clear that their presence in the atmosphere contributes to SBS. In particular, it is important to avoid products with emissions that are too great to be diffused by standard ventilation.

Chapter Fourteen

COMFORT

Comfort includes a range of issues addressed by ADA requirements (particularly Title I) and further modifications to meet the needs of disabled people. Added to this chapter's code and ADA requirements and recommendations to meet the need are nationwide case examples of problems resolved in this area. Also refer to the new Compliance Product Selection Guide at the back of this book. Section B of the Guide describes products, including furniture, that enhance the comfort and productivity of disabled people.

Comfort Definitions

1. Designs that fit equipment to people, not people to equipment.
2. Designs that allow choice of orientation and viewing.
3. Policies and procedures to ensure independence and dignity.

Meeting the Code

(ADA Title I, ANSI/HFS 100.1988) Meeting the requirements of Title I of the ADA involves providing not only access for job applicants, but also a user-friendly environment in which disabled employees can effectively perform their job functions. The appropriate modifications can provide comfort, while increasing productivity.

Following are examples of comfort-related cases settled with the involvement of the Department of Justice.

- *A Texas police department agreed to change its policies and procedures on public contact after an individual with severe physical disabilities was treated in a demeaning manner at the scene of an automobile accident. The police officer involved received a reprimand and was required to attend sensitivity training.*
- *A famous entertainer, who was performing in New York, allowed a man with a hearing impairment to move closer to the stage so that he could read the entertainer's lips during the concert, and provided him with printed lyrics for all of the songs to be performed.*
- *City of Fargo, North Dakota — The City of Fargo agreed to resolve complaints against its sports stadium and general entertainment facility, the Fargodome. The City will adopt a formal policy that provides for ticket prices for individuals with disabilities who need*

special seating to attend events in the Fargodome that are equivalent to ticket prices charged to others. The City also agreed to publicize its new policy, appoint an ADA coordinator for the Fargodome, develop an ADA grievance procedure, and conduct an evaluation of its policies and practices as required by Title II.

- A baseball stadium agreed to make its ticket counters, seating, rest rooms, and concessions accessible for people who have mobility impairments.

Proper Seating Position for Work

The entire primary viewing area should allow the display/work to be located between 0 and 60 degrees below the horizontal plane at eye level. Figure 14.1 shows proper seating positions, with dimensions.

Considerations for disabled people when seating and positioning for work should include a contoured seat cushion of 1/2″ to 1″ in depth. This allows for proper weight distribution of the pelvic bone, and also maintains proper circulation to the legs. Backrests should extend from the lower back to the shoulders and should be contoured for a minimum of 12 inches.

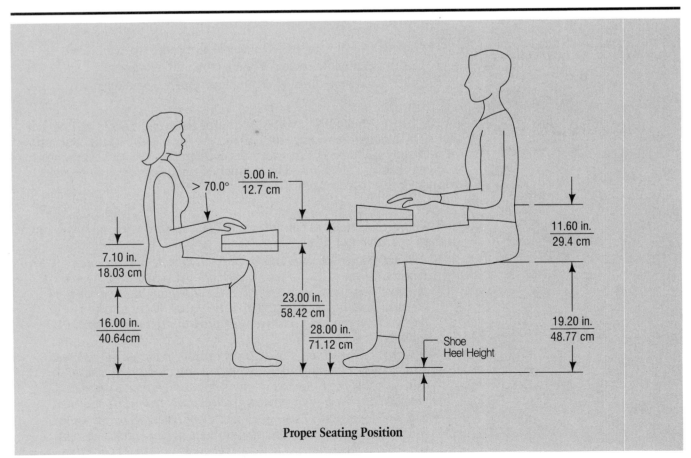

Proper Seating Position

Figure 14.1

An ergonomic chair with breathable fabric is recommended. The following specifications accommodate most office workers and can be interchanged between work sites. They allow independent posture and positioning through the day. (See Figure 14.2 with parts labeled to coincide with those listed below.)

a. Adjustable seat tilting 10 degrees forward, 20 degrees backward.
b. Headrest: 15 inches wide by 6 inches high, by 3 inches thick.
c. Neck rest to meet the contour of the cervical spine.
d. Back height above seat: between 22–31 inches.
e. Back width at shoulders of 14–19 inches.
f. Seat pan: 17–20 inches wide by 14–22 inches deep.
g. Arm height: 6–9 inches above the seat.
h. Armrest length: 6–9 inches up to front curve.
i. Armrest: 2-1/2–5 inches wide and 3/4 inch thick.
j. Lateral side supports (fabric with padding).
k. Distance of armrest to front of seat: 5–7 inches.
l. Diameter of base: 27 inches, with 5 casters.
m. Seat height adjustment: 19"–24" and 17"–20-1/2".
n. Lumbar pad range of 5 inches.
o. Fabric: site dependent.

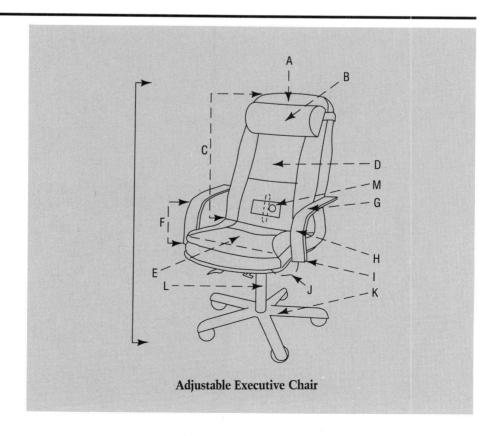

Adjustable Executive Chair

Figure 14.2

Meeting the Need

Meeting the need for comfort and safety is an issue for disabled people who have either a partial or total loss of sensation due to stroke, motor loss, or paralysis. Tactile sensitivity also declines with age. Sources of heat and abrasion are of particular concern. It is important to insulate any sources of heat that can be contacted (e.g., hot pipes). Maintain hot water temperatures to an upper limit of 120 degrees. Wall, equipment, and surface finishes should be rounded and non-abrasive. Lighting can also enhance comfort by making it easier to negotiate within a space. Comfort can be enhanced when the range of motion necessary (kneeling, bending, reaching, or leaning) is not at full extension using a leverage joint as a hinge pin (elbow or knee). Comfort and range of motion can be achieved when the range of access to controls, shelving, drawers, and equipment begins at 2'-6" above grade, and does not exceed 4'-0". The depth of access should not exceed 18". Wheels on chairs and work surfaces and height adjustments also promote comfort. Mechanical aids are available to compensate for strength, grasp, and reach limitations.

Meeting the needs of people who have hearing impairments means designing environments that minimize the acoustic interference of background noise and reverberation. Furniture configuration should be organized to enhance face-to-face communication for lip reading. Hearing aids work best in face-to-face communication away from large groups. Another factor to keep in mind is that rugs and low humidity environments (which are highly charged with static) can interfere with high frequency and low frequency interpretation of sounds.

Chapter Fifteen

COMMUNICATION

This chapter focuses not only on the requirements of the ADA, but also on other actions that can be taken to improve the quality of life and productivity of disabled people. Case examples have been added, describing ways in which some states and cities have addressed communications issues.

Communication enhancements include lighting that aids lip reading and sign language interpreters who are signing for audiences or one person. Assistive devices should also be available so that deaf or hard of hearing people can access and use such devices as TDD's, close-captioned decoders, telephone amplifiers, and listening systems.

Communication Definitions

1. The availability of quiet rooms and appropriate modes of communication to fit the strengths of the person.
2. Call systems in place for the medically fragile.
3. Support for language needs, such as international symbols.

Meeting the Code

(ANSI 117.1, ADA Titles I, II, III & IV) Meeting the codes for communications means providing devices in accessible locations that allow disabled people to communicate fully. Public telephones are a good example.

- *A western state department of corrections agreed to provide a sign language interpreter for a deaf inmate's parole hearing.*
- *A Michigan State district court agreed to provide an assistive listening device for an upcoming court date for an individual who is hard of hearing.*
- *A city in Texas agreed to provide additional microphones during city council meetings to ensure more effective communication with persons who have hearing impairments.*
- *Pinellas County, Florida—The Sixth Judicial District of Florida entered into an agreement requiring the courts in that district to establish a written policy on providing qualified interpreters for participants, including parties, witnesses, jurors, and spectators, who are deaf or hard of hearing; secure the services of a qualified interpreter when necessary to ensure effective communication; notify the public about the policy; and inform and instruct all appropriate district court officials to comply with the policy.*

Telephones

Public telephones must be accessible in all public areas, lobbies, and public spaces for use by people with disabilities. For wheelchair users, telephones can be mounted on the wall or as part of a quad that is designed for circular access. The clearance dimension is 2'-6" wide by 4' long, with a mounting to access the coin slot of no higher than 4'-6". Receiver handset cords should be 2'-6" long. To allow for conversation, phones should be in locations with the least noise. Privacy baffles should be provided where high traffic areas may impede phone conversation.

Additional assistive hearing devices should include signaling devices that use light or vibration to communicate an emergency alarm, door bells, or wake-up systems. Listening devices, such as close-captioned decoders for television, should be available for use with public address systems in auditoriums. Telephone headsets should be capable of increasing volume and TDD's should be available for communication with the deaf. An example of ADA compliance:

> • *An Arizona hotel agreed to purchase additional TDD's and closed-captioning decoders to implement a better system for responding to guests with hearing impairments who request the use of this equipment during their stay in the hotel.*

It is recommended that the work telephone be a speaker phone. The features of the phone should be large keys, memory and re-dial, and an intercom function for inter-office communications. A telephone-based call system may be useful to prevent sickness or an accident from becoming an emergency.

Meeting the Need

Work areas should be reorganized as needed to allow access to communication systems outfitted with meaningful system supports such as touch-tone dialing, amplifiers and hand-free speaking and listening. Commercial or sales establishments should lower the height of phones to provide access, and have staff assigned to aid and assist people with stamina difficulties when necessary. In addition, the public relations strategy should include providing information (a visible listing) of the support services available (e.g., a sign language interpreter). Lighting should directly illuminate telephone areas to support dialing and information retrieval.

Further, to go beyond code requirements and better meet the needs of the hearing impaired, employees may be informed of the following guidelines.

Deaf people use a variety of methods to communicate. Finger spelling and sign language are two ways. Many deaf people also use speech reading, oral communication, and writing. Here are some suggestions for communication with a deaf person who is especially comfortable with oral communication.

- Get the deaf person's attention before speaking. A light touch on the shoulder, a wave, or other visual signals will help.
- Look directly at the deaf person when speaking, even when an interpreter is present.
- Speak slowly and clearly without shouting, do not exaggerate or over-emphasize lip movements.
- Use body language and facial expression to supplement your communication.
- Maintain eye contact.
- If you encounter difficulty, try rephrasing a thought using different words.

- Keep your hands away from your face and mouth while speaking.
- Make sure lighting makes your face clearly visible.
- Long mustaches, gum chewing, cigarette smoking, pencil biting and similar obstructions of the lips will lessen the effectiveness of your communication.

Figure 15.1 is an illustration of the alphabet in sign language.

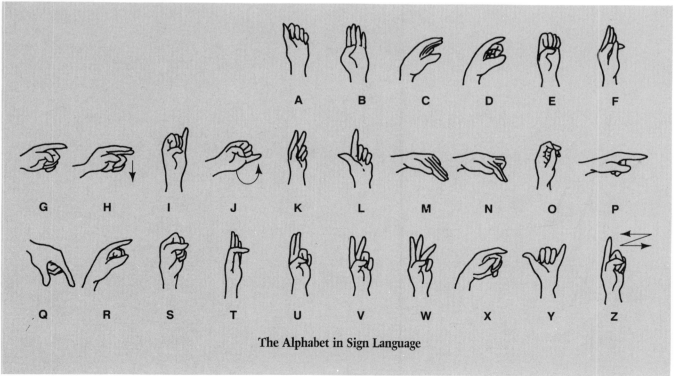

The Alphabet in Sign Language

Figure 15.1

Chapter Sixteen

DENSITY

For people with disabilities, it is important to create densities within areas that allow the maximum maneuverability and safety. For example, space should be wide enough to allow adequate passage for egress in emergencies. Independent function is critical to maintain one's dignity and self-esteem. The density of a space can either foster or impede not only independence, but communication. For example, if furniture groupings are too dense, then a wheelchair cannot access an area. A deaf person in a crowded seating arrangement cannot have the possibility of an intimate conversation. People who are blind or have low vision avoid dense spaces because it confuses and disorients them. Spaces that are too dense also present the problem of requiring that the person be able to perform multiple activities, such as open a door at the top of a stair or maneuver between two doors.

While codes such as NFPA and the law (ADA) have certain requirements for space allowance, additional modifications can be made to properly accommodate people with disabilities.

Density Definitions

1. An appropriate ratio of people and equipment to available space for optimum efficiency and minimal accidents.
2. A proper allowance of space per person for maneuverability.

Meeting the Code

[(National Fire Protection Association (NFPA), ADA Titles I & III)] Important considerations for density include local fire codes which limit occupancy, NFPA codes which set forth fire protection requirements, and ADA Titles I and III which state clearances for accessibility.

The following paragraphs include recommendations that not only meet the code requirements, but also increase the productivity and efficiency of the space.

One case of a modification made to address a density issue:

- *A 12-theater complex in Colorado agreed to provide additional seating throughout its theaters for people who use wheelchairs.*

Assembly Areas

The room should have a four foot wide clearance around furniture as well as an unobstructed area with a minimum radius of five feet for maneuvering the wheelchair. (See Figure 16.1.) A feeling of spaciousness and high visibility are also desirable. Carpeted floors should be low profile, but high density to provide a cushion for falls, while not offering resistance which may impair mobility. All hanging signs and lights must be a minimum of seven feet from the floor.

Meeting the Need

Maneuverability in the office is essential. Space should be rearranged to accommodate access to the staff, while maintaining staff and visitor access to the disabled person. The older the clientele, the less dense space should be within minimum standards to facilitate ambulation and access to items.

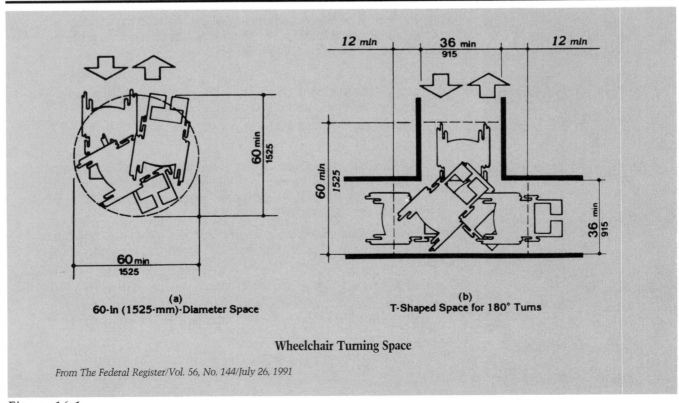

Wheelchair Turning Space

(a) 60-in (1525-mm)-Diameter Space

(b) T-Shaped Space for 180° Turns

From *The Federal Register/Vol. 56, No. 144/July 26, 1991*

Figure 16.1

Chapter Seventeen

DIVISION OF SPACE

Proper division of space means making maximum use of a facility's layout to promote utility. An example is reducing the amount of travel time required by a person with a mobility impairment to get from the entrance to the front desk, and then to the elevators. The division of a space should support people with limitations of strength and stamina with mechanical aids. For people with intellectual impairments, the division of space is critical. It should be simply and clearly organized with signage and visual cues.

Division of Space Definitions

1. Proper layout that integrates employees around the use of shared equipment.
2. Employee work spaces located based on reduction of barriers to access.
3. Flexibility within a space that facilitates rearrangement of orientations.

Meeting the Code

(ADA Title I, ANSI 7.1) Meeting the ADA Title I requirements means providing layouts that allow disabled people to apply for jobs and demonstrate their skills, as well as performing the necessary job functions on a regular basis.

Meeting the Code and the Need: Cases Settled

- *Two fast food restaurants agreed to relocate their accessible parking spaces to make them closer to the front door.*
- *A California department store agreed to make its rest rooms and fitting rooms accessible for people with manual or mobility impairments, to lower the height of its public telephones and drinking fountains to make them accessible for people who use wheelchairs, and to upgrade its elevators and install signage to make the store accessible for people who have vision impairments.*

Layout Considerations

Following are layout considerations and recommendations for accessible office designs.

1. What types of services and activities will be provided?
2. What size will the group be?
3. What times of the day will the room be in use?

4. Where will the site be located?

5. What are the physical features of the space?

6. What is the size of the available space?

7. What are the contours?

8. How much and what kind of space is needed for specific activities, special furniture, equipment, electrical service, plumbing fixtures, exhaust and ventilation requirements and storage?

9. Safety is an overall concern.

Meeting the Need

Design and layout of space should seek to enhance productivity for all staff and create a centralized resource area for all shared equipment (copier, postage meter, etc.). Layout changes may be necessary to access items in order to facilitate more productive and efficient use of time in an area. In addition, landmarks, such as the beginning and end of aisles, should be consistent if environments are to support efficient use of space. Dramatic spatial changes are an excellent way to indicate access passages.

Office Design

People with disabilities do not need more floor space to facilitate mobility, but the space needs to be managed differently. The office design shown in Figure 17.1 illustrates proper access arrangements. This office space was developed for a typical office using the five foot radius requirement. While the ADA requires a 36″ minimum aisle width, barrier-free design standards recommend that aisles be a minimum of 42″ wide to allow for the movement of wheelchairs and walkers. Consideration should also be given to the type of activities and the number of participants who will engage in these activities. Group and individual participation rooms should be designed for access, participation, and productivity.

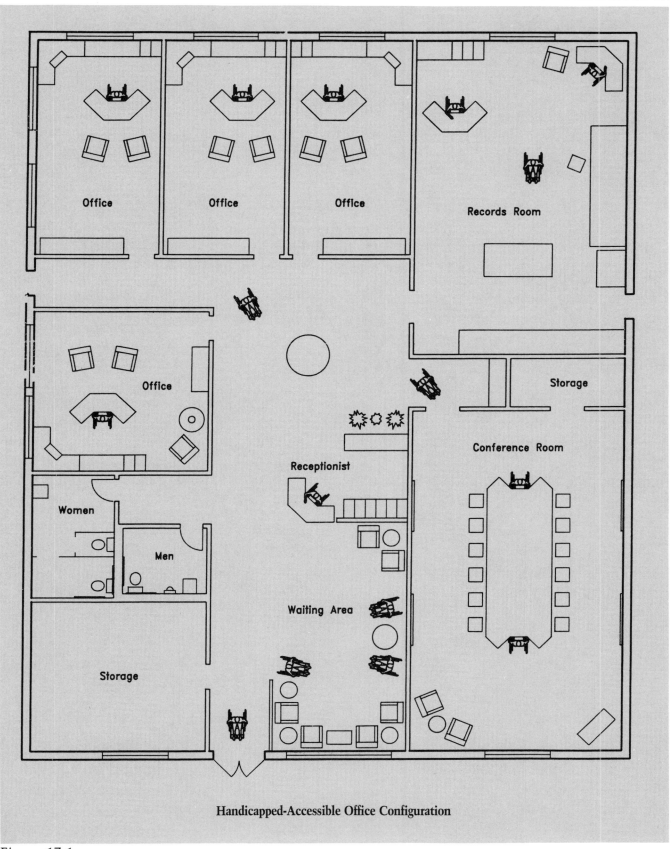

Handicapped-Accessible Office Configuration

Figure 17.1

Chapter Eighteen

EQUIPMENT

Equipment Definitions

1. Technology that enhances capability without emphasizing disability.
2. Adaptive and assistive devices that increase the opportunity to be independent.
3. Meeting safety requirements, in particular, the ergonomic standard.

Meeting the Code

(U.L. NFPA 101, ADA Title I) Meeting the code for equipment means addressing NFPA's requirements for safety equipment at the workplace. The ADA requires the provision of necessary assistive devices to enable disabled employees to effectively perform job functions. In some cases, the ADA requires standard equipment to be modified to make it accessible to disabled people.

All equipment should meet this criteria:

1. User-friendly in operation.
2. Durable.
3. Easy to install.
4. In keeping with standards for electrical code approvals.
5. Easy to maintain.
6. Easy to identify problems and service.

The following are examples of cases settled with the participation of the Department of Justice. In each case, equipment was used or modified to address the rights and needs of disabled people.

- *A health club agreed to install a lift to enable a wheelchair user to participate in an arthritis rehabilitation program in the club's swimming pool.*
- *A credit union agreed to lower an ATM machine to make it accessible for persons who use wheelchairs.*
- *A committee of bar examiners of a west coast state agreed to allow a severely visually impaired individual to use a personal computer with a high resolution monitor to take the bar exam.*

Meeting the Need

Proper position and posture are required to access equipment and use it effectively. Any equipment has to be user-friendly and within reach (on average within 12 inches and not weighing more than 2 lbs. if it must be moved).

Equipment should not require:

Poor operator posture:
- Shoulders elevated and/or one higher than the other.
- Wrists flexed or extended during work routine.
- Elbows elevated more than 30 degrees.
- Back bent and head unsupported by spine.

Excess force, including:
- Work that requires a constant, pinching grasp.
- Instrument handles that are too smooth. Provide non-slip gripping surface.

Excess mechanical stresses, such as:
- Diameter of instrument too small, difficult to grasp.
- Instrument handles hexagonal.
- Cords on handpieces short or curly.
- Handpieces unbalanced.
- Gloves ill-fitting.

Figure 18.1 shows some examples of equipment commonly used to meet the needs of the physically challenged.

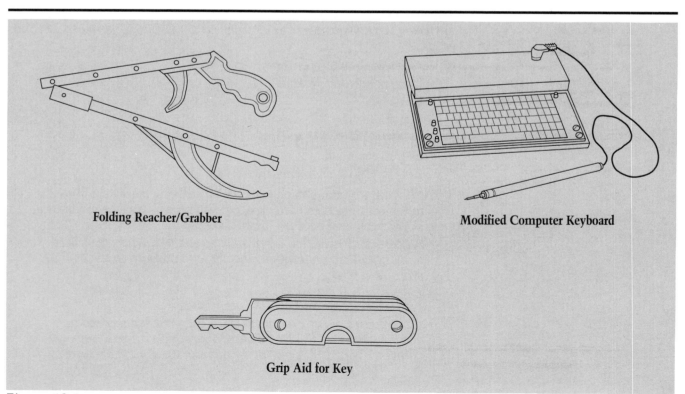

Folding Reacher/Grabber

Modified Computer Keyboard

Grip Aid for Key

Figure 18.1

Chapter Nineteen

FINISHES

People with disabilities require finishes that support mobility; for example, provide rugs that do not impede mobility with excessive pile depth. Also, busy patterns should be avoided, as they often cause confusion. Wall surfaces should be smooth to prevent abrasions to people leaning on hand rails. Furniture should have smooth surfaces with rounded corners.

Finishes Definition

Surface coverings that support the health and safety of individuals, no matter what the functional limitations of those individuals (for example: gait and instability problems).

Meeting the Code

(ADA Titles I, II & III; National Fire Protection Act 101) Finishes offer an important opportunity to create an environment that fully integrates people with disabilities. Meeting the codes for finishes means providing high contrasts for visual acuity, slip-resistant finishes for ramps and floor coverings, and warning strips for changes in level or to indicate the approach to stairs or hazardous areas.

Finishes

All surfaces should be easily maintainable with smooth wall coverings and/or laminated surfaces.

Floors

(All flooring and flooring materials must meet National Fire Code, Class I.) A level loop carpeting should be used in spaces where people walk to provide a pleasant walking surface and reduce glare and noise. Direct-glue carpeting should be used to prevent slipping and rolling resistance to wheelchairs. Where water absorbency is an issue, jute backing is safest. Floors should be relatively light in color, with 30 to 50 percent reflectance.

All floors must have a non-slip surface, preferably with patterns and edgings that can guide people with low vision. See ADA-AG Sections 4.3.6 and 4.5.3 in Appendix A.

Color Schemes for Flooring
- Cool colors (blues and greens)
- Pastel colors (like light blue)
- Warm colors (yellow and reds)
- Subdued colors with intense color accents

- Neutral colors (like beige, putty, or tan)
- White
- Intense colors (fire engine red, kelly green)
- Grays

Walls

Brick, concrete and tile are the most resistant to abuse from contact. Surfaces should be smooth to prevent abrasions, and glare should be minimized whenever possible. Reflectance should be 40 to 60 percent.

Color schemes for wall finishes are basically the same as for floors, with a wider choice of patterns and materials.

Ceilings

These can be textured, pattern-painted or fabric-covered to provide visual relief and serve as an aid to orientation. Reflectance should be 70 to 90 percent. Ceiling colors are typically in the ranges of off-white, light winter sky color, and beige.

Meeting the Need

The choice of finish is determined by the individual's specific functional limitations (e.g., enhancing visual acuity contrasts on shelving may be critical for someone with a visual impairment).

Flooring

To maintain a high level of productivity, a desirable image, and clean, level work surfaces, the following two steps must be taken:

Step 1: Proper Specification of Work Areas

An effective ergonomic program begins with proper flooring specifications—with both people and maintenance in mind.

- A good understanding of the intended use and expectation of people and performance is imperative when specifying: 1) matting, 2) carpet, 3) wood, 4) concrete for each work area.

Examples: Mattings

1. Chemical-resistant matting should provide safety and comfort in dry areas where people may be exposed to chemicals, oil, or grease. Shipping and receiving areas where people stand on hard, cold floors may also need chemical-resistant matting to prevent mat breakdown from de-icing salts. Black mat, 9/16" thick, with beveled yellow safety edges, is important to prevent accidents when stepping on or off the mat.

2. Kitchen matting should provide relief for workers in areas that require frequent floor surface cleaning. It should lift for floor cleaning in kitchens, cafeterias, and food preparation areas. Liquids should drain under matting to pool areas. Slippery food spills should be trapped in the mat holes for later cleaning. 1/2" thick grease-resistant mats should connect together to custom fit requirements along food preparation stations.

3. Drainage area matting is heavy-duty and designed to prevent slips and falls while reducing leg and lower back stress. Surface ribs and drainage holes help keep the surface of the mat free of metal shavings and cutting fluids in metal working areas. 7/8" thick mats resist most common chemicals, lubricants, and solvents. Again, black with yellow safety edge is important for safety.

Today's market-driven flooring choices have been designed in consideration of cost, image, and maintenance *before* people. For example, when considering carpet, the typical facilities factors have been:

Aesthetics and Pattern Types
- Cut pile or loop pile
- Solid color or multi-color
- Pattern
- Broadloom or Modular

When the Americans with Disabilities Act and Workers' Compensation are taken into account, aesthetics and pattern types should also support comfort and visual acuity for low vision people.

Fiber
- Soil-hiding fiber characteristics
- Stain resistance and stain removal characteristics
- Resiliency and crush resistance
- Light-fastness characteristics

With people in mind, fibers should also be chosen that provide minimum resistance to walking.

Backing System
- Tuft-bind strength
- Edge-ravel resistance
- Delamination resistance
- Moisture resistance

Backing systems should also prevent ravel which can cause trips, slips, and falls.

Maintenance
- Permanent resistance to 99% of all common stains
- Superior fade resistance to sunlight and gas
- Environmentally safe
- Ease of stain removal
- Lower maintenance cost
- Long lasting durability and resistance to soiling

Keeping worn areas to a minimum is critical to prevent accidents.

Always consider proper specification and product performance in terms of job tasks and people:

Examples:
1. Wood floors with polyurethane finishes are often slippery when wet.

Color is an important factor in the long-term appearance retention and maintenance of any installation.

Example:
1. Carpet: A light color cut carpet pile product is a poor choice in heavy traffic entrance type areas, whereas a darker color in a loop construction will retain its resilience and cushioning effect longer.
2. Concrete can be painted to create clarity of use (e.g., passageways for material handling).

Step #2 – Definition and Mapping of Traffic Areas and Patterns

Using a blueprint of the facility layouts, outline heavy, medium, and light traffic areas.

- Heavy: outside entrances, corridors, stairways, and main aisles.
- Medium: secondary aisles, office space, meeting rooms, atriums.
- Light: back office, conference rooms, executive areas.

Note: Lighting is a major consideration in matching traffic and task patterns.

Chapter Twenty

FURNISHINGS

Properly chosen or modified furnishings for disabled people can allow or enhance mobility with safety and comfort, and have the opportunity to increase productivity as well. Attributes of furnishings are ease of access and operation (usually with one hand). For example, the drawer pulls on cabinets or dressers should be a single, center pull that eliminates the need for two-hand operation. Drawer slides should accommodate ease of use and access.

Along with the code and ADA requirements for furnishings, this chapter also describes some examples of items currently available and their important features. (Section B of the Product Selection Guide at the back of this book contains other furnishings ideas.) Two case studies show examples of how businesses are responding to the challenge of meeting the ADA and disabled people's needs.

Furnishings Definitions

1. Adaptable, flexible, designed to enhance the strengths of a person and increase their capacity.
2. Maintaining image and privacy with dignity.

Meeting the Code

(ANSI 100, 1988; ADA Titles I & III) Two compliance cases:
- *An insurance company in Massachusetts agreed to provide new furnishings for six people with multiple sclerosis.*
- *Pinnick vs. International House of Pancakes (IHOP), California — Upon notice by the Federal district court that the constitutionality of a Federal law was being challenged, the Department intervened in this case to defend the constitutionality of Title III of the ADA. The suit had been filed by a private individual asserting that the California pancake restaurant had failed to undertake readily achievable barrier removal (access to tables) and to provide auxiliary aids and services. The court adopted the Department's views and upheld Title III's constitutionality. The defendant has appealed the court's ruling*

Seating and Tables

Title III of the ADA clearly specifies provisions for built-in seating and tables [See ADA-AG Sections 4.1.3 (18) and 4.32]. Specific seating requirements are also provided for dressing and fitting rooms (4.35.4), restaurants and cafeterias (5.1 and 5.2), and libraries (8.2). Title I requires whatever modifications are necessary, including furnishings, to enable disabled employees to perform their job functions.

Office Furniture **Adjustable Height and Tilt Desks**

This type of desk should be designed with electronic lifters to raise and tilt work surfaces to a comfortable height and angle to reduce work fatigue and increase productivity. (See Figure 20.1.)

The functional features of an adjustable desk should include:

1. Height adjustment of between 28 and 46 inches to access any wheelchair or accommodate a person working either seated or standing.
2. Easy assembly and breakdown into portable sets to accommodate job changes, movement to training sites or home.
3. It is recommended that work station components not weigh more than 40 lbs.
4. It is recommended that adaptive aids should not weigh more than 40 lbs.
5. Electronic switch panels should support adaptive aids.
6. Work station surfaces should ideally accommodate shelves angled forward, backward, down and up to 180 degrees.
7. Equipment supports should have the flexibility to allow adjustments during work sessions to reduce stress and fatigue.

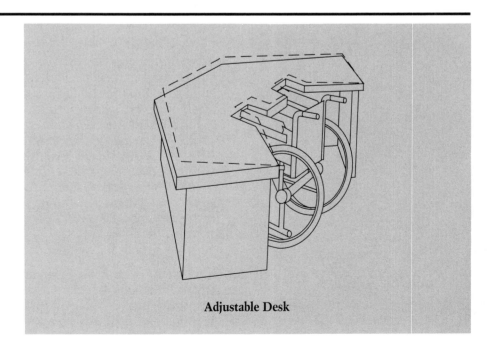

Adjustable Desk

Figure 20.1

8. Clocks and timers can be used to alert workers of time—by task and necessary breaks.

9. Storage areas should be available for adaptive aids, supplies, data, finished work, and files.

10. Computers should have touch-sensitive keyboards and key guards to reduce strength requirements.

Accessible File

A fold-down front is useful for access from a wheelchair, and a fold-up top provides access from a standing position. The file should also roll to any work area. It could hold one drawer of legal size information. (See Figure 20.2.)

Rotating File

A carousel-like cube, revolving files are designed so that the backs of standard book binders and files extend one inch (1.3 cm) beyond the edge for grasping access.

Adaptive Chair

Designed for the fragile person who needs mobility within a room for ease of accessibility. The chair is custom-cushioned for lumbar and seat pan support to any bodily dimension. The L-shaped armrests allow a closer fit to any work surface and may be used to position the arms and wrists for ease of movement when rising from the chair. Chair has a height adjustment range of 6 to 12 inches (15 to 30 cm).

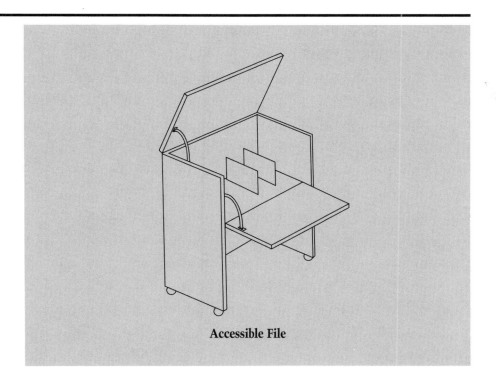

Accessible File

Figure 20.2

Adjustable Height Chair

These custom-designed chairs have an electronic height adjustment capability of from 12 to 36 inches. The control box is customized for any disabling condition, thus providing access to varying table heights. Armrests can be raised for ease of transfer. A seat belt provides user security. There are large casters positioned at the bottom for ease of mobility, with locks that can be accessible from a seated position. (See Figure 20.3.)

Meeting the Need

1. Work surfaces should be redesigned if necessary to accommodate a person's height and reach requirements while supporting a vocational strategy to increase work life opportunities.
2. Work stations should promote productivity and efficiency while reducing stress and fatigue.

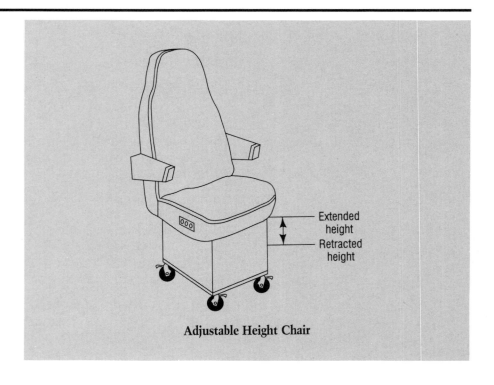

Adjustable Height Chair

Figure 20.3

Chapter Twenty-One

IMAGE

To properly meet the needs of people with disabilities, it is important to consider the relationship between image and design. To the extent possible, consider each disability and the effect of design on independence and dignity. For example, if a person has a mobility or vision impairment, then designs that reduce the length of passage one has to travel (and the attendant barriers) increase his or her ability to move within the space without being conspicuous. Designing special furnishings that match existing decor allow people to fit in with similar status. Installing sinks inside handicap-accessible bathroom stalls allows a disabled person to manage personal hygiene with dignity.

Along with a review of code and ADA requirements, this chapter includes summaries of cases settled showing how states, counties, and businesses have resolved problems in this area.

Image Definitions

1. Coordination of color and furnishings to enhance image and comfort.
2. Privacy to prevent unwanted visual access.
3. Acoustical and door control in private rooms, such as toilet areas.
4. Equipment that enhances independence and dignity.

Meeting the Code

(ADA Titles I & II; 29 CFR Part 1630) To the extent possible, the attributes of image to be considered are:

1. Adaptive designs that integrate into existing decor without creating conspicuous changes that call attention to a disability.
2. Finishes that enhance visual acuity and are of equal quality and standard to the norm.
3. Accessibility to all areas of a facility in the pattern of normal traffic.
4. Equipment of equal standard to the norm.

Note 1: Office workers place a great deal of importance on the physical office environment to facilitate their productivity. Nearly seven in ten (69%) claim it is "very important" to have the right kind of physical office environment to enable them to do as much work as they are reasonably able to do.

Note 2: This appears to be especially true for workers in technical jobs (77% claim it is "very important"). The proper environment is also important to union members (76%), government workers (73%), and workers who have not attended college and earn $35,000 or less per year (74%). While 69% of office workers say the physical environment is very important, only 60% of top executives and 58% of facilities managers think their office workers would say this.

Following are examples of cases involving image that were settled with intervention from the Department of Justice.

- *A national retail chain agreed to provide accessible parking at its stores nationwide.*
- *A major rental car company agreed to provide accessible parking at a major metropolitan airport and to institute valet parking service when needed by customers with disabilities.*
- *Van Buren County, Arkansas—Van Buren County agreed to relocate county court activities to an accessible site upon request; develop a self-evaluation and a transition plan; adopt a grievance procedure; and place public notices of its nondiscrimination policy and responsibilities under the ADA on county bulletin boards and in local newspapers.*
- *Clearwater, Florida—The complaint alleged that the police department had failed to provide an interpreter in the arrest of an individual who is deaf. The Clearwater police department agreed to establish and publicize a written policy for providing interpreters whenever necessary for effective communication.*
- *Paulding County, Ohio—In response to a complaint that the county courtroom was inaccessible to individuals with mobility impairments, the county Board of Commissioners agreed to relocate court activities to an accessible site upon request, if the request is made in a reasonable period of time before the scheduled court date. The county board also agreed to publicize its new policy.*

Meeting the Need

The best match between environments, equipment, and people is that which maintains the image of the facility and the dignity of the employee. If your employee or customer is lost, confused, or embarrassed in your facility, then your image and their independence and dignity are compromised.

Chapter Twenty-Two

LIGHTING

Proper lighting is important to all users of facilities, but particularly to people with disabilities as a design factor to increase their mobility within a space. For example, a well-lit ramp with well-lit signage increases the likelihood of safe passage. Lighting is critical to people with low vision who need illumination to read signs and negotiate environments. Disabled employees often use task lighting to accommodate their work lighting needs, as they change positions in wheelchairs.

This chapter includes code and ADA requirements, as well as recommendations for better meeting the needs of disabled people. A new section outlines the "Green Lights Program," the Environmental Protection Agency's initiative to encourage use of energy-efficient lighting.

Lighting Definitions

1. Illumination as needed to prevent fatigue.
2. Full spectrum total room lighting.
3. Glare control.

Meeting the Code

(Illumination Engineers, U.L., ADA Titles I, II & III) Generally, lighting requirements under ADA involve the provision of accessible controls. The following paragraphs present the basic requirements, as well as recommendations to enhance the disabled employee's productivity.

Efficiency Standards

These standards, incorporated in both the National Appliance Energy Conservation Act of 1988 and The National Energy Policy Act of 1992 (EPACT), are designed to eliminate inefficient lighting products. The Appliance Act deals with ballasts and the EPACT deals with lamps and luminaries. The following is a summary of the ASHRAE/IES Standard 90.1-1989, "Energy Efficient Design of New Buildings Except Low-Rise Residential Buildings."

Purpose of Standard

- To set minimum requirements for the energy efficient design of new buildings without constraining the building function, nor the comfort or productivity of the occupants.

- To provide criteria for energy efficient design.
- To provide sound guidance for energy efficient design. (This is not a design procedure.)

The Green Lights Program

Green Lights is a voluntary, non-regulatory program sponsored by the U.S. Environmental Protection Agency (EPA). Its purpose is to encourage major U.S. corporations to install energy-efficient lighting technologies wherever they are profitable and maintain or improve lighting quality.

The underlying principle of the Green Lights program is "Environmental Protection at a Profit." Corporations that make the commitment to Green Lights will profit by lowering their electricity bills, improving lighting quality, and increasing worker productivity. They will also reduce the air pollution caused by electricity generation, which includes carbon dioxide, sulfur dioxide, and nitrogen oxides. EPA launched the Green Lights program to help U.S. companies realize their potential to profit while preventing pollution by installing energy-efficient lighting designs and technologies.

For more information:

Green Lights General Hotline:
(202) 775-6650
Fax: (202) 775-6680

Green Lights Technical Hotline:
(202) 862-1145
Fax: (202) 862-1144

Green Lights Ally Hotline:
(202) 293-4527
Fax: (202) 223-9534

Green Lights Electronic Bulletin Board:
(202) 775-6671

Lighting Requirements

There should be strong overhead lighting, as well as full spectrum and task lights for individual tasks. Task lights should be adjustable in intensity, location, and direction. Special sensitivity to glare should be taken into account, avoiding highly reflective surfaces. Screens, baffles, shades or curtains should be used wherever sunlight enters. In general, indirect lighting should be used except where task lighting is required.

Automatic lighting sensors respond to the presence of individuals by turning the lights on and off as a person enters and exits the space. Skylights maximize the level of natural light in the work space, and are also an excellent source of natural daylight.

The range of illumination recommended by the Illuminating Engineers Society for persons whose vision depends on good illumination is 60 to 140 footcandles. Reflectors should be as close as possible to ceilings to enhance the effectiveness of ceiling light fixtures. To further reduce eyestrain and fatigue, colors should contrast and be equally illuminated. Controls and operating mechanisms should be placed within the reach ranges specified in ADA-AG 4.2.5 and 4.2.6. They should be operable with one hand, and not require tight grasping, pinching or twisting of the wrist. (See 4.27.)

Meeting the Need

Illumination levels must focus people's attention on the most important objects (e.g., the product and the price in a retail establishment). The level of illumination must be set to increase the eyes' ability to see forms, symbols, and objects from 6 inches to 6 feet. The illumination range, according to the Illuminating Engineers Society, should be 60 to 140 footcandles. Individual task lighting should be provided in order to furnish a higher level of illumination for specific areas.

Quality lighting can now be provided for even the most visually demanding task. Incandescent, fluorescent, halogen, high-intensity and natural lighting methods are being used in efficient and highly ergonomic variations. This aids in eliminating the "gloomy" feeling that many experience during the winter (low light) months.

Epilepsy Warning

A very small percentage of individuals may experience epileptic seizures when exposed to certain light patterns or flashing lights. Exposure to certain light patterns or backgrounds on a television screen or while playing video games may induce an epileptic seizure in these individuals. Certain conditions may induce undetected epileptic symptoms even in persons who have no history of prior seizures or epilepsy: dizziness, altered vision, eye or muscle twitches, loss of awareness, disorientation, any involuntary movement, or convulsions.

- *One example of compliance is a city in Illinois that agreed to reinstate an individual with epilepsy who had lost his position as custodian as a result of his disability.*

Vision Enhancements

Vision impairments are often the accompanying disabilities of diabetes and head injuries. The types of impairments may include low vision, loss of peripheral vision, reduced color sensitivity, and/or increased sensitivity to bright light. Therefore, lighting, coordination of color and the use of magnification become critical to maintain the visual acuity of persons with disabilities. Solutions to these impairments should be developed by assessing the vision loss.

Because the lens of the eye thickens and yellows over time, by the age of 60 it receives just one-third of the light it did when that person was 20 years old. The older person is also more sensitive to glare and reduced depth perception. Because the lens of the eye yellows, colors are no longer perceived as they were when the person was younger. There is also an increased incidence of color blindness.

Lighting should take into consideration the following factors to reduce the stress and fatigue of eye strain:

1. Illumination high enough to allow the individual to perform the required tasks of the job.
2. The types of forms, symbols, and objects used on the job.
3. The amount of reading necessary and in what form the text is in—handwriting versus books or blueprints.
4. The amount of time spent on computer terminals.
5. The amount of time the person must spend working with objects near or far.
6. Sensitivity to glare.
7. The narrowing visual field.

8. Contrasts in colors. For example: pale pastel colors tend to wash out; blue and green can be easily confused; and dark gray, black, and brown may appear muddy. Use of contrasting colors is recommended. Selection of colors for a low-vision or aging population might be more effective if choices are viewed through yellow-brown acetate.

Lighting in Parking Lots

A well-lighted parking lot is an important feature of a shopping center, a business park, an apartment complex, or a factory. Good lighting can attract customers, facilitate traffic and pedestrian safety, deter crime and vandalism, and create a sense of personal security. As with any lighting design, incorporating the appropriate luminaire in a parking lot lighting system is important. See Figure 22.1.

Occupancy Sensors

Occupancy sensors are motion-sensing devices that automatically turn on luminaires (light fixtures) when motion is detected, keep luminaires on when motion detection is maintained, and turn off luminaires when motion is not detected. They usually are used as an energy-saving measure to eliminate "wasted light" when rooms are unoccupied.

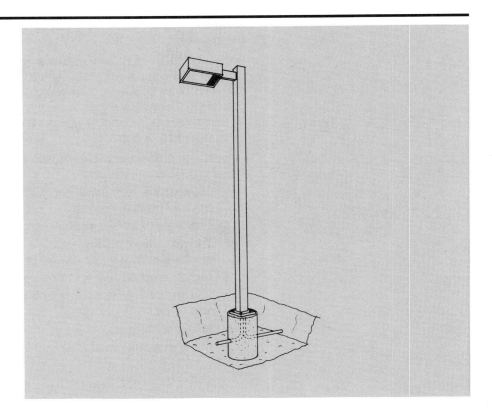

Figure 22.1

The most appropriate application for occupancy sensors is in spaces where occupancy is infrequent or unpredictable such as private offices, conference rooms, classrooms, hallways, service corridors, warehouses, toilet rooms, storage closets, or copy rooms. The two most common motion-sensing technologies used in occupancy sensors are passive infrared and ultrasonic. Some manufacturers combine the two into one product, which is referred to as a *hybrid sensor*. See Figure 22.2 for an example of motion detector technology, a ceiling-mounted passive infrared occupancy sensor.

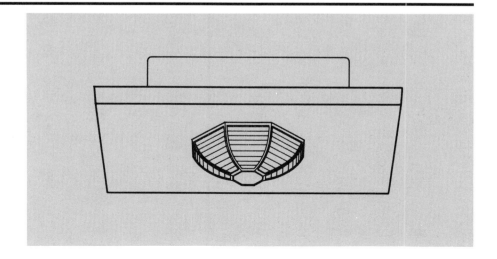

Figure 22.2

Chapter Twenty-Three

MAINTENANCE

It is important to design a building and develop maintenance schedules that allow people with disabilities to safely and efficiently use facilities—beginning with an accessible entrance and throughout the facility. Proper maintenance includes the following:

- designing enough storage areas so that volume buys of items do not overflow into areas that affect passage
- specifying finishes and furnishings that when cleaned do not have a slippery residue
- keeping walkways clear of hazards (e.g., ice and debris)
- changing flickering lights that reduce illumination, thereby creating a hazard for the visually impaired (and even causing seizures in some individuals)
- keeping toilet areas fully supplied
- providing adequate staff to maintain facilities

Maintenance Definitions

1. Minimum maintenance requirements include a clear method for problem identification and availability of accessible, serviceable equipment.
2. The maintenance program must be an organizational priority, since disabled people are dependent on both equipment (such as wheelchairs, elevators, and automatic door openers) and unobstructed passageways to utilize their full capabilities.

Meeting the Code

(ADA, Title I) Maintaining an area or a piece of equipment is usually part of every person's job. People with disabilities do not have to be excluded from these functions and, in many cases, prefer to take care of their own area and equipment. Reasonable accommodation for maintenance may mean reviewing expectations to determine what is possible for each person. The chart in Figure 23.1 has proven useful in making such a review.

Settled Cases

The following is an example, from a Department of Justice update, of a maintenance-related case.

- *A New England town agreed to build a roof over the ramp leading to its 150-year-old town hall to ensure that the ramp does not become blocked by snow.*

Meeting the Need

Proper maintenance should focus on avoiding equipment breakdowns. Equipment failure not only can cause capability breakdowns, but in some cases, can be life-threatening (e.g., where back-up generators are not functional, to provide power for respirators, lifts, etc.).

Environments where customers interact with employees to conduct business should be set up in such a way that they are not consistently "damaged" by customers (e.g., passages that are constantly scarred because people are misjudging corridors). This means incorporating effective visual cues, and using elements such as handrails and bumper guards.

Epilepsy Warning to Maintenance Personnel

This information, first noted in the lighting chapter, bears repeating here.

- *A small percentage of individuals may experience epileptic seizures when exposed to certain light patterns or flashing lights. Certain conditions may also induce undetected epileptic symptoms, even in persons who have no history of prior seizures or epilepsy. The person may experience any of the following symptoms: dizziness, altered vision, eye or muscle twitches, loss of awareness, disorientation, any involuntary movement, or convulsions. Therefore, IMMEDIATELY change any flickering lights.*

Job Description For Maintenance

Name: _____   Job Title: _____

Date: _____   Interviewer: _____

Physical Requirements	Weight/ Reach	% of Time	Required Adaptations	Remarks
Carrying				
Cleaning				
Driving				
Holding				
Lifting				
Opening				
Pulling				
Pushing				
Removing				
Threading				
Walking				

Figure 23.1

Following are some maintenance guidelines, in the context of safety for disabled people and all facility users.

Step 1 — Routine Maintenance

- Frequency: Varies with conditions — a general guideline follows:
  - Heavy traffic areas: daily
  - Medium traffic areas: every other day
  - Light traffic areas: once or twice per week
- Provide equipment that supports wet and dry cleaning strategies based on flooring type and safety considerations.
- Determine cleaning extraction strategy.
- Provide appropriate equipment for each floor.
- Identify acceptable cleaning methods and standards.
- Establish rules for maintenance personnel and employees.

Step 2 — First Spill Response

- React to all spills immediately.
- If possible, establish a "hot line" for employees to call for immediate response to spills.

Step 3 — Preventive Maintenance

- Establish a preventive maintenance (PM) program with an outside contractor for equipment such as elevators and wheelchair lifts.
- Establish internal PM programs for attending to items such as battery replacement in automatic faucets and valves, replacement of fluorescent bulbs, and lubrication of hinges.

Step 4 — Monitoring Results

Once the initial program is established, monitoring results is critical to achieving your safety expectations. Adjustment of frequencies and spot cleaning may be necessary to meet your maintenance objectives. A walk-through inspection of work areas should be made at least monthly and accident logs reviewed.

Chapter Twenty-Four

NOISE

Controlling noise is a benefit to everyone. The quieter an environment, the less fatiguing and more comfortable it tends to be, particularly for older people. In general, noise should be minimized, except that which provides an auditory cue to people with visual impairments, such as the sound of automatic doors. The goal is to provide acoustic supports that enhance communication by minimizing the interference (from background noise and reverberation).

Noise Management Definitions

1. A reduction of unwanted sound that distracts and causes fatigue.
2. Controlling variable noise that lowers everyone's resistance to stress.

Meeting the Code

(OSHA, ADA Titles I, II, III & IV) The Department of Labor states that noise is not to exceed 90 decibels in an 8-hour day. The normal level is 25 decibels for frequencies of 1000, 2000 and 3000 hertz.

The following standards are published by The American Society for Testing and Materials (ASTM) Committee D-33 on Environmental Acoustics and Subcommittee E.33.02 on Open Plan Office published in ASTM volume 04.06. This list is an updated version from the book "Noise Control Manual," Harris, pages 92 to 93, Van Nostrand Reinhold (Now Chapman & Hall), 1992.

ASTM E1041 – Guide for Measurement of Masking Sound in Open Offices.

ASTM E1110 – Classification for Determination of Articulation Class.

ASTM E1111 – Test Method for Measuring the Interzone Attenuation of Ceiling Systems.

ASTM E1130-90 – Method for Objective Measurement of Speech Privacy in Open Offices Using Articulation Index.

ASTM E1374-90 – Guide to Open Office Acoustics and Applicable ASTM Standards.

ASTM E1375-90 – Method for Measuring the Interzone Attenuation of Furniture Panels Used as Acoustical Barriers.

E1376-90 – Method for Measuring Interzone Attenuation of Sound Reflected by Wall Finishes & Furniture Panels.

E1414-91a—Text Method for Airborne Sound Attenuation Between Rooms Sharing a Common Ceiling Plenum.

Exposure to constant noise can not only lead to loss of hearing, but can also lower one's tolerance to noise. The result is interference with reception of other sounds and disturbance of work performance. The goal should be to reduce general background noise with floor, wall, and ceiling sound-reduction materials. In large rooms, noise can be mitigated with baffling, wall hangings, banners, panels, and partitions. (See Figure 24.1.)

As much as possible, sound absorption panels should be used to enhance productivity in the environment. Floors should be carpeted, curtains or noise-absorbing materials hung on all windows; partitions should be available; and printers should be housed in sound-proof covers. If noise pollution is a problem that cannot be solved with these measures, then a white noise diversion machine might be added.

In response to the ADA:

- *A city in Texas agreed to provide additional microphones during city council meetings to ensure more effective communication with persons who have hearing impairments.*

This solution, in part, addressed the problem of background noise by amplifying the proceedings.

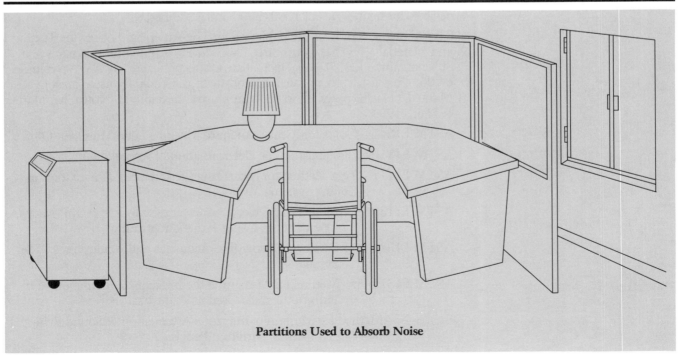

Partitions Used to Absorb Noise

Figure 24.1

Meeting the Need

Hearing difficulties, coupled with noise, increase the need for repositioning to hear sounds. This is more difficult when wheelchairs are used for mobility. Therefore, redundant cueing safety systems should always be used, particularly in noisy environments. For example, fire and smoke alarms should have both an audible and visual mode to ensure safety. (See ADA-AG 4.28 and 4.29.)

The older a population of employees/customers, the more sensitive they are to environmental distraction (background noise). Therefore, it is important to address this issue when evaluating a facility for reasonable accommodation.

People are also less able to hear high pitched sounds due to degenerative changes in the auditory system. This condition, known as *Presbycusis*, begins around age 50, but becomes more noticeable after age 65. Without a high pitched hearing capacity, speech becomes less clear.

Chapter Twenty-Five

PASSAGES

Safe, clear passages are essential for people who have disabilities such as a partial or total loss of mobility due to stroke, spinal cord injury, or paralysis. Passages should be designed or modified to support people with mobility, vision, hearing, and stamina difficulties. Passages are safe when well lit and free of obstacles. Proper signage is critical in passages to guide people with these limitations. Travel distances should also be considered when designing passages for people who tire easily due to their disability.

This chapter reviews code and ADA requirements related to passages, and suggests modifications that will better support the needs of disabled people. Some case examples show how various local governments and institutions resolved related issues.

Passages Definitions

1. Ability to negotiate within an environment safely.
2. Ability to map a building properly for easy access to all centralized resources.

Meeting the Code

(ATBCB 1190.13, UFAS 4.13, ADA Titles I, II & III) Passages are a key issue addressed by the ADA. The following entries list ADA provisions and corresponding reference numbers for doors and doorways, corridors, walkways, and tactile cues.

Doors and Doorways

Doors should have a clear opening of between 32 and 36 inches onto a level surface for a minimum distance of five feet in the direction the door swings. The level surface must extend one foot beyond the strike jamb side of the doorway. The threshold must be no higher than 1/2", with no sharp inclines or abrupt changes. The door closer must not impair the use of the door to the handicapped. On all swinging doors with hinges, the pressure required to open doors with door closures should be limited to three to six foot-pounds, with a check action of four to six seconds before closing. Pocket doors with push plates are the best type of door because they do not swing in the way of the wheelchair user, thereby creating obstructions. (See Figure 25.1.) Refer to ADA-AG in Appendix A, Sections 4.1.3 (7-9), 4.1.6 (1.g), 4.1.6 (3), 4.13, and 4.3.3.

Following are examples of passage related issues from a Department of Justice update.

- *Hickman County, Kentucky—Hickman County agreed to develop a compliance plan to provide access to the services, programs, and activities conducted in its courthouse, thus resolving a complaint alleging that a man using a wheelchair was unable to enter the circuit clerk's office to renew his driver's license because the doors were too narrow.*
- *Livingston v. Guice, North Carolina— A person who uses a wheelchair filed a lawsuit in Federal district court against the State of North Carolina and a state court judge charging that they had violated Title II of the ADA by preventing her from entering a courtroom through the only accessible entrance known to her. The Department argued in an amicus brief that states may be sued for damages under Title II. The court has not yet issued a ruling.*
- *An Illinois bank agreed to install automatic doors at its front entrance to make it easier for people with visual, manual, and mobility impairments to gain access.*

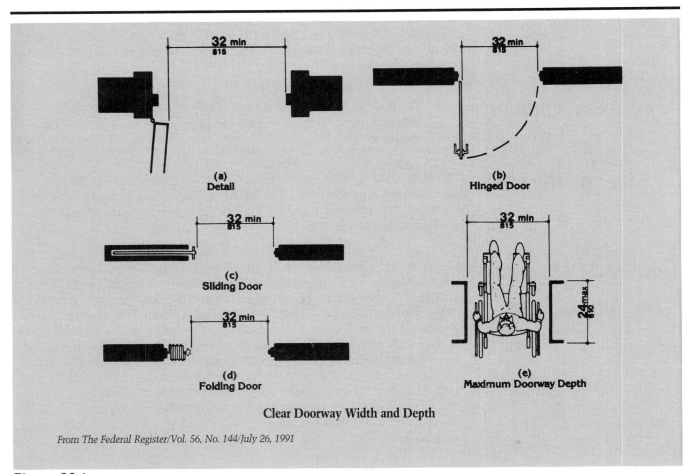

Clear Doorway Width and Depth

From The Federal Register/Vol. 56, No. 144/July 26, 1991

Figure 25.1

• *In Iowa, a board of elections agreed to move a polling place to an accessible location.*

Tactile Cues

(ATBCB 1190.190) Raised grooves, handrails, aggregated concrete and rubber strips are among the items used for sensory identification of various areas to visually impaired individuals in environments. The use of tactile cueing raises the individual's self-esteem by providing an avenue for independent participation.

Handrails should have tactile cues for mapping an area, and be weight-bearing for support up to 100 pounds. Tactile cues are differentiations in texture used to alert visually impaired persons to such hazards as floor-level changes, stairs, approaching pedestrians and vehicular traffic. They can also be incorporated into the design of levers, door handles, appliance and fixture controls (raised grooves, exposed concrete and rubber strips).

Figures 25.2 – 25.4 show handrail dimension requirements, a cushioned handrail, and protruding obstruction limitations. Refer to ADA-AG Section 4.29 for details. (See the update on Tactile Warnings at the end of Appendix A, following the ADA-AG.)

Walkways

(ATBCB 1190.50) Inclined walks must have a level platform at the top and bottom. Walkways should be at least 48 inches wide with a gradient no more than 5%. A non-slip surface should be used. Level areas should be placed at regular intervals. For all walkways, a curb ramp must be provided at any intersection. The curb ramp must be four feet wide and have a slope no greater than one inch of rise for every foot. Transitions between two surfaces must

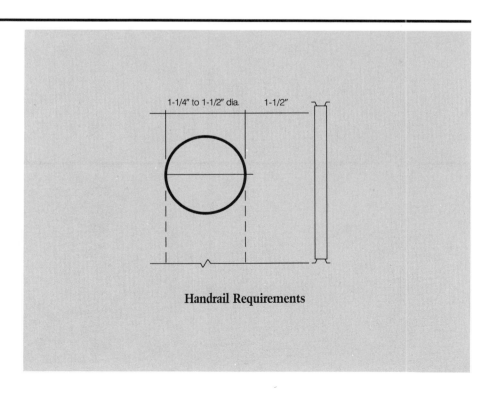

1-1/4" to 1-1/2" dia.   1-1/2"

Handrail Requirements

Figure 25.2

be smooth. Curb ramps must also have non-slip surfaces. Figure 25.5 provides more detail on stairway and handrail requirements. Refer to ADA-AG Sections 4.1.6 (3a), 4.1.7 (3a), 4.5, 4.8, and 4.26 for walkway requirements.

Corridors

(ATBCB 1190.50, ADA Title III) Corridors should, ideally, be a minimum of 42 inches wide, no longer than 75 feet, and lit with indirect lighting to prevent glare — to accommodate physically challenged people. Wall surfaces should have blends of contrasted colors to add to visual acuity. Figure 25.6 shows width requirements for corridors, in the context of turns around obstructions. Figure 25.7 shows width and length requirements for straight hallways. Refer to ADA-AG, Section 4.1.3, 4.3.2 (4), 4.1.7 (3b), 4.3, 4.4.1, 4.4.2, and 4.5.2 for details on corridor requirements.

- *A California convenience store of a well-known franchise agreed to make three of its checkout aisles, including one express lane, accessible for people who use mobility devices.*

Meeting the Need

Safety and passages are critically interactive. Wide corridors are essential to passage for those with either mobility or vision impairments. Provisions for access and egress are paramount and are supported by uniformity of length, space, lighting, signage, and safety measures.

The following should be kept in mind when designing or modifying passages that will be used by older people.

With age, the center of balance moves forward, putting more weight on the toes. The upper back and spine condense and round, with the shoulders and spine curving inward. Reflexes are slower. From the age of 40 into the seventies, there is about 45 percent decline in muscular output and endurance, and energy levels decline. Therefore, a design for a facility used by people in this age range would benefit from the same approaches taken in designing for ADA compliance.

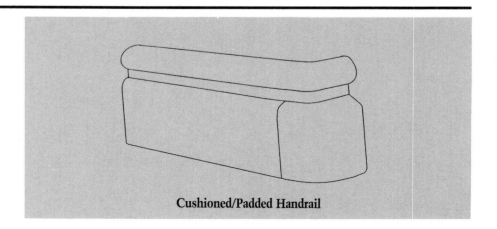

Cushioned/Padded Handrail

Figure 25.3

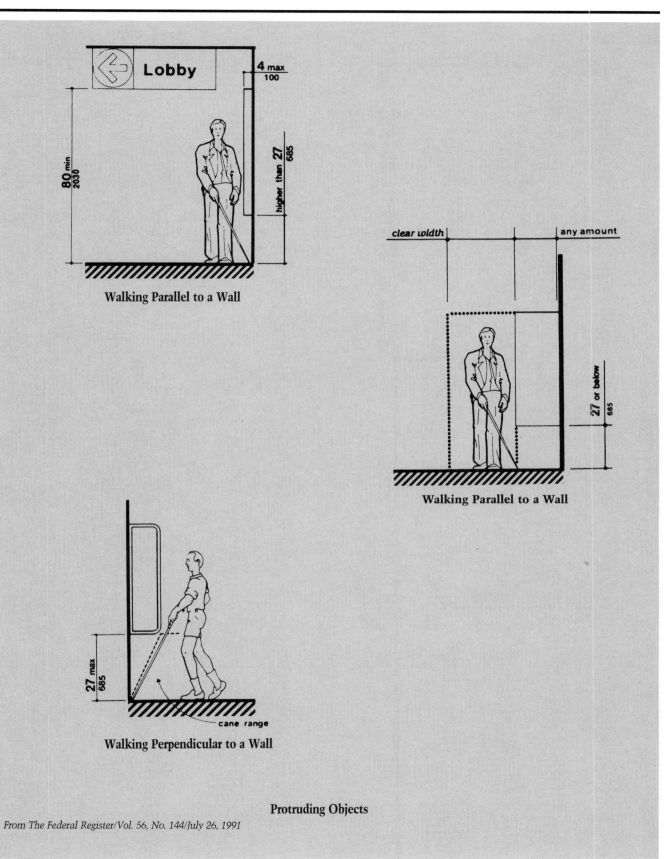

Walking Parallel to a Wall

Walking Parallel to a Wall

Walking Perpendicular to a Wall

Protruding Objects

From The Federal Register/Vol. 56, No. 144/July 26, 1991

Figure 25.4

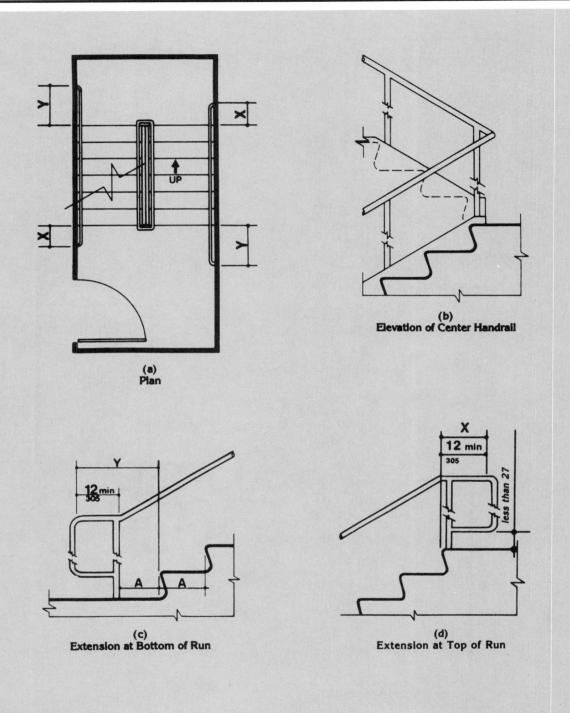

(a)
Plan

(b)
Elevation of Center Handrail

(c)
Extension at Bottom of Run

(d)
Extension at Top of Run

NOTE:
X is the 12 in. minimum handrail extension required at each top riser.
Y is the minimum handrail extension of 12 in. plus the width of one tread that is required at each bottom riser.

Stair Handrails

From The Federal Register/Vol. 56, No. 144/July 26, 1991

Figure 25.5

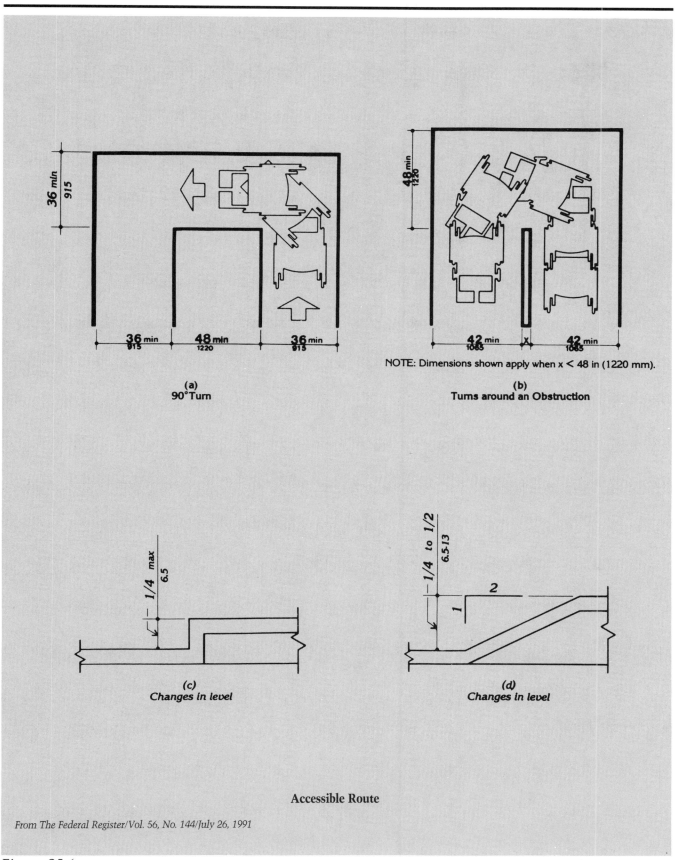

(a)
90° Turn

(b)
Turns around an Obstruction

NOTE: Dimensions shown apply when x < 48 in (1220 mm).

(c)
Changes in level

(d)
Changes in level

Accessible Route

From *The Federal Register/Vol. 56, No. 144/July 26, 1991*

Figure 25.6

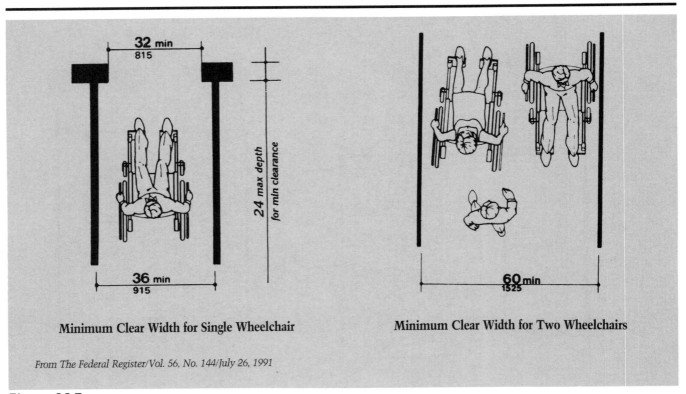

Minimum Clear Width for Single Wheelchair

Minimum Clear Width for Two Wheelchairs

From The Federal Register/Vol. 56, No. 144/July 26, 1991

Figure 25.7

Chapter Twenty-Six

SAFETY

Safety and security measures are of the utmost concern to designers of environments in which disabled people participate as employees, guests, citizens, and patrons. Safety interacts with each factor discussed in this book, and should be a key indicator of a successful design. Safety for a mobility-impaired person is often contingent on proper maintenance of passages. Safety for a hearing-impaired person is the ability to rely on visual cues. Safety for a vision-impaired person may be adequate illumination of signage or availability of Braille markers. The total environment should be evaluated by functional limitation to ensure proper safety provisions.

Safety Definitions

Measures that protect people from harm due to environmental conditions, equipment, and other people. An established program that promotes a feeling of security.

Meeting the Code

(ADA Titles I, II, III & IV; OSHA General Guidelines, NFPA 101) *All office injuries can be prevented; unsafe action causes unsafe conditions.*

The following guidelines are derived from the aforementioned codes.

1. Electrical equipment must be grounded.
2. No long extension cords may be stretched over the floor.
3. Heavy equipment or furniture must be properly secured.
4. Safe smoking areas and practices must be implemented.
5. Safety instructions must be posted for emergency use.
6. Carpets must be firmly secured.
7. Basic safety principles must be followed at all times.
8. Temperature should be moderated via accessible controls.
9. Harmful noise should be eliminated, none higher than 85 decibels without ear protection.
10. Hazardous materials must be contained and/or eliminated.
11. Handrails should be used when necessary to accommodate individuals with disabilities.
12. Corridors should be clearly marked.
13. Protective equipment should be provided in accordance with job hazards.

14. Safety equipment, with clearly posted instructions, must be on hand for emergencies.
15. Equipment should have protective guards.
16. Glare must be reduced wherever possible.
17. Surfaces should be maintained so that there are no dangers, such as loose tile. Rooms should be free of sharp corners, projections and slippery surfaces. All exits should conform to the NFPA Life Safety Code (No. 101).

The following are examples of settled cases that involve safety issues.

- *A State Department of Corrections agreed to relocate an inmate with a disability to a facility 400 miles closer to his mother's home so that his mother could visit him and monitor his medical condition.*
- *Inter-Continental Hotel, New York, New York – The Department of Justice entered a wide-ranging formal settlement agreement with the Inter-Continental Hotel in midtown New York, a member of a chain of prestigious hotels in major cities. The hotel will make numerous changes to its 691-room facility and procedures over the next five years, including removing physical barriers in public areas such as the front entrance, lobby, and ballroom, as well as in 21 guest rooms; providing television decoders, telephone handset amplifiers, visual smoke alarms, and visual door knock and telephone indicators in 35 guest rooms; making elevator modifications to provide access for persons with vision impairments; and modifying reservation and room assignment policies to ensure that accessible rooms are made available to those who request them.*
- *A drugstore chain agreed to modify its policy against permitting animals in its stores by making an exception in the case of service animals such as guide dogs.*

Alarms and Tactile Warnings

ADA 4.28.1. Alarm systems that are required to be accessible by 4.1 shall comply with 4.28.

ADA 4.28.2 Audible Alarms. If provided, audible emergency alarms shall produce a sound that exceeds the prevailing equivalent sound level in the room or space by at least 15 decibels, or exceeds any maximum sound level with a duration of 60 seconds by 5 decibels, whichever is louder. Sound levels for alarm signals shall not exceed 120 decibels.

ADA 4.28.3 Visual Alarms. If provided, electrically powered, internally illuminated emergency exit signs shall flash as a visual emergency alarm in conjunction with audible emergency alarms. The flashing frequency of visual alarm devices shall be a minimum of 1 Hz. and a maximum of 3 Hz. per the NFPA, if such alarms use electricity from the building as a power source, then they shall be installed on the same system as the audible emergency alarms.

ADA 4.29 Tactile Warnings. Tactile warnings are required on walking surfaces at hazardous vehicular areas and reflection pools. Doors that lead to areas that might prove dangerous to a blind person (for example, doors to loading platforms, boiler rooms, stages, and the like) shall be made identifiable to the touch by a textured surface on the door handle, knob, pull, or other operating hardware. This textured surface may be made by knurling or roughing or by a material applied to the contact surface. Such textured surfaces shall not be provided for emergency exit doors or any doors other than those to hazardous areas. Textured surfaces for tactile door warnings shall be standardized within a building, facility, site, or complex of buildings. Tactile warnings at stairs are not specified by ADA. Refer to ADA-AG, Section 4.29 for other details on tactile warnings.

See the Department of Justice update at the end of Appendix A for revisions/clarifications regarding tactile warning requirements.

Meeting the Need

Designing for Safety

Safety measures must provide extra protection for people who are able to offer less resistance to harm, and therefore may incur greater injury. Safety in the office is just as important as it is in any other environment. It should be the designer's concern, just as it is the concern of those people using the office. Some principles to consider in evaluating any office environment are listed below. The principles are more important when physically challenged and fully ambulatory people are working together, because disabled people are vulnerable.

1. People, not objects, cause accidents.
2. Many accidents occur while a person is moving—slipping, falling, and tripping.
3. The body parts most frequently injured in the office are the hands and fingers.

Safety Issues for an Aging Population

Physical change is a major aspect of aging as the five senses—vision, touch, hearing, smell and taste—lose their sharpness. Changes in flexibility and strength also deteriorate in varying degrees. These changes are very gradual and the cumulative effects might not be obvious until a person enters his or her eighties. Notably, these changes affect every individual differently and to varying degrees. Only seven percent of the older population live in institutions, which is an indication of the percentage of the general population severely impacted by the physical changes of aging.

In designing for safety in an environment, it is important to consider the following physical changes that occur with age.

- Eye lens turns yellow
- Color blindness increases
- Sense of touch is not greatly reduced
- Lens thickens, less light penetrates
- Pupil reflex is slower
- Susceptibility to glare increases
- Strength and flexibility decrease
- Sense of balance changes
- Reflexes are slower
- Walking gait changes
- Sense of balance changes
- Reaction time becomes slower
- High-pitched sounds are more difficult to hear

A Final Word

Whether addressing code requirements or the needs of individuals, safety is a concern of all citizens. In additional to the value of preventing harm to human beings it must be remembered that lost time due to accidents is costly from both an insurance and productivity standpoint. Money spent correcting safety deficiencies is always well spent.

Chapter Twenty-Seven

SIGNAGE

Signage is visual access to public areas (lobbies and public spaces) for people with disabilities. For wheelchair users, signs can be mounted on the wall or as part of a four-way view set at intersections of passages. The important evaluative criteria for signage is that it can be viewed by people with low vision from 30 feet away. Low vision is 20% of normal (or 100% vision) with proper lighting, high contrast, and 6″ lettering. Some low vision people can see signs from 30′.

Proper signage, at a minimum, guides people to places with independence, and it may also save lives. That is why every functional limitation should be considered when designing and using signage. This includes additional assistive hearing devices such as signals that use light or vibration to communicate an emergency alarm, as well as doorbells and wake-up systems.

Meeting the Code and the Need

The following sample case illustrates signage along with other solutions for ADA compliance.

- *Omaha Zoological Society, Omaha, Nebraska – The Omaha Zoological Society, a nonprofit corporation that operates and manages the Henry Doorly Zoo, Lied Jungle indoor rain forest, and its Treetops Restaurant, agreed to provide a variety of auxiliary aids and services, including audiotape recordings of the Lied Jungle Trail guide and information about the rain forest contained on signs located throughout the jungle. Staff will be available to serve as guides to visitors with visual impairments upon request.*

Signage Definitions

1. Clear guidance for the newest person to any area of the building.
2. Luminescence and lettering that provide clarity.
3. Contrasted colors used to enhance legibility.

Definitions as Used in ADA

1. *Commerce:* Means travel, trade, traffic, commerce, transportation or communication.
2. *Public Accommodation: Operations affect commerce.* The definition of public accommodation incorporates the categories listed below:
   a. Places of lodging

b. Establishments serving food or drink
   c. Places of exhibition or entertainment
   d. Places of public gathering
   e. Sales or rental establishments
   f. Service establishments
   g. Stations used for specified public transportation
   h. Places of public display or collection
   i. Places of recreation
   j. Places of education
   k. Social service center establishment
3. *Commercial Facilities:* Facilities that are intended for nonresidential use by private entity and whose operations affect commerce.
4. *Tactile:* Describes an object that can be perceived using the sense of touch.
5. *Signage:* Displayed verbal, symbolic, tactile and pictorial information.
6. *Accessible:* Readily approachable and usable by disabled people.
7. *Hoistway:* The shaft in which an elevator operates.
8. *Eggshell:* The finish of the lettering or sign (in this case it is not a color).
9. *Braille:* Grade 2 Braille is required by ADA. Grade 2 Braille uses the same characters as Grade 1 but utilizes combinations of characters or symbols to form contractions or represent combinations of letters. For instance, in Grade 2 the word "men" (in all lower case) does not require three Braille tiles (characters), but only two. Each tile is comprised of a potential six raised dots. The number and location of the dots indicates the character(s) it represents.

Raised and Braille Characters and Pictorial Symbol Signs

- Letters and numbers shall be raised a minimum of 1/32", upper case, sanserif or simple serif type. Raised characters shall be at least 5/8" (16 mm) high, but no higher than 2" (50 mm). An eggshell (matte) finish is recommended. Character proportions shall have a width to height ratio between 3:5 and 1:1 and a stroke width to height ratio between 1:5 and 1:10.
- Contrast between characters and background is recommended to be at least 70%. The greatest readability is usually achieved through the use of light-colored characters or symbols on a dark background, or dark on light.
- Braille Characters: Must be Grade 2. Standard dimensions for literary Braille are: Dot diameter (.059"). Inter-dot spacing (.090"), horizontal separation between cells (.241") and vertical separation between cells (.395").

Meeting the Code

(ATBCB 1190.200, UFAS 4.30, ADA Titles I, II & III; U.L., International Standards Organization) Signage is a key issue in the ADA, due to its importance in allowing people to access all parts of a facility. Issues such as character proportion, color contrast, and mounting location are spelled out in specific terms in the ADA. Applicable law sections are 4.30.1 through 4.30.8. The ADA requires:

1. For signs that designate permanent rooms and spaces: signage must have raised lettering, Braille and pictograms (where applicable), as well as being mounted in a specific location.

2. For signs that provide direction to, or information about, functional spaces of the building: signs must comply with character proportion, height, finish and contrast rules. Lower case is acceptable, tactile-lettering and Braille are not required. Fire evacuation signs that direct building users to the fire exit would fall into this category except that they do not have the requirement for 5/8″ minimum lettering (lettering might be smaller in this instance).

3. Elements and spaces of accessible facilities (accessible by a disabled person) that shall be identified by the International Symbol of Accessibility (appropriate such as wheelchair, TDD symbol, etc.) are:

   a. Parking spaces designated as reserved for individuals with disabilities.

   b. Accessible passenger loading zones.

   c. Accessible entrances when not all are accessible (inaccessible entrances shall have directional signage to indicate the route to the nearest accessible entrance).

   d. Accessible toilet and bathing facilities, when all the facilities in the building are not accessible (inaccessible toilet and bathing facilities shall have directional signage to indicate the route to the nearest accessible rest room).

4. Overhead and Protruding Signs: a minimum character height of 3″ is required, lower case can be used, raised and Braille characters are not required. Overhead and right angle signs must allow a minimum clear head room of 80″.

Labeling

Entrances

The international symbol of access must be displayed at facility and vehicle entrances that are wheelchair accessible. (See Figures 27.1–27.4.)

Composition

All signs should be graphics with large lettering in high contrast colors as designated by the International Standards Organization.

Exterior Signage

Symbols of Accessibility

If any of the entrances to the building are not accessible, then inaccessible entrances should be so labeled with directions to the nearest accessible entrance. The accessible entrances should be designated with the international symbol. (Figure 27.1.) Refer to 4.30.7 and 4.1.2 (7)(c) of ADA-AG.

Parking Spaces

Accessible parking spaces shall be designated as reserved by a sign showing the symbol of accessibility (Figure 27.1). Such signs shall be located in such a way that they cannot be obscured by a vehicle parked in the space. Refer to ADA-AG 4.1.2 (7a) and 4.6.4.

Interior Signage

In general, all the signs used in a facility, including directional and informational signage, should meet the following requirements. (To meet the need, attention should also be given to modifications of building directories and menu boards.)

Accessible Check-out Aisles

Sign Required: International Symbol of Accessibility

Mounting: Above the check-out aisle in the same location where the check-out aisle number or type of check-out is displayed.

Character Proportion

Letters and numbers on signage shall have a width-to-height ratio of between 3:5 and 1:1, and a stroke-width-to-height ratio of between 1:5 and 1:10. Refer to Section 4.30.2 of ADA-AG.

Character Height

Characters and numbers on signs shall be sized according to the viewing distance from which they are to be read. For signs higher than 80", the minimum letter height shall be three inches. The minimum height is measured using an upper case X. Lower case letters are permitted.

Color Contrast & Sign Finish

The colors used for characters and symbols should provide high contrast to the sign background to meet the needs of those with low vision. The characters and backgrounds of signs shall be non-glare. Refer to ADA-AG 4.30.5.

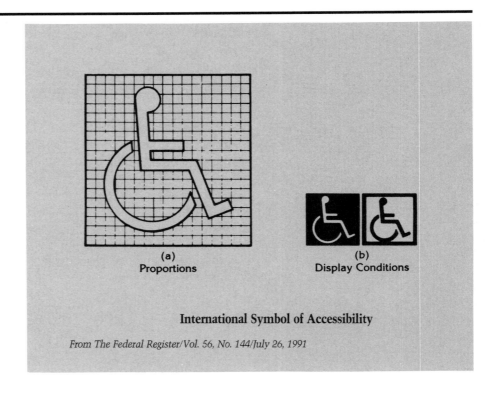

(a)
Proportions

(b)
Display Conditions

International Symbol of Accessibility

From The Federal Register/Vol. 56, No. 144/July 26, 1991

Figure 27.1

Assembly Areas

The international symbol of access for hearing loss must be displayed where assistive listening systems are required. (See Figure 27.5.)

Public Telephones

Text telephones must be identified with the TDD symbol. Volume control telephones must be identified by the international symbol for hearing loss.

Permanent Room or Space Identification

Signs for permanent rooms or spaces (such as numbers on hotel guest rooms, hospital patient rooms, and office suites, as well as signs designating men's and women's rest rooms) must have raised and Braille characters and must also meet the requirements listed under "General Specifications." Refer to 4.1.2 (7), and 4.1.3 (16a) in ADA-AG.

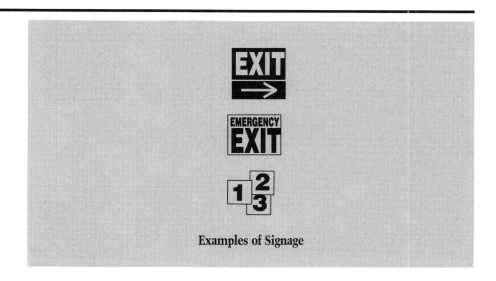

Examples of Signage

Figure 27.2

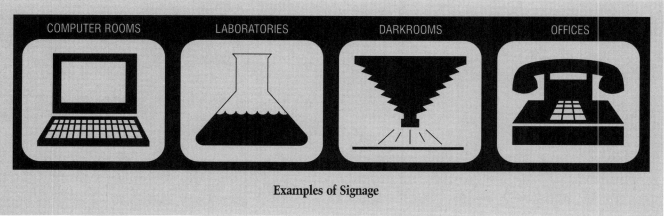

Examples of Signage

Figure 27.3

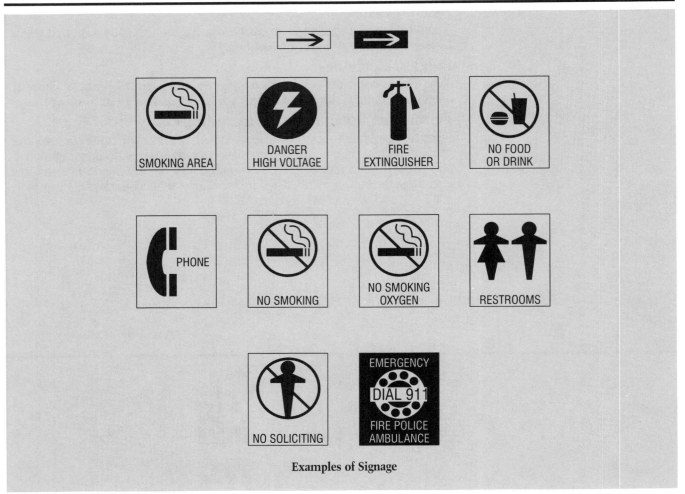

Examples of Signage

Figure 27.4

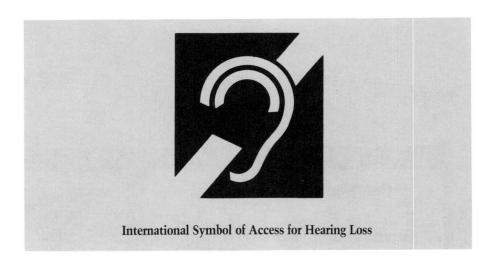

International Symbol of Access for Hearing Loss

Figure 27.5

Raised and Braille Characters and Pictograms

Raised characters shall be raised 1/32", upper-case, sans serif or simple serif type. The letter height shall be between 5/8" and 2". Grade 2 Braille shall be accompanied by the equivalent verbal description placed directly below the pictogram. The border dimension of the pictogram shall be a minimum of 6" in height. Refer to 4.30.4 of ADA-AG.

Signage Locations and Measurements

- The accessible pictogram is required only when not all rest rooms in the building are accessible. Non-accessible toilet or bathing facilities should have signage provided indicating the location of the nearest accessible toilet or bathing facility within the building.
- The center of a mounted sign should measure 60" from the floor. The ADA-AG also recommends mounting 2" from the latch side of the door. To comply with ADA the accessible symbol and description with the Braille translation must be mounted on the latch side of the door. The MAN/WOMAN symbol is not required in this position, and therefore may be mounted directly to the door.
- Hoistway (elevator) Entrances: All elevator hoistway entrances shall have raised and Braille floor designations provided on both jambs. The centerline of the characters shall be 60" (1525 mm) above finish floor. Such characters shall be 2" (50 mm) high and must conform to requirements of signage. Permanently applied plates are acceptable if they are permanently fixed to the jambs.
- Elevator Two-Way Communication Systems: The highest operable part of the system shall be a maximum of 48" (1220 mm) from the floor of the car. It shall be identified by a raised symbol and lettering, and located adjacent to the device.
- Areas of rescue shall be identified by a sign which states "AREA OF RESCUE ASSISTANCE," and should display the International Symbol of Accessibility. The sign shall be illuminated when exit sign illumination is required. Instructions on the use of the area under emergency conditions shall be posted adjoining the two-way communication system. See 4.30.6 and 4.4.2 of ADA-AG.

Overhead Signage

Overhead signage includes ceiling, perpendicular, and soft-mounted signs.

Meeting the Need

Redundant cuing (e.g., maps that are easily read, with signs that are consistent in high contrast colors and with large lettering) is an essential aid to help customers, clients, and employees negotiate environments.

Mapping a Building

Persons with disabling conditions often experience changes in sensory or cognitive abilities which may include loss of short term memory. Therefore, the physical environment should promote re-orientation using simple design with repetitive architectural elements, fixtures, and finishes.

Mapping a Room

Room signage should be organized with identifying directional and informational signage that has significant color contrasts and features large lettering (two inches).

Chapter Twenty-Eight

STORAGE

People with disabilities require storage areas that allow the maximum of maneuverability and safety. For example, space must be wide enough to allow passage for access to resources. Reach and stamina are also important concerns. For example, if closet shelves and clothing rods are too high, a person in a wheelchair cannot access or store items. Independent function is critical to maintain one's dignity and self-esteem. Access to stored items can either foster or impede self-reliance. If storage areas are not accessible, additional staff must be available to compensate for lack of reasonable accommodation.

This chapter reviews ADA requirements for storage and provides further guidance for meeting the needs of people with disabilities. See Section B of the Compliance Product Selection Guide at the back of this book for storage product sources.

Storage Definitions

Items in an accessible location; an uncluttered space that allows independent access to stored items.

Meeting the Code

(ATBCB 1190.240, ADA 4.25, ADA Title I) Storage is an important code issue because it involves the provision of access without requiring the assistance of others. Meeting the code for storage means adhering to the reach and hardware requirements spelled out by the ADA.

Storage Areas

Storage areas should be accessible and uncluttered to allow independent access to supplies.

General

Fixed storage facilities such as cabinets, shelves, closets, and drawers required to be accessible by ADA-AG 4.1.3 (12) and 4.1.7 (3e) shall comply with 4.25.

Clear Floor Space

A clear floor space at least 30 inches by 48 inches (760 mm by 1220 mm) complying with 4.2.4 that allows either a forward or parallel approach by a person using a wheelchair shall be provided at accessible storage facilities. Refer to ADA-AG 4.25.2 in Appendix A.

Height

Accessible storage spaces shall be within at least one of the reach ranges specified in 4.2.5 and 4.2.6. Clothes rods shall be a maximum of 54 inches (1370 mm) from the floor. Refer to ADA-AG 4.25.3.

Hardware

Hardware for accessible storage facilities shall comply with ADA-AG 4.27.4. Touch latches and U-shaped pulls are acceptable.

Figure 28.1 is an illustration of reach requirements and limits.

The design of storage should include accessible shelving that allows access from a height of 29 inches and does not exceed a depth of 12 inches. There should be areas for individual storage and units for project maintenance.

Meeting the Need   Shelving for storage or display of inventory should provide flexibility—whether for the employees maintaining supplies and inventory, or for customers who need access to products (e.g., a revolving display that allows the person access without movement).

The following guidelines should be considered.

1. Reach should not require overhead or extended arms.
2. The weight of items should not exceed five pounds.
3. There should be minimal vibration from adjacent equipment.
4. No sharp edges should contact the hand or wrist.
5. No finger or pinch grasp should be necessary.
6. Accessing an item should not take more than two minutes.
7. Removing an item should take no more than 30 seconds.

See Chapter Twenty, "Furnishings," for examples of furniture that provides accessible storage solutions.

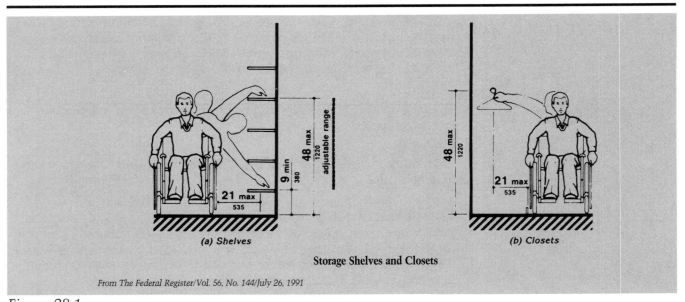

(a) Shelves   (b) Closets

Storage Shelves and Closets

From The Federal Register/Vol. 56, No. 144/July 26, 1991

Figure 28.1

Chapter Twenty-Nine

TEMPERATURE

A number of variables, including personal activity levels, uniformity of temperature, radiant heat gain or loss and humidity, interact to determine whether people are comfortable with the temperature of the indoor air. Frequently the medical conditions of people with disease, injury, disability or aging may result in temperature sensitivities. Temperature sensitivity is complicated by the fact that it may vary during the course of a day for the same person. Any excesses of cold or heat can aggravate the symptoms of a person's condition. Therefore, designs should minimize temperature extremes in the overall facility and, to the extent possible, allow moderation of hot and cold in some zoned areas. For example, guests in hotels should be able to moderate room temperature. Large gathering rooms should be modified based on the density of anticipated crowds.

Meeting the Code

Temperature Control & Humidity

The following chart is the ASHRAE Standard 55-1981, "Thermal Environmental Conditions for Human Occupancy, Acceptable Ranges of Temperature and Relative Humidity During Summer and Winter."

Relative Humidity	Winter Temperature	Summer Temperature
30%	68.5°F – 76.0°F	74.0°F – 80.0°F
40%	68.5°F – 75.5°F	73.5°F – 79.5°F
50%	68.5°F – 74.5°F	73.0°F – 79.0°F
60%	68.0°F – 74.0°F	72.5°F – 78.0°F

Applies for persons clothed in typical summer and winter clothing, at light, mainly sedentary activity.

In general, the range of humidity levels recommended seems to be 30% to 60% RH. Relative humidities below this level may produce discomfort from dryness. On the other hand, maintaining relative humidities at the lowest possible level helps to restrict the growth of mold and mildew. The concerns (comfort for the most part) associated with dry air must be balanced against the risk (enhanced microbiological growth) associated with humidification. If temperatures are maintained at the lower end of the comfort range (68 – 70°F) during heating periods, relative humidity in most climates will not fall much below 30% (also within the comfort range) in occupied buildings.

A properly designed and functioning HVAC system:
- provides thermal comfort
- distributes adequate amounts of outdoor air (number of air exchanges per hour) to meet ventilation needs of all building occupants
- isolates and removes odors and contaminants through pressure control, filtration, and exhaust fans

Meeting the Need

Thermal comfort and ventilation needs are met by supplying "conditioned" air (a blend of outdoor and recirculated air that has been filtered, heated or cooled, and sometimes humidified or dehumidified).

A number of variables interact to determine whether people are comfortable with the temperature of the indoor air. The activity level, age, and physiology of each person affect the thermal comfort requirements of that individual.

Uniformity of temperature is important to comfort. When the heating and cooling needs of rooms within a single zone change at different rates, rooms that are served by a single thermostat may be at different temperatures. Temperature stratification is a common problem caused by convection (the tendency of light, warm air to rise and heavier, cooler air to sink). If air is not properly mixed by the ventilation system, the temperature near the ceiling can be several degrees warmer than at floor level. Even if air is properly mixed, uninsulated floors over unheated spaces can create discomfort in some climate zones. Large fluctuations of indoor temperature can also occur when controls have a wide "dead band" (a temperature range within which neither heating nor cooling mechanisms are activated).

Radiant heat transfer may cause people located near very hot or very cold surfaces to be uncomfortable even though the thermostat setting and the measured air temperature are within the comfort range. Buildings with large window areas sometimes have acute problems of discomfort due to radiant heat gains and losses, with the locations of complaints shifting during the day as the sun angle changes. Large vertical surfaces can also produce a significant flow of naturally-convecting air, producing complaints of draftiness. Adding insulation to walls helps to moderate the temperature of interior wall surfaces. Closing curtains also reduces heating from direct sunlight and isolates building occupants from exposure to window surfaces (which, lacking insulation, are likely to be much hotter or colder than the walls).

Humidity is a factor in thermal comfort. Raising relative humidity reduces a person's ability to lose heat through perspiration and evaporation, so that the effect is similar to raising the temperature.

Generally, people work more comfortably in settings that are cooler and drier, versus warm, humid environments. However, heating, ventilation and air-conditioning systems should be set by three criteria:
1. Activity levels (static versus dynamic work).
2. Age of the population (the older the population, the higher the temperature needs).
3. The likelihood of disease susceptibility and transmission.

Temperature is a design issue when disabled people are involved because it is more difficult to maintain normal body temperature in a wheelchair than when fully ambulatory. Designs must consider both tactile and thermal sensitivity. For example, there should be no hot radiators for a person to run into, or air that drafts or blows extremes of hot or cold. The ability to control one's own comfort is an important psychological boost to anyone, challenged or not.

Designs for heating, ventilating and air-conditioning should take into consideration the wide range of comfort bands that exist for individuals based on their unique size, weight, and disabling conditions. Many people are susceptible to the loss of body heat and have little tolerance even for transient swings in ambient temperature.

Double-paned window units and reflective "shields" are excellent methods of both preventing heat loss and promoting cooling during the appropriate seasons.

If thermal discomfort is a problem,
- Check HVAC condition and operation.
- Measure indoor and outdoor temperature and humidity. See if extreme conditions exceed design of HVAC equipment.
- Check for drafts and stagnant areas.
- Check for excessive radiant heat gain or loss.

Current Concerns

Managers of office work forces, and designers and facility managers are concerned with the following issues regarding temperature and air quality in their offices:

- **Variable temperatures:** The energy crisis of the late 1970s led to attempts to legislate energy efficiency (for example, the wide "dead-band" on the thermostats in government buildings, and the never-adopted Building Energy Performance Standards) and to an increased energy consciousness in building owners and the design professions. The legacy of this period has been an expansion of the thermal "comfort zone" in office buildings. Before this expansion, workers were used to offices with energy inefficient (but highly effective) heating and air-conditioning systems, that provided a constant and narrow band of temperatures and air quality. The band is now considerably wider, and the fluctuations are probably more frequent and greater. Do these workers notice the increase in temperature fluctuations? Are they bothered by them? Do these swings affect performance or satisfaction?

- **Open offices and homogeneous thermal and air quality experience:** The rapid growth of open offices in this country has been accompanied by a loss of control over temperature and air quality for many people who were formally in private offices or in small group offices. Full floors are often a single temperature zone to ensure that everybody gets the same temperature. But is everybody (or even large numbers of people) comfortable at the same temperature? How strongly do other factors moderate people's thermal experience? Can thermal problems be largely solved through environmental means, or must a more complex strategy be developed?

- **Air quality:** The past decade has seen a substantial shift in national health attitudes, with more people taking personal responsibility for their health. Evidence for this is an enormous increase in the number of people exercising regularly, a substantial reduction in fat intake, and a major decrease in smoking, the latter through both legislation and personal initiatives. While many organizations have fitness programs and see self-help health as an investment, many have still not banned smoking in the workplace. While the thermal comfort zone has been extended because of energy consciousness, there has not been a substantial increase in fresh air in office space. Given the increased sensitivity by both smokers and non-smokers, air quality may have become a more important issue. (See Chapter 13 for more on air quality.)

What Factors Affect Responses to Thermal Comfort?

Since responses to temperatures are known to be affected by activities and by body type, as well as by the ambient conditions themselves, it is useful to examine responses by job type and sex (as a surrogate for body type).

Since VDT equipment gives off localized heat, temperature responses can be compared for equipment users and non-users. In a study on this subject, we also wished to examine a hypothesis that recently designed energy-conscious buildings would appear to be "underconditioned," with many more people being too warm in the summer and too cool in the winter, clearly affected by outside conditions. For some of these analyses we used a special data base of nine geographically dispersed regional centers of one company, with almost 800 respondents. This data base provides information about summer and winter thermal conditions.

Sex (or size) differences: There are significant and stable differences between men and women's responses to temperature and air quality. Women are far more likely (1) to be too cool, (2) to notice temperature fluctuations, and (3) to have a lower tolerance to smoke or odors. Both temperature results are explainable not as a sex difference per se, but as a size difference between males and females.

The 50th percentile male is a bit over 5'-9" and weighs 162 pounds, while the 50th percentile female is a bit over 5'-3" and weighs 135 pounds. The larger the person (the more a person looks like a sphere), the less surface area per unit of volume there is, since area increases as the square of a number of volume increases as its cube. Smaller people, with their high surface-area-to-volume ratio (lots of heat-losing surface) generally have higher sensitivity to cold and somewhat higher sensitivity to temperature fluctuation, although this is less true of heat gain or feelings of warmth.

Even when air quality is generally good, 10% of the general population may experience poor air quality "frequently" or "constantly." Of these, women are significantly more likely than men to notice smoke or odors.

Summer and winter differences: Results show that buildings generally tend to be only slightly underconditioned, that is, a bit too warm in the summer and too cool in the winter. In fact, many people seem to experience problems of overconditioning, and say it is too cool in the summer and too warm in the winter. This same pattern, with more or less equal winter-summer responses, holds for temperature fluctuations and for air quality. In fact, the largest group of responses are for individuals who give exactly the same responses both summer and winter. That is, if these individuals report it is too cool "constantly" in the winter, they report it is too cool "constantly" in the summer as well. Others will report it is "never" too cool in the summer and "never" too cool in the winter.

For example, 55% have identical responses about too warm and too cool for the summer and winter, while 68% have identical responses to the temperature fluctuation question for both summer and winter.

We examined three hypotheses to explain this:

1. It may be that those people who are over or under sensitive to specific temperature are over or under sensitive independent of actual conditions.
2. The HVAC systems operate to make interior climate fairly independent of external conditions so that summer and winter are thermally irrelevant.
3. People are not differentiating sufficiently among the summer versus winter questions on the survey.

The third hypothesis seems unsupported, for analysis shows that respondents are discerning among the summer versus winter questions and that their answers have a conceptual consistency.

The second hypothesis, that buildings act as "closed systems," independent of seasonal pressures, is only partly true, for our analysis shows they are a bit "underconditioned," cooler in the winter and warmer in the summer.

The first hypothesis seems highly probable: that there are people whose metabolism and other factors make them either relatively insensitive or oversensitive to temperature and temperature fluctuations. Analysis shows that these differences are very strongly related to body type, with large people relatively insensitive to and small people very sensitive to temperatures that are too cool or that fluctuate too much.

While analysis of body types is best done using height and weight and the DuBois Nomograph, ours was done by sex, after establishing that (a) height correlates with weight and (b) our samples' height averages for men and women are 5'-11" and 5'-4", respectively, with little overlap of the two sexes in height categories.

Recommendations

It is clear, both from the responses in the above study and in the concerns expressed by facility managers, that providing for an ideal building temperature is an ongoing challenge. It is also evident that temperature is felt subjectively so that even if building conditions and temperatures were uniform, building occupants would respond differently. As a result, the best solution appears to be providing, to the greatest extent possible, localized temperature modification solutions, such as fans, unit heaters, operable windows, and adjustable heating and cooling vents.

Chapter Thirty

WINDOWS

Windows and window treatments should be designed such that people with disabilities can enjoy access to the outside world, as employees and guests in facilities. For visual access to people in wheelchairs, windows should have low sills (two feet from the floor). To compensate for limited hand strength and stamina, a maximum force of 5 pounds should be required to turn a handle, slide a window open, or move a drapery by pulling the fabric or using a rod.

The need for natural illumination is great, even though windows may need to be shaded to reduce glare. They should be positioned to provide as much natural light and access to the outside environment as possible. Optimum window sill height should be 15 to 20 inches from the floor.

Casement windows combine an easily accessible bottom-mounted lever locking handle that incorporates a single-handed opening crank. The crank is located at the lowest point on the window and should be easily maneuvered with one hand. This provides security and control to the disabled person. (See Figure 30.1.)

Currently, the ADA does not address windows or window hardware. Requirements for these items have been "reserved."

Windows Definitions

1. Provisions of optimum natural light.
2. High levels of illumination which also provide a view and a feeling of spaciousness.

Meeting the Code

(ATBCB 1190.140, UFAS 4.12, ADA Title I) While Title III of the ADA offers no specific provisions for windows, Title I requires that the facility accommodate disabled employees, including the provision of adequate light and ventilation.

Meeting the Need

Visual access to the outside allows a space to be perceived as less confined no matter how small the space. People are inclined to stay longer in spaces with windows. Reducing a sense of confinement is critical to maintaining creativity and comfort, independence, and dignity.

For people with mobility impairments, windows become most critical. The following is a rank order of most frequent reasons for operable, accessible windows.

1. Access to daylight
2. A view of the external environment
3. Ventilation, if the window opens
4. Sunlight and heat
5. A dynamic, interesting change to the panorama
6. A way to monitor weather and seasonal changes
7. Visual relief in the form of distant objects which provide a contrast to the typical "close work" found in offices
8. A feeling of not being "closed in"
9. Light for work
10. Reduction in sensory deprivation
11. Increased feeling of expanded view
12. Sense of safety through visual access

The greatest benefits of windows are natural light and a sense of space. The installation of new exterior windows is generally a costly solution. However, installing new interior windows, e.g., between individual offices and an atrium is a less expensive alternative, which, in some cases, will provide a sense of space and additional light.

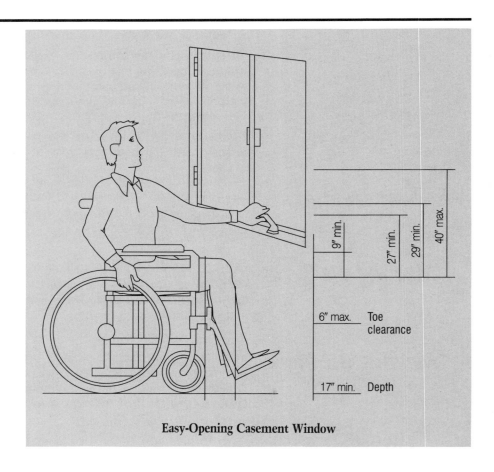

Easy-Opening Casement Window

Figure 30.1

246

Chapter Thirty-One

25 LOW-COST COMPLIANCE SOLUTIONS

According to Job Accommodation Network's (JAN) ongoing survey of Title I costs (accommodations for disabled employees), 32% of the costs of accommodations have been between $1.00 and $500. Despite this relatively low cost overall, some modifications can be costly. In selected cases, a creative approach can be used to properly meet the needs of disabled people without causing an organization undue hardship.

Whether accommodations are made in the "standard" way, or by means of a creative, less costly alternative, the goal of accommodation must always be the same—to meet the need, the code, and the ADA for individuals with disabilities so that they may function safely with independence and dignity. Understanding the functional limitations of the people for whom a reasonable accommodation is to be made is critical to designing effective environments. It is therefore important to obtain guidance from those who are experienced in this area before undertaking compliance solutions. Embarking on modifications without correct or adequate information can lead to expensive errors in terms of projects that have to be redone, and/or fines or lawsuits for failing to correctly comply with the law.

The following solutions are a sampling of the kinds of ideas available through an expert on ADA and barrier-free design (such as Work Stations, Inc.). The Compliance Product Selection Guide at the back of this book contains sources for many of the products described in this section. Again, professional guidance is key to selecting the right product for your situation.

Accessibility:
- Portable aluminum ramps can be used to allow wheelchair users to roll up one step to access a facility. A portable ramp not only provides versatility and cost effectiveness in that it can be used in more than one location as needed, but it also can be removed, unlike a permanent ramp, to avoid problems such as traffic obstruction. Cost: $420.00 versus $500 or more to install each permanent concrete ramp.
- Swing-clear door hinges can be used to replace existing hinges in some cases when a door opening is marginally undersized per ADA requirements. Cost: $368 per door versus approximately $1000 to widen the door opening and install a new, appropriately sized door.

- A swimming pool can be made accessible with a lifter that allows disabled users access to pool recreation and therapy. This is an alternative to remodeling the pool with a costly built-in ramp that occupies valuable space. Cost of the lift: approximately $1,000.

Adaptability:

- A standard doorknob can be converted to an ADA-compliant lever handle using an adapter kit, in lieu of replacing the entire cylinder lockset. Cost: $12.00 for an adapter kit, complete with the one required tool, versus $50.00 for new lockset (plus installation). A standard knob-operated mortise lockset can also be retrofitted to accommodate ADA lever requirements. Cost: Mortise lock retrofit kit: $110–$147 versus $175–$250 for a new mortise lockset (plus installation).
- A paper cup dispenser can be added adjacent to a drinking fountain at the proper height from the floor. This solution enables wheelchair users to use the drinking fountain without the expense of replacing the existing appliance with a $900 dual-height drinking fountain.
- An existing toilet at a height that does not comply with ADA requirements can be replaced with a new toilet specially designed with water and sewer connections to match existing plumbing, and a compliant seat height. This fixture allows compliance without the much greater expense of repiping. Cost for replacement toilet: approximately $400, versus $1400 for toilet, repiping and finishes repair.
- Writing aids, most costing less than $10.00, can help people who suffer from arthritis and other hand crippling conditions by providing wrist supports and comfortable grip designs. Aids include pen holders, specially designed pens, and ball-shaped holders for pens or utensils. Not only does this approach provide people with greater independence, but helps avoid more expensive alternatives, such as dictating notes and having them transcribed.

Air Quality:

- Portable air filtration units can be used for individual offices and discreet spaces. This alternative to a costly air filtration system for the entire facility addresses individual needs at less than $200 per unit.

Comfort:

- Existing seating can often be modified with specially designed supports such as ergonomic cushions or leg rests, at relatively low cost. For some disabilities, however, the best solution is a specialized ergonomic chair. For example, a chair with a split seat and many adjustment capabilities might be chosen to accommodate someone who has had one leg amputated. Cost: $750.00.

Communication:

- A portable telephone amplifier increases the volume of telephone conversation to a comfortable listening level with an adjustable volume control. Cost: $26.00. While it is difficult to quantify the cost of alternative solutions, this low-cost aid helps make it possible for valued employees/patrons to participate fully and productively. Compromising their ability to communicate is a costly alternative. Cordless headset telephones, adaptive speakerphones, and remote control emergency message telephones are other relatively low-cost communications aids that support communications for people with limited hearing and/or motor function.

Division of Space:

- Resources (copier, mail, files) can be placed to accommodate a person with a mobility impairment. Cost: $0. This solution is planned as part of a space planning redesign of an office. The alternative is the new "creative office" designs, costing roughly $1000 per 100 square feet.

Equipment:

- A voice-activated computer can be provided for a writer with limited use of hands. Cost: $995, plus the upgrade to the computer. This solution saves the cost of providing an administrative assistant for word processing.
- An automatic page-turner is another relatively low-cost device that fosters independence and productivity. The alternative is having someone available to turn pages or read to the disabled person.

Finishes:

- Paint in high contrast colors allows a vision-impaired person to more easily locate corners and handrails. Cost: interior latex paint $20.00 per gallon. The more expensive alternative is wallpaper and/or carpet with a border pattern, both of which also have a higher maintenance cost.

Furniture:

- Low-cost accommodations to existing furniture include adding casters to the legs of desks and lowering desk legs, and putting files on lazy susans to increase access. This approach can provide a workable solution in many cases without the investment in specialized furniture.

Image:

- All accommodations should consider how to maximize the person's dignity by the design. For example, locating a disabled person closer to resources is an inconspicuous and low-cost way of accommodating for the fatigue that may be part of a disease such as chronic heart condition. Another approach to support image for disabled people is using devices such as an environmental control unit that operates electrical devices and a telephone, enabling the user to control these aspects of his/her environment.

Lighting:

- Installing motion sensors that turn lights on when a person enters a room or area is a cost-effective alternative to moving light switches. Cost: $35 per sensor plus installation. Touch or rocker switches allow people with grip problems easier access to lighting. Cost: $2.35 per unit for materials, plus installation.

Maintenance:

- Ease of maintenance should be a design criterion for all equipment specified. Heat coils in exterior ramps (in areas of the country with significant snow and ice accumulation) can be designed in and the cost may be justified by the labor savings for maintenance. Cost: $8.85 per square foot for installation of electric heating cables in a new concrete ramp. (Energy costs should also be considered.)

Noise:

- Acoustical accommodation in panel systems can allow people with hearing impairments to maximize their hearing opportunity. Cost varies between $100 to $400 per system. In appropriate circumstances, standard hearing protection such as ear plugs or gun muffs can reduce the distraction of unwanted sound.

Safety:

- Fluorescent safety tape affixed to the top and bottom stair to mark the beginning and ending of a set of stairs is a low-cost way to enhance the safety of vision-impaired people. Cost: $5.00.

Signage:

- The use of pictures as well as word signs offers an important benefit in accommodating all abilities and disabilities. While pictures are not required by ADA for every signage situation, the cost (approximately $5.00 per pictogram) is minimal, and the benefit significant for people with limited vision or learning disabilities.

Storage:

- Providing both high and low access to closet poles and shelves is a fairly simple way to make storage space accessible. Cost: $10.00 per pole for materials. In cabinets and closets, consider adding roll-out trays ($400 to furnish a closet with a full range of accessible features). Add wire racks to walls ($28.00 per unit).

Temperature:

- Installing low-cost small fans helps to circulate air and improve its quality for those whose disabilities may involve temperature and air quality sensitivity. Cost: $15.00 per fan.
- Installing scald controls in bathrooms not only reduces the risk of burns to those who have motor control impairments, but can reap savings in energy costs. Unit cost: approximately $75.

Windows:

- An expensive solution to the problem of a windowless office might be remodeling the facility to incorporate an atrium or skylights. Less costly alternatives that expand the space and feeling of contact with the outside include interior design elements and art; the use of fans and air filtration systems; and upgraded lighting, including the use of full spectrum lightbulbs, and fixtures designed to counteract the effects of Seasonal Affective Disorder. (See the Compliance Product Selection Guide for examples of these kinds of products.)

TITLE I
CASE STUDIES—
EMPLOYMENT

INTRODUCTION

Title I, the employment title of the ADA, prohibits discrimination by a covered entity against qualified persons with disabilities. Accordingly, employers are required to make reasonable accommodations for applicants or employees with disabilities. The ADA does not interfere with the employer's right to hire the best qualified applicant. Further, the ADA does not impose affirmative action obligations.

General Rule

A covered entity may not discriminate against a qualified individual who has a disability in any employment practice. The employer must make a reasonable accommodation that will allow the individual to perform the job, unless such accommodation causes an undue hardship for the employer.

Who is a Covered Entity?

- Private Employers
- State and Local Governments
- Employment Agencies
- Labor Organizations
- Labor/Management
- Communities

All employers with 25 or more employees must comply after July 26, 1992. Employers with 15 to 24 employees must comply after July 26, 1994. Employers with fewer than 15 employees are not covered entities.

Who is Protected?

Title I protects qualified people with disabilities who can perform the essential job functions, with or without a reasonable accommodation.

Essential Job Functions

A job's essential functions are considered to be the fundamental duties that one must be able to perform with or without a reasonable accommodation. An employer may not refuse to hire an applicant because their disability prevents them from performing the nonessential duties of the job. (See Chapter 4 for more information about evaluating job functions.)

Employment Practices Covered

The ADA makes it unlawful to discriminate against people with disabilities in all employment practices, including recruitment, hiring, training, job assignments, pay, layoffs, firing, promotions, leave, benefits and all other employment-related activities. It is also unlawful for an employer to retaliate against an applicant for asserting his/her rights under the ADA.

Enforcement

The ADA's employment provisions are enforced by the Equal Employment Opportunity Commission (EEOC). If an individual wishes to file a complaint with the EEOC, he or she should contact the nearest EEOC regional office. To find out the location of that office, call 1-800-669-4000 (Voice/TDD).

Private lawsuits are permissible under Title I of the ADA, and the remedies available under Title VII of the Civil Rights Act of 1964 apply to ADA employment claims. Currently, those remedies include back pay, reinstatement, lost benefits, and in cases of intentional discrimination, compensatory damages up to $300,000, depending on the size of the employer.

The following case studies are examples of facilities that required reasonable accommodation under Title I of the ADA. While the range of physical limitations, facility layouts, and job functions creates a tremendous variety of requirements and solutions under Title I—Employment, these studies are intended to provide an overview—from office and manufacturing employees to a disabled student. (Note: classroom modifications would also apply under Title III.)

Chapter Thirty-Two

NURSING HOME

The following nursing home case study is of a facility in New England with multiple patient rooms and various other in-house areas that required reviewing. The following areas were evaluated and recommendations made: reception, patient day rooms, patient bedrooms, bathrooms, and occupational therapy. In addition, one nurses' station was reviewed for ergonomic fit to tasks and equipment relative to productivity and fatigue.

Work Site Analysis typically evaluated:
- Job tasks
- Expected productivity rates
- Causes of stress and fatigue
- Musculoskeletal considerations
- Dimensions of the working area
- Employees' use of shared equipment
- Design of the employees' work station and areas
- Seating, posture and positioning
- Accessories and equipment

The total work environment was also reviewed.

Evaluation by Factors

Accessibility

Access into the building is currently accomplished from the parking lot areas to ground level doors. The doors are heavy and the door knobs difficult to use (both to open and position the door). This makes access difficult both when trying to push a person or wheel oneself, and when carrying articles and opening the doors. The existing valet areas and electric-eye door openings are excellent access options, as long as signage clearly directs people to these areas.

Recommendations

Weather conditions make access difficult during the winter months. Recommendations include heated canopies and ramps.

Adaptability

The existing work site area for nursing staff had not taken nursing feedback into consideration, and had thereby diminished their productivity. The fixed-to-the-floor and fixed-to-the-wall work surfaces observed allowed no adaptability or flexibility to accommodate a variety of body types, nor for the reconfiguration of space to add new equipment. Also, visual access to patient areas is limited. The ability of the person (in a wheelchair) to see over the nurses' station counter was limited by their height in a seated position. Furthermore, the nurses' station counter access requires passersby to overreach and bend to gather materials. Work surface organization does not appear to be supported with either visual storage aids or ease of access to materials. Seating offers minimal support of staff working postures.

Recommendations

Perform a task analysis of the work areas at the nursing stations. Organize the stations into functional areas: charting, medical records, medication, and inventory. Conduct work site analyses in selected areas to facilitate the match between people, equipment, and work sites to maintain productivity without creating stress and fatigue. The design should accommodate height and reach requirements, while supporting a strategy to prevent known occupational hazards in patient care facilities (back injury, carpal tunnel syndrome, injuries to hands and fingers, head and neck fatigue).

Air Quality

Review and apply the latest standards on air quality from the EPA (Environmental Protection Agency), ANSI and ARI (Air-Conditioning and Refrigeration Institute).

Comfort

The visitor lounge areas are configured with chairs, couches, lamps, rugs, and tables to create a "waiting area" that facilitates a break from the patient room and a place for people to rest and talk. The mix of utility of these areas has often made visitors uncomfortable.

Recommendations

Re-zone the visitor waiting areas to accommodate the needs of patients and visitors. Evaluate visitor needs by conducting a survey (using volunteer staff) and make data-based decisions as to how to reconfigure areas for comfort (separate spaces to rest, talk, or be distracted).

Communication

Communication with visitors was available on the floor with telephones that appeared to be accessible to the ambulatory, but not to people in wheelchairs, children, or people who may need assistance (hearing impaired, visually impaired, learning disabled). The internal communication system was not evaluated.

Recommendations

Telephone placement for visitors was reviewed to meet the standards for access.

Density

The density of patient care areas (e.g., bathing) was not planned to accommodate equipment, support accessories, and space to work and to move quickly. In addition, there was no clear thought given to the flexibility and adaptability of space configurations. It maintained the highest quality of patient care, but it appeared to be inefficient and disorganized from the staff's point of view (though the space was not observed on a time-by-task analysis).

Recommendations

Continue to ask the caregivers' input into space designs, taking into consideration that adaptability and flexibility are critical to prevent injury to both patients and caregivers.

Division of Space

The nursing station was designed in a linear fashion to accommodate work areas by function, access to resources, co-workers and equipment. The layout of the work environment appeared to accommodate staff mostly by allowing each to stay out of the others' way. Although the space was well positioned for access to two hallways, the adaptability and ergonomic fit to people were not evident. Observation revealed that staff had not yet been fitted to their work stations nor had work site supports been integrated into the work surfaces.

Recommendations

Redesign the layout to enhance productivity for all staff. Create a resource area for all shared equipment (copier, patient notes, medications) to save steps in the preparation and processing of paperwork.

Equipment

All equipment should include aids to support functional limitations. Nursing homes accommodating patients should review equipment for vertical and horizontal reach. For example, self-contained beverage counters, in dining areas, should allow reach with safety to access drinks. Hot soups should be in containers that do not tip. Food display equipment should have visual aids such as mirrors to assist in viewing food, and tray slides to aid food management.

Recommendations

1. All dinnerware and utensils should be easy to use by people with limited strength, grip, and grasp. Four-pronged forks are easier to use than three-pronged ones. Larger handled accessories give a larger grip surface. Handles on wide mugs are easier than tea cups. Condiments should be available on the table. Overall, design must balance between accommodating disabilities and meeting image requirements.
2. Supplemental lighting may be required for patients with low vision.
3. Telephones are typically available in nursing homes. The telephone should be equipped with volume control, flashing lights (as a visual signal), and have TDD's available for people who are deaf. All phones should be equipped with large push button controls to allow function with hand limitations.
4. Emergency signal systems should include visual and auditory alarms. Visual alarms should flash in conjunction with other building emergency systems. Audible alarms should be installed for visually impaired patients (and for patients for whom the staff have extra concerns).

Finishes

All finishes are to provide support for grip/grasp and stability difficulties, as well as maintaining safety, comfort and independence.

Recommendations

1. Carpets should be a low pile and high density fiber glued directly to the slab or high density pad.
2. Tile in bathrooms should have a non-skid surface to prevent slips and falls.
3. Color contrasts between different surfaces should be distinct between furniture and rugs, walls and ceilings.

4. Protection of finishes should include low corner guards to a height of four feet, kick plates on doors, and vinyl edgings on surface edges.

Furniture

The guest reception area of the nursing home was laid out to be the most home-like in terms of atmosphere. However, the lack of privacy in the area has limited its utility. The furnishings are traditional. The front reception area is the primary market area for the facility and should be upgraded.

Recommendations

Redesign the reception area to serve as an educational area for patients, staff, and visitors in the continuous understanding of the nursing home's system of medical management. The new designs should accommodate the functional limitations that affect the aging (limitations of gait and stability, hearing, vision, grip, and grasp).

Image

The nursing home image is standard in terms of professional space that supports the work effort of staff. However, it could improve its image with designs that exemplify the "state of the art" in reasonable accommodations.

Recommendations

1. Use a design that is a "working model" of the spirit of independence and dignity for the elderly. This is especially significant since the nursing home is filling needs along the rehabilitation continuum. This facility could serve as a model for the enhancement of people's capabilities with design and technologies.

2. Increase opportunities to enhance staff, visitor, and patient self-image. Utilize capacity-building technologies to increase patient capability and staff productivity, while reducing Workers' Compensation claims and stress and fatigue.

3. In keeping with the mission of occupational therapy, design a fully functional therapeutic area to support skill plans (with the objective of teaching skills of daily living).

4. Accommodate bathrooms for independent toileting for residents, and reduction of back strain for staff.

Lighting

Current lighting is fluorescent in ceiling mounts shaded to diffuse the light and cause less glare. No task lighting is individually positioned for staff. The available lighting adds a lux intensity that keeps the room consistently bright (an approximate lux of between 60,000 to 80,000) with a minimum of shadowing.

Recommendations

To complement the effect of fluorescent lighting (which is limited spectrum and reduces the eyes' ability to see a full spectrum of primary colors), areas around the nursing home were evaluated. Determinations were made to ascertain which areas to contrast for brightness, and which should be glare-coded to increase visual acuity.

Maintenance

Maintenance and material handling are always major issues for nursing homes. Observation of current carts (for linens, medication, cleaning supplies) showed a state-of-the art approach at this facility, but still require modifications for handling and management of the carts in transport. Handling of hazardous materials was an occupational issue.

Recommendations

Evaluate staff for aches and strains on the job. Aches become pains, pains become injuries.

Noise

The facility operates as a people-based environment with equipment humming and people making normal conversation (background noise is 40 to 55 decibels). Noise can be a problem, in terms of interfering with rest.

Recommendations

Offer noise reducers to patients in the form of ear plugs. Provide headphones for radio or television use, or place speakers adjacent to listening area. Noise sensitivity is often increased for people in discomfort or pain.

Passages

The facility is accessible via main passageways from main lobbies which access all areas on the patient floor. Passages are wide and accommodating because the space was designed to move people and resources throughout the building.

Recommendations

The corridor configurations accommodate most passage with ease (people and equipment). The maintenance of passages is, however, an issue. More corner guards on walls, and bumper pads on equipment were needed to protect corners from passing carts. It may be easier to modify the carts than the walls.

Safety

The nursing home is a safety-oriented environment designed to meet the NFPA Life Safety Code and all local building requirements. The in-house engineering/maintenance department endeavors to meet all the above standards and to implement the guidelines established by ADA to accommodate patients and workers. An outstanding question is whether a documented and well-rehearsed evacuation procedure exists.

Recommendations

1. Clearly define evacuation procedures by floor. While a plan may be in place, fire evacuation procedures and staff responsibility are not evident. Maintain clear corridors at all times.
2. Provide protective equipment, such as fire extinguishers at an accessible height.
3. Install more handrails, but without the square-cornered edge. Add soft bumper guards to the existing railings.

Signage

The facility is departmentalized, with access by visitors of varying capabilities. Signage is not well coordinated in the home. Existing signs are not visibly useful for mapping one's passage independently through the building.

Recommendations

1. Develop a color coding system that can guide visitors and patients no matter what their language, age, or disability.
2. Use international symbols in addition to color coding.
3. Make signs visible from four sides, not two.
4. Use high contrast colors that allow low-vision people to read them from twenty feet away.

Storage

Existing systems for storage of forms and medical necessity materials needs improvement. It must be worked out (under-counter form storage accessed from the front of the nursing station and cart storage in between rooms).

Recommendations

Make files accessible by organized frequency of use. The ideal solution is a book shelf area deep enough for files to be accessed easily by staff in various work areas.

Temperature

Temperature is not zoned, but is on a building system. Temperature difficulties are not evident.

Recommendations

Request the most recent OSHA guidelines.

Windows

The windows are fixed to maintain a consistent temperature.

Recommendations

None.

Chapter Thirty-Three

MACHINE SHOP

The machine shop is a 1500 square foot metal shop. It contains three Bridgeports and one lathe. The bench grinding area is set up with tables for materials and allows the passage of stock.

Evaluation by Factors

Accessibility

Access into the building is accomplished by means of one step up to ground level, double doors. The doors are heavy and difficult to use (both to open and position the door). The front doors are a problem to access and maneuver, particularly when one is carrying materials necessary for work. From the main reception area, hallways are used to access the shop. Corridors require a minimum of maneuverability in order to maintain clear passage. The bathroom is accessible and reported to be safe for independent toileting.

Recommendations

1. Change the cam on the entrance door most frequently accessed to allow a lighter pull to open and a longer open time for entering the building.
2. Always maintain clear corridors and passages.

Adaptability

The work area was designed with furniture arranged for visual access to the front of the room, and drafting access to the computer and drafting tables. The shop area was designed in conformance with standard OSHA guidelines and in typical shop flow (materials to machine/machine to work table for inspection/materials to finish machine). Tasks are computerized for drawing which aids employee coordination of assignments. The main need for adaptability concerns making provisions to enable disabled employees to completely master all aspects of machines. This requires adaptations to enable reach to parts of the machines, as well as visibility to change parts.

Adaptations to the current machine shop site should be systemized to fit employees' current computers and the management of tool designs in the shop.

Recommendations

The shop site currently can be adapted with supports that will increase employees' capabilities to bring all work within easy reach so that it requires less grip and grasp strength, and will allow it to be accessed at a comfortable height. All shop supports should be flexible and moveable so they may be accessed when needed.

Comfort

The comfort requirements for employees should incorporate reach requirements and weight maximums. (See Chapter 14). They should be standard minimums that do not stress and fatigue the body with difficult postures and positioning. Currently, the shop configuration has a few of the essentials within reach (e.g., lathe with platform foot control stop).

Recommendations

1. Retrofit the lathe to allow employees to exert force of no more than two lbs. for less than five seconds to stop the lathe.
2. Redesign so that no postures are required which involve over-extension.
3. Provide rest periods that refresh workers.
4. An example piece of support equipment is shown in Figure 33.1. This safety platform allows the worker to stand at a comfortable height, using the handles for support, and to sit when necessary to relieve fatigue.

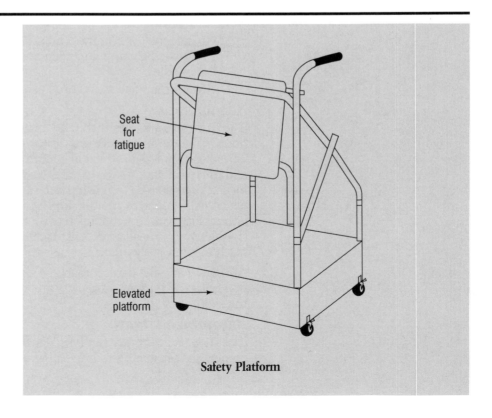

Seat for fatigue

Elevated platform

Safety Platform

Figure 33.1

Communication

Currently, communication is managed internally with close proximate interaction between employees, peers, and supervisor. There is no telephone communication which requires access for an employee to do his/her current work (ordering parts, customer relations).

Recommendations

Telephone placement should always be within arm's length of the computer. The telephone should either have a headset installed or a soft phone pad added to the hand-held receiver. Correspondence and/or essential reading material should be organized for employees in summary forms that allow them to stay informed but not overburdened.

Density

The density in the employees' work area could be a problem. The area is large and accommodating for ease of mobility between machines and the access aisles. However, the movement of materials within the space may be a problem for some employees. Proper organization and handling of materials are essential. The space for each is tight.

Recommendations

First, the space should be rearranged to allow more access to shelving that would be utilitarian if set at a height that provides easy reach to stock. Secondly, a material-handling cart will be necessary for employees to access stock and move it as they move themselves.

Division of Space

The office environment is designed in a linear fashion to accommodate work areas by function and access to resources, supervisor, and equipment. The layout of the shop environment appears to accommodate workers as they work at each machine. The division of this area could be improved with layout changes that increase access to the inspection table. (See Figure 33.2, a machine shop work station.)

Recommendations:

Redesign the layout to enhance productivity for all workers. Create a resource area for all shared materials, tools, inspection tables, and cleaning aids to save steps in the preparation and processing of stock to finished goods. Such a change would:

1. increase visibility
2. increase access, and
3. reduce the number of turns necessary to negotiate the space.

Furniture

The current chair and computer surfaces create the necessary professional image, and are adequately positioned given the layout of the floor space. However, the actual utility of the furnishings could be enhanced to increase productivity and safety while reducing stress and fatigue. The furnishings currently are not flexible enough to support the work effort with ease. There is no ergonomic fit, because the work surface cannot accommodate employees' reach requirements.

Recommendations

1. Provide an adjustable-height desk to accommodate any reach necessity.
2. Provide a finished surface on the desk that adds contrast for reading.

3. Add an electronic switch panel to accommodate desk-top access to electrical power for support equipment.
4. Provide flexible shelving on the work surface to accommodate all reading material and support papers.
5. Provide a clock and timer.
6. Add a storage area with access for file management.

Image

Image is standard in terms of professional machine shop space that supports custom work. To enhance the professional image, the environment can be streamlined for increased productivity, thereby reflecting enhanced "job readiness."

Recommendations

Consider these features:

1. Designs for each area (passages, zoned common areas, and conference space) should encompass the attributes that create "job readiness."

2. Incorporate capacity-building technologies to increase productivity while reducing stress and fatigue (e.g., mechanical supports, computer technologies, communication systems, etc.).

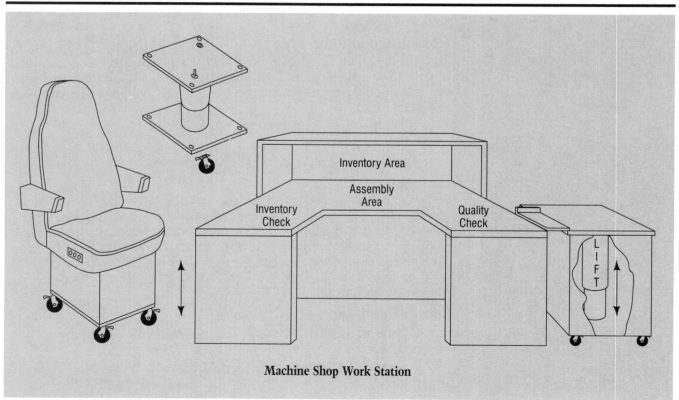

Machine Shop Work Station

Figure 33.2

Lighting

Current lighting is fluorescent in ceiling mounts that are screened to diffuse the light and cause less glare. No task lighting is individually positioned for workers. The available lighting adds a lux intensity which keeps the room consistently bright (approx. lux between 60,000 to 80,000), with a minimum of shadowing.

Recommendations

To complement the effect of fluorescent lighting (which is limited spectrum and therefore reduces the eyes' ability to see a full spectrum of primary colors), the computer that employees use should be contrasted for brightness, and glare-coded to increase visual acuity. Task lighting should be available.

Maintenance

Maintenance in this environment primarily concerns clean-up on a daily basis and the observation of the supervisor oiling the machines monthly.

Recommendations

None.

Noise

The shop operates as a standard machine shop with grinders, Bridgeports, and normal conversation as the background noise (55 to 65 decibels). As a noise filter, employees can use their ear muffs to reduce the shop distractions, as long as safety is maintained.

Recommendations

None.

Passages

The facility is accessible down one main passageway from the front doors to the receptionist's lobby and into other rooms. For employees, the facility is mostly on ground level, where full ambulation with ease is attained.

Recommendations

None.

Safety

The supervisor and the facility are very concerned with the safety of the employees in the shop as exemplified by their desire to meet all of the standards and guidelines necessary to accommodate for employee capabilities. One question is how the evacuation procedure would be carried out in the event of a fire.

Recommendations

1. Clear corridors of any items that can be stored.
2. Provide protective equipment for fire safety.
3. Clearly define evacuation procedures and perform at least one fire drill to train staff.
4. Establish a safe smoking area and safety procedure.

Signage

The facility is departmentalized with access only by employees and supervisors who are in assigned areas at designated times all day.

Recommendations

Hang signage from the ceilings to identify where staff are located, so that visitors can easily map the office.

Storage

Resources are racked and shelved, which requires reach to access. Physically challenged employees must ask for help from peers, which requires dependence at all times. Some storage should be accessible in employee areas for personal and professional items.

Recommendations

Make shelves accessible by organized frequency of use. Ideally, provide a book shelf area deep enough for papers that can be accessed by employees and supervisors.

Temperature/Air Quality

Temperature is not zoned, but is on a building system. Temperature difficulties were not noted.

Recommendations

None.

Windows

The window bank is a clear positive in this shop environment. The availability of natural light is uplifting and gives a feeling of spaciousness to the shop.

Recommendations

None.

Chapter Thirty-Four

INDUSTRIAL WORKER (FACTORY)

This worker is employed by a glass company that manufactures custom windows for residential installations. The employee has limited right hand movement, strength and stamina, and is returning to work as an aluminum cutter and assembler. The evaluation includes some considerations and recommendations to improve safety and productivity for all employees.

Evaluation by Factors

Accessibility

Access into the building is accomplished via level outside doors leading directly into the building. Access to the manufacturing area is a linear pathway, guided with yellow lines, OSHA standard width. The areas of access are difficult to determine from the outline of the floor.

Recommendations

Repaint the floors with access zones color-coded by work areas and pathways of travel for product as it moves through the manufacturing area. Post signs at the entrance to the shop floor.

Adaptability

The work site areas are configured and aligned in squares to manage material handling and production. Work areas have fixed-height tables on which work is either cut by machine or assembled. All tasks require that the hand be used as a tool. For example, the hand acts as a guide and pressure source for cutting tubing for window frames. The hand is used as a pressure surface (the palm) as window frames are assembled into fixed box shapes.

Recommendations

Customization of the work surface should accommodate the individual's capabilities. This means designing tools that do the work of the hand at the functional level of other employees, such as "tubing pad," a flat cut-resistant piece of plexiglass that has been padded on one side to hold tubing in place no matter what the circumference. The "tubing pad" also has been fitted with a support strap and pad to conform to one's palm. The strap and pad protect the worker from stress to the hand from pressing it fully flat (to create the pressure needed to align the tubing for cutting).

Figure 34.1 illustrates a systems approach to integrating the worker's tasks: cutting, assembling, adding desiccant, and final assembly.

Air Quality

The open cylinder of desiccant may be absorbing moisture from the air.

Recommendations

Close the desiccant to prevent moisture absorption.

Comfort

The limitations of posture and positioning are critical issues in accommodating persons who work in manufacturing on hard floors. Reach requirements and weight maximums were calculated for employees and found to be of no concern at this job. Anti-fatigue mats in the saw area would reduce fatigue, and shoe inserts would cushion feet against the hard floor.

Recommendations

None.

Communication

Currently, communication is managed internally with close proximate interaction between co-workers and supervisors.

Recommendations

None.

Density

Staff are assigned work areas which adequately accommodate their equipment, support accessories and offer space to work, but do not guide material handling.

Recommendations

Redesign of work space to minimize material handling within areas from a linear to circular radius. For example, pairing people on job tasks to minimize travel and transfer of material would increase efficiency.

Division of Space

The total work environment at this facility is designed in a linear fashion to order the work areas by function and access to resources, coworkers, and equipment. The layout of the work environment is departmentalized by work areas using machines to delineate space.

Recommendations

A redesign of the layout to enhance productivity for all staff and employees would be to create a mid-access corridor for walking only and corridors

INVENTORY				
Position 1	**Position 2**	**Position 3**	**Position 4**	**Position 5**
1. Cutting 2. Transfer to co-worker	Assembly on surface with backstop	Cart with wheels 1. Step-wide bottom acts as backstop 2. Load cart	1. Move cart 2. Load desiccant to tubes and seal	Final assembly

Figure 34.1

specifically designated for material handling. This would increase safe movement of staff within the plant and reduce the amount of concentration necessary for safe material handling.

Finishes

Low reflectance (30–50%) and high contrast colors are used.

Furniture

Not relevant.

Recommendations

None.

Image

Image is not an issue at the manufacturing site as it does not have customers on the manufacturing floor.

Recommendations

None.

Lighting

Current lighting is fluorescent in ceiling mounts, with some task lighting at machines. This accommodates most lighting needs.

Recommendations

None.

Maintenance

There are no maintenance issues in this job.

Noise

The noise level is tolerable at an estimated 60 decibels in employees' area. They report not being bothered by noise.

Recommendations

None.

Passages

Facility is an open floor plan with passages configured to access the building and one's work area. The passages are adequate between the office and manufacturing areas.

Recommendations

None.

Safety

The facility reports a safety-oriented manufacturing environment, meeting all standards and guidelines to prevent further injury with work place accommodations. Evacuation procedures in case of emergency were not reviewed.

Recommendations

Review potential areas of soft tissue injury. Establish training to prevent injury and reduce lost time difficulties. Review the evacuation procedure with supervisors and staff in case of emergency.

Signage

The facility is departmentalized with access only by employees who circulate through the same areas each day. Signage for pathways is unnecessary. No signage for safety was noted.

Recommendations

Coordinate signage with the floor plan to aid material handling and safety.

Storage

Resources are stored at each work area, which require refilling, but are considered by employees to be accessible.

Recommendations

None.

Temperature

Temperature is not zoned, but is on a building system. Temperature difficulties were not reported.

Recommendations

None

Windows

The facility's environment is not lit with natural light at the work site levels. Employees did not identify any difficulties associated with lack of windows.

Recommendations

None.

Chapter Thirty-Five

OFFICE WORKER/ARCHITECT

A thirty-four-year-old male with severe back injury (inoperable disk problems) must reposition from sitting to standing every 20 minutes to avoid disk compression. He is also a chronic pain patient. The facility is a one-story office building.

Evaluation by Factors

Accessibility

Access to the building is acceptable. Site is completely handicapped accessible. Parking for this person is a designated spot very near the entrance door. Parking spaces for handicapped drivers and/or clients comply with the regulations of the ADA and State Architectural Barriers Board, Sections 23.5–23.9. Available and reserved parking is proximate to the building and offers an unobstructed entry/exit. An interior elevator provides access to the lower level area.

Adaptability

The work site area was evaluated and redesigned to incorporate a more efficient work flow pattern for the injured worker. Drawing tables, work surfaces, computers and tools necessary for daily tasks and activities were reviewed.

Air Quality

A small fan was installed to maintain optimum air circulation.

Comfort

A new chair was recommended for the disabled employee to allow for height adjustment between the drafting table, general work surface, and computer area. Work surfaces for drafting were made adjustable in height in order to allow for repositioning (sit to stand) at person's level.

Communication

Work was brought to the person and due to the routine of the tasks and years of experience, required supervision was limited. The telephone was a necessary part of this person's environment to facilitate research.

Density

The work area was designed with consideration given to the man's back condition. Pathways were adequate for transportation. Flow pattern was redesigned to reduce the number of steps between tasks. A more direct linear configuration was installed.

Division of Space
Space was arranged for ease of access to central resources and ease of access to others for supervision, direction, and interaction.

Equipment
A tilt board was installed for additional, flexible writing space. (See Figure 35.1.)

Finishes
A padded work surface was used to prevent injury when leaning.

Furnishings
An adjustable-height work station was designed and sized to accommodate the size and shape of large architectural projects. A self-regulating load cart was introduced in order to avoid unnecessary bending to move books and drafting materials.

Image
Available furnishings were adapted and repositioned to allow better access and ease of task completion. If tasks are difficult and hard to access, a poor self-image can result.

Lighting
Overhead lighting was installed with full spectrum fluorescence to reduce glare. Additional individual task lighting was added to the desk and drafting table.

Maintenance
No special maintenance was required.

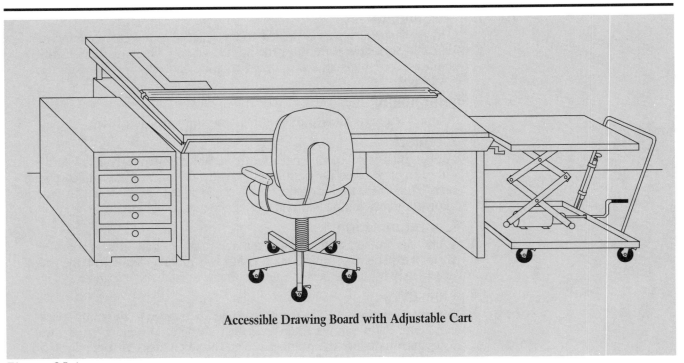

Accessible Drawing Board with Adjustable Cart

Figure 35.1

Noise

Actuator (electronic lift) used to angle the work surface is limited to 45 decibels.

Passages

All passages are adequate.

Safety

Safety was enhanced with the addition of locking casters on all rolling tables and delivery carts. All floor areas were inspected for loose rugs or tiles.

Signage

Signage is more than adequate.

Storage

Individual lockers were installed in the immediate area, both for the injured worker and others. None were available previously.

Temperature

Temperature control is adequate.

Windows

Due to lower level placement of the area, no windows are accessible to this person.

Additional Considerations

Due to the difficulties this person was experiencing, fellow employees and supervisors were made aware and accepted the necessary repositioning. Also, positive response was expressed concerning occasional rest periods.

TITLE II
CASE STUDIES —
PUBLIC SERVICES

Part Six

INTRODUCTION

Title II of the ADA states that no qualified individual with a disability shall be subject to discrimination by a public entity. Many functions of state and local governments were previously prohibited from discriminating because they received federal funds. Under Section 504 of the Rehabilitation Act of 1973, any entity that accepted money from any federal agency was not permitted to discriminate on the basis of disability. The ADA expands this coverage to all services provided by state and local governments, regardless of whether they receive federal money.

Who is Covered?

As of January 26, 1992, Title II of the ADA prohibits discrimination on the basis of disability by "public entities." Public entities include any state or local government and any of its departments, agencies, or other instrumentalities.

All activities, services and programs of public entities are covered, including employment, activities of state legislatures and courts, town meetings, police and fire departments, and motor vehicle licensing.

Who is Protected?

Title II of the ADA provides comprehensive civil rights protections for "qualified individuals with disabilities." An individual with a disability is a person who has a physical or mental impairment that substantially limits a major life activity, has a record of such an impairment or is regarded as having such an impairment.

A qualified individual is a person with a disability who meets the essential eligibility requirements for the program or activity offered by a public entity. The essential eligibility requirements will depend on the type of service or activity involved.

Program Access

State and local governments:

- Must ensure that individuals with disabilities are not excluded from services, programs and activities because buildings are inaccessible.
- Need not remove physical barriers, such as stairs, in all existing buildings, as long as they make their programs accessible to individuals who are unable to use an inaccessible existing facility.

- Can provide the services, programs, and activities offered in the facility to individuals with disabilities through alternative methods, if physical barriers are not removed, such as relocating a service to an accessible facility, providing an aide or personal assistant to enable the individual with a disability to obtain the service, or providing benefits or services in an individual's home or alternative accessible site.

Integrated Programs

Public entities may not provide services or benefits to individuals with disabilities through programs that are separate or different, unless the separate programs are necessary to ensure that the benefits and services are equally effective. Even when separate programs are permitted, an individual with a disability still has the right to choose to participate in the regular program.

State and local governments may not require an individual with a disability to accept a special accommodation or benefit if the individual chooses not to accept it.

Enforcement

Private parties may bring lawsuits to enforce their rights under Title II of the ADA. The remedies available are the same as those provided under Section 504 of the Rehabilitation Act of 1973. A reasonable attorney's fee may be provided to the prevailing party.

Complaints may be filed within 180 days of alleged discrimination with any federal agency that provides financial assistance to the program in question or with the Department of Justice (DOJ), which will refer the complaint to the appropriate agency. Any complaints filed with DOJ should be sent to:

U.S. Department of Justice
Civil Rights Division
Coordination and Review Section
P.O. Box 66118
Washington, DC 20035-6118
   (202) 307-2222 (Voice)
   (202) 307-2676 (TDD)

Part Six contains two Public Services (Title II) case studies, a municipal building and a government-sponsored residence for medically fragile individuals. Once again, recommended modifications are organized by factors, and include guidance for better meeting the needs of disabled people, as well as the ADA requirements.

Chapter Thirty-Six

GOVERNMENT BUILDINGS AND MUNICIPAL AREAS

Title II of the Americans with Disabilities Act, 1990 prohibits discrimination on the basis of disability in the full and equal use of public services. The case studies presented in Part VI illustrate the modifications to achieve the overall integration of people with disabilities who may wish to participate in these entities. Each site should be evaluated to determine if all limitations have been "reasonably accommodated," both environmentally and in policy, procedure, and practice.

Again, meeting the need is accommodating for all functional limitations, but understanding that:

1. All disabilities are not observable.
2. The observable disability may not be the actual barrier to receiving services. For example, a person in a wheelchair may also be blind and need Braille assistance.
3. It is therefore critical to design for the range of limitations which must be accommodated at specific sites.
4. Figure 36.1 is a list of critical sites that must be analyzed in government facilities.

- Parking Areas
- Entrances
- Loading/Unloading Areas
- Lobbies
- Information Areas
- Administrative Services
- Public Bathrooms
- Outside Landscaped Areas
- Meeting and Conference Rooms
- Administrative Offices

Government Facilities Critical Sites

Figure 36.1

Evaluation by Factors

Accessibility

Access to federal, state and local buildings that serve citizens should be designed to accommodate disabled as well as nondisabled people. Citizens should be able to park and access buildings no matter what their functional limitation. Access is particularly important because people who have disabilities may have more frequent need of government services. Citizens in general should be able to expect better accommodation in buildings that are supported by their tax dollars.

Recommendations

1. Drive-up windows may be a "reasonable accommodation" for buildings that have little or no parking and are difficult to access. (As governments have consolidated services to maximize space utilization, accessibility to buildings and lobby areas has become more congested.)

2. At least one entrance into the building should be evident by appearance, signage, and access. Minimum entrance requirements should be met for width, operating force, and maneuvering clearance. Automatic doors are recommended as doors in a series if weather vestibules are necessary for northern climates.

3. Accommodations for varying weather conditions are essential. Awnings and canopies are an important consideration given the additional time access to buildings may require. Recommended minimum height is 9'-6".

4. A heated ramp may reduce the maintenance and increase safety for citizens, by preventing the accumulation of snow and ice.

5. Lighting should clearly illuminate the entrance into the buildings with a minimum of five footcandles.

6. Flush transitions from driveways to sidewalks are recommended to aid in the transfer from the street to the walk. These transitions aid in mobility of people using aids such as walkers, canes, crutches and wheelchairs.

7. Colored curbings may be contrasted for visual acuity. Raised edgings at the end of a flush transition can prevent slippage for persons in wheelchairs who may be visually impaired. Definitions of edgings and transitions are important. *Note: Detectable warning strips should be provided for safety. These strips are 3' wide and 1" deep. The grooved strips permit people to sense the transition through a raised rounded surface (ANSI 4.7, 4.27).*

8. Construction materials used for outdoor walkways should provide for a non-slip surface that is smooth. Any transition between walkways should be smooth. Gratings in walkways should be relocated.

9. Layout of the access to the entrance from parking lots should be clearly delineated with crosswalks.

10. Underground parking must be able to accommodate wheelchair vans which need a minimum clearance of 9' to enter the area and typically require extra-wide parking of 8'-6" of side clearance. 16'-6" is the minimum recommended length for vans.

11. Any steps should conform to ANSI 4.9 with exterior steps having a rise of 5-3/4" to 6".

Adaptability

Adaptability in the lobbies of most government buildings is critical to the use of services. Since cultural diversity and disability create a wide range of needs, the access to services through adaptations is a necessity. For example, access to stamps bought either at stamp machines or at counters requires adaptations. Stamp vending machines should have Braille-imbedded signage to guide the person to use the machine successfully and independently. Adaptability in the government buildings is based on citizens' needs. This means planning for flexibility within the environment at each bureaucratic service, and planning for the citizens' functional limitations. Census data can be used to guide the extent of adaptations necessary, to begin to prioritize needs.

Recommendations

1. Provide flexibility to allow for the reconfiguration of space—to add either new furnishings or equipment.
2. Create visual access within a given space, such as the front desk or the lobby. This is essential to foster communication between staff and visitors.
3. Offer some variety in seating options at varying heights, with different posture supports for a range of body types.
4. Provide clipboards as writing surfaces for people to fill out forms.
5. Offer audio tapes of how to use services for people who cannot read or have limitations of sight.
6. Design voting stations to accommodate people's functional limitations.
7. Make sure designs accommodate staff height and reach requirements to support their work and their interaction with visitors.
8. Ensure that controls on any equipment used by visitors are easy to operate with limited hand function. Mounting at a height of 4' is ideal for most people with limitations of stature.
9. The ability to operate all fixtures and equipment (e.g., for light switches) provided by the facility by remote control is an excellent adaptation for people with disabilities.
10. Provide adaptive seating for people with disabilities to use the public toilet.

Comfort

The visitor lobby areas are typically outfitted with benches and located in noisy hallways. The atmosphere of most bureaucratic buildings is cold and uninviting, which tends to prevent people from staying longer than business requires. Terrazzo floors are cold and noisy. The noise level should be low enough to promote conversation. The light should be high enough for reading and filling out necessary forms. Access to each area should include use of space for a given period of time.

Recommendations

1. Rezone the visitor lobby areas to accommodate visitor access to services. Comfort is enhanced by designs with the following characteristics:
   - The ability to find and use information about government services.
   - A sense of safety and security (e.g., ability to cognitively map a space).

- A sense of independence and dignity (e.g., organization of space to find essential services such as public bathrooms).
- The simplicity of design and usability (e.g., configuration of furniture to create passages).
- Cues that support disability (e.g., signage with large lettering).
- A sense that time is available to complete a task.

Communication

Citizens should be able to call a government facility for emergencies and to obtain information on everyday issues. They should be able to communicate both from the outside and inside in any government building. Communication for disabled citizens should be available in the form of people and equipment. For example, telephones with adaptations should be accessible to both the ambulatory and to people in wheelchairs, as well as people who may need help (hearing impaired, visually impaired, learning disabled). The internal communication system should be evaluated from both a service and an information perspective.

Recommendations

1. Public telephones for citizens should be reviewed to meet the standards for access.
2. Face-to-face access for communication (e.g., counters that separate staff from citizens) should allow ease of contact and communication.
3. Communication of information should be available in several forms — e.g., verbal, maps of the building, signage, and color coding of the space.
4. The speed at which communication supports are given should accommodate for varying disabilities. Communications systems used by police operators should have an indicator that signals the operator that they may need to modify their communication to a particular citizen's needs. Operators receiving calls from citizens with hearing impairments should know how to listen and respond.

Density

The density of government buildings has presented difficulties in accommodating equipment, support accessories, and space to work and to move quickly. With ADA, there must be a clarity of design to the flexibility and adaptability of space configurations.

Recommendations

1. The density of furnishings should be set for maximum use of the space with the minimum of obstacles and obstructions to usability.
2. Circulation routes should be organized with clear passages around dense visitor gathering areas to promote independence and prevent injury.
3. Density calculations should be based on census data by geographic areas to represent the need for services by different populations.

Division of Space

The division of space in government buildings should accommodate visitors' needs based on access and utilization reviews. Layouts of government buildings should accommodate the functions by need. The most frequent services should be located along lobby areas on the first floor. The less frequent the service need, the higher up it may be in the building, at the farthest distance from the elevator access. Division of space is different if the services are for a primarily geriatric population, versus the registry of motor vehicles. The following list is of the primary spaces.

- Entrances and Vestibules
- Front Desk
- Information Coordinator
- Administrative/Business
- Public Rest Rooms
- Vending Services

Division of space is critical to allow visitors to use the space with comfort, safety, and independence.

Recommendations

1. Required widths for maneuverability must be met, and are particularly important at the entrance to a service area. A width of two feet is recommended on the pull side of the door to allow for wheelchairs and assistive devices to be positioned clear of the door's path as it opens. This width also allows for an angled approach to the door to access handles and use security.

2. Clearances become the critical variable in the division of space in crowded areas where services require that payment be made, such as the registry of motor vehicles. Clearance to the sides of objects should allow a minimum of 3' between desks and counters. Clearance to the front of objects must allow access to machines. Clearances for maneuverability are those that allow a disabled person to move into an office and up to a table or desk, and to access forms for filing papers and signing documents.

3. Public bathrooms must provide access to the toilet and sinks. Specific requirements include:
   - Toilets should provide a clear access to transfer (ANSI 4.16).
   - The top of the toilet should be 17 – 19″.
   - Grab bars and toilet paper holders should be installed for access at 24″ (ANSI 4.16.4 and .6).
   - Vanities should include access with minimum dimensions of 2'-3″ in height, 2-1/2' wide, and 1'-7″ in depth. Hot water pipes should be insulated to prevent scalding.
   - The top of the basin should be no higher than 2'-10″. The basin should be no deeper than 6-1/2″ (ANSI 4.19).
   - All vanity tops should be rounded on the edges, with a maximum depth of 1 – 2″.
   - Mirrors should be mounted with the lowest edge of reflectance no higher than 3'-4″ (ANSI 4.19).
   - Faucets should operate with lever handles or single lever controls (ANSI 4.19). Another option is infrared automatic faucets.
   - Any items for hanging should have mounts of a maximum height of 4'-6″.
   - Lighting should be 70 footcandles to allow sufficient light for fine hand function, personal hygiene, and make-up application.

Equipment

Standard to every building is equipment that must be accommodated for citizens with disabilities.

Recommendations

1. Televisions should be set on "lazy susan" turntables to allow visual access and should be operable with remote control units. Screens should be a minimum of 21". The location of the set should facilitate viewing from benches in lobby areas and should be at a minimum height of 48" from the floor.

2. Displays, signals, and warning systems that communicate information should be in both visual and audible form.

3. Telephones are critical to safety and independence. There should be outside telephones to access information in case a visitor comes less than fully prepared to conduct business. The telephone should be equipped with volume control, flashing lights to signal incoming calls and messages, and a TDD for people who are deaf. All telephones should be equipped with large push button controls to allow function with hand limitations.

4. Emergency signal systems should include visual and auditory alarms. Visual alarms should flash in conjunction with other building emergency systems. Audible alarms should be installed for visually impaired citizens. Citizens for whom the staff have extra concerns should be given extra assistance. A wheelchair may be available, for example, to aid mobility.

Finishes

It is important to consider the finishes of walls, ceilings, and surfaces in all buildings from the standpoint of safety, comfort, and independence.

Recommendations

1. Carpet should be a low pile and high density fiber glued directly to the slab or a high density pad.

2. Tile in bathrooms should have a non-skid surface to prevent slips and falls.

3. Color contrasts between different surfaces should be distinct between furniture, rugs and walls, and ceilings.

4. Protection of finishes should include low corner guards to a height of 4', kick plates on doors, and vinyl edgings on surface edges.

Furniture

The furnishings can be standard in most areas of the building, with the exception of special considerations in the lobby areas. The design and location of furnishings becomes crucial for safety, comfort, and independence. All furnishings should be strong and sturdy, since citizens use the furniture to support them during transfer as well as for mobility.

Recommendations

1. Benches should be easy to access, and set at a height low enough to facilitate transfer for people with limited mobility (18 – 20").

2. Writing stands should be positioned near information and forms, as well as away from the wall to provide access at a height of approximately 28" above the benches. The writing stand surface should be large enough to accommodate special devices.

3. Chairs should be designed for comfort and ease of rise.

4. Display racks and desks should have drawer access to allow the full use of hands or hooks to open and close. This requires a clear grasping area a minimum of 4" wide and 1-1/2" deep. Desk and writing surface depths should be no more than 18" for full usability.

Image

The government facility image is best maintained by integrating adaptive accommodations into the existing decor with colors and finishes that support all visitors comfortably and are easy to maintain by staff. Image should include interventions and designs that exemplify the "state of the art" in reasonable accommodations. A public relations strategy might be incorporated into image design that is a "working model" of the spirit of *independence and dignity for the physically challenged.* This is especially significant since the government is financed by the people. The capabilities of disabled citizens should be enhanced with design and technologies.

Recommendations

The attributes of image to be considered are:

1. Designs for each service area, passages, zoned common areas, and conference space that encompass the 20 factors that create reasonable accommodation.

- Accessibility
- Adaptability
- Air Quality
- Comfort
- Communication
- Density
- Division of Space
- Equipment
- Finishes
- Furniture
- Image
- Lighting
- Maintenance
- Noise
- Passages
- Safety
- Signage
- Storage
- Temperature
- Windows

2. Capacity-building technologies to increase visitor capability and staff productivity while reducing Workers' Compensation claims, stress and fatigue.

3. In keeping with the mission of service and comfort, a fully functional lobby area should be designed with equipment to support skill and capacity for all people with disabilities.

Lighting

Lighting is typically a key image and atmosphere design factor that often limits the activity of people with disabilities. Lighting should be available as an aid to people with low vision, in particular, to support their ability to communicate through speech reading, sign language, gestures, and body movements. Lighting should be a minimum brightness of 50 footcandles in order to illuminate any paperwork and information that is necessary for visitors to use the facility. Important areas to consider are the entrance, lobby, service areas, and passages. Illumination (approximate lux between 60,000 to 80,000) should be accomplished with minimum shadowing.

Recommendations

1. To complement the effect of fluorescent lighting (which is limited spectrum and therefore reduces the eyes' ability to see a full spectrum of primary colors), areas around the facility should be evaluated. Certain areas should be contrasted for brightness, and glare-coded to increase visual acuity.

2. Lamps on writing surfaces should have transluscent shades to reduce contrast and glare and increase the uniformity of lighting. Lamps should be mounted to allow adjustability on the walls and prevent accidents. The ability to increase and decrease light for tasks is essential to accommodate for vision needs. Touch

controls or remote switches are recommended for lamps. Lamps should be positioned at every task area.

Maintenance

Maintenance and material handling are always an issue for buildings serving people with disabilities. The key maintenance issue in government facilities is the ability to maintain equipment in all areas so as not to interfere with the utility to visitors or employees.

Recommendations

1. Design for maintenance (e.g., consider maintenance efficiencies when planning the size and layout of service areas).
2. Select equipment supports that require a minimum of maintenance.
3. Require service contracts on safety-related equipment that has a potential for breakdown (e.g., talking computers).
4. Keep extra remote control units on hand for all equipment.

Noise

Environments that accommodate people with disabilities should incorporate "acoustically sound" designs, with the goal of minimizing interference, background noise, and reverberation (created by equipment humming and people making normal conversation to a 40 – 55 decibel level). Noise is often the reason for people's discomfort in unfamiliar environments.

Recommendations

1. Use acoustical intervention like noise-absorbing insulation and partitions to reduce the noise between rooms and in conference locations.
2. Use listening systems to increase the opportunity to participate in meetings and conferences.
3. Locate heating and cooling units away from the areas that service visitors so that auditory interference does not occur.

Passages

Government designs must allow accessibility from main lobbies through main passageways that access all areas in the building from floor to floor. Passages must be wide enough to access two people passing in wheelchairs and with equipment.

Recommendations

The corridor configurations should accommodate most passages with ease (people and equipment). The maintenance of passages should be considered. More corner guards on walls and bumper pads on equipment may be needed to protect corners. It may be easier to modify the carts with bumper guards than the walls.

Safety

Safety and security are two design considerations that interact to improve visitor services. People can function with independence and dignity when safety and security procedures are in place to reduce their vulnerability to injury, crime, and/or violence. Safety and security is best when service areas have lock systems that are accessible and user-friendly. Staff should be aware of the special needs of employees and visitors in case of emergencies. The design should support fast staff reactions to emergencies.

Recommendations

1. Control night-time access to buildings.
2. Provide appropriate lighting at access points.

3. Use television monitors in areas where security may be an issue.
4. Train staff in the safe evacuation of people with disabilities.
5. Use locks that have an electric eye, providing access for opening a lock without the use of keys or difficult hand positions.
6. Clear corridors.
7. Provide protective equipment.
8. Clearly define evacuation procedures by floor.
9. Consider fire separation areas that create refuge on each floor. These can be the ideal solution where egress is difficult due to stairs, elevators, and distances to egress points.
10. Provide visual and auditory communications for display signals and warning systems.
11. Identify *hazardous* areas by disability. This includes steps in corridors for people who are blind or have low vision.
12. Keep doors to hazardous or private areas locked.

Signage

Graphics and the use of international symbols meet the needs of both people with disabilities and visitors from all parts of the country and the world. Graphics and lettering should effectively communicate both the location and the purpose of a space. Very often existing signs are not visually useful for mapping one's way throughout a building with independence.

Recommendations

1. Consult ANSI 4.28 for the minimum requirement for signage as a guide.
2. Note that signage should be a guide to people, places, and things in a building.
3. Develop a color coding system for the building to guide visitors and employees no matter what their language, age, or disability.
4. Use international symbols in addition to color coding.
5. Make maps and staff assistance available to visitors.
6. Ensure that signs are well lit or back lit.
7. Place signs perpendicular to the line of travel.
8. Ensure that signs are visible from four sides, not two, if traffic approaches from four sides.
9. Use high contrast colors that allow people with low vision to read the signs from 20 feet away.
10. Install tactile surfaces on door knobs, pulls, and handles to alert people that they may be entering a hazardous area.
11. Recessed lettering on door jambs can also be used to alert people to hazardous areas.

Storage

Accommodations for storage of clothing and personal items may be essential for employees with disabilities. Access to closets and stored supplies are important considerations.

Recommendations

1. Bi-fold doors are recommended for maximum access to storage in closets because they are easy to operate, move out of the line of vision and access, plus they do not interfere with mobility.

2. Closets should be located with a minimum of 2-1/2'–4' of available space in front of the closet. To maneuver around the closet, a minimum of 5' of turning space is ideal.
3. Storage of coats is best facilitated with low-hanging rods and shelving built into the closet. The pole for hanging clothes should be set at approximately 4'-6" to allow for front and side reach from a wheelchair. To accommodate all disabilities, a split closet is recommended.
4. Clothes hangers should be removable and replaceable.
5. The closet should be lit for ease of utility.

Temperature

Temperature is typically not zoned in government buildings to prevent people from tampering with HVAC systems.

Recommendations

1. Vestibules are recommended to maintain temperature continuity, heating and cooling and must have a minimum of 5' of turning radius to allow for wheelchair access.
2. Care should be taken to prevent cold drafting by heating and ventilation systems.

Windows

Windows in government buildings should provide visual access to the outdoor environment, and should have accessible controls for window coverings. Visual access at the 3-1/2' level is accomplished if the sill is set at 2'. Double-hung windows are most difficult to operate.

Recommendations

1. Windows should have hardware that is easy to reach. If sills are too large, then access is difficult. (See Chapter 30 for more detail on window recommendations.)
2. Minimize the infiltration of drafting at the installation.
3. Use handles that can be operated by a person with grip and grasp difficulties. A maximum of five pounds of force is recommended.
4. Sliding windows on good rollers are the easiest to operate.
5. Casement windows with cranks can be operated as long as the latch is easy to engage.
6. Window treatments, such as draperies and blinds, should be accessible with rods that are long enough to operate for full closing and opening. Drawstrings attached to the wall must be accessible without removing furnishings to reach them. Motorized controls are an expensive last resort.

Chapter Thirty-Seven

RESIDENCE FOR THE MEDICALLY FRAGILE

This facility is a staffed residence in which medically fragile people can live and do contract work. It is a single-story, fully sprinklered duplex residence, comprised of two essentially separate four-person units. Each separate unit of the duplex contains 2,100 square feet, for a total of 4,200 square feet per duplex. Each unit has its own kitchen, bathrooms, bedrooms, living and dining spaces, driveway, parking area and identity. The two units share a common roof, foundation and outdoor yard space. Moderately sloping sites were selected so that each unit is on a different level. Each unit has all entrances and all exterior pathways at grade.

Though functionally separate, the two units were connected to each other. Options for interconnectors include:

- a fully heated sun room
- a fire door or passageway in a common wall

Minimum Requirements

The facility was designed for the medically fragile and includes the following accommodations:

Overall Size of Duplex

A total of 4,200 s.f., net usable area, with each unit of the duplex having 2,100 s.f.

Lot Size

Lots of legal size according to local codes, and of the size and dimensions typical of the surrounding neighborhood. The lot allows for an outdoor recreation area.

Outside Premises

A usable and well-landscaped, relatively level "backyard" area, of sufficient size and appearance was designed to allow residents and staff to participate in normal outdoor home activities, such as cookouts, gardening, and recreation. Each unit of the duplex has its own separately delineated outdoor area. In addition, the outdoor areas are surrounded by a privacy fence.

A wheelchair-accessible paved patio, terrace, or deck (preferably located directly off the kitchen/dining area or optional sun room) was included for each unit of the duplex.

Layout and/or landscaping allowed for some privacy and separation from adjoining homes, to the extent typical of the neighborhood.

The home conforms to all setback requirements for its location.

General Build-out Specifications

All work performed, all materials and equipment furnished, and the installation thereof conforms to all applicable standards, codes, and rules and regulations for the type of work involved, including, but not limited to:

- the State Building Code
- the State Electrical Code
- the State Fuel Code
- the State Gas Code
- the State Plumbing Code
- the State Architectural Access Bureau
- the Underwriters Laboratories, Inc.
- the National Electrical Manufacturers' Association
- the National Fire Protection Association.

Evaluation by Factors

Accessibility

Available Parking: Parking spaces readily available for use by clients, staff, and visitors, immediately proximate to the building.

Handicapped Parking: Parking spaces for handicapped drivers and/or clients comply with the regulations of the State Architectural Barriers Board.

Reserved Parking: On-site parking spaces for authorized vehicles. This parking accommodates overnight and weekend parking, and has unlimited entry and exit privileges.

The home and grounds are free of barriers preventing access to any space by handicapped persons.

Adaptability

Number/size of bathrooms. Each unit of the duplex contains:

One full bathroom (min. size: 150 s.f.)
One half bathroom (min. size: 60 s.f.)

The full bathroom was designed to conform to the particular special needs of the disabled residents of the home, including extra heating capacity and installation of a large therapeutic whirlpool tub with access on both sides. Specific design criteria for the full bathroom included:

One accessible shower (min. dimensions: 5' x 5'): A "roll-in" shower, designed to enable bathing in a seated position.

One installed "therapeutic bath" (approx. dimensions of 8'-6" x 2'-6") to accommodate bathing in a supine position. Space was designed to allow walking access around both sides of the tub for staff to assist residents in using the tub.

A fully accessible toilet and sink, both of which must meet ADA and state code (in this case, the Architectural Access Board (AAB)) accessibility criteria and allow for a 5' turning radius. Grab bars should also be installed on either side of the toilet.

An auxiliary heating source: Ceiling-mounted radiant heating panels over the shower/tub area, with separate controls and timers.

Adequate ventilation, allowing a desirable air change of 1/minute or 250 c.f.m. with a variable-speed exhaust fan.

Storage space including medicine cabinet over sink, with mirror at wheelchair height, and open shelves at side of sink to provide accessible storage of toiletries.

The half bathroom (consisting of accessible toilet and sink) provides a 5' turning radius for wheelchair users. The design of this bathroom conforms to ADA and AAB accessibility criteria. All adaptations are custom fitted to the individuals' capabilities.

Air Quality

Harmful materials: The building and premises are free of hazardous friable asbestos-containing material and lead paint. Where asbestos-containing material had been present, the builder provided written certification by an approved asbestos removal inspector that the building was free from hazardous asbestos-containing material (ACM) and that any ACM has been encapsulated, enclosed, or maintained in good repair. The landlord is required to protect the health of the employees and house residents and clients during the term of lease by maintaining the house in a safe condition.

Stove fans to remove smoke and particles are installed in the kitchen.

Air contaminants (dust, vapor, fumes, gases, including Radon gas, etc.) are contained at less than harmful levels by means of ventilation, filtration, and/or removal of the contaminant.

Comfort

Chairs were adapted with pillows to provide lateral and side support. The chair arms were modified to extend the level of support from the elbow to the wrist in order to maintain a level hand at computer keyboards. Seat belts were installed on the chairs for safety and security. ADA reach requirements and weight maximums were applied, with the standard maximum weight being no more than one pound.

Communication

Work is brought to the residents by staff in order to minimize fatigue from moving about the rooms. The telephone is located four feet off the ground.

Density

Room areas were designed with consideration to each resident's specific need for orientation for viewing and location for work and leisure.

Division of Space

Number/size of bedrooms: Each unit of the duplex structure houses four individuals, in a combination of single occupancy and double occupancy bedrooms.

Single bedrooms are a minimum of 170 s.f. each; double bedrooms are a minimum of 250 s.f. each. Double bedrooms were designed with two means of entry, with doors. All bedrooms provide a 5' turning radius for wheelchair accessibility.

Bedroom space is important because of the need to accommodate specialized medical equipment used by all residents of the duplexes. This equipment includes both a customized, full-size wheelchair (max. dimensions: 3' x 5'-6") and a side-lyer (max. dimensions: 3' x 6'-6"). Other bulky equipment (such as wheelchair lifts) are required, much of which will be transported frequently to and from the bedroom.

Each bedroom includes an individual closet and shelf/storage areas for each occupant, preferably along one wall. The closet and storage area are required both to maximize storage space for wheelchairs and/or other ambulatory equipment and to enable disabled residents to see and have easy access to clothing and personal items.

The *closet* contains a combination of installed shelves, bins, and clothes-hanging area (closet pole) to hold a variety of clothing. The closet has bi-fold louvered doors. The shelf/storage area includes a shelf with space beneath to accommodate a "side-lyer" (horizontal wheelchair) of the following dimensions: 30" wide, 6'-6" long, and 40" high. The space above this area includes shelves.

Kitchen/dining area (including food storage area): The kitchen and dining area for the physically challenged has a combined minimum of 300 s.f., as required, in each unit of the duplex. Access to the kitchen is through a doorway from the outside. The door is on an actuated arm to allow it to be opened without the use of one's body. Once in the kitchen, a moveable lift transfer cart is available to allow the transfer of groceries and other items within the household.

The kitchen was designed to accommodate cooking by the staff (two to three adults) and to include wall and base cabinets, stove, oven, refrigerator, and dishwasher. All appliances were sized to meet the needs of four adult residents. To increase access, the space was modified into zones to allow for the processes of preparation, cooking, and cleaning. The kitchen doors and passageways were designed for wheelchair access. Accessible counters, stoves, and other equipment were installed.

The dining area allows comfortable dining space for six adults, including people who use large, specially-adapted wheelchairs (six feet long), as well as others who do not require supportive devices.

A separate pantry room or area (min. 70 s.f.) with shelves and counter cabinet space for food storage was provided adjacent to the kitchen food preparation area. The pantry area includes a small countertop and small sink for any required medication preparations, etc. In addition, the pantry includes a small lockable wall cabinet above the counter and space for a small cube refrigerator on or below the counter, for medication storage.

The kitchen and dining area were designed to maximize open interior space and natural light using an open floor plan with a kitchen counter island or peninsula separating kitchen and dining areas.

Living rooms/communal areas: Each unit of the duplex has two rooms suitable for the residents' communal activity, e.g., living room and den of sufficient size to allow four to six adults comfortable communal space. The living room (180 s.f.) is suitable for more "noisy" communal activity, and is adjacent to the kitchen and dining area in an open design rather than a separate room.

The den (150 s.f.) was designed as a separate room to allow quieter, more private/separate activity, such as visiting or listening to music/T.V. It also includes an alcove with a small built-in countertop to serve as a desk area with room for a two-drawer file cabinet beneath it and two to three shelves built above it. A closet with a lockable door was provided, of sufficient depth (min. 3' deep) to accommodate an additional 5 drawer file cabinet.

Sun room: The design for each unit of the duplex provided for a sun room. This room serves as a third living space (in addition to the living room and den required above). The sun room's desirable location is off the kitchen or other communal spaces. It is a large (200 s.f.), heated room with many windows and/or skylights, designed to provide maximum natural light. The room has at least partial southern exposure and was designed to access the outdoor patio or deck area.

Basement: A full basement was designed for each unit of the duplex, to allow space for industrial-capacity washers and dryers, a utility sink, large freezer, HVAC system, hot water tanks and heaters, electrical panel, and other mechanical needs. The basement is used for general storage of food and hygiene items purchased in bulk, as well as seasonal clothing and equipment. Basements are connected by means acceptable to building code provisions, and each unit has at least one means of egress to grade. Each basement includes a side-by-side utilities hook-up for washer and dryer, along with outside ventilation outlets for dryers. Gas dryers were required. Basement laundry areas provide counter space for sorting and folding, and shelf space for supplies.

Equipment

Television and lighting are on remote controls. Each duplex unit has a backup generator for emergency heating and electrical needs. The refrigerator is a side-by-side double door type. The door handles were modified to allow ease of opening with a leverage tool. All refrigerator shelves were re-tooled to allow them to slide out for ease of access. The stove was installed as part of a center island work surface to allow access to the four burners in the front. For health and safety, ceramic tops covered the burners. A can opener was positioned for ease of access and set for a leverage point to allow ease of attachment of canned goods. A jar opener was fixed to the underside of a cabinet to allow jars to be opened with mechanical advantage. A microwave oven was positioned at the optimum access height for the individual in order to increase button sensitivity. A toaster oven was installed with ease of access through push button controls. Nonbreakable dishes were selected, and silverware is stored in an "on the counter" holder. The dishwasher is accessible from the side and raised one foot from the floor to increase access.

Finishes

In communal living areas, kitchen/dining area, and corridors, vinyl wall coverings were selected, with colors and design selected for high contrast, ease of maintenance, and low reflectance. Counters were covered in high contrast formica with colored trim. In bathrooms, floor-to-ceiling ceramic tile was installed in the shower and tub area. Bathroom wall backing is at least 1 layer (1/2" min.) Wonderboard, plus appropriate wood blocking for installed grab bars. Elsewhere, two coats of paint; finishes and colors to be high contrast for visual acuity. Paints used were toxic-free and lead-free. All painted and vinyl covered surfaces are annually repainted or replaced.

Floor finish: Level looped carpet with an embedded high contrast border was chosen to define the travel way. Hardwood floors and rubberized tiles in one foot squares for ease of installation, maintenance, and repair.

Living, family and bedroom areas: Wall-to-wall carpeting (.28 oz. face weight per square yard, cut pile, five-year guarantee, anti-static warranty) to conform to State Building Code and AAB regulations.

Dining/kitchen area: Hardwood and terrazzo, unglazed ceramic or quarry tile, or sheet vinyl.

Bathroom/laundry areas: All surfaces were required to be water resistant, including but not limited to: terrazzo, unglazed ceramic or quarry tile.

Furnishings

Adjustable-height and tilt work stations were designed and sized to accommodate individual computer systems. Additional side tables were added to expand work surfaces. All counters were built to be accessed from the side, with bread board panels that extend out for additional work space, and set to accommodate bar stools.

Image

Room furniture was adapted, with lift systems on computer and work surfaces to allow ease of access and task completion. All fixtures and case goods were designed in contrasts, thereby allowing the maximum use of visual supports.

Lighting

Overhead lighting was installed with full spectrum fluorescence to reduce glare. Additional individual task lighting was added as needed in reading areas, kitchen, sun room, living room, and bedrooms and positioned to highlight each work area. Dimmer switches allow each area to be zoned for brightness.

Maintenance

The premises are maintained in good repair and tenantable condition. Maintenance includes, but is not limited to: repair and replacement of broken glass; repair and replacement of roofs and ceiling leaks; repair and replacement of floors, walls, ceilings, plumbing, locks, fire protection equipment, lighting fixtures, heating, ventilation, and air conditioning systems, structural or exterior components, staircases, counter surfaces, appliances, and all other fixtures and equipment provided by the landlord. In addition, duplex exteriors are to be kept clean, painted and in good repair and the grounds and landscaping receive proper care and maintenance annually. All maintenance services are provided on a timely basis within hours and days of need.

All appliances are set for ease of service by the virtue of zoned space. Ease of cleaning is further supported by the three-sided access to all appliances.

Noise

All noise levels are kept at 45 – 55 decibels.

All appliances are below the 45 decibel level.

Passages

Corridors are six feet wide with grab rails. Access and turning radius were designed for five feet and 180 degree turns. The corridors were centralized to reduce the "institutional look" of the units.

The entryways were designed as staging areas large enough to accommodate two to three residents awaiting assistance with coats, vehicle boarding, etc.

Interior Doors are solid core, 3' wide, full height (6'-8" or higher), with the exception of bedroom closet doors which must be bi-fold. All doors and hardware meet ADA standards. To avoid damage from impact of wheelchairs and other adaptive devices, all interior door frames are fitted with protective door frame guides of rigid PVC or equal, and meet all fire safety standards.

Safety

Emergency Generator: Duplexes are provided with a built-in backup emergency generator of sufficient capacity to meet heating and electrical needs, to ensure the use of medical equipment in case of power failure. Specifically, an 8-kilowatt capacity generator was provided, to ensure sufficient emergency capacity to power the following equipment:

- oxygen concentrator – 6 amps
- suction machine – 3 amps
- air compressor – 8 amps
- feeding compressor – 3/16 amps

Fire Alarm System: This home was constructed to meet Section 636 of the Massachusetts State Building Code regarding limited group residences (780 CMR: State Board of Building Regulations and Standards). All fire protection equipment and materials are maintained by the landlord in accordance with applicable codes and ordinances, as well as all applicable licensing standards. This includes, but is not limited to, fire doors, fire walls, fire stops, fire extinguishers, fire escapes, exit route diagrams, and alarm/sprinkler systems and their testing. The kitchen is furnished with fire extinguishers.

All grounds, entrances, means of egress, walkways, and parking areas are adequately lit (min. 5 footcandles) to ensure night-time security and safety of residents and staff. Sprinkler systems were required to comply with Chapter 21 of the NFPA Life Safety Code, 1985 edition (NFPA 101, Chapter 21, Small Facilities, "impractical evacuation").

Domestic Water: Adequate continuous hot and cold water into the homes is provided by city water. The hot water tanks are accessible and controlled by staff, and are capable of being regulated not to exceed 130 degrees Fahrenheit. The hot water supply is sufficient to provide hot water needs for eight adults on a daily basis. The minimum acceptable size is 120 gallon capacity for each unit of the duplex.

Specialized Tubs in Bathroom: A therapeutic tub was required in each full bathroom of each unit of the duplex.

Signage

Braille signage was provided for a blind resident who required a wheelchair.

Storage

Each unit of the duplex includes the following: At least one *large closet* (8-12 s.f.) with bi-fold door, was provided at the main entry, to accommodate outdoor clothing and other personal items for up to six adults. One large (10 s.f.) *linen closet* is also available with bi-fold door to hold bed linens, towels, and bathroom supplies. All cabinets are adjustable height for ease of access with visual inspection through glass-paneled door fronts. Interior paint of the cabinets enhanced the contrast between the objects and goods stored.

Temperature

Heating/Air conditioning: Central HVAC was required for all duplexes, with separate controls for each unit. The gas-fired heating system is capable of maintaining the temperature in all rooms as follows: minimum 68 degrees, maximum 78 degrees Fahrenheit throughout home on a 24-hour basis. Thermostats are controlled by on-site staff.

Zone control, electrical distribution, lighting switches: See CMR (Code of Mass. Regulations) residential code requirements and AAB (Architectural Access Board) accessibility criteria for type of light switches and number of fixtures required. A minimum of four double outlets are required in single bedrooms, and six double outlets in double bedrooms.

Windows

The design of the communal areas provided lower, larger windows than in conventional housing, to allow people seated in wheelchairs greater access to light and views. Casement windows were chosen, with easy-to-operate lever handles.

Weatherstripped interior windows with double storm windows are present. All glazing had to comply with "Safety Standard for Architectural Glazing and Sealing Systems," issued by the Consumer Product Safety Commission. Windows are low-E glass to promote energy efficiency.

As new construction, double-paned insulated windows were installed throughout. All glazing had to comply as above. The home was constructed with energy-efficient windows (low-E glass) to minimize heating costs.

Figure 37.1 is an illustration of an accessible office, with recommendations for individual components. Figure 37.2 shows the features of an accessible kitchen for a residence.

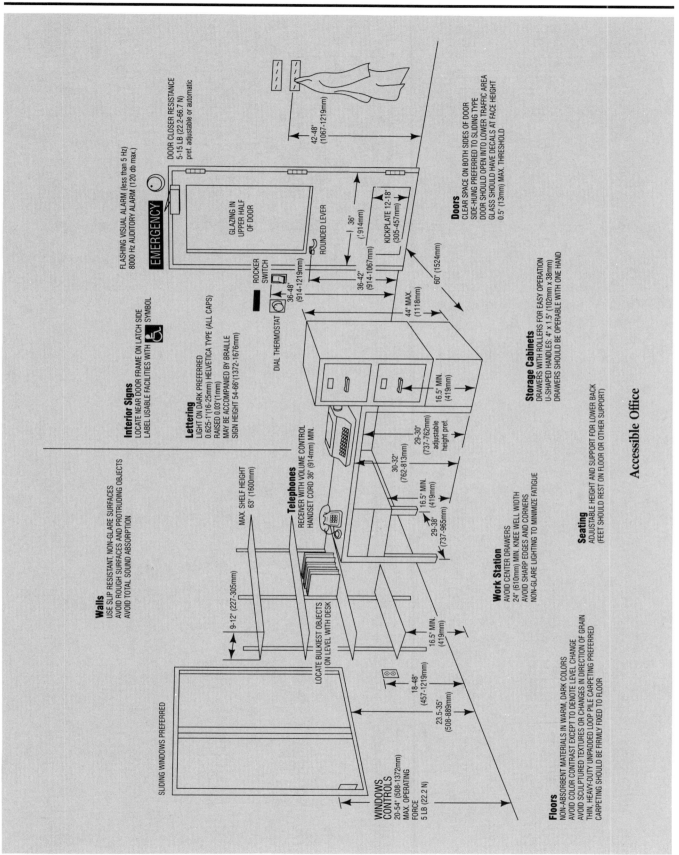

Figure 37.1

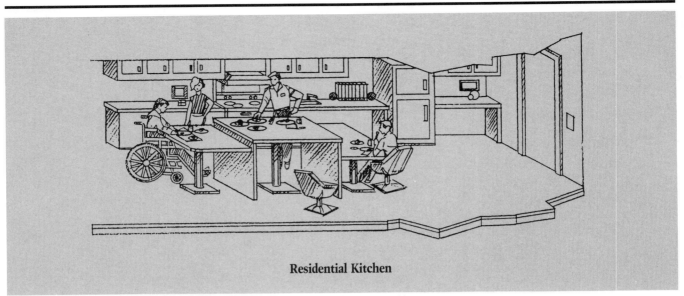

Residential Kitchen

Figure 37.2

TITLE III CASE STUDIES – PUBLIC ACCOMMODATION

Part Seven

INTRODUCTION

Title III of the Americans with Disabilities Act (ADA) states that no individual with a disability shall be discriminated against because of his or her disability in the full and equal enjoyment of the goods, services, facilities, privileges, advantages and accommodations of any places of public accommodation. The intent of the ADA is to make places of public accommodation as accessible as possible and to ensure that goods and services are provided in an integrated manner. The ADA's prohibition on discrimination applies to the owners and operators of the public accommodation, and anyone who leases (or leases to) a place of public accommodation.

What Is a Public Accommodation?

A place of public accommodation is defined as a facility operated by a private entity that affects interstate commerce and falls within at least one of these categories:

- Places of lodging, such as inns, hotels and motels, except establishments in which the proprietor resides and rents out no more than five rooms.
- Establishments serving food or drink, such as restaurants and bars.
- Places of public gathering, such as auditoriums, convention centers and lecture halls.
- Sales or rental establishments, such as grocery stores, bakeries, clothing stores and shopping centers.
- Service establishments, such as dry cleaners, banks, beauty shops, hospitals and offices of health care professionals, lawyers and accountants.
- Stations used for specified public transportation, such as terminals and depots.
- Places of public display, such as museums, libraries and galleries.
- Places of exhibition or entertainment, such as theaters, concert halls or stadiums.
- Places of recreation, such as parks, zoos or amusement parks.
- Places of education, such as nursery, elementary, secondary, undergraduate and postgraduate private schools.
- Social service centers, such as day-care or senior citizen centers, adoption programs, food banks and homeless shelters.

- Places of exercise or recreation, such as gymnasiums, health spas, bowling alleys or golf courses.

Both landlords and tenants are subject to Title III requirements for new construction and alterations. Examples of commercial facilities include factories, warehouses, office buildings and wholesale establishments that sell exclusively to other businesses.

Private clubs and religious organizations are exempt from public accommodation requirements.

What Is Necessary to Comply?

Places of public accommodation must take certain steps to comply with the ADA. Unless noted elsewhere, the general effective date of the provisions concerning public accommodations is January 26, 1992.

A public accommodation may not discriminate against a person with a disability by *refusing service or denying participation* in an activity. To achieve the goal of equal participation, services, goods and activities must be provided in the most integrated setting possible. Individuals with disabilities cannot be required to accept separate or special services.

Title III Enforcement

Individuals who encounter a violation of this section may file a complaint with the Department of Justice. DOJ will investigate and seek a resolution. Complaints and requests for investigation may be filed at:

U.S. Department of Justice
Civil Rights Division
Public Access Section
P.O. Box 66738
Washington, DC 20035-6738

The Attorney General of the United States may also bring suit to enforce the ADA's public accommodations provision. Civil penalties not to exceed $50,000 for a first violation and $100,000 for any subsequent violation may be assessed in cases brought by the Attorney General. Individuals may bring private lawsuits to obtain court orders to stop discrimination, but money damages cannot be awarded in these cases.

The following case studies contain examples with recommendations for modifications to achieve public accommodation (Title III). Each case is evaluated by factor (See Part IV for more on the 20 audit factors). Specific guidance is given for code-required modifications. Further recommendations go beyond the ADA, identifying cost-effective ways in which to better meet the needs of the physically challenged. These measures not only allow the owner/facility manager to more fully comply with the spirit of the ADA, but also provide financial returns in the form of enhanced productivity, reduced accidents/Workers' Compensation claims, and increased sales.

Chapter Thirty-Eight

HOTEL

Title III of ADA prohibits discrimination on the basis of disability in the full and equal enjoyment of goods, services, facilities, privileges, advantages, or accommodations of any place of public accommodation and services operated by private entities. The goods, services, and accommodations must be offered in the most appropriate integrated setting.

The case studies presented reflect the overall integration of people who may wish to participate in these entities with their particular functional limitations. Each site should be evaluated to determine if all limitations have been "reasonably accommodated," both environmentally and in policy, procedure, and practice.

To meet the needs of the physically challenged, one should accommodate for all functional limitations, but understand that:

1. All disabilities are not observable.
2. The observable disability may not be the barrier to receiving services; for example, a person in a wheelchair may also be blind and need Braille assistance.

It is therefore critical to design for the range of limitations which may affect specific sites. The list in Figure 38.1 identifies the key sites in a hotel to evaluate. Figure 38.2 is a checklist of disabilities that can be used as a guide to analyze the accessibility of critical areas, and whether these areas require accommodation.

The ADA Guidelines state that hotels and motels must provide accessible sleeping rooms in the quantities listed in Figure 38.3. See Sections 9.1–9.3 in Appendix A for complete requirements.

Evaluation by Factors

Accessibility

Access into the building should be designed to accommodate participants in and patrons of the hospitality business. Guests should be able to arrive from airports, train stations, cabs, and cars to the main entrance, and they should be able to unload and load their luggage. Luggage should be included in a plan for access to the registration and guest areas. *Note: By July 26, 1992, transportation vehicles that are made available to guests must have accommodations for people with disabilities; for example, wheelchair lifts in vans.*

Access can be very difficult when trying to either push a person or wheel oneself, or carrying parcels and opening the doors. The valet areas and electric-eye door openings are excellent access options as long as signage clearly directs people to these areas. Once disabled patrons have unloaded from personal vehicles, parking areas should be close to the entrance and meet all of the standards set by the state and federal access boards. Valet parking is an acceptable alternative in cases where the only available parking is off-site.

Recommendations

1. A clear entrance into the facility should be evident by appearance, signage, and access.
2. Accommodations for varying weather conditions are essential. Awnings and canopies at the offloading and entry areas are an important consideration given the additional time required for disabled persons to gain access to the buildings. Recommended minimum awning height is 9'-6".
3. A heated ramp may reduce the maintenance and increase safety for patrons by preventing ice and snow accumulation.
4. Passenger loading and unloading zones must allow room for vehicles and patrons with their luggage.
5. Lighting should clearly illuminate the entrance into the facility.
6. Flush transitions from driveways to sidewalks are required to aid in the transfer from the street to the walk. These transitions aid in the mobility of people and luggage, especially when curbs are color contrasted for visual acuity. Raised edgings at the end of a flush transition can prevent slippage for persons in wheelchairs who may be visually impaired. It is important to distinguish all edgings and transitions. *Note: Detectable warning strips should be provided for safety. These strips are 3' wide and 1" deep. Grooved strips alert people to a transition by creating a raised rounded surface (ANSI 4.7, 4.27).*

- Parking Areas
- Entrances
- Lobbies
- Information Areas: Front Desk, Concierge, Bell Captain Station
- Administrative Offices
- Retail
- Meeting/Conference Rooms
- Public Bathrooms
- Loading/Unloading Areas
- Administrative Offices
- Business Services
- Guest Rooms
- Recreation Areas

Hotel Critical Sites

Figure 38.1

ANALYSIS BY STRENGTHS AND LIMITATIONS

CRITICAL AREA: _____

Function	Manageable/Disability	Accommodation Required
Sight	[ ] Visually Impaired	_____
	[ ] Blind	_____
Hearing	[ ] Hearing Impaired	_____
Speech	[ ] Deaf	_____
Interpretation of Information	[ ] Mental/Psychological Impairment	_____
Coordination	[ ] _____	_____
	Susceptibility to:	
	[ ] Fainting	_____
	[ ] Seizures	_____
	[ ] Dizziness	_____
Stamina	[ ] Respiratory Limitation	_____
	[ ] Cardiovascular Limitation	_____
	[ ] Muscular/Skeletal Limitation	_____
Head Movement	[ ] Limited Movement	_____
Sensation	[ ] Absence of Sensation	_____
	[ ] Chronic Pain	_____
Lifting	[ ] _____	_____
Reaching	[ ] _____	_____
Reach and Grasp:	[ ] _____	_____
Left	[ ] _____	_____
Right	[ ] _____	_____
Respiration	[ ] _____	_____
Sitting	[ ] _____	_____
Standing	[ ] _____	_____
Mobility	[ ] _____	_____
Self-care	[ ] _____	_____

This checklist is used to review a critical area to evaluate its accessibility in terms of specific disabilities. For example, for "sight," determine the area's accessibility to blind and visually-impaired people, whether it is manageable as is, and what, if any, accommodation is needed. If a site needs to accommodate other known disabilities (in addition to those listed), these should be noted in the proper category in the "Manageable/Disability" column, and the type of accommodation listed.

Figure 38.2

7. Construction materials for outdoor walkways should allow for smooth, but non-slip surfaces. Any transitions between walkways should be smooth, and drainage gratings should be removed.

8. Layout of the access areas from entrances to the lobby and front desk should allow ease of passage, and a short distance of travel that is clearly marked with lit signage.

9. Layout of the access to the entrance from parking lots should be clearly delineated with crosswalks.

10. Underground parking must be able to accommodate wheelchair vans which need a minimum height clearance of 9' to enter the area and typically require extra wide parking with 8'-6" of side clearance. 16'-6" is the minimum recommended length allowed for vans.

11. Any steps should conform to ANSI 4.9, with exterior steps having a rise of 5-3/4" to 6", and a run of 11".

12. Elevators should have a 20 second time delay on door closing for easier access.

Number of Rooms	Accessible Rooms	Rooms with Roll-in Showers	Number of Elements	Accessible Elements
1 to 25	1		1 to 25	1
26 to 50	2		26 to 50	2
51 to 75	3	1	51 to 75	3
76 to 100	4	1	76 to 100	4
101 to 150	5	2	101 to 150	5
151 to 200	6	2	151 to 200	6
201 to 300	7	3	201 to 300	7
301 to 400	8	4	301 to 400	8
401 to 500	9	4 plus one for each additional 100 over 400	401 to 500	9
501 to 1000	2% of total		501 to 1000	2% of total
1001 and over	20 plus 1 for each 100 over 1000		1001 and over	20 plus 1 for each 100 over 1000

In addition to those accessible sleeping rooms and suites required by 9.1.2, sleeping rooms and suites that comply with 9.3 (Visual Alarms, Notification Devices, and Telephones) shall be provided in conformance with the following table:

Sleeping Accommodations for Persons with Hearing Impairments

From The Federal Register/Vol. 56, No. 144/July 26, 1991

Figure 38.3

Adaptability

The areas where adaptability is critical are environments used for a variety of people with special needs, for example: people of all heights and conditions of vision, with and without full mobility. Adaptability in the hospitality industry means acquiring the ability to service guests based on their needs. This means planning for flexibility within the environment at specific sites.

Recommendations

1. Provide flexibility to reconfigure space to add either new furnishings or equipment.
2. Create visual access within a given space such as the front desk or lobby. This is essential to foster communication between staff and guests, and between people in general.
3. Provide a variety of seating options at varying heights and with different posture supports for a range of body types and conditions.
4. Recognize that planning for peoples' equipment needs was a boon for business travelers, and planning for people with disabilities can also be a boon to the hospitality industry. An example of thoughtful planning is having a walk-out area for guests with seeing eye dogs.
5. Design to accommodate the staff's height and reach requirements, while supporting a prevention strategy of the known occupational hazards in hospitality facilities (back injury, carpal tunnel syndrome, injuries to hands and fingers, head and neck fatigue).
6. Adapt the guest rooms with extra electrical outlets to accommodate assistive and adaptive devices. Many people need to recharge their equipment every night. Have outlets positioned above the floor with enough floor space to recharge a wheelchair, walker, or respirator.
7. Make sure controls, including thermostats, are easy to operate with limited hand function. Mounting at a height of 4 feet is ideal for most people with limitations of stature.
8. Provide for remote operation of fixtures and equipment (e.g., remote for the light switches — on/off and dimming).
9. Provide seats for bathtubs as an aid and assist for guests who need support in the bathroom.
10. Make adjustable-height seats available for toilets.

Air Quality

Air quality is a crucial element in the hotel business, especially with the commitment to customer service to provide both smoking areas and smoke-free areas in lobbies, restaurants and retail space. HVAC systems now bear a higher burden of ventilation and circulation requirements based on the *usage* of each particular area within a building. Buildings can no longer be viewed as a single entity where air quality is concerned.

Recommendations

Evaluate the HVAC system's capacity to manage the categories of airborne contaminants that can occur in the hotel environment. Expect to specify by usage areas for inorganic compounds such as carbon dioxide, sulfer dioxide, carbon monoxide, nitrous oxide, ammonia, and radon. Pay attention to the industries' expectations on percent of airborne fibers from clothing, bed and bath and furnishings. Each system should also be qualified for its sufficiency in ventilation and humidity management as relates to temperature and seasonal variations. The system must accomplish more than air exchange. In closed environments, air quality systems must be specified to the full range of contaminants, not a single source or one point in time, because air quality problems are cumulative in effect.

Comfort

The visitor lobby areas are configured with chairs, couches, lamps, rugs, and tables to create a "reception area" that images a facility, creates an atmosphere, invites relaxation, and provides a place for communication and observation for people outside of their rooms. The extent to which people are comfortable using the lobby as a gathering point is based on how well it fits their mix of utility. Access to and from elevators is important. The light should be high enough to promote reading. How comfortable is the access to the area and use of the space for a given period of time?

Recommendations

Re-zone the visitor lobby areas to accommodate the needs of guests and visitors. Evaluate guests' needs by conducting a survey using guest services staff to make data-based decisions as to how to reconfigure areas for comfort (a place to rest, talk, or be distracted). Comfort is enhanced by designs with the following characteristics:

1. A sense of safety and security, e.g., ability to cognitively map a space.
2. A sense of independence and dignity, e.g., organization of space to find essential services such as public bathrooms.
3. Simplicity of design and usability, e.g., configuration of furniture to create passages.
4. Cues that support disability, e.g., signage with large lettering.
5. A sense that time is available to complete a task.

Communication

Communication for patrons and staff should be available in the form of both people and equipment. For example, telephones with adaptations should be accessible to both the ambulatory and people in wheelchairs, as well as children and people who may need assistance (hearing impaired, visually impaired, learning disabled). The internal communication system should be evaluated from a service and safety perspective. Can a person in a guest room call for help, if necessary, from all points in the room or bathroom?

Recommendations

1. Volume controls must be available in permanently installed telephones in accessible rooms. Electrical outlets must be available within four feet of the telephone connection.
2. Auxiliary alarms (in compliance with ADA-AG Ref. 4.28) must be provided in accessible rooms.
3. Separate devices should be available to alert guests to door knocks or telephone calls.
4. Public phones for guests should be reviewed to meet the ADA standards for access. (See Chapters 11, "Accessibility," and 15, "Communication.")
5. Access for communication should be face to face, e.g., counters that separate staff from guests should allow ease of contact and communication.
6. Communication of information should be available in several forms, e.g., verbal, maps of the building, signage, color coding of space.
7. The speed at which communication supports are given should accommodate varying disabilities. Guest telephones should have

an indicator that signals the operator that they may need to modify their communication to a particular guest's needs.

Density

The density of visitor and guest areas must be planned to accommodate equipment, support accessories, and space to work and to move quickly. The design process should focus on the flexibility and adaptability of space configurations.

Recommendations

1. The density of furnishings should be set for maximum use of the space with the minimum of obstacles and obstructions to usability.
2. Circulation routes should be organized with clear passages around dense visitor gathering areas to promote independence and prevent injury.
3. Density calculations should allow for 10% of the expected occupancy to be disabled in order to meet fire codes.

Division of Space

The division of space in the hospitality industry has to accommodate guest services and guest rooms. The layout of the hospitality environment should accommodate the access to functions by need. As is traditional, checking in and out should be located as close to the entrance as possible. After a guest's access to the hotel has been accomplished, access to the services of the hotel become critical. The areas of services to consider are:

- Entrances and Vestibules
- Front Desk
- Lobby and Reception
- Concierge and Bell Captain
- Retail Areas
- Restaurants
- Public Rest Rooms
- Laundry Areas
- Vending Services
- Administrative and Business

Of all the areas, the most important is the guest room in terms of division of space. *Division of space* refers to where the rooms are located, as well as the layout within the room to accommodate bathing, storage, dressing, sleeping, eating, and working. Division of space is critical to allow guests to use the space with comfort, safety, and independence.

Recommendations for Guest Rooms and Guest Bathrooms

1. Widths for maneuverability are critical, particularly at the entrance to a guest room. An allowance of two feet is recommended on the pull side of the door to allow for wheelchairs and assistive devices to be positioned clear of the door's path as it opens. This width also allows for an angled approach to the door to access door handles and use security devices. Refer to the ADA Guidelines, 4.13, for specific requirements.
2. Clearance becomes the critical variable in the division of space in guest rooms. Considerations include:
   - Clearance to the sides of objects (e.g., a minimum of three feet between walls and beds).
   - Clearance to the front of objects (e.g., clearance to access the closet).

- Clearances for maneuverability (e.g., to move in the bathroom, to position oneself properly at the table or desk, and to access the drawers for storage of clothing).
- Critical to guest bathrooms is the ability to maneuver between the toilet, sink, and bathing areas.

3. The following are specific dimensional requirements for the bathroom.
   - Toilets should provide a clear access to transfer (ANSI 4.16).
   - The top of the toilet should be between 17" and 19" from the floor.
   - Grab bars and toilet paper should be installed for access at 24" (ANSI 4.16.4 and .6).
   - Vanities should include access of minimum dimensions of 2'-3" high; 2-1/2' wide; and 1'-7" deep. Hot water pipes should be insulated to prevent scalding.
   - The top of the basin should be no higher than 2'-10". The basin should also be no deeper than 6-1/2" (ANSI 4.19).
   - All vanity tops should be rounded on the edges with a maximum depth of 1 – 2".
   - Mirrors should be mounted with the lowest edge of reflectance no higher than 3'-4" (ANSI 4.19).
   - Faucets should operate with lever handles or single lever controls (ANSI 4.19). Hand spray attachments are recommended, with remote drain controls added that are level with the vanity.
   - Tubs and showers should meet ANSI 4.20 for clearances. Where possible, roll-in showers are recommended with grab bars, and accessible to towels and toiletries (ANSI 4.24).
   - Any items for hanging should have mounts of a maximum height of 4'-6".
   - Bathroom lighting should be 70 footcandles to allow sufficient light for fine hand function, shaving, and makeup.
   - All bathroom controls should have offset levers and remote controls for the drain.

Equipment

Standard to every guest room is equipment that needs to be accommodated for guests with disabilities. In addition, there may be a need for special transfer devices for guests who need assistance in lifting and transferring.

Recommendations

1. Televisions should be set on lazy susan turntables to allow flexible visual access and operation by remote control. Screens should be large with a minimum of 21" of viewing space. Location of the set should facilitate viewing from the bed, and the set should be at a minimum height of 48" from the floor.
2. Radios should have visual signals.
3. Telephones are critical to safety and independence. There should be two in each guest room, one in the bathroom and one in the guest's living/sleeping areas. While the ADA requires volume control and flashing lights to signal incoming calls and messages, a TDD should be available for guests who are deaf. All phones should be equipped with large push button controls to allow function with hand limitations.
4. ADA requires emergency signal systems (visual and auditory), with visual alarms that flash in conjunction with other building emergency systems. For guests for whom the staff have extra

concern, bed alarms (within the bed) that vibrate for the benefit of the hearing impaired may be useful to have as an option.

Furnishings

The furnishings can be standard in most areas of the facility with the exception of special considerations in the guest rooms. The design and location of furnishings in guest rooms becomes critical for safety, comfort, and independence. All furnishings should be strong, sturdy, and stable since guests often use the furniture to support themselves during transfers and for mobility.

Recommendations

1. Beds should be easy to access and set at a height low enough to facilitate transfer for people with limited mobility. A height of 18 – 20″ is recommended. This allows the person ease of transfer and assist when rising. Below the box spring, a kick space of 3″ in height and 3″ in depth facilitates movement. Medium-to-firm mattresses are recommended. If possible, assistive mattress supports (e.g., egg crate mattress inserts) can be available to guests with back problems.

2. Night stands should be positioned between beds or next to the bed away from the wall to provide access at a height of above the mattress (approximately 24″ from the floor). The night stand surface should be large enough to accommodate special devices and the necessary telephone and radio alarms. The night stand should be wide and shallow, not square, with an 18″ depth and 4′ of width ideal.

3. Chairs should be designed for comfort and have locking casters to allow the chair to be used as a "scoot chair" within a guest room. Chair should have arms to facilitate rising and lowering during seating.

4. Portable suitcase stands on wheels allow the guest to position clothing as is necessary in any part of the room.

5. Dressers and desks should have drawer pulls that allow the full use of hands or hooks to open and close. This requires a clear grasping area with a minimum of 4″ wide by 1-1/2″ deep. Desk and dresser surface depths should be no more than 18″ deep for full usability.

6. The ADA requires at least one of each type of storage (e.g., shelves, closets, drawers) to be accessible according to the ADA reach ranges.

Finishes

Finishes of walls, ceilings, and surfaces are crucial to proper accommodation in all guest areas to maintain safety, comfort, and independence.

Recommendations

1. Carpet should be a low pile and high density fiber glued directly to the slab or a high density pad.

2. Tile in bathrooms should have a non-skid surface to prevent slips and falls.

3. Color contrasts between different surfaces should be distinct to differentiate between furniture, rugs, walls, and ceilings.

4. Protection of finishes should include low corner guards to a height of 4′, kick plates on doors, and vinyl edgings on surface edges.

Image

The hospitality image is best maintained by integrating adaptive accommodations into the existing decor with color and finishes that support all guests comfortably and are easy to maintain by staff. Another aspect of image is having interventions and designs that exemplify the "state of the art" in reasonable accommodations. A public relations strategy might be incorporated into the imaged design, showing that the facility is a "working model" of the spirit of independence and dignity for the physically challenged. This would be especially significant since the industry is a service business that is defined by its "home away from home" feeling. Guest relations reach a new standard of excellence when people whose capabilities are enhanced with design and technologies are fully integrated.

Recommendations

The attributes of image to be considered are:

1. Design for each guest room, passages, zoned common areas, and conference spaces to encompass the 20 factors that create "reasonable accommodation."

   - Accessibility
   - Adaptability
   - Air Quality
   - Comfort
   - Communication
   - Density
   - Division of Space
   - Equipment
   - Finishes
   - Furniture
   - Image
   - Lighting
   - Maintenance
   - Noise
   - Passages
   - Safety
   - Signage
   - Storage
   - Temperature
   - Windows

2. Use capacity-building technologies to increase guest capability and staff productivity while reducing Workers' Compensation claims, stress, and fatigue.

3. In keeping with the mission of service and comfort, design for fully functional hospitality areas, with equipment to support skill and capacity for all people with disabilities.

Lighting

Lighting is typically a critical image and atmosphere design factor that often limits people with disabilities. Lighting should be available as an aid to people with low vision in particular, to enhance their ability to communicate through speech reading, sign language, gestures, and body movements. Lighting should be a minimum brightness of 50 footcandles in order to illuminate any hotel paperwork and information that is necessary for guests using the facility. Critical areas to consider are: the front desk, the concierge, doorways, and passages. Illuminate (approximate lux between 60,000 to 80,000) with a minimum of shadowing.

Recommendations

1. To complement the effect of fluorescent lighting (which is limited spectrum and reduces the eyes' ability to see a full spectrum of primary colors), areas around the facility should be evaluated. Determinations should be made to ascertain which areas should be contrasted for brightness, and which should be glare-coded to increase visual acuity.

2. Lamps in guest rooms should have translucent shades to reduce contrast and glare and increase the uniformity of lighting. Lamps should be mounted on the walls to allow adjustability and prevent accidents. The ability to increase and decrease light for tasks is essential to accommodate for vision needs. Touch controls or remote switches are recommended for lamps. Lamps should be positioned at every task area: bedside, desk, table, sink, and bathtub/shower.

Maintenance

Maintenance and material handling are always issues for facilities serving guests with disabilities. The critical issue in hospitality is the ability to maintain equipment and hospitality areas so as not to interfere with the utility to guests.

Recommendations

1. Design for maintenance (e.g., use the size and layout of guest rooms as an additional boon to staff maintenance).
2. Select equipment supports that require a minimum of maintenance.
3. Require service contracts on equipment that has a potential for a safety breakdown (e.g., a portable lift).
4. Keep extra remotes on hand for all equipment.

Noise

Environments that incorporate people with disabilities need to incorporate "acoustically sound" designs with the goal of minimizing interference, background noise, and reverberation created by equipment humming, and people making normal conversation to 40 – 55 decibels. Noise is often why people feel uncomfortable in unfamiliar environments.

Recommendations

1. Use acoustical intervention to reduce the noise between rooms and in conference locations.
2. Use listening systems to increase the opportunity to participate in meetings and conferences.
3. In the guests' rooms, it is important to locate heating and cooling units away from the television so that auditory interference does not occur.

Passages

Hospitality designs must allow accessibility through main passageways from main lobbies to access all areas in the facility from floor to floor. Passages must be wide enough to accommodate two people passing in wheelchairs with luggage, because the space is designed to move people and resources throughout the facility.

Recommendations

Standard corridor configurations accommodate most passages with ease (people and equipment). The maintenance of passages is an issue. More corner guards on walls and bumper pads on equipment are needed to protect corners. It may be easier to modify equipment than the walls.

Safety

Safety and security are two design considerations that interact to improve guest services. Guests can function with independence and dignity when safety and security procedures have been developed to reduce their vulnerability to injury, crime, and/or violence. Guests' safety and security is best when their rooms have lock systems that are accessible and user-friendly. Staff should be aware of the unique needs of guests in cases of emergencies. Designs should support the need for fast reactions to emergencies on the part of staff.

Recommendations

1. Control night access to buildings.
2. Provide appropriate lighting at access points.
3. Use television monitors in areas where security may be an issue.
4. Train staff in the safe evacuation of people with disabilities.
5. Use guest locks that have an electric eye for room access, opening a lock without the use of keys or difficult hand positions.
6. Clear corridors.
7. Provide protective equipment.
8. Clearly define evacuation procedures by floor.
9. Fire separation areas can be provided that create refuge on each floor. This may be the ideal when egress is difficult due to stairs, elevators, and distances to egress points.
10. Provide display signals and warning systems with information communicated both visually and auditorily.
11. It is particularly important to identify hazardous areas as well as steps in corridors with tactile or other cues, depending on the disability, for people who are blind or with low vision.
12. Keep doors to hazardous or private areas locked.

Signage

Graphics and the use of international symbols meet the needs of both people with disabilities and visitors from all parts of the country and the world. Graphics and lettering should be able to communicate location and purpose of space. Very often, existing signs are not visually useful for mapping one's way throughout a facility with independence.

1. ANSI 4.28 is the minimum requirement for signage as a guide.
2. Make signage a guide to people, places, and things in a facility.
3. Develop a color coding system for the hotel that can guide the visitors and guests no matter what their language, age, or disability.
4. Use international symbols, in addition to color coding.
5. Provide maps, as well as staff assistance.
6. Make sure signs are well lit or back lit.
7. Place signs perpendicular to the line of travel.
8. Make sure signs are visible from four sides, not two, if traffic approaches from four sides.
9. Provide signs with high contrast colors that allow people with low vision to read them from 20 feet away.
10. Install tactile surfaces on door knobs, pulls, and handles to alert people that they may be entering a hazardous area.
11. Recessed lettering on door jambs can also be used to alert people to hazardous areas.

Storage

Accommodation for storage areas of clothing and personal hygiene items is essential for people with disabilities. Access to closets and bathroom supplies are important considerations.

Recommendations

1. Bi-fold doors are recommended for maximum access to storage in closets because they are easy to operate, move out of the line of vision, provide access, plus they do not interfere with mobility.
2. Locate closets to allow a minimum of 2-1/2' – 4' of space in front of the closet. To maneuver around the closet, a minimum of 5' of turning space is ideal.
3. Storage of clothing is best facilitated with low-hanging rods and shelving built into the closet. The pole for hanging clothes should be set at approximately 4'-6" to allow for front and side reach from a wheelchair. To accommodate all disabilities, a split closet is recommended.
4. Clothes hangers should be able to be removed and replaced.
5. The closet should be lit for ease of utility.

Temperature

Temperature is typically zoned in hotels to allow guests to modify their room temperature based on their individual needs.

Recommendations

1. Vestibules are recommended to maintain temperature continuity, heating, and cooling.
2. Make sure room temperature controls are accessible in height and have dials that are user-friendly (e.g., large digits).
3. Position controls in a normal passageway location (e.g., inside the door to the room).
4. Take care to prevent cold drafting by heating and ventilation systems.

Windows

Windows in the hospitality industry should provide access to a large environment with an opportunity to choose privacy or access. Visual access at the 3-1/2' level is accomplished if the sill is set at 2'. Double-hung windows are the most difficult to operate.

Recommendations

1. Provide window hardware that is easy to reach. If sills are too large (deep), then access is difficult.
2. Minimize the infiltration of drafts at the installation.
3. Use handles that can be operated by a person with grip and grasp difficulties. A maximum of five pounds of force is recommended.
4. Sliding windows on good rollers are the easiest to operate.
5. Casement windows with cranks can be operated as long as the catch to the latch is easy to engage.
6. Make window treatments, such as draperies and blinds, accessible with rods that are long enough to operate for full closing and opening. Drawstrings that are attached to the wall must be accessible without removing furnishings to reach them. Motorized controls are an expensive last resort.

Chapter Thirty-Nine

RETAIL STORE

For employees, the goal of a design for "reasonable accommodation" should be to maintain their productivity and efficiency, while reducing stress and fatigue within the job description (essential job functions). For customers, "reasonable accommodation" should allow people to be able to independently use environmental supports to accomplish their objectives.

Evaluation by Factors

Accessibility
The design should allow for approach, entrance, and exit to and from buildings, with minimal dependence on staff for assistance. For example, electric-eye doors are often used in spaces that require a turn to a second entrance that is difficult to maneuver. Any bathrooms, kitchens, or personal areas are especially important to review.

Adaptability
Maps are essential to show shoppers or visitors to public access buildings the shortest routes to meet their objectives.

Air Quality
Air quality is critical to the retail business as the HVAC system is charged with the management of a larger than normal volume of airborne fibers from clothing and people. HVAC systems in retail areas, particularly those in closed malls, bear a higher burden of ventilation and circulation requirements. This is particularly true when the outside air exchange may be compromised by automobile exhaust fumes.

Recommendations
Evaluate the HVAC system's capacity to manage the categories of airborne contaminants that can occur in the retail environment. Expect to find and test for inorganic compounds such as carbon dioxide, sulfur dioxide, carbon monoxide, nitrous oxide, ammonia and radon. Pay attention to the percent of airborne fibers from clothing (new to the market) and customers. In addition, the HVAC system must accommodate fumes from detergents, pesticides, wall paints, and the dust and debris from ceiling systems. It is necessary to specify the system by volume of people and the actual facility. Air quality becomes critical for workers who may be continuously exposed to the illnesses of customers. The ventilation system must also be evaluated for its capacity to manage humidity and air exchange. In closed environments,

air quality systems must be specified to the full range of contaminants, not a single source or one point in time, because air quality problems are cumulative in effect.

Comfort

People who have difficulty with ambulation will do business more frequently in a place that has a designated rest area.

Communication

Stores that use phones instead of staff to guide customers should lower the phones' access height and have staff assigned to aid and assist people with stamina difficulties. In addition, the public relations strategy should include identification of the available supports. Physically challenged consumers need to be assured in advance that assistance is available prior to arrival at a site.

Density

The older the clientele, the less dense the retail space should be to facilitate ambulation and access to items.

Division of Space

Layout changes may be necessary to access items more efficiently. This may be based on a market analysis of the frequency of purchase by particular groups. In addition, landmarks, such as the beginning and end of aisles, should be redundant if environments are to support efficient use of space. Dramatic spatial changes are an excellent indicator to access (e.g., offsetting the beginning of aisles by one foot to show the store depth).

Equipment

Position and posture required to access equipment is critical to its effective use by customers. Any equipment has to be user-friendly and within reach (on average, within 12 inches and not weighing more than 2 lbs.) to move.

Finishes

Finish is determined by functional limitations, (e.g., contrasts used to enhance visual acuity on shelving).

Image

The match must be between maintaining the image of the facility and the dignity of your customer. For example, if your customer is lost or confused by your facility, then your image and their dignity are compromised.

Lighting

Illumination levels must focus peoples' attention on the most important items (e.g., the product and the price).

Maintenance

Environments where customers interact with employees to conduct business should be designed in such a way that they are not consistently "damaged" by customers (e.g., passages that are constantly scarred because people are misjudging corridors).

Noise

The older your population of customers, the fewer distractions can be tolerated. Therefore, background noise should be minimized.

Passages

Safety and passages are an interactive issue. Wide corridors (that enable two wheelchairs to pass) are important.

Safety

This is the number one concern when catering to customers. Safety is best defined by a complete understanding of the functional limitations of stamina, mobility, and visual acuity.

Signage

Redundant cuing is an essential aid to help customers negotiate environments (e.g., maps that are easily read with signs that are consistent—in high contrast colors with large lettering). The use of scents as an olfactory cue is a type of signage. For example, cooked food in delicatessen departments of supermarkets.

Storage

Shelving for display of inventory should accommodate the need for flexibility both for employees maintaining inventory and customer access (e.g., revolving displays that allow the person access without movement).

Temperature

People usually move faster through a setting that is cooler. Modification of temperature depends on the needs of clientele. Generally, the older the population, the higher the temperature (68°F minimum) should be.

Windows

Visual access to the outside allows a space to be perceived as less crowded, no matter how small the interior space. People tend to stay longer in spaces with windows.

Chapter Forty

HOSPITAL/CLINIC

This case study concerns a medical center with low-vision employees in a data processing area dedicated to patient billing. The work area is composed of cubicles.

Evaluation by Factors

Accessibility

Access into the building is accomplished from the parking lot areas to ground-level doors. The doors are heavy, and the door knobs are difficult to use (both for opening and positioning the door). One ramp was a switchback, high-railed and uncovered. This makes access difficult when trying to push a person or wheel oneself, or when carrying parcels and opening the doors.

Recommendations

The existing valet areas and electric-eye door openings are excellent access options as long as signage clearly directs people to these areas and the electric doors are always operational. Cover all ramps, at least during the winter. (Sun damage is actually worse for awnings than winter weather abuse.) Add railings at a height that can be accessed by people in wheelchairs— approximately 27 inches.

Adaptability

The work site area for nursing staff has taken nursing feedback into consideration and allowed for designs that fit the "tasks at hand." However, the work surfaces being fixed to the floor and fixed to the wall allow for no adaptability or flexibility for a variety of body types, nor for reconfiguration of space to add new equipment.

In addition, visual access to patient areas is limited. A person's ability to see over the nurses' station counter is limited by his or her height. Also, the nurses' station counter access, as a person passes by, requires over-reaching and bending to gather materials. Organization of the work surface itself did not appear to be supported with either visual storage aids or ease of access to materials. Seating was minimally supporting the working postures of staff.

Recommendations

The work areas at the nursing stations would benefit from a task analysis that would organize the stations into functional areas: charting, medical records, medication and inventory. (See Figure 40.1.) The counter should have multiple levels, with work surfaces at 2'-7" to 3'-6". The cut-out and knee space should be 2'-6" to 3' wide. Counters there should be 2'-10" and 1'-7" deep.

Air Quality

Air quality in health care settings is governed by the greatest number of legal constraints. HVAC systems are regulated by the Environmental Protection Agency. ASHRAE guidelines and the critical consideration of the OSHA regulations on both airborne and blood-borne pathogens. Air quality to health care standards is a prerequisite to providing an environment for both workers and patients and the visitor population.

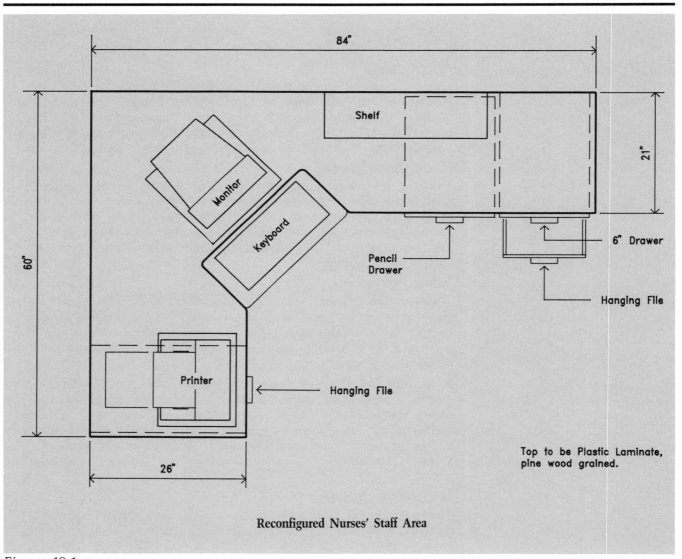

Reconfigured Nurses' Staff Area

Figure 40.1

Recommendations

Evaluate the HVAC system's capacity to manage the categories of airborne pathogens and contaminants that can occur in the health care environment. Use all federal and association guidelines to cross reference regulatory points. Specify the system from the perspective of *how testing will occur.* Define what tests of the system will be expected and design appropriate points of access. Design for ventilation management of inorganic compounds such as carbon dioxide, sulfur dioxide, carbon monoxide, nitrous oxide, ammonia and radon. Pay attention to the percent of airborne fibers from clothing, bed and bath, and furnishings. Evaluate to ensure the sufficiency of the ventilation system for managing humidity and air exchange by usage area (from common areas to surgical suites in which sterilization of instruments occurs). In closed environments air quality systems must be specified to the full range of contaminants, not a single source or one point in time, because air quality problems are cumulative in effect.

Comfort

The visitor lounge areas are configured with chairs, television, phones, and tables to create a "waiting area" that facilitates a break from the patient rooms and a place for people to rest and talk. The mix of utility of these areas is what makes visitors uncomfortable.

Recommendations

Re-zone the visitor waiting areas to accommodate the needs of both patients and visitors. Evaluate visitor needs by conducting a visitor survey (using volunteer staff) and make data-based decisions as to how to reconfigure areas for comfort (offering a place to rest, talk, or be distracted).

Communication

Communication for visitors is available on every floor with pay phones that appear to be accessible to the ambulatory, but not to people in wheelchairs, children, or those who may need assistance (hearing impaired, visually impaired, learning disabled). The internal hospital communication system was not evaluated.

Recommendations

Phone placement for visitors should be reviewed to meet the standards for access. See "Communication," Chapter 15.

Density

The density of patient care areas (e.g., ICU, premie) was excellently planned to accommodate equipment, support accessories, and space to work and to move quickly. In addition, there was a clear thoughtfulness to the flexibility and adaptability of space configurations. It maintains the highest quality of patient care with the least stress to caregivers. The space was observed without a time-by-task analysis, but it appeared efficient and organized.

Recommendations

No recommendations. Maintain regular communication with caregivers to get their input into space designs, taking into consideration that the overhead shelves often require over-reaching and can be a hazard in ICU.

Division of Space

The office environment at the center is linearly designed to accommodate work areas by function, access to resources, co-workers and equipment. The layout of the work environment appears to accommodate staff by status. Although the space is newly renovated and is being outfitted with new paneled areas and furnishings, the adaptability and ergonomic fit to people is not evident. Observation reveals that staff have not yet been fitted to their work stations, nor have work site supports been integrated into the new location.

Recommendations

Redesign the layout to enhance productivity for all staff, creating a resource area for all shared equipment (copier, postage meter, mail station) to save steps in the preparation and processing of paperwork. In addition, an office layout map, which the front receptionist can use to direct visitors, would allow the workers' areas to be rearranged to facilitate the work without compromising access to materials.

Equipment

A large magnifier screen reader and CRT valet are used for the computer, with a tilt board for angling documents to accommodate low vision. Adjustable shelving is installed, as well as a large dial and speaker for the telephone system.

Finishes

Finishes are high contrast and low glare to accommodate employees with low vision.

Furnishings

Work sites are currently in various stages of being installed and completed for staff in many areas of the center. Ergonomic fittings to create work sites that enhance the productivity standard have not yet been put into place. The furnishings are well imaged in many parts of the center, but the question is whether image and intervention are both being served.

Recommendations

Work site analysis should be conducted in selected areas to facilitate the match between people, equipment, and work sites—to maintain productivity without creating stress and fatigue. Designs should accommodate height and reach requirements, while supporting a strategy to prevent the known occupational hazards in patient care facilities (back injury, carpal tunnel syndrome, injuries to hands and fingers, head and neck fatigue).

Image

The center's image is standard in terms of professional space that supports the work effort of staff. However, it could improve its image in terms of office designs that exemplify the "state-of-the-art" in reasonable accommodations. A public relations strategy might be incorporated into the office design, making it a "working model" of the spirit of the Americans with Disabilities Act. Total redesign would be especially significant since the center's office not only employs people with disabilities, but is visited by disabled patients—all of whose capabilities could be enhanced with design and technologies. In particular, the front lobby reception area station should be redone to allow visual access for the persons behind the desk to greet visitors, especially those who are in wheelchairs.

Recommendations

The goals of image to be considered are:

1. Design offices, passages, zoned common areas, and conference space to encompass the 20 factors that create "reasonable accommodation."
2. Incorporate capacity-building technologies to increase productivity, while reducing stress and fatigue (for example, mechanical supports, computer technologies, and communication systems).

Lighting

Current lighting is fluorescent in ceiling mounts that are shaded to diffuse the light and reduce glare. No task lighting is individually positioned for staff. The available lighting adds a lux intensity which keeps the room consistently bright (approximately 60,000 to 80,000 lux) with a minimum of shadowing.

Recommendations

Areas around the hospital should be evaluated and methods examined to complement the effect of fluorescent lighting (which is limited spectrum and reduces the eyes' ability to see a full spectrum of primary colors). Determinations should be made as to which areas should be contrasted for brightness and glare-coded to increase visual acuity. Areas in use by patients who may suffer from seasonal affective disorders (SAD) should be under special consideration for lighting.

Maintenance

Maintenance and material handling are always an issue for hospitals. Currently used carts are state of the art, but no modifications have been made for safer handling and management of the carts in transport. Material handling is an occupational issue.

Recommendations

Evaluate staff for aches and strains on the job. Aches become pains, pains become injuries.

Noise

The hospital operates as a technology-based environment. With equipment humming and people making normal conversation, the background noise is 40 to 55 decibels. Noise is the reason most people have trouble resting in hospitals.

Recommendations

Offer noise reducers to the patients in the form of ear plugs, or recommend they use the radio or TV with earphones. Noise sensitivity is often increased for people in discomfort or pain.

Passages

The medical center is accessible down main passageways from lobbies which access elevators to each patient floor. Passages are wide and accommodating, because the space is designed to move people and resources throughout the facility.

Recommendations

The corridor configurations accommodate most passage (people and equipment) with ease. However, the maintenance of passages is an issue. Install more corner guards on walls, and bumper pads on equipment to protect corners. It may be easier to modify the carts than the walls.

Safety

The medical center is currently a safety-oriented environment for all workers. This is exemplified by engineering controls which endeavor to meet all of the standards and guidelines necessary to accommodate disabled patients and workers. One remaining question is how evacuation procedures would be carried out in the event of a fire.

Recommendations

Continue to install handrails, but without the square-cornered edge. Add a soft bumper guard to the existing railings. Clear corridors. Clearly define evacuation procedures for each floor. While they may exist, fire evacuation procedures were not observable. Establish a safe smoking area and enforce safety procedures to prevent, for example, smoking on the elevators.

Signage

The center is departmentalized with a volume of access by visitors of varying capabilities. Signage is not well coordinated in the hospital. Existing signs are not visibly useful for mapping one's independent passage through the hospital.

Recommendations

Develop a color coding system for the hospital that can guide the visitors, no matter what their language, age, or disability. Signs should use international symbols in addition to color coding. They should also be visible from four sides, not just two. Signs should be in high contrast colors that allow people with low vision to read them from 20 feet away.

Storage

Storage of forms and items of medical necessity appears to have been very well thought out (under-counter form storage accessed from the front of the nursing station, and cart storage in between rooms). Storage appears to be handled well. Access to frequently used items is easy.

Recommendations

Files should be made accessible in an organized way based on frequency of use. A book shelf (or the use of a carousel or rotary file) deep enough for files, and easily accessed by staff in various work areas represents the ideal.

Temperature

Temperature is not zoned, but is on a building system. Temperature difficulties were not noted.

Recommendations

Request and follow the most recent OSHA guidelines.

Windows

The windows are fixed to maintain a regulated temperature.

Recommendations

None.

Chapter Forty-One

THERAPY ROOM

Therapy rooms should be designed to maximize the use of time, energy, floor space, and equipment. An optimum design affords staff the opportunity to help restore the patients' functional abilities through the use of various physical and occupational therapies.

Physical: This room should be equipped with special exercise equipment that promotes activity and independent use.

Occupational: This room should facilitate group use of activities which focus on improving manipulation skills (e.g., eye/hand coordination). Storage of supplies and products/projects in progress must be addressed in the design process. Occupational therapy rooms should be designed with continuing care in mind. They should foster a sense of independence and strive to provide a visible increase in patient capability from the onset of rehabilitation through recovery. The highest level of independence should be the ultimate goal of a therapy room.

Key Design Goal

The design should accommodate limitations, while fostering increased capability in mobility, strength and stamina, visual acuity, hearing, tactile and thermal sensitivity, and psychology.

Rooms should be:
- flexible: furniture/equipment easily moved
- accommodating: for all physical disabilities
- adaptable: for all clients, staff/clinicians

Evaluation by Factors

The following checklists bring up key issues from the viewpoints of facilities managers, clinicians, and patients. These checklists can be used to interview representatives of each group, to obtain their input for design.

1. **Facilities Managers:** Does the room design make the best use of:
   - aesthetics and image
   - ease of maintenance and operations
   - function and fitness
   - lowered first costs and life cycle costs
   - responsiveness of a status marking system

- bulk purchase agreements or existing inventory
- integration with other work places.

2. **Clinicians:** Does the room maintain your expectations and needs in the following areas:
   - Accessibility
   - Adaptability
   - Air Quality
   - Comfort
   - Communication
   - Density
   - Division of Space
   - Equipment
   - Finishes
   - Furnishings
   - Image
   - Lighting
   - Maintenance
   - Noise
   - Passages
   - Safety
   - Signage
   - Storage
   - Temperature
   - Windows

3. **Patients participating in therapy:** Are you able to independently use therapy supports and accomplish therapeutic objectives through:
   - redundant cuing
   - landmarks: water, decorating, dramatic spatial changes
   - personalized areas
   - accessibility
   - illumination levels
   - sounds
   - smells

4. **In general,** does the room provide an atmosphere which:
   - increases opportunities for individual choice
   - encourages independence
   - compensates for changes in patient perception and sensory acuity
   - decreases unnecessary mobility
   - encourages social interaction
   - stimulates participation in activities offered
   - reduces conflict and distraction
   - provides a safe environment
   - makes activities accessible
   - improves client, staff, and facility image
   - plans for growth and change in individuals

Figure 41.1 is a chart summarizing the chief design considerations from the perspective of the facility manager, the therapist, and the patient. All three views are important from the early planning stages.

Areas to Consider in Design

Accessibility
Access often requires the assistance of aids in the beginning of therapy.

Adaptability
Adaptations are site- and therapy-specific to clinical disciplines (e.g., speech, physical therapy, occupational therapy, etc.).

Interactive Design Factors	Facility Manager	Clinic Staff	Patient Need
Accessibility	✔	✔	✔
Adaptability	✔	✔	✔
Comfort	✔	✔	✔
Communication	✔	✔	✔
Density		✔	✔
Division of Space		✔	✔
Equipment	✔	✔	✔
Finishes			✔
Furnishings	✔	✔	✔
Lighting	✔		✔
Maintenance	✔		
Noise	✔	✔	✔
Passages	✔	✔	✔
Safety	✔	✔	✔
Signage	✔	✔	✔
Storage	✔	✔	✔
Temperature/Air Quality	✔	✔	✔
Windows	✔	✔	✔

Design Considerations from the Perspective of the Facility Manager, Therapist and Patient

Figure 41.1

Air Quality

Air quality is critical in therapy rooms which bring people of varying degrees of wellness together for rehabilitation. Airborne pathogens and contaminants must be reviewed, especially if the therapy room includes any hydro-therapy. As therapy rooms are often windowless for more privacy, there is a higher burden of ventilation and circulation requirements.

Recommendations

Evaluate the HVAC system's capacity to manage the categories of airborne pathogens and contaminants that can occur in therapy rooms. Expect to specify the system for organic and inorganic compounds such as carbon dioxide, sulfur dioxide, carbon monoxide, nitrous oxide, ammonia and radon. Pay attention to the percent of airborne fibers from clothing, bath and furnishings. Evaluate the ventilation system for its capacity to manage humidity and air exchange. In closed environments air quality systems must be specified to the full range of contaminants, not a single source or one point in time, because air quality problems are cumulative in effect.

Consultation Rooms

These should be private rooms next to the therapy area and equipped for doctors and clinicians, for screening and consulting with patients. These rooms should include an examination table, desk, chair, and side chair. Storage areas/cabinets should be available.

Comfort and Seating

Seating should accommodate people who are in recovery and may have poor blood circulation or difficulty transferring into and out of seats. Major functional considerations should be:

1. Ease of getting in and out
2. Comfort and support while sitting or reclining
3. Safety

Density

Consideration should be given to the type of activities and the number of participants who will engage in the activities for which each type of room is used. Group and individual participation rooms should be a minimum of 60 square feet. Each individual should have at least a five square foot area for access to the room and enough additional space allotted for comfortable participation in various therapies and/or activities.

Division of Space to Encourage Mapping the Room

Persons in rehabilitation often experience changes in sensory or cognitive abilities which may include loss of short-term memory. Therefore, the physical environment should promote re-orientation, by means of a simple design with repetitive architectural elements, fixtures and finishes.

Finishes

All surfaces should be easily maintainable with either vinyl wall covering and/or laminated surfaces. Reflectance should be 40 to 60 percent.

Floors

A level loop carpeting should be used in spaces where people walk to provide a pleasant walking surface and reduce glare and noise. Direct-glue carpeting should be used to prevent slipping and rolling resistance to wheelchairs. Where water absorbency is an issue, jute backing is safest. Floors should be relatively light in tone with 30 to 50 percent reflectance.

Walls

Brick, concrete and tile are the most resistant to abuse from contact. Surfaces should be smooth to prevent slippage and glare should be minimized whenever possible.

Ceilings

These can be textured, pattern-painted, or fabric-covered to provide visual relief and to serve as an aid to orientation. Reflectance should be 70 to 90 percent.

Furnishings

Furniture should support the activities of the room and be easily arranged into new configurations. Desk and table tops should have light non-glare surfaces with a reflectance range of 30 to 50 percent. High contrasts are desirable for changes in surfaces.

Lighting

There should be strong full spectrum overhead lighting, with task lights for individual tasks. Task lights should be adjustable in intensity, location, and direction. Special sensitivity to glare should be taken into account, and use of highly reflective surfaces avoided. Wherever sunlight enters, screens, baffles, shades, or curtains should be used. In general, indirect lighting should be used whenever possible.

Noise

Reduce general background noise with floor, wall, and ceiling sound-reduction materials. In large therapy rooms, sound can be moderated with baffling, wall hangings, banners and panels.

Safety

Rooms should be free of sharp corners, projections and slippery surfaces.

Safety and Tactile Cues

Raised grooves, hand rails, aggregate concrete and rubber strips, etc., provide necessary sensory identification of various areas to individuals in therapy. The use of tactile cuing raises the individual's self-esteem by providing an avenue for independent participation.

Signage

Rooms should be organized with identifying, directional and informational signs that have significant color contrasts and feature large lettering.

Storage and Display Space

The design of storage should include accessible shelving that allows access from 29 inches and does not exceed a depth of 12 inches. There should be areas for individual storage of work in progress and facility storage of therapy items. Movable storage units are useful. The design should include areas for display of individual projects and accomplishments. The display areas can also be used as clinical training tools to explain how therapies work.

Temperature Control

Design heating, ventilating and air-conditioning should take into consideration the narrow range of comfort for recovering patients. Many patients are susceptible to the loss of body heat and have little tolerance for even transient swings in ambient temperature. Care should be taken to avoid drafts of either hot or cool air.

Layout Considerations for all Therapy Rooms

The following factors need to be considered from the perspective of each party's interest when designing rooms to serve multiple needs.

1. What type of services and activities will be provided?
2. What size will the group be?
3. What times of the day will the room be in use?
4. Where will the room be located?
5. What physical features are required in the room?
6. How much space is needed for specific activities, special furniture, equipment, electrical service, plumbing fixtures, exhaust and ventilation requirements and storage?
7. What are the room contours?
8. What is the required room size?
9. What safety measures will be incorporated?

Figure 41.2 is an illustration of an accessible configuration for a therapy room.

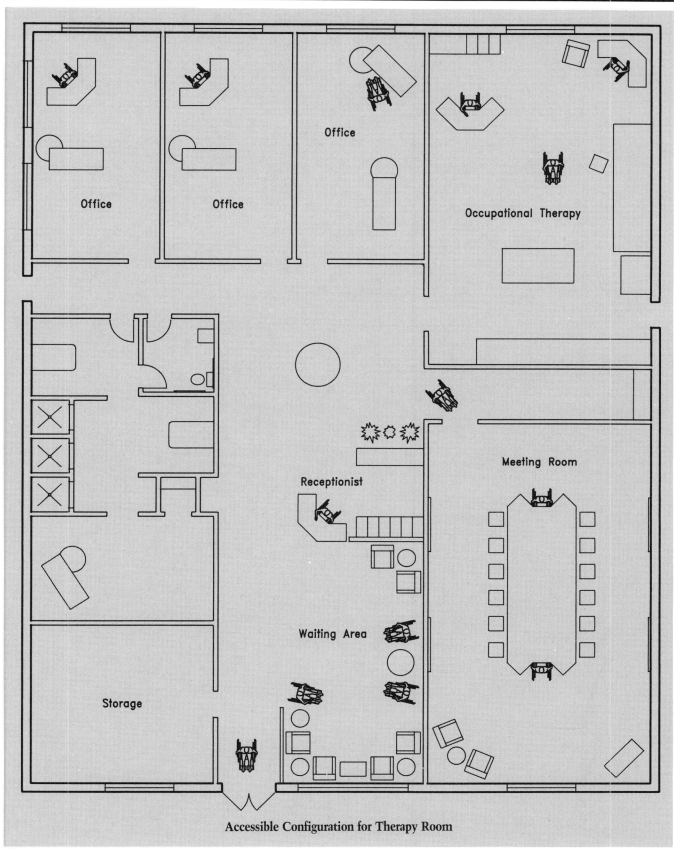

Accessible Configuration for Therapy Room

Figure 41.2

Chapter Forty-Two

AUDITORIUMS

Title III of the Americans with Disabilities Act prohibits discrimination on the basis of disability in the full and equal enjoyment of goods, services, facilities, privileges, advantages, or accommodations of any place of public accommodation and services operated by private entities. The goods, services, and accommodations must be offered in the most appropriate integrated setting. Auditoriums, museums, theatres, sports arenas and convention centers have their own special concerns regarding accomodation and the ADA.

The "case study" format is useful in this section to indicate areas that should be evaluated in this type of facility and recommended modifications. The goal is the overall integration of people who may wish to participate in activities within these facilities, and have certain functional limitations. Each site should be evaluated to determine if physical limitations have been "reasonably accommodated" according to ADA, both environmentally and in terms of policy, procedure, and practice. Meeting the need means accommodating for functional limitations, but understanding that:

1. All disabilities are not observable.
2. The observable disability may not be the one that causes a barrier to receiving services; for example, a person in a wheelchair may also be blind and need Braille assistance. It is therefore important to design for the range of limitations which may affect specific sites.

The list of critical sites (below) may be used to analyze these types of public gathering places.

- Entrances
- Reception Area
- Seating
- Concession
- Public Bathrooms
- Event Sales
- Focal Point of the Event

Evaluation by Factors

Accessibility

Access to buildings that serve large functions and gatherings of people should be designed to accommodate people management in varying numbers. Patrons should be able to arrive comfortably whether as individuals, couples, or in groups. They should be able to purchase or use passes and tickets through human ticket sellers or machines. They should be able to gain entry and be routed to seating easily. *Note: Any transportation vehicles that are made available to patrons must have accommodations for people with disabilities; for example, wheelchair lifts in vans.* Access to events can be facilitated by design and crowd management techniques which allow people to fully participate.

Recommendations for Outside Access

1. Use appearance, signage, and access to clearly identify the entrance to the facility.

2. Use lighting to clearly illuminate the entrance to the facility.

3. Provide accommodations for varying weather conditions. Awnings and canopies are an important consideration given the additional time access to buildings may take. Recommended minimum height for awnings is 9'-6".

4. Provide room for vehicles and patrons with their luggage at passenger loading and unloading zones.

5. Clearly delineate the layout of the access to the entrance from parking lots with marked crosswalks.

6. Provide proper accommodation for wheelchair vans in underground parking areas (a minimum clearance of 9' to enter the area and extra wide parking, typically 8'-6" of side clearance; 16'-6" is the minimum recommended length for vans).

7. Avoid changes in level from the outside to the inside. When a level change of more than 1/4" does occur, then transition strips should be installed with a transition slope of 1–2".

8. Provide smooth transitions from driveways to sidewalks. These transitions aid in mobility of people and luggage. Curbings should also be color-contrasted for visual acuity. Raised edgings of 1/2" at the end of a flush transition can prevent slippage for persons in wheelchairs who may be visually impaired. Defining edgings and transitions is important. *Note: Detectable warning strips should be provided for safety. These raised strips are 3' wide and 1" high. They provide a sense of transition by creating a raised rounded surface (ANSI 4.7, 4.27)*

9. Use non-slip surface materials for the construction of outdoor walkways. Any transitions between walkways should be smooth, and gratings should be relocated.

10. Any part of an accessible route with a slope greater than 1" in 20" shall be considered a ramp, and shall comply with the following provisions: The maximum slope for ramps of 30' or less is 1" in 12". The maximum slope of a ramp 50' or longer is reduced as the length of the ramp increases. 50' is the longest continuous ramp without a landing, with a total vertical rise of no more than 2'-6". When the fixed rise is 30", slope and length can vary 30' and can have a slope of 1" in 12" or 1" in 15"; 40' can have a slope of 1" in 20". A minimum clearance width of 3' measured from the inside handrail. A maximum clear width of 5' allows two-way traffic for people in wheelchairs.

11. Provide curbs, walls, and a railing for ramps that have a vertical rise exceeding 6" with a length greater than 6'.

12. Consider a heated ramp, which may reduce maintenance by preventing ice and snow accumulation, and increase safety for patrons.

13. Make sure any steps conform to ANSI 4.9 with exterior steps having a rise of between 5-3/4″ and 6″. Non-slip treads should have a minimum depth of 11″. Nosings should be sloped, beveled, or rounded and not project more than 1-1/2″.

14. Provide handrails on both sides of the stairs at a height of 2′-6″ to 2′-10″ for adults, and 2′ to 2′-4″ for children to ensure left- and right-handed support and passage up and down. Handrails should be continuous to support weight and balance during the whole elevation, and should extend 12 – 14″ beyond the landing or last step. Handrails should end in an L-shape fixed to the wall for support. The hand contact surface of the handrail should be 1-1/4–1-1/2″. Wall-mounted handrails should provide a grip surface of 1-1/2″.

15. Provide landings the width of the ramp, 5′ in length, wherever a change in direction takes place. Landings should accommodate door openings.

16. Manual doors that can be positioned as an open station of access are best for crowd management when they have double widths of 7′ to accommodate people and staff (ticket takers, pass reviewers, counters). The manual doors should be as close to the access ramp as possible to minimize travel time.

17. Thresholds at the door should not exceed a height of 1/4″ tapered to a slope of 1–2″.

18. Layout of the access areas from entrances to the lobby and front desk should allow ease of passage, a short distance of travel that is clearly marked with lit signage.

Adaptability

For this type of facility, adaptability is most critical in the area(s) where crowds gather for a learning or entertainment experience. Adaptability for large gatherings is the ability to deliver a learning or entertainment experience for all people regardless of their special needs. This means planning for flexibility within the environment at specific sites.

Recommendations

1. Make it possible to reconfigure space to add, remove or modify furnishings, seating, and equipment. Integration of people is essential.

2. Provide participants with the opportunity to maintain visual and auditory access to a focal point (film, lecture, event, display) for both learning and entertainment experiences. This means providing visual and auditory aids. For example, a lecture should have sign language interpretation, Braille-supported materials, or double-screen access to slides.

3. It may also be important to facilitate communication between people conducting events and the audience. This may mean having staff and equipment that can be mobilized in a "question and answer session" using mobile microphones. Stands may be required for mobile microphones for people who have grip and grasp problems. Lapel microphones are also recommended.

4. Provide a variety of seating options at varying heights to accommodate a variety of posture supports for a range of body

types (e.g., booster seats for young children).

5. Plan for peoples' equipment needs, both spatially and electronically. Controls on any equipment provided by the facility to increase interaction should have panel buttons arranged in an understandable order (e.g., change in volume: low to high). No buttons should be higher than 4' above the floor for a front approach in a wheelchair, or 4'-6" for a side approach. All buttons should have a raised tactile surface. Buttons should light up when engaged.

6. Equip hazard areas (bathrooms, elevators) with call buttons to allow emergency communication.

7. Install mirrors to facilitate the use of space, both for turning corners and adding visual access (e.g., reading the floor numbers from the back of an elevator).

8. Design to accommodate staffs' height and reach requirements, while supporting a strategy to prevent the known occupational hazards in hospitality facilities (back injury, carpal tunnel syndrome, injuries to hands and fingers, head and neck fatigue).

9. Adapt the 5% of the seating (UFAS) that accommodates wheelchairs with electrical outlets to power assistive and adaptive devices used by people with disabilities. In case of adaptive equipment battery failure, have outlets positioned 4' above the floor for access.

10. Ensure that controls on any listening devices are easy to operate with limited hand function. Mounting at 4' is ideal for most people with limited stature.

11. The ability to operate all fixtures and equipment provided by the facility is particularly important to teachers and trainers. Remote mechanisms are an excellent adaptation for people with disabilities (e.g., for the light switches — on/off and dimming, and management of audio visual equipment).

12. Handicapped seats for toilets should be available as an aid and assist for patrons who need support in the bathroom. See Chapter 11, "Accessibility," for detailed bathroom requirements.

13. Adjustable height seats should be available for toilets.

Air Quality
Air quality is a major factor in the design of densely packed spaces like auditoriums. This is especially true when space is "sold" to service groups of people, whether it be 20 or 500. Air quality is a part of the customer service.

Recommendations
Evaluate the HVAC system's capacity to manage the categories of airborne contaminants that can occur in "crowded" environments. Expect to find and test for inorganic compounds such as carbon dioxide, sulfur dioxide, carbon monoxide, nitrous oxide, ammonia and radon. Pay attention to the percent of airborne fibers from clothing and furnishings. Evaluate the ventilation system for its capacity to manage humidity and air exchange. In closed environments air quality systems must be specified to the full range of contaminants, not a single source or one point in time, because air quality problems are cumulative.

Comfort
The visitor/patron reception areas should be designed for ease of access. They may be intended as standing room only, or configured with chairs, couches, lamps, rugs, and tables to create a more relaxed "intermission" area. Consistent with image, large function space creates an atmosphere that

invites interaction, time for purchases from shops and concessions, and a transition time for food and rest room visits. The extent to which people are comfortable using the retail or reception areas as a gathering point depends on how well it allows access without the "push of the crowd," and the provisions of food, drink, and souvenirs. Access to and from elevators is important. The light should be high enough to promote mobility, viewing of displays, and the opportunity to purchase items.

Recommendations

Zone the patron reception areas in a circular fashion to accommodate the needs of said patrons. Evaluate their access needs by defining what opportunities and services the facility is providing. Re-configure areas for comfort (a place to rest, talk, or purchase, or view people and displays). Comfort is enhanced by designs with the following characteristics:

1. A sense of safety and security, e.g., cognitively mapped space.
2. A sense of independence and dignity, e.g., organization of space to find essential services such as public bathrooms.
3. Simplicity of design and usability in the configuration of furniture, displays, and service areas to create passages.
4. Cues that support the disability, e.g., signage with large lettering.
5. A sense that time is available to complete a task.

Communication

Communication for patrons should be available in the form of support for people and equipment. For example, listening and visual systems should be available to support the "learning or entertainment experience." Communication is critical to the success of the facility for people with special needs. Communication systems must assist all peoples' enjoyment of a facility's entertainment, learning, retail, and services goals.

Recommendations

1. Provide listening systems for audio amplification to provide assistance for people with hearing impairments. These systems might be hard-wired headphones with individual volume controls. To maximize the effectiveness of listening systems, they should be provided with seats that are within 50' of the speaker, and located in areas where there is the least amount of distracting background noise, echoes, or reverberation. Additional listening supports may be in the form of induction loops, wireless FM, and infrared systems that rebroadcast sound in the form of light. Each system should be usable with or without hearing aids. Induction loops are connected to the speaker's microphone system. Wireless FM is broadcast to headsets. Infrared systems broadcast using light to transmit sound to headsets. The point from which patrons begin to receive service should cater to their particular disability (for example, discussion of seating preference based on accessibility and the determination of what menu should be available, e.g., Braille).
2. Provide sign language interpreters with seating near speakers, set above the crowd, to promote visual access. They should have a light shining on them to illuminate their hands and facial expressions.
3. Provide visual systems to enhance viewing. Screens should be as large as possible and set at a height over the crowd for the best visual access. The more projection surfaces, the better.

4. Make communication of information available in several forms, e.g., verbal, maps of the facility (to include the areas of independent access—retail, rest rooms), signage, and color coding of display areas.

5. Review public telephones for patrons to make sure they meet the ADA requirements for access and control.

6. Make facility staff accessible for face-to-face communication so that all patrons can purchase and receive tickets, exchange money, and receive food or retail purchases.

7. Microphone access to staff (e.g., at ticket windows) should be positioned for talking and listening at 3'-6" for mobile (wheelchair) traffic.

Density

The density requirement of seating for the disabled as required by the Uniform Federal Standard of Accessibility (UFSA) is a minimum of 5% of the total. Seating should not be in a segregated area, but along parameters to allow for a maximum of choices.

Seating should accommodate visual access to the focal points of the event. There should be a minimum of travel time required between areas of where events are held and seating, rest rooms, vending and self-service drink or retail areas.

Recommendations

1. Design to accommodate equipment (respirators), support accessories (lap trays on wheelchairs), and space for staff and patrons to use the space safely.

2. Make the space flexible and adaptable in configuration to allow the integration of people with disabilities into groups of varying size (1 – 20 other patrons). People want to sit with their family and friends, not be segregated behind the bleachers or on a ramp in front of the stands.

3. The relationship of aisles to seating in meeting rooms should be set for maximum use of the space with the minimum of obstacles and obstructions to usability. For example, aisles to seating should be 3' wide with double the clearance (6') in meeting rooms where parallel tables are set in a linear design. *Note: 2'-6" of clearance behind wheelchairs is advised to accommodate for positioning under tables. This clearance allows wheelchairs to negotiate out of a space by rolling backwards to reposition.*

4. Promote independence and safety for people with disabilities with crowd management plans that meet fire codes and egress standards, and are staffed properly.

5. When assigning seating for vision and hearing impairments, 50' within the podium makes for the best visual and listening access.

Division of Space

The division of space for gatherings or functions has to accommodate patrons' services to meet objectives for learning or entertainment. The layout of focal points and display areas should accommodate access irrespective of special needs.

The registration/greeting area should be located as close to the entrance as possible. Once access to the facility has been accomplished, access to the event is the next crucial issue. Design for service and division of space should always consider the safe environment of patrons in case of emergency.

The divisions of space to consider are:
- Entrance and Vestibules
- Display Areas
- Lobby and Reception
- Self-Service Areas
- Administration and Business
- Food Service
- Lounges/Bars
- Rest rooms
- Main Event Areas

Proper division of space is essential to allow patrons to participate in events with safety and independence.

Recommendations

1. Design entrances to accommodate independent entry into the event with ease of access. Entrances should meet the minimum operating requirements (discussed in "Accessibility") for width, operating force (not to exceed eight pounds of pull force, which is defined by the weight of the door and the tension applied to closers).

2. Entrances can accommodate most disabilities with one of three door choices. Automatic doors operated by scanners are ideal because they eliminate the need for operating mats and guardrails (ANSI/BHMA 156.10-1985). Accessible revolving doors should include the maneuver space with a front approach of 1'-6" from a front approach area of 5'. Manual swinging doors require a latch pull on the side of the door and maneuverability space of 90 degrees. Thresholds on all entrances should not exceed 1/2" in height and should be beveled at 1/4". For safety, mats should be slip-resistant with a minimum friction coefficient of 6.

3. It is recommended that the reception of patrons sets the service tones for an event. Designs may incorporate reception areas for the purchase and sale of tickets.

4. Clearance widths are key considerations in the division of space for events. Clearance to the sides of walls and seating sections should be a minimum of 3'. Clearance should also be considered in spaces that are set as display areas and for movement underneath writing surfaces.

5. Locate retail areas centrally to all services within the facility, with maximum visual access to the points of interest to patrons, e.g., food, vending, souvenirs.

6. Design self-service operations to support limitations of reach for people with disabilities. Service areas, e.g., vending, food purchase, condiment stands, and drink bars, should have a minimum aisle width of 3', with service levels for tray slides being 2'-10" high and a maximum of 12" deep. Reach should be aided by the ability to move selections of food toward one's body to take a portion of food. Safety is critical at self-serve counters where hot foods and drinks may be accessed.

7. Rest rooms should be accessed within a short distance from the entrance since patrons often use the rest rooms before and after eating.

8. Public rest rooms:
   - Toilets should provide a clear access to transfer (ANSI 4.16).

- The top of the toilet should be between 17" and 19" above the floor.
- Grab bars and toilet paper should be installed for access at 24" (ANSI 4.16.4 and .6).
- Vanities should include access at minimum dimensions of 2'-3" high, 2-1/2' wide, and 1'-7" deep. Hot water pipes should be insulated to prevent scalding.
- The top of the basin should be no higher than 2'-10" and basin depth no deeper than 6-1/2" (ANSI 4.19).
- All vanity tops should be rounded on the edges with a maximum depth of 1 – 2".
- Mirrors should be mounted with the lowest edge of reflectance no higher than 3'-4" (ANSI 4.19).
- Faucets should operate with offset lever handles or single lever controls (ANSI 4.19). Another option is infrared-controlled automatic faucets.
- Any items for hanging should have mounts at a maximum height of 4'-6".
- Bathroom lighting should be 70 footcandles to allow for fine hand function, such as applying makeup.

9. Lounges and bars should be located between the reception areas and the event areas, since people often begin and end their event experience in this area.

Equipment

Standard equipment for every event should be positioned to accommodate the disabled. In addition, there may be a need for special transfer devices for patrons who need assistance in lifting and transfer.

Recommendations

1. Review any equipment that is needed to access an event for safety and independence. For example, ticket machines need to be accessible at a 3'-6" height. Turnstiles, which regulate traffic into an event, may need to be modified to accommodate wheelchair or walker width. Push power required to make the turnstile move must be no more than 8 pounds.
2. Provide visual equipment.
3. Consider using machines that talk (e.g., to convey that more money for a purchase is required, notifying the customer that correct change only will be accepted or advising a patron how to begin operation).
4. Provide supplemental lighting for patrons with low vision.
5. Sports events should accommodate visual and auditory access for patrons by positioning screens, speakers, etc. for optimum viewing and listening.
6. Telephones should be equipped with volume controls, flashing lights (as a visual signal), and have a TDD available for people who are deaf. All phones should be equipped with large push button controls to allow function by those with hand limitations.
7. Emergency signal systems should include both visual and auditory alarms. Visual alarms should flash in conjunction with other building emergency systems. Audible alarms should be installed for visually-impaired guests and for patrons for whom the staff have extra concern.

Furniture

Seating is the key furniture issue and can be standard in most areas of event facilities. The design and location of seating is directly related to safety, comfort, and independence. All seating should be strong, stable, and sturdy, since patrons' comfort is critical to participation. Seating may include writing surface tops (without aprons) to facilitate learning experiences. Raised leaves on seating are often the best option for large gathering seating. Built-in seating should accommodate people of varying widths and heights. Accommodation is for varying disabilities and the special equipment disabled people may bring.

Recommendations

1. Allow for space to integrate a wheelchair into existing areas of seating. This can be accomplished with removable sections of seating that can accommodate wheelchairs. Aisles between rows of seating should be a minimum of 20″ to allow access to rows of seating for people with crutches and leg braces.

2. Writing surfaces for seats should include a knee space of at least 2′-3″ in height and 2′-6″ in width, 1′-7″ in depth. Seat height should be set at 18″ to accommodate most people.

3. Seats should be lightweight, padded for comfort, with arm rests 7 – 8″ above the seat, inclined backwards to add support. Recommended seat depth and width is 16″ square. The height should be low enough to facilitate transfer for people with limited mobility. A height of 15 – 20″ is recommended, as this allows the person ease of transfer and assist when rising.

Finishes

Finishes of walls should reduce reverberation and echo in event areas and add to the focal points. Carpet should support comfortable mobility without creating resistance to equipment supports (walkers, canes, wheelchairs). Hard floor surfaces should be slip-resistant (.6 coefficient wet/dry). Ceilings should minimize reflectance.

Recommendations

1. Carpet should be low pile and high density fiber glued directly to the slab or high density pad.

2. Tile in bathrooms should have a non-skid surface to prevent slips and falls.

3. Color contrasts between different surfaces should be distinct between furniture and rugs, walls and ceilings.

4. Colors should guide the eye from dark to light to the focal points of events. The lightest areas in an event area should be where speakers, movies, and events are positioned.

5. Protection of finishes should include low corner guards to a height of 4′, kick plates on doors, and vinyl edgings on surface edges of aisle seating.

Image

The best layout for large event facilities provides obstacle-free access from the entrance to full participation in an event. Pace is very important in the sense that crowd management is under control for all participants. Patrons must feel that design and staff understand their service needs, and that as a patron, their event experience can be managed with independence. The best imaged adaptive accommodations in event arenas are those which are consistent with one's sensory expectations, e.g., "I can hear, see, smell, feel and communicate at this event. I can cheer the ball game, cry at the movie, ask questions of the lecturer, and use the rest room. I can read the signs to get to the rest room."

Image should be enhanced by interventions and designs that exemplify the "state of the art" in public accommodations. For large events, image involves the ability to serve the whole age continuum, no matter what their capabilities.

Recommendations

Consider the following attributes of image:

1. Designs that present a facility for use by all create accessible environments that adapt to people's special needs for comfort, communication, equipment, furnishings, and lighting.
2. Capacity-building technologies increase patron capability and staff productivity, while reducing Workers' Compensation claims, stress, and fatigue.
3. Image is a result of a total plan of service to include all of the design factors.

Lighting

Lighting is a key image and atmosphere design factor that often limits people with disabilities. Lighting should be available as an aid to people with low vision, in particular, to support their ability to communicate through speech reading, sign language, gestures, and body movements.

Lighting should be a minimum brightness of 50 footcandles in order to illuminate both display areas and information necessary for patrons to participate in learning or entertainment.

Recommendations

1. Provide higher levels of illumination for older patrons of an event.
2. Lighting changes throughout display areas should not require the eyes to adjust to rapid changes. This is particularly important for people with mobility problems negotiating differing spaces.
3. To complement the effect of fluorescent lighting (which is limited spectrum and reduces the eye's ability to see a full spectrum of primary colors), areas around the function hall should be evaluated and determinations made to ascertain which areas should be contrasted for brightness, and which should be glare-coded to increase visual acuity.
4. Lamps at podiums and desks should have translucent shades to reduce contrast and glare and increase the uniformity of lighting. Lamps should be mounted to allow adjustability on the walls and prevent accidents. The ability to increase and decrease light during an event is essential to accommodate for vision needs. Touch controls or remote switches are recommended for lamps.
5. Glare reduction from windows and skylights is essential for visual acuity and fatigue reduction.

Maintenance

One of the biggest maintenance issues involved in servicing large events is frequently waste management. It is essential that physical plant staff maintain clear passages for patrons with mobility problems.

Recommendations

1. Include the needs of the disabled in a design for maintenance and waste management. For example, access to trash receptacles allows people to maintain a clean area during an event.
2. Select equipment supports that require a minimum of maintenance.
3. Require service contracts on equipment that has a potential for a safety breakdown, e.g., beverage bars that serve hot liquids.

Noise

The success of an event may be strongly affected by the comfort level (volume and clarity) at which communication can occur (announcers, lecturers). Noise should be maintained at a minimum for echo, reverberation, and background noise created by equipment humming and people making normal conversation to a 40 – 55 decibel level.

Recommendations

1. Use acoustical intervention to reduce the noise between people in different focused listening locations by adding acoustical panels to walls, having folding panels on hand to separate patrons, and having walls sound-insulated between meeting rooms.
2. Use listening systems to increase the opportunity to participate in meetings and conferences.

Passages

Typical of large function areas are the tiered aisles of auditoriums, theaters, and lecture halls. The slope of the passages should integrate the slope for accessible ramps. Passages and aisles that provide the greatest access for visual and auditory acuity are those which allow the choice of front, middle, or back row seating. Cross aisles in the middle with a minimum width of 3' and access to seating, integrate disabled persons into the normal seating, thereby removing a sense of segregation.

Recommendations

1. Even if aisle configurations accommodate most passages with ease (people and equipment), maintenance of passages is an important issue. Install more corner guards on walls and bumper pads on equipment to protect corners.
2. Aisles to event areas should be 3' wide with 6' of clearance between back row seating. Access should accommodate the passage of people in wheelchairs and equipment.

Safety

Safety and security are two design considerations which interact to improve patron experiences. For example, if events are held at night, then lighting and security are design issues. What areas need to be well lit and where should security be positioned? The point is to reduce patrons' vulnerability to injury from equipment, other patrons or passages, vehicles or criminal activity, within the event areas and in parking areas.

Recommendations

1. Control night access to buildings with locked security.
2. Provide appropriate lighting at access points.
3. Use television monitors in areas where security may be an issue.
4. Train staff in the safe evacuation of people with disabilities.
5. Keep passages cleared at all times.
6. Clearly define evacuation procedures.

7. Install fire separation areas that create refuge where events are not on ground level. These are ideal when egress is difficult due to stairs, elevators, and distances to egress points.
8. Display signals and warning systems should have information that is communicated visually and auditorily.
9. Identify hazardous areas by disability. For example, provide warnings of steps in corridors for people who are blind or have low vision.
10. Keep doors to hazardous or private areas locked.

Signage

Signage at events should guide the person through the event experience from the entrance, to reception, to focal gathering points, to the rest rooms. Graphics, together with the use of international symbols, meet the needs of both people with disabilities and patrons from all parts of the country and the world. Graphics and lettering should effectively communicate location and the purpose of the space. Very often existing signs are not visually useful for mapping one's way throughout a facility with independence.

Recommendations

1. Follow ANSI 4.28 as the minimum requirement for signage.
2. Make signage a practical guide to people, places, and things in a facility.
3. Develop a color coding system for the facility that can guide the visitors and guests, no matter what their language, age, or disability.
4. Use international symbols in addition to color coding. (See Figure 42.1.)
5. Signs should be well lit.
6. Signs should be placed perpendicular to the main line of travel if there are a minimum number of approaches.
7. Signs should be visible from four sides, not just two, if traffic approaches from four sides.
8. Signs should be in high contrast colors that allow low-vision people to read the signs from twenty feet away.
9. Door knobs, pulls, and handles should have tactile surfaces that alert people that they may be entering a hazardous area.
10. Recessed lettering on door jambs can also be used to alert people to hazardous areas.

Storage

Storage should accommodate personal belongings that make event participation easier when stored, e.g., coats and umbrellas. If storage is self-service, then accessible hooks should be installed. If there is a coat room, the counter height must accommodate disabled patrons.

Recommendations

1. Access to storage for coats must be easy to operate, in the line of vision, and not interfere with mobility.
2. Coat areas should be located with an availability of space in front of the closet of a minimum of 2-1/2'–4'. To maneuver, a minimum of 5' of turning space is ideal.
3. Storage of clothing is best facilitated with built-in low-hanging rods and shelving for hats. The pole for hanging clothes should be set at approximately 4'-6" to allow for front and side reach from

a wheelchair. To accommodate all disabilities, a split closet is recommended.

4. Coat hangers should be able to be removed and replaced.
5. The space should be lit for ease of utility.

Temperature

Temperature and air quality are critical in the event business, particularly with the advent of non-smoking areas. This impacts on the division of space because 5% of the areas in both smoking and non-smoking areas must be set aside for people with disabilities.

Recommendations

1. Vestibules that separate the outside entrance from the building interior are recommended as an insulator to maintain temperature continuity, heating, and cooling. They must provide a minimum of 5' of turning radius for wheelchairs.
2. Room temperature controls should be accessible to staff to modify temperature for people who may be temperature-sensitive.

Examples of Signage

Figure 42.1

3. Care should be taken to prevent cold drafting by heating and ventilation systems.

Windows

Windows are rare in large event areas. Access to the large environment is not important or desired by people at events that take place in these facilities.

Recommendations

If staff and patrons have access to windows, then:

1. Windows should have hardware that is easy to reach. If sills are too deep, then access is difficult.
2. Minimize the infiltration of drafts.
3. Use handles that can be operated by a person with grip and grasp difficulties. A maximum of five pounds of required force is recommended.
4. Sliding windows on good rollers are the easiest to operate.
5. Casement windows with cranks can be operated as long as the catch to the latch is easy to engage.
6. Window treatments, such as draperies and blinds, should be accessible with rods that are long enough for a person in a wheelchair to operate for full closing and opening. Drawstrings must be accessible without removing furnishings to reach them. Again, motorized controls are an expensive last resort.

Chapter Forty-Three

RESTAURANT

Restaurants, whether their seating capacity is 15 or 150, should have a commitment to designs that will enhance their business. Barrier-free access is critical to the enjoyment of one's dining experience. The restaurant represented in this case study details the factors that are critical to public accommodation of people with a range of disabling conditions.

The following is a list of key areas to be analyzed for accessibility. The hotel checklist (Figure 38.1) may also be used as an information-gathering tool for analyzing the critical sites in a restaurant.

- Parking Areas
- Entrances
- Reception
- Dining Areas
- Public Bathrooms
- Self-Service Areas
- Lounge & Bar
- Retail

Evaluation by Factors

Accessibility

Access into the restaurant should be designed to accommodate patrons of the service business. Guests should be able to arrive in cabs and cars to the main entrance of the facility. *Note: Any transportation vehicles that are made available to guests must have accommodations for people with disabilities; for example, wheelchair lifts in vans.*

Opening doors for access can be very difficult when trying to either push a person or wheel oneself. Electric-eye door openers are excellent access options, as long as signage clearly directs people to these areas.

Recommendations

1. A clear entrance into the restaurant should be evident by appearance, signage and access. Button-activated doors can be useful. Accommodations for varying weather conditions are essential. Awnings and canopies at the off-loading and entry areas are an important consideration for people with disabilities who require additional time to access buildings. Recommended minimum height for awnings to accommodate van off-loading is 9'-6".

2. A heated ramp may reduce the maintenance and increase safety for patrons, by preventing ice and snow accumulation.

3. Passenger loading and unloading zones must allow room for vehicles, patrons, and their equipment.

4. Lighting should clearly illuminate the entrance into the restaurant.

5. Flush transitions from driveways to sidewalks are recommended to aid in the transfer from the street to the walk. These transitions aid in the mobility of people and equipment when the curbs are color contrasted for visual acuity. Raised edgings at the end of a flush transition can prevent slippage for persons in wheelchairs who may be visually impaired. Definitions of edgings and transitions are important. *Note: Detectable warning strips should be provided for safety. These strips are 3' wide and 1" deep. Grooves maintain a sense of transition if laid in strips that create a raised, rounded surface (ANSI 4.7, 4.27).*

6. Layout of the access areas from entrances into the restaurant should allow for ease of passage, and maintain a short distance of travel that is clearly marked with lit signage.

7. Construction materials of outdoor walkways should allow for a non-slip surface that is smooth. Any transitions between walkways should be smooth and drainage gratings should be removed.

8. Layout of the access to entrances from parking lots should be clearly delineated with crosswalks.

9. Underground parking must be able to accommodate wheelchair vans which need a minimum clearance of 9' to enter the area and typically require extra-wide parking of 8'-6" of side clearance. 16'-6" is the minimum recommended length for vans.

10. Any steps should conform to ANSI 4.9 with exterior steps having a rise of 5-3/4"–6".

Adaptability

The areas where adaptability is critical are environments used by a variety of people with special needs — for example, people of all heights and conditions of vision, with and without the ability to use their extremities. Adaptability in the restaurant industry means acquiring the ability to service guests based on their needs. This means planning for flexibility within the environment at specific sites.

Recommendations

1. Provide flexibility to reconfigure space to add either new furnishings or equipment.

2. Create visual access within a given space, such as dining areas or the lobby. This is essential to foster communication between staff and patrons, and between people in general.

3. Provide some variety of seating options (e.g., some chairs with arms) at varying heights and with different postures. This allows support for a range of body types and conditions.

4. Designs should accommodate the staff's height and reach requirements while supporting a prevention strategy of the known occupational hazards in service facilities (back injury, carpal tunnel syndrome, injuries to hands and fingers, head and neck fatigue).

Air Quality

Air quality is a crucial element in the restaurant business, especially with the commitment to customer service, e.g., providing smoking areas and smoke-free areas within the same room. HVAC systems that have to be managed for a range of customer densities and smoking now bear a higher burden of ventilation and circulation requirements.

Recommendations

Evaluate the HVAC system's capacity to manage the categories of airborne contaminants that can occur in the restaurant environment. Expect to specify and provide access for testing for inorganic compounds such as carbon dioxide, sulfur dioxide, carbon monoxide, nitrous oxide, ammonia and radon. Consider the percent of airborne fibers from clothing and furnishings. In addition, air quality in restaurants is affected by detergents, pesticides, sterilizing agents, wall paints, carpeting and ceiling and tile systems. Kitchens present the unique problems of odors that travel through plumbing vents, air ducts, and boiler stacks. The ventilation system must be capable of managing humidity and air exchange sufficiently. Remember that in closed environments air quality systems must be specified to the full range of contaminants, not a single source or one point in time, because air quality problems are cumulative.

Comfort

The patron reception areas should be designed for ease of access to announce arrival for dining services and support a comfortable waiting area for seating. This area should allow for the integration of people with "functional limitations." It is necessary to create a reception area that is consistent with the restaurant's atmosphere, whether elegant or fast food. Comfort in a restaurant is determined by the ease with which a person requests and receives the full measure of dining services.

Recommendations

Re-zone the visitor lobby areas to accommodate the needs of guests and visitors. Evaluate guests' needs by conducting a survey using guest services staff to make data-based decisions as to how to re-configure areas for comfort (a place to rest, talk, or be distracted). Comfort is enhanced by designs with the following characteristics:

1. A sense of safety and security, e.g., ability to cognitively map a space.
2. A sense of independence and dignity, e.g., organization of space to find essential services such as public bathrooms.
3. Simplicity of design and usability, e.g., configuration of furniture to create passages.
4. Cues that support disability, e.g., signage with large lettering.
5. A sense that time is available to complete a task.

Communication

Communication for patrons should be available in the form of people and equipment. How people are greeted and seated in a restaurant is the first important interaction in service industries. Communication adaptations should be available to help people with disabilities express their enjoyment of the restaurant's atmosphere and food.

Recommendations

1. Access for communication should be face to face. For example, at the podium that the maitre d' uses to review reservations, patrons should begin to receive service that caters to their disability (for

example, discussion of seating preference to locations designed for accessibility and a determination of what menus should be made available, (e.g., Braille).

2. Communication of information should be available in several forms, e.g., verbal, maps of the restaurant (including the areas of independent access — salad bars and rest rooms), signage, and color coding of space.

3. Telephone hook-ups should be installed near seating areas for people with disabilities who may receive calls at the restaurant.

Density

The density requirement for some seating according to the Uniform Federal Standard of Accessibility is a minimum of 5%. Seating should not be in a segregated area, but along parameters to allow for a maximum of choice. Designs of dining areas should minimize travel time between areas where orders are taken or given, seating, rest rooms, vending, and self-service drink/salad bars.

Recommendations

1. Designs should accommodate supportive equipment, and accessories (lap trays on wheelchairs), and should allow enough space for staff and patrons to use the space safely.

2. The space should be flexible and adaptable in configuration to allow the integration of people with disabilities into groups of varying size (1–20 other patrons).

3. The relationship of aisles to furnishings should be set for maximum use of the space, with the minimum of obstacles and obstructions to usability. For example, aisles to seating should be 3' wide, with double the clearance (6') if parallel tables are set in a linear design. *Note: 2'-6" of clearance behind wheelchairs is advised to accommodate for positioning under tables. This clearance allows wheelchairs to negotiate out of a space by rolling backwards to reposition at the table or leave.*

Division of Space

The division of space in a restaurant should accommodate access to all services and, in addition, account for the safe evacuation of patrons in case of emergency. Therefore, designs should consider the division of space as a service and safety opportunity for both patrons and staff. The divisions of space to consider are:

- Reception of Patrons
- Self-Service Areas
- Lounge and Bars
- Entrance to the Restaurant Lobby
- Dining Area
- Rest rooms

Division of space is critical to allow patrons to dine with comfort, safety, and independence.

Recommendations

1. Entrances should be designed to accommodate independent entry into the restaurant with ease of access. Entrances should meet the minimum operating requirements (discussed previously under "Accessibility") for width, operating force (not to exceed 8 pounds of pull force which is defined by the weight of the door and the tension applied to closers). Entrances can accommodate

most disabilities with one of four choices of doors. Automatic doors operated by scanners are ideal because they eliminate the need for operating mats and guardrails (ANSI/BHMA 156.10-1985). Button-actuated door openers provide automatic access for the disabled, and standard (manual) access for others. Accessible revolving doors should include the maneuver space 1'-6" from a front approach of five feet. Manual swing doors require a latch pull on the side of the door and a maneuverability space of 90 degrees. Thresholds on all entrances should not exceed in height, and should be beveled to 1/4". Any matting at thresholds should be flush to the floor surface. For safety, mats should be slip-resistant, with a minimum coefficient of friction at .6.

2. The quality of patrons' reception sets the tone for service. The design should incorporate a reception for reservations and order taking, and should provide a place to process the check by either patrons or staff. The reception counter should be multi-leveled or equipped with a podium that allows a work height of between 2'-6" and 3'-6". This height allows for visual and reach access by patrons with disabilities.

3. Dining areas should be located centrally to all services within the restaurant with maximum visual access to the "points of interest to patrons", e.g., ocean views, entertainment, self-service centers.

4. Self-service areas are the areas of access that must be designed primarily to support limitations of reach for people with disabilities. Service areas, e.g., salad bars, buffet lines, condiment stands, drink bars and vending areas, should have a minimum aisle space of 3', with service levels for tray slides being 2' by 10" high and a maximum of 12" deep. Reach should be aided by the ability to move selections of food toward one's body to take a portion. Safety is critical at self-serve counters where hot foods and drinks may be accessed.

5. Rest rooms should be accessed within a short distance from the entrance since patrons often use the rest rooms before and after eating. The following are specific dimension requirements for bathrooms (See Chapter 11, "Accessibility" for more detail on ADA requirements.)

    - Toilets should provide a clear access to transfer (ANSI 4.16).
    - The top of the toilet should be 17–19" above the floor.
    - Grab bars and toilet paper holders should be installed for access at 24" above the floor (ANSI 4.16.4 and .6).
    - Lavatories should be designed to minimum dimensions of 2'-3" high, 2-1/2' wide, and 1'-7" deep (space provided underneath lavatory). Hot water pipes should be insulated to prevent scalding.
    - The top of the basin should be no higher than 2'-10" and the depth should be no greater than 6-1/2" (ANSI 4.19).
    - All vanity tops should be rounded on the edges with a maximum depth of 1–2".
    - Mirrors should be mounted with the lowest edge of reflectance at no higher than 3'-4" (ANSI 4.19).
    - Faucets should operate with lever handles or single lever controls (ANSI 4.19). Handspray attachments are recommended, with remote drain controls added that are level with the vanity.

- Any items for hanging should have mounts of a maximum height of 4'-6".
- Bathroom lighting should be 70 footcandles to allow sufficient light for fine hand function, shaving and makeup.
- All bathroom controls for the disabled should have offset levers and remote controls for the drains.

6. Lounges and bars should be located between the reception areas and dining areas, since people often begin and end their dining experience in these areas.

Equipment

Restaurants accommodating patrons should review equipment for vertical and horizontal reach. For example, self-contained beverage counters should allow reach with safety to access drinks. Hot soups should be in containers that do not tip. Food service equipment should include visual aids, such as mirrors, as part of food display areas to assist in viewing food. Tray slides should be provided to aid food management.

Recommendations

1. Dinnerware and utensils should be easy to use by people with limited strength, as well as grip and grasp problems. Four-pronged forks are easier to use than three-pronged ones. Larger handled accessories give a larger grip surface. Wide handles on mugs are easier than small tea cup handles. Condiments should be available on the table. Designs must accommodate the balance between providing for disabilities and ambiance.
2. Supplemental lighting may be required for guests with low vision.
3. Sports bars should accommodate for visual and auditory access of patrons by positioning equipment for optimum viewing and listening of all patrons.
4. Telephones are typically available in restaurants, and should be equipped with volume controls, flashing lights (as a visual signal), and have TDD for people who are deaf. All phones should be equipped with large push button controls to allow function with hand limitations.
5. Emergency signal systems must include visual and auditory alarms. Visual alarms should flash in conjunction with other building emergency systems. Audible alarms should be installed for visually impaired guests, as well as for patrons for whom the staff have extra concerns.

Furniture

Furnishings for restaurants (tables, chairs, and built-in seating) should accommodate people of varying configurations, heights, and postures. Accommodation should include provisions for persons with varying disabilities and the attendant equipment. The design and location of furnishings becomes critical for safety, comfort, and independence. All furnishings should be strong, sturdy and stable, since patrons may use chairs or tables to support themselves during transfers and for mobility.

Recommendations

1. Tables should provide a surface large enough to accommodate full servings with condiment access on lazy susans. Minimum recommended table service area is 3'-6" per side per square foot or for narrow/long tables, a minimum of 3' in width. Pedestal tables should have a recommended surface of 4'. Tables may have built-in bread boards to allow additional eating areas for people

in wheelchairs who need extra space. Table tops should be 10–12″ above the seat height of chairs to clear most armrests.

2. Chairs should be lightweight, padded for comfort, with armrests 7 – 8″ above the seat, inclined backs to add support, and have a recommended seat depth and width of 16″ square. The height should be low enough to facilitate transfers of people with limited mobility. A height of 15–20″ is recommended. This allows the person ease of transfer and assists when rising. Chairs with locking casters are also recommended to allow patrons the flexibility of repositioning at the table with the safety of the caster locks if necessary.

3. Chairs and tables should allow a minimum seating of four per table, and accommodate wheelchair kick plates 8″ in length. 1′-7″ of foot room is recommended per person per table with 2′-6″ of clearance side to side.

Finishes

Wall finishes should absorb noise in restaurants and add to the ambiance. Carpet should support comfortable mobility without creating resistance to equipment supports (walkers, canes, wheelchairs). Hard floor surfaces should be slip-resistant (.6 coefficient wet/dry). Ceilings should minimize reflectance.

Recommendations

1. Carpet should be low pile and high density fiber glued directly to the slab or high density pad.

2. Tile in bathrooms should have a non-skid surface to prevent slips and falls.

3. Color contrasts should differentiate between furniture and rugs, walls and ceilings.

4. Protection of finishes should include low corner guards to a height of 4′, kick plates on doors, and vinyl edgings on surface edges.

Image

Restaurants, whether elegant or fast food, are successful when they deliver a sensory experience to their patrons. The image that succeeds for people with disabilities is the ease of access, understanding of their service needs, and the expectation that as a patron, the dining experience can be managed without being conspicuous. The best imaged adaptive accommodations in restaurants are those which are consistent with the expected finishes that support all patrons comfortably and are easy to maintain by staff.

Image should include interventions and designs that exemplify the "state of the art" in reasonable accommodations. For restaurants, the ability to serve the whole age continuum, no matter what their capabilities, is the true test of "service."

Recommendations

The attributes of image to be considered are:

1. Menu designs that incorporate the needs of all people's reading capacities. For example, for patrons with vision difficulties, it is recommended that menus be printed in 14 point type that is clearly contrasted. To the extent possible, if illustrations can be incorporated without compromising image, pictures are useful.

2. If lighting is deliberately low to create atmosphere, then add task lighting to tables that need extra light without losing image.

3. Capacity-building technologies to increase patron capability and staff productivity (and self-image) while reducing Workers' Compensation claims, stress and fatigue.
4. Image is a function of a total plan of service to include all of the design factors.

Lighting

Lighting is typically an image and atmosphere design factor that often limits people with disabilities. Lighting should be available as an aid to people with low vision, particularly, if it aids their ability to communicate through speech reading, sign language, gestures, and body movements.

Lighting should be a minimum brightness of 50 footcandles in order to illuminate any menus and information that is necessary for patrons to order food.

Recommendations

1. The older the patrons of a restaurant, the higher the level of illumination should be.
2. Lighting changes throughout a restaurant should not be sudden, thereby requiring a rapid adjustment for the eyes. This is particularly important for people with mobility problems negotiating differing spaces.
3. To complement the effect of fluorescent lighting (which is limited spectrum and reduces the eye's ability to see a full spectrum of primary colors), areas around the restaurant should be evaluated. Determinations should be made to ascertain which areas should be contrasted for brightness and glare-coded to increase visual acuity.
4. Lamps at tables should have translucent shades to reduce contrast and glare and increase the uniformity of lighting. Lamps should be mounted on walls to allow adjustability and prevent accidents. The ability to increase and decrease light for eating areas is essential to accommodate vision needs. Touch controls or remote switches are recommended for lamps.
5. Provide as much natural light as possible in seating areas, while controlling glare from windows and skylights to promote visual acuity and to reduce fatigue.

Maintenance

Maintenance and food handling are always an issue for restaurants serving patrons with disabilities. The critical issue in food service is the ability to maintain equipment in food service areas so as not to interfere with the restaurant's atmosphere.

Recommendations

1. Design for maintenance, e.g., use size and layout of the dining area as an advantage to staff maintenance.
2. Select equipment supports that require a minimum of maintenance.
3. Require service contracts on equipment that has a potential for safety breakdown, e.g., beverage bars that serve hot liquids.

Noise

Restaurants are most comfortable when communication between patrons is enhanced by design. Noise is reduced in restaurants by division of space (e.g., kitchens away from dining areas, busing done after patrons leave), and acoustical interventions. For people with disabilities, the design goal should be to minimize interference, background noise and reverberation created by equipment humming and people making normal conversation to a 40 – 55 decibel level.

Recommendations

1. Use acoustical interventions such as acoustical panels added to walls, folding panels on hand to separate patrons, and sound-insulated walls between banquet rooms to reduce the noise between people and serving locations.

Passages

Passages in restaurants are access aisles that allow patrons to negotiate space between service areas and dining areas. The ease with which people can move is the criteria for passage. Passages should be designed to move people and dining services throughout the restaurant.

Recommendations

1. The aisle configurations should accommodate most passages (people and equipment) with ease. Maintenance of passages requires corner guards on walls and bumper pads on equipment to protect corners. It may be easier to modify dining carts than the walls.
2. Aisles to dining areas should be 3' wide with 6' of clearance between accessible seating. Access should accommodate the passage of people in wheelchairs and support equipment.

Safety

Safety and security are two design considerations which interact to improve patron experiences. For example, if the image of the restaurant is enhanced with plants as decoration, then, for safety reasons, overhanging plants should be trimmed to a height of 7'. Serving areas and independent serving should accommodate railings and tray guides to the needs of people with disabilities. The point is to reduce patrons' vulnerability to injury from equipment, staff, or self-service within the restaurant, and to possible crime/violence outside the restaurant.

Recommendations

1. Provide access to hot food items with attention to safety.
2. Use safety-oriented containers for hot food (e.g., pitchers with lids that lock).
3. Provide appropriate lighting at access points.
4. Use television monitors in areas where security may be an issue.
5. Train staff in the safe evacuation of people with disabilities.
6. Clear passages of any items that can be stored.
7. Clearly define evacuation procedures.
8. Provide fire separation areas that create refuge on floors where restaurants are not on ground level. These are ideal when egress is difficult due to stairs, elevators, and distances to egress points.
9. Provide display signals and warning systems with visual and audible information.
10. It is particularly important to identify hazardous areas (e.g., steps in corridors for people who are blind or who have low vision).
11. Doors to hazardous or private areas should be kept locked.

Signage

Signage in restaurants should guide the person through the dining experience from the entrance, to reception, to lounges/bars, and to rest rooms. Graphics and the use of international symbols meet the needs of people with disabilities and patrons from all parts of the country and the world. Graphics and lettering should communicate the location and purpose of a space. Very often, existing signs are not visually useful for mapping one's way throughout a facility with independence.

Recommendations

1. ANSI 4.28 is the minimum requirement for signage as a guide.
2. Signage should be a guide to people, places, and things in a facility.
3. Develop a color coding system for the restaurant that can guide the patrons no matter what their language, age, or disability.
4. Signs should use international symbols in addition to color coding (see international symbols in previous case study).
5. Orientation signs should be well lit, and emergency signs back-lit.
6. Signs should be placed perpendicular to the line of travel.
7. Signs should be visible from four sides, not two.
8. Signs should be in high contrast colors that allow low-vision people to read them from twenty feet away.
9. Door knobs, pulls, and handles should have tactile surfaces that alert people that they may be entering a hazardous area.
10. Recessed lettering on door jambs can also be used to alert people to hazardous areas.

Storage

Storage should accommodate personal belongings (e.g., coats and umbrellas) that make dining easier when stored. If storage is self-service, then accessible hooks should be installed. If there is a coat room, the counter height should accommodate all patrons.

Recommendations

1. Access to storage for coats must be easy, in the line of vision and access, and not interfere with mobility.
2. Coat areas should be located with a minimum of 2-1/2'–4' of space available in front. To maneuver, a minimum of 5' of turning space is ideal.
3. Storage of clothing is best facilitated with low-hanging rods and shelving for hats built in. The pole for hanging clothes should be set at approximately 4'-6" to allow for front and side reach from a wheelchair. To accommodate all disabilities, a split closet is again recommended.
4. Coat hangers should be removable and replaceable. The space should be lit for ease of utility.

Temperature

Temperature and air quality are critical in the restaurant business, particularly with the advent of non-smoking areas. This impacts on the division of space when setting aside 5% of the restaurant for access to people with disabilities.

Recommendations

1. Vestibules are recommended to maintain temperature continuity, heating, and cooling, and must have a minimum of 5' of turning radius to allow for wheelchair access.
2. Room temperature controls should be accessible to staff to modify temperature for people who may be temperature-sensitive.

3. Care should be taken to prevent cold drafting by heating and ventilation systems.

Windows

Windows with a view are the cornerstone of image in restaurants. Access to the large outdoor environment is important to most patrons. Large panoramic windows are ideal. If accommodating for visual access at the 3-1/2' window level, the sill must be set at 2'.

Recommendations

If staff and patrons have access to windows, then:

1. Windows should have hardware that is easy to reach. If sills are too deep, then access is difficult.
2. Minimize the infiltration of drafting at the installation.
3. Use handles that can be operated by a person with grip and grasp difficulties. *A maximum of five pounds of force is recommended.*
4. Sliding windows on good rollers are the easiest to operate.
5. Casement windows with cranks can be operated as long as the catch to the latch is easy to disengage.
6. Window treatments, such as draperies and blinds, should be accessible with rods that are long enough to operate for full closing and opening. Drawstrings that are attached to the wall must be accessible without removing furnishings to reach them. Motorized controls are, once again, an expensive last resort.

Chapter Forty-Four

SCHOOL/STUDENT

The subject of this case study is a 12-year-old female with impaired gait and reach, in remission from cancer. She attends middle school. The building has two floors, and is 10 years old.

Evaluation by Factors

Accessibility

Access to the building was up a ramp in the front of the building. For protection from the elements, the ramp was covered with an awning. Access within the building was aided by the school nurse who was available to hold the door to allow the child to enter with a walker.

Adaptability

The work station area was rearranged easily for ease of access to necessary classroom materials, with furniture placed on wheels.

Air Quality

In general: The building's HVAC system should be inspected semi-annually and cleaned. Ventilation rates should be checked to ensure compliance with the ASHRAE level of 20 cfm per person. If necessary, air distribution should be modified. The HVAC unit and filter-holding frames should be checked for air-tightness, and the filter efficiency checked against ASHRAE standards. Outside air intake locations should be reviewed to ensure adequate distance from pollutants.

A specific recommendation for the disabled student was to purchase a small portable fan to maintain optimal air circulation.

Comfort

The student's chair was adapted with pillows to provide lateral and side support. Orthotics (foot/leg supports) were prescribed to support the feet and prevent pronation.

Communication

A communication system was not necessary for this child.

Density

The class area was designed to accommodate the student's walker, which was 28 inches wide.

Division of Space

People and space were arranged for ease of access to central resources (blackboards, bookshelves, paper, etc.) and ease of access to each other for supervision, direction, and interaction.

Equipment

Sliding book shelves were mounted to the student's desk for ease of reach.

Finishes

A non-glare contrasted color work surface top of black Formica, trimmed in light oak was used.

Furnishings

An adjustable-height and tilt work station was designed and sized to accommodate school work.

Image

Available classroom furniture was adapted with lift systems and roll bars to allow this student to maintain an integrated classroom look to the extent possible.

Lighting

Overhead lighting was installed with full-spectrum fluorescence to reduce glare.

Maintenance

No maintenance was required.

Noise

Actuator (electronic lift) on the desk is limited to 45 decibels.

Passages

All passages were able to accommodate the student's walker. The bathroom door was modified with a ball bearing strip to increase ease of movement over the floor surface.

Safety

Safety was enhanced with the addition of locking casters on all rolling furniture. All floor areas were inspected for loose rugs or tiles. Handrails were installed at strategic locations to prevent falling when repositioning with the walker.

Signage

All signage in use was adequate.

Storage

A school locker was assigned which was convenient for this student. Personal items were stored in a backpack on the walker to allow for easy access all day.

Temperature

Current temperature control was adequate.

Windows

All windows were located along the outside wall and were not accessible to this student.

Additional Considerations

Due to the student's gait impairment, other students and teachers endeavored to schedule meetings either in this student's area or at the beginning or end of the day to accommodate her mobility needs.

Figure 44.1 shows the features of an accessible classroom.

Classroom with Modifications

Figure 44.1

Part Eight

ADA COMPLIANCE PRODUCT SELECTION GUIDE

Part Eight

INTRODUCTION

The Americans with Disabilities Act gives facility management, safety management and human resources professionals an opportunity to design solutions for compliance with specific ADA requirements, and to focus on an overall approach that fosters independent and dignified use of their facility. Meeting high ADA standards should not be viewed as an overhead cost, but rather as an investment in greater success and productivity for any facility, be it a school, office, restaurant, shop, library, theater or courthouse.

Section A of this Product Selection Guide is intended to provide examples of products that comply with specific elements of the ADA-AG. Section B of the guide covers products that, while not necessarily addressing specific ADA-AG requirements, enhance the productivity and quality of life of disabled people. Many of these products, such as ergonomic office furniture, also provide solutions for compliance with Title I of the ADA.

Standards for Product Evaluation

Products should be purchased that meet building codes, the ADA, and the human factors needs of people. (See Part IV for a factor-by-factor analysis) There are nine recommended standards for evaluating sales professionals and products before making purchasing decisions to meet ADA requirements. While the case example is signage, all ADA factors can be evaluated by these nine basic standards.

1. Sales professionals should have **knowledge of their product's price and performance, as well as the rules, regulations, standards and statutes at the federal, state and local levels that affect the product's use in your business.** For example, if you manage a grocery store and require accessible check-out aisles, your signage sales representative should be familiar with the check-out signage requirements:
   - A sign with the International Symbol of Accessibility should be mounted above the check-out aisle in the same location where the check-out number or type is displayed.

2. **Definitions as used in the ADA** are an important factor in a sales professional's knowledge of their products. For example, signage is required for commercial business.
   - *Commerce* is defined as travel, trade, traffic, retail, transportation or communication.

- *Public Accommodations* are operations that affect commerce as incorporated into the following 12 categories.
  a. Places of lodging
  b. Establishments serving food or drink
  c. Places of exhibition or entertainment
  d. Places of public gathering
  e. Sales or rental establishments
  f. Service establishments
  g. Stations used for specified public transportation
  h. Places of public display or collection
  i. Places of recreation
  j. Places of education
  k. Social service center establishment
- *Commercial Facilities* are facilities that are intended for nonresidential use by a private entity, and whose operations affect commerce.
- *Accessible,* as it relates to signage, refers to the accessibility of the location by disabled persons, and signs are required to locate accommodations and accessible routes.

3. All sales professionals should be able to **define and commit to delivery and installation procedures**, to ensure that **product locations and measurements** are in compliance. For example:

   Location/Illumination:
   - Areas of Rescue shall be identified by a sign which states "AREA OF RESCUE ASSISTANCE" and shall display the International Symbol of Accessibility. The sign shall be illuminated when exit sign illumination is required. Instructions on the use of the area under emergency conditions shall be posted adjoining the two-way communication system.

   Measurements:
   - Signage for room identification door numbers shall be mounted 60" from the floor to the center line of the sign on the latch side of the door. If space is not available, sign is to be mounted to the closest adjoining wall.

4. **Commitment to post-delivery evaluation of an installation** can, where practical, be an important vendor qualification. For example, the ADA often has "interactive" factors such as signs and lighting. Illumination levels on the sign's surface shall be in the 100 to 300 lux range (10 to 30 footcandles) and shall be uniform over the sign surface. Signs shall be located such that the illumination level on the surface of the sign is not significantly exceeded by the ambient light or visible bright lighting source behind or in front of the sign. The sign surface should also appear in a matte finish.

5. **Commitment to future modifications to meet changing employee needs** is also significant, as accommodations have to be made to address specific disabilities. For example, not all rest rooms may be modified at one time. However, appropriate signage must be installed to direct disabled people to the correct accessible rest room.
   - The accessible pictogram is required only when not all rest rooms in the building are accessible. Non-accessible toilet or

bathing facilities should have signage provided indicating the location of the nearest accessible toilet or bathing facility within the building.

6. **Commitment to meet the needs of your facility's changing environment.** Depending on your wall finishes and illumination, raised borders around signs containing raised characters may make them confusing to read unless the border is set far away from the characters. This is a recommendation only as it is referenced in the appendix of the ADA-AG. **Your sales professional should be familiar with all appendices and additions to the ADA-AG.**

7. Sales professionals **should be able to coordinate and understand corporate contingencies as represented by human resources, safety officers, purchasing agents and specific site supervisors.** For example:

   • Pictograms other than the accessible symbol are not required. However, pictograms are a necessity for people with learning disabilities. It is recommended that when pictograms are used, they should be accompanied by the equivalent verbal description placed directly below the pictogram. The border dimension of the pictogram shall be 6″ (152mm) minimum in height. Any descriptive or Braille translation must not be within the 6″ vertical field of the pictogram. There is no thickness requirement for pictograms.

8. Sales representatives should have **knowledge of the forms that may be required by regulatory agencies,** and how these forms are managed. It is also important that they understand the ADA from a legal perspective, such as:

   • Where signs designate permanent rooms and spaces, regulations require that signage has raised lettering, braille and pictograms (where applicable), as well as requirements for mounting in a specific location. Also, when to specify signs which provide direction to or information about functional spaces of the building. Further, they should know the regulations that require signs to comply with character proportion, height, finish and contrast rules. (Lowercase is acceptable, tactile lettering and Braille are not required.) Fire evacuation signs that direct users to the fire exit would fall into this category except that they do not have the requirement for 5/8″ minimum lettering (lettering might be smaller in this instance). A signage sales professional should also know what elements and spaces of accessible facilities (accessible by disabled persons) shall be identified by the International Symbol of Accessibility (as appropriate, such as wheelchair, TDD symbol, etc.):

     a. Parking spaces designed as reserved for individuals with disabilities.

     b. Accessible passenger loading zones.

     c. Accessible entrances when not all are accessible. (Inaccessible entrances shall have directional signage to indicate the route to the nearest accessible entrance.)

   • And finally, they should know where to specify overhead and protruding signs: (A minimum character height of 3″ is required, lowercase can be used, raised and Braille characters are not required. Overhead and right angle signs must allow a minimum clear headroom of 80″.)

9. The ability to provide **expert representation in the event of a legal challenge** is the sales professional's guarantee, in a sense, which, in the case of signage requirements, means proven compliance with the applicable laws, sections 4.30.1 through 4.30.8.

Qualifying a Product for ADA Compliance

Qualifying a product, not only for ADA compliance, but for meeting the needs of users and building codes involves eight criteria:

1. **Adaptability:** For example, in the case of signage, visible in both day and night conditions.
2. **Flexibility:** Signage on the elevator two-way communication systems: The highest operable part of the system shall be a maximum of 48" (1220mm) from the floor of the car. It shall be identified by a raised symbol and lettering and located adjacent to the device.
3. **Free from defects in design**
4. **Free from defects in manufacturing**
5. **Clear standards of use**
6. **Meets all regulatory standards and will upgrade to meet future and pending standards.** For example: Parking spaces for disabled people have a requirement for a sign with the International Symbol of Accessibility, with mounting to be seen from a driver's seat. It must be mounted high enough from the ground and located at the front of a parking space to be visible from any vehicle. Also, for wider aisles for vans, a sign is required to alert van users to the presence of a wider aisle and must be indicated by a "Van Accessible" sign. Future standards may include a requirement that signs also state, "tow away zone" or "$500.00 fine if abused."
7. **Ease of use by disabled people of any functional limitation.** To meet this goal for signage, signs should have raised and Braille characters *and* a Pictorial Symbol, though ADA does not *require* the latter. Signs should meet the following specifications.
   a. Letters and numbers shall be raised a minimum of 1/32", uppercase, sanserif or simple serif type. Raised characters shall be at least 5/8" (16mm) high, but no higher than 2" (50mm). An eggshell (matte) finish is recommended. Character proportions shall have a width to height ratio of between 3:5 and 1:1 and a stroke width to height ratio between 1:5 and 1:10 (Scott-ADA letters conform to these requirements).

      Contrast between characters and background is recommended to be at least 70%. The greatest readability is usually achieved through the use of light-colored characters or symbols on a dark background, or dark on light.
   b. Braille Characters: Must be Grade 2. Standard dimensions for literary Braille are: Dot diameter (.059"), inter-dot spacing (.090"), horizontal separation between cells (.241") and vertical separation between cells (.395"). Scott Braille conforms to these requirements.
8. **Ease of maintenance** is the final criterion in specifying ADA products. If the cost of maintenance is higher than the initial cost of the product, it is too much.

Section A

PRODUCTS FOR COMPLIANCE WITH TITLE III

Section A of the Compliance Product Selection Guide lists and describes products that meet specific requirements of the ADA Act Guidelines (Title III). Readers who have had some experience addressing ADA compliance in remodeling or new construction may be familiar with some of the items and manufacturers in this section. However, several of the products have been included because while they offer valuable, sometimes unique features and solutions, they may be less familiar, and can be difficult to locate and price without the assistance of an accessibility expert.

Hands-Free Lavatory Systems

Manufactured by:
Bradley Corporation
9101 Fountain Blvd.
Menomonee Falls, WI 53051
(414) 251-6000

Type of Products Manufactured:
Modular multiple lavatory systems

Compliance with ADA-AG:
4.19, 4.27

Bradley Express® is a complete modular lavatory system designed for high usage washrooms.

With a single specification, universally accessible "no-touch" handwashing stations can be provided for up to three users. The modular fixture installs with less than 30 connections, compared to over 90 for three conventional lavatories. Bowl design is one continuous surface with rounded corners for easy cleaning, and Bradley's Accu-Zone® electronic metering control means valves are virtually maintenance free.

Bradley's Terreon™ material, similar to natural stone, is a solid surface, not just a coating, and has the look of polished granite. Unlike natural stone, Terreon™ resists stains, burns and impact. It's repairable with everyday cleaners or fine grit abrasives.

The Express® system is equipped with Accu-Zone® infrared metering control, to provide water conservation along with universal accessibility.

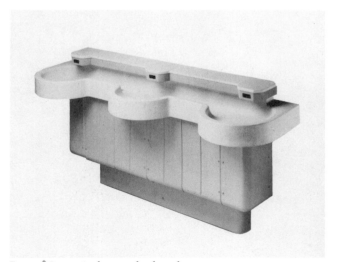

Express® Lavatories have no knobs or buttons.

Hands-Free, Sensor-Operated Faucets

Manufactured by:
Toto Kiki USA, Inc.
415 West Taft Avenue, Unit A
Orange, CA 92665
(714) 282-8686

Type of Products Manufactured:
Water-related products and equipment for residential and commercial facilities.

Compliance with ADA-AG:
4.19.5

Toto Kiki's contemporary-styled, hands-free, automatic faucets are designed for busy restrooms requiring high-end fittings. Both AC-powered (12V, DC) and battery-operated (6V, DC) configurations are available in either single hole, 4" or 8" cover plate.

The faucets utilize less than 0.25 gallons per cycle and provide several integral features for safety and durability, including: anti-scald thermal mixing chamber; waterproof electronic components; vandal-proof assembly; removable strainer; and automatic shutoff.

A self-adjusting sensor automatically sets the detection range according to conditions, preventing water from being discharged by false detection. This "smart sensor" technology eliminates installation and cycling problems.

Toto's battery-powered faucets were specially designed for retrofit applications, to provide ease of installation without the cost and downtime involved in implementing power supplies and wiring.

TOTO's Hands-Free, Sensor-Operated Faucet

Single-Handle Lavatory Faucet

Manufactured by:
Delta Faucet Company
55 East 111th Street
P.O. Box 40980
Indianapolis, IN 46280
(317) 848-1812

Type of Products Manufactured:
Residential and commercial plumbing products

Compliance with ADA-AG:
4.24.7

Delta Faucet Company's single-handle lever offers an easy grip and an on/off pattern that will be familiar to most users. Chrome and special finishes are available, all protected with an epoxy coating.

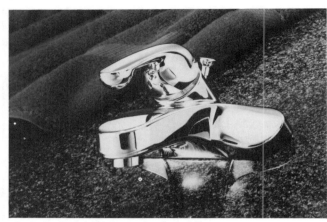

The Delta Faucet Company's Single-Handle Lavatory Faucet

Pull-Out Spray Kitchen Faucets

Manufactured by:
Delta Faucet Company
55 East 111th Street
P.O. Box 40980
Indianapolis, IN 46280
(317) 848-1812

Type of Products Manufactured:
Residential and commercial plumbing products

Compliance with ADA-AG:
4.24.7

Delta's Gourmet Pull-Out Spray™ Faucet Model #466 has a retractable 59-inch hose and is available in chrome with a white sprayhead, white and almond. Its lever handle is ADA-approved.

The restyled Waterfall™ Kitchen Faucet line, available in single-handle and widespread versions, is ADA-compliant and features an elevated spout that swings 360° to allow easy clean-ups for large pots. Its high arc is also suitable for multiple-bowl sinks.

The Delta Gourmet Pull-Out Spray™ Faucet

The Waterfall™ Kitchen Faucet

Pull-Out Spray Kitchen Faucet

Manufactured by:
Grohe America, Inc.
241 Covington Dr.
Bloomingdale, IL 60108
(800) 323-9660

Type of Products Manufactured:
Faucets and controls

Compliance with ADA-AG:
4.24.7

The EuroPlus pull-out spray kitchen faucet is ADA-compliant. Its features include a fingertip control that allows a choice between two finely-controlled water flow patterns (regular or spray).

The EuroPlus kitchen faucet line also features a long-reach 10″ cast spout model with or without side spray. Optional 10″ escutcheon and soap/lotion dispensers in matching finishes allow several alternatives for customizing the work space at the kitchen sink.

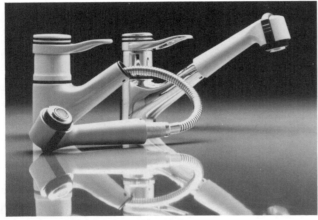

EuroPlus™ Pull-Out Spray Head Kitchen Faucets, Models 33.853-X and 33.853

Valve and Lavatory Faucet

Manufactured by:
Grohe America, Inc.
241 Covington Dr.
Bloomingdale, IL 60108
(800) 323-9660

Type of Products Manufactured:
Faucets and controls

Compliance with ADA-AG:
4.24.7

The EuroPlus lavatory faucet, a European style faucet that meets ADA requirements, is available in both cast spout and pull-out spout versions. The pull-out spout model is designed to add convenience to everyday tasks such as rinsing the sink bowl, washing hair, or bathing infants. An optional feature available with the pull-out is the EuroPlus Toothbrush Kit attachment. Using a connector on the bottom of the faucet spout, water flows through the toothbrush for dental hygiene.

EuroPlus finishes, color accents, and styling are matched in faucets and shower/tub valves.

EuroPlus Valve with EuroPlus Lavatory Faucet Models 33.683-L and 33.083-L

Accessible Showers/Baths

Manufactured by:

National Fiber Glass Products
5 Greenwood Avenue
Romeoville, IL 60441
(708) 257-3300

Type of Products Manufactured:

ADA-compliant showers and baths, designed for new construction and remodeling.

Compliance with ADA-AG:

4.20, 4.21

National Fiber Glass Products offers one-piece and multi-piece remodeling baths that are designed for luxury and safety. Each unit has a sanitary Ever-Brite™ finish and is structurally reinforced with mounting flanges, walls and floor. National products are available in colors that coordinate with those of all major plumbing manufacturers. Optional features include: custom support blocking and grab bar installation, sanitary molded folding seat with stainless steel hardware, therapeutic White Water™ Whirlpool system, enclosure bonnet, bonnet light and a chrome-plated soap dish. All of these ADA-accepted options allow products to be built to specifications.

Model No. 820F, 62″ × 35″ × 78″

Accessible Shower Stalls and Bathroom Accessories

Manufactured by:

SafeTek International, Inc.
P.O. Box 23
Melbourne, FL 32902
(407) 952-1300

Type of Products Manufactured:

Thermoplastic grab bars, folding shower and tub benches, hand-held shower heads mounted on a gliding safety bar, one-piece and knock-down accessible shower stalls, barrier-free shower bases.

Compliance with ADA-AG:

4.20, 4.21, 4.23, 4.26

SafeTek offers accessible fixtures and accessories in a range of color choices. SafeTek products are designed to withstand deterioration in a moist environment, and require low maintenance. SafeTek products meet or exceed ADA standards, as well as all commercial codes.

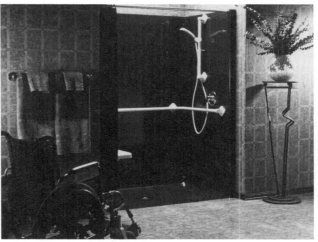

Barrier-Free Shower

Barrier-Free Shower Door

Manufactured by:
Tub-Master Corp.
413 Virginia Drive
Orlando, FL 32803-1892
(800) 327-1911

Type of Products Manufactured:
Bath and shower fixtures and accessories.

Compliance with ADA-AG:
4.21.8, 4.13, 4.13.11

Tub-Master's barrier-free shower door folds completely out of the way for easy access to the showering area. Close the doors for a watertight shower, keeping the water splash out of the rest of the bathroom. The special bottom track creates a small dam, but still allows easy rollover of wheelchairs.

This product meets or exceeds national safety standards and conforms to ADA. Panels are translucent Polystyrene that won't crack or shatter but will allow light into bathing area. The door can be fabricated to fit any opening and space.

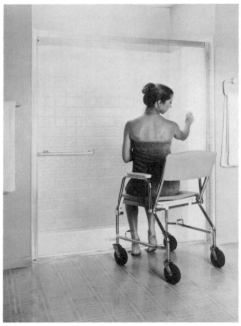

Tub-Master Barrier-Free Shower Door

Barrier-Free Shower Packages

Manufactured by:
Tub-Master Corp.
413 Virginia Drive
Orlando, FL 32803-1892
(800) 327-1911

Type of Products Manufactured:
Bath and shower fixtures and accessories.

Compliance with ADA-AG:
4.21.8, 4.13, 4.13.11

The Tub-Master barrier-free shower door, used in hospitals, nursing homes, and private residences, is now combined with a specially designed fiberglass shower base that allows easy access. Fiberglass wall surrounds are available for all sizes. The 32" × 60" model will replace a standard 5' tub.

Grab bars, fold-up shower seats and hand-held showers are available to complete the package.

The How-Handi handicapped accessible fiberglass shower base is designed to be installed on an existing floor or recessed into the floor. All units have a 1/2" high water dam at the front edge. This water dam is sloped to the inside and allows for easy wheelchair removal. The shower bases meet ADA requirements, ANSI Z124-2-1987 and HUD/FHA UM 734.

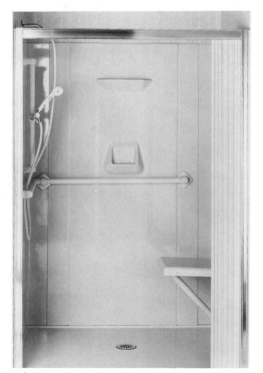

Tub-Master Barrier-Free Shower Package

Barrier-Free Washroom Planning Guide

Manufactured by:
Bobrick Washroom Equipment, Inc.
11611 Hart Street
North Hollywood, CA 91605-5882

Type of Products Manufactured:
Washroom Equipment

Compliance with ADA-AG:
Guidance for complying with 4.16 – 4.24

Bobrick, a provider of a line of washroom accessories and toilet compartments that meet the ADA-AG, has created a planning guide with the assistance of Ronald L. Mace, FAIA, president of Barrier-Free Environments, Inc.

The guide includes detailed layout designs for large and small public washrooms, with specific requirements for accessories such as soap dispensers, hand dryers, partition-mounted combination units, paper towel dispensers and waste receptacles, grab bars, toilet tissue dispensers, shower seats and toilet compartments.

Also available on request are a Wheelchair Maneuverability Drawing Template and a list of Bobrick accessories and toilet compartments that comply with ADA-AG.

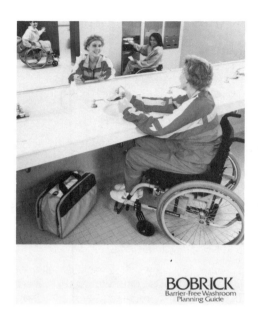

Bobrick's 20-Page Barrier-Free Washroom Planning Guide

Telecommunication Devices for the Deaf (TDD/TTY)

Manufactured by:
Compu-TTY, Inc.
3309 Winthrop
Suite 85
Fort Worth, TX 76116-5600
(817) 738-2485

Type of Products Manufactured:
Telecommunication Devices for the Deaf (TDD/TTY): printing and non-printing models; Public Pay Phone TDDs; Trident Technology Personal Communication Terminal (PCT)

Compliance with ADA-AG:
4.1.3 (17), 4.31.9

Compu-TTY, Inc. offers several low-cost, low-profile solutions to the ADA requirements. The Telecommunication Devices for the Deaf (TDD/TTY) offered by Compu-TTY range from basic, non-printing TTYs to the advanced Memory Printer MP2000D and PCT. All machines are user-friendly. Each comes with a one-year warranty and can be serviced at the company's service repair center. Available features offered throughout the product line include keyboard dialing, memory dialing, auto answer, remote message retrieval, direct connect, built-in printer, and acoustic cups which accommodate both square and round handsets to simple, two-way communication via TDD/TTY.

The Compu-TTY MP2000D offers 32K memory and multi-wide printer.

Infrared Listening System

Manufactured by:
Sennheiser Electronic Corporation
6 Vista Drive
P.O. Box 987
Old Lyme, CT 06371
(203) 434-9190

Type of Products Manufactured:
Microphones, headphones, boom sets, RF wireless, infra-red technology

Compliance with ADA-AG:
4.1.3 (19) (b), 4.33

The SI20-R and SZI20-R are medium area infrared listening system components designed to maximize flexibility and ease of installation. They provide a cost effective solution for ADA compliance for the hard-of-hearing, simultaneous translation, and other assistive listening applications.

The SZI20-R slave emitters are unobtrusive and easy to mount. Each floods an area of 750 square feet (mono mode) or 375 square feet (two channel/stereo mode) with invisible infrared light. Using the IZK20 and IZM20 clamping accessories, up to four SZI20-R's can be clustered together at a single mounting point and individually aimed to cover the listening area evenly.

This system can be used with the RI100-A and RI100-J under-the-chin receivers for mono/channel 1 operation, or the H200 under-the-chin and HDI452-P over-the-head receivers for stereo operation. The advanced electronic and ergonomic design of Sennheiser infrared receivers provides both fidelity and comfort.

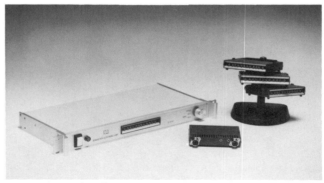

SI20R/SZI20R Infrared Listening System Components

Adapter to Convert Door Knobs to Lever Handles

Manufactured by:
Extend, Inc.
P.O. Box 864
Moorhead, MN 56560-0864
(800) 425-3837

Type of Products Manufactured:
Door hardware

Compliance with ADA-AG:
4.13.9

The Handi-Lever Slim from Extend, Inc. requires no modification to the existing door knob. It is constructed of heavy-duty cast aluminum and is available in seven sizes and eight color finishes. The Handi-Lever Slim is an inexpensive and effective way for businesses, institutions, and individuals to convert existing hardware to ADA-compliant lever handles.

The Handi-Lever Slim

Lever Adapter Kit for Doorknobs

Manufactured by:
Lindustries, Inc.
21 Shady Hill Road
Weston, MA 02193
(617) 237-8177

Type of Product Manufactured:
Lever adapters for doorknobs.

Compliance with ADA-AG:
4.13.9

Lindustries, Inc.'s Leveron fits all standard doorknobs and converts them to lever handles. Leveron offers an inexpensive alternative to replacing existing locksets. No rekeying or replacement of existing locksets is necessary. Installment is simple and requires no tools other than the custom wrench included with every Leveron. One size fits all standard doorknobs, right or left hand doors, and can be used outside as well as in.

The lever handle eliminates the need for grasping or turning doorknobs for people with arthritis or other disabilities. Unlike standard lever locksets, the Leveron may be positioned at any angle the user prefers.

Made of high performance polymer in the U.S., it withstands the impact of heavy traffic and will not rust or corrode in salt air like metal levers. Because it is a polymer, it is electric shock-resistant and won't freeze or heat up in any climate. Leveron comes in six colors including Hi-Glow which glows in the dark.

Lindustries, Inc. states that Leveron has been approved by the Veterans Administration and the Arthritis Foundation and complies with ANSI standards. It has been used in housing under FHAA and UFAS constraints.

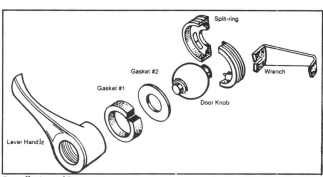

Installation of Leveron

Cylindrical Lever Lockset

Manufactured by:
Corbin Russwin Architectural Hardware
225 Episcopal Road
Berlin, CT 06037
(203) 225-7411

Type of Products Manufactured:
Locksets, exit devices, door closers, and key systems.

Compliance with ADA-AG:
4.13.9

Corbin Russwin's economy-priced Grade 2 CL3800 Series standard duty lever lockset is designed to meet operational, security and finish standards as well as code requirements with full compliance with ANSI A117.1, Accessibility for the Physically Handicapped. Available in a wide range of architectural finishes, it is designed for new or retrofit light commercial and heavy duty residential applications.

Solid levers are standard on the CL3800 Series, with no plastic appliques riveted to the lever. Independent return springs prevent lever sag and an interlocking tubular chassis and latch bolt design provides alignment for strength, durability, and smooth operation.

The CL3800 Series is compatible with existing Corbin Russwin 6 pin key systems. In addition, several options are available, including a high security cylinder, construction master keying, visual key control, Corbin Russwin interchangeable core, and competitive cylinder compatibility. The CL3800 is available through authorized Corbin Russwin distributors nationwide.

Corbin Russwin Architectural Hardware is a full line supplier of locksets, exit devices, door closers, and key systems.

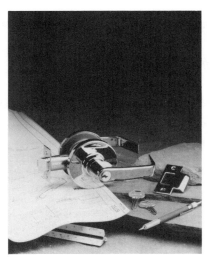

The CL3800 Series

Accessible Lockset

Manufactured by:
Yale Security Inc.
P.O. Box 25288
Charlotte, NC 28229-8010
(800) 438-1951

Type of Products Manufactured:
Accessible locksets.

Compliance with ADA-AG:
4.13.9

Yale Security's 5400LN Heavy Duty Cylindrical Key-In-Lever lockset provides ease of accessibility for handicapped persons. All three available lever designs are easy to grip and depress for entry.

The 5400LN lockset is designed for industrial, commercial, and institutional use and features rugged construction with independent lever return springs to prevent lever sag. The 5400LN meets accessibility guidelines of the ADA, the Uniform Federal Accessibilities Standards, and ANSI 117.1.

All 5400LN locksets are uniform in size, to simplify architectural specifications and installation procedures. The 5400LN is self-aligning and may be used to retrofit existing bored locksets with a 2-3/4" backset.

All three lever designs accept a standard 6 or 7-pin 1802 cylinder, and may be specified to accept the Yale 1210 6-pin or 1220 7-pin interchangeable core cylinder. The 5400 LN Series is available for use with Schlage cylinders or Best interchangeable core cylinders.

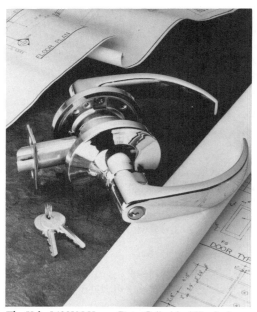

The Yale 5400LN Heavy Duty Cylindrical Key-In-Lever Lockset

Mortise Lock Retrofit Kit

Manufactured by:
Yale Security Inc.
P.O. Box 25288
Charlotte, NC 28229-8010
(800) 438-1951

Type of Products Manufactured:
Mortise lock retrofit kits

Compliance with ADA-AG:
4.13.9

The Yale 87FL Mortise Lock Retrofit Kit contains all internal components necessary to convert Yale 8700/8600/4600 Series mechanical, electrified, and electronic mortise locks from knob trim to lever trim. The kit provides an inexpensive method of conversion to meet requirements of the ADA without replacing the entire lock.

The kit may be used with any of Yale's lever handle sets. Existing roses or escutcheon plates need not be replaced. Complete illustrated instructions are included with the kit. The 87FL Kit is U.L. approved; locks converted according to the instructions will maintain U.L. listing.

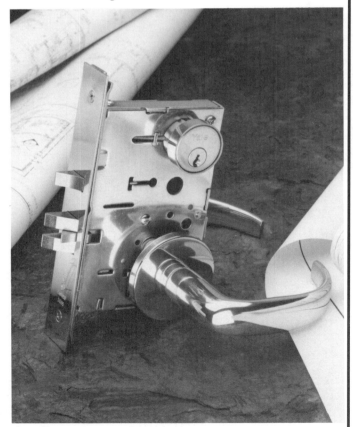

The Yale 87FL Mortise Lock Retrofit Kit

Commercial Hinges and Hardware

Manufactured by:
Hager Hinge Company
139 Victor Street
St. Louis, MO 63104
(800) 325-9995

Type of Products Manufactured:
Commercial grade hinges, Roton continuous geared hinges, trim and auxiliary hardware, thresholds and weatherstripping for use in general commercial construction projects.

Compliance with ADA-AG:
Assists with compliance with 4.13

Hager's commercial hinges will aid in the accessibility of all personnel using a facility, no matter what the requirements. Full Mortise type hinges with wide throw or swing-clear designs are available in a variety of weights and styles. These hinges swing the door completely out of the opening, in some cases providing the needed extra width to meet ADA door width requirements without having to widen the doorway.

The Roton Continuous geared hinges prevent the uneven wear that results from high-traffic, heavy doors by distributing the weight of the door over the full length of the hinge. The continuous gear eliminates stress points and allows the door to open a full 180° in most applications.

Hager manufactures a full line of thresholds: saddle, half-saddle, exit device type, interlocking, and abrasive safety tread thresholds, all of which can improve accessibility to various facilities.

Hager also manufactures a full line of trim and auxiliary hardware which includes cast door pulls, push plates, bar units, door edgings, corner guards, door protection plates, and wall stops to help bring doors into full compliance with the ADA-AG.

Hager Swing-Clear Hinges

Door Closer

Manufactured by:
Yale Security, Inc.
P.O. Box 25288
Charlotte, NC 28229-8010
(800) 438-1951

Type of Products Manufactured:
Door closers

Compliance with ADA-AG:
4.13.11

The 400/4400 Series Door Closers feature backcheck cushioning and backcheck positioning in the door's opening cycle, and closing and latch speed control in the door's closing cycle. In addition, they feature spring power adjustment to permit the closer's power to be fine tuned to each door, frame, and environmental condition.

4400BF (barrier-free) series closers are adjustable in a 1–4 size range. They are lighter powered than the 4400 Series, with reduced door opening resistance to comply with ADA standards.

The Yale 4400BF and 4420BF Series door closers are designed to comply with requirements of the ADA and ANSI A117.1. They may be installed regular arm, top jamb, or parallel arm.

The Yale 4400 Series Door Closer

Automatic Door Operator

Manufactured by:
Dor-O-Matic
7350 West Wilson Ave.
Hardwood Heights, IL 60656
(708) 867-7400

Type of Product Manufactured:
Low energy door operators for handicapped access

Compliance with ADA-AG:
4.13

The Senior-Swing™ handicap access door operator meets ADA requirements for providing equal access for people with disabilities at exterior and interior entryways. Senior-Swing is Dor-O-Matic's versatile, heavy duty, two-in-one door operator with smooth electro-mechanical operation. It also features advanced microprocessor controls. The handicap access door operator opens the door automatically for the disabled, and can be used in its manual mode for other traffic. Senior-Swing is concealed overhead or surface applied. Meets ANSI/BHMA Standard A156.19, and meets UL requirements.

Dor-O-Matic Handicap Access Door Operator

Automatic Door Operator

Manufactured by:
The Dorma Group
Dorma Drive
Reamstown, PA 17567
(800) 523-8483

Type of Products Manufactured:
Surface and concealed door closers, door pivots and fire/life safety products.

Compliance with ADA-AG:
4.13.10, 4.13.11, 4.13.12

The Dorma ED-800, a surface closer-based, low-energy power operator, precisely senses the door environment and responds appropriately. Both ADA- and NFPA 80-compliant, it fulfills the universal need for constant, reliable control of normally closed doors, and the need to power them open for disabled people.

The ED-800 design can be configured for left or right hand doors, push-side or pull-side mount, power-assist or low-energy operation.

In its standard mode of operation, the ED-800 has all the features of an ANSI/BHMA Grade 1 door closer. When used as a low-energy power-open operator, ED-800 will open the door with a force than never exceeds 15 lbs. When configured as a power assist unit, ED-800 allows the door to be opened by lightly pushing on it with a force of approximately 1.5 lbs.

An optional "push and go" mode is also available for special situations in which every pedestrian is physically challenged. In this mode, a slight movement of the door itself triggers the power-opening cycle.

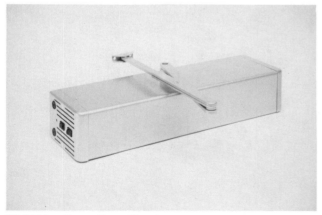

ED-800 Low Energy Power Operator

Automatic Door Operators

Manufactured by:
Horton Automatics
A Division of Overhead Door Corp.
4242 Baldwin Blvd.
Corpus Christi, TX 78405-3399
(800) 531-3111

Type of Products Manufactured:
Automatic swinging, sliding, bifolding, and revolving doors

Compliance with ADA-AG:
4.13.12

The Series 7000 and Series 4000 LE are low-powered, slow-opening operators for barrier-free door openings. They are designed for ease of installation on existing doors, and require no structural changes. The slow speed eliminates the need for guide rails and floor switch mats. The operators comply with ANSI A117 and A156.19 standards. A pushbutton switch opens the door, which can also be used manually. A wireless remote control switch is also available.

The Series 4000 heavy-duty operator is activated by motion detectors for fast traffic and the high cycle usually found in supermarkets, department stores, post offices and hospitals. Guide rails are a requirement for this operator. Complies with ANSI A156.10 when installed and adjusted properly.

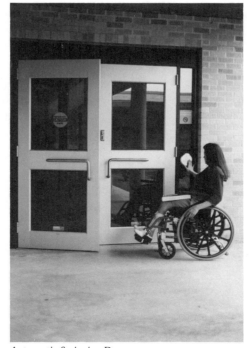

Automatic Swinging Doors

Automatic Revolving Doors

Manufactured by:

Horton Automatics
A Division of Overhead Door Corp.
4242 Baldwin Blvd.
Corpus Christi, TX 78405-3399
(800) 531-3111

Type of Products Manufactured:

Automatic swinging, sliding, bifolding, and revolving doors

Compliance with ADA-AG:

4.13.2

The 20 foot wide Grand™ II automatic revolving door has an opening large enough for wheelchairs, up to four pedestrians to walk through side-by-side, and for shopping carts, luggage carts, and even stretchers.

This door allows businesses the climate-control "always open/always closed" feature that only revolving doors offer. With three wings, the door is activated by motion detectors that detect pedestrians from four to 10 feet in front of the door opening. The door can also be set for continuous rotation. To accommodate slow-moving pedestrians or persons pushing large carts, gurneys or other hard to maneuver items, the Grand™ II has four push buttons that slow the door. After one revolution at the slower speed, the door automatically returns to three RPM.

Safety features include StopGuard™, a safety sensing system that electronically slows the door when it detects an object 18 – 24" from the wing and turns off the operator when an object is 6 – 10" from the wing, and ToeGuard™, a cushioned edge that minimizes potential foot contact. Wings fold toward the core for emergency egress.

Automatic Grand™ II Revolving Door

Automatic Sliding Doors

Manufactured by:

Horton Automatics
A Division of Overhead Door Corp.
4242 Baldwin Blvd.
Corpus Christi, TX 78405-3399
(800) 531-3111

Type of Products Manufactured:

Automatic swinging, sliding, bifolding, and revolving doors

Compliance with ADA-AG:

4.13.12

The sliding door package provides for a barrier-free entrance. This model is made to interface with storefront and curtain-wall construction. The sliding doors open automatically and are designed to swing out in case of emergency.

These doors offer adjustable astragal and full-nose weatherstripping. Double mohair weatherstripping is used around the perimeter of the door. For seasonal adjustments, a switch is available to limit the opening size. A spring keeps the swing panel closed.

UL-listed sliding panels with emergency breakout have a thumb turn lock inside and standard key cylinders outside. Biparting sliding panels with emergency breakout panels are provided with a two-point deadlock hook bolt for panel and a threshold drop bolt.

Automatic Sliding Doors

Automatic Swing-Door Operator

Manufactured by:
Gyro Tech
S82 W18717 Gemini Drive
Muskego, WI 53150
(414) 679-0045

Type of Products Manufactured:
Automatic swing-door operators for people unable
to operate manual doors.

Compliance with ADA-AG:
4.13.12

The System 710 was designed for low-maintenance operation. At
36″ it is compact, allowing for easy surface mounting to existing
doors. The system is built with solid-state electronic controls.

The System 710 operates in both automatic and manual modes.
It has a 2–60 second hold-open range for an adjustable safe-passage
time, an automatic "recycle" feature to safely stop, then close
the door if an obstruction is encountered, and a "push 'n' go" feature
to automatically open the door when activated by the pedestrian.
It also features an easy manual mode operation with door closer

in the event of a power failure, and adjustable closing speeds for
safety and energy savings.

The door closes slowly by means of spring energy, and closing
force is controlled by a manual closer independent of the motor
and electric control. The complete automatic door cycle is 8–20
seconds. Closing speed is fully adjustable. Manual door operation
requires less than 12 pounds of force applied to the door stile.

The GT System 710 Gemini by Gyro Tech

Free Guide for ADA Evaluation of Elevators

Manufactured by:
Dover Elevator Systems, Inc.
P.O. Box 2177
Memphis, TN 38101
(601) 393-2110

Type of Product Manufactured:
Free guide for ADA evaluation of elevators.

Compliance with ADA-AG:
Provides guidance for compliance with 4.10.

A free guide from Dover Elevators provides a detailed summary of ADA guidelines for elevators. The handbook covers the 12 basic elevator components, including automatic operation, hall call buttons, hall lanterns, Braille jamb pads, door reopening devices, door/signal timing, elevator floor plan, inside car illumination, car controls, car position indicator, and emergency communication.

It includes a checklist for evaluating elevators.

Dover representatives will answer questions about the evaluation and help accomplish an upgrade, providing suggestions for appropriate actions available to you if you are not in compliance.

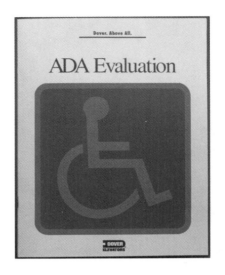

Dover ADA Elevator Evaluation Guide.

Elevator Compliance Brochure

Manufactured by:
Montgomery KONE, Inc.
One Montgomery Court
Moline, IL 61265
(309) 764-6771

Type of Products Manufactured:
Elevators – modernization, service

Compliance with ADA-AG:
Offers guidance for compliance with 4.10

This brochure offers guidelines to assist in reviewing existing equipment for compliance with the ADA. It addresses buildings which require elevators, specific regulations, and offers guidance on how to obtain professional, expert assistance. This brochure also contains an easy-to-follow ADA audit form to help determine equipment compliance.

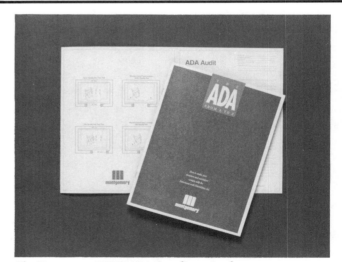

The Montgomery KONE ADA Compliance Brochure

Elevator Upgrades

Manufactured by:
Schindler Elevator Corporation
20 Whippany Road
P.O. Box 1935
Morristown, NJ 07962-1935
(201) 984-9500

Type of Products Manufactured:
Elevator accessibility improvements including lowered pushbuttons, Braille plates, audible signals and announcements, communications systems and door edge guards.

Compliance with ADA-AG:
4.10

Schindler offers upgrades to improve accessibility of existing elevator systems. The GT fixture line features elongated covers for corridor pushbuttons (shown below), which can introduce lowered buttons at ADAAG-required height while concealing old wall cutouts without cutting or patching. Designs fit various architectural styles. Braille number plates can be installed adjacent to car buttons and on door jambs.

Audible signal systems provide floor-passing chimes or audible announcements. Other systems activate hall lantern chimes with ADAAG-required "one ring up, two rings down" tones.

Communications systems provide the preferred hands-free operation, and can be programmed to communicate with the emergency control center.

Door edge systems use dozens of invisible light beams to detect persons or objects in the door path, and can reverse closing doors without physical contact.

For a free elevator upgrade booklet with checklist, write to "ADA Handbook, ML-255" at the above address.

With GT fixtures Schindler can introduce lowered buttons while avoiding costly rewiring or wall refinishing.

Hydraulic and Cable Drum Elevators

Manufactured by:
Access Industries, Inc.
Accessibility Products
4001 East 138th Street
Grandview, MO 64030-2840
(800) 925-3100

Type of Products Manufactured:
Elevators, inclined platform lifts

Compliance with ADA-AG:
4.11

The Flexi-Lift® is a 2:1 roped hydraulic elevator that may be equipped with fully automatic doors to provide unassisted access for the disabled. It is ideal for public buildings where space and cost constraints are an issue. The Flexi-Lift® is designed for easy, cost-efficient installation in retrofit applications. Travel is limited to 5 floors. Rated load capacity is 1,400 lbs. Standard car size is 42" by 60". Options are available.

The Classique® is a winding cable drum drive elevator that is commonly found in churches, lodges, and other public facilities where usage is limited and local codes permit its installation. Travel is limited to 6 floors. Rated load capacity is 750 lbs. Standard car size is 36" by 48". Options are available.

Classique® Elevator

Wheelchair Lifts

Manufactured by:
Access Industries, Inc.
Accessibility Products
4001 East 138th Street
Grandview, MO 64030-2840
(800) 925-3100

Type of Products Manufactured:
Vertical platform lifts, inclined platform lifts and elevators

Compliance with ADA-AG:
4.11

Vertical Platform Lifts: Porch-Lift® and VPL® Series 2000 vertical platform lifts install adjacent to a landing and can carry a person in a wheelchair from one level to another. These lifts may be installed with or without a hoistway. Enclosed models come with a modular hoistway comprised of a metal frame and clear acrylic panels. A portable model is available.

For commercial or residential, indoor or outdoor applications, vertical platform lifts are an excellent alternative to ramps and elevators. Eight different models and an array of options make these vertical platform lifts a flexible and cost/space efficient means of providing access to disabled people.

Inclined Platform Lifts: Carrier-Lift® inclined platform lifts can transport a person in a wheelchair, or a seated person, up and down curved or straight stairways with multiple landings. The lift runs on custom-designed rails mounted on the inside wall, and can accommodate 180° turns. A power system folds the platform for compact storage at the top and bottom landings. The passenger can operate the lift using the operating panel or pendant controls.

Porch-Lift® Vertical Platform Lift

Portable Wheelchair Lift

Manufactured by:
Ascension, L.C.
P.O. Box 40020
Tucson, AZ 85717-0020
(800) 459-0400

Type of Products Manufactured:
A portable lifting device which provides access to stages or risers for individuals with disabilities.

Compliance with ADA-AG:
4.11

The SPECT-A-LIFT® Model SLA-2050 complies with all applicable requirements of the ADA. It is suitable for auditoriums, arenas, schools, churches, courtrooms, and meeting and banquet rooms in hotels and convention centers.

Requiring 11 feet of linear space, the SPECT-A-LIFT replaces up to 55 feet of linear ramp, saving the cost of a ramp and the space it takes up, and the repeated labor cost of installing and removing the ramp.

When not in use, the SPECT-A-LIFT can be stored in a space 4 feet wide by 5 feet long. It can be moved by one person (rolled on its built-in casters), or transported by forklift.

The SPECT-A-LIFT can lift up to 650 pounds to a maximum height of 50 inches. A stage sensor box automatically stops the car at any stage level and a dockplate spans the gap between the car and the stage.

Safety features include a toe guard, gate interlock, and a safety skirting. SPECT-A-LIFT operates on 110-volt power and draws 9 amps.

A free 8-minute demonstration video is available.

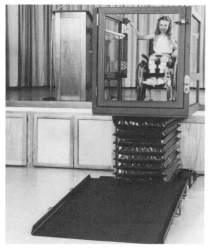

SPECT-A-LIFT® Model SLA-2050

Wheelchair Lift, Stair Climb

Manufactured by:
The Flinchbaugh Co., Inc.
390 Eberts Lane
York, PA 17403-0330
(800) 326-2418

Type of Products Manufactured:
Wheelchair Lifts, Stair Climbs

Compliance with ADA-AG:
4.11.2

The Butler Wheelchair Lift was designed to accommodate a narrower than average width stairway, to meet aesthetic needs, and to simplify installation. It is compact, smooth operating, and has a range of built-in safeties. A variety of accessories are available to meet the requirements and configurations of a home or public building.

The Butler Stairclimb fits any straight stairway up to 19 feet in length, with the track supplied. This standard model of stair climb is available from stock and does not have to be ordered to size.

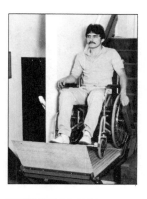

Flinchbaugh's Butler™ Wheelchair Lift

Flinchbaugh's Butler™ Imperial Stairclimb

Platform Wheelchair Lift

Manufactured by:
Garaventa (Canada) Ltd.
7505 - 134A Street,
Surrey, BC V3W 7B3
or
P.O. Box 1769
Blaine, WA 98231-1769
(800) 663-6556

Type of Products Manufactured:
Platform (wheelchair) lifts and other stairway access and egress products for people with disabilities. Permanent and portable devices available.

Compliance with ADA-AG:
3.5, 4.11

The Garaventa Stair-Lift is a wheelchair platform lift that travels along straight or turning stairways, providing access to multi-story buildings, indoors or outdoors. The platform is supported by two smooth tubes that are mounted to the central core or the outside wall of a stairway. When not in use, the platform folds and can be stored off the stairway, out of the way.

Unlike an elevator or vertical platform lift, the Garaventa Stair-Lift does not require much space or the construction of a hoistway. It can also be installed in a stairway in as little as nine weeks.

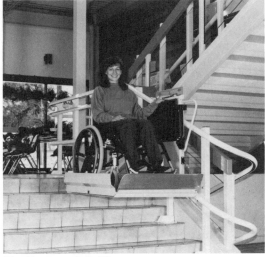

The Garaventa Stair-Lift

Mobile Modular Furniture

Manufactured by:
Anthro Corporation
10450 SW Manhasset Dr.
Tualatin, OR 97062
(800) 325-3841

Type of Products Manufactured:
Mobile modular furniture

Compliance with ADA-AG:
4.32.3, 4.32.4

The mobile, adjustable AdjustaCart is comfortable to use, especially for those who work in both a standing and a seated position.

With a squeeze of the control pad, the front surface can be positioned anywhere within a 12.75″ travel range. When the control pad is released, the system locks in place. The surface can also be tilted as far as 9 degrees toward the user and 15 degrees away.

The AdjustaCart is available in 2 widths (36″ wide and 48″ wide) and three colors (black, bone, and light grey). And like all AnthroCarts, over 50 accessories can be added. Call for our free Anthro catalog.

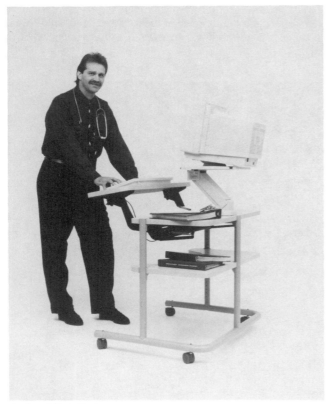

Anthro AdjustaCart

Adjustable Work Surfaces

Manufactured by:
Flex-Y-Plan Industries, Inc.
6960 West Ridge Road
P.O. Box CC
Fairview, PA 16415-0829
(800) 458-0552

Type of Products Manufactured:
Adjustable work surfaces

Compliance with ADA-AG:
4.32.3, 4.32.4

The Versa Height Adjustable Worksurface allows ample width and clearance under the work surface to accommodate wheelchair access, and it adjusts within a 25″ travel range. A unique spring-assist mechanism allows fingertip height control without difficult crank mechanisms, sensitive pneumatic cylinders, or costly electrical controls. Flex-Y-Plan offers an extensive 10-year warranty. Whether standing or seated on a drafting stool, in a task chair or in a wheelchair, the Adjusta Surface conforms to the individual user. Call for a free brochure and specification sheet.

The Versa Height Adjustable Worksurface

Adjustable Height Work Surfaces

Manufactured by:

Haworth, Inc.
One Haworth Center
Holland, MI 49423-9576
(800) 344-2600

Type of Products Manufactured:

Office furniture including panel and beam systems, link desks, wood and steel casegoods and storage files, tables, seating, ergonomic accessories.

Compliance with ADA-AG:

4.32.3, 4.32.4

The Tango Desking System can be adjusted in height at installation or by the user to accommodate wheelchairs, variously sized people, and alternative work styles. The hand crank is located in the work surface for comfortable access and minimal intrusion into the work space.

The Tango System also features a pedestal with loop pulls, allowing easy access to storage for those with limited motion. Pedestals can be attached to maximize clear toe space and improve worker mobility. The overhead storage unit is height-adjustable to accommodate reach ranges. Haworth also offers adjustable height tables and work surfaces which can be adjusted at installation or by the user.

Haworth provides a brochure, *The ADA and the Workplace,* and an Office Ergonomics Disk (an IBM-compatible computer disk that links ADA legislation to office design).

The Tango Desking System

Handrails

Manufactured by:

The C/S Group
Box 380, Route 405
Muncy, PA 17756
(800) 233-8493

Type of Products Manufactured:
Handrails and handrail/crash rails

Compliance with ADA-AG:
4.26

Acrovyn® Handrails provide a safe, sure grip and conform to the ADA, ANSI, OSHA and national building codes. All Acrovyn products are U.L.® Classified and Labeled, Class I Fire Rated.

Acrovyn's ergonomically styled railings include three profiles: Models HR-8C, HRB-10C and HRB-16C. By dividing the railing's height into individual sections, the new designs are intended to provide a sleek appearance and are available in up to five different color options in one railing. Model HR-12C is a dual rail system which has been re-designed specifically for children, geriatrics, and wheelchair-bound patient areas. All Acrovyn Handrails employ a unique bumper action to cushion vehicular traffic impacts.

Also available is the Renaissance Rail Collection™, a group of wood and wood/Acrovyn Handrails and Crash Rails. The Renaissance Collection allows all components to be easily removed for repair or refinishing without having to remove the entire rail assembly from the wall.

Acrovyn HRB-10C Handrail

Modular Ramp Systems

Manufactured by:
AlumiRamp, Inc.
90 Taylor Street
Quincy, MI 49082
(800) 800-3864

Type of Products Manufactured:
Modular ramp systems

Compliance with ADA-AG:
4.8

Modular Ramp System

AlumiRamp has designed a ramping system that offers versatility in both straight ramps and ramp systems with turn platforms. This allows customization of a system to fit many applications.

Modular ramp systems offered by AlumiRamp have the following features: anodized welded aluminum construction; extruded skid-resistant surface; black finish; modular design that provides the ability to change or relocate the system; quick installations; and versatility in possible designs.

Audible/Visible Alarm Systems

Manufactured by:
Cerberus Pyrotronics
8 Ridgedale Avenue
Cedar Knolls, NJ 07927
(201) 267-1300

Types of Products Manufactured:
Strobes and audible/visible combination signals such as electronic mini-horns, multitone signals, chimes and voice evacuation speakers.

Compliance with ADA-AG:
2.2, 4.28

Cerberus Pyrotronics provides a complete line of strobe and audible/visible combination signals consisting of high output electronic mini-horns, versatile multitone signals and chimes, and voice evacuation speakers.

These strobe products, when properly specified and installed in accordance with NFPA/ANSI standards, can provide the Equivalent Facilitation outlined under ADA-AG Gen. Section 2.2 by meeting or exceeding the illumination of 75 Candela at 50 feet.

Each strobe product is made with a durable Lexan lens and housing for extra protection and increased service. In addition, each strobe series offers a convenient strobe/plate retrofit assembly for upgrading existing signaling devices to meet the latest visible signaling requirements.

Cerberus Pyrotronics MT Multitone Strobe Series offers a choice of eight nationally and internationally recognized alerting sounds.

Audible and Visual Fire Alarms

Manufactured by:
Gentex Corp
10985 Chicago Drive
Zeeland, MI 49464
(800) 436-8391

Type of Products Manufactured:
Audible and Visual Fire Alarm Products

Compliance with ADA-AG:
4.28.3

The Gentex GXS 1575 complies with 4.28.3 visual alarms by offering xenon strobe light at a 75 candela output, minimum 1 Hz flash rate regardless of voltage and clear lens. Available with a beige or fire alarm red faceplate. Gentex Corporation also manufactures audible and visual alarms and smoke detectors/visual alarms for the hearing impaired.

The Gentex GXS 1575

Raised Character and Braille Signage

Manufactured by:
Advance Corporation/Braille-Tac™ Div.
327 E. York Ave.
St. Paul, MN 55101
(800) 328-9451

Type of Products Manufactured:
1. Chemically etched, magnesium metal, ADA-compliant, Braille and tactile signage.
2. Injection molded plastic, ADA-compliant, Braille and tactile signage.

Compliance with ADA-AG:
4.30

Braille-Tac™ Chemcast™ signs are durable, one-piece magnesium signs in which all components (graphics, raised characters, and Braille dots) are integral to the sign itself. The baked acrylic polyurethane finish has been tested for durability in an accelerated weathering test and retains its color and gloss in accordance with ASTM D523 and ASTM D224. Chemcast™ signs are graffiti remover resistant and have been tested according to the ASTM 4752 Solvent Resist Test.

Chemcast™ signs are available in varying thicknesses and can be etched, machined, or shaped. They can be decorated with any of 22 standard colors or can be custom matched.

Injection molded plastic signs are economical stock signs. Pictograms, pictograms with copy, and copy signs have been designed and molded to assist in compliance efforts. Injection molded plastic signs are an alternative for all facilities that require ADA-compliant, generic signage.

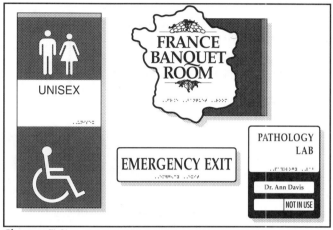

Chemcast™ Signs

ADA-Compliant Signage

Manufactured by:
APCO
388 Grant Street, SE
Atlanta, GA 30312
(404) 688-9000

Type of Products Manufactured:
Braille and raised character signage

Compliance with ADA-AG:
4.30

APCO offers a broad range of sign products to make facilities accessible to the visually impaired. In their ADA Process 1 feature (shown here) the background of thin photosensitive plastic is etched away, leaving raised characters and braille. The tactile plastic is then laminated to a rigid plastic backplate or standard molded insert for stability.

ADA Process 2 features braille which is embossed from the back of a scuff-resistant plastic, with a background color applied beneath. Printed graphics may also be applied. The plastic is then laminated to a rigid acrylic backplate or standard molded insert. Individual dimensional characters are applied to the face.

Metal Etch™ is a durable, vandal-resistant ADA sign, suitable for interior and exterior applications.

APCO's ADA sign products are available in a variety of colors, and graphics, and feature the Grade 2 braille characters and 1/32-inch raised letters required by the ADA.

IM System® Sign with ADA Process 1 feature.

ADA Signage

Manufactured by:

Garnett/AccuBraille
30 Cleveland Street
San Francisco, CA 94103
(415) 863-8450

Type of Products Manufactured:

High end modular ADA signage for facilities that require an architectural presentation of building graphics and directionals.

Compliance with ADA-AG:

4.1, 4.30.1, 4.30.4, 4.30.5, 4.30.6

Garnett/AccuBraille manufactures sign products using materials such as brass, aluminum, and Plexiglas in a wide variety of architectural finishes. Three product lines are designed to complement existing sign packages. Garnett/AccuBraille's modular signs are the result of nearly 50 years in the sign business, and 6 years of manufacturing braille and raised letter signage.

Garnett/AccuBraille ADA Signage

Modular, Changeable Signage

Manufactured by:

Innerface Architectural Signage Inc.
5320 Webb Parkway
Lilburn, GA 30247
(800) 445-4796

Type of Products Manufactured:

Modular, changeable signage

Compliance with ADA-AG:

4.30

INNERFACE, a producer of architectural signage and wayfinding for 24 years, provides modular, changeable interior and exterior signage. The company also offers a professional signage planning service which includes on-site studies, wayfinding and ADA signage planning.

As with all INNERFACE signage, the Adapt signage system is unconditionally guaranteed. Call for a free brochure, video, or to contact a local representative.

INNERFACE Architectural Signage

Interior Sign Systems

Manufactured by:

Kroy Sign Systems
14555 North Hayden Road
Scottsdale, AZ 85260
(800) 733-5769

Type of Products Manufactured:
Comprehensive interior sign systems; employee, room and departmental identification; regulatory signs, overheads; directionals; non-illuminated and illuminated directories. Full sign design and ADA-compliant programming service.

Compliance with ADA-AG:
4.30, 4.30.1, 4.30.1.2, 4.30.3, 4.30.4 – 4.30.8, 4.1.2 (7) (d), 4.1.3 (8) (d), 4.1.6 (1) (h), 4.3.11

Kroy offers a full range of standard and custom-built products that combine ADA code tactile letters, Grade 2 Braille, pictograms and contrasting colors to suit a facility's unique requirements. An innovator of in-house updateable signs, Kroy Sign Systems communicate both image and function in design and crafting.

Find out more about ADA signage regulations by calling for Kroy's free ADA Signage Information Booklet™.

Kroy Sign System's ADA Signage

Signage, Braille and Raised Letters

Manufactured by:

Lettering Specialists, Inc.
P.O. Box 3410
8020 N. Lawndale Ave.
Skokie, IL 60076
(708) 674-3414

Type of Products Manufactured:
Architecturally designed signage for room and building identification.

Compliance with ADA-AG:
4.30

Lettering Specialists, Inc. has been manufacturing interior signage for over 30 years. Their complete signage system includes nameplates, directional signs, ceiling banners, and directories.

The 11000 Series tactile signage system (raised letter/symbols and Grade 2 Braille) features:

- a vandal-resistant sign
- impossible to scratch off background or letter color
- no exposed painted surface
- all surfaces non-glare, mar-resistant
- rounded Braille dots
- all symbols as specified by the US Department of Transportation and the Americans with Disabilities Act.

Call for a complete brochure on the 11000 Series, including examples of over 80 symbols, partial representation of over 200 letter styles and 320 colors.

Tactile Sign with Raised Letter/Symbols with Grade 2 Braille

ADA-Compliant Signage

Manufactured by:
Quartet Manufacturing Company
5700 Old Orchard Road
Skokie, IL 60077
(708) 965-0600

Type of Products Manufactured:
ADA-compliant signage.

Compliance with ADA-AG:
4.30, A4.30

Quartet's ADA Signs comply with all ADA requirements for critical signage. Contemporary radius cornered, international signage with easy-to-read messages, clear graphics and Grade 2 Braille. Durable 1/8" injection-molded plastic with white raised tactile graphics on gray (accessible sign on blue). Sign dimensions: 6"w × 9"h. Includes mounting instructions and double-sided adhesive tape.

ADA-Compliant Signage

Modular Signage, Braille, Raised Letters

Manufactured by:
Scott Sign Systems, Inc.
P.O. Box 1047
Tallevast, FL 34270-1047
(800) 237-9447

Type of Products Manufactured:
Modular signage, braille, raised letters

Compliance with ADA-AG:
4.30.1 through 4.30.8

SCOTT Sign Systems, Inc.® manufactures and supplies the signage elements needed to comply with the ADA requirements. Scott-ADA™ letters and specially molded plaques have been designed to conform with tactile signing requirements.

For a changeable or permanent application, specify BraillDots™ applied to the Snap Plate System mounted within a frame. Clear or solid color, Snap Plates are available with a variety of lettering applications, in standard sizes and colors, or custom colored.

The SCOTT ONE® Architectural Sign System combines frames in various shapes and sizes and can incorporate BraillDots.

BraillDots™ can be incorporated into many substrates including: granites and solid surface materials, acrylics, metals, and engraving materials.

The SCOTT ONE® Architectural Sign System

Elevator and Building Interior Signage

Manufactured by:

SCS CO•SINES
Div. of Stencil Cutting and Supply Co.
1700 Gervais Avenue
Maplewood, MN 55109
(612) 770-2123

Type of Products Manufactured:
Elevator and building interior signage.

Compliance with ADA-AG:
4.10.12, 4.28.6.2, 4.30, 4.30.2, 4.30.5

SCS company manufactures code-compliant braille markings for both elevators and building interiors which meets or exceeds NEII, ANSI, CABO ANSI, ADA-AG and UFAS codes. Their products are manufactured with high quality materials using methods of die casting, water etching, metal embossing, stainless, bronze, photopolymer, and a complete line of acrylic materials.

Cast Elevator Markings

Embosser for Producing Braille Signage

Manufactured by:

Enabling Technologies Company
3102 S.E. Jay Street
Stuart, FL 34997
(407) 283-4817

Type of Products Manufactured:
A complete line of braille embossers, including a braille embosser able to produce braille on heavier plastic for signs.

Compliance with ADA-AG:
4.30.4

The Thomas Brailler is a desktop machine that handles a full range of tractor-feed paper from 20 to 100 pounds in weight, and up to 15 inches in width. It also produces high quality braille on heavy plastics and light metals. Its operating speed of 40 characters per second allows it to produce more than one hundred and twenty pages per hour. Or it can be loaded with vinyl and aluminum sheets to produce signs with braille markings.

Among the Thomas Brailler's capabilities:

- High resolution graphics: lets you combine text and graphics on a single page without stopping.
- Multi-strike feature: places well defined braille on heavy plastics and some light metals. The quality is suitable for making braille signs or adding braille to printed ones.
- Single-sheet operation: allows braille to be placed on loose sheets of paper, plastic or metal foils.
- Raised print characters: in conjunction with an optional software package, embosses print characters which can be read either tactually or visually.

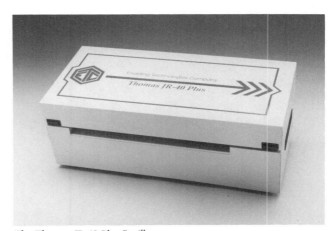

The Thomas JR-40 Plus Brailler

Audible Signage

Manufactured by:

Talking Signs, Inc.
812 North Blvd.
Baton Rouge, LA 70802

Type of Products Manufactured:

Infrared remote signage. Informational and wayfinding systems for the visually impaired and print handicapped.

Compliance with ADA-AG:

4.34.4

Talking Signs® transmitters emit a voice message continuously carried on an infrared light wave. The visually impaired person carries a receiver that he or she uses to scan an environment to locate features such as escalators, elevators, public telephones, information counters and restrooms.

When the receiver senses a Talking Signs® transmission, it converts it to spoken voice from a speaker. An ear loop is also available. Using Talking Signs® receivers, the visually impaired person can independently travel through transit stations, airports, shopping centers, public buildings, parks, etc. Talking Signs® assist in the development of a cognitive map of one's surroundings. Approaching buses can be identified as well.

Margie Donovan uses Talking Signs® at Powell Street Station in San Francisco (Photo: Gretchen Hildner, S.F. Muni)

Alerting System for Hotel Rooms

Manufactured by:

Harc™ Mercantile, Ltd.
1111 West Centre Avenue
P.O. Box 3055
Kalamazoo, MI 49003
(800) 445-9968

Type of Products Manufactured:
Visual alerting and annunciation systems for hotel and motel rooms.

Compliance with ADA-AG:
9.1, 4.28

The Harc™ Room Valet is a supervised, permanently installed hardwired visual/tactile alerting system designed specifically for hotel/motels, senior communities, health care, and university housing. The features and performance of the Room Valet meet and/or exceed the current ADA standards. Its design is flexible to adapt to future changes or specific regulations. The indicator panel has a flashing strobe light, and back light icons which shows signal source. The Room Valet alerts to five conditions: in-room smoke alarm, phone ring, wake up, door bell or push button, and house/central fire alarm, which interfaces to ADA standard visual house alarm in room signal.

The design is unique, the self-contained strobe light and bed shaker combine to wake the sleeping person. The direct connection to signal sources is designed to eliminate false alarms. The remote annunciators are suited for suites, bathrooms, etc.

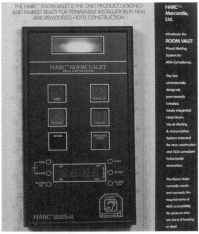

The Harc™ Room Valet

Barrier-Free Water Cooler

Manufactured by:
EBCO Manufacturing Company
265 N. Hamilton Rd.
P.O. Box 13150
Columbus, OH 43213-0150
(614) 861-1350

Type of Products Manufactured:
Water coolers, dehumidifiers

Compliance with ADA-AG:
4.1, 4.2, 4.4

The Versacooler™ can be installed as original equipment or used to replace most brands of water coolers. The versatility of its open back design allows connection to most waterways without changing plumbing locations.

The design includes a smooth rounded cabinet appearance without exposed fasteners or openings. Lightly pressing one of the three touch pads activates a continuous flow bubbler that supplies a steady stream of cold water.

The P8AM satisfies ANSI Standard A117.1 (1986) and when properly installed, allows a facility to comply with ADA requirements.

Standard features:

• Waterways are lead-free in materials and construction
• Stainless steel top
• Heavy-gauge galvanized steel frame
• High-efficiency cooling tank and coil
• Limited 5-year warranty

The Versacooler™ P8AM

Compliant Water Coolers and Drinking Fountains

Manufactured by:
Halsey Taylor
P.O. Box 9001
Oak Brook, IL
(708) 574-3500

Type of Products Manufactured:
Deluxe wall-mounted water coolers

Compliance with ADA-AG:
4.15

Halsey Taylor offers a wide range of water coolers and drinking fountains for just about any application—from stone and steel outdoor drinking fountains, to contemporary CFC-free water coolers.

The HAC8FS-Q shown here features a large open-back design for easier rough-ins and easy-to-operate pushbars with raised letters for the visually impaired. The standard platinum vinyl finish blends with any decor. Optional finishes include Slate Vinyl, Almond Vinyl, Stainless Steel and Golden Bronzetone. The HAC is also available with an electronic sensor (Model HAC8EE-Q).

The Halsey-Taylor Barrier-Free HAC

Section B

PRODUCTS FOR TITLE I COMPLIANCE AND LIFESTYLE ENHANCEMENTS

Section B describes products that support efforts to meet Title I requirements (for example, office furniture and visual or speech-enhancing software for disabled employees). Often, these products provide a direct solution to an access problem that not only affords the disabled employee maximum independence and productivity, but also simplifies management's involvement and reduces the required expense. Other included products enhance productivity and/or the quality of life for disabled people in a variety of ways, with solutions such as full spectrum lighting, a preset thermostat that automatically adjusts water temperature, and a lightweight, take-apart scooter.

Thermostat Valve for Faucets

Manufactured by:

Grohe America, Inc.
241 Covington Dr.
Bloomingdale, IL 60108
(800) 323-9660

Type of Products Manufactured:
Faucets and controls

The Grohmix Thermostat allows users to safely pre-set bath or shower water temperature by dialing a thermostat, in the same way as for home heat or air conditioning. The Grohmix system promotes bathing safety for everyone, but is particularly important for physically impaired people. Accurate to within one degree Fahrenheit, the temperature is selected by dialing the Grohmix handle within the 60° to 100° comfort zone. Hotter temperatures can only be achieved by pressing the red override button.

Fluctuations in the water pressure and variations in the cold and hot water supply temperature are automatically compensated for by the thermo-element. In the event of a cold water supply failure, the unit shuts off automatically, thus avoiding any hazard of scalding. Constant manual adjustments to correct water temperature fluctuations are eliminated. By means of this exact and rapid control, Grohmix thermostats also help to save water and energy.

Grohmix Thermostat/Pressure Balance Valve, Model 34.434

Computer Magnification System

Manufactured by:
TeleSensory
455 N. Bernardo Ave.
Mountain View, CA 94043
(800) 804-8004

Type of Products Manufactured:
Products for visually impaired people

Vista, a computer magnification system, allows a person with low vision to magnify information on the computer screen. It magnifies text and graphics up to 16 times. Vista is designed for IBM PC compatible computers and is fully compatible with the Windows environment.

Vista is the only screen-enlarging system completely mouse-controlled for convenience and to avoid keyboard conflict. Vista has screen navigation, cursor tracking and a wide range of special presentation views that magnify text and graphics up to 16 times. Vista is compatible with networks and terminal emulation systems. Vista can magnify a single line, vary the size of the enlarged window, vary the enlargement and enlarge a single "ruler" line while moving around the screen. Vista comes complete with a circuit board, software and a 3-button mouse that connects directly to the Vista circuit board.

Vista Computer Magnification System

Software Speech Recognition Systems

Manufactured by:
Dragon Systems, Inc.
320 Nevada Street
Newton, MA 02160
(800) 825-5897

Type of Products Manufactured:
Hands-free speech recognition software

DragonDictate for Windows can help users create everything from business letters to complex documents and spreadsheets—entirely by voice. Allows users to work directly within their favorite Windows applications.

Speak rather than type—Dictate text and say commands without remembering awkward keystrokes.

Use the computer hands-free—Move the mouse, dictate text and enter data without touching the keyboard.

Work independently—Create documents from start to finish. Bypass transcription services and support personnel to save valuable time and money.

DragonDictate Classic Edition has a 30,000-word active vocabulary, and works directly with word processing, spreadsheet, and database programs. This full-featured program adapts to voice, vocabulary, and environment requirements. Additional versions include *DragonDictate Starter Edition* with a 5,000-word vocabulary and *DragonDictate Power Edition,* offering a 60,000-word vocabulary.

DragonDictate, Available for Windows or DOS

Speech Processing System

Manufactured by:
Voice Connexion
17835 Skypark Circle, Suite C
Irvine, CA 92714
(714) 261-2366

Type of Products Manufactured:
Voice products and software

Micro IntroVoice is a complete voice input/output system which provides voice recognition of 1,000 words with an accuracy of better than 98%, and unlimited text-to-speech synthesis or fixed vocabulary recorded speech. Micro IntroVoice listens to command or data input, then responds by sending keystrokes via the serial port, and text to the on-board synthesizer for audio prompting and verification.

From large networks to small hand-helds, Micro IntroVoice provides DOS compatibility for use with IBM AT, 80XXX and compatibles. Using the supplied "C" library, the system may also be used with OS/2, UNIX, DEC, dumb terminals, emulators, or custom OEM applications.

Vocabulary creation, editing, voice training, testing, and maintenance are easily accomplished from a standard IBM AT, 80XXX or compatible computer with the supplied software.

The Micro IntroVoice is shipped complete with microphone, system software and sample vocabularies, AC adapter, serial cable, and documentation.

The Micro IntroVoice Voice Recognition and Synthesis System

Automatic Lift Chair

Manufactured by:
 ALC, Inc.
 P.O. Box 126
 1825 Mayfield Rd.
 Richfield, WI 53076
 (800) 783-4178

Type of Products Manufactured:
 Automatic lift chairs

People who have arthritis, muscular dystrophy, Parkinson's Disease or other disabilities that make it difficult to reach a standing or sitting position know what it feels like to always be dependent on someone else for assistance. Often, the pain and discomfort of moving or the fear of falling discourages one from moving at all, further restricting the mobility of lower limbs and back.

The Action-Lift Chair is designed to provide comfort, convenience, mobility, and independence. A switch activates a gear-driven motor which safely and gently raises the chair to a wide variety of positions. Not just the seat, but the complete chair rises, providing both arm and back support.

- Available in a choice of fabrics and colors.
- Meets flammability requirements of California Bulletin 117.
- A solid hardwood frame and durable no-sag seat construction
- A control that can be held in your hand, or placed on your lap.
- A lift mechanism constructed of formed steel and welded steel tubing, then powder-coated for long lasting protection.
- Linear actuator with a thermal overload protector for safety and long life.

Action-Lift Chair

Ergonomic Chair for Individuals with Impaired Mobility

Manufactured by:
 Work Stations, Inc.
 11 Silver Street
 South Hadley, MA 01075
 (413) 535-3340

Type of Products Manufactured:
 Adaptive and assistive devices and furnishings, including custom designed furnishings for individual clients and major manufacturing, industrial, educational, health care and commercial organizations.

The Chariot Chair was designed for the fragile person who requires mobility within a room to access various materials and perform needed functions. The chair is custom cushioned for lumbar and seat pan support to any body dimensions. The L-shaped armrests allow a closer fit to any work surface, and may be used to position the arms and wrists to support a person rising from the chair. The chair is adjustable in height from 6 – 12″ (15 – 30cm).

Chariot Chair

Ergonomic Seating

Manufactured by:
BodyBilt Seating, Inc.
One BodyBilt Place
Navasota, TX 77868
(409) 825-1700

Type of Products Manufactured:
Ergonomic seating designed to help employers accommodate employees with chronic and/or temporary neuromusculoskeletal disorders, repetitive stress injuries (RSI), or other sitting-related activities that result in conditions which substantially limit major life activities.

BodyBilt seating is based on the principle of natural, zero-gravity posture. BodyBilt's system of 10-Point Posture Control™ (ten ergonomic adjustments) helps users emulate the body's most stress-free posture. Since employers must accommodate employees with even temporary RSIs, BodyBilt offers ergonomic seating for a variety of job functions. BodyBilt's J-Series Task Seating accommodates workers who perform task-oriented jobs, such as industrial and assembly work, secretarial work, data entry, etc. K-Series Management Seating is available for workers who must perform a variety of job functions, from computer work to teleconferencing and interviewing. The S-Series Big & Tall Seating offers ergonomic accommodation for workers above the 80th percentile, with reinforced components, a 26.5-inch seat structure, and a full warranty for users up to 350 lbs. Optional features include Air Lumbar™ (inflatable backrest), the Linear Tracking™ (articulating) Arm, and the Pivot™ Arm. CleanRoom and ESD models are available. All BodyBilt models are fully prescriptable.

BodyBilt ergonomic seating is designed to accommodate workers disabled by RSIs.

Ergonomic Seating

Manufactured by:
GRAHL Office Ergonomics
One Grahl Drive
Coldwater, MI 49036
(517) 278-8011

Type of Products Manufactured:
Ergonomic seating and office furniture

The Xellence Duo-Seat was designed with the input of physicians and ergonomists for people with special needs such as: congenital defects, back or hip injuries, knee and hip surgery or replacement, Muscular Dystrophy and others. Each section of the split seat can be adjusted individually to relieve pressure to legs or hips resulting from working in a seated position. Changing positions is beneficial to both the healing process and comfort.

The Hugger Duo-Back backrests are mounted on pivots, enabling them to move in all three axes: backward and forward, up and down, and left to right. As a result, the back is supported in many positions. The shape and mobility of these backrests enables them to follow the contours of the back as it moves, varying the support needed, and stimulating muscle tone and blood circulation without any pressure to the spinal column.

The Triple-Y-Base is designed to provide greater stability without a larger diameter.

Different backrest designs and arm supports are available to fit individual needs, preferences and task requirements.

The Grahl Xellence Duo-Seat

Adjustable Height Desk

Manufactured by:

Work Stations, Inc.
11 Silver Street
South Hadley, MA 01075
(413) 535-3340

Type of Products Manufactured:

Adaptive and assistive devices and furnishings, including custom designed furnishings for individual clients and major manufacturing, industrial, educational, health care and commercial organizations.

This U-shaped desk was designed to accommodate a disabled person who uses a wheelchair. Touch- and pressure-sensitive controls (in the form of a hand switch, joy stick, and head switch) are available for independent functioning, no matter what the impairment. The work surface height is adjustable from 23 – 48" (58 – 122cm). (Individual work stations are available with height ranges of 6, 12 or 18".) Surfaces can tilt to 30 degrees.

Design features include: electronic height and tilt, solid hardwood construction, low sheen finish to minimize glare and eye fatigue, and easy assembly and breakdown into portable sections.

Ergonomic features include: surface shaped to bring work closer, easy accommodation of wheelchairs and other special needs, unrestricted leg space, electronic switch panel to support adaptive aids and environmental control, storage for adaptive aids, supplies, and adaptable equipment supports.

Adjustable Height Desk, Rotofile, Accessifile, Bookcase

Full Spectrum Fluorescent Tubes

Manufactured by:
Ott bioLightsystems
28 Parker Way
Santa Barbara, CA 93101
(800) 234-3724

Type of Products Manufactured:
Biologically beneficial lighting, lighting retrofit specialists.

Ergonomically correct, full spectrum light is beneficial for anyone with a visual impairment because it is designed for the way the eye sees naturally and it provides the highest visual acuity. This means improved readability and increased productivity.

The human eye is a light sensing system that utilizes both photopic (luminance) and scotopic (spectral) lumens. Scotopically rich light provides the eye with more usable light so that a person can actually see more efficiently. Full spectrum lighting combines high Kelvin temperature and optimum color rendition. Cathode radiation shielding is an added safety component to provide biologically beneficial indoor lighting.

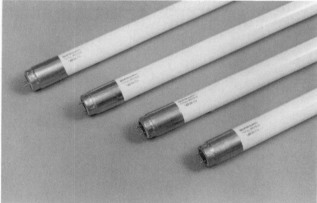

The bioLightube is ergonomic, energy efficient fluorescent lighting.

Full Spectrum Incandescent Lightbulb

Manufactured by:
Ott bioLightsystems
28 Parker Way
Santa Barbara, CA 93101
(800) 234-3724

Type of Products Manufactured:
Biologically beneficial lighting, light retrofit specialists

The full spectrum, neodymium lightbulb is beneficial for anyone with a visual impairment because it provides the highest visual acuity of any incandescent bulb. Neodymium, a rare earth element used in laser technology, has the capability of absorbing excessive yellows and other dulling components. The result is balanced, purified spectral light. The bioLightbulb has a life of 3500 hours.

The bioLightbulb provides maximum visual acuity, glare-free lighting.

Therapeutic Lighting Fixtures

Manufactured by:

Ott bioLightsystems
28 Parker Way
Santa Barbara, CA 93101
(800) 234-3724

Type of Products Manufactured:

Biologically beneficial lighting, lighting retrofit specialists.

The bioLightsystem has several applications. For example:

Phototherapy (light therapy): As a therapeutic lighting device, it is often effective in the treatment of seasonal affective disorder, clinical depression, and fatigue-related ailments.

For the computer operator: The fixture is designed to counteract the negative effects of the VDT screen. According to the manufacturer, electromagnetic radiation from the computer screen magnetizes the red blood cells, causing them to clump together, inhibiting blood flow. Full spectrum light rays, entering the retina, are converted into electrical impulses (photocurrent) which the brain can interpret. This photocurrent regulates body chemistry and allows the magnetized blood cells to return to their natural streaming pattern with replenished oxygen supply.

The Full Spectrum, Radiation-Shielded bioLightsystem

Overhead Storage

Manufactured by:
The Knoll Group
1235 Water Street
East Greenville, PA 18041
(800) 445-5045

Type of Products Manufactured:
Ergonomic furniture/furnishings

Reuter Overhead Storage combines technological advances with aesthetics to provide ergonomic, accessible furnishings. Reuter overheads are equipped with a pneumatic-action door that opens at the touch of a finger, even if the user is seated. With the optional ADA pull, doors can also be closed from a seated position.

The Reuter door pivots out of the way; inside, movable horizontal and vertical partitions let users adjust their own spaces. A unique integral wire management system accommodates electrical cords for items such as clocks and radios in a trough in the back of the unit.

Knoll Interaction Tables work with other office furnishings to respond to changing needs, moment by moment or day by day. To expand a desk or add a secondary worksurface—Interaction Tables go wherever they are needed. They can be configured in various ways and move on bases that glide or roll and then lock into place.

With biomorphic shapes and soft, rounded edges, Interaction Tables can be used as worktables, personal tables, or group meeting tables, on their own or with other pieces.

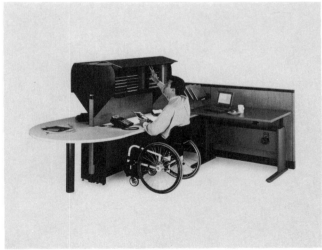

The Reuter Overhead Storage System

Accessible Files and Bookcase

Manufactured by:
Work Stations, Inc.
11 Silver Street
South Hadley, MA 01075
(413) 535-3340

Type of Products Manufactured:
Adaptive and assistive devices and furnishings, including custom designed furnishings for individual clients and major manufacturing, industrial, educational, health care and commercial organizations.

The Roto-file is a carousel-like cube which revolves 360 degrees for full accessibility. It is designed so that the backs of standard book binders and files extend 1/2″ (1.3cm) beyond the edge for grasping access.

The Accessifile is a file containment system that has a fold-down front for access from a wheelchair, and a fold-up top for standing access. The file rolls easily to any work area. It holds one drawer of legal size material.

The custom bookcase is designed to be positioned at the correct height for optimum access. Internal dividers help safely support books or other materials. Drawers are also available for additional storage.

Rotofile

Accessifile

Interactive Driving Simulator

Manufactured by:

Virtual Worlds, Inc.
5050 Newport Dr., Suite #10
Rolling Meadows, IL 60008
(800) 354-3659

Type of Products Manufactured:

Interactive driving simulators intended to re-educate and rehabilitate driving skills in individuals whose abilities have been adversely affected.

This driving training can help those whose disabilities have been affected by stroke, brain trauma, impaired vision, physical limitations, and aging to regain driving skills essential for personal or occupational needs.

The Virtual Worlds, Inc. Simulator allows for the objective measurement of driving capabilities through a graphic user interface, driving performance analysis, and custom-tailored programmable driving scenarios.

It satisfies the needs of many physically challenged individuals to receive quality driving training without the potential risk of on-road hazards.

Virtual World's® Interactive Driving Simulator

Low Vision Reading Systems

Manufactured by:

OPTELEC
P.O. Box 729
Westford, MA 01886
(800) 828-1056

Types of Products Manufactured:

Low vision reading systems for the visually impaired and large print computer software.

Optelec specializes in providing independence through products for the visually impaired. They offer a complete line of video magnifiers for all applications, size and space requirements. All desktop reading systems will magnify books, newspapers, and medicine bottles up to 60 times. Also enables users to write letters, checks and even view photographs. Video magnifiers are available in a 14″ or 20″ either black or white, color or multi-color monitor. The control panel is easy to use.

Optelec's portable video magnifier weighs less than 25 lbs. and can be operated with a rechargeable battery pack or plugged into a power source. Virtual screen technology provides a field of view eqivalent to a 14″ monitor. The innovative screen design offers privacy and tilts for comfortable viewing. The magnification range is from 3–40 times.

LPDOS computer software will magnify text from 2–8 times in DOS and 2–16 times in windows. It is compatible with IBM, PC, network systems and notebooks.

Optelec Spectrum JR. provides true color for photographs and sharp black and white text for reading.

Electric Scooters and Powerchairs

Manufactured by:

Electric Mobility Corp.
1 Mobility Plaza
Sewell, NJ 08080
(800) 662-4548

Type of Products Manufactured:

Products for personal, independent mobility for the aged and handicapped.

Electric Mobility has provided independent mobility to over 100,000 users. Their line of 3-wheel and 4-wheel scooters and 4-wheel electric powerchairs — from the Littlest Rascal for small riders or confined spaces up to the Electric Xpress "Super Scooter" for longer-range, higher-speed outdoor travel — addresses a range of mobility needs and price ranges. The "Take-Apart" frame allows easier transportation, with the heaviest component weighing only 29.5 lbs. Every "Take-Apart" Rascal features the patented ConvertAble Option that allows conversion from an outdoor 3-wheeler to an indoor 4-wheeler . . . without tools. The Model 200 is similar and less expensive, but does not have the take-apart feature. For rougher terrain, riders can choose the Quantum 300 or 400 four-wheeled scooter. Rascals are available in a Deluxe

version for standard applications and a Heavy-Duty version for larger riders and rougher usage. Every Rascal carries a 5-year limited warranty on components and a Lifetime Frame Warranty.

1996 Rascal 240 carries up to 400 lbs. and goes 20 miles on a single charge.

APPENDIX

Table of
Contents

Appendix A

THE AMERICANS WITH DISABILITIES ACT GUIDELINES

Federal Register / Vol. 56, No. 144 / Friday, July 26, 1991 / Rules and Regulations   35605

Appendix A to Part 36—Standards for Accessible Design

ADA ACCESSIBILITY GUIDELINES
FOR BUILDINGS AND FACILITIES
TABLE OF CONTENTS

i

35606   Federal Register / Vol. 56, No. 144 / Friday, July 26, 1991 / Rules and Regulations

Federal Register / Vol. 56, No. 144 / Friday, July 26, 1991 / Rules and Regulations   **35607**

1. PURPOSE.

This document sets guidelines for accessibility to places of public accommodation and commercial facilities by individuals with disabilities. These guidelines are to be applied during the design, construction, and alteration of such buildings and facilities to the extent required by regulations issued by Federal agencies, including the Department of Justice, under the Americans with Disabilities Act of 1990.

The technical specifications 4.2 through 4.35, of these guidelines are the same as those of the American National Standard Institute's document A117.1-1980, except as noted in this text by italics. However, sections 4.1.1 through 4.1.7 and sections 5 through 10 are different from ANSI A117.1 in their entirety and are printed in standard type.

The illustrations and text of ANSI A117.1 are reproduced with permission from the American National Standards Institute. Copies of the standard may be purchased from the American National Standards Institute at 1430 Broadway, New York, New York 10018.

2. GENERAL.

2.1 Provisions for Adults. *The specifications in these guidelines are based upon adult dimensions and anthropometrics.*

2.2* Equivalent Facilitation. *Departures from particular technical and scoping requirements of this guideline by the use of other designs and technologies are permitted where the alternative designs and technologies used will provide substantially equivalent or greater access to and usability of the facility.*

3. MISCELLANEOUS INSTRUCTIONS AND DEFINITIONS.

3.1 Graphic Conventions. Graphic conventions are shown in Table 1. Dimensions that are not marked minimum or maximum are absolute, unless otherwise indicated in the text or captions.

Table 1
Graphic Conventions

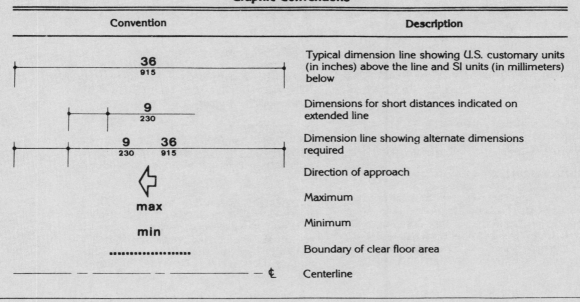

Convention	Description
36 / 915	Typical dimension line showing U.S. customary units (in inches) above the line and SI units (in millimeters) below
9 / 230	Dimensions for short distances indicated on extended line
9 / 230 36 / 915	Dimension line showing alternate dimensions required
⇦	Direction of approach
max	Maximum
min	Minimum
....	Boundary of clear floor area
———— ¢	Centerline

1

3.4 General Terminology

3.2 Dimensional Tolerances. All dimensions are subject to conventional building industry tolerances for field conditions.

3.3 Notes. The text of *these guidelines* does not contain notes or footnotes. Additional information, explanations, and advisory materials are located in the Appendix. Paragraphs marked with an asterisk have related, nonmandatory material in the Appendix. In the Appendix, the corresponding paragraph numbers are preceded by an A.

3.4 General Terminology.

comply with. Meet one or more specifications of *these guidelines.*

if, if ... then. Denotes a specification that applies only when the conditions described are present.

may. Denotes an option or alternative.

shall. Denotes a mandatory specification or requirement.

should. Denotes an advisory specification or recommendation.

3.5 Definitions.

Access Aisle. An accessible pedestrian space between elements, such as parking spaces, seating, and desks, that provides clearances appropriate for use of the elements.

Accessible. Describes a site, building, facility, or portion thereof that complies with *these guidelines.*

Accessible Element. An *element* specified by *these guidelines* (for example, telephone, controls, and the like).

Accessible Route. A continuous unobstructed path connecting all accessible elements and spaces of a building or facility. Interior accessible routes may include corridors, floors, ramps, elevators, lifts, and clear floor space at fixtures. Exterior accessible routes may include parking access aisles, curb ramps, *crosswalks at vehicular ways*, walks, ramps, and lifts.

Accessible Space. Space that complies with these guidelines.

Adaptability. The ability of certain building spaces and elements, such as kitchen counters, sinks, and grab bars, to be added or altered so as to accommodate the needs of *individuals with or without disabilities* or to accommodate the needs of persons with different types or degrees of disability.

Addition. An expansion, extension, or increase in the gross floor area of a building or facility.

Administrative Authority. A governmental agency that adopts or enforces regulations and *guidelines* for the design, construction, or *alteration* of buildings and facilities.

Alteration. An alteration is a change to a building or facility made by, on behalf of, or for the use of a public accommodation or commercial facility, that affects or could affect the usability of the building or facility or part thereof. Alterations include, but are not limited to, remodeling, renovation, rehabilitation, reconstruction, historic restoration, changes or rearrangement of the structural parts or elements, and changes or rearrangement in the plan configuration of walls and full-height partitions. Normal maintenance, reroofing, painting or wallpapering, or changes to mechanical and electrical systems are not alterations unless they affect the usability of the building or facility.

Area of Rescue Assistance. An area, which has direct access to an exit, where people who are unable to use stairs may remain temporarily in safety to await further instructions or assistance during emergency evacuation.

Assembly Area. A room or space accommodating a *group of* individuals for recreational, educational, political, social, or amusement purposes, or for the consumption of food and drink.

Automatic Door. A door equipped with a power-operated mechanism and controls that open and close the door automatically upon receipt of a momentary actuating signal. The switch that begins the automatic cycle may be a photoelectric device, floor mat, or manual switch (see power-assisted door).

2

Federal Register / Vol. 56, No. 144 / Friday, July 26, 1991 / Rules and Regulations **35609**

3.5 Definitions

Building. Any structure used and intended for supporting or sheltering any use or occupancy.

Circulation Path. An exterior or interior way of passage from one place to another for pedestrians, including, but not limited to, walks, hallways, courtyards, stairways, and stair landings.

Clear. Unobstructed.

Clear Floor Space. *The minimum unobstructed floor or ground space required to accommodate a single, stationary wheelchair and occupant.*

Closed Circuit Telephone. *A telephone with dedicated line(s) such as a house phone, courtesy phone or phone that must be used to gain entrance to a facility.*

Common Use. Refers to those interior and exterior rooms, spaces, or elements that are made available for the use of a restricted group of people (for example, *occupants of a homeless shelter*, the occupants of an office building, or the guests of such occupants).

Cross Slope. The slope that is perpendicular to the direction of travel (see running slope).

Curb Ramp. A short ramp cutting through a curb or built up to it.

Detectable Warning. *A standardized surface feature built in or applied to walking surfaces or other elements to warn visually impaired people of hazards on a circulation path.*

Dwelling Unit. A single unit which provides a kitchen or food preparation area, in addition to rooms and spaces for living, bathing, sleeping, and the like. *Dwelling units include a single family home or a townhouse used as a transient group home; an apartment building used as a shelter; guestrooms in a hotel that provide sleeping accommodations and food preparation areas; and other similar facilities used on a transient basis. For purposes of these guidelines, use of the term "Dwelling Unit" does not imply the unit is used as a residence.*

Egress, Means of. *A continuous and unobstructed way of exit travel from any point in a building or facility to a public way. A means of egress comprises vertical and horizontal travel and may include intervening room spaces, doorways, hallways, corridors, passageways, balconies, ramps, stairs, enclosures, lobbies, horizontal exits, courts and yards. An accessible means of egress is one that complies with these guidelines and does not include stairs, steps, or escalators. Areas of rescue assistance or evacuation elevators may be included as part of accessible means of egress.*

Element. *An architectural or mechanical component of a building, facility, space, or site, e.g., telephone, curb ramp, door, drinking fountain, seating, or water closet.*

Entrance. *Any access point to a building or portion of a building or facility used for the purpose of entering. An entrance includes the approach walk, the vertical access leading to the entrance platform, the entrance platform itself, vestibules if provided, the entry door(s) or gate(s), and the hardware of the entry door(s) or gate(s).*

Facility. *All or any portion of buildings, structures, site improvements, complexes, equipment, roads, walks, passageways, parking lots, or other real or personal property located on a site.*

Ground Floor. *Any occupiable floor less than one story above or below grade with direct access to grade. A building or facility always has at least one ground floor and may have more than one ground floor as where a split level entrance has been provided or where a building is built into a hillside.*

Mezzanine or Mezzanine Floor. *That portion of a story which is an intermediate floor level placed within the story and having occupiable space above and below its floor.*

Marked Crossing. A crosswalk or other identified path intended for pedestrian use in crossing a vehicular way.

Multifamily Dwelling. Any building containing more than two dwelling units.

Occupiable. *A room or enclosed space designed for human occupancy in which individuals congregate for amusement, educational or similar purposes, or in which occupants are engaged at labor, and which is equipped with means of egress, light, and ventilation.*

3

Appendix A

3.5 Definitions

Operable Part. A part of a piece of equipment or appliance used to insert or withdraw objects, or to activate, deactivate, or adjust the equipment or appliance (for example, coin slot, pushbutton, handle).

Path of Travel. *(Reserved).*

Power-assisted Door. A door used *for human passage* with a mechanism that helps to open the door, or relieves the opening resistance of a door, upon the activation of a switch or a continued force applied to the door itself.

Public Use. Describes interior or exterior rooms or spaces that are made available to the general public. Public use may be provided at a building or facility that is privately or publicly owned.

Ramp. A walking surface which has a running slope greater than 1:20.

Running Slope. The slope that is parallel to the direction of travel (see cross slope).

Service Entrance. An entrance intended primarily for delivery of goods or services.

Signage. *Displayed* verbal, symbolic, *tactile*, and pictorial information.

Site. A parcel of land bounded by a property line or a designated portion of a public right-of-way.

Site Improvement. Landscaping, paving for pedestrian and vehicular ways, outdoor lighting, recreational facilities, and the like, added to a site.

Sleeping Accommodations. Rooms in which people sleep; for example, dormitory and hotel or motel guest rooms or suites.

Space. *A definable area, e.g., room, toilet room, hall, assembly area, entrance, storage room, alcove, courtyard, or lobby.*

Story. *That portion of a building included between the upper surface of a floor and upper surface of the floor or roof next above. If such* portion of a building does not include occupiable space, it is not considered a story for purposes of these guidelines. There may be more than one floor level within a story as in the case of a mezzanine or mezzanines.

Structural Frame. The structural frame shall be considered to be the columns and the girders, beams, trusses and spandrels having direct connections to the columns and all other members which are essential to the stability of the building as a whole.

Tactile. Describes an object that can be perceived using the sense of touch.

Text Telephone. *Machinery or equipment that employs interactive graphic (i.e., typed) communications through the transmission of coded signals across the standard telephone network. Text telephones can include, for example, devices known as TDD's (telecommunication display devices or telecommunication devices for deaf persons) or computers.*

Transient Lodging. *A building, facility, or portion thereof, excluding inpatient medical care facilities, that contains one or more dwelling units or sleeping accommodations. Transient lodging may include, but is not limited to, resorts, group homes, hotels, motels, and dormitories.*

Vehicular Way. A route intended for vehicular traffic, such as a street, driveway, or parking lot.

Walk. An exterior pathway with a prepared surface intended for pedestrian use, including general pedestrian areas such as plazas and courts.

NOTE: Sections 4.1.1 through 4.1.7 are different from ANSI A117.1 in their entirety and are printed in standard type (ANSI A117.1 does not include scoping provisions).

Federal Register / Vol. 56, No. 144 / Friday, July 26, 1991 / Rules and Regulations **35611**

4.0 Accessible Elements and Spaces: Scope and Technical Requirements

4. ACCESSIBLE ELEMENTS AND SPACES: SCOPE AND TECHNICAL REQUIREMENTS.

4.1 Minimum Requirements

4.1.1* Application.

(1) General. All areas of newly designed or newly constructed buildings and facilities required to be accessible by 4.1.2 and 4.1.3 and altered portions of existing buildings and facilities required to be accessible by 4.1.6 shall comply with these guidelines, 4.1 through 4.35, unless otherwise provided in this section or as modified in a special application section.

(2) Application Based on Building Use. Special application sections 5 through 10 provide additional requirements for restaurants and cafeterias, medical care facilities, business and mercantile, libraries, accessible transient lodging, and transportation facilities. When a building or facility contains more than one use covered by a special application section, each portion shall comply with the requirements for that use.

(3)* Areas Used Only by Employees as Work Areas. Areas that are used only as work areas shall be designed and constructed so that individuals with disabilities can approach, enter, and exit the areas. These guidelines do not require that any areas used only as work areas be constructed to permit maneuvering within the work area or be constructed or equipped (i.e., with racks or shelves) to be accessible.

(4) Temporary Structures. These guidelines cover temporary buildings or facilities as well as permanent facilities. Temporary buildings and facilities are not of permanent construction but are extensively used or are essential for public use for a period of time. Examples of temporary buildings or facilities covered by these guidelines include, but are not limited to: reviewing stands, temporary classrooms, bleacher areas, exhibit areas, temporary banking facilities, temporary health screening services, or temporary safe pedestrian passageways around a construction site. Structures,

sites and equipment directly associated with the actual processes of construction, such as scaffolding, bridging, materials hoists, or construction trailers are not included.

(5) General Exceptions.

(a) In new construction, a person or entity is not required to meet fully the requirements of these guidelines where that person or entity can demonstrate that it is structurally impracticable to do so. Full compliance will be considered structurally impracticable only in those rare circumstances when the unique characteristics of terrain prevent the incorporation of accessibility features. If full compliance with the requirements of these guidelines is structurally impracticable, a person or entity shall comply with the requirements to the extent it is not structurally impracticable. Any portion of the building or facility which can be made accessible shall comply to the extent that it is not structurally impracticable.

(b) Accessibility is not required to (i) observation galleries used primarily for security purposes; or (ii) in non-occupiable spaces accessed only by ladders, catwalks, crawl spaces, very narrow passageways, or freight (non-passenger) elevators, and frequented only by service personnel for repair purposes; such spaces include, but are not limited to, elevator pits, elevator penthouses, piping or equipment catwalks.

4.1.2 Accessible Sites and Exterior Facilities: New Construction. An accessible site shall meet the following minimum requirements:

(1) At least one accessible route complying with 4.3 shall be provided within the boundary of the site from public transportation stops, accessible parking spaces, passenger loading zones if provided, and public streets or sidewalks, to an accessible building entrance.

(2) At least one accessible route complying with 4.3 shall connect accessible buildings, accessible facilities, accessible elements, and accessible spaces that are on the same site.

(3) All objects that protrude from surfaces or posts into circulation paths shall comply with 4.4.

5

Appendix A

4.1.2 Accessible Sites and Exterior Facilities: New Construction

(4) Ground surfaces along accessible routes and in accessible spaces shall comply with 4.5.

(5) (a) If parking spaces are provided for self-parking by employees or visitors, or both, then accessible spaces complying with 4.6 shall be provided in each such parking area in conformance with the table below. Spaces required by the table need not be provided in the particular lot. They may be provided in a different location if equivalent or greater accessibility, in terms of distance from an accessible entrance, cost and convenience is ensured.

Total Parking in Lot	Required Minimum Number of Accessible Spaces
1 to 25	1
26 to 50	2
51 to 75	3
76 to 100	4
101 to 150	5
151 to 200	6
201 to 300	7
301 to 400	8
401 to 500	9
501 to 1000	2 percent of total
1001 and over	20 plus 1 for each 100 over 1000

Except as provided in (b), access aisles adjacent to accessible spaces shall be 60 in (1525 mm) wide minimum.

(b) One in every eight accessible spaces, but not less than one, shall be served by an access aisle 96 in (2440 mm) wide minimum and shall be designated "van accessible" as required by 4.6.4. The vertical clearance at such spaces shall comply with 4.6.5. All such spaces may be grouped on one level of a parking structure.

EXCEPTION: Provision of all required parking spaces in conformance with "Universal Parking Design" (see appendix A4.6.3) is permitted.

(c) If passenger loading zones are provided, then at least one passenger loading zone shall comply with 4.6.6.

(d) At facilities providing medical care and other services for persons with mobility impairments, parking spaces complying with 4.6 shall be provided in accordance with 4.1.2(5)(a) except as follows:

(i) Outpatient units and facilities: 10 percent of the total number of parking spaces provided serving each such outpatient unit or facility;

(ii) Units and facilities that specialize in treatment or services for persons with mobility impairments: 20 percent of the total number of parking spaces provided serving each such unit or facility.

(e) Valet parking: Valet parking facilities shall provide a passenger loading zone complying with 4.6.6 located on an accessible route to the entrance of the facility. Paragraphs 5(a), 5(b), and 5(d) of this section do not apply to valet parking facilities.

(6) If toilet facilities are provided on a site, then each such public or common use toilet facility shall comply with 4.22. If bathing facilities are provided on a site, then each such public or common use bathing facility shall comply with 4.23.

For single user portable toilet or bathing units clustered at a single location, at least 5% but no less than one toilet unit or bathing unit complying with 4.22 or 4.23 shall be installed at each cluster whenever typical inaccessible units are provided. Accessible units shall be identified by the International Symbol of Accessibility.

EXCEPTION: Portable toilet units at construction sites used exclusively by construction personnel are not required to comply with 4.1.2(6).

(7) Building Signage. Signs which designate permanent rooms and spaces shall comply with 4.30.1, 4.30.4, 4.30.5 and 4.30.6. Other signs which provide direction to, or information about, functional spaces of the building shall comply with 4.30.1, 4.30.2, 4.30.3, and 4.30.5. Elements and spaces of accessible facilities which shall be identified by the International Symbol of Accessibility and which shall comply with 4.30.7 are:

(a) Parking spaces designated as reserved for individuals with disabilities;

6

4.1.3 Accessible Buildings: New Construction

(b) Accessible passenger loading zones;

(c) Accessible entrances when not all are accessible (inaccessible entrances shall have directional signage to indicate the route to the nearest accessible entrance);

(d) Accessible toilet and bathing facilities when not all are accessible.

4.1.3 Accessible Buildings: New Construction. Accessible buildings and facilities shall meet the following minimum requirements:

(1) At least one accessible route complying with 4.3 shall connect accessible building or facility entrances with all accessible spaces and elements within the building or facility.

(2) All objects that overhang or protrude into circulation paths shall comply with 4.4.

(3) Ground and floor surfaces along accessible routes and in accessible rooms and spaces shall comply with 4.5.

(4) Interior and exterior stairs connecting levels that are not connected by an elevator, ramp, or other accessible means of vertical access shall comply with 4.9.

(5)* One passenger elevator complying with 4.10 shall serve each level, including mezzanines, in all multi-story buildings and facilities unless exempted below. If more than one elevator is provided, each full passenger elevator shall comply with 4.10.

EXCEPTION 1: Elevators are not required in facilities that are less than three stories or that have less than 3000 square feet per story unless the building is a shopping center, a shopping mall, or the professional office of a health care provider, or another type of facility as determined by the Attorney General. The elevator exemption set forth in this paragraph does not obviate or limit in any way the obligation to comply with the other accessibility requirements established in section 4.1.3. For example, floors above or below the accessible ground floor must meet the requirements of this section except for elevator service. If toilet or bathing facilities are provided on a level not served by an elevator, then toilet or bathing facilities must be provided on the accessible ground floor. In new construction if a building or facility is eligible for this exemption but a full passenger elevator is nonetheless planned, that elevator shall meet the requirements of 4.10 and shall serve each level in the building. A full passenger elevator that provides service from a garage to only one level of a building or facility is not required to serve other levels.

EXCEPTION 2: Elevator pits, elevator penthouses, mechanical rooms, piping or equipment catwalks are exempted from this requirement.

EXCEPTION 3: Accessible ramps complying with 4.8 may be used in lieu of an elevator.

EXCEPTION 4: Platform lifts (wheelchair lifts) complying with 4.11 of this guideline and applicable state or local codes may be used in lieu of an elevator only under the following conditions:

(a) To provide an accessible route to a performing area in an assembly occupancy.

(b) To comply with the wheelchair viewing position line-of-sight and dispersion requirements of 4.33.3.

(c) To provide access to incidental occupiable spaces and rooms which are not open to the general public and which house no more than five persons, including but not limited to equipment control rooms and projection booths.

(d) To provide access where existing site constraints or other constraints make use of a ramp or an elevator infeasible.

(6) Windows: (Reserved).

(7) Doors:

(a) At each accessible entrance to a building or facility, at least one door shall comply with 4.13.

(b) Within a building or facility, at least one door at each accessible space shall comply with 4.13.

(c) Each door that is an element of an accessible route shall comply with 4.13.

7

Appendix A

4.1.3 Accessible Buildings: New Construction

(d) Each door required by 4.3.10, Egress, shall comply with 4.13.

(8) In new construction, at a minimum, the requirements in (a) and (b) below shall be satisfied independently:

(a)(i) At least 50% of all public entrances (excluding those in (b) below) must be accessible. At least one must be a ground floor entrance. Public entrances are any entrances that are not loading or service entrances.

(ii) Accessible entrances must be provided in a number at least equivalent to the number of exits required by the applicable building/fire codes. (This paragraph does not require an increase in the total number of entrances planned for a facility.)

(iii) An accessible entrance must be provided to each tenancy in a facility (for example, individual stores in a strip shopping center).

One entrance may be considered as meeting more than one of the requirements in (a). Where feasible, accessible entrances shall be the entrances used by the majority of people visiting or working in the building.

(b)(i) In addition, if direct access is provided for pedestrians from an enclosed parking garage to the building, at least one direct entrance from the garage to the building must be accessible.

(ii) If access is provided for pedestrians from a pedestrian tunnel or elevated walkway, one entrance to the building from each tunnel or walkway must be accessible.

One entrance may be considered as meeting more than one of the requirements in (b).

Because entrances also serve as emergency exits whose proximity to all parts of buildings and facilities is essential, it is preferable that all entrances be accessible.

(c) If the only entrance to a building, or tenancy in a facility, is a service entrance, that entrance shall be accessible.

(d) Entrances which are not accessible shall have directional signage complying with 4.30.1, 4.30.2, 4.30.3, and 4.30.5, which indicates the location of the nearest accessible entrance.

(9)* In buildings or facilities, or portions of buildings or facilities, required to be accessible, accessible means of egress shall be provided in the same number as required for exits by local building/life safety regulations. Where a required exit from an occupiable level above or below a level of accessible exit discharge is not accessible, an area of rescue assistance shall be provided on each such level (in a number equal to that of inaccessible required exits). Areas of rescue assistance shall comply with 4.3.11. A horizontal exit, meeting the requirements of local building/life safety regulations, shall satisfy the requirement for an area of rescue assistance.

EXCEPTION: Areas of rescue assistance are not required in buildings or facilities having a supervised automatic sprinkler system.

(10)* Drinking Fountains:

(a) Where only one drinking fountain is provided on a floor there shall be a drinking fountain which is accessible to individuals who use wheelchairs in accordance with 4.15 and one accessible to those who have difficulty bending or stooping. (This can be accommodated by the use of a "hi-lo" fountain; by providing one fountain accessible to those who use wheelchairs and one fountain at a standard height convenient for those who have difficulty bending; by providing a fountain accessible under 4.15 and a water cooler; or by such other means as would achieve the required accessibility for each group on each floor.)

(b) Where more than one drinking fountain or water cooler is provided on a floor, 50% of those provided shall comply with 4.15 and shall be on an accessible route.

(11) Toilet Facilities: If toilet rooms are provided, then each public and common use toilet room shall comply with 4.22. Other toilet rooms provided for the use of occupants of specific spaces (i.e., a private toilet room for the occupant of a private office) shall be adaptable. If bathing rooms are provided, then each public and common use bathroom shall comply with 4.23. Accessible toilet rooms and bathing facilities shall be on an accessible route.

8

4.1.3 Accessible Buildings: New Construction

(12) Storage, Shelving and Display Units:

(a) If fixed or built-in storage facilities such as cabinets, shelves, closets, and drawers are provided in accessible spaces, at least one of each type provided shall contain storage space complying with 4.25. Additional storage may be provided outside of the dimensions required by 4.25.

(b) Shelves or display units allowing self-service by customers in mercantile occupancies shall be located on an accessible route complying with 4.3. Requirements for accessible reach range do not apply.

(13) Controls and operating mechanisms in accessible spaces, along accessible routes, or as parts of accessible elements (for example, light switches and dispenser controls) shall comply with 4.27.

(14) If emergency warning systems are provided, then they shall include both audible alarms and visual alarms complying with 4.28. Sleeping accommodations required to comply with 9.3 shall have an alarm system complying with 4.28. Emergency warning systems in medical care facilities may be modified to suit standard health care alarm design practice.

(15) Detectable warnings shall be provided at locations as specified in 4.29.

(16) Building Signage:

(a) Signs which designate permanent rooms and spaces shall comply with 4.30.1, 4.30.4, 4.30.5 and 4.30.6.

(b) Other signs which provide direction to or information about functional spaces of the building shall comply with 4.30.1, 4.30.2, 4.30.3, and 4.30.5.

EXCEPTION: Building directories, menus, and all other signs which are temporary are not required to comply.

(17) Public Telephones:

(a) If public pay telephones, public closed circuit telephones, or other public telephones are provided, then they shall comply with 4.31.2 through 4.31.8 to the extent required by the following table:

Number of each type of telephone provided on each floor	Number of telephones required to comply with 4.31.2 through 4.31.8[1]
1 or more single unit	1 per floor
1 bank[2]	1 per floor
2 or more banks[2]	1 per bank. Accessible unit may be installed as a single unit in proximity (either visible or with signage) to the bank. At least one public telephone per floor shall meet the requirements for a forward reach telephone[3].

[1] Additional public telephones may be installed at any height. Unless otherwise specified, accessible telephones may be either forward or side reach telephones.

[2] A bank consists of two or more adjacent public telephones, often installed as a unit.

[3] EXCEPTION: For exterior installations only, if dial tone first service is available, then a side reach telephone may be installed instead of the required forward reach telephone (i.e., one telephone in proximity to each bank shall comply with 4.31).

(b)* All telephones required to be accessible and complying with 4.31.2 through 4.31.8 shall be equipped with a volume control. In addition, 25 percent, but never less than one, of all other public telephones provided shall be equipped with a volume control and shall be dispersed among all types of public telephones, including closed circuit telephones, throughout the building or facility. Signage complying with applicable provisions of 4.30.7 shall be provided.

(c) The following shall be provided in accordance with 4.31.9:

(i) if a total number of four or more public pay telephones (including both interior and exterior phones) is provided at a site, and at least one is in an interior location, then at least one interior public text telephone shall be provided.

(ii) if an interior public pay telephone is provided in a stadium or arena, in a convention center, in a hotel with a convention center, or

9

4.1.3 Accessible Buildings: New Construction

in a covered mall, at least one interior public text telephone shall be provided in the facility.

(iii) if a public pay telephone is located in or adjacent to a hospital emergency room, hospital recovery room, or hospital waiting room, one public text telephone shall be provided at each such location.

(d) Where a bank of telephones in the interior of a building consists of three or more public pay telephones, at least one public pay telephone in each such bank shall be equipped with a shelf and outlet in compliance with 4.31.9(2).

(18) If fixed or built-in seating or tables (including, but not limited to, study carrels and student laboratory stations), are provided in accessible public or common use areas, at least five percent (5%), but not less than one, of the fixed or built-in seating areas or tables shall comply with 4.32. An accessible route shall lead to and through such fixed or built-in seating areas, or tables.

(19)* Assembly areas:

(a) In places of assembly with fixed seating accessible wheelchair locations shall comply with 4.33.2, 4.33.3, and 4.33.4 and shall be provided consistent with the following table:

Capacity of Seating in Assembly Areas	Number of Required Wheelchair Locations
4 to 25	1
26 to 50	2
51 to 300	4
301 to 500	6
over 500	6, plus 1 additional space for each total seating capacity increase of 100

In addition, one percent, but not less than one, of all fixed seats shall be aisle seats with no armrests on the aisle side, or removable or folding armrests on the aisle side. Each such seat shall be identified by a sign or marker. Signage notifying patrons of the availability of such seats shall be posted at the ticket office. Aisle seats are not required to comply with 4.33.4.

(b) This paragraph applies to assembly areas where audible communications are integral to the use of the space (e.g., concert and lecture halls, playhouses and movie theaters, meeting rooms, etc.). Such assembly areas, if (1) they accommodate at least 50 persons, or if they have audio-amplification systems, and (2) they have fixed seating, shall have a permanently installed assistive listening system complying with 4.33. For other assembly areas, a permanently installed assistive listening system, or an adequate number of electrical outlets or other supplementary wiring necessary to support a portable assistive listening system shall be provided. The minimum number of receivers to be provided shall be equal to 4 percent of the total number of seats, but in no case less than two. Signage complying with applicable provisions of 4.30 shall be installed to notify patrons of the availability of a listening system.

(20) Where automated teller machines (ATMs) are provided, each ATM shall comply with the requirements of 4.34 except where two or more are provided at a location. then only one must comply.

EXCEPTION: Drive-up-only automated teller machines are not required to comply with 4.27.2, 4.27.3 and 4.34.3.

(21) Where dressing and fitting rooms are provided for use by the general public, patients, customers or employees, 5 percent, but never less than one, of dressing rooms for each type of use in each cluster of dressing rooms shall be accessible and shall comply with 4.35.

Examples of types of dressing rooms are those serving different genders or distinct and different functions as in different treatment or examination facilities.

4.1.4 (Reserved).

4.1.5 Accessible Buildings: Additions.

Each addition to an existing building or facility shall be regarded as an alteration. Each space or element added to the existing building or facility shall comply with the applicable provisions of 4.1.1 to 4.1.3, Minimum Requirements (for New Construction) and the applicable technical specifications of 4.2 through 4.35 and sections 5 through 10. Each addition that

10

Federal Register / Vol. 56, No. 144 / Friday, July 26, 1991 / Rules and Regulations

affects or could affect the usability of an area containing a primary function shall comply with 4.1.6(2).

4.1.6 Accessible Buildings: Alterations.

(1) General. Alterations to existing buildings and facilities shall comply with the following:

(a) No alteration shall be undertaken which decreases or has the effect of decreasing accessibility or usability of a building or facility below the requirements for new construction at the time of alteration.

(b) If existing elements, spaces, or common areas are altered, then each such altered element, space, feature, or area shall comply with the applicable provisions of 4.1.1 to 4.1.3 Minimum Requirements (for New Construction). If the applicable provision for new construction requires that an element, space, or common area be on an accessible route, the altered element, space, or common area is not required to be on an accessible route except as provided in 4.1.6(2) (Alterations to an Area Containing a Primary Function.)

(c) If alterations of single elements, when considered together, amount to an alteration of a room or space in a building or facility, the entire space shall be made accessible.

(d) No alteration of an existing element, space, or area of a building or facility shall impose a requirement for greater accessibility than that which would be required for new construction. For example, if the elevators and stairs in a building are being altered and the elevators are, in turn, being made accessible, then no accessibility modifications are required to the stairs connecting levels connected by the elevator. If stair modifications to correct unsafe conditions are required by other codes, the modifications shall be done in compliance with these guidelines unless technically infeasible.

(e) At least one interior public text telephone complying with 4.31.9 shall be provided if:

(i) alterations to existing buildings or facilities with less than four exterior or interior public pay telephones would increase the total number to four or more telephones with at least one in an interior location; or

(ii) alterations to one or more exterior or interior public pay telephones occur in an existing building or facility with four or more public telephones with at least one in an interior location.

(f) If an escalator or stair is planned or installed where none existed previously and major structural modifications are necessary for such installation, then a means of accessible vertical access shall be provided that complies with the applicable provisions of 4.7, 4.8, 4.10, or 4.11.

(g) In alterations, the requirements of 4.1.3(9), 4.3.10 and 4.3.11 do not apply.

(h)*Entrances: If a planned alteration entails alterations to an entrance, and the building has an accessible entrance, the entrance being altered is not required to comply with 4.1.3(8), except to the extent required by 4.1.6(2). If a particular entrance is not made accessible, appropriate accessible signage indicating the location of the nearest accessible entrance(s) shall be installed at or near the inaccessible entrance, such that a person with disabilities will not be required to retrace the approach route from the inaccessible entrance.

(i) If the alteration work is limited solely to the electrical, mechanical, or plumbing system, or to hazardous material abatement, or automatic sprinkler retrofitting, and does not involve the alteration of any elements or spaces required to be accessible under these guidelines, then 4.1.6(2) does not apply.

(j) EXCEPTION: In alteration work, if compliance with 4.1.6 is technically infeasible, the alteration shall provide accessibility to the maximum extent feasible. Any elements or features of the building or facility that are being altered and can be made accessible shall be made accessible within the scope of the alteration.

Technically Infeasible. Means, with respect to an alteration of a building or a facility, that it has little likelihood of being accomplished because existing structural conditions would require removing or altering a load-bearing member which is an essential part of the structural frame; or because other existing physical or site constraints prohibit modification or

11

4.1.6 Accessible Buildings: Alterations

addition of elements, spaces, or features which are in full and strict compliance with the minimum requirements for new construction and which are necessary to provide accessibility.

(k) EXCEPTION:

(i) These guidelines do not require the installation of an elevator in an altered facility that is less than three stories or has less than 3,000 square feet per story unless the building is a shopping center, a shopping mall, the professional office of a health care provider, or another type of facility as determined by the Attorney General.

(ii) The exemption provided in paragraph (i) does not obviate or limit in any way the obligation to comply with the other accessibility requirements established in these guidelines. For example, alterations to floors above or below the ground floor must be accessible regardless of whether the altered facility has an elevator. If a facility subject to the elevator exemption set forth in paragraph (i) nonetheless has a full passenger elevator, that elevator shall meet, to the maximum extent feasible, the accessibility requirements of these guidelines.

(2) Alterations to an Area Containing a Primary Function: In addition to the requirements of 4.1.6(1), an alteration that affects or could affect the usability of or access to an area containing a primary function shall be made so as to ensure that, to the maximum extent feasible, the path of travel to the altered area and the restrooms, telephones, and drinking fountains serving the altered area, are readily accessible to and usable by individuals with disabilities, unless such alterations are disproportionate to the overall alterations in terms of cost and scope (as determined under criteria established by the Attorney General).

(3) Special Technical Provisions for Alterations to Existing Buildings and Facilities:

(a) Ramps: Curb ramps and interior or exterior ramps to be constructed on sites or in existing buildings or facilities where space limitations prohibit the use of a 1:12 slope or less may have slopes and rises as follows:

(i) A slope between 1:10 and 1:12 is allowed for a maximum rise of 6 inches.

(ii) A slope between 1:8 and 1:10 is allowed for a maximum rise of 3 inches. A slope steeper than 1:8 is not allowed.

(b) Stairs: Full extension of handrails at stairs shall not be required in alterations where such extensions would be hazardous or impossible due to plan configuration.

(c) Elevators:

(i) If safety door edges are provided in existing automatic elevators, automatic door reopening devices may be omitted (see 4.10.6).

(ii) Where existing shaft configuration or technical infeasibility prohibits strict compliance with 4.10.9, the minimum car plan dimensions may be reduced by the minimum amount necessary, but in no case shall the inside car area be smaller than 48 in by 48 in.

(iii) Equivalent facilitation may be provided with an elevator car of different dimensions when usability can be demonstrated and when all other elements required to be accessible comply with the applicable provisions of 4.10. For example, an elevator of 47 in by 69 in (1195 mm by 1755 mm) with a door opening on the narrow dimension, could accommodate the standard wheelchair clearances shown in Figure 4.

(d) Doors:

(i) Where it is technically infeasible to comply with clear opening width requirements of 4.13.5, a projection of 5/8 in maximum will be permitted for the latch side stop.

(ii) If existing thresholds are 3/4 in high or less, and have (or are modified to have) a beveled edge on each side, they may remain.

(e) Toilet Rooms:

(i) Where it is technically infeasible to comply with 4.22 or 4.23, the installation of at least one unisex toilet/bathroom per floor, located in the same area as existing toilet facilities, will be permitted in lieu of modifying existing toilet facilities to be accessible. Each unisex toilet room shall contain one water closet complying with 4.16 and one lavatory complying with 4.19, and the door shall have a privacy latch.

12

4.1.7 Accessible Buildings: Historic Preservation

(ii) Where it is technically infeasible to install a required standard stall (Fig. 30(a)), or where other codes prohibit reduction of the fixture count (i.e., removal of a water closet in order to create a double-wide stall), either alternate stall (Fig. 30(b)) may be provided in lieu of the standard stall.

(iii) When existing toilet or bathing facilities are being altered and are not made accessible, signage complying with 4.30.1, 4.30.2, 4.30.3, 4.30.5, and 4.30.7 shall be provided indicating the location of the nearest accessible toilet or bathing facility within the facility.

(f) Assembly Areas:

(i) Where it is technically infeasible to disperse accessible seating throughout an altered assembly area, accessible seating areas may be clustered. Each accessible seating area shall have provisions for companion seating and shall be located on an accessible route that also serves as a means of emergency egress.

(ii) Where it is technically infeasible to alter all performing areas to be on an accessible route, at least one of each type of performing area shall be made accessible.

(g) Platform Lifts (Wheelchair Lifts): In alterations, platform lifts (wheelchair lifts) complying with 4.11 and applicable state or local codes may be used as part of an accessible route. The use of lifts is not limited to the four conditions in exception 4 of 4.1.3(5).

(h) Dressing Rooms: In alterations where technical infeasibility can be demonstrated, one dressing room for each sex on each level shall be made accessible. Where only unisex dressing rooms are provided, accessible unisex dressing rooms may be used to fulfill this requirement.

4.1.7 Accessible Buildings: Historic Preservation.

(1) Applicability:

(a) General Rule. Alterations to a qualified historic building or facility shall comply with 4.1.6 Accessible Buildings: Alterations, the applicable technical specifications of 4.2 through 4.35 and the applicable special application sections 5 through 10 unless it is determined in accordance with the procedures in 4.1.7(2) that compliance with the requirements for accessible routes (exterior and interior), ramps, entrances, or toilets would threaten or destroy the historic significance of the building or facility in which case the alternative requirements in 4.1.7(3) may be used for the feature.

EXCEPTION: (Reserved).

(b) Definition. A qualified historic building or facility is a building or facility that is:

(i) Listed in or eligible for listing in the National Register of Historic Places; or

(ii) Designated as historic under an appropriate State or local law.

(2) Procedures:

(a) Alterations to Qualified Historic Buildings and Facilities Subject to Section 106 of the National Historic Preservation Act:

(i) Section 106 Process. Section 106 of the National Historic Preservation Act (16 U.S.C. 470 f) requires that a Federal agency with jurisdiction over a Federal, federally assisted, or federally licensed undertaking consider the effects of the agency's undertaking on buildings and facilities listed in or eligible for listing in the National Register of Historic Places and give the Advisory Council on Historic Preservation a reasonable opportunity to comment on the undertaking prior to approval of the undertaking.

(ii) ADA Application. Where alterations are undertaken to a qualified historic building or facility that is subject to section 106 of the National Historic Preservation Act, the Federal agency with jurisdiction over the undertaking shall follow the section 106 process. If the State Historic Preservation Officer or Advisory Council on Historic Preservation agrees that compliance with the requirements for accessible routes (exterior and interior), ramps, entrances, or toilets would threaten or destroy the historic significance of the building or facility, the alternative requirements in 4.1.7(3) may be used for the feature.

13

439

35620   Federal Register / Vol. 56, No. 144 / Friday, July 26, 1991 / Rules and Regulations

4.2 Space Allowance and Reach Ranges

(b) Alterations to Qualified Historic Buildings and Facilities Not Subject to Section 106 of the National Historic Preservation Act. Where alterations are undertaken to a qualified historic building or facility that is not subject to section 106 of the National Historic Preservation Act, if the entity undertaking the alterations believes that compliance with the requirements for accessible routes (exterior and interior), ramps, entrances, or toilets would threaten or destroy the historic significance of the building or facility and that the alternative requirements in 4.1.7(3) should be used for the feature, the entity should consult with the State Historic Preservation Officer. If the State Historic Preservation Officer agrees that compliance with the accessibility requirements for accessible routes (exterior and interior), ramps, entrances or toilets would threaten or destroy the historical significance of the building or facility, the alternative requirements in 4.1.7(3) may be used.

(c) Consultation With Interested Persons. Interested persons should be invited to participate in the consultation process, including State or local accessibility officials, individuals with disabilities, and organizations representing individuals with disabilities.

(d) Certified Local Government Historic Preservation Programs. Where the State Historic Preservation Officer has delegated the consultation responsibility for purposes of this section to a local government historic preservation program that has been certified in accordance with section 101(c) of the National Historic Preservation Act of 1966 (16 U.S.C. 470a (c)) and implementing regulations (36 CFR 61.5), the responsibility may be carried out by the appropriate local government body or official.

(3) Historic Preservation: Minimum Requirements:

(a) At least one accessible route complying with 4.3 from a site access point to an accessible entrance shall be provided.

EXCEPTION: A ramp with a slope no greater than 1:6 for a run not to exceed 2 ft (610 mm) may be used as part of an accessible route to an entrance.

(b) At least one accessible entrance complying with 4.14 which is used by the public shall be provided.

EXCEPTION: If it is determined that no entrance used by the public can comply with 4.14, then access at any entrance not used by the general public but open (unlocked) with directional signage at the primary entrance may be used. The accessible entrance shall also have a notification system. Where security is a problem, remote monitoring may be used.

(c) If toilets are provided, then at least one toilet facility complying with 4.22 and 4.1.6 shall be provided along an accessible route that complies with 4.3. Such toilet facility may be unisex in design.

(d) Accessible routes from an accessible entrance to all publicly used spaces on at least the level of the accessible entrance shall be provided. Access shall be provided to all levels of a building or facility in compliance with 4.1 whenever practical.

(e) Displays and written information, documents, etc., should be located where they can be seen by a seated person. Exhibits and signage displayed horizontally (e.g., open books), should be no higher than 44 in (1120 mm) above the floor surface.

NOTE: The technical provisions of sections 4.2 through 4.35 are the same as those of the American National Standard Institute's document A117.1-1980, except as noted in the text.

4.2 Space Allowance and Reach Ranges.

4.2.1* Wheelchair Passage Width. The minimum clear width for single wheelchair passage shall be 32 in (815 mm) at a point and 36 in (915 mm) continuously (see Fig. 1 and 24(e)).

4.2.2 Width for Wheelchair Passing. The minimum width for two wheelchairs to pass is 60 in (1525 mm) (see Fig. 2).

4.2.3* Wheelchair Turning Space. The space required for a wheelchair to make a 180-degree turn is a clear space of 60 in (1525 mm)

14

4.2.4* Clear Floor or Ground Space for Wheelchairs

diameter (see Fig. 3(a)) or a T-shaped space (see Fig. 3(b)).

4.2.4* Clear Floor or Ground Space for Wheelchairs.

4.2.4.1 Size and Approach. The minimum clear floor or ground space required to accommodate a single, stationary wheelchair and occupant is 30 in by 48 in (760 mm by 1220 mm) (see Fig. 4(a)). The minimum clear floor or ground space for wheelchairs may be positioned for forward or parallel approach to an object (see Fig. 4(b) and (c)). Clear floor or ground space for wheelchairs may be part of the knee space required under some objects.

4.2.4.2 Relationship of Maneuvering Clearance to Wheelchair Spaces. One full unobstructed side of the clear floor or ground space for a wheelchair shall adjoin or overlap an accessible route or adjoin another wheelchair clear floor space. If a clear floor space is located in an alcove or otherwise confined on all or part of three sides, additional maneuvering clearances shall be provided as shown in Fig. 4(d) and (e).

4.2.4.3 Surfaces for Wheelchair Spaces. Clear floor or ground spaces for wheelchairs shall comply with 4.5.

4.2.5* Forward Reach. If the clear floor space only allows forward approach to an object, the maximum high forward reach allowed shall be 48 in (1220 mm) (see Fig. 5(a)). *The minimum low forward reach is 15 in (380 mm).* If the high forward reach is over an obstruction, reach and clearances shall be as shown in Fig. 5(b).

4.2.6* Side Reach. If the clear floor space allows parallel approach by a person in a wheelchair, the maximum high side reach allowed shall be 54 in (1370 mm) and the low side reach shall be no less than 9 in (230 mm) above the floor (Fig. 6(a) and (b)). If the side reach is over an obstruction, the reach and clearances shall be as shown in Fig 6(c).

4.3 Accessible Route.

4.3.1* General. All walks, halls, corridors, aisles, *skywalks, tunnels,* and other spaces

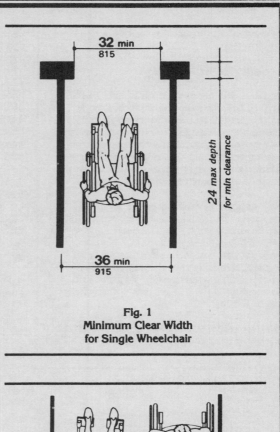

Fig. 1
Minimum Clear Width
for Single Wheelchair

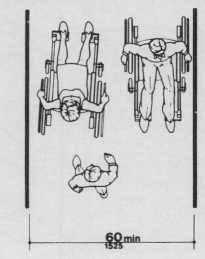

Fig. 2
Minimum Clear Width
for Two Wheelchairs

15

Appendix A

4.3 Accesssible Route

that are part of an accessible route shall comply with 4.3.

4.3.2 Location.

(1) At least one accessible route *within the boundary of the site* shall be provided from public transportation stops, accessible parking, and accessible passenger loading zones, and public streets or sidewalks to the accessible building entrance they serve. *The accessible route shall, to the maximum extent feasible, coincide with the route for the general public.*

(2) At least one accessible route shall connect accessible buildings, facilities, elements, and spaces that are on the same site.

(3) At least one accessible route shall connect accessible building or facility entrances with all accessible spaces and elements and with all accessible dwelling units within the building or facility.

(4) An accessible route shall connect at least one accessible entrance of each accessible

dwelling unit with those exterior and interior spaces and facilities that serve the accessible dwelling unit.

4.3.3 Width. The minimum clear width of an accessible route shall be 36 in (915 mm) except at doors (see 4.13.5 and 4.13.6). If a person in a wheelchair must make a turn around an obstruction, the minimum clear width of the accessible route shall be as shown in Fig. 7(a) and (b).

4.3.4 Passing Space. If an accessible route has less than 60 in (1525 mm) clear width, then passing spaces at least 60 in by 60 in (1525 mm by 1525 mm) shall be located at reasonable intervals not to exceed 200 ft (61 m). A T-intersection of two corridors or walks is an acceptable passing place.

4.3.5 Head Room. Accessible routes shall comply with 4.4.2.

4.3.6 Surface Textures. The surface of an accessible route shall comply with 4.5.

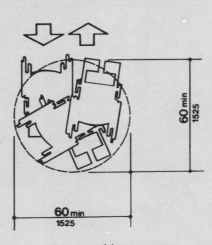

(a)
60-in (1525-mm)-Diameter Space

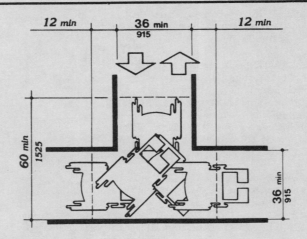

(b)
T-Shaped Space for 180° Turns

Fig. 3
Wheelchair Turning Space

16

Federal Register / Vol. 56, No. 144 / Friday, July 26, 1991 / Rules and Regulations   **35623**

4.3 Accessible Route

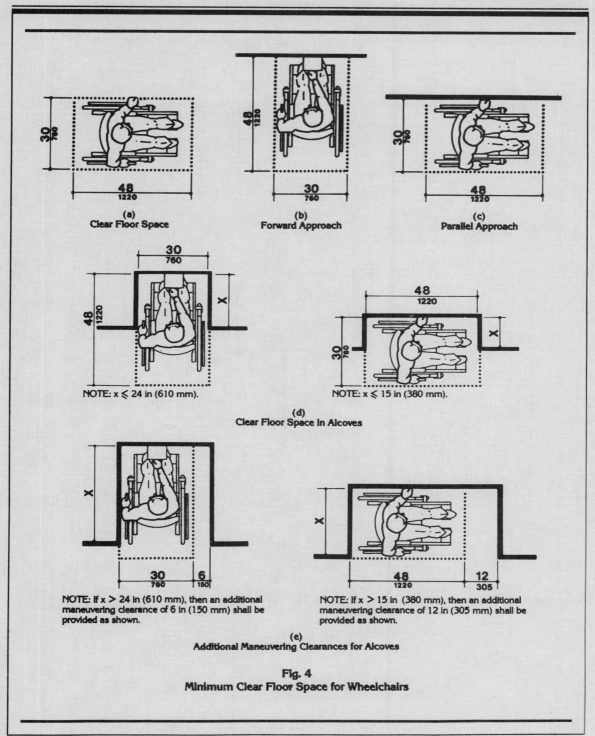

(a)
Clear Floor Space

(b)
Forward Approach

(c)
Parallel Approach

NOTE: x ≤ 24 in (610 mm).

NOTE: x ≤ 15 in (380 mm).

(d)
Clear Floor Space in Alcoves

NOTE: If x > 24 in (610 mm), then an additional maneuvering clearance of 6 in (150 mm) shall be provided as shown.

NOTE: If x > 15 in (380 mm), then an additional maneuvering clearance of 12 in (305 mm) shall be provided as shown.

(e)
Additional Maneuvering Clearances for Alcoves

Fig. 4
Minimum Clear Floor Space for Wheelchairs

17

Appendix A

4.3 Accessible Route

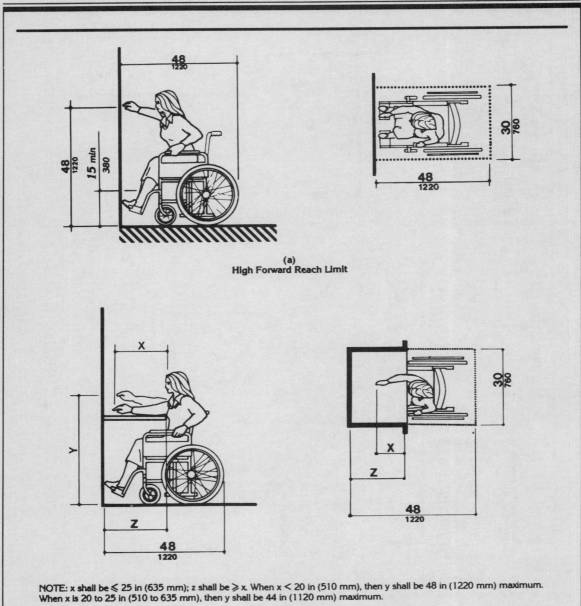

(a)
High Forward Reach Limit

NOTE: x shall be ≤ 25 in (635 mm); z shall be ≥ x. When x < 20 in (510 mm), then y shall be 48 in (1220 mm) maximum. When x is 20 to 25 in (510 to 635 mm), then y shall be 44 in (1120 mm) maximum.

(b)
Maximum Forward Reach over an Obstruction

Fig. 5
Forward Reach

4.3.7 Slope

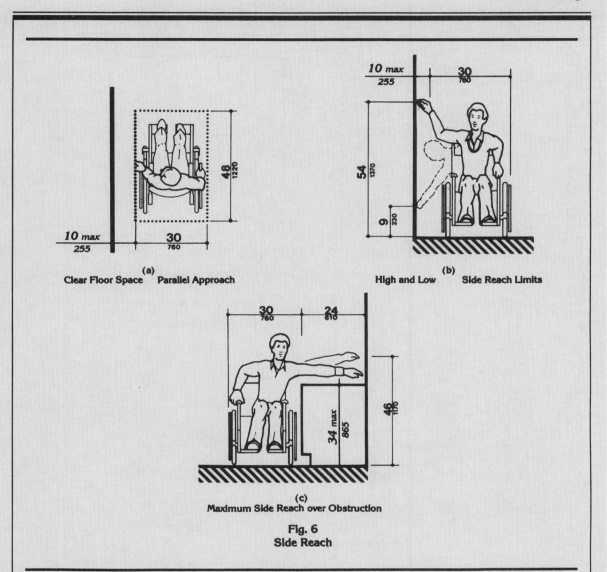

(a)
Clear Floor Space   Parallel Approach

(b)
High and Low   Side Reach Limits

(c)
Maximum Side Reach over Obstruction

Fig. 6
Side Reach

4.3.7 Slope. An accessible route with a running slope greater than 1:20 is a ramp and shall comply with 4.8. Nowhere shall the cross slope of an accessible route exceed 1:50.

4.3.8 Changes in Levels. Changes in levels along an accessible route shall comply with 4.5.2. If an accessible route has changes in level greater than 1/2 in (13 mm), then a curb ramp, ramp, elevator, or platform lift *(as permitted in 4.1.3 and 4.1.6)* shall be provided that complies with 4.7, 4.8, 4.10, or 4.11, respectively. An accessible route does not include stairs, steps, or escalators. See definition of "egress, means of" in 3.5.

4.3.9 Doors. Doors along an accessible route shall comply with 4.13.

19

Appendix A

4.3.10* Egress

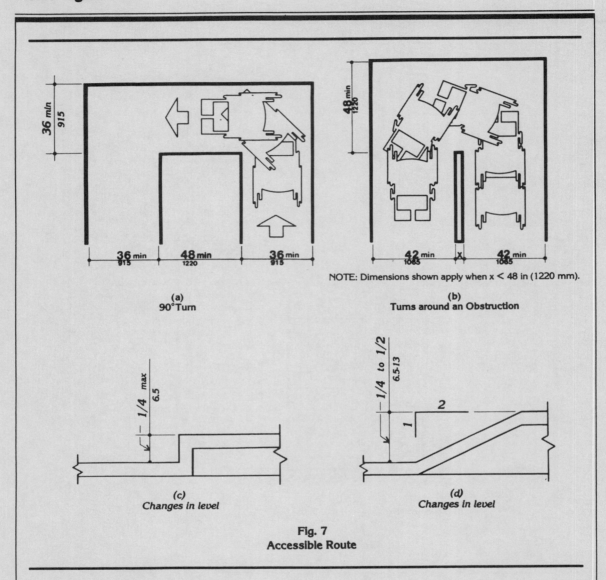

NOTE: Dimensions shown apply when x < 48 in (1220 mm).

(a)
90° Turn

(b)
Turns around an Obstruction

(c)
Changes in level

(d)
Changes in level

Fig. 7
Accessible Route

4.3.10* Egress. Accessible routes serving any accessible space or element shall also serve as a means of egress for emergencies or connect to an accessible area of *rescue assistance*.

4.3.11 Areas of Rescue Assistance.

4.3.11.1 Location and Construction. An area of rescue assistance shall be one of the following:

(1) A portion of a stairway landing within a smokeproof enclosure (complying with local requirements).

(2) A portion of an exterior exit balcony located immediately adjacent to an exit stairway when the balcony complies with local requirements for exterior exit balconies. Openings to the interior of the building located within 20 feet (6 m) of the

20

Federal Register / Vol. 56, No. 144 / Friday, July 26, 1991 / Rules and Regulations   **35627**

4.4 Protruding Objects

area of rescue assistance shall be protected with fire assemblies having a three-fourths hour fire protection rating.

(3) A portion of a one-hour fire-resistive corridor (complying with local requirements for fire-resistive construction and for openings) located immediately adjacent to an exit enclosure.

(4) A vestibule located immediately adjacent to an exit enclosure and constructed to the same fire-resistive standards as required for corridors and openings.

(5) A portion of a stairway landing within an exit enclosure which is vented to the exterior and is separated from the interior of the building with not less than one-hour fire-resistive doors.

(6) When approved by the appropriate local authority, an area or a room which is separated from other portions of the building by a smoke barrier. Smoke barriers shall have a fire-resistive rating of not less than one hour and shall completely enclose the area or room. Doors in the smoke barrier shall be tight-fitting smoke- and draft-control assemblies having a fire-protection rating of not less than 20 minutes and shall be self-closing or automatic closing. The area or room shall be provided with an exit directly to an exit enclosure. Where the room or area exits into an exit enclosure which is required to be of more than one-hour fire-resistive construction, the room or area shall have the same fire-resistive construction, including the same opening protection, as required for the adjacent exit enclosure.

(7) An elevator lobby when elevator shafts and adjacent lobbies are pressurized as required for smokeproof enclosures by local regulations and when complying with requirements herein for size, communication, and signage. Such pressurization system shall be activated by smoke detectors on each floor located in a manner approved by the appropriate local authority. Pressurization equipment and its duct work within the building shall be separated from other portions of the building by a minimum two-hour fire-resistive construction.

4.3.11.2 Size. Each area of rescue assistance shall provide at least two accessible areas each being not less than 30 inches by 48 inches (760 mm by 1220 mm). The area of rescue

assistance shall not encroach on any required exit width. The total number of such 30-inch by 48-inch (760 mm by 1220 mm) areas per story shall be not less than one for every 200 persons of calculated occupant load served by the area of rescue assistance.

EXCEPTION: The appropriate local authority may reduce the minimum number of 30-inch by 48-inch (760 mm by 1220 mm) areas to one for each area of rescue assistance on floors where the occupant load is less than 200.

4.3.11.3* Stairway Width. Each stairway adjacent to an area of rescue assistance shall have a minimum clear width of 48 inches between handrails.

4.3.11.4* Two-way Communication. A method of two-way communication, with both visible and audible signals, shall be provided between each area of rescue assistance and the primary entry. The fire department or appropriate local authority may approve a location other than the primary entry.

4.3.11.5 Identification. Each area of rescue assistance shall be identified by a sign which states "AREA OF RESCUE ASSISTANCE" and displays the international symbol of accessibility. The sign shall be illuminated when exit sign illumination is required. Signage shall also be installed at all inaccessible exits and where otherwise necessary to clearly indicate the direction to areas of rescue assistance. In each area of rescue assistance, instructions on the use of the area under emergency conditions shall be posted adjoining the two-way communication system.

4.4 Protruding Objects.

4.4.1* General. Objects projecting from walls (for example, telephones) with their leading edges between 27 in and 80 in (685 mm and 2030 mm) above the finished floor shall protrude no more than 4 in (100 mm) into walks, halls, corridors, passageways, or aisles (see Fig. 8(a)). Objects mounted with their leading edges at or below 27 in (685 mm) above the finished floor may protrude any amount (see Fig. 8(a) and (b)). Free-standing objects mounted on posts or pylons may overhang 12 in (305 mm) maximum from 27 in to 80 in (685 mm to 2030 mm) above the ground or

21

35628   Federal Register / Vol. 56, No. 144 / Friday, July 26, 1991 / Rules and Regulations

4.4 Protruding Objects

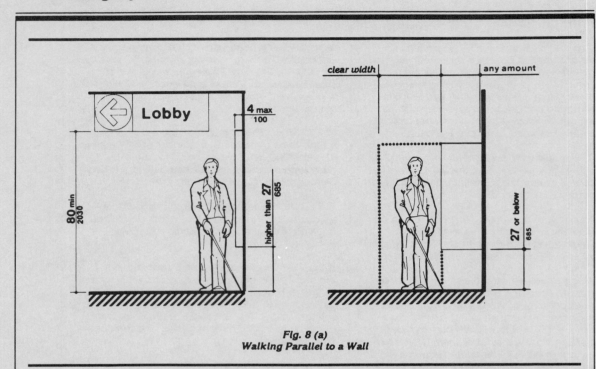

Fig. 8 (a)
Walking Parallel to a Wall

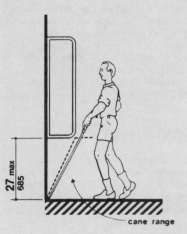

Fig. 8 (b)
Walking Perpendicular to a Wall

Fig. 8
Protruding Objects

finished floor (see Fig. 8(c) and (d)). Protruding objects shall not reduce the clear width of an accessible route or maneuvering space (see Fig. 8(e)).

4.4.2 Head Room. Walks, halls, corridors, passageways, aisles, or other circulation spaces shall have 80 in (2030 mm) minimum clear head room (see Fig. 8(a)). *If vertical clearance of an area adjoining an accessible route is reduced to less than 80 in (nominal dimension), a barrier to warn blind or visually-impaired persons shall be provided (see Fig. 8(c-1)).*

4.5 Ground and Floor Surfaces.

4.5.1* General. Ground and floor surfaces along accessible routes and in accessible rooms and spaces including floors, walks, ramps, stairs, and curb ramps, shall be stable, firm, slip-resistant, and shall comply with 4.5.

4.5.2 Changes in Level. Changes in level up to 1/4 in (6 mm) may be vertical and without edge treatment *(see Fig. 7(c))*. Changes in level between 1/4 in and 1/2 in (6 mm and 13 mm)

Federal Register / Vol. 56, No. 144 / Friday, July 26, 1991 / Rules and Regulations   35629

4.4 Protruding Objects

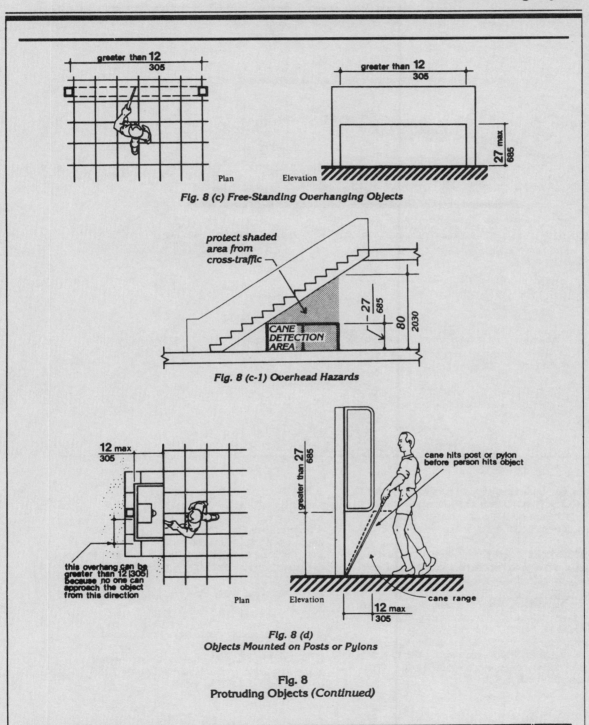

Fig. 8 (c) Free-Standing Overhanging Objects

Fig. 8 (c-1) Overhead Hazards

Fig. 8 (d)
Objects Mounted on Posts or Pylons

Fig. 8
Protruding Objects *(Continued)*

23

4.5 Ground and Floor Surfaces

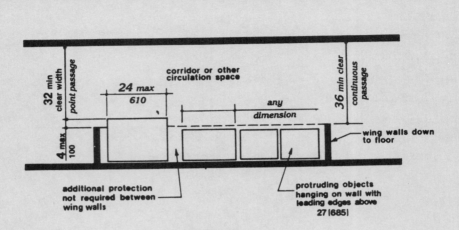

Fig. 8 (e)
Example of Protection around Wall-Mounted Objects and Measurements of Clear Widths

Fig. 8
Protruding Objects *(Continued)*

shall be beveled with a slope no greater than 1:2 *(see Fig. 7(d))*. Changes in level greater than 1/2 in (13 mm) shall be accomplished by means of a ramp that complies with 4.7 or 4.8.

4.5.3* Carpet. If carpet or carpet tile is used on a ground or floor surface, then it shall be securely attached; have a firm cushion, pad, or backing, or no cushion or pad; and have a level loop, textured loop, level cut pile, or level cut/uncut pile texture. The maximum pile *thickness* shall be 1/2 in (13 mm) (see Fig. 8(f)). Exposed edges of carpet shall be fastened to floor surfaces and have trim along the entire length of the exposed edge. Carpet edge trim shall comply with 4.5.2.

4.5.4 Gratings. If gratings are located in walking surfaces, then they shall have spaces no greater than 1/2 in (13 mm) wide in one direction *(see Fig. 8(g))*. If gratings have elongated openings, then they shall be placed so that the long dimension is perpendicular to the dominant direction of travel *(see Fig. 8(h))*.

4.6 Parking and Passenger Loading Zones.

4.6.1 Minimum Number. *Parking spaces required to be accessible by 4.1 shall comply with 4.6.2 through 4.6.5. Passenger loading zones required to be accessible by 4.1 shall comply with 4.6.5 and 4.6.6.*

4.6 Parking and Passenger Loading Zones

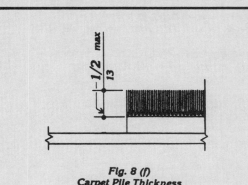

**Fig. 8 (f)
Carpet Pile Thickness**

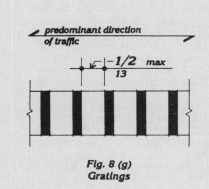

predominant direction
of traffic

**Fig. 8 (g)
Gratings**

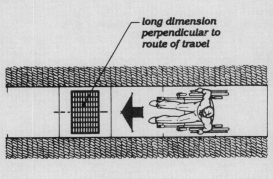

long dimension
perpendicular to
route of travel

**Fig. 8 (h)
Grating Orientation**

4.6.2 Location. *Accessible parking spaces serving* a particular building shall be located on the shortest accessible route of travel *from adjacent parking* to an accessible entrance. *In parking facilities* that do not serve a particular building, *accessible parking* shall be located on the shortest accessible route *of travel* to an accessible pedestrian entrance of the parking facility. *In buildings with multiple accessible entrances with adjacent parking, accessible parking spaces shall be dispersed and located closest to the accessible entrances.*

4.6.3* Parking Spaces. *Accessible* parking spaces shall be at least 96 in (2440 mm) wide. Parking access aisles shall be part of an accessible route to the building or facility entrance and shall comply with 4.3. Two accessible parking spaces may share a common access aisle (see Fig. 9). Parked vehicle overhangs shall not reduce the clear width of an accessible route. *Parking spaces and access aisles shall be level with surface slopes not exceeding 1:50 (2%) in all directions.*

4.6.4* Signage. Accessible parking spaces shall be designated as reserved by a sign showing the symbol of accessibility (see 4.30.7). *Spaces complying with 4.1.2(5)(b) shall have an additional sign "Van-Accessible" mounted below the symbol of accessibility.* Such signs shall *be located so they cannot be obscured by a vehicle parked in the space.*

4.6.5* Vertical Clearance. *Provide minimum vertical clearance of 114 in (2895 mm) at accessible passenger loading zones and along at least one vehicle access route to such areas from site entrance(s) and exit(s). At parking spaces complying with 4.1.2(5)(b), provide minimum vertical clearance of 98 in (2490 mm) at the parking space and along at least one vehicle access route to such spaces from site entrance(s) and exit(s).*

4.6.6 Passenger Loading Zones. Passenger loading zones shall provide an access aisle at least 60 in *(1525 mm)* wide and 20 ft *(240 in) (6100 mm)* long adjacent and parallel to the vehicle pull-up space (see Fig. 10). If there are curbs between the access aisle and the vehicle pull-up space, then a curb ramp complying with 4.7 shall be provided. *Vehicle standing spaces and access aisles shall be level with*

25

4.7 Curb Ramps

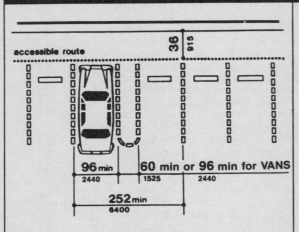

Fig. 9
Dimensions of Parking Spaces

surface slopes not exceeding 1:50 (2%) in all directions.

4.7 Curb Ramps.

4.7.1 Location. Curb ramps complying with 4.7 shall be provided wherever an accessible route crosses a curb.

4.7.2 Slope. Slopes of curb ramps shall comply with 4.8.2. The slope shall be measured as shown in Fig. 11. *Transitions from ramps to walks, gutters, or streets shall be flush and free of abrupt changes. Maximum slopes of adjoining gutters, road surface immediately adjacent to the curb ramp, or accessible route shall not exceed 1:20.*

4.7.3 Width. The minimum width of a curb ramp shall be 36 in (915 mm), exclusive of flared sides.

4.7.4 Surface. Surfaces of curb ramps shall comply with 4.5.

4.7.5 Sides of Curb Ramps. If a curb ramp is located where pedestrians must walk across the ramp, *or where it is not protected by handrails or guardrails*, it shall have flared sides; the maximum slope of the flare shall be 1:10 (see Fig. 12(a)). Curb ramps with returned curbs

may be used where pedestrians would not normally walk across the ramp (see Fig. 12(b)).

4.7.6 Built-up Curb Ramps. Built-up curb ramps shall be located so that they do not project into vehicular traffic lanes (see Fig. 13).

4.7.7 *Detectable Warnings*. A curb ramp shall have a *detectable* warning complying with 4.29.2. *The detectable warning shall extend* the full width and depth of the curb ramp.

4.7.8 Obstructions. Curb ramps shall be located or protected to prevent their obstruction by parked vehicles.

4.7.9 Location at Marked Crossings. Curb ramps at marked crossings shall be wholly contained within the markings, excluding any flared sides (see Fig. 15).

4.7.10 Diagonal Curb Ramps. If diagonal (or corner type) curb ramps have returned curbs or other well-defined edges, such edges shall be parallel to the direction of pedestrian flow. The bottom of diagonal curb ramps shall have 48 in (1220 mm) minimum clear space as shown in Fig. 15(c) and (d). If diagonal curb ramps are provided at marked crossings, the 48 in (1220 mm) clear space shall be within the markings (see Fig. 15(c) and (d)). If diagonal curb ramps have flared sides, they shall also have at least a 24 in (610 mm) long segment of straight curb located on each side of the curb ramp and within the marked crossing (see Fig. 15(c)).

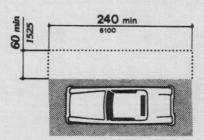

Fig. 10
Access Aisle at Passenger Loading Zones

26

4.8 Ramps

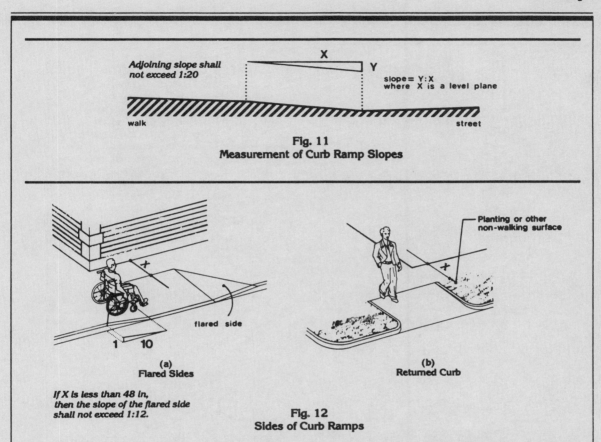

Fig. 11
Measurement of Curb Ramp Slopes

(a)
Flared Sides

(b)
Returned Curb

If X is less than 48 in, then the slope of the flared side shall not exceed 1:12.

Fig. 12
Sides of Curb Ramps

4.7.11 Islands. Any raised islands in crossings shall be cut through level with the street or have curb ramps at both sides and a level area at least 48 in (1220 mm) long between the curb ramps in the part of the island intersected by the crossings (see Fig. 15(a) and (b)).

4.8 Ramps.

4.8.1* General. Any part of an accessible route with a slope greater than 1:20 shall be considered a ramp and shall comply with 4.8.

4.8.2* Slope and Rise. The least possible slope shall be used for any ramp. The maximum slope of a ramp in new construction shall be 1:12. The maximum rise for any run shall be 30 in (760 mm) (see Fig. 16). Curb ramps

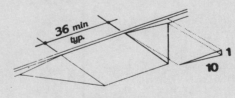

Fig. 13
Built-Up Curb Ramp

and ramps to be constructed on existing sites or in existing buildings or facilities may have slopes and rises as *allowed in 4.1.6(3)(a)* if space limitations prohibit the use of a 1:12 slope or less.

27

35634   Federal Register / Vol. 56, No. 144 / Friday, July 26, 1991 / Rules and Regulations

4.8 Ramps

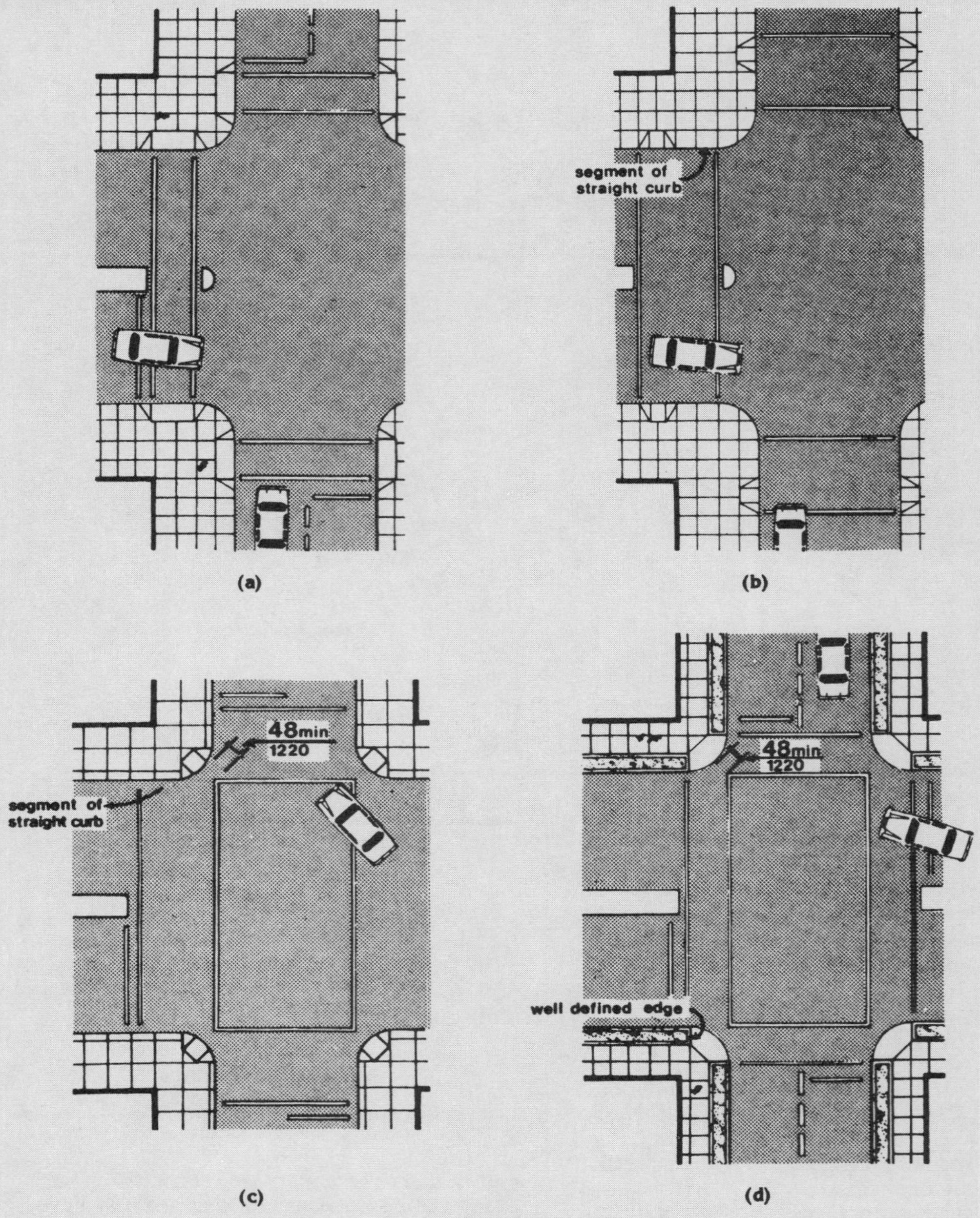

(a)

(b)

segment of
straight curb

(c)

48min.
1220

segment of
straight curb

(d)

48min.
1220

well defined edge

Fig. 15
Curb Ramps at Marked Crossings

28

454

4.8 Ramps

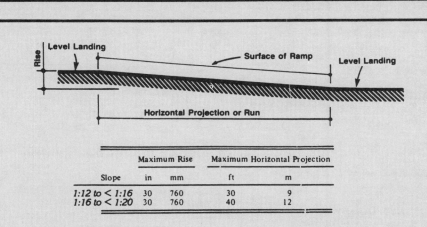

Slope	Maximum Rise		Maximum Horizontal Projection	
	in	mm	ft	m
1:12 to < 1:16	30	760	30	9
1:16 to < 1:20	30	760	40	12

Fig. 16
Components of a Single Ramp Run and Sample Ramp Dimensions

4.8.3 Clear Width. The minimum clear width of a ramp shall be 36 in (915 mm).

4.8.4* Landings. Ramps shall have level landings at bottom and top of *each ramp and each ramp* run. Landings shall have the following features:

(1) The landing shall be at least as wide as the ramp run leading to it.

(2) The landing length shall be a minimum of 60 in (1525 mm) clear.

(3) If ramps change direction at landings, the minimum landing size shall be 60 in by 60 in (1525 mm by 1525 mm).

(4) If a doorway is located at a landing, then the area in front of the doorway shall comply with 4.13.6.

4.8.5* Handrails. If a ramp run has a rise greater than 6 in (150 mm) or a horizontal projection greater than 72 in (1830 mm), then it shall have handrails on both sides. Handrails are not required on curb ramps *or adjacent to seating in assembly areas.* Handrails shall comply with 4.26 and shall have the following features:

(1) Handrails shall be provided along both sides of ramp segments. The inside handrail on switchback or dogleg ramps shall always be continuous.

(2) If handrails are not continuous, they shall extend at least 12 in (305 mm) beyond the top and bottom of the ramp segment and shall be parallel with the floor or ground surface (see Fig. 17).

(3) The clear space between the handrail and the wall shall be 1 - 1/2 in (38 mm).

(4) Gripping surfaces shall be continuous.

(5) *Top of handrail gripping surfaces shall be mounted between 34 in and 38 in (865 mm and 965 mm) above ramp surfaces.*

(6) *Ends of handrails shall be either rounded or returned smoothly to floor, wall, or post.*

(7) *Handrails shall not rotate within their fittings.*

4.8.6 Cross Slope and Surfaces. The cross slope of ramp surfaces shall be no greater than 1:50. Ramp surfaces shall comply with 4.5.

29

Appendix A

4.9 Stairs

4.8.7 Edge Protection. Ramps and landings with drop-offs shall have curbs, walls, railings, or projecting surfaces that prevent people from slipping off the ramp. Curbs shall be a minimum of 2 in (50 mm) high (see Fig. 17).

4.8.8 Outdoor Conditions. Outdoor ramps and their approaches shall be designed so that water will not accumulate on walking surfaces.

4.9 Stairs.

4.9.1* Minimum Number. *Stairs required to be accessible by 4.1 shall comply with 4.9.*

4.9.2 Treads and Risers. On any given flight of stairs, all steps shall have uniform riser heights and uniform tread widths. Stair treads shall be no less than 11 in (280 mm) wide, measured from riser to riser (see Fig. 18(a)). *Open risers are not permitted.*

4.9.3 Nosings. The undersides of nosings shall not be abrupt. The radius of curvature at the leading edge of the tread shall be no greater than 1/2 in (13 mm). Risers shall be sloped or the underside of the nosing shall have an angle not less than 60 degrees from the horizontal. Nosings shall project no more than 1-1/2 in (38 mm) (see Fig. 18).

4.9.4 Handrails. Stairways shall have handrails at both sides of all stairs. Handrails shall comply with 4.26 and shall have the following features:

(1) Handrails shall be continuous along both sides of stairs. The inside handrail on switchback or dogleg stairs shall always be continuous (see Fig. 19(a) and (b)).

(2) If handrails are not continuous, they shall extend at least 12 in (305 mm) beyond the top riser and at least 12 in (305 mm) plus the width of one tread beyond the bottom riser. At the top, the extension shall be parallel with the floor or ground surface. At the bottom, the handrail shall continue to slope for a distance of the width of one tread from the bottom riser; the remainder of the extension shall be horizontal (see Fig. 19(c) and (d)). Handrail extensions shall comply with 4.4.

(3) The clear space between handrails and wall shall be 1-1/2 in (38 mm).

(4) Gripping surfaces shall be uninterrupted by newel posts, other construction elements, or obstructions.

(5) *Top of handrail gripping surface shall be mounted between 34 in and 38 in (865 mm and 965 mm) above stair nosings.*

(6) *Ends of handrails shall be either rounded or returned smoothly to floor, wall or post.*

(7) *Handrails shall not rotate within their fittings.*

4.9.5 Detectable Warnings at Stairs. (Reserved).

4.9.6 Outdoor Conditions. Outdoor stairs and their approaches shall be designed so that water will not accumulate on walking surfaces.

4.10 Elevators.

4.10.1 General. *Accessible* elevators shall be on an accessible route and shall comply with 4.10 and with the *ASME A17.1-1990*, Safety Code for Elevators and Escalators. *Freight elevators shall not be considered as meeting the requirements of this section unless the only elevators provided are used as combination passenger and freight elevators for the public and employees.*

4.10.2 Automatic Operation. Elevator operation shall be automatic. Each car shall be equipped with a self-leveling feature that will automatically bring the car to floor landings within a tolerance of 1/2 in (13 mm) under rated loading to zero loading conditions. This self-leveling feature shall be automatic and independent of the operating device and shall correct the overtravel or undertravel.

4.10.3 Hall Call Buttons. Call buttons in elevator lobbies and halls shall be centered at 42 in (1065 mm) above the floor. Such call buttons shall have visual signals to indicate when each call is registered and when each call is answered. Call buttons shall be a minimum of 3/4 in (19 mm) in the smallest dimension. The button designating the up direction shall be on top. (See Fig. 20.) *Buttons shall be raised or flush. Objects mounted beneath hall call buttons shall not project into the elevator lobby more than 4 in (100 mm).*

30

456

Federal Register / Vol. 56, No. 144 / Friday, July 26, 1991 / Rules and Regulations   **35637**

4.10 Elevators

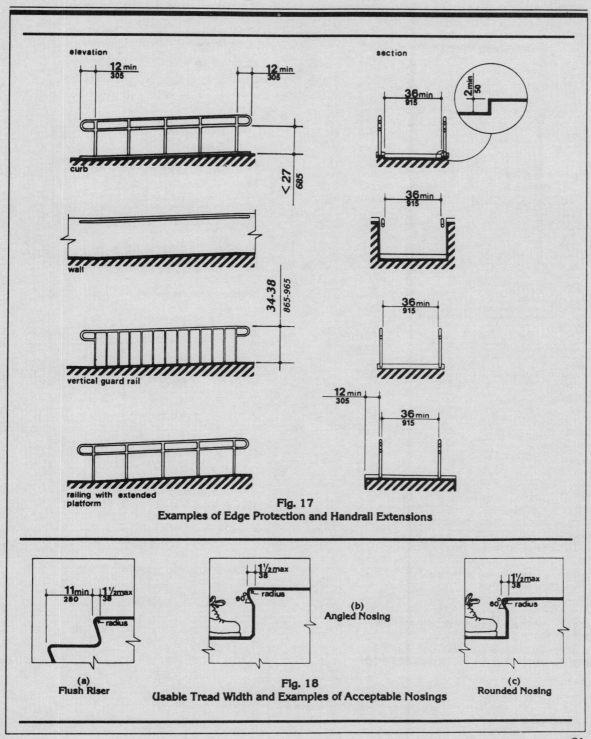

Fig. 17
Examples of Edge Protection and Handrail Extensions

Fig. 18
Usable Tread Width and Examples of Acceptable Nosings

31

35638   Federal Register / Vol. 56, No. 144 / Friday, July 26, 1991 / Rules and Regulations

4.10 Elevators

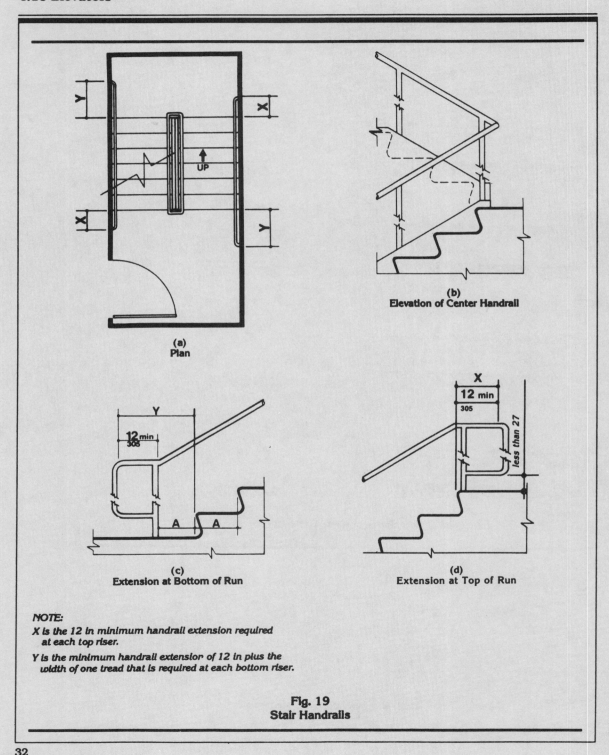

(a)
Plan

(b)
Elevation of Center Handrail

(c)
Extension at Bottom of Run

(d)
Extension at Top of Run

NOTE:

X is the 12 in minimum handrail extension required at each top riser.

Y is the minimum handrail extension of 12 in plus the width of one tread that is required at each bottom riser.

Fig. 19
Stair Handrails

32

4.10 Elevators

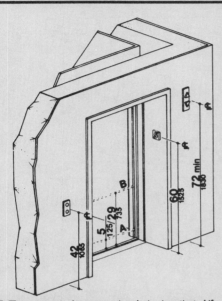

NOTE: The automatic door reopening device is activated if an object passes through either line A or line B. Line A and line B represent the vertical locations of the door reopening device not requiring contact.

**Fig. 20
Hoistway and Elevator Entrances**

4.10.4 Hall Lanterns. A visible and audible signal shall be provided at each hoistway entrance to indicate which car is answering a call. Audible signals shall sound once for the up direction and twice for the down direction or shall have verbal annunciators that say "up" or "down." Visible signals shall have the following features:

(1) Hall lantern fixtures shall be mounted so that their centerline is at least 72 in (1830 mm) above the lobby floor. (See Fig. 20.)

(2) Visual elements shall be at least 2-1/2 in (64 mm) in the smallest dimension.

(3) Signals shall be visible from the vicinity of the hall call button (see Fig. 20). In-car lanterns located in cars, visible from the vicinity of hall call buttons, and conforming to the above requirements, shall be acceptable.

4.10.5 *Raised and Braille* Characters on Hoistway Entrances. All elevator hoistway entrances shall have *raised and Braille* floor designations provided on both jambs. The centerline of the characters shall be 60 in (1525 mm) *above finish* floor. Such characters shall be 2 in (50 mm) high and shall comply with 4.30.4. Permanently applied plates are acceptable if they are permanently fixed to the jambs. (See Fig. 20).

4.10.6* Door Protective and Reopening Device. Elevator doors shall open and close automatically. They shall be provided with a reopening device that will stop and reopen a car door and hoistway door automatically if the door becomes obstructed by an object or person. The device shall be capable of completing these operations without requiring contact for an obstruction passing through the opening at heights of 5 in and 29 in (125 mm and 735 mm) above finish floor (see Fig. 20). Door reopening devices shall remain effective for at least 20 seconds. After such an interval, doors may close in accordance with the requirements of *ASME A17.1-1990.*

4.10.7* Door and Signal Timing for Hall Calls. The minimum acceptable time from notification that a car is answering a call until the doors of that car start to close shall be calculated from the following equation:

$$T = D/(1.5 \text{ ft/s}) \text{ or } T = D/(445 \text{ mm/s})$$

where T total time in seconds and D distance (in feet or millimeters) from a point in the lobby or corridor 60 in (1525 mm) directly in front of the farthest call button controlling that car to the centerline of its hoistway door (see Fig. 21). For cars with in-car lanterns, T begins when the lantern is visible from the vicinity of hall call buttons and an audible signal is sounded. *The minimum acceptable notification time shall be 5 seconds.*

4.10.8 Door Delay for Car Calls. The minimum time for elevator doors to remain fully open in response to a car call shall be 3 seconds.

4.10.9 Floor Plan of Elevator Cars. The floor area of elevator cars shall provide space for wheelchair users to enter the car, maneuver

33

4.10.12 Car Controls

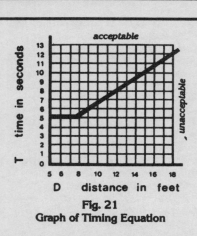

Fig. 21
Graph of Timing Equation

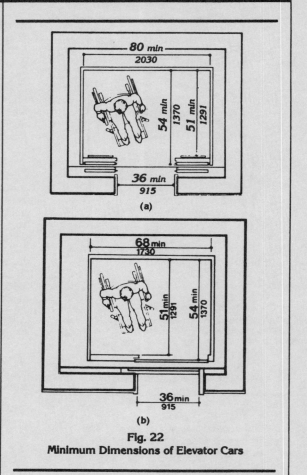

Fig. 22
Minimum Dimensions of Elevator Cars

within reach of controls, and exit from the car. Acceptable door opening and inside dimensions shall be as shown in Fig. 22. The clearance between the car platform sill and the edge of any hoistway landing shall be no greater than 1-1/4 in (32 mm).

4.10.10 Floor Surfaces. Floor surfaces shall comply with 4.5.

4.10.11 Illumination Levels. The level of illumination at the car controls, platform, and car threshold and landing sill shall be at least 5 footcandles (53.8 lux).

4.10.12* Car Controls. Elevator control panels shall have the following features:

(1) Buttons. All control buttons shall be at least 3/4 in (19 mm) in their smallest dimension. They *shall* be *raised* or flush.

(2) Tactile, *Braille*, and Visual Control Indicators. All control buttons shall be designated by *Braille and by raised* standard alphabet characters for letters, arabic characters for numerals, or standard symbols as shown in Fig. 23(a), and as required in *ASME A17.1-1990*. *Raised and Braille* characters and symbols shall comply with 4.30. The call button for the main entry floor shall be designated by a *raised* star at the left of the floor designation (see Fig. 23(a)). All raised designations for control buttons shall be placed immediately to the left of the button to which they apply. Applied plates,

permanently attached, are an acceptable means to provide raised control designations. Floor buttons shall be provided with visual indicators to show when each call is registered. The visual indicators shall be extinguished when each call is answered.

(3) Height. All floor buttons shall be no higher than 54 in (1370 mm) above the *finish floor for side approach and 48 in (1220 mm) for front approach.* Emergency controls, including the emergency alarm and emergency stop, shall be grouped at the bottom of the panel and shall have their centerlines no less than 35 in (890 mm) above the finish floor (see Fig. 23(a) and (b)).

Federal Register / Vol. 56, No. 144 / Friday, July 26, 1991 / Rules and Regulations   35641

4.10.13* Car Position Indicators

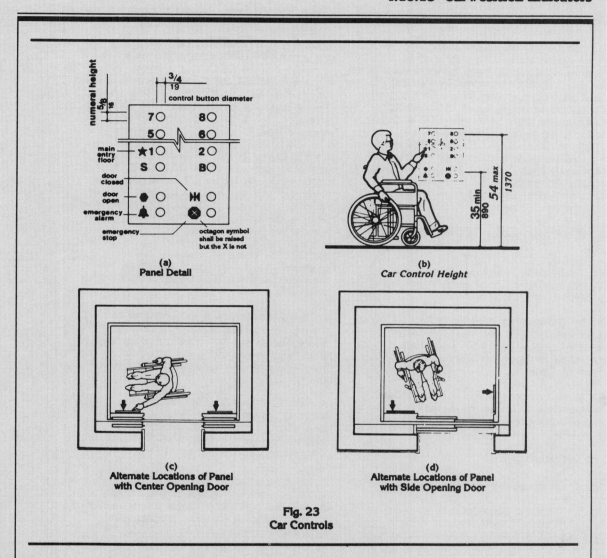

(a)
Panel Detail

(b)
Car Control Height

(c)
**Alternate Locations of Panel
with Center Opening Door**

(d)
**Alternate Locations of Panel
with Side Opening Door**

**Fig. 23
Car Controls**

(4) **Location.** Controls shall be located on a front wall if cars have center opening doors, and at the side wall or at the front wall next to the door if cars have side opening doors (see Fig. 23(c) and (d)).

4.10.13* Car Position Indicators. In elevator cars, a visual car position indicator shall be provided above the car control panel or over the door to show the position of the elevator in the hoistway. As the car passes or stops at a floor served by the elevators, the corresponding numerals shall illuminate,

and an audible signal shall sound. Numerals shall be a minimum of 1/2 in (13 mm) high. The audible signal shall be no less than 20 decibels with a frequency no higher than 1500 Hz. An automatic verbal announcement of the floor number at which a car stops or which a car passes may be substituted for the audible signal.

4.10.14* Emergency Communications. If provided, emergency two-way communication systems between the elevator and a point outside the hoistway shall comply with *ASME*

35

35642   Federal Register / Vol. 56, No. 144 / Friday, July 26, 1991 / Rules and Regulations

4.11 Platform Lifts (Wheelchair Lifts)

A17.1-1990. The highest operable part of a two-way communication system shall be a maximum of *48 in (1220 mm)* from the floor of the car. It shall be identified by a raised symbol and lettering complying with 4.30 and located adjacent to the device. If the system uses a handset then the length of the cord from the panel to the handset shall be at least 29 in (735 mm). *If the system is located in a closed compartment the compartment door hardware shall conform to 4.27, Controls and Operating Mechanisms. The emergency intercommunication system shall not require voice communication.*

4.11 Platform Lifts (Wheelchair Lifts).

4.11.1 Location. *Platform lifts (wheelchair lifts) permitted by 4.1 shall comply with the requirements of 4.11.*

4.11.2* Other Requirements. If platform lifts *(wheelchair lifts)* are used, they shall comply with 4.2.4, 4.5, 4.27, and *ASME A17.1 Safety Code for Elevators and Escalators, Section XX, 1990.*

4.11.3 Entrance. *If platform lifts are used then they shall facilitate unassisted entry, operation, and exit from the lift in compliance with 4.11.2.*

4.12 Windows.

4.12.1* General. *(Reserved).*

4.12.2* Window Hardware. *(Reserved).*

4.13 Doors.

4.13.1 General. *Doors required to be accessible by 4.1 shall comply with the requirements of 4.13.*

4.13.2 Revolving Doors and Turnstiles. Revolving doors or turnstiles shall not be the only means of passage at an accessible entrance or along an accessible route. *An accessible gate or door shall be provided adjacent to the turnstile or revolving door and shall be so designed as to facilitate the same use pattern.*

4.13.3 Gates. Gates, including ticket gates, shall meet all applicable specifications of 4.13.

4.13.4 Double-Leaf Doorways. If doorways have two *independently operated* door leaves, then at least one leaf shall meet the specifications in 4.13.5 and 4.13.6. That leaf shall be an active leaf.

4.13.5 Clear Width. Doorways shall have a minimum clear opening of 32 in (815 mm) with the door open 90 degrees, measured between the face of the door and the *opposite* stop (see Fig. 24(a), (b), (c), and (d)). Openings more than 24 in (610 mm) in depth shall comply with 4.2.1 and 4.3.3 (see Fig. 24(e)).

EXCEPTION: Doors not requiring full user passage, such as shallow closets, may have the clear opening reduced to 20 in (510 mm) minimum.

4.13.6 Maneuvering Clearances at Doors. Minimum maneuvering clearances at doors that are not automatic or power-assisted shall be as shown in Fig. 25. The floor or ground area within the required clearances shall be level and clear.

EXCEPTION: Entry doors to acute care hospital bedrooms for in-patients shall be exempted from the requirement for space at the latch side of the door (see dimension "x" in Fig. 25) if the door is at least 44 in (1120 mm) wide.

4.13.7 Two Doors in Series. The minimum space between two hinged or pivoted doors in series shall be 48 in (1220 mm) plus the width of any door swinging into the space. Doors in series shall swing either in the same direction or away from the space between the doors (see Fig. 26).

4.13.8* Thresholds at Doorways. Thresholds at doorways shall not exceed 3/4 in (19 mm) in height for exterior sliding doors or 1/2 in (13 mm) for other types of doors. Raised thresholds and floor level changes at accessible doorways shall be beveled with a slope no greater than 1:2 (see 4.5.2).

4.13.9* Door Hardware. Handles, pulls, latches, locks, and other operating devices on accessible doors shall have a shape that is easy

36

Federal Register / Vol. 56, No. 144 / Friday, July 26, 1991 / Rules and Regulations   **35643**

4.13 Doors

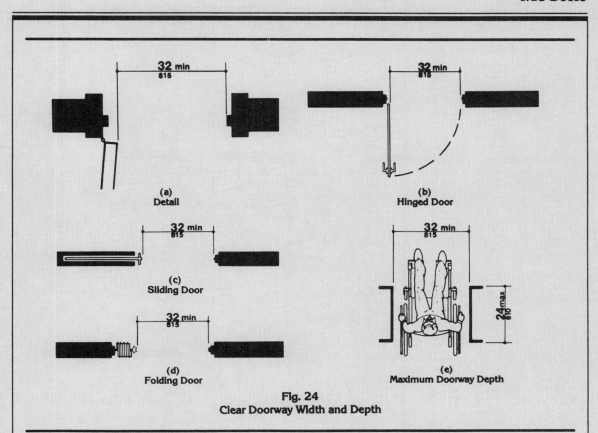

**Fig. 24
Clear Doorway Width and Depth**

to grasp with one hand and does not require tight grasping, tight pinching, or twisting of the wrist to operate. Lever-operated mechanisms, push-type mechanisms, and U-shaped handles are acceptable designs. When sliding doors are fully open, operating hardware shall be exposed and usable from both sides. *Hardware required for accessible door passage shall be mounted no higher than 48 in (1220 mm) above finished floor.*

4.13.10* Door Closers. If a door has a closer, then the sweep period of the closer shall be adjusted so that from an open position of 70 degrees, the door will take at least 3 seconds to move to a point 3 in (75 mm) from the latch, measured to the leading edge of the door.

4.13.11* Door Opening Force. The maximum force for pushing or pulling open a door shall be as follows:

(1) Fire doors shall have the minimum opening force allowable by the appropriate administrative authority.

(2) Other doors.

(a) exterior hinged doors: *(Reserved).*

(b) interior hinged doors: 5 lbf (22.2N)

(c) sliding or folding doors: 5 lbf (22.2N)

These forces do not apply to the force required to retract latch bolts or disengage other devices that may hold the door in a closed position.

35644 Federal Register / Vol. 56, No. 144 / Friday, July 26, 1991 / Rules and Regulations

4.13 Doors

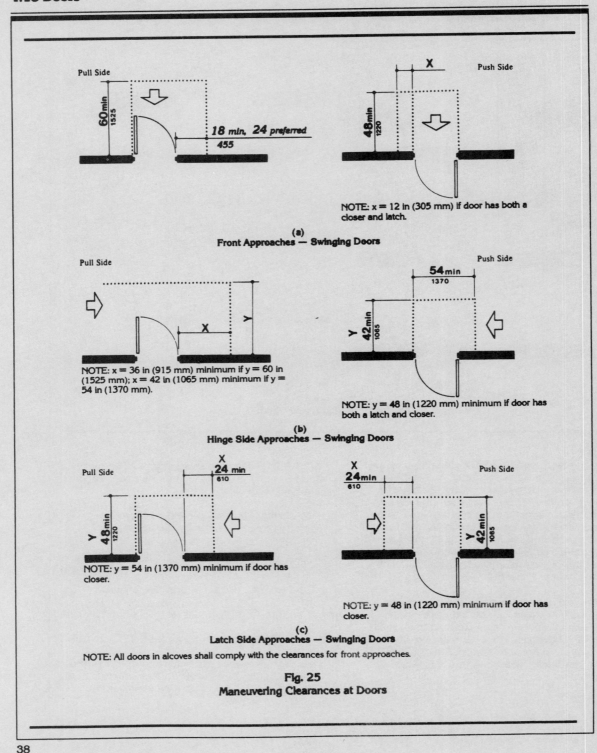

Fig. 25
Maneuvering Clearances at Doors

Federal Register / Vol. 56, No. 144 / Friday, July 26, 1991 / Rules and Regulations

4.13 Doors

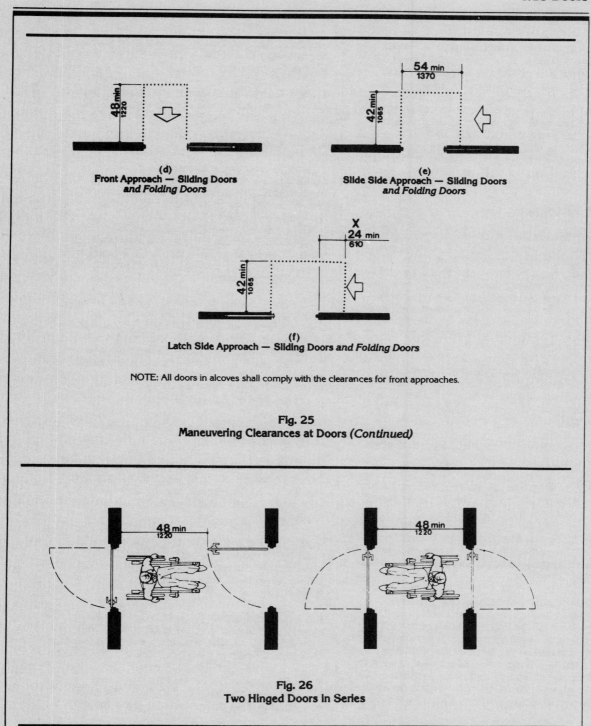

NOTE: All doors in alcoves shall comply with the clearances for front approaches.

Fig. 25
Maneuvering Clearances at Doors *(Continued)*

Fig. 26
Two Hinged Doors in Series

35646   Federal Register / Vol. 56, No. 144 / Friday, July 26, 1991 / Rules and Regulations

4.14 Entrances

4.13.12* Automatic Doors and Power-Assisted Doors. If an automatic door is used, then it shall comply with *ANSI/BHMA A156.10-1985.* Slowly opening, low-powered, automatic doors shall *comply with ANSI A156.19-1984.* Such doors shall not open to back check faster than 3 seconds and shall require no more than 15 lbf (66.6N) to stop door movement. If a power-assisted door is used, its door-opening force shall comply with 4.13.11 and its closing shall conform to the requirements in *ANSI A156.19-1984.*

4.14 Entrances.

4.14.1 Minimum Number. *Entrances required to be accessible by 4.1* shall be part of an accessible route complying with 4.3. Such entrances shall be connected by an accessible route to public transportation stops, to accessible parking and passenger loading zones, and to public streets or sidewalks if available (see 4.3.2(1)). They shall also be connected by an accessible route to all accessible spaces or elements within the building or facility.

4.14.2 Service Entrances. A service entrance shall not be the sole accessible entrance unless it is the only entrance to a building or facility (for example, in a factory or garage).

4.15 Drinking Fountains and Water Coolers.

4.15.1 Minimum Number. *Drinking fountains or water coolers required to be accessible by 4.1* shall comply with 4.15.

4.15.2* Spout Height. Spouts shall be no higher than 36 in (915 mm), measured from the floor or ground surfaces to the spout outlet (see Fig. 27(a)).

4.15.3 Spout Location. The spouts of drinking fountains and water coolers shall be at the front of the unit and shall direct the water flow in a trajectory that is parallel or nearly parallel to the front of the unit. The spout shall provide a flow of water at least 4 in (100 mm) high so as to allow the insertion of a cup or glass under the flow of water. *On an accessible drinking fountain with a round or oval bowl, the spout must be positioned so the flow of water is within 3 in (75 mm) of the front edge of the fountain.*

4.15.4 Controls. Controls shall comply with 4.27.4. *Unit controls shall be front mounted or side mounted near the front edge.*

4.15.5 Clearances.

(1) Wall- and post-mounted cantilevered units shall have a clear knee space between the bottom of the apron and the floor or ground at least 27 in (685 mm) high, 30 in (760 mm) wide, and 17 in to 19 in (430 mm to 485 mm) deep (see Fig. 27(a) and (b)). Such units shall also have a minimum clear floor space 30 in by 48 in (760 mm by 1220 mm) to allow a person in a wheelchair to approach the unit facing forward.

(2) Free-standing or built-in units not having a clear space under them shall have a clear floor space at least 30 in by 48 in (760 mm by 1220 mm) that allows a person in a wheelchair to make a parallel approach to the unit (see Fig. 27(c) and (d)). This clear floor space shall comply with 4.2.4.

4.16 Water Closets.

4.16.1 General. Accessible water closets shall comply with 4.16.

4.16.2 Clear Floor Space. Clear floor space for water closets not in stalls shall comply with Fig. 28. Clear floor space may be arranged to allow either a left-handed or right-handed approach.

4.16.3* Height. The height of water closets shall be 17 in to 19 in (430 mm to 485 mm), measured to the top of the toilet seat (see Fig. 29(b)). *Seats shall not be sprung to return to a lifted position.*

4.16.4* Grab Bars. Grab bars for water closets not located in stalls shall comply with 4.26 and Fig. 29. *The grab bar behind the water closet shall be 36 in (915 mm) minimum.*

4.16.5* Flush Controls. Flush controls shall be hand operated *or automatic* and shall comply with 4.27.4. Controls for flush valves

4.17 Toilet Stalls

shall be mounted on the wide side of toilet areas no more than 44 in (1120 mm) above the floor.

4.16.6 Dispensers. Toilet paper dispensers shall be installed within reach, as shown in Fig. 29(b). *Dispensers that control delivery, or that do not permit continuous paper flow, shall not be used.*

4.17 Toilet Stalls.

4.17.1 Location. Accessible toilet stalls shall be on an accessible route and shall meet the requirements of 4.17.

4.17.2 Water Closets. Water closets in accessible stalls shall comply with 4.16.

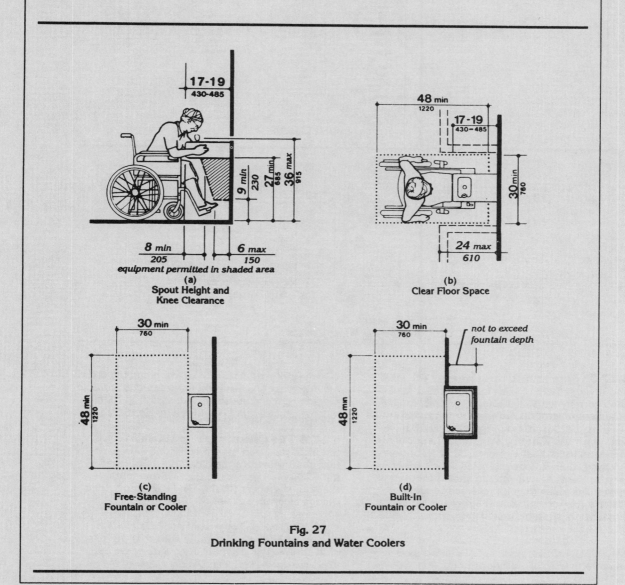

(a)
Spout Height and
Knee Clearance

(b)
Clear Floor Space

(c)
Free-Standing
Fountain or Cooler

(d)
Built-In
Fountain or Cooler

Fig. 27
Drinking Fountains and Water Coolers

41

Appendix A

4.17 Toilet Stalls

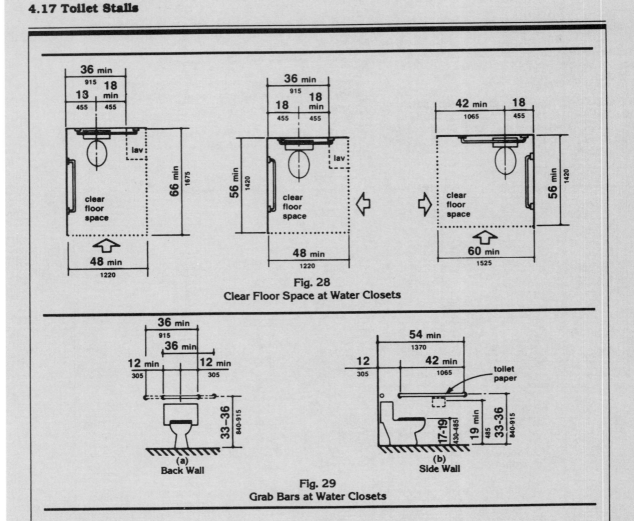

Fig. 28
Clear Floor Space at Water Closets

Fig. 29
Grab Bars at Water Closets

4.17.3* Size and Arrangement. The size and arrangement of the standard toilet stall shall comply with Fig. 30(a), *Standard Stall.* Standard toilet stalls with a minimum depth of 56 in (1420 mm) (see Fig. 30(a)) shall have wall-mounted water closets. If the depth of a standard toilet stall is increased at least 3 in (75 mm), then a floor-mounted water closet may be used. Arrangements shown for standard toilet stalls may be reversed to allow either a left- or right-hand approach. Additional stalls shall be provided in conformance with 4.22.4.

EXCEPTION: *In instances of alteration work where provision of a standard stall (Fig. 30(a)*

is technically infeasible or where plumbing code requirements prevent combining existing stalls to provide space, either alternate stall (Fig. 30(b)) may be provided in lieu of the standard stall.

4.17.4 Toe Clearances. In standard stalls, the front partition and at least one side partition shall provide a toe clearance of at least 9 in (230 mm) above the floor. If the depth of the stall is greater than 60 in (1525 mm), then the toe clearance is not required.

4.17.5* Doors. Toilet stall doors, *including door hardware,* shall comply with 4.13. If toilet stall approach is from the latch side of the stall door, clearance between the door side of the

42

4.17 Toilet Stalls

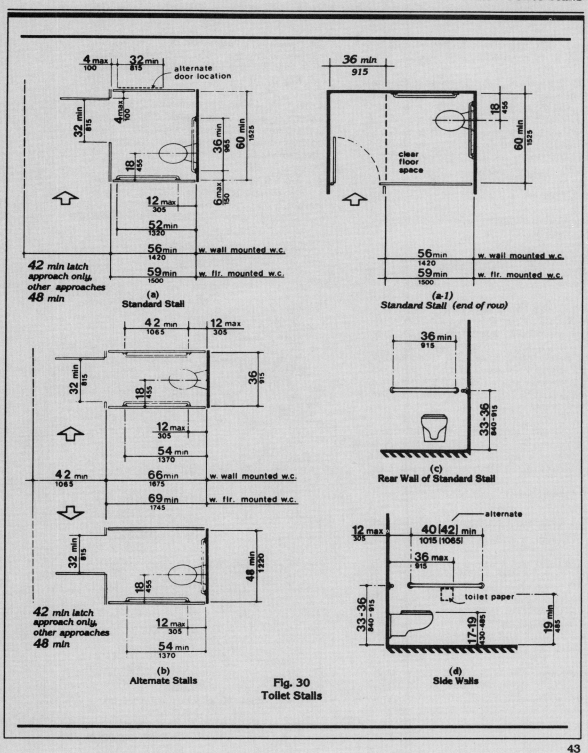

42 min latch approach only, other approaches 48 min

(a)
Standard Stall

(a-1)
Standard Stall (end of row)

(c)
Rear Wall of Standard Stall

42 min latch approach only, other approaches 48 min

(b)
Alternate Stalls

Fig. 30
Toilet Stalls

(d)
Side Walls

35650   Federal Register / Vol. 56, No. 144 / Friday, July 26, 1991 / Rules and Regulations

4.19 Lavatories and Mirrors

stall and any obstruction may be reduced to a minimum of 42 in (1065 mm) (Fig. 30).

4.17.6 Grab Bars. Grab bars complying with the length and positioning shown in Fig. 30(a), (b), (c), and (d) shall be provided. Grab bars may be mounted with any desired method as long as they have a gripping surface at the locations shown and do not obstruct the required clear floor area. Grab bars shall comply with 4.26.

4.18 Urinals.

4.18.1 General. Accessible urinals shall comply with 4.18.

4.18.2 Height. Urinals shall be stall-type or wall-hung with an elongated rim at a maximum of 17 in (430 mm) above the finish floor.

4.18.3 Clear Floor Space. A clear floor space 30 in by 48 in (760 mm by 1220 mm) shall be provided in front of urinals to allow forward approach. This clear space shall adjoin or overlap an accessible route and shall comply with 4.2.4. Urinal shields that do not extend beyond the front edge of the urinal rim may be provided with 29 in (735 mm) clearance between them.

4.18.4 Flush Controls. Flush controls shall be hand operated or automatic, and shall comply with 4.27.4, and shall be mounted no more than 44 in (1120 mm) above the finish floor.

4.19 Lavatories and Mirrors.

4.19.1 General. The requirements of 4.19 shall apply to lavatory fixtures, vanities, and built-in lavatories.

4.19.2 Height and Clearances. Lavatories shall be mounted with the rim or counter surface no higher than 34 in (865 mm) above the finish floor. Provide a clearance of at least 29 in (735 mm) above the finish floor to the bottom of the apron. Knee and toe clearance shall comply with Fig. 31.

4.19.3 Clear Floor Space. A clear floor space 30 in by 48 in (760 mm by 1220 mm) complying with 4.2.4 shall be provided in front of a lavatory to allow forward approach. Such

clear floor space shall adjoin or overlap an accessible route and shall extend a maximum of 19 in (485 mm) underneath the lavatory (see Fig. 32).

4.19.4 Exposed Pipes and Surfaces. Hot water and drain pipes under lavatories shall be insulated or otherwise configured to protect against contact. There shall be no sharp or abrasive surfaces under lavatories.

4.19.5 Faucets. Faucets shall comply with 4.27.4. Lever-operated, push-type, and electronically controlled mechanisms are examples of acceptable designs. If self-closing valves are

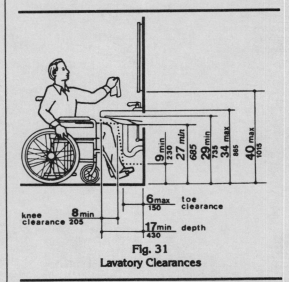

Fig. 31
Lavatory Clearances

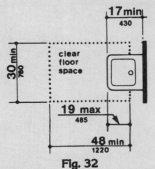

Fig. 32
Clear Floor Space at Lavatories

44

Federal Register / Vol. 56, No. 144 / Friday, July 26, 1991 / Rules and Regulations   **35651**

4.20 Bathtubs

used the faucet *shall remain* open for at least 10 seconds.

4.19.6* Mirrors. Mirrors shall be mounted with the bottom edge *of the reflecting surface* no higher than 40 in (1015 mm) *above the finish* floor (see Fig. 31).

4.20 Bathtubs.

4.20.1 General. Accessible bathtubs shall comply with 4.20.

4.20.2 Floor Space. Clear floor space in front of bathtubs shall be as shown in Fig. 33.

4.20.3 Seat. An in-tub seat or a seat at the head end of the tub shall be provided as shown in Fig. 33 and 34. The structural strength of seats and their attachments shall comply with 4.26.3. Seats shall be mounted securely and shall not slip during use.

4.20.4 Grab Bars. Grab bars complying with 4.26 shall be provided as shown in Fig. 33 and 34.

4.20.5 Controls. Faucets and other controls complying with 4.27.4 shall be located as shown in Fig. 34.

4.20.6 Shower Unit. A shower spray unit with a hose at least 60 in (1525 mm) long that can be used *both* as a fixed shower head *and* as a hand-held shower shall be provided.

4.20.7 Bathtub Enclosures. If provided, enclosures for bathtubs shall not obstruct controls or transfer from wheelchairs onto bathtub seats or into tubs. Enclosures on bathtubs shall not have tracks mounted on their rims.

4.21 Shower Stalls.

4.21.1* General. Accessible shower stalls shall comply with 4.21.

4.21.2 Size and Clearances. Except as specified in 9.1.2, shower stall size and clear floor space shall comply with Fig. 35(a) or (b). The shower stall in Fig. 35(a) shall be 36 in by 36 in (915 mm by 915 mm). Shower stalls required by 9.1.2 shall comply with Fig. 57(a)

or (b). The shower stall in Fig. 35(b) will fit into the space required for a bathtub.

4.21.3 Seat. A seat shall be provided in shower stalls 36 in by 36 in (915 mm by 915 mm) and shall be as shown in Fig. 36. The seat shall be mounted 17 in to 19 in (430 mm to 485 mm) from the bathroom floor and shall extend the full depth of the stall. In a 36 in by 36 in (915 mm by 915 mm) shower stall, the seat shall be on the wall opposite the controls. *Where a fixed seat is provided in a 30 in by 60 in minimum (760 mm by 1525 mm) shower stall, it shall be a folding type and shall be mounted on the wall adjacent to the controls as shown in Fig. 57.* The structural strength of seats and their attachments shall comply with 4.26.3.

4.21.4 Grab Bars. Grab bars complying with 4.26 shall be provided as shown in Fig. 37.

4.21.5 Controls. Faucets and other controls complying with 4.27.4 shall be located as shown in Fig. 37. In shower stalls 36 in by 36 in (915 mm by 915 mm), all controls, faucets, and the shower unit shall be mounted on the side wall opposite the seat.

4.21.6 Shower Unit. A shower spray unit with a hose at least 60 in (1525 mm) long that can be used *both* as a fixed shower head *and* as a hand-held shower shall be provided.

EXCEPTION: In unmonitored facilities where vandalism is a consideration, a fixed shower head mounted at 48 in (1220 mm) above the shower floor may be used in lieu of a hand-held shower head.

4.21.7 Curbs. If provided, curbs in shower stalls 36 in by 36 in (915 mm by 915 mm) shall be no higher than 1/2 in (13 mm). Shower stalls that are 30 in by 60 in (760 mm by 1525 mm) minimum shall not have curbs.

4.21.8 Shower Enclosures. If provided, enclosures for shower stalls shall not obstruct controls or obstruct transfer from wheelchairs onto shower seats.

4.22 Toilet Rooms.

4.22.1 Minimum Number. *Toilet facilities required to be accessible by 4.1 shall comply*

45

Appendix A

4.21 Shower Stalls

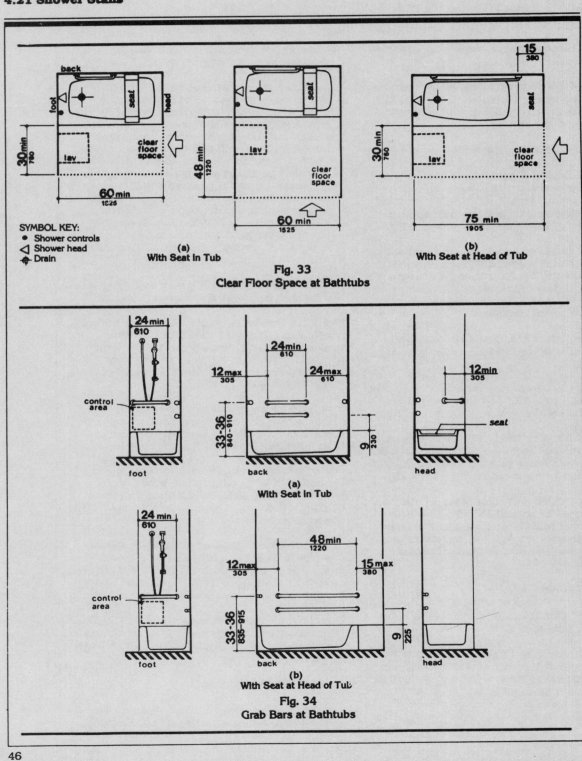

SYMBOL KEY:
- Shower controls
- Shower head
- Drain

(a)
With Seat in Tub

(b)
With Seat at Head of Tub

Fig. 33
Clear Floor Space at Bathtubs

(a)
With Seat in Tub

(b)
With Seat at Head of Tub

Fig. 34
Grab Bars at Bathtubs

46

4.22 Toilet Rooms

with 4.22. Accessible toilet rooms shall be on an accessible route.

4.22.2 Doors. All doors to accessible toilet rooms shall comply with 4.13. Doors shall not swing into the clear floor space required for any fixture.

4.22.3° Clear Floor Space. The accessible fixtures and controls required in 4.22.4, 4.22.5, 4.22.6, and 4.22.7 shall be on an accessible route. An unobstructed turning space complying with 4.2.3 shall be provided within an accessible toilet room. The clear floor space at fixtures and controls, the accessible route, and the turning space may overlap.

4.22.4 Water Closets. If toilet stalls are provided, then at least one shall be a standard toilet stall complying with 4.17; *where 6 or more stalls are provided, in addition to the stall complying with 4.17.3, at least one stall 36 in (915 mm) wide with an outward swinging, self-closing door and parallel grab bars complying with Fig. 30(d) and 4.26 shall be provided. Water closets in such stalls* shall comply with 4.16. If water closets are not in stalls, then at least one shall comply with 4.16.

4.22.5 Urinals. If urinals are provided, *then* at least one shall comply with 4.18.

4.22.6 Lavatories and Mirrors. If lavatories and mirrors are provided, *then* at least one of each shall comply with 4.19.

4.22.7 Controls and Dispensers. If controls, dispensers, receptacles, or other

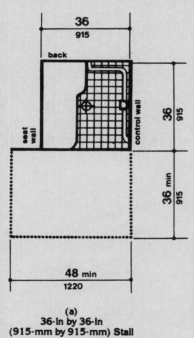

(a)
36-in by 36-in
(915-mm by 915-mm) Stall

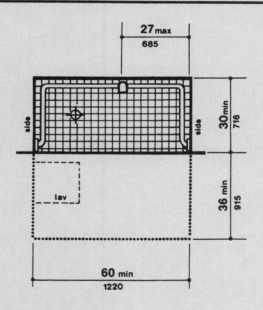

(b)
30-in by 60-in
(760-mm by 1525-mm) Stall

Fig. 35
Shower Size and Clearances

35654   **Federal Register** / Vol. 56, No. 144 / Friday, July 26, 1991 / Rules and Regulations

4.23 Bathrooms, Bathing Facilities, and Shower Rooms

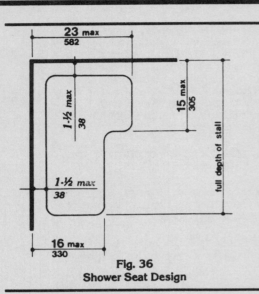

Fig. 36
Shower Seat Design

equipment are provided, *then* at least one of each shall be on an accessible route and shall comply with 4.27.

4.23 Bathrooms, Bathing Facilities, and Shower Rooms.

4.23.1 Minimum Number. Bathrooms, bathing facilities, or shower rooms *required to be accessible by 4.1* shall comply with 4.23 and shall be on an accessible route.

4.23.2 Doors. Doors to accessible bathrooms shall comply with 4.13. Doors shall not swing into the floor space required for any fixture.

4.23.3* Clear Floor Space. The accessible fixtures and controls required in 4.23.4, 4.23.5, 4.23.6, 4.23.7, 4.23.8, and 4.23.9 shall be on an accessible route. An unobstructed turning

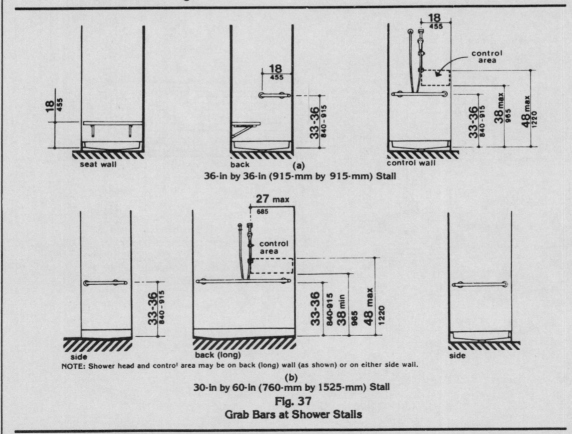

(a)
36-in by 36-in (915-mm by 915-mm) Stall

NOTE: Shower head and control area may be on back (long) wall (as shown) or on either side wall.

(b)
30-in by 60-in (760-mm by 1525-mm) Stall

Fig. 37
Grab Bars at Shower Stalls

48

space complying with 4.2.3 shall be provided within an accessible bathroom. The clear floor spaces at fixtures and controls, the accessible route, and the turning space may overlap.

4.23.4 Water Closets. If toilet stalls are provided, then at least one shall be a standard toilet stall complying with 4.17; *where 6 or more stalls are provided, in addition to the stall complying with 4.17.3, at least one stall 36 in (915 mm) wide with an outward swinging, self-closing door and parallel grab bars complying with Fig. 30(d) and 4.26 shall be provided. Water closets in such stalls* shall comply with 4.16. If water closets are not in stalls, then at least one shall comply with 4.16.

4.23.5 Urinals. If urinals are provided, then at least one shall comply with 4.18.

4.23.6 Lavatories and Mirrors. If lavatories and mirrors are provided, then at least one of each shall comply with 4.19.

4.23.7 Controls and Dispensers. If controls, dispensers, receptacles, or other equipment *are* provided, *then* at least one of each shall be on an accessible route and shall comply with 4.27.

4.23.8 Bathing and Shower Facilities. If tubs or showers are provided, then at least one accessible tub that complies with 4.20 or at least one accessible shower that complies with 4.21 shall be provided.

4.23.9* Medicine Cabinets. If medicine cabinets are provided, at least one shall be located with a usable shelf no higher than 44 in (1120 mm) above the floor space. The floor space shall comply with 4.2.4.

4.24 Sinks.

4.24.1 General. Sinks *required to be accessible by 4.1* shall comply with 4.24.

4.24.2 Height. Sinks shall be mounted with the counter or rim no higher than 34 in (865 mm) *above the finish* floor.

4.24.3 Knee Clearance. Knee clearance that is at least 27 in (685 mm) high, 30 in (760 mm) wide, and 19 in (485 mm) deep shall be pro-

vided underneath sinks.

4.24.4 Depth. Each sink shall be a maximum of 6-1/2 in (165 mm) deep.

4.24.5 Clear Floor Space. A clear floor space at least 30 in by 48 in (760 mm by 1220 mm) complying with 4.2.4 shall be provided in front of a sink to allow forward approach. The clear floor space shall be on an accessible route and shall extend a maximum of 19 in (485 mm) underneath the sink (see Fig. 32).

4.24.6 Exposed Pipes and Surfaces. Hot water and drain pipes exposed under sinks shall be insulated or otherwise *configured so as to protect against contact.* There shall be no sharp or abrasive surfaces under sinks.

4.24.7 Faucets. Faucets shall comply with 4.27.4. Lever-operated, push-type, touch-type, or electronically controlled mechanisms are acceptable designs.

4.25 Storage.

4.25.1 General. *Fixed* storage facilities such as cabinets, shelves, closets, and drawers *required to be accessible by 4.1* shall comply with 4.25.

4.25.2 Clear Floor Space. A clear floor space at least 30 in by 48 in (760 mm by 1220 mm) complying with 4.2.4 that allows either a forward or parallel approach by a person using a wheelchair shall be provided at accessible storage facilities.

4.25.3 Height. Accessible storage spaces shall be within at least one of the reach ranges specified in 4.2.5 and 4.2.6 *(see Fig. 5 and Fig. 6).* Clothes rods or shelves shall be a maximum of 54 in (1370 mm) *above the finish floor for a side approach. Where the distance from the wheelchair to the clothes rod or shelf exceeds 10 in (255 mm) (as in closets without accessible doors) the height and depth to the rod or shelf shall comply with Fig. 38(a) and Fig. 38(b).*

4.25.4 Hardware. Hardware for accessible storage facilities shall comply with 4.27.4. Touch latches and U-shaped pulls are acceptable.

Appendix A

4.26 Handrails, Grab Bars, and Tub and Shower Seats

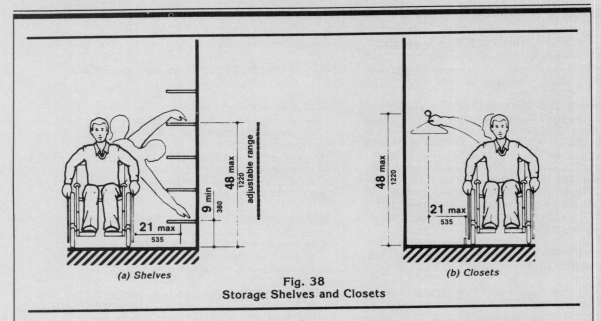

(a) Shelves

Fig. 38
Storage Shelves and Closets

(b) Closets

4.26 Handrails, Grab Bars, and Tub and Shower Seats.

4.26.1* General. All handrails, grab bars, and tub and shower seats *required to be accessible by 4.1, 4.8, 4.9, 4.16, 4.17, 4.20 or 4.21* shall comply with 4.26.

4.26.2* Size and Spacing of Grab Bars and Handrails. The diameter or width of the gripping surfaces of a handrail or grab bar shall be 1-1/4 in to 1-1/2 in (32 mm to 38 mm), or the shape shall provide an equivalent gripping surface. If handrails or grab bars are mounted adjacent to a wall, the space between the wall and the grab bar shall be 1-1/2 in (38 mm) (see Fig. 39(a), (b), (c), and (e)). Handrails may be located in a recess if the recess is a maximum of 3 in (75 mm) deep and extends at least 18 in (455 mm) above the top of the rail (see Fig. 39(d)).

4.26.3 Structural Strength. The structural strength of grab bars, tub and shower seats, fasteners, and mounting devices shall meet the following specification:

(1) Bending stress in a grab bar or seat induced by the maximum bending moment from the application of 250 lbf (1112N) shall

be less than the allowable stress for the material of the grab bar or seat.

(2) Shear stress induced in a grab bar or seat by the application of 250 lbf (1112N) shall be less than the allowable shear stress for the material of the grab bar or seat. If the connection between the grab bar or seat and its mounting bracket or other support is considered to be fully restrained, then direct and torsional shear stresses shall be totaled for the combined shear stress, which shall not exceed the allowable shear stress.

(3) Shear force induced in a fastener or mounting device from the application of 250 lbf (1112N) shall be less than the allowable lateral load of either the fastener or mounting device or the supporting structure, whichever is the smaller allowable load.

(4) Tensile force induced in a fastener by a direct tension force of 250 lbf (1112N) plus the maximum moment from the application of 250 lbf (1112N) shall be less than the allowable withdrawal load between the fastener and the supporting structure.

(5) Grab bars shall not rotate within their fittings.

Federal Register / Vol. 56, No. 144 / Friday, July 26, 1991 / Rules and Regulations **35657**

4.26 Handrails, Grab Bars, and Tub and Shower Seats

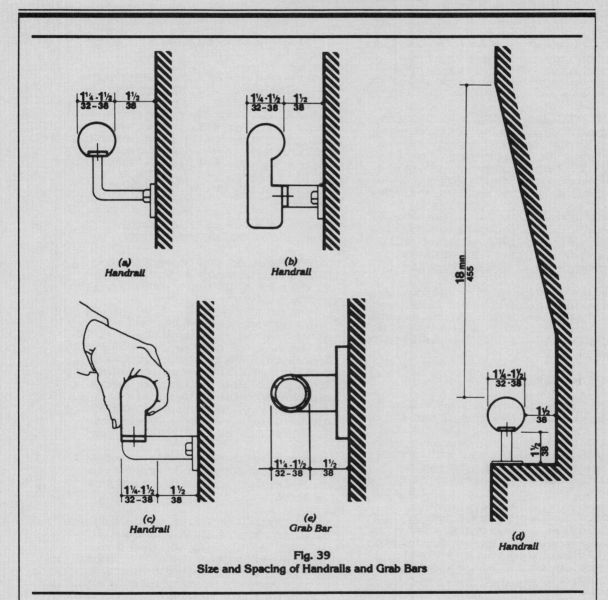

Fig. 39
Size and Spacing of Handrails and Grab Bars

4.26.4 Eliminating Hazards. A handrail or grab bar and any wall or other surface adjacent to it shall be free of any sharp or abrasive elements. Edges shall have a minimum radius of 1/8 in (3.2 mm).

4.27 Controls and Operating Mechanisms.

4.27.1 General. Controls and operating mechanisms *required to be accessible by 4.1* shall comply with 4.27.

51

477

Appendix A

4.28 Alarms

4.27.2 Clear Floor Space. Clear floor space complying with 4.2.4 that allows a forward or a parallel approach by a person using a wheelchair shall be provided at controls, dispensers, receptacles, and other operable equipment.

4.27.3* Height. The highest operable part of controls, dispensers, receptacles, and other operable equipment shall be placed within at least one of the reach ranges specified in 4.2.5 and 4.2.6. Electrical and communications system receptacles on walls shall be mounted no less than 15 in (380 mm) above the floor.

EXCEPTION: These requirements do not apply where the use of special equipment dictates otherwise or where electrical and communications systems receptacles are not normally intended for use by building occupants.

4.27.4 Operation. Controls and operating mechanisms shall be operable with one hand and shall not require tight grasping, pinching, or twisting of the wrist. The force required to activate controls shall be no greater than 5 lbf (22.2 N).

4.28 Alarms.

4.28.1 General. *Alarm systems required to be accessible by 4.1 shall comply with 4.28. At a minimum, visual signal appliances shall be provided in buildings and facilities in each of the following areas: restrooms and any other general usage areas (e.g., meeting rooms), hallways, lobbies, and any other area for common use.*

4.28.2* Audible Alarms. If provided, audible emergency alarms shall produce a sound that exceeds the prevailing equivalent sound level in the room or space by at least 15 dbA or exceeds any maximum sound level with a duration of 60 seconds by 5 dbA, whichever is louder. Sound levels for alarm signals shall not exceed 120 dbA.

4.28.3* Visual Alarms. *Visual alarm signal appliances shall be integrated into the building or facility alarm system. If single station audible alarms are provided then single station visual alarm signals shall be provided. Visual alarm signals shall have the following minimum photometric and location features:*

(1) The lamp shall be a xenon strobe type or equivalent.

(2) The color shall be clear or nominal white (i.e., unfiltered or clear filtered white light).

(3) The maximum pulse duration shall be two-tenths of one second (0.2 sec) with a maximum duty cycle of 40 percent. The pulse duration is defined as the time interval between initial and final points of 10 percent of maximum signal.

(4) The intensity shall be a minimum of 75 candela.

(5) The flash rate shall be a minimum of 1 Hz and a maximum of 3 Hz.

(6) The appliance shall be placed 80 in (2030 mm) above the highest floor level within the space or 6 in (152 mm) below the ceiling, whichever is lower.

(7) In general, no place in any room or space required to have a visual signal appliance shall be more than 50 ft (15 m) from the signal (in the horizontal plane). In large rooms and spaces exceeding 100 ft (30 m) across, without obstructions 6 ft (2 m) above the finish floor, such as auditoriums, devices may be placed around the perimeter, spaced a maximum 100 ft (30 m) apart, in lieu of suspending appliances from the ceiling.

(8) No place in common corridors or hallways in which visual alarm signalling appliances are required shall be more than 50 ft (15 m) from the signal.

4.28.4* Auxiliary Alarms. *Units and* sleeping accommodations shall have a visual alarm connected to the building emergency alarm system or shall have a standard 110-volt electrical receptacle into which such an alarm can be connected *and a means by which a signal from the building emergency alarm system can trigger such an auxiliary alarm. When visual alarms are in place the signal shall be visible in all areas of the unit or room.* Instructions for use of the auxiliary alarm or receptacle shall be provided.

Federal Register / Vol. 56, No. 144 / Friday, July 26, 1991 / Rules and Regulations

4.29 Detectable Warnings.

4.29.1 General. *Detectable warnings required by 4.1 and 4.7 shall comply with 4.29.*

4.29.2* Detectable Warnings on Walking Surfaces. *Detectable warnings shall consist of raised truncated domes with a diameter of nominal 0.9 in (23 mm), a height of nominal 0.2 in (5 mm) and a center-to-center spacing of nominal 2.35 in (60 mm) and shall contrast visually with adjoining surfaces, either light-on-dark, or dark-on-light.*

The material used to provide contrast shall be an integral part of the walking surface. Detectable warnings used on interior surfaces shall differ from adjoining walking surfaces in resiliency or sound-on-cane contact.

4.29.3 Detectable Warnings on Doors To Hazardous Areas. *(Reserved).*

4.29.4 Detectable Warnings at Stairs. *(Reserved).*

4.29.5 Detectable Warnings at Hazardous Vehicular Areas. If a walk crosses or adjoins a vehicular way, *and the walking surfaces are not separated by* curbs, railings, or other elements *between the pedestrian areas and vehicular areas*, the boundary between the areas shall be defined by a continuous *detectable* warning *which is* 36 in (915 mm) wide, complying with 4.29.2.

4.29.6 Detectable Warnings at Reflecting Pools. The edges of reflecting pools shall be protected by railings, walls, curbs, or *detectable* warnings complying with 4.29.2.

4.29.7 Standardization. *(Reserved).*

4.30 Signage.

4.30.1* General. Signage *required to be accessible by 4.1 shall comply with the applicable provisions of 4.30.*

4.30.2* Character Proportion. Letters and numbers on signs shall have a width-to-height ratio between 3:5 and 1:1 and a stroke-width-to-height ratio between 1:5 and 1:10.

4.30.3 Character Height. *Characters and numbers on signs shall be sized according to the viewing distance from which they are to be read. The minimum height is measured using an upper case X. Lower case characters are permitted.*

Height Above Finished Floor	*Minimum Character Height*
Suspended or Projected Overhead in compliance with 4.4.2	*3 in. (75 mm) minimum*

4.30.4* Raised and Brailled Characters and Pictorial Symbol Signs (Pictograms). Letters and numerals shall be raised 1/32 in, upper case, sans serif or simple serif type and shall be accompanied with Grade 2 Braille. Raised characters shall be at least 5/8 in (16 mm) high, but no higher than 2 in (50 mm). *Pictograms shall be accompanied by the equivalent verbal description placed directly below the pictogram. The border dimension of the pictogram shall be 6 in (152 mm) minimum in height.*

4.30.5* Finish and Contrast. *The characters and background of signs shall be eggshell, matte, or other non-glare finish.* Characters and symbols shall contrast with their background — either light characters on a dark background or dark characters on a light background.

4.30.6 Mounting Location and Height. *Where permanent identification is provided for rooms and spaces, signs shall be installed on the wall adjacent to the latch side of the door. Where there is no wall space to the latch side of the door, including at double leaf doors, signs shall be placed on the nearest adjacent wall. Mounting height shall be 60 in (1525 mm) above the finish floor to the centerline of the sign. Mounting location for such signage shall be so that a person may approach within 3 in (76 mm) of signage without encountering protruding objects or standing within the swing of a door.*

4.30.7* Symbols of Accessibility.

(1) Facilities and elements required to be identified as accessible by 4.1 shall use the international symbol of accessibility. The

53

Appendix A

4.30 Signage

(a)
Proportions
International Symbol of Accessibility

(b)
Display Conditions
International Symbol of Accessibility

(c)
International TDD Symbol

(d)
International Symbol of Access for Hearing Loss

Fig. 43
International Symbols

symbol shall be displayed as shown in Fig. 43(a) and (b).

(2) *Volume Control Telephones. Telephones required to have a volume control by 4.1.3(17)(b) shall be identified by a sign containing a depiction of a telephone handset with radiating sound waves.*

(3) *Text Telephones. Text telephones required by 4.1.3 (17)(c) shall be identified by the international TDD symbol (Fig 43(c)). In addition, if a facility has a public text telephone, directional signage indicating the location of the nearest text telephone shall be placed adjacent to all banks of telephones which do not contain a text telephone. Such directional signage shall include the international TDD symbol. If a facility has no banks of telephones, the directional signage shall be provided at the entrance (e.g., in a building directory).*

(4) *Assistive Listening Systems. In assembly areas where permanently installed assistive listening systems are required by 4.1.3(19)(b) the availability of such systems shall be identified with signage that includes the international symbol of access for hearing loss (Fig 43(d)).*

4.30.8* Illumination Levels. (Reserved).

4.31 Telephones.

4.31.1 General. Public telephones *required to be accessible by 4.1* shall comply with 4.31.

4.31.2 Clear Floor or Ground Space. A clear floor or ground space at least 30 in by 48 in (760 mm by 1220 mm) that allows either a forward or parallel approach by a person using a wheelchair shall be provided at telephones (see Fig. 44). The clear floor or ground space shall comply with 4.2.4. Bases, enclosures, and fixed seats shall not impede approaches to telephones by people who use wheelchairs.

4.31.3* Mounting Height. The highest operable part of the telephone shall be within the reach ranges specified in 4.2.5 or 4.2.6.

4.31.4 Protruding Objects. *Telephones shall comply with 4.4.*

Federal Register / Vol. 56, No. 144 / Friday, July 26, 1991 / Rules and Regulations

4.31 Telephones

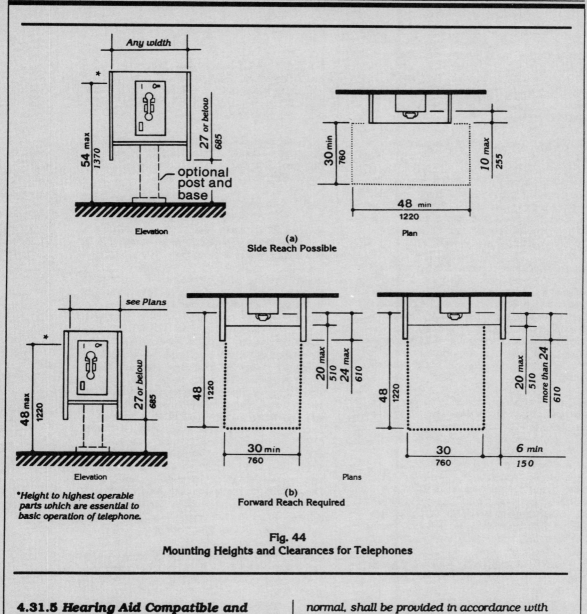

Fig. 44
Mounting Heights and Clearances for Telephones

4.31.5 Hearing Aid Compatible and Volume Control Telephones Required by 4.1.

(1) Telephones shall be hearing aid compatible.

(2) Volume controls, *capable of a minimum of 12 dbA and a maximum of 18 dbA above*

normal, shall be provided in accordance with 4.1.3. If an automatic reset is provided then 18 dbA may be exceeded.

4.31.6 Controls. Telephones shall have pushbutton controls where service for such equipment is available.

55

481

35662   Federal Register / Vol. 56, No. 144 / Friday, July 26, 1991 / Rules and Regulations

4.32 Fixed or Built-in Seating and Tables

4.31.7 Telephone Books. Telephone books, if provided, shall be located *in a position that complies with the reach ranges specified in 4.2.5 and 4.2.6.*

4.31.8 Cord Length. The cord from the telephone to the handset shall be at least 29 in (735 mm) long.

4.31.9* Text Telephones Required by 4.1.

(1) Text telephones used with a pay telephone shall be permanently affixed within, or adjacent to, the telephone enclosure. If an acoustic coupler is used, the telephone cord shall be sufficiently long to allow connection of the text telephone and the telephone receiver.

(2) Pay telephones designed to accommodate a portable text telephone shall be equipped with a shelf and an electrical outlet within or adjacent to the telephone enclosure. The telephone handset shall be capable of being placed flush on the surface of the shelf. The shelf shall be capable of accommodating a text telephone and shall have 6 in (152 mm) minimum vertical clearance in the area where the text telephone is to be placed.

(3) Equivalent facilitation may be provided. For example, a portable text telephone may be made available in a hotel at the registration desk if it is available on a 24-hour basis for use with nearby public pay telephones. In this instance, at least one pay telephone shall comply with paragraph 2 of this section. In addition, if an acoustic coupler is used, the telephone handset cord shall be sufficiently long so as to allow connection of the text telephone and the telephone receiver. Directional signage shall be provided and shall comply with 4.30.7.

4.32 Fixed or Built-in Seating and Tables.

4.32.1 Minimum Number. Fixed or built-in seating or tables *required to be accessible by 4.1* shall comply with 4.32.

4.32.2 Seating. If seating spaces for people in wheelchairs are provided at *fixed* tables or counters, clear floor space complying with 4.2.4 shall be provided. Such clear floor space shall not overlap knee space by more than 19 in (485 mm) (see Fig. 45).

4.32.3 Knee Clearances. If seating for people in wheelchairs is provided at tables *or* counters, knee spaces at least 27 in (685 mm) high, 30 in (760 mm) wide, and 19 in (485 mm) deep shall be provided (see Fig. 45).

4.32.4* Height of Tables or Counters. The tops of *accessible* tables and *counters* shall be from 28 in to 34 in (710 mm to 865 mm) *above the finish* floor or ground.

4.33 Assembly Areas.

4.33.1 Minimum Number. Assembly *and associated* areas *required to be accessible by 4.1 shall comply with 4.33.*

4.33.2* Size of Wheelchair Locations. Each wheelchair location shall provide minimum clear ground or floor spaces as shown in Fig. 46.

4.33.3* Placement of Wheelchair Locations. Wheelchair areas shall be an integral part of any fixed seating plan and shall be *provided so as to provide people with physical disabilities a choice of admission prices and lines of sight comparable to those for members of the general public.* They shall adjoin an accessible route that also serves as a means of egress in case of emergency. *At least one companion fixed seat shall be provided next to each wheelchair seating area. When the seating capacity exceeds 300, wheelchair spaces shall be provided in more than one location. Readily removable seats may be installed in wheelchair spaces when the spaces are not required to accommodate wheelchair users.*

EXCEPTION: Accessible viewing positions may be clustered for bleachers, balconies, and other areas having sight lines that require slopes of greater than 5 percent. Equivalent accessible viewing positions may be located on levels having accessible egress.

4.33.4 Surfaces. The ground or floor at wheelchair locations shall be level and shall comply with 4.5.

4.33 Assembly Areas

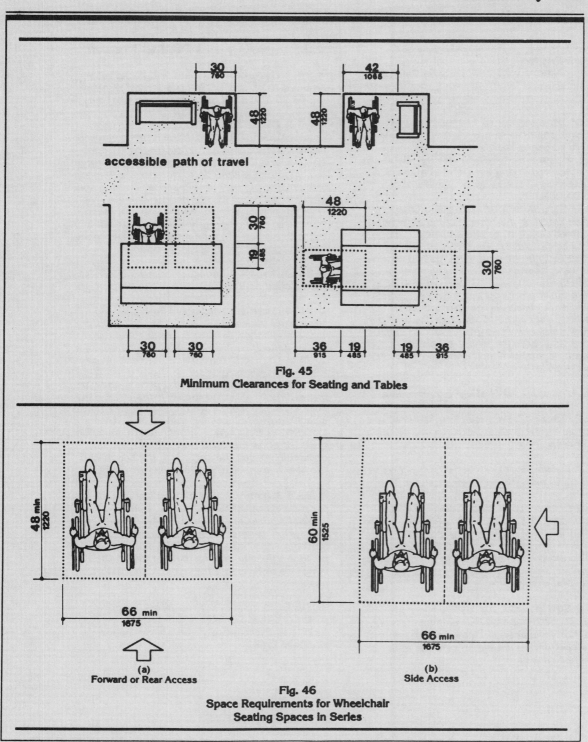

**Fig. 45
Minimum Clearances for Seating and Tables**

(a)
Forward or Rear Access

(b)
Side Access

**Fig. 46
Space Requirements for Wheelchair
Seating Spaces in Series**

57

4.34 Automated Teller Machines

4.33.5 Access to Performing Areas.
An accessible route shall connect wheelchair seating locations with performing areas, including stages, arena floors, dressing rooms, locker rooms, and other spaces used by performers.

4.33.6* Placement of Listening Systems.
If the listening system provided serves individual fixed seats, then such seats shall be located within a 50 ft (15 m) viewing distance of the stage or playing area and shall have a complete view of the stage or playing area.

4.33.7* Types of Listening Systems.
Assistive listening systems (ALS) are intended to augment standard public address and audio systems by providing signals which can be received directly by persons with special receivers or their own hearing aids and which eliminate or filter background noise. The type of assistive listening system appropriate for a particular application depends on the characteristics of the setting, the nature of the program, and the intended audience. Magnetic induction loops, infra-red and radio frequency systems are types of listening systems which are appropriate for various applications.

4.34 Automated Teller Machines.

4.34.1 General. *Each machine required to be accessible by 4.1.3 shall be on an accessible route and shall comply with 4.34.*

4.34.2 Controls. *Controls for user activation shall comply with the requirements of 4.27.*

4.34.3 Clearances and Reach Range.
Free standing or built-in units not having a clear space under them shall comply with 4.27.2 and 4.27.3 and provide for a parallel approach and both a forward and side reach to the unit allowing a person in a wheelchair to access the controls and dispensers.

4.34.4 Equipment for Persons with Vision Impairments. *Instructions and all information for use shall be made accessible to and independently usable by persons with vision impairments.*

4.35 Dressing and Fitting Rooms.

4.35.1 General. *Dressing and fitting rooms required to be accessible by 4.1 shall comply with 4.35 and shall be on an accessible route.*

4.35.2 Clear Floor Space. *A clear floor space allowing a person using a wheelchair to make a 180-degree turn shall be provided in every accessible dressing room entered through a swinging or sliding door. No door shall swing into any part of the turning space. Turning space shall not be required in a private dressing room entered through a curtained opening at least 32 in (815 mm) wide if clear floor space complying with section 4.2 renders the dressing room usable by a person using a wheelchair.*

4.35.3 Doors. *All doors to accessible dressing rooms shall be in compliance with section 4.13.*

4.35.4 Bench. *Every accessible dressing room shall have a 24 in by 48 in (610 mm by 1220 mm) bench fixed to the wall along the longer dimension. The bench shall be mounted 17 in to 19 in (430 mm to 485 mm) above the finish floor. Clear floor space shall be provided alongside the bench to allow a person using a wheelchair to make a parallel transfer onto the bench. The structural strength of the bench and attachments shall comply with 4.26.3. Where installed in conjunction with showers, swimming pools, or other wet locations, water shall not accumulate upon the surface of the bench and the bench shall have a slip-resistant surface.*

4.35.5 Mirror. *Where mirrors are provided in dressing rooms of the same use, then in an accessible dressing room, a full-length mirror, measuring at least 18 in wide by 54 in high (460 mm by 1370 mm), shall be mounted in a position affording a view to a person on the bench as well as to a person in a standing position.*

NOTE: Sections 4.1.1 through 4.1.7 and sections 5 through 10 are different from ANSI A117.1 in their entirety and are printed in standard type.

5.0 Restaurants and Cafeterias

5. RESTAURANTS AND CAFETERIAS.

5.1* General. Except as specified or modified in this section, restaurants and cafeterias shall comply with the requirements of 4.1 to 4.35. Where fixed tables (or dining counters where food is consumed but there is no service) are provided, at least 5 percent, but not less than one, of the fixed tables (or a portion of the dining counter) shall be accessible and shall comply with 4.32 as required in 4.1.3(18). In establishments where separate areas are designated for smoking and non-smoking patrons, the required number of accessible fixed tables (or counters) shall be proportionally distributed between the smoking and non-smoking areas. In new construction, and where practicable in alterations, accessible fixed tables (or counters) shall be distributed throughout the space or facility.

5.2 Counters and Bars. Where food or drink is served at counters exceeding 34 in (865 mm) in height for consumption by customers seated on stools or standing at the counter, a portion of the main counter which is 60 in (1525 mm) in length minimum shall be provided in compliance with 4.32 or service shall be available at accessible tables within the same area.

5.3 Access Aisles. All accessible fixed tables shall be accessible by means of an access aisle at least 36 in (915 mm) clear between parallel edges of tables or between a wall and the table edges.

5.4 Dining Areas. In new construction, all dining areas, including raised or sunken dining areas, loggias, and outdoor seating areas, shall be accessible. In non-elevator buildings, an accessible means of vertical access to the mezzanine is not required under the following conditions: 1) the area of mezzanine seating measures no more than 33 percent of the area of the total accessible seating area; 2) the same services and decor are provided in an accessible space usable by the general public; and, 3) the accessible areas are not restricted to use by people with disabilities. In alterations, accessibility to raised or sunken dining areas, or to all parts of outdoor seating areas is not required provided that the same services and decor are provided in an accessible space usable by the general public and are not restricted to use by people with disabilities.

5.5 Food Service Lines. Food service lines shall have a minimum clear width of 36 in (915 mm), with a preferred clear width of 42 in (1065 mm) to allow passage around a person using a wheelchair. Tray slides shall be mounted no higher than 34 in (865 mm) above the floor (see Fig. 53). If self-service shelves

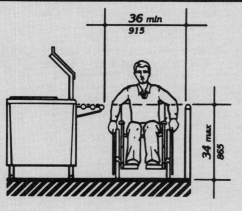

Fig. 53
Food Service Lines

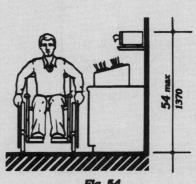

Fig. 54
Tableware Areas

59

485

35666   Federal Register / Vol. 56, No. 144 / Friday, July 26, 1991 / Rules and Regulations

6.0 Medical Care Facilities

are provided, at least 50 percent of each type must be within reach ranges specified in 4.2.5 and 4.2.6.

5.6 Tableware and Condiment Areas. Self-service shelves and dispensing devices for tableware, dishware, condiments, food and beverages shall be installed to comply with 4.2 (see Fig. 54).

5.7 Raised Platforms. In banquet rooms or spaces where a head table or speaker's lectern is located on a raised platform, the platform shall be accessible in compliance with 4.8 or 4.11. Open edges of a raised platform shall be protected by placement of tables or by a curb.

5.8 Vending Machines and Other Equipment. Spaces for vending machines and other equipment shall comply with 4.2 and shall be located on an accessible route.

5.9 Quiet Areas. (Reserved).

6. │ MEDICAL CARE FACILITIES.

6.1 General. Medical care facilities included in this section are those in which people receive physical or medical treatment or care and where persons may need assistance in responding to an emergency and where the period of stay may exceed twenty-four hours. In addition to the requirements of 4.1 through 4.35, medical care facilities and buildings shall comply with 6.

(1) Hospitals - general purpose hospitals, psychiatric facilities, detoxification facilities — At least 10 percent of patient bedrooms and toilets, and all public use and common use areas are required to be designed and constructed to be accessible.

(2) Hospitals and rehabilitation facilities that specialize in treating conditions that affect mobility, or units within either that specialize in treating conditions that affect mobility — All patient bedrooms and toilets, and all public use and common use areas are required to be designed and constructed to be accessible.

(3) Long term care facilities, nursing homes — At least 50 percent of patient bedrooms and toilets, and all public use and common use areas are required to be designed and constructed to be accessible.

(4) Alterations to patient bedrooms.

(a) When patient bedrooms are being added or altered as part of a planned renovation of an entire wing, a department, or other discrete area of an existing medical facility, a percentage of the patient bedrooms that are being added or altered shall comply with 6.3. The percentage of accessible rooms provided shall be consistent with the percentage of rooms required to be accessible by the applicable requirements of 6.1(1), 6.1(2), or 6.1(3), until the number of accessible patient bedrooms in the facility equals the overall number that would be required if the facility were newly constructed. (For example, if 20 patient bedrooms are being altered in the obstetrics department of a hospital, 2 of the altered rooms must be made accessible. If, within the same hospital, 20 patient bedrooms are being altered in a unit that specializes in treating mobility impairments, all of the altered rooms must be made accessible.) Where toilet/bath rooms are part of patient bedrooms which are added or altered and required to be accessible, each such patient toilet/bathroom shall comply with 6.4.

(b) When patient bedrooms are being added or altered individually, and not as part of an alteration of the entire area, the altered patient bedrooms shall comply with 6.3, unless either: a) the number of accessible rooms provided in the department or area containing the altered patient bedroom equals the number of accessible patient bedrooms that would be required if the percentage requirements of 6.1(1), 6.1(2), or 6.1(3) were applied to that department or area; or b) the number of accessible patient bedrooms in the facility equals the overall number that would be required if the facility were newly constructed. Where toilet/bathrooms are part of patient bedrooms which are added or altered and required to be accessible, each such toilet/bathroom shall comply with 6.4.

Federal Register / Vol. 56, No. 144 / Friday, July 26, 1991 / Rules and Regulations

7.0 Business and Mercantile

6.2 Entrances. At least one accessible entrance that complies with 4.14 shall be protected from the weather by canopy or roof overhang. Such entrances shall incorporate a passenger loading zone that complies with 4.6.6.

6.3 Patient Bedrooms. Provide accessible patient bedrooms in compliance with 4.1 through 4.35. Accessible patient bedrooms shall comply with the following:

(1) Each bedroom shall have a door that complies with 4.13.

EXCEPTION: Entry doors to acute care hospital bedrooms for in-patients shall be exempted from the requirement in 4.13.6 for maneuvering space at the latch side of the door if the door is at least 44 in (1120 mm) wide.

(2) Each bedroom shall have adequate space to provide a maneuvering space that complies with 4.2.3. In rooms with 2 beds, it is preferable that this space be located between beds.

(3) Each bedroom shall have adequate space to provide a minimum clear floor space of 36 in (915 mm) along each side of the bed and to provide an accessible route complying with 4.3.3 to each side of each bed.

6.4 Patient Toilet Rooms. Where toilet/bath rooms are provided as a part of a patient bedroom, each patient bedroom that is required to be accessible shall have an accessible toilet/bath room that complies with 4.22 or 4.23 and shall be on an accessible route.

7. BUSINESS AND MERCANTILE.

7.1 General. In addition to the requirements of 4.1 to 4.35, the design of all areas used for business transactions with the public shall comply with 7.

7.2 Sales and Service Counters, Teller Windows, Information Counters.

(1) In department stores and miscellaneous retail stores where counters have cash registers and are provided for sales or distribution of goods or services to the public, at least one of each type shall have a portion of the counter which is at least 36 in (915 mm) in length with a maximum height of 36 in (915 mm) above the finish floor. It shall be on an accessible route complying with 4.3. The accessible counters must be dispersed throughout the building or facility. In alterations where it is technically infeasible to provide an accessible counter, an auxiliary counter meeting these requirements may be provided.

(2) At ticketing counters, teller stations in a bank, registration counters in hotels and motels, box office ticket counters, and other counters that may not have a cash register but at which goods or services are sold or distributed, either:

(i) a portion of the main counter which is a minimum of 36 in (915 mm) in length shall be provided with a maximum height of 36 in (915 mm); or

(ii) an auxiliary counter with a maximum height of 36 in (915 mm) in close proximity to the main counter shall be provided; or

(iii) equivalent facilitation shall be provided (e.g., at a hotel registration counter, equivalent facilitation might consist of: (1) provision of a folding shelf attached to the main counter on which an individual with disabilities can write, and (2) use of the space on the side of the counter or at the concierge desk, for handing materials back and forth).

All accessible sales and service counters shall be on an accessible route complying with 4.3.

(3)° Assistive Listening Devices. (Reserved)

61

487

8.0 Libraries

7.3* Check-out Aisles.

(1) In new construction, accessible check-out aisles shall be provided in conformance with the table below:

Total Check-out Aisles of Each Design	Minimum Number of Accessible Check-out Aisles (of each design)
1 – 4	1
5 – 8	2
8 – 15	3
over 15	3, plus 20% of additional aisles

EXCEPTION: In new construction, where the selling space is under 5000 square feet, only one check-out aisle is required to be accessible.

EXCEPTION: In alterations, at least one check-out aisle shall be accessible in facilities under 5000 square feet of selling space. In facilities of 5000 or more square feet of selling space, at least one of each design of check-out aisle shall be made accessible when altered until the number of accessible check-out aisles of each design equals the number required in new construction.

Examples of check-out aisles of different "design" include those which are specifically designed to serve different functions. Different "design" includes but is not limited to the following features - length of belt or no belt; or permanent signage designating the aisle as an express lane.

(2) Clear aisle width for accessible check-out aisles shall comply with 4.2.1 and maximum adjoining counter height shall not exceed 38 in (965 mm) above the finish floor. The top of the lip shall not exceed 40 in (1015 mm) above the finish floor.

(3) Signage identifying accessible check-out aisles shall comply with 4.30.7 and shall be mounted above the check-out aisle in the same location where the check-out number or type of check-out is displayed.

7.4 Security Bollards.
Any device used to prevent the removal of shopping carts from store premises shall not prevent access or egress to people in wheelchairs. An alternate entry that is equally convenient to that provided for the ambulatory population is acceptable.

---

8. | LIBRARIES.

8.1 General. In addition to the requirements of 4.1 to 4.35, the design of all public areas of a library shall comply with 8, including reading and study areas, stacks, reference rooms, reserve areas, and special facilities or collections.

8.2 Reading and Study Areas. At least 5 percent or a minimum of one of each element of fixed seating, tables, or study carrels shall comply with 4.2 and 4.32. Clearances between fixed accessible tables and between study carrels shall comply with 4.3.

8.3 Check-Out Areas. At least one lane at each check-out area shall comply with 7.2(1). Any traffic control or book security gates or turnstiles shall comply with 4.13.

8.4 Card Catalogs and Magazine Displays. Minimum clear aisle space at card catalogs and magazine displays shall comply with Fig. 55. Maximum reach height shall comply with 4.2, with a height of 48 in (1220 mm) preferred irrespective of approach allowed.

8.5 Stacks. Minimum clear aisle width between stacks shall comply with 4.3, with a minimum clear aisle width of 42 in (1065 mm) preferred where possible. Shelf height in stack areas is unrestricted (see Fig. 56).

9.0 Accessible Transient Lodging

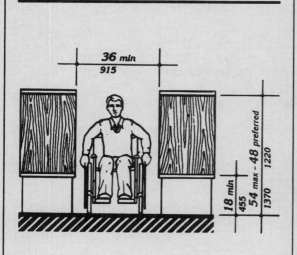

**Fig. 55
Card Catalog**

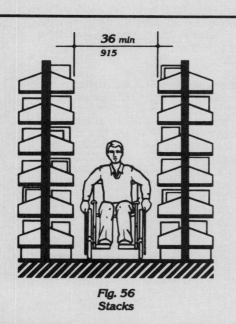

**Fig. 56
Stacks**

9. ACCESSIBLE TRANSIENT LODGING.

(1) Except as specified in the special technical provisions of this section, accessible transient lodging shall comply with the applicable requirements of 4.1 through 4.35. Transient lodging includes facilities or portions thereof used for sleeping accommodations, when not classed as a medical care facility.

9.1 Hotels, Motels, Inns, Boarding Houses, Dormitories, Resorts and Other Similar Places of Transient Lodging.

9.1.1 General. All public use and common use areas are required to be designed and constructed to comply with section 4 (Accessible Elements and Spaces: Scope and Technical Requirements).

EXCEPTION: Sections 9.1 through 9.4 do not apply to an establishment located within a building that contains not more than five rooms for rent or hire and that is actually occupied by the proprietor of such establishment as the residence of such proprietor.

9.1.2 Accessible Units, Sleeping Rooms, and Suites. Accessible sleeping rooms or suites that comply with the requirements of 9.2 (Requirements for Accessible Units, Sleeping Rooms, and Suites) shall be provided in conformance with the table below. In addition, in hotels, of 50 or more sleeping rooms or suites, additional accessible sleeping rooms or suites that include a roll-in shower shall also be provided in conformance with the table below. Such accommodations shall comply with the requirements of 9.2, 4.21, and Figure 57(a) or (b).

63

35670   Federal Register / Vol. 56, No. 144 / Friday, July 26, 1991 / Rules and Regulations

9.1.3 Sleeping Accommodations for Persons with Hearing Impairments

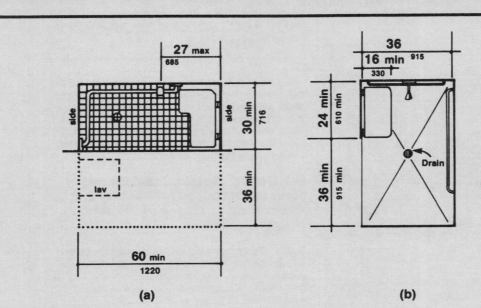

Fig. 57
Roll-in Shower with Folding Seat

Number of Rooms	Accessible Rooms	Rooms with Roll-in Showers
1 to 25	1	
26 to 50	2	
51 to 75	3	1
76 to 100	4	1
101 to 150	5	2
151 to 200	6	2
201 to 300	7	3
301 to 400	8	4
401 to 500	9	4 plus one for each additional 100 over 400
501 to 1000	2% of total	
1001 and over	20 plus 1 for each 100 over 1000	

9.1.3 Sleeping Accommodations for Persons with Hearing Impairments.

In addition to those accessible sleeping rooms and suites required by 9.1.2, sleeping rooms and suites that comply with 9.3 (Visual Alarms, Notification Devices, and Telephones) shall be provided in conformance with the following table:

Number of Elements	Accessible Elements
1 to 25	1
26 to 50	2
51 to 75	3
76 to 100	4
101 to 150	5
151 to 200	6
201 to 300	7
301 to 400	8
401 to 500	9
501 to 1000	2% of total
1001 and over	20 plus 1 for each 100 over 1000

Federal Register / Vol. 56, No. 144 / Friday, July 26, 1991 / Rules and Regulations   **35671**

9.2 Requirements for Accessible Units, Sleeping Rooms and Suites

9.1.4 Classes of Sleeping Accommodations.

(1) In order to provide persons with disabilities a range of options equivalent to those available to other persons served by the facility, sleeping rooms and suites required to be accessible by 9.1.2 shall be dispersed among the various classes of sleeping accommodations available to patrons of the place of transient lodging. Factors to be considered include room size, cost, amenities provided, and the number of beds provided.

(2) Equivalent Facilitation. For purposes of this section, it shall be deemed equivalent facilitation if the operator of a facility elects to limit construction of accessible rooms to those intended for multiple occupancy, provided that such rooms are made available at the cost of a single-occupancy room to an individual with disabilities who requests a single-occupancy room.

9.1.5. Alterations to Accessible Units, Sleeping Rooms, and Suites.
When sleeping rooms are being altered in an existing facility, or portion thereof, subject to the requirements of this section, at least one sleeping room or suite that complies with the requirements of 9.2 (Requirements for Accessible Units, Sleeping Rooms, and Suites) shall be provided for each 25 sleeping rooms, or fraction thereof, of rooms being altered until the number of such rooms provided equals the number required to be accessible with 9.1.2. In addition, at least one sleeping room or suite that complies with the requirements of 9.3 (Visual Alarms, Notification Devices, and Telephones) shall be provided for each 25 sleeping rooms, or fraction thereof, of rooms being altered until the number of such rooms equals the number required to be accessible by 9.1.3.

9.2 Requirements for Accessible Units, Sleeping Rooms and Suites.

9.2.1 General. Units, sleeping rooms, and suites required to be accessible by 9.1 shall comply with 9.2.

9.2.2 Minimum Requirements. An accessible unit, sleeping room or suite shall be on an accessible route complying with 4.3 and have the following accessible elements and spaces.

(1) Accessible sleeping rooms shall have a 36 in (915 mm) clear width maneuvering space located along both sides of a bed, except that where two beds are provided, this requirement can be met by providing a 36 in (915 mm) wide maneuvering space located between the two beds.

(2) An accessible route complying with 4.3 shall connect all accessible spaces and elements, including telephones, within the unit, sleeping room, or suite. This is not intended to require an elevator in multi-story units as long as the spaces identified in 9.2.2(6) and (7) are on accessible levels and the accessible sleeping area is suitable for dual occupancy.

(3) Doors and doorways designed to allow passage into and within all sleeping rooms, suites or other covered units shall comply with 4.13.

(4) If fixed or built-in storage facilities such as cabinets, shelves, closets, and drawers are provided in accessible spaces, at least one of each type provided shall contain storage space complying with 4.25. Additional storage may be provided outside of the dimensions required by 4.25.

(5) All controls in accessible units, sleeping rooms, and suites shall comply with 4.27.

(6) Where provided as part of an accessible unit, sleeping room, or suite, the following spaces shall be accessible and shall be on an accessible route·

(a) the living area.

(b) the dining area.

(c) at least one sleeping area.

(d) patios, terraces, or balconies.

EXCEPTION: The requirements of 4.13.8 and 4.3.8 do not apply where it is necessary to utilize a higher door threshold or a change in level to protect the integrity of the unit from wind/water damage. Where this exception results in patios, terraces or balconies that are not at an accessible level, equivalent facilitation

65

Appendix A

9.3 Visual Alarms, Notification Devices and Telephones

shall be provided. (E.g., equivalent facilitation at a hotel patio or balcony might consist of providing raised decking or a ramp to provide accessibility.)

(e) at least one full bathroom (i.e., one with a water closet, a lavatory, and a bathtub or shower).

(f) if only half baths are provided, at least one half bath.

(g) carports, garages or parking spaces.

(7) Kitchens, Kitchenettes, or Wet Bars. When provided as accessory to a sleeping room or suite, kitchens, kitchenettes, wet bars, or similar amenities shall be accessible. Clear floor space for a front or parallel approach to cabinets, counters, sinks, and appliances shall be provided to comply with 4.2.4. Countertops and sinks shall be mounted at a maximum height of 34 in (865 mm) above the floor. At least fifty percent of shelf space in cabinets or refrigerator/freezers shall be within the reach ranges of 4.2.5 or 4.2.6 and space shall be designed to allow for the operation of cabinet and/or appliance doors so that all cabinets and appliances are accessible and usable. Controls and operating mechanisms shall comply with 4.27.

(8) Sleeping room accommodations for persons with hearing impairments required by 9.1 and complying with 9.3 shall be provided in the accessible sleeping room or suite.

9.3 Visual Alarms, Notification Devices and Telephones.

9.3.1 General. In sleeping rooms required to comply with this section, auxiliary visual alarms shall be provided and shall comply with 4.28.4. Visual notification devices shall also be provided in units, sleeping rooms and suites to alert room occupants of incoming telephone calls and a door knock or bell. Notification devices shall **not** be connected to auxiliary visual alarm signal appliances. Permanently installed telephones shall have volume controls complying with 4.31.5; an accessible electrical outlet within 4 ft (1220 mm) of a telephone connection shall be provided to facilitate the use of a text telephone.

9.3.2 Equivalent Facilitation. For purposes of this section, equivalent facilitation shall include the installation of electrical outlets (including outlets connected to a facility's central alarm system) and telephone wiring in sleeping rooms and suites to enable persons with hearing impairments to utilize portable visual alarms and communication devices provided by the operator of the facility.

9.4 Other Sleeping Rooms and Suites.
Doors and doorways designed to allow passage into and within all sleeping units or other covered units shall comply with 4.13.5.

9.5 Transient Lodging in Homeless Shelters, Halfway Houses, Transient Group Homes, and Other Social Service Establishments.

9.5.1 New Construction. In new construction all public use and common use areas are required to be designed and constructed to comply with section 4. At least one of each type of amenity (such as washers, dryers and similar equipment installed for the use of occupants) in each common area shall be accessible and shall be located on an accessible route to any accessible unit or sleeping accommodation.

EXCEPTION: Where elevators are not provided as allowed in 4.1.3(5), accessible amenities are not required on inaccessible floors as long as one of each type is provided in common areas on accessible floors.

9.5.2 Alterations.

(1) Social service establishments which are not homeless shelters:

(a) The provisions of 9.5.3 and 9.1.5 shall apply to sleeping rooms and beds.

(b) Alteration of other areas shall be consistent with the new construction provisions of 9.5.1.

(2) Homeless shelters. If the following elements are altered, the following requirements apply:

10.0 Transportation Facilities

(a) at least one public entrance shall allow a person with mobility impairments to approach, enter and exit including a minimum clear door width of 32 in (815 mm).

(b) sleeping space for homeless persons as provided in the scoping provisions of 9.1.2 shall include doors to the sleeping area with a minimum clear width of 32 in (815 mm) and maneuvering space around the beds for persons with mobility impairments complying with 9.2.2(1).

(c) at least one toilet room for each gender or one unisex toilet room shall have a minimum clear door width of 32 in (815 mm), minimum turning space complying with 4.2.3, one water closet complying with 4.16, one lavatory complying with 4.19 and the door shall have a privacy latch; and, if provided, at least one tub or shower shall comply with 4.20 or 4.21, respectively.

(d) at least one common area which a person with mobility impairments can approach, enter and exit including a minimum clear door width of 32 in (815 mm).

(e) at least one route connecting elements (a), (b), (c) and (d) which a person with mobility impairments can use including minimum clear width of 36 in (915 mm), passing space complying with 4.3.4, turning space complying with 4.2.3 and changes in levels complying with 4.3.8.

(f) homeless shelters can comply with the provisions of (a)-(e) by providing the above elements on one accessible floor.

9.5.3. Accessible Sleeping Accommodations in New Construction.
Accessible sleeping rooms shall be provided in conformance with the table in 9.1.2 and shall comply with 9.2 Accessible Units, Sleeping Rooms and Suites (where the items are provided). Additional sleeping rooms that comply with 9.3 Sleeping Accommodations for Persons with Hearing Impairments shall be provided in conformance with the table provided in 9.1.3.

In facilities with multi-bed rooms or spaces, a percentage of the beds equal to the table provided in 9.1.2 shall comply with 9.2.2(1).

10. TRANSPORTATION FACILITIES. (Reserved).

APPENDIX

This appendix contains *materials of an advisory nature* and provides additional information that should help the reader to understand the minimum requirements of the *guidelines* or to design buildings or facilities for greater accessibility. The paragraph numbers correspond to the sections or paragraphs of the *guideline* to which the material relates and are therefore not consecutive (for example, A4.2.1 contains additional information relevant to 4.2.1). Sections *of the guidelines* for which additional material appears in this appendix have been indicated by an asterisk. *Nothing in this appendix shall in any way obviate any obligation to comply with the requirements of the guidelines itself.*

A2.2 Equivalent Facilitation. *Specific examples of equivalent facilitation are found in the following sections:*

4.1.6(3)(c)	*Elevators in Alterations*
4.31.9	*Text Telephones*
7.2	*Sales and Service Counters, Teller Windows, Information Counters*
9.1.4	*Classes of Sleeping Accommodations*
9.2.2(6)(d)	*Requirements for Accessible Units, Sleeping Rooms, and Suites*

A4.1.1 Application.

A4.1.1(3) Areas Used Only by Employees as Work Areas. *Where there are a series of individual work stations of the same type (e.g., laboratories, service counters, ticket booths), 5%, but not less than one, of each type of work station should be constructed so that an individual with disabilities can maneuver within the work stations. Rooms housing individual offices in a typical office building must meet the requirements of the guidelines concerning doors, accessible routes, etc. but do not need to allow for maneuvering space around individual desks. Modifications required to permit maneuvering within the work area may be accomplished as a reasonable accommodation to individual employees with disabilities under Title I of the ADA. Consideration should also be given to placing shelves in employee work areas at a convenient height for accessibility or installing commercially available shelving that is adjustable so that reasonable accommodations can be made in the future.*

If work stations are made accessible they should comply with the applicable provisions of 4.2 through 4.35.

A4.1.2 Accessible Sites and Exterior Facilities: New Construction.

A4.1.2(5)(e) Valet Parking. *Valet parking is not always usable by individuals with disabilities. For instance, an individual may use a type of vehicle controls that render the regular controls inoperable or the driver's seat in a van may be removed. In these situations, another person cannot park the vehicle. It is recommended that some self-parking spaces be provided at valet parking facilities for individuals whose vehicles cannot be parked by another person and that such spaces be located on an accessible route to the entrance of the facility.*

A4.1.3 Accessible Buildings: New Construction.

A4.1.3(5) *Only full passenger elevators are covered by the accessibility provisions of 4.10. Materials and equipment hoists, freight elevators not intended for passenger use, dumbwaiters, and construction elevators are not covered by these guidelines. If a building is exempt from the elevator requirement, it is not necessary to provide a platform lift or other means of vertical access in lieu of an elevator.*

Under Exception 4, platform lifts are allowed where existing conditions make it impractical to install a ramp or elevator. Such conditions generally occur where it is essential to provide access to small raised or lowered areas where space may not be available for a ramp. Examples include, but are not limited to, raised pharmacy platforms, commercial offices raised above a sales floor, or radio and news booths.

A4.1.3(9) *Supervised automatic sprinkler systems have built in signals for monitoring features of the system such as the opening and closing of water control valves, the power supplies for needed pumps, water tank levels, and for indicating conditions that will impair the satisfactory operation of the sprinkler system.*

A1

Federal Register / Vol. 56, No. 144 / Friday, July 26, 1991 / Rules and Regulations

A4.2 Space Allowances and Reach Ranges

Because of these monitoring features, supervised automatic sprinkler systems have a high level of satisfactory performance and response to fire conditions.

__A4.1.3(10)__ If an odd number of drinking fountains is provided on a floor, the requirement in 4.1.3(10)(b) may be met by rounding down the odd number to an even number and calculating 50% of the even number. When more than one drinking fountain on a floor is required to comply with 4.15, those fountains should be dispersed to allow wheelchair users convenient access. For example, in a large facility such as a convention center that has water fountains at several locations on a floor, the accessible water fountains should be located so that wheelchair users do not have to travel a greater distance than other people to use a drinking fountain.

__A4.1.3(17)(b)__ In addition to the requirements of section 4.1.3(17)(b), the installation of additional volume controls is encouraged. Volume controls may be installed on any telephone.

__A4.1.3(19)(a)__ Readily removable or folding seating units may be installed in lieu of providing an open space for wheelchair users. Folding seating units are usually two fixed seats that can be easily folded into a fixed center bar to allow for one or two open spaces for wheelchair users when necessary. These units are more easily adapted than removable seats which generally require the seat to be removed in advance by the facility management.

Either a sign or a marker placed on seating with removable or folding arm rests is required by this section. Consideration should be given for ensuring identification of such seats in a darkened theater. For example, a marker which contrasts (light on dark or dark on light) and which also reflects light could be placed on the side of such seating so as to be visible in a lighted auditorium and also to reflect light from a flashlight.

A4.1.6 Accessible Buildings: Alterations.

__A4.1.6(1)(h)__ When an entrance is being altered, it is preferable that those entrances being altered be made accessible to the extent feasible.

A4.2 Space Allowances and Reach Ranges.

A4.2.1 Wheelchair Passage Width.

(1) Space Requirements for Wheelchairs. Many persons who use wheelchairs need a 30 in (760 mm) clear opening width for doorways, gates, and the like, when the latter are entered head-on. If the *person* is unfamiliar with a building, if competing traffic is heavy, if sudden or frequent movements are needed, or if the wheelchair must be turned at an opening, then greater clear widths are needed. For most situations, the addition of an inch of leeway on either side is sufficient. Thus, a minimum clear width of 32 in (815 mm) will provide adequate clearance. However, when an opening or a restriction in a passageway is more than 24 in (610 mm) long, it is essentially a passageway and must be at least 36 in (915 mm) wide.

(2) Space Requirements for Use of Walking Aids. Although people who use walking aids can maneuver through clear width openings of 32 in (815 mm), they need 36 in (915 mm) wide passageways and walks for comfortable gaits. Crutch tips, often extending down at a wide angle, are a hazard in narrow passageways where they might not be seen by other pedestrians. Thus, the 36 in (915 mm) width provides a safety allowance both for the person *with a disability* and for others.

(3) Space Requirements for Passing. Able-bodied *persons* in winter clothing, walking

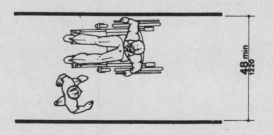

Fig. A1
Minimum Passage Width for One Wheelchair and One Ambulatory Person

35676   Federal Register / Vol. 56, No. 144 / Friday, July 26, 1991 / Rules and Regulations

A4.2 Space Allowances and Reach Ranges

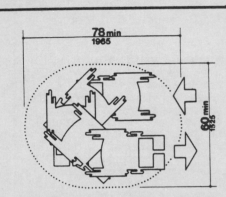

Fig. A2
Space Needed for Smooth U-Turn in a Wheelchair

straight ahead with arms swinging, need 32 in (815 mm) of width, which includes 2 in (50 mm) on either side for sway, and another 1 in (25 mm) tolerance on either side for clearing nearby objects or other pedestrians. Almost all wheelchair users and those who use walking aids can also manage within this 32 in (815 mm) width for short distances. Thus, two streams of traffic can pass in 64 in (1625 mm) in a comfortable flow. Sixty inches (1525 mm) provides a minimum width for a somewhat more restricted flow. If the clear width is less than 60 in (1525 mm), two wheelchair users will not be able to pass but will have to seek a wider place for passing. Forty-eight inches (1220 mm) is the minimum width needed for an ambulatory person to pass a nonambulatory or semi-ambulatory person. Within this 48 in (1220 mm) width, the ambulatory person will have to twist to pass a wheelchair user, a person with a *service animal*, or a

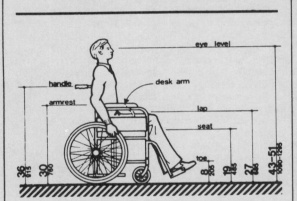

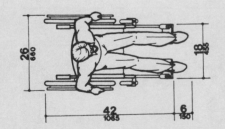

NOTE: Footrests may extend further for tall people

Fig. A3
Dimensions of Adult-Sized Wheelchairs

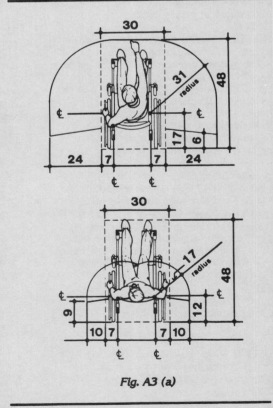

Fig. A3 (a)

A3

Federal Register / Vol. 56, No. 144 / Friday, July 26, 1991 / Rules and Regulations

A4.3 Accessible Route

semi-ambulatory person. There will be little leeway for swaying or missteps (see Fig. A1).

A4.2.3 Wheelchair Turning Space.
These guidelines specify a minimum space of 60 in (1525 mm) diameter *or a 60 in by 60 in (1525 mm by 1525 mm) T-shaped space* for a pivoting 180-degree turn of a wheelchair. This space is usually satisfactory for turning around, but many people will not be able to turn without repeated tries and bumping into surrounding objects. The space shown in Fig. A2 will allow most wheelchair users to complete U-turns without difficulty.

A4.2.4 Clear Floor or Ground Space for Wheelchairs.
The wheelchair and user shown in Fig. A3 represent typical dimensions for a large adult male. The space requirements in this *guideline* are based upon maneuvering clearances that will accommodate most wheelchairs. Fig. A3 provides a uniform reference for design not covered by this *guideline*.

A4.2.5 & A4.2.6 Reach.
Reach ranges for persons seated in wheelchairs may be further clarified by Fig. A3(a). These drawings approximate in the plan view the information shown in Fig. 4, 5, and 6.

A4.3 Accessible Route.

A4.3.1 General.

(1) Travel Distances. Many people with mobility impairments can move at only very slow speeds; for many, traveling 200 ft (61 m) could take about 2 minutes. This assumes a rate of about 1.5 ft/s (455 mm/s) on level ground. It also assumes that the traveler would move continuously. However, on trips over 100 ft (30 m), disabled people are apt to rest frequently, which substantially increases their trip times. Resting periods of 2 minutes for every 100 ft (30 m) can be used to estimate travel times for people with severely limited stamina. In inclement weather, slow progress and resting can greatly increase a disabled person's exposure to the elements.

(2) Sites. Level, indirect routes or those with running slopes lower than 1:20 can sometimes provide more convenience than direct routes with maximum allowable slopes or with ramps.

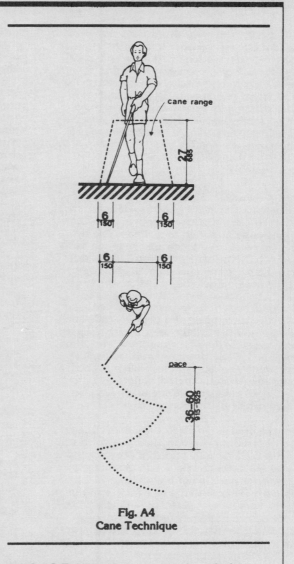

**Fig. A4
Cane Technique**

A4.3.10 Egress. Because people with disabilities may visit, be employed or be a resident in any building, emergency management plans with specific provisions to ensure their safe evacuation also play an essential role in fire safety and life safety.

A4.3.11.3 Stairway Width. *A 48 inch (1220 mm) wide exit stairway is needed to allow assisted evacuation (e.g., carrying a person in a wheelchair) without encroaching on the exit path for ambulatory persons.*

A4

35678 **Federal Register** / Vol. 56, No. 144 / Friday, July 26, 1991 / Rules and Regulations

A4.5 Ground and Floor Surfaces

A4.3.11.4 Two-way Communication. *It is essential that emergency communication not be dependent on voice communications alone because the safety of people with hearing or speech impairments could be jeopardized. The visible signal requirement could be satisfied with something as simple as a button in the area of rescue assistance that lights, indicating that help is on the way, when the message is answered at the point of entry.*

A4.4 Protruding Objects.

A4.4.1 General. *Service animals* are trained to recognize and avoid hazards. However, most people with severe impairments of vision use the long cane as an aid to mobility. The two principal cane techniques are the touch technique, where the cane arcs from side to side and touches points outside both shoulders; and the diagonal technique, where the cane is held in a stationary position diagonally across the body with the cane tip touching or just above the ground at a point outside one shoulder and the handle or grip extending to a point outside the other shoulder. The touch technique is used primarily in uncontrolled areas, while the diagonal technique is used primarily in certain limited, controlled, and familiar environments. Cane users are often trained to use both techniques.

Potential hazardous objects are noticed only if they fall within the detection range of canes (see Fig. A4). Visually impaired people walking toward an object can detect an overhang if its lowest surface is not higher than 27 in (685 mm). When walking alongside *protruding* objects, they cannot detect overhangs. Since proper cane and *service animal* techniques keep people away from the edge of a path or from walls, a slight overhang of no more than 4 in (100 mm) is not hazardous.

A4.5 Ground and Floor Surfaces.

A4.5.1 General. *People who have difficulty walking or* maintaining balance *or who use crutches, canes, or walkers,* and those with restricted gaits are particularly sensitive to slipping and tripping hazards. For such people, a stable and regular surface is necessary for safe walking, particularly on stairs. Wheelchairs can be propelled most easily on surfaces that are hard, stable, and regular. Soft loose surfaces such as shag carpet, loose sand or gravel, wet clay, and irregular surfaces such as cobblestones can significantly impede wheelchair movement.

Slip resistance is based on the frictional force necessary to keep a shoe heel or crutch tip from slipping on a walking surface under conditions likely to be found on the surface. *While the* dynamic *coefficient of friction during walking varies in a complex and non-uniform way, the* static *coefficient of friction, which can be measured in several ways, provides a close approximation of the slip resistance of a surface. Contrary to popular belief, some slippage is* necessary *to walking, especially for persons with restricted gaits; a truly "non-slip" surface could not be negotiated.*

The Occupational Safety and Health Administration recommends that walking surfaces have a static coefficient of friction of 0.5. A research project sponsored by the Architectural and Transportation Barriers Compliance Board (Access Board) conducted tests with persons with disabilities and concluded that a higher coefficient of friction was needed by such persons. A static coefficient of friction of 0.6 is recommended for accessible routes and 0.8 for ramps.

It is recognized that the coefficient of friction varies considerably due to the presence of contaminants, water, floor finishes, and other factors not under the control of the designer or builder and not subject to design and construction guidelines and that compliance would be difficult to measure on the building site. Nevertheless, many common building materials suitable for flooring are now labeled with information on the static coefficient of friction. While it may not be possible to compare one product directly with another, or to guarantee a constant measure, builders and designers are encouraged to specify materials with appropriate values. As more products include information on slip resistance, improved uniformity in measurement and specification is likely. The Access Board's advisory guidelines on Slip Resistant Surfaces provides additional information on this subject.

Cross slopes on walks and ground or floor surfaces can cause considerable difficulty in propelling a wheelchair in a straight line.

A5

Federal Register / Vol. 56, No. 144 / Friday, July 26, 1991 / Rules and Regulations   35679

A4.6 Parking and Passenger Loading Zones

A4.5.3 Carpet. Much more needs to be done in developing both quantitative and qualitative criteria for carpeting (*i.e., problems associated with texture and weave need to be studied*). However, certain functional characteristics are well established. When both carpet and padding are used, it is desirable to have minimum movement (preferably none) between the floor and the pad and the pad and the carpet which would allow the carpet to hump or warp. In heavily trafficked areas, a thick, soft (plush) pad or cushion, particularly in combination with long carpet pile, makes it difficult for individuals in wheelchairs and those with other ambulatory disabilities to get about. Firm carpeting can be achieved through proper selection and combination of pad and carpet, sometimes with the elimination of the pad or cushion, and with proper installation. *Carpeting designed with a weave that causes a zig-zag effect when wheeled across is strongly discouraged.*

A4.6 Parking and Passenger Loading Zones.

A4.6.3 Parking Spaces. *The increasing use of vans with side-mounted lifts or ramps by persons with disabilities has necessitated some revisions in specifications for parking spaces and adjacent access aisles. The typical accessible parking space is 96 in (2440 mm) wide with an adjacent 60 in (1525 mm) access aisle. However, this aisle does not permit lifts or ramps to be deployed and still leave room for a person using a wheelchair or other mobility aid to exit the lift platform or ramp. In tests conducted with actual lift/van/wheelchair combinations, (under a Board-sponsored Accessible Parking and Loading Zones Project) researchers found that a space and aisle totaling almost 204 in (5180 mm) wide was needed to deploy a lift and exit conveniently. The "van accessible" parking space required by these guidelines provides a 96 in (2440 mm) wide space with a 96 in (2440 mm) adjacent access aisle which is just wide enough to maneuver and exit from a side mounted lift. If a 96 in (2440 mm) access aisle is placed between two spaces, two "van accessible" spaces are created. Alternatively, if the wide access aisle is provided at the end of a row (an area often unused), it may be possible to provide the wide access aisle without additional space (see Fig. A5(a)).*

A sign is needed to alert van users to the presence of the wider aisle, but the space is not intended to be restricted only to vans.

"Universal" Parking Space Design. An alternative to the provision of a percentage of spaces with a wide aisle, and the associated need to include additional signage, is the use of what has been called the "universal" parking space design. Under this design, all accessible spaces are 132 in (3350 mm) wide with a 60 in (1525 mm) access aisle (see Fig. A5(b)). One

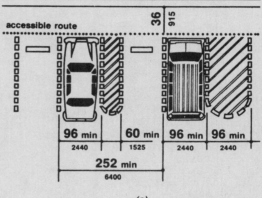

(a)
Van Accessible Space at End Row

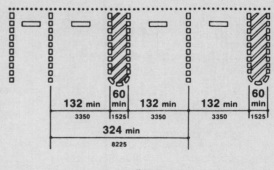

(b)
Universal Parking Space Design

Fig. A5
Parking Space Alternatives

Appendix A

A4.8 Ramps

advantage to this design is that no additional signage is needed because all spaces can accommodate a van with a side-mounted lift or ramp. Also, there is no competition between cars and vans for spaces since all spaces can accommodate either. Furthermore, the wider space permits vehicles to park to one side or the other within the 132 in (3350 mm) space to allow persons to exit and enter the vehicle on either the driver or passenger side, although, in some cases, this would require exiting or entering without a marked access aisle.

An essential consideration for any design is having the access aisle level with the parking space. Since a person with a disability, using a lift or ramp, must maneuver within the access aisle, the aisle cannot include a ramp or sloped area. The access aisle must be connected to an accessible route to the appropriate accessible entrance of a building or facility. The parking access aisle must either blend with the accessible route or have a curb ramp complying with 4.7. Such a curb ramp opening must be located within the access aisle boundaries, not within the parking space boundaries. Unfortunately, many facilities are designed with a ramp that is blocked when any vehicle parks in the accessible space. Also, the required dimensions of the access aisle cannot be restricted by planters, curbs or wheel stops.

A4.6.4 Signage. Signs designating parking places for disabled people can be seen from a driver's seat if the signs are mounted high enough above the ground and located at the front of a parking space.

A4.6.5 Vertical Clearance. High-top vans, which disabled people or transportation services often use, require higher clearances in parking garages than automobiles.

A4.8 Ramps.

A4.8.1 General. Ramps are essential for wheelchair users if elevators or lifts are not available to connect different levels. However, some people who use walking aids have difficulty with ramps and prefer stairs.

A4.8.2 Slope and Rise. *Ramp slopes between 1:16 and 1:20 are preferred.* The ability to manage an incline is related to both its slope and its length. Wheelchair users with

disabilities affecting *their* arms or with low stamina have serious difficulty using inclines. Most ambulatory people and most people who use wheelchairs can manage a slope of 1:16. Many people cannot manage a slope of 1:12 for 30 ft (9 m).

A4.8.4 Landings. *Level landings are essential toward maintaining an aggregate slope that complies with these guidelines. A ramp landing that is not level causes individuals using wheelchairs to tip backward or bottom out when the ramp is approached.*

A4.8.5 Handrails. The requirements for stair and ramp handrails in this *guideline* are for adults. When children are principal users in a building or facility, a second set of handrails at an appropriate height can assist them and aid in preventing accidents.

A4.9 Stairs.

A4.9.1 Minimum Number. *Only interior and exterior stairs connecting levels that are not connected by an elevator, ramp, or other accessible means of vertical access have to comply with 4.9.*

A4.10 Elevators.

A4.10.6 Door Protective and Reopening Device. The required door reopening device would hold the door open for 20 seconds if the doorway remains obstructed. After 20 seconds, the door may begin to close. However, if designed in accordance with *ASME A17.1-1990*, the door closing movement could still be stopped if a person or object exerts sufficient force at any point on the door edge.

A4.10.7 Door and Signal Timing for Hall Calls. This paragraph allows variation in the location of call buttons, advance time for warning signals, and the door-holding period used to meet the time requirement.

A4.10.12 Car Controls. Industry-wide standardization of elevator control panel design would make all elevators significantly more convenient for use by people with severe visual impairments. In many cases, it will be possible to locate the highest control on elevator panels within 48 in (1220 mm) from the floor.

A7

Federal Register / Vol. 56, No. 144 / Friday, July 26, 1991 / Rules and Regulations

A4.11 Platform Lifts (Wheelchair Lifts)

A4.10.13 Car Position Indicators. A special button may be provided that would activate the audible signal within the given elevator only for the desired trip, rather than maintaining the audible signal in constant operation.

A4.10.14 Emergency Communications. A device that requires no handset is easier to use by people who have difficulty reaching. *Also, small handles on handset compartment doors are not usable by people who have difficulty grasping.*

Ideally, emergency two-way communication systems should provide both voice and visual display intercommunication so that persons with hearing impairments and persons with vision impairments can receive information regarding the status of a rescue. A voice intercommunication system cannot be the only means of communication because it is not accessible to people with speech and hearing impairments. While a voice intercommunication system is not required, at a minimum, the system should provide both an audio and visual indication that a rescue is on the way.

A4.11 Platform Lifts (Wheelchair Lifts).

A4.11.2 Other Requirements. *Inclined stairway chairlifts, and inclined and vertical platform lifts (wheelchair lifts) are available* for short-distance, vertical transportation of people with disabilities. Care should be taken in selecting lifts *as some lifts are not equally suitable for use by both wheelchair users and semi-ambulatory individuals.*

A4.12 Windows.

A4.12.1 General. *Windows intended to be operated by occupants in accessible spaces should comply with 4.12.*

A4.12.2 Window Hardware. *Windows requiring pushing, pulling, or lifting to open (for example, double-hung, sliding, or casement and awning units without cranks) should require no more than 5 lbf (22.2 N) to open or close. Locks, cranks, and other window hardware should comply with 4.27.*

A4.13 Doors.

A4.13.8 Thresholds at Doorways. Thresholds and surface height changes in doorways are particularly inconvenient for wheelchair users who also have low stamina or restrictions in arm movement because complex maneuvering is required to get over the level change while operating the door.

A4.13.9 Door Hardware. Some disabled persons must push against a door with their chair or walker to open it. Applied kickplates on doors with closers can reduce required maintenance by withstanding abuse from wheelchairs and canes. To be effective, they should cover the door width, less approximately 2 in (51 mm), up to a height of 16 in (405 mm) from its bottom edge and be centered across the *width of the door.*

A4.13.10 Door Closers. Closers with delayed action features give a person more time to maneuver through doorways. They are particularly useful on frequently used interior doors such as entrances to toilet rooms.

A4.13.11 Door Opening Force. Although most people with disabilities can exert at least 5 lbf (22.2N), both pushing and pulling from a stationary position, a few people with severe disabilities cannot exert 3 lbf (13.13N). Although some people cannot manage the allowable forces in this guideline and many others have difficulty, door closers must have certain minimum closing forces to close doors satisfactorily. Forces for pushing or pulling doors open are measured with a push-pull scale under the following conditions:

(1) Hinged doors: Force applied perpendicular to the door at the door opener or 30 in (760 mm) from the hinged side, whichever is farther from the hinge.

(2) Sliding or folding doors: Force applied parallel to the door at the door pull or latch.

(3) Application of force: Apply force gradually so that the applied force does not exceed the resistance of the door. In high-rise buildings, air-pressure differentials may require a modification of this specification in order to meet the functional intent.

Appendix A

A4.15 Drinking Fountains and Water Coolers

A4.13.12 Automatic Doors and Power-Assisted Doors. Sliding automatic doors do not need guard rails and are more convenient for wheelchair users and visually impaired people to use. If slowly opening automatic doors can be reactivated before their closing cycle is completed, they will be more convenient in busy doorways.

A4.15 Drinking Fountains and Water Coolers.

A4.15.2 Spout Height. *Two drinking fountains, mounted side by side or on a single post, are usable by people with disabilities and people who find it difficult to bend over.*

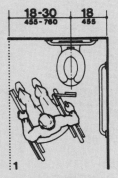 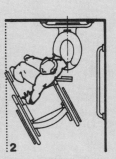 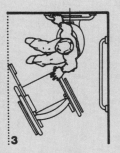 

1. Takes transfer position, swings footrest out of the way, sets brakes.

2. Removes armrest, transfers.

3. Moves wheelchair out of the way, changes position (some people fold chair or pivot it 90° to the toilet).

4. Positions on toilet, releases brake.

**(a)
Diagonal Approach**

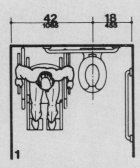  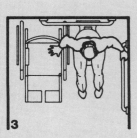

1. Takes transfer position, removes armrest, sets brakes.

2. Transfers.

3. Positions on toilet.

**(b)
Side Approach**

**Fig. A6
Wheelchair Transfers**

A9

A4.16 Water Closets

A4.16 Water Closets.

A4.16.3 Height. Height preferences for toilet seats vary considerably among disabled people. Higher seat heights may be an advantage to some ambulatory disabled people, but are often a disadvantage for wheelchair users and others. Toilet seats 18 in (455 mm) high seem to be a reasonable compromise. Thick seats and filler rings are available to adapt standard fixtures to these requirements.

A4.16.4 Grab Bars. Fig. A6(a) and (b) show the diagonal and side approaches most commonly used to transfer from a wheelchair to a water closet. Some wheelchair users can transfer from the front of the toilet while others use a 90-degree approach. Most people who use the two additional approaches can also use either the diagonal approach or the side approach.

A4.16.5 Flush Controls. Flush valves and related plumbing can be located behind walls or to the side of the toilet, or a toilet seat lid can be provided if plumbing fittings are directly behind the toilet seat. Such designs reduce the chance of injury and imbalance caused by leaning back against the fittings. Flush controls for tank-type toilets have a standardized mounting location on the left side of the tank (facing the tank). Tanks can be obtained by special order with controls mounted on the right side. If administrative authorities require flush controls for flush valves to be located in a position that conflicts with the location of the rear grab bar, then that bar may be split or shifted toward the wide side of the toilet area.

A4.17 Toilet Stalls.

A4.17.3 Size and Arrangement. *This section requires use of the 60 in (1525 mm) standard stall (Figure 30(a)) and permits the 36 in (915 mm) or 48 in (1220 mm) wide alternate stall (Figure 30(b)) only in alterations where provision of the standard stall is technically infeasible or where local plumbing codes prohibit reduction in the number of fixtures. A standard stall provides a clear space on one side of the water closet to enable persons who use wheelchairs to perform a side or diagonal transfer from the wheelchair to the water closet. However, some persons with disabilities who use mobility aids such as walkers, canes or crutches*

are better able to use the two parallel grab bars in the 36 in (915 mm) wide alternate stall to achieve a standing position.

In large toilet rooms, where six or more toilet stalls are provided, it is therefore required that a 36 in (915 mm) wide stall with parallel grab bars be provided in addition to the standard stall required in new construction. The 36 in (915 mm) width is necessary to achieve proper use of the grab bars; wider stalls would position the grab bars too far apart to be easily used and narrower stalls would position the grab bars too close to the water closet. Since the stall is primarily intended for use by persons using canes, crutches and walkers, rather than wheelchairs, the length of the stall could be conventional. The door, however, must swing outward to ensure a usable space for people who use crutches or walkers.

A4.17.5 Doors. To make it easier for wheelchair users to close toilet stall doors, doors can be provided with closers, spring hinges, or a pull bar mounted on the inside surface of the door near the hinge side.

A4.19 Lavatories and Mirrors.

A4.19.6 Mirrors. If mirrors are to be used by both ambulatory people and wheelchair users, then they must be at least 74 in (1880 mm) high at their topmost edge. A single full length mirror can accommodate all people, including children.

A4.21 Shower Stalls.

A4.21.1 General. Shower stalls that are 36 in by 36 in (915 mm by 915 mm) wide provide additional safety to people who have difficulty maintaining balance because all grab bars and walls are within easy reach. Seated people use the walls of 36 in by 36 in (915 mm by 915 mm) showers for back support. Shower stalls that are 60 in (1525 mm) wide and have no curb may increase usability of a bathroom by wheelchair users because the shower area provides additional maneuvering space.

A4.22 Toilet Rooms.

A4.22.3 Clear Floor Space. *In many small facilities, single-user restrooms may be the only*

Appendix A

A4.22 Toilet Rooms

facilities provided for all building users. In addition, the guidelines allow the use of "unisex" or "family" accessible toilet rooms in alterations when technical infeasibility can be demonstrated. Experience has shown that the provision of accessible "unisex" or single-user restrooms is a reasonable way to provide access for wheelchair users and any attendants, especially when attendants are of the opposite sex. Since these facilities have proven so useful, it is often considered advantageous to install a "unisex" toilet room in new facilities in addition to making the multi-stall restrooms accessible, especially in shopping malls, large auditoriums, and convention centers.

Figure 28 (section 4.16) provides minimum clear floor space dimensions for toilets in accessible "unisex" toilet rooms. The dotted lines designate the minimum clear floor space, depending on the direction of approach, required for wheelchair users to transfer onto the water closet. The dimensions of 48 in (1220 mm) and 60 in (1525 mm), respectively, correspond to the space required for the two common transfer approaches utilized by wheelchair users (see Fig. A6). It is important to keep in mind that the placement of the lavatory to the immediate side of the water closet will preclude the side approach transfer illustrated in Figure A6(b).

To accommodate the side transfer, the space adjacent to the water closet must remain clear of obstruction for 42 in (1065 mm) from the centerline of the toilet (Figure 28) and the lavatory must not be located within this clear space. A turning circle or T-turn, the clear floor space at the lavatory, and maneuvering space at the door must be considered when determining the possible wall locations. A privacy latch or other accessible means of ensuring privacy during use should be provided at the door.

RECOMMENDATIONS:

1. In new construction, accessible single-user restrooms may be desirable in some situations because they can accommodate a wide variety of building users. However, they cannot be used in lieu of making the multi-stall toilet rooms accessible as required.

2. Where strict compliance to the guidelines for accessible toilet facilities is technically infeasible in the alteration of existing facilities, accessible "unisex" toilets are a reasonable alternative.

3. In designing accessible single-user restrooms, the provisions of adequate space to allow a side transfer will provide accommodation to the largest number of wheelchair users.

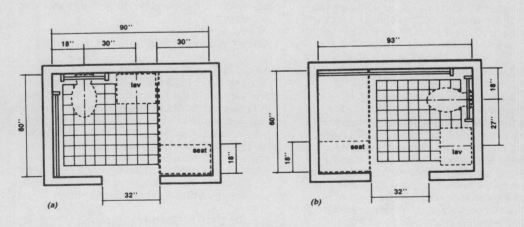

Fig. A7

A11

Federal Register / Vol. 56, No. 144 / Friday, July 26, 1991 / Rules and Regulations **35685**

A4.23 Bathrooms, Bathing Facilities, and Shower Rooms

A4.23 Bathrooms, Bathing Facilities, and Shower Rooms.

A4.23.3 Clear Floor Space. *Figure A7 shows two possible configurations of a toilet room with a roll-in shower. The specific shower shown is designed to fit exactly within the dimensions of a standard bathtub. Since the shower does not have a lip, the floor space can be used for required maneuvering space. This would permit a toilet room to be smaller than would be permitted with a bathtub and still provide enough floor space to be considered accessible. This design can provide accessibility in facilities where space is at a premium (i.e., hotels and medical care facilities). The alternate roll-in shower (Fig. 57b) also provides sufficient room for the "T-turn" and does not require plumbing to be on more than one wall.*

A4.23.9 Medicine Cabinets. Other alternatives for storing medical and personal care items are very useful to disabled people. Shelves, drawers, and floor-mounted cabinets can be provided within the reach ranges of disabled people.

A4.26 Handrails, Grab Bars, and Tub and Shower Seats.

A4.26.1 General. Many disabled people rely heavily upon grab bars and handrails to maintain balance and prevent serious falls. Many people brace their forearms between supports and walls to give them more leverage and stability in maintaining balance or for lifting. The grab bar clearance of 1-1/2 in (38 mm) required in this guideline is a safety clearance to prevent injuries resulting from arms slipping through the openings. It also provides adequate gripping room.

A4.26.2 Size and Spacing of Grab Bars and Handrails. This specification allows for alternate shapes of handrails as long as they allow an opposing grip similar to that provided by a circular section of 1-1/4 in to 1-1/2 in (32 mm to 38 mm).

A4.27 Controls and Operating Mechanisms.

A4.27.3 Height. *Fig. A8 further illustrates*

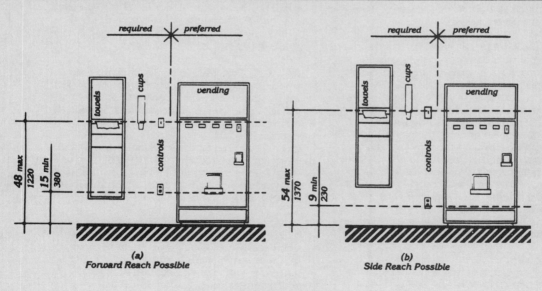

(a)
Forward Reach Possible

(b)
Side Reach Possible

Fig. A8
Control Reach Limitations

mandatory and advisory control mounting height provisions for typical equipment.

Electrical receptacles installed to serve individual appliances and not intended for regular or frequent use by building occupants are not required to be mounted within the specified reach ranges. Examples would be receptacles installed specifically for wall-mounted clocks, refrigerators, and microwave ovens.

A4.28 Alarms.

A4.28.2 Audible Alarms. Audible emergency signals must have an intensity and frequency that can attract the attention of individuals who have partial hearing loss. People over 60 years of age generally have difficulty perceiving frequencies higher than 10,000 Hz. An alarm signal which has a periodic element to its signal, such as single stroke bells (clang-pause-clang-pause), hi-low (up-down-up-down) and fast whoop (on-off-on-off) are best. Avoid continuous or reverberating tones. Select a signal which has a sound characterized by three or four clear tones without a great deal of "noise" in between.

A4.28.3 Visual Alarms. The specifications in this section do not preclude the use of zoned or coded alarm systems.

A4.28.4 Auxiliary Alarms. Locating visual emergency alarms in rooms where persons who are deaf may work or reside alone can ensure that they will always be warned when an emergency alarm is activated. To be effective, such devices must be located and oriented so that they will spread signals and reflections throughout a space or raise the overall light level sharply. *However, visual alarms alone are not necessarily the best means to alert sleepers. A study conducted by Underwriters Laboratory (UL) concluded that a flashing light more than seven times brighter was required (110 candela v. 15 candela, at the same distance) to awaken sleepers as was needed to alert awake subjects in a normal daytime illuminated room.*

For hotel and other rooms where people are likely to be asleep, a signal-activated vibrator placed between mattress and box spring or under a pillow was found by UL to be much more effective in alerting sleepers. Many readily available devices are sound-activated so that they could respond to an alarm clock, clock

radio, wake-up telephone call or room smoke detector. Activation by a building alarm system can either be accomplished by a separate circuit activating an auditory alarm which would, in turn, trigger the vibrator or by a signal transmitted through the ordinary 110-volt outlet. Transmission of signals through the power line is relatively simple and is the basis of common, inexpensive remote light control systems sold in many department and electronic stores for home use. So-called "wireless" intercoms operate on the same principal.

A4.29 Detectable Warnings.

A4.29.2 Detectable Warnings on Walking Surfaces. *The material used to provide contrast should contrast by at least 70%. Contrast in percent is determined by:*

$$Contrast = [(B_1 - B_2)/B_1] \times 100$$

*where B_1 = light reflectance value (LRV) of the lighter area
and B_2 = light reflectance value (LRV) of the darker area.*

Note that in any application both white and black are never absolute; thus, B_1 never equals 100 and B_2 is always greater than 0.

A4.30 Signage.

A4.30.1 General. In building complexes where finding locations independently on a routine basis may be a necessity (for example, college campuses), tactile maps or prerecorded instructions can be very helpful to visually impaired people. Several maps and auditory instructions have been developed and tested for specific applications. The type of map or instructions used must be based on the information to be communicated, which depends highly on the type of buildings or users.

Landmarks that can easily be distinguished by visually impaired individuals are useful as orientation cues. Such cues include changes in illumination level, bright colors, unique patterns, wall murals, location of special equipment or other architectural features.

Many people with disabilities have limitations in movement of their heads and reduced peripheral vision. Thus, signage positioned

Federal Register / Vol. 56, No. 144 / Friday, July 26, 1991 / Rules and Regulations   35687

A4.30 Signage

perpendicular to the path of travel is easiest for them to notice. People can generally distinguish signage within an angle of 30 degrees to either side of the centerlines of their faces without moving their heads.

A4.30.2 Character Proportion. The legibility of printed characters is a function of the viewing distance, character height, the ratio of the stroke width to the height of the character, the contrast of color between character and background, and print font. The size of characters must be based upon the intended viewing distance. A severely nearsighted person may have to be much closer to recognize a character of a given size than a person with normal visual acuity.

A4.30.4 Raised and Brailled Characters and Pictorial Symbol Signs (Pictograms). *The standard dimensions for literary Braille are as follows:*

Dot diameter	*.059 in.*
Inter-dot spacing	*.090 in.*
Horizontal separation between cells	*.241 in.*
Vertical separation between cells	*.395 in.*

Raised borders around *signs containing* raised characters may make them confusing to read unless the border is set far away from the characters. *Accessible signage with descriptive materials about public buildings, monuments, and objects of cultural interest may not provide sufficiently detailed and meaningful information. Interpretive guides, audio tape devices, or other methods may be more effective in presenting such information.*

A4.30.5 Finish and Contrast. *An eggshell finish (11 to 19 degree gloss on 60 degree glossimeter) is recommended. Research indicates that signs are more legible for persons with low vision when characters contrast with their background by at least 70 percent. Contrast in percent shall be determined by:*

$$Contrast = [(B_1 - B_2)/B_1] \times 100$$

*where B_1 = light reflectance value (LRV) of the lighter area
and B_2 = light reflectance value (LRV) of the darker area.*

Note that in any application both white and black are never absolute; thus, B_1 never equals 100 and B_2 is always greater than 0.

The greatest readability is usually achieved through the use of light-colored characters or symbols on a dark background.

A4.30.7 Symbols of Accessibility for Different Types of Listening Systems. *Paragraph 4 of this section requires signage indicating the availability of an assistive listening system. An appropriate message should be displayed with the international symbol of access for hearing loss since this symbol conveys general accessibility for people with hearing loss. Some suggestions are:*

*INFRARED
ASSISTIVE LISTENING SYSTEM
AVAILABLE
——PLEASE ASK——*

*AUDIO LOOP IN USE
TURN T-SWITCH FOR
BETTER HEARING
——OR ASK FOR HELP——*

*FM
ASSISTIVE LISTENING
SYSTEM AVAILABLE
——PLEASE ASK——*

The symbol may be used to notify persons of the availability of other auxiliary aids and services such as: real time captioning, captioned note taking, sign language interpreters, and oral interpreters.

A4.30.8 Illumination Levels. *Illumination levels on the sign surface shall be in the 100 to 300 lux range (10 to 30 footcandles) and shall be uniform over the sign surface. Signs shall be located such that the illumination level on the surface of the sign is not significantly exceeded by the ambient light or visible bright lighting source behind or in front of the sign.*

A14

35688   Federal Register / Vol. 56, No. 144 / Friday, July 26, 1991 / Rules and Regulations

A4.31 Telephones.

A4.31.3 Mounting Height. In localities where the dial-tone first system is in operation, calls can be placed at a coin telephone through the operator without inserting coins. The operator button is located at a height of 46 in (1170 mm) if the coin slot of the telephone is at 54 in (1370 mm). A generally available public telephone with a coin slot mounted lower on the equipment would allow universal installation of telephones at a height of 48 in (1220 mm) or less to all operable parts.

***A4.31.9 Text Telephones.** A public text telephone may be an integrated text telephone pay phone unit or a conventional portable text telephone that is permanently affixed within, or adjacent to, the telephone enclosure. In order to be usable with a pay phone, a text telephone which is not a single integrated text telephone pay phone unit will require a shelf large enough (10 in (255mm) wide by 10 in (255 mm) deep with a 6 in (150 mm) vertical clearance minimum) to accommodate the device, an electrical outlet, and a power cord. Movable or portable text telephones may be used to provide equivalent facilitation. A text telephone should be readily available so that a person using it may access the text telephone easily and conveniently. As currently designed pocket-type text telephones for personal use do not accommodate a wide range of users. Such devices would not be considered substantially equivalent to conventional text telephones. However, in the future as technology develops this could change.*

A4.32 Fixed or Built-in Seating and Tables.

A4.32.4 Height of Tables or Counters. Different types of work require different *table or counter* heights for comfort and optimal performance. Light detailed work such as writing requires a *table or counter* close to elbow height for a standing person. Heavy manual work such as rolling dough requires *a counter or table* height about 10 in (255 mm) below elbow height for a standing person. This principle of *high/low table or counter heights* also applies for seated persons; however, the limiting condition for seated manual work is clearance under the *table or counter.*

Table A1 shows convenient *counter heights* for seated persons. The great variety of heights for comfort and optimal performance indicates a need for alternatives or a compromise in height if people who stand and people who sit will be using the same counter area.

Table A1
Convenient Heights of Tables and Counters for Seated People[1]

Conditions of Use	Short Women in mm		Tall Men in mm	
Seated in a wheelchair:				
Manual work–				
Desk or removeable armrests	26	660	30	760
Fixed, full-size armrests[2]	32[3]	815	32[3]	815
Light detailed work:				
Desk or removable armrests	29	735	34	865
Fixed, full-size armrests[2]	32[3]	815	34	865
Seated in a 16-in. (405-mm)				
High chair:				
Manual work	26	660	27	685
Light detailed work	28	710	31	785

[1] All dimensions are based on a work-surface thickness of 1 1/2 in (38 mm) and a clearance of 1 1/2 in (38 mm) between legs and the underside of a work surface.

[2] This type of wheelchair arm does not interfere with the positioning of a wheelchair under a work surface.

[3] This dimension is limited by the height of the armrests: a lower height would be preferable. Some people in this group prefer lower work surfaces, which require positioning the wheelchair back from the edge of the counter.

A4.33 Assembly Areas.

A4.33.2 Size of Wheelchair Locations. Spaces large enough for two wheelchairs allow people who are coming to a performance together to sit together.

A4.33.3 Placement of Wheelchair Locations. The location of wheelchair areas can be planned so that a variety of positions

Federal Register / Vol. 56, No. 144 / Friday, July 26, 1991 / Rules and Regulations   35689

Table A2. Summary of Assistive Listening Devices

within the seating area are provided. This will allow choice in viewing and price categories.

Building/life safety codes set minimum distances between rows of fixed seats with consideration of the number of seats in a row, the exit aisle width and arrangement, and the location of exit doors. "Continental" seating, with a greater number of seats per row and a

commensurate increase in row spacing and exit doors, facilitates emergency egress for all people and increases ease of access to mid-row seats especially for people who walk with difficulty. Consideration of this positive attribute of "continental" seating should be included along with all other factors in the design of fixed seating areas.

Table A2. Summary of Assistive Listening Devices

System	Advantages	Disadvantages	Typical Applications
Induction Loop Transmitter: Transducer wired to induction loop around listening area. Receiver: Self-contained induction receiver or personal hearing aid with telecoil.	Cost-Effective Low Maintenance Easy to use Unobtrusive May be possible to integrate into existing public address system. Some hearing aids can function as receivers.	Signal spills over to adjacent rooms. Susceptible to electrical interference. Limited portability Inconsistent signal strength. Head position affects signal strength. Lack of standards for induction coil performance.	Meeting areas Theaters Churches and Temples Conference rooms Classrooms TV viewing
FM Transmitter: Flashlight-sized worn by speaker. Receiver: With personal hearing aid via DAI or induction neck-loop and telecoil; or self-contained with earphone(s).	Highly portable Different channels allow use by different groups within the same room. High user mobility Variable for large range of hearing losses.	High cost of receivers Equipment fragile Equipment obtrusive High maintenance Expensive to maintain Custom fitting to individual user may be required.	Classrooms Tour groups Meeting areas Outdoor events One-on-one
Infrared Transmitter: Emitter in line-of-sight with receiver. Receiver: Self-contained. Or with personal hearing aid via DAI or induction neckloop and telecoil.	Easy to use Insures privacy or confidentiality Moderate cost Can often be integrated into existing public address system.	Line-of-sight required between emitter and receiver. Ineffective outdoors Limited portability Requires installation	Theaters Churches and Temples Auditoriums Meetings requiring confidentiality TV viewing

Source: <u>Rehab Brief</u>, National Institute on Disability and Rehabilitation Research, Washington, DC, Vol. XII, No. 10, (1990).

A5.0 Restaurants and Cafeterias

A4.33.6 Placement of Listening Systems. A distance of 50 ft (15 m) allows a person to distinguish performers' facial expressions.

A4.33.7 Types of Listening Systems. *An assistive listening system appropriate for an assembly area for a group of persons or where the specific individuals are not known in advance, such as a playhouse, lecture hall or movie theater, may be different from the system appropriate for a particular individual provided as an auxiliary aid or as part of a reasonable accommodation. The appropriate device for an individual is the type that individual can use, whereas the appropriate system for an assembly area will necessarily be geared toward the "average" or aggregate needs of various individuals.* A listening system that can be used from any seat in a seating area is the most flexible way to meet this specification. Earphone jacks with variable volume controls can benefit only people who have slight hearing loss and do not help people who use hearing aids. At the present time, *magnetic induction* loops are the most feasible type of listening system for people who use hearing aids *equipped with "T-coils,"* but people without hearing aids or those with hearing aids not equipped with inductive pick-ups cannot use them *without special receivers.* Radio frequency systems can be extremely effective and inexpensive. People without hearing aids can use them, but people with hearing aids need a special receiver to use them as they are presently designed. If hearing aids had a jack to allow a by-pass of microphones, then radio frequency systems would be suitable for people with and without hearing aids. Some listening systems may be subject to interference from other equipment and feedback from hearing aids of people who are using the systems. Such interference can be controlled by careful engineering design that anticipates feedback sources in the surrounding area.

Table A2, reprinted from a National Institute of Disability and Rehabilitation Research "Rehab Brief," shows some of the advantages and disadvantages of different types of assistive listening systems. In addition, the Architectural and Transportation Barriers Compliance Board (Access Board) has published a pamphlet on Assistive Listening Systems which lists demonstration centers across the country where technical assistance can be obtained in selecting and installing appropriate systems. The state of New York has also adopted a detailed technical specification which may be useful.

A5.0 Restaurants and Cafeterias.

A5.1 General. *Dining counters (where there is no service) are typically found in small carry-out restaurants, bakeries, or coffee shops and may only be a narrow eating surface attached to a wall. This section requires that where such a dining counter is provided, a portion of the counter shall be at the required accessible height.*

A7.0 Business and Mercantile.

A7.2(3) Assistive Listening Devices. *At all sales and service counters, teller windows, box offices, and information kiosks where a physical barrier separates service personnel and customers, it is recommended that at least one permanently installed assistive listening device complying with 4.33 be provided at each location or series. Where assistive listening devices are installed, signage should be provided identifying those stations which are so equipped.*

A7.3 Check-out Aisles. *Section 7.2 refers to counters without aisles; section 7.3 concerns check-out aisles. A counter without an aisle (7.2) can be approached from more than one direction such as in a convenience store. In order to use a check-out aisle (7.3), customers must enter a defined area (an aisle) at a particular point, pay for goods, and exit at a particular point.*

Tuesday
April 12, 1994

Part III

Department of Justice
Office of the Attorney General
28 CFR Part 36

Architectural and Transportation Barriers Compliance Board
36 CFR Part 1191

Department of Transportation
Office of the Secretary
49 CFR Part 37

Americans With Disabilities Act Accessibility Guidelines; Detectable Warnings; Joint Final Rule

17442   **Federal Register** / Vol. 59, No. 70 / Tuesday, April 12, 1994 / Rules and Regulations

DEPARTMENT OF JUSTICE

Office of the Attorney General

28 CFR Part 36

[A.G. Order No. 1852–94]

ARCHITECTURAL AND TRANSPORTATION BARRIERS COMPLIANCE BOARD

36 CFR Part 1191

[Docket 93–3]

RIN 3014–AA15

DEPARTMENT OF TRANSPORTATION

Office of the Secretary

49 CFR Part 37

Americans With Disabilities Act Accessibility Guidelines; Detectable Warnings

AGENCIES: Architectural and Transportation Barriers Compliance Board, Department of Justice and Department of Transportation.

ACTION: Joint final rule.

SUMMARY: The Architectural and Transportation Barriers Compliance Board is conducting research during fiscal year 1994 on whether detectable warnings are needed at curb ramps and hazardous vehicular areas and their effect on persons with mobility impairments and other pedestrians. Depending on the results of this research, the Access Board may conduct additional research during fiscal year 1995 to refine the scoping provisions and technical specifications for detectable warnings at these locations. Because of the issues that have been raised about the use of detectable warnings at curb ramps and curbless entranceways to retail stores and other places of public accommodation, the Access Board, the Department of Justice, and the Department of Transportation are suspending temporarily until July 26, 1996 the requirements for detectable warnings at curb ramps, hazardous vehicular areas, and reflecting pools in the Americans With Disabilities Act Accessibility Guidelines (ADAAG) so that the agencies can consider the results of the research and determine whether any changes in the requirements are warranted.

EFFECTIVE DATE: May 12, 1994.

FOR FURTHER INFORMATION CONTACT: Access Board: James J. Raggio, General Counsel, Architectural and Transportation Barriers Compliance Board, 1331 F Street NW., suite 1000,

Washington, DC 20004–1111. Telephone (202) 272–5434 (voice) or (202) 272–5449 (TTY).

Department of Justice: Stewart B. Oneglia, Chief, Coordination and Review Section, Civil Rights Division, Department of Justice, Post Office Box 66118, Washington, DC 20035. Telephone (202) 307–2222 (voice or TTY).

Department of Transportation: Robert C. Ashby, Deputy Assistant General Counsel for Regulation and Enforcement, Department of Transportation, 400 7th Street SW., room 10424, Washington, DC 20590. Telephone (202) 366–9306 (voice) or (202) 755–7687 (TTY).

The telephone numbers listed above are not toll-free numbers.

This document is available in the following alternate formats: cassette tape, braille, large print, and computer disc. Copies may be obtained from the Access Board by calling (202) 272–5434 (voice) or (202) 272–5449 (TTY). The document is also available on electronic bulletin board from the Department of Justice at (202) 514–6193.

SUPPLEMENTARY INFORMATION:

Background

On July 9, 1993, the Access Board published a notice in the **Federal Register** announcing that it planned to conduct research during fiscal year 1994 on whether detectable warnings are needed at curb ramps and hazardous vehicular areas and their effect on persons with mobility impairments and other pedestrians.[1] 58 FR 37058. On the same day, the Access Board, the Department of Justice, and the Department of Transportation (hereinafter referred to as "the agencies") published a joint notice of the proposed rulemaking (NPRM) in the **Federal Register** to suspend temporarily the requirements for detectable warnings at curb ramps, hazardous vehicular areas, and reflecting pools in the Americans with Disabilities Act Accessibility Guidelines (ADAAG) pending the research. 58 FR 37052. In issuing the NPRM, the agencies noted

[1] Detectable warnings are a pattern of closely spaced, small truncated domes that are built in or applied to a walking surface to alert persons who are blind or who have low vision of hazards on a circulation path. 36 CFR Part 1191, Appendix A, Section 4.29.2. Research has shown that the truncated dome pattern is highly detectable both by cane and under foot. The truncated dome pattern has been used as a detectable warning along transit platform edges for over five years by the Bay Area Rapid Transit (BART) system in California and by the Metro-Dade Transit Agency in Florida. The truncated dome pattern has also been used in Great Britain, Japan, and other countries as a detectable warning.

that blind persons and their organizations had taken differing positions regarding whether detectable warnings are needed at these locations; that persons with mobility impairments had expressed concern that installing detectable warnings on the entire length of curb ramps would adversely affect their ability to safely negotiate the sloped surfaces; and that a national association of retail stores had asserted that installing detectable warnings on curb ramps and curbless entranceways to the stores would pose a tripping hazard for their customers. The agencies stated in the NPRM that because of these potential safety issues they believed that it would be in the public interest to suspend temporarily the ADAAG requirements for detectable warnings at the locations noted above until the research provides additional information to address the issues.

Over 150 comments were received on the July 9, 1993 NPRM. Another 110 comments concerning detectable warnings were received in response to a NPRM published by the Access Board in the **Federal Register** on December 21, 1992 which proposed to reserve detectable warnings provisions for curb ramps installed in the public right-of-way by State and local governments. 58 FR 60612. The comments received in response to both the July 9, 1993 NPRM and the December 21, 1992 NPRM have been considered in this rulemaking. The comments came from blind persons and their organizations (132 comments); State and local government agencies (54 comments); manufacturers of detectable warnings (14 comments); professional and trade associations (11 comments); businesses (4 comments); organizations representing persons with mobility impairments (4 comments); mobility specialists (13 comments); and other individuals (17 comments) and entities (14 comments). About 25 persons submitted comments in response to both NPRM's.

The comments centered around three issues: whether detectable warnings are needed at curb ramps and other locations; their effect on persons with mobility impairments and other pedestrians; and their durability, maintainability, and cost. The comments are further discussed below.

Need for Detectable Warnings at Curb Ramps and Other Locations

The National Federation of the Blind (NFB), ten NFB chapters, and 31 blind individuals submitted comments supporting the proposed suspension of the ADAAG requirements for detectable warnings at curb ramps, hazardous vehicular areas, and reflecting pools.

Federal Register / Vol. 59, No. 70 / Tuesday, April 12, 1994 / Rules and Regulations **17443**

NFB further recommended that detectable warnings be eliminated eventually from ADAAG, including at transit platform edges. NFB asserted that blind persons are responsible for using effective travel methods (i.e., cane or guide dog) and that public policy should be based on an "individual responsibility" standard. NFB pointed out that blind persons move about safely every day without detectable warnings; and stated that fears of blind persons falling or being injured are based on emotional responses and not factual information. NFB claimed that there are sufficient cues already available in the environment to alert blind persons of hazards on a circulation path and that if only some hazards are marked by detectable warnings, the inconsistency is likely to defeat their intended purpose and could create a threat rather than an aid to safe mobility for blind persons.

The American Council of the Blind (ACB), 18 ACB chapters, the Council of Citizens with Low Vision International and two of its chapters, the Guide Dog Users of Massachusetts and Pennsylvania, the National Alliance of Blind Students, the American Foundation for the Blind, the Association for Education and Rehabilitation of the Blind and Visually Impaired, 15 other State and local organizations representing persons who are blind or who have vision impairments, 49 blind individuals, and eight mobility specialists submitted comments opposing the suspension. These commenters recounted incidents of blind persons approaching curb ramps and stepping into the street without stopping; walking into reflecting pools; and falling from transit platforms. News articles were submitted reporting the deaths of three blind persons who fell from subway platforms in Boston and New York and from a commuter rail platform in Maryland during 1993.[2] Another news article reported an incident of a blind person who was severely injured from falling in front of an oncoming train in Baltimore in December 1992.

ACB submitted a report of a recent research project which studied cues used by blind persons to detect streets. Barlow, J. and Bentzen, B.L., *Cues Blind Travelers Use to Detect Streets*, Washington, DC: American Council of the Blind (1993). Eight cities were included in the research project. In each city, ten blind persons who use canes to

travel approached ten unfamiliar intersections with curb ramps without detectable warnings. They were asked to stop when they believed their next step would be into the street and to report the cues which they used to determine where to stop. Of the 80 blind persons who participated in the research project, 75% were considered good-to-excellent travellers by self-report and through assessment by orientation and mobility specialists; and two-thirds reported travelling independently a minimum of five times a week.

Of the 800 street approaches, the participants walked down the center of the curb ramps in 557 instances and stopped before the street in 360 cases (65%). Of the 22 cues reportedly used to detect the street, the two most frequently mentioned cues were the downslope of the ramp and the presence of traffic on the street perpendicular to the participant's line of travel. Other cues frequently mentioned were the upslope or texture change at the street, the end of the building line or shoreline, and the presence of traffic on the street parallel to the participant's line of travel. The participants stated that they usually used a combination of cues to identify the street.

In the 197 instances (35%) where the participants walked down the curb ramp and did not stop before the street:

• There was traffic on the street perpendicular to the participant's line of travel in 116 cases (59%). The traffic was moving in 75 cases and idling in 41 cases.

• The participants took two or more steps into the street in 151 cases (76%).

Although the participants reported the presence of the traffic on the street perpendicular to their line of travel and the upslope or texture change at the street as frequently used cues to detect the street, the research data indicate that these cues are not sufficient to consistently and dependably identify the street.[3]

The research data suggest that there is a strong relationship between the slope of the curb ramp and the detection of the street.[4]

---

[3] The research project also analyzed participant variables such as frequency of travel, travel proficiency, cane lengthen in relation to stride length, cane technique, hearing, and organizational membership. Travel proficiency and cane technique were found to be marginally significant factors in detecting the street. The other factors were not significant.

[4] The research data also suggest that there is a strong relationship between the rate of change in slope between the walkway leading up to the curb ramp and the ramp itself. The participants had a greater rate (85%) of detecting the street were the change in slope was abrupt and a lower rate (57%) where the change in slope was gradual.

• Where the slope was 6° or more (1:10 or more), the participants stopped before the street in 172 of 194 instances (89%).

• Where the slope was 5° (1:11 to 1:13), the participants stopped before the street in 31 of 44 instances (70%).

• Where the slope was 4° or less (1:14 or less), the participants stopped before the street in 157 of 319 instances (49%).[5]

The report made the following recommendations for additional research:

[F]uture research could more precisely measure the curb ramps included in this project, and analyze performance with relationship to these more accurate measurements. It may be possible that ramps which have 1:12 slopes facilitate high detection rates, while ramps of lesser slopes (e.g., 1:15) may be clearly associated with low detection rates. If ramps of 1:12 facilitate high street detection rates, then it is possible that the [ADAAG] requirement for detectable warnings on curb ramps could be limited, e.g., to ramps having slopes less than 1:12. The requirement that detectable warnings extend over the entire surface of curb ramps is not supported by empirical evidence that such an extensive tactile cue is necessary to alert blind travellers to the end of a curb ramp and the beginning of a street. It is possible that a lesser amount of warning (24" or 36") may be sufficient. If so, the optimal placement of the warning still remains to be determined. Suggested locations are (1) on the lower end of the ramp, immediately adjoining the street; (2) on the upper end of the ramp; and (3) around the sides and at the top of the ramp. Dimensions and location of detectable warnings need further empirical research.

Effect of Detectable Warnings on Persons With Mobility Impairments and Other Pedestrians

Eastern Paralyzed Veterans Association, Paralyzed Veterans of America, and two State organizations representing persons with mobility impairments expressed concern that detectable warnings could have an adverse effect on persons who use wheelchairs and other mobility aids,

---

[5] The ten most difficult streets to detect (i.e., where most participants stepped into the street without stopping) had a ramp with a slope of 4° or less and at least one of the following characteristics: a curb ramp parallel to the participant's line of travel; a very quiet street or busy street with surges of traffic and gaps in traffic cues; no building line or a building line that was different from others on the route; and little or no texture change or upslope at the street or a change which was considered gradual. At one blended curb, all ten participants stepped into the street without stopping and five of them crossed the entire street without detecting it despite an abrupt end to the shore line, a surface texture change, and a slight lip where the street pavement overlapped the sidewalk.

---

[2] None of the transit platform edges had detectable warnings that conform to the ADAAG requirements. The New York subway platform edge was marked by a yellow stripe and an abrasive material.

Appendix A

especially on sloped surfaces.[6] They generally supported suspending the ADAAG requirements for detectable warnings at curb ramps, hazardous vehicular areas, and reflecting pools while additional research is conducted.

The International Mass Retail Association, the National Grocers Association, the Food Marketing Association, the Building Owners and Managers Association International, a regional commercial real estate association, 37 State and local government agencies, and four businesses expressed concern that detectable warnings would pose a tripping hazard to other pedestrians and supported the suspension. Commenters who opposed the suspension stated that concerns about the safety of others are speculative and unsubstantiated. Several manufacturers commented that there have been no reported incidents of trips or falls attributable to their products. A bank and a retail store chain stated that they had installed detectable warnings on curb ramps at their sites and had received complaints from wheelchair users and elderly customers. Only one commenter, a local school district, reported that an adult and some students had tripped while running over a curb ramp with detectable warnings.

The Federal Transit Administration and Project ACTION of the National Easter Seal Society have recently

---

[6] Eastern Paralyzed Veterans Association (EPVA) initially supported the ADAAG requirements for detectable warnings and explained that it had changed its position after reviewing the data from the earlier Bay Area Rapid Transit (BART) and Metro-Dade Transit Agency studies. The BART study conducted tests on level platform surfaces with 24 persons with mobility impairments, including four manual wheelchair users. Five participants (21%) responded that the detectable warnings would be helpful; eight (33%) responded that they were "not affected"; seven (29%) responded that they would be "insignificantly affected"; four (17%) responded that they would be "moderately impaired"; and none responded that they would be "seriously impaired." Three of the manual wheelchair users responded that they would be "insignificantly affected" and the other one responded that he or she would be "moderately impaired." Peck, A.F. and Bentzen, B.L., Tactile Warnings to Promote Safety in the Vicinity of Transit Platform Edges, Cambridge, MA: Transportation Systems Center (1987). The Metro-Dade Transit Agency conducted tests with seven wheelchair users on level platform surfaces. Five of the participants responded that they were "not affected" or "insignificantly affected." The other two had difficulty with the detectable warnings but their specific responses are not reported in the study. Mitchell, M., Pathfinder Tactile Tile Demonstration Test Project, Miami, FL: Metro-Dade Transit Agency (1988). Carsonite International, the manufacturer of the detectable warning materials used in the BART and Metro-Dade Transit Agency systems, submitted a letter from BART stating that in over five years experience with detectable warnings on its rail system, no problems have been observed with wheelchair users entering or exiting the trains.

sponsored a research project on detectable warnings which among other things tested detectable warnings on curb ramps for safety and negotiability by persons with mobility impairments. Bentzen, B.L., Nolin, T.L., Easton, R.D., and Desmarais, L., Detectable Warning Surfaces: Detectability by Individuals with Visual Impairments, and Safety and Negotiability for Individuals with Physical Impairments, Cambridge, MA: Transportation Systems Center (1993). The study tested a variety of detectable warning materials with 40 persons having a wide range of physical disabilities. The participants included 15 persons who use mobility aids with wheels (power and manual wheelchairs, and three- and four-wheeled scooters); 18 persons who use mobility aids with tips (canes, crutches and walkers); and seven persons who do not use any mobility aid. The participants travelled up and down ramps that were six feet long and four feet wide with a 1:12 slope, the maximum slope permitted by ADAAG for new construction. Detectable warnings were installed on the entire six foot length of the ramps. For comparison, participants also travelled up and down a brushed concrete ramp of the same dimensions. Subjective and objective measurements were collected.

Of the 40 participants, the objective data showed that:

• 14 participants (35%) exhibited no difficulty negotiating the ramp;

• 19 participants (47.5%) exhibited few difficulties; and

• 7 participants (17.5%) exhibited numerous difficulties.

The latter group included four persons who used manual wheelchairs; two persons who used walkers with wheels (rollators); and one person who wore leg braces and used a quad cane.

A physical therapist who observed the participants reported that persons using no mobility aids performed consistently well on all the ramps with detectable warnings and that even those with protheses or braces showed good negotiability. Persons using power wheelchairs, and three- and four-wheeled scooters demonstrated few, if any difficulties, on any of the ramps with detectable warnings. However, four of the five manual wheelchair users exhibited numerous difficulties negotiating the ramps with detectable warnings, including exerting additional effort to go up the ramps, and the small, narrow front wheels getting caught in the groves between the domes. Participants using canes, crutches, or walkers were observed to have the most difficulties on the ramps with detectable warnings. Mobility aids with small tips

(canes or walkers) appeared to get caught between the domes or lay on an angle between the grove and the dome, causing the participant to feel less stable. Participants who used crutches with larger tips appeared more safe and generally negotiated the ramps with detectable warnings better than those who used canes or walkers.

The research project report recommended that "given even the moderately increased level of difficulty and decrease in safety which detectable warnings on slopes pose for persons with physical disabilities, it is desirable to limit the width of detectable warnings to no more than that required to provide an effective warning for persons with visual impairments." The report suggested that a standard width of 24, 30 or 36 inches be established for detectable warning surfaces and indicated that such widths would provide an effective stopping distance for 90 to 95% of blind persons and persons with low vision.

Durability, Maintainability, and Cost

Many of the commenters who supported suspending the ADAAG requirements for detectable warnings at curb ramps, hazardous vehicular areas, and reflecting pools also expressed concern about the durability and maintainability of detectable warning materials, especially under certain climatic conditions (e.g., snow and ice, and the need for snow and ice removal).

One commenter stated that a member of the ANSI A117 Committee recently visited the Bay Area Rapid Transit (BART) system and observed a 50 to 60% "failure rate" with the corners of the detectable warning titles "turning up and creating tripping hazards." The commenter also cited a magazine article on the use of detectable warnings in Japan as evidence that they are prone to breakage and deterioration.

Manufacturers of various detectable warning materials responded with information about their products. Carsonite International, the manufacturer of the detectable warning materials used in the BART system, stated that in its ten years of experience, it is rare that the product or the adhesive fails. Where loosening or delamination has occurred, it was due to a failure to properly prepare the substrate. Carsonite International also submitted a letter from BART stating that annual costs for maintaining the detectable warnings at its 34 stations are $10,800 for materials and 8,160 hours of labor.

Another detectable warning manufacturer stated that its product has been in use for the past two winters in the Boston area and that there have been no notable difficulties with snow and ice removal. The commenter also mentioned sites in Ontario, Canada where detectable warnings have been installed and have performed well under tough winter conditions. Other commenters who opposed the suspension noted that there were snow and ice removal techniques that could be used with detectable warnings without adversely affecting the efficiency of the overall snow removal operation such as hot-air blowers, stiff brooms, and de-icing materials.

A few commenters who supported the suspension objected to the cost of detectable warnings but did not provide any specific data. There are currently a variety of detectable warning products on the market, including ceramic, hard composite, and resilient tiles; cast pavers; pre-cast concrete and concrete stamping systems; stamped metal; rubber mats; and resilient coatings. The costs of these products range from three to twenty dollars per square foot. One commenter mentioned that a university had installed detectable warnings on 25 to 30 new curb ramps on its campus at an added cost of $5,000 for the entire project.

Other Issues

The Washington Metropolitan Area Transit Authority (WMATA) submitted comments on the July 9, 1993 NPRM stating that based on a comparison of trackbed falling accidents for the WMATA and BART systems, it believed that the granite edges on its platforms are superior to truncated domes. Based on this analysis, WMATA requested that the ADAAG requirements for detectable warnings be changed from truncated domes to granite edges. The truncated dome pattern was adopted in ADAAG because research has shown that it is highly detectable both by cane and underfoot. WMATA did not submit any information showing that its granite edge is equally detectable both by cane and underfoot. As WMATA noted in its comments, the number of trackbed falling accidents involving blind persons and persons with low vision are relatively small in comparison to the millions of passenger miles traveled annually on our nation's rail systems to do any statistically meaningful analysis.

WMATA also recommended that research be conducted on the safety of the truncated dome pattern for other passengers and that the ADAAG requirements for detectable warnings in key stations and in newly constructed and altered rail stations be suspended indefinitely. The truncated dome pattern has been used as a detectable

warning on the platform edges of all rail stations in the BART and Metro-Dade Transit Agency systems for over five years and no safety problems have been reported by persons with mobility impairments or other passengers. The Access Board is conducting additional research because questions have been raised whether experience from the rail station environment is transferable to sloped curb ramps and curbless entranceways to retail stores. Additional research on the use of the truncated dome pattern in rail stations is not necessary.

The New York Metropolitan Transportation Authority (MTA) and the Southeastern Pennsylvania Transportation Authority (SEPTA) referenced a NPRM published by the Department of Transportation on November 17, 1992 (57 FR 54210) which proposed to extend the deadline for retrofitting key rail stations with detectable warnings until January 26, 1995. MTA and SEPTA stated that they did not believe that the proposed extension provided sufficient time for them to complete testing products and to purchase and install the detectable warnings. MTA and SEPTA requested that the deadline for retrofitting key rail stations with detectable warnings be delayed until the Access Board's research on use of detectable warnings on curb ramps and hazardous vehicular areas is completed.

The Department of Transportation published a final rule on November 30, 1993 (58 FR 63092) extending the deadline for retrofitting key rail stations with detectable warnings until July 26, 1994. In the final rule, the Department of Transportation stated that "[t]he drop-offs at the edges of rail station platforms create a clear, documented, and unacceptable hazard to persons with visual impairments" and that detectable warnings as specified in ADAAG will mitigate this hazard. The Department of Transportation noted that many rail systems have been working with detectable warning manufacturers to address concerns about durability and maintainability and that the extension provided for in the final rule was adequate to permit an aggressive effort by rail systems to address concerns about installation.

The American Public Transit Association (APTA) submitted a comment stating that, if as a result of the additional research conducted by the Access Board on the use of detectable warnings at curb ramps and hazardous vehicular areas, the technical specifications for detectable warnings should be changed, rail systems could be placed in a position of installing

material which could be found to be unsafe in other applications, and having to replace the material later. If the research shows that detectable warnings are needed at curb ramps and hazardous vehicular areas, it is possible that some refinements may be made to the scoping provisions and technical specification for detectable warnings (e.g., the location and width of detectable warnings for curb ramps; the types of hazardous vehicular areas where detectable warnings will be required). However, substantial change to the basic pattern of raised truncated domes is not anticipated. The Department of Transportation has indicated in its final rule extending the deadline for retrofitting key rail stations with detectable warnings that if the technical specifications for detectable warnings change in the future, the grandfathering provision in its regulations (49 CFR 37.9) could apply in appropriate situations to avoid making rail systems reinstall detectable warnings meeting the revised specifications.

Final Common Rule

This rulemaking raises some difficult issues. It involves making decisions about the safety needs of blind persons and persons with low vision and considering their needs in light of the concerns expressed by persons with mobility impairments and other commenters. The task is all the more complicated by the fact that blind persons and their organizations have taken differing positions on the matter.

After carefully reviewing the comments received on the July 9, 1993 and December 21, 1992 NPRM's and the reports of the two recent research projects discussed above, the agencies believe that it is in the public interest to suspend temporarily the ADAAG requirements for detectable warnings at curb ramps, hazardous vehicular areas, and reflecting pools while additional research is conducted on the need for detectable warnings at these locations and their effect on persons with mobility impairments and other pedestrians.

The July 9, 1993 NPRM proposed that the suspension remain in effect until January 26, 1995. This date was first proposed by the Access Board in November 1992. At the time, the Access Board envisioned that the additional research would be completed in fiscal year 1994 and that the agencies would have an opportunity to review the results of the research and, if necessary, initiate further rulemaking on detectable warnings before January 26, 1995. In subsequent planning for the research project, the Access Board has divided

17446   Federal Register / Vol. 59, No. 70 / Tuesday, April 12, 1994 / Rules and Regulations

the project into two phases. The first phase, which is scheduled for completion in fiscal year 1994, will focus on whether detectable warnings are needed at curb ramps and hazardous vehicular areas and their effect on persons with mobility impairments and other pedestrians. Depending on the results of the first phase, an optional second phase may be conducted during fiscal year 1995 to refine the scoping provisions and technical specifications for detectable warnings at these locations. If the second phase of the research project is conducted, the agencies will conduct further rulemaking to amend the scoping provisions and technical specifications based upon the recommendations of the research project. Allowing nine months for the rulemaking process from the end of fiscal year 1995, the joint final rule provides for the suspension to remain in effect until July 26, 1996. Of course, depending on the results of the first phase of the research project, the agencies could decide to conduct further rulemaking earlier. The July 26, 1996 date is the outside period by which the agencies expect to complete all rulemaking on this matter.

Several commenters requested that the agencies provide guidance in this rulemaking on whether entities may be required to retrofit existing curb ramps, hazardous vehicular areas, and reflecting pools with detectable warnings at a future date under the program accessibility requirements for State and local governments (28 CFR 35.150) and the readily achievable barrier removal requirements for public accommodations (28 CFR 36.304). At this time, it is premature to provide such guidance. The agencies will further address these questions after the research project is completed and further rulemaking on the matter is conducted.

Regulatory Analyses and Notices

The agencies have independently determined that this final rule is not a significant regulatory action and that a regulatory assessment is not required

under Executive Order 12866. It is a significant rule under the Department of Transportation's Regulatory Policies and Procedures since it amends the agency's ADA regulations, which are a significant rule. The Department of Transportation expects the economic impacts to be minimal and has not prepared a full regulatory evaluation.

The agencies hereby independently certify that this proposed rule is not expected to have a significant economic impact on a substantial number of small entities. Accordingly, a regulatory flexibility analysis is not required.

The agencies have also independently determined that there are no Federalism impacts sufficient to warrant the preparation of a Federalism assessment under Executive Order 12612.

Text of Final Common Rule

The text of the final common rule appears below.
§ ____ Temporary suspension of certain detectable warning requirements.

The requirements contained in sections 4.7.7, 4.29.5, and 4.29.6 of Appendix A to this part are suspended temporarily until July 26, 1996.

Adoption of Final Common Rule

The agency specific proposals to adopt the final common rule, which appears at the end of the common preamble, are set forth below.

DEPARTMENT OF JUSTICE

Office of the Attorney General

28 CFR Part 36

List of Subjects in 28 CFR Part 36

Administrative practice and procedure, Alcoholism, Buildings and facilities, Business and industry, Civil rights, Consumer protection, Drug abuse, Historic preservation, Individuals with disabilities, Reporting and recordkeeping requirements.

Authority and Issuance

By the authority vested in me as Attorney General by 28 U.S.C. 509, 510; 5 U.S.C. 301; and 42 U.S.C. 12186(b),

and for the reasons set forth in the common preamble, part 36 of chapter I of title 28 of the Code of Federal Regulations is amended as follows:

PART 36—NONDISCRIMINATION ON THE BASIS OF DISABILITY BY PUBLIC ACCOMMODATIONS AND IN COMMERCIAL FACILITIES

1. The authority citation for 28 CFR part 36 is revised to read as follows:

Authority: 5 U.S.C. 301; 28 U.S.C. 509, 510; 42 U.S.C. 12186(b).

2. Section 36.407 is added to read as set forth at the end of the common preamble.

Dated: February 23, 1994.

Janet Reno,
Attorney General.

ARCHITECTURAL AND TRANSPORTATION BARRIERS COMPLIANCE BOARD

36 CFR Part 1191

List of Subjects in 36 CFR Part 1191

Buildings and facilities, Civil rights, Individuals with disabilities.

Authority and Issuance

For the reasons set forth in the common preamble, part 1191 of title 36 of the Code of Federal Regulations is amended as follows:

PART 1191—AMERICANS WITH DISABILITIES ACT (ADA) ACCESSIBILITY GUIDELINES FOR BUILDINGS AND FACILITIES

1. The authority citation for 36 CFR part 1191 continues to read as follows:

Authority: Americans with Disabilities Act of 1990 (42 U.S.C. 12204).

2. Section 1191.2 is added to read as set forth at the end of the common preamble.

Authorized by vote of the Access Board on November 10, 1993.

Judith E. Heumann,
Chairperson, Architectural and Transportation Barriers Compliance Board.

DEPARTMENT OF TRANSPORTATION

Office of the Secretary

49 CFR Part 37

List of Subjects in 49 CFR Part 37

Buildings and facilities, Buses, Civil rights, Individuals with disabilities, Mass transportation, Railroads, Reporting and recordkeeping requirements, Transportation.

Authority and Issuance

For the reasons set forth in the common preamble, part 37 of title 49 of the Code of Federal Regulations is amended as follows:

PART 37—TRANSPORTATION SERVICES FOR INDIVIDUALS WITH DISABILITIES (ADA)

1. The authority citation for 49 CFR part 37 continues to read as follows:

Authority: Americans with Disabilities Act of 1990 (42 U.S.C. 12101–12213); 49 U.S.C. 322.

2. Section 37.15 is added to read as set forth at the end of the common preamble.

Dated: April 6, 1994.

Federico Peña,

Secretary of Transportation.

[FR Doc. 94–8676 Filed 4–11–94; 8:45 am]

BILLING CODE 4410–01–P; 8150–01–P; 4910–62–P

Appendix A

Tuesday
January 18, 1994

Part VI

Department of Justice

Office of the Attorney General

28 CFR Part 36
Americans With Disabilities Act;
Transportation Facilities and Accessible
Automated Teller Machines (ATMs); Final
Rule

2674   **Federal Register** / Vol. 59, No. 11 / Tuesday, January 18, 1994 / Rules and Regulations

DEPARTMENT OF JUSTICE

Office of the Attorney General

28 CFR PART 36

[Order No. 1836–94]

Nondiscrimination on the Basis of Disability by Public Accommodations and in Commercial Facilities: Amendments to the Americans With Disabilities Act Accessibility Guidelines (Accessible Automated Teller Machines and Transportation Facilities)

AGENCY: Department of Justice.

ACTION: Final rule.

SUMMARY: This final rule amends Appendix A to the Department of Justice regulation implementing title III of the Americans with Disabilities Act (ADA) by incorporating the accessibility guidelines for transportation facilities issued by the Architectural and Transportation Barriers Compliance Board (Access Board), and by adopting the amendments to the reach range requirement for accessible automated teller machines (ATMs) and fare vending machines jointly issued by the Access Board and the Department of Transportation.

EFFECTIVE DATE: February 17, 1994.

FOR FURTHER INFORMATION CONTACT: Stewart B. Oneglia, Chief, Coordination and Review Section, Civil Rights Division, U.S. Department of Justice, Washington, DC 20530, (202) 514–0301 (Voice), (202) 514–0383 (TDD) (the Division's ADA Information Line). These telephone numbers are not toll-free numbers.

Copies of this rule are available in the following alternate formats: large print, Braille, electronic file on computer disk, and audio-tape. Copies may be obtained from the Coordination and Review Section at (202) 514–0301 (Voice) or (202) 514–0383 (TDD). The rule is also available on electronic bulletin board at (202) 514–6193. These telephone numbers are not toll-free numbers.

SUPPLEMENTARY INFORMATION:

Background

On July 26, 1991 (56 FR 35544), the Department of Justice (Department) published its final regulation implementing title III of the Americans with Disabilities Act of 1990 (ADA) Public Law 101–336, which prohibits discrimination on the basis of disability by private entities that own, lease, lease to, or operate a place of public accommodation, and requires that all new places of public accommodation

and commercial facilities, and all alterations to such facilities, be designed and constructed so as to be readily accessible to and usable by persons with disabilities.

Section 36.406 of the regulation, "Standards for new construction and alterations," provides that new construction and alterations subject to the regulation shall comply with the standards for accessible design published as appendix A to the regulation. Appendix A contains the Americans with Disabilities Act Accessibility Guidelines for Buildings and Facilities (ADAAG), which was separately published by the Architectural and Transportation Barriers Compliance Board (Access Board) as a final guideline on July 26, 1991 (56 FR 35408). On April 5, 1993, the Department issued a final rule containing technical amendments to appendix A (58 FR 17521), which incorporated technical corrections to ADAAG made by the Access Board on January 14, 1992 (57 FR 1393).

Section 36.406 of the title III regulation implements sections 306(b) and 306(c) of the ADA, which require the Attorney General to promulgate standards for accessible design for buildings and facilities subject to the ADA, and require those standards to be consistent with the supplemental minimum guidelines and requirements for accessible design published by the Access Board pursuant to section 504 of the ADA. Sections 5 through 9 of appendix A are special application sections and contain additional requirements for restaurants and cafeterias, medical care facilities, business and mercantile facilities, libraries, and transient lodging. Section 10 of ADAAG, which was intended to establish special access requirements for transportation facilities, was reserved when the Department's final rule was published because the Access Board had not yet published that section of its minimum guidelines.

On September 6, 1991 (56 FR 45500), the Access Board published a final rule amending the guidelines by adding final guidelines for transportation facilities as a new section 10, and on January 14, 1992 (57 FR 1393), the Access Board published a final rule making corrections to that section.

On September 8, 1992 (57 FR 41006), the Access Board published a Notice of Proposed Rulemaking (NPRM) proposing to amend the reach range requirements for accessible ATMs under ADAAG based on new information received in connection with a petition for rulemaking. The Access Board's proposed amendment set out the reach

ranges for controls when a person using a wheelchair could make a forward approach only, a parallel approach only, or both a forward and parallel approach to an ATM. To address the reach over an obstruction resulting from recessed controls and the installation of fixtures called "surrounds" (which contain writing counters and bins for envelopes and waste paper), in front of ATMs, the proposed amendment included a table of reach depths and maximum heights for the placement of the controls where the reach depth to any control is more than 10 inches from a parallel approach. A detailed discussion of the proposed amendment is contained in the Access Board's proposed rule. On November 17, 1992 (57 FR 54210), the Department of Transportation issued an NPRM to amend its ADA regulations in several respects, including conforming the standards for transportation facilities to incorporate the reach range requirements for ATMs. The amendment is relevant to transportation facilities because fare vending machines are required to comply with the same requirements as ATMs. See ADAAG 10.3.1(7). On July 15, 1993 (58 FR 38204), the Access Board and the Department of Transportation published a joint final rule adopting the proposed changes to the reach range requirements for ATMs and fare vending machines.

On April 5, 1993 (58 FR 17558), this Department published a proposed rule to amend appendix A to its title III regulation to include section 10 of the Access Board's final guidelines, as amended (transportation facilities), and to adopt the changes relating to the reach range requirements applicable to automated teller machines proposed by the Access Board in its September 8, 1992 (57 FR 41006) proposed rule. In the Department's proposed rule, it sated that "[a]ll timely comments received by the Board on the proposed transportation rule issued by the Board on March 20, 1991 (56 FR 11874), and on the proposed rule relating to ATM reach ranges issued by the Board on September 8, 1992 (57 FR 41006), will be deemed by the Department to have been submitted in response to this proposed rule and will be thoroughly analyzed and considered by the Department prior to the adoption of any final rule. Therefore, it is not necessary for any timely comments submitted to the Board on those proposed rules to be resubmitted to the Department." Any new comments on the Department's proposed rule were due on or before May 5, 1993.

Appendix A

Summary of Rule and Comments

The Department of Justice is adopting as a final rule the accessibility guidelines for transportation facilities published by the Access Board as a final rule on September 6, 1991, as amended by the Access Board on January 14, 1992, and as further jointly amended on July 15, 1993, by the Access Board and the Department of Transportation, to reflect changes relating to reach range requirements.

The Department is also adopting as a final rule the proposed amendment to the reach range requirement for ATMs. As stated in the Department's NPRM, all timely comments received by the Access Board on the proposed transportation and ATM rules have been analyzed by the Department in connection with this final rule. An analysis of these comments is contained in the final rules issued by the Access Board and referenced above, and the Department concurs with the Access Board's analysis. In addition to the comments previously received by the Access Board, the Department directly received seven comments in response to its NPRM. Of these seven comments, three substantially duplicated comments on the proposed revisions to ATM requirements previously sent to the Access Board by the same commenters, and two addressed issues not covered by the NPRM. Of the two new comments on issues raised by the NPRM, one expressed support for both the proposed transportation and the proposed ATM provisions without discussing any rationale for such support, and on comment, submitted by an advocacy group, opposed the changes to ATM reach range requirements on the ground that the changes would not make ATMs readily accessible to and usable by individuals with disabilities, but did not include any additional documentation.

Regulatory Process Matters

The Department has determined that this final rule is not a major rule under E.O. 12291. Accordingly, a regulatory impact statement is not required.

The Department has determined that this final rule will not have a significant economic impact on a substantial number of small business entities. Therefore, it is not subject to the Regulatory Flexibility Act.

The Department also has determined that there are no Federalism impacts sufficient to warrant the preparation of a Federalism assessment under Executive Order 12612.

List of Subjects in 28 CFR Part 36

Administrative practice and procedure, Alcoholism, Americans with disabilities, Buildings and facilities, Business and industry, Civil rights, Consumer protection, Drug abuse, Historic preservation, Reporting and recordkeeping requirements.

Dated: January 5, 1994.

By the authority vested in me as Attorney General by 28 U.S.C. 509, 510, 5 U.S.C. 301, and section 306(b) of the Americans with Disabilities Act, Pub. L. 101–336, and for the reasons set forth in the preamble, chapter I of title 28 of the Code of Federal Regulations is amended as follows:

Janet Reno,

Attorney General.

PART 36—NONDISCRIMINATION ON THE BASIS OF DISABILITY BY PUBLIC ACCOMMODATIONS AND IN COMMERCIAL FACILITIES

1. The authority citation for 28 CFR part 36 is revised to read as follows:

Authority: Americans With Disabilities Act of 1990 (42 U.S.C. 12186).

2. The appendix to § 36.406 is amended by removing "[10, Reserved]" in the last line of the third column and adding, in lieu thereof, "10".

3. Appendix A to part 36 is amended by revising paragraph 20 in section 4.1.3, by revising section 4.43 and sections 4.34.1 through 4.34.4, by adding 4.34.5, by revising the heading of section 10, by adding the text to section 10, and by adding sections A10.3 and A10.3.1(7) to the appendix to appendix A. Pages 10, 58, 67, and A17 are republished with the revisions and additions included, and pages 58A and 68 through 71 are added, to read as follows:

Appendix A to Part 36—Standards for Accessible Design

*　　*　　*　　*　　*

BILLING CODE 4410-01-M

2676 Federal Register / Vol. 59, No. 11 / Tuesday, January 18, 1994 / Rules and Regulations

4.1.3 Accessible Buildings: New Construction

in a covered mall, at least one interior public text telephone shall be provided in the facility.

(iii) if a public pay telephone is located in or adjacent to a hospital emergency room, hospital recovery room, or hospital waiting room, one public text telephone shall be provided at each such location.

(d) Where a bank of telephones in the interior of a building consists of three or more public pay telephones, at least one public pay telephone in each such bank shall be equipped with a shelf and outlet in compliance with 4.31.9(2).

(18) If fixed or built-in seating or tables (including, but not limited to, study carrels and student laboratory stations), are provided in accessible public or common use areas, at least five percent (5%), but not less than one, of the fixed or built-in seating areas or tables shall comply with 4.32. An accessible route shall lead to and through such fixed or built-in seating areas, or tables.

(19)* Assembly areas:

(a) in places of assembly with fixed seating accessible wheelchair locations shall comply with 4.33.2, 4.33.3, and 4.33.4 and shall be provided consistent with the following table:

Capacity of Seating in Assembly Areas	Number of Required Wheelchair Locations
4 to 25	1
26 to 50	2
51 to 300	4
301 to 500	6
over 500	6, plus 1 additional space for each total seating capacity increase of 100

In addition, one percent, but not less than one, of all fixed seats shall be aisle seats with no armrests on the aisle side, or removable or folding armrests on the aisle side. Each such seat shall be identified by a sign or marker. Signage notifying patrons of the availability of such seats shall be posted at the ticket office. Aisle seats are not required to comply with 4.33.4.

(b) This paragraph applies to assembly areas where audible communications are integral to the use of the space (e.g., concert and lecture halls, playhouses and movie theaters, meeting rooms, etc.). Such assembly areas, if (1) they accommodate at least 50 persons, or if they have audio-amplification systems, and (2) they have fixed seating, shall have a permanently installed assistive listening system complying with 4.33. For other assembly areas, a permanently installed assistive listening system, or an adequate number of electrical outlets or other supplementary wiring necessary to support a portable assistive listening system shall be provided. The minimum number of receivers to be provided shall be equal to 4 percent of the total number of seats, but in no case less than two. Signage complying with applicable provisions of 4.30 shall be installed to notify patrons of the availability of a listening system.

(20) Where automated teller machines are provided, each machine shall comply with the requirements of 4.34 except where two or more machines are provided at a location, then only one must comply.

EXCEPTION: Drive-up-only automated teller machines are not required to comply with 4.34.2 and 4.34.3.

(21) Where dressing and fitting rooms are provided for use by the general public, patients, customers or employees, 5 percent, but never less than one, of dressing rooms for each type of use in each cluster of dressing rooms shall be accessible and shall comply with 4.35.

Examples of types of dressing rooms are those serving different genders or distinct and different functions as in different treatment or examination facilities.

4.1.4 (Reserved).

4.1.5 Accessible Buildings: Additions.
Each addition to an existing building or facility shall be regarded as an alteration. Each space or element added to the existing building or facility shall comply with the applicable provisions of 4.1.1 to 4.1.3, Minimum Requirements (for New Construction) and the applicable technical specifications of 4.2 through 4.35 and sections 5 through 10. Each addition that

4.33.5 Access to Performing Areas

4.33.5 Access to Performing Areas.
An accessible route shall connect wheelchair seating locations with performing areas, including stages, arena floors, dressing rooms, locker rooms, and other spaces used by performers.

4.33.6* Placement of Listening Systems.
If the listening system provided serves individual fixed seats, then such seats shall be located within a 50 ft (15 m) viewing distance of the stage or playing area and shall have a complete view of the stage or playing area.

4.33.7* Types of Listening Systems.
Assistive listening systems (ALS) are intended to augment standard public address and audio systems by providing signals which can be received directly by persons with special receivers or their own hearing aids and which eliminate or filter background noise. The type of assistive listening system appropriate for a particular application depends on the characteristics of the setting, the nature of the program, and the intended audience. Magnetic induction loops, infra-red and radio frequency systems are types of listening systems which are appropriate for various applications.

4.34 Automated Teller Machines.

4.34.1 General. *Each automated teller machine required to be accessible by 4.1.3 shall be on an accessible route and shall comply with 4.34.*

4.34.2 Clear Floor Space. *The automated teller machine shall be located so that clear floor space complying with 4.2.4 is provided to allow a person using a wheelchair to make a forward approach, a parallel approach, or both, to the machine.*

4.34.3 Reach Ranges.

(1) Forward Approach Only. If only a forward approach is possible, operable parts of all controls shall be placed within the forward reach range specified in 4.2.5.

(2) Parallel Approach Only. If only a parallel approach is possible, operable parts of controls shall be placed as follows:

(a) Reach Depth Not More Than 10 in (255 mm). Where the reach depth to the operable parts of all controls as measured from the vertical plane perpendicular to the edge of the unobstructed clear floor space at the farthest

protrusion of the automated teller machine or surround is not more than 10 in (255 mm), the maximum height above the finished floor or grade shall be 54 in (1370 mm).

(b) Reach Depth More Than 10 in (255 mm). Where the reach depth to the operable parts of any control as measured from the vertical plane perpendicular to the edge of the unobstructed clear floor space at the farthest protrusion of the automated teller machine or surround is more than 10 in (255 mm), the maximum height above the finished floor or grade shall be as follows:

Reach Depth		Maximum Height	
In	*Mm*	*In*	*Mm*
10	255	54	1370
11	280	53½	1360
12	305	53	1345
13	330	52½	1335
14	355	51½	1310
15	380	51	1295
16	405	50½	1285
17	430	50	1270
18	455	49½	1255
19	485	49	1245
20	510	48½	1230
21	535	47½	1205
22	560	47	1195
23	585	46½	1180
24	610	46	1170

(3) Forward and Parallel Approach. If both a forward and parallel approach are possible, operable parts of controls shall be placed within at least one of the reach ranges in paragraphs (1) or (2) of this section.

(4) Bins. Where bins are provided for envelopes, waste paper, or other purposes, at least one of each type provided shall comply with the applicable reach ranges in paragraph (1), (2), or (3) of this section.

EXCEPTION: Where a function can be performed in a substantially equivalent manner by using an alternate control, only one of the controls needed to perform that function is required to comply with this section. If the controls are identified by tactile markings, such markings shall be provided on both controls.

4.34.4 Controls. *Controls for user activation shall comply with 4.27.4.*

4.35 Dressing and Fitting Rooms

4.34.5 Equipment for Persons with Vision Impairments. *Instructions and all information for use shall be made accessible to and independently usable by persons with vision impairments.*

4.35 Dressing and Fitting Rooms.

4.35.1 General. *Dressing and fitting rooms required to be accessible by 4.1 shall comply with 4.35 and shall be on an accessible route.*

4.35.2 Clear Floor Space. *A clear floor space allowing a person using a wheelchair to make a 180-degree turn shall be provided in every accessible dressing room entered through a swinging or sliding door. No door shall swing into any part of the turning space. Turning space shall not be required in a private dressing room entered through a curtained opening at least 32 in (815 mm) wide if clear floor space complying with section 4.2 renders the dressing room usable by a person using a wheelchair.*

4.35.3 Doors. *All doors to accessible dressing rooms shall be in compliance with section 4.13.*

4.35.4 Bench. *Every accessible dressing room shall have a 24 in by 48 in (610 mm by 1220 mm) bench fixed to the wall along the longer dimension. The bench shall be mounted 17 in to 19 in (430 mm to 485 mm) above the finish floor. Clear floor space shall be provided alongside the bench to allow a person using a wheelchair to make a parallel transfer onto the bench. The structural strength of the bench and attachments shall comply with 4.26.3. Where installed in conjunction with showers, swimming pools, or other wet locations, water shall not accumulate upon the surface of the bench and the bench shall have a slip-resistant surface.*

4.35.5 Mirror. *Where mirrors are provided in dressing rooms of the same use, then in an accessible dressing room, a full-length mirror, measuring at least 18 in wide by 54 in high (460 mm by 1370 mm), shall be mounted in a position affording a view to a person on the bench as well as to a person in a standing position.*

NOTE: Sections 4.1.1 through 4.1.7 and sections 5 through 10 are different from ANSI A117.1 in their entirety and are printed in standard type.

58A

Appendix A

(a) at least one public entrance shall allow a person with mobility impairments to approach, enter and exit including a minimum clear door width of 32 in (815 mm).

(b) sleeping space for homeless persons as provided in the scoping provisions of 9.1.2 shall include doors to the sleeping area with a minimum clear width of 32 in (815 mm) and maneuvering space around the beds for persons with mobility impairments complying with 9.2.2(1).

(c) at least one toilet room for each gender or one unisex toilet room shall have a minimum clear door width of 32 in (815 mm), minimum turning space complying with 4.2.3, one water closet complying with 4.16, one lavatory complying with 4.19 and the door shall have a privacy latch; and, if provided, at least one tub or shower shall comply with 4.20 or 4.21, respectively.

(d) at least one common area which a person with mobility impairments can approach, enter and exit including a minimum clear door width of 32 in (815 mm).

(e) at least one route connecting elements (a), (b), (c) and (d) which a person with mobility impairments can use including minimum clear width of 36 in (915 mm), passing space complying with 4.3.4, turning space complying with 4.2.3 and changes in levels complying with 4.3.8.

(f) homeless shelters can comply with the provisions of (a)-(e) by providing the above elements on one accessible floor.

9.5.3. Accessible Sleeping Accommodations in New Construction.

Accessible sleeping rooms shall be provided in conformance with the table in 9.1.2 and shall comply with 9.2 Accessible Units, Sleeping Rooms and Suites (where the items are provided). Additional sleeping rooms that comply with 9.3 Sleeping Accommodations for Persons with Hearing Impairments shall be provided in conformance with the table provided in 9.1.3.

In facilities with multi-bed rooms or spaces, a percentage of the beds equal to the table provided in 9.1.2 shall comply with 9.2.2(1).

10. TRANSPORTATION FACILITIES.

10.1 General. Every station, bus stop, bus stop pad, terminal, building or other transportation facility, shall comply with the applicable provisions of 4.1 through 4.35, sections 5 through 9, and the applicable provisions of this section. The exceptions for elevators in 4.1.3(5), exception 1 and 4.1.6(1)(k) do not apply to a terminal, depot, or other station used for specified public transportation, or an airport passenger terminal, or facilities subject to Title II.

10.2 Bus Stops and Terminals.

10.2.1 New Construction.

(1) Where new bus stop pads are constructed at bus stops, bays or other areas where a lift or ramp is to be deployed, they shall have a firm, stable surface; a minimum clear length of 96 inches (measured from the curb or vehicle roadway edge) and a minimum clear width of 60 inches (measured parallel to the vehicle roadway) to the maximum extent allowed by legal or site constraints; and shall be connected to streets, sidewalks or pedestrian paths by an accessible route complying with 4.3 and 4.4. The slope of the pad parallel to the roadway shall, to the extent practicable, be the same as the roadway. For water drainage, a maximum slope of 1:50 (2%) perpendicular to the roadway is allowed.

(2) Where provided, new or replaced bus shelters shall be installed or positioned so as to permit a wheelchair or mobility aid user to enter from the public way and to reach a location, having a minimum clear floor area of 30 inches by 48 inches, entirely within the perimeter of the shelter. Such shelters shall be connected by an accessible route to the boarding area provided under paragraph (1) of this section.

(3) Where provided, all new bus route identification signs shall comply with 4.30.5. In addition, to the maximum extent practicable, all new bus route identification signs shall comply with 4.30.2 and 4.30.3. Signs

67

2680 Federal Register / Vol. 59, No. 11 / Tuesday, January 18, 1994 / Rules and Regulations

10.3 Fixed Facilities and Stations

that are sized to the maximum dimensions permitted under legitimate local, state or federal regulations or ordinances shall be considered in compliance with 4.30.2 and 4.30.3 for purposes of this section.

EXCEPTION: Bus schedules, timetables, or maps that are posted at the bus stop or bus bay are not required to comply with this provision.

10.2.2 Bus Stop Siting and Alterations.

(1) Bus stop sites shall be chosen such that, to the maximum extent practicable, the areas where lifts or ramps are to be deployed comply with section 10.2.1(1) and (2).

(2) When new bus route identification signs are installed or old signs are replaced, they shall comply with the requirements of 10.2.1(3).

10.3 Fixed Facilities and Stations.

10.3.1 New Construction. New stations in rapid rail, light rail, commuter rail, intercity bus, intercity rail, high speed rail, and other fixed guideway systems (e.g., automated guideway transit, monorails, etc.) shall comply with the following provisions, as applicable:

(1) Elements such as ramps, elevators or other circulation devices, fare vending or other ticketing areas, and fare collection areas shall be placed to minimize the distance which wheelchair users and other persons who cannot negotiate steps may have to travel compared to the general public. The circulation path, including an accessible entrance and an accessible route, for persons with disabilities shall, to the maximum extent practicable, coincide with the circulation path for the general public. Where the circulation path is different, signage complying with 4.30.1, 4.30.2, 4.30.3, 4.30.5, and 4.30.7(1) shall be provided to indicate direction to and identify the accessible entrance and accessible route.

(2) In lieu of compliance with 4.1.3(8), at least one entrance to each station shall comply with 4.14, Entrances. If different entrances to a station serve different transportation fixed routes or groups of fixed routes, at least one entrance serving each group or route shall comply with 4.14, Entrances. All accessible entrances shall, to the maximum extent practicable, coincide with those used by the majority of the general public.

(3) Direct connections to commercial, retail, or residential facilities shall have an accessible route complying with 4.3 from the point of connection to boarding platforms and all transportation system elements used by the public. Any elements provided to facilitate future direct connections shall be on an accessible route connecting boarding platforms and all transportation system elements used by the public.

(4) Where signs are provided at entrances to stations identifying the station or the entrance, or both, at least one sign at each entrance shall comply with 4.30.4 and 4.30.6. Such signs shall be placed in uniform locations at entrances within the transit system to the maximum extent practicable.

EXCEPTION: Where the station has no defined entrance, but signage is provided, then the accessible signage shall be placed in a central location.

(5) Stations covered by this section shall have identification signs complying with 4.30.1, 4.30.2, 4.30.3, and 4.30.5. Signs shall be placed at frequent intervals and shall be clearly visible from within the vehicle on both sides when not obstructed by another train. When station identification signs are placed close to vehicle windows (i.e., on the side opposite from boarding) each shall have the top of the highest letter or symbol below the top of the vehicle window and the bottom of the lowest letter or symbol above the horizontal mid-line of the vehicle window.

(6) Lists of stations, routes, or destinations served by the station and located on boarding areas, platforms, or mezzanines shall comply with 4.30.1, 4.30.2, 4.30.3, and 4.30.5. A minimum of one sign identifying the specific station and complying with 4.30.4 and 4.30.6 shall be provided on each platform or boarding area. All signs referenced in this paragraph shall, to the maximum extent practicable, be placed in uniform locations within the transit system.

Appendix A

Federal Register / Vol. 59, No. 11 / Tuesday, January 18, 1994 / Rules and Regulations   **2681**

10.3 Fixed Facilities and Stations

(7)* Automatic fare vending, collection and adjustment (e.g., add-fare) systems shall comply with 4.34.2, 4.34.3, 4.34.4, and 4.34.5. At each accessible entrance such devices shall be located on an accessible route. If self-service fare collection devices are provided for the use of the general public, at least one accessible device for entering, and at least one for exiting, unless one device serves both functions, shall be provided at each accessible point of entry or exit. Accessible fare collection devices shall have a minimum clear opening width of 32 inches; shall permit passage of a wheelchair; and, where provided, coin or card slots and controls necessary for operation shall comply with 4.27. Gates which must be pushed open by wheelchair or mobility aid users shall have a smooth continuous surface extending from 2 inches above the floor to 27 inches above the floor and shall comply with 4.13. Where the circulation path does not coincide with that used by the general public, accessible fare collection systems shall be located at or adjacent to the accessible point of entry or exit.

(8) Platform edges bordering a drop-off and not protected by platform screens or guard rails shall have a detectable warning. Such detectable warnings shall comply with 4.29.2 and shall be 24 inches wide running the full length of the platform drop-off.

(9) In stations covered by this section, rail-to-platform height in new stations shall be coordinated with the floor height of new vehicles so that the vertical difference, measured when the vehicle is at rest, is within plus or minus 5/8 inch under normal passenger load conditions. For rapid rail, light rail, commuter rail, high speed rail, and intercity rail systems in new stations, the horizontal gap, measured when the new vehicle is at rest, shall be no greater than 3 inches. For slow moving automated guideway "people mover" transit systems, the horizontal gap in new stations shall be no greater than 1 inch.

EXCEPTION 1: Existing vehicles operating in new stations may have a vertical difference with respect to the new platform within plus or minus 1-1/2 inches.

EXCEPTION 2: In light rail, commuter rail and intercity rail systems where it is not operationally or structurally feasible to meet the horizontal gap or vertical difference

requirements, mini-high platforms, car-borne or platform-mounted lifts, ramps or bridge plates, or similar manually deployed devices, meeting the applicable requirements of 36 CFR part 1192, or 49 CFR part 38 shall suffice.

(10) Stations shall not be designed or constructed so as to require persons with disabilities to board or alight from a vehicle at a location other than one used by the general public.

(11) Illumination levels in the areas where signage is located shall be uniform and shall minimize glare on signs. Lighting along circulation routes shall be of a type and configuration to provide uniform illumination.

(12) Text Telephones: The following shall be provided in accordance with 4.31.9:

(a) If an interior public pay telephone is provided in a transit facility (as defined by the Department of Transportation) at least one interior public text telephone shall be provided in the station.

(b) Where four or more public pay telephones serve a particular entrance to a rail station and at least one is in an interior location, at least one interior public text telephone shall be provided to serve that entrance. Compliance with this section constitutes compliance with section 4.1.3(17)(c).

(13) Where it is necessary to cross tracks to reach boarding platforms, the route surface shall be level and flush with the rail top at the outer edge and between the rails, except for a maximum 2-1/2 inch gap on the inner edge of each rail to permit passage of wheel flanges. Such crossings shall comply with 4.29.5. Where gap reduction is not practicable, an above-grade or below-grade accessible route shall be provided.

(14) Where public address systems are provided to convey information to the public in terminals, stations, or other fixed facilities, a means of conveying the same or equivalent information to persons with hearing loss or who are deaf shall be provided.

69

2682 **Federal Register** / Vol. 59, No. 11 / Tuesday, January 18, 1994 / Rules and Regulations

10.3.2 Existing Facilities: Key Stations.

(15) Where clocks are provided for use by the general public, the clock face shall be uncluttered so that its elements are clearly visible. Hands, numerals, and/or digits shall contrast with the background either light-on-dark or dark-on-light. Where clocks are mounted overhead, numerals and/or digits shall comply with 4.30.3. Clocks shall be placed in uniform locations throughout the facility and system to the maximum extent practicable.

(16) Where provided in below grade stations, escalators shall have a minimum clear width of 32 inches. At the top and bottom of each escalator run, at least two contiguous treads shall be level beyond the comb plate before the risers begin to form. All escalator treads shall be marked by a strip of clearly contrasting color, 2 inches in width, placed parallel to and on the nose of each step. The strip shall be of a material that is at least as slip resistant as the remainder of the tread. The edge of the tread shall be apparent from both ascending and descending directions.

(17) Where provided, elevators shall be glazed or have transparent panels to allow an unobstructed view both in to and out of the car. Elevators shall comply with 4.10.

EXCEPTION: Elevator cars with a clear floor area in which a 60 inch diameter circle can be inscribed may be substituted for the minimum car dimensions of 4.10, Fig. 22.

(18) Where provided, ticketing areas shall permit persons with disabilities to obtain a ticket and check baggage and shall comply with 7.2.

(19) Where provided, baggage check-in and retrieval systems shall be on an accessible route complying with 4.3, and shall have space immediately adjacent complying with 4.2. If unattended security barriers are provided, at least one gate shall comply with 4.13. Gates which must be pushed open by wheelchair or mobility aid users shall have a smooth continuous surface extending from 2 inches above the floor to 27 inches above the floor.

10.3.2 Existing Facilities: Key Stations.

(1) Rapid, light and commuter rail key stations, as defined under criteria established by the Department of Transportation in subpart C of 49 CFR part 37 and existing intercity rail stations shall provide at least one accessible route from an accessible entrance to those areas necessary for use of the transportation system.

(2) The accessible route required by 10.3.2(1) shall include the features specified in 10.3.1 (1), (4)-(9), (11)-(15), and (17)-(19).

(3) Where technical infeasibility in existing stations requires the accessible route to lead from the public way to a paid area of the transit system, an accessible fare collection system, complying with 10.3.1(7), shall be provided along such accessible route.

(4) In light rail, rapid rail and commuter rail key stations, the platform or a portion thereof and the vehicle floor shall be coordinated so that the vertical difference, measured when the vehicle is at rest, is within plus or minus 1-1/2 inches under all normal passenger load conditions, and the horizontal gap, measured when the vehicle is at rest, is no greater than 3 inches for at least one door of each vehicle or car required to be accessible by 49 CFR part 37.

EXCEPTION 1: Existing vehicles retrofitted to meet the requirements of 49 CFR 37.93 (one-car-per-train rule) shall be coordinated with the platform such that, for at least one door, the vertical difference between the vehicle floor and the platform, measured when the vehicle is at rest with 50% normal passenger capacity, is within plus or minus 2 inches and the horizontal gap is no greater than 4 inches.

EXCEPTION 2: Where it is not structurally or operationally feasible to meet the horizontal gap or vertical difference requirements, mini-high platforms, car-borne or platform mounted lifts, ramps or bridge plates, or similar manually deployed devices, meeting the applicable requirements of 36 CFR part 1192, or 49 CFR part 38, shall suffice.

70

Appendix A

10.4 Airports

(5) New direct connections to commercial, retail, or residential facilities shall, to the maximum extent feasible, have an accessible route complying with 4.3 from the point of connection to boarding platforms and all transportation system elements used by the public. Any elements provided to facilitate future direct connections shall be on an accessible route connecting boarding platforms and all transportation system elements used by the public.

10.3.3 Existing Facilities: Alterations.

(1) For the purpose of complying with 4.1.6(2) Alterations to an Area Containing a Primary Function, an area of primary function shall be as defined by applicable provisions of 49 CFR 37.43(c) (Department of Transportation's ADA Rule) or 28 CFR 36.403 (Department of Justice's ADA Rule).

10.4. Airports.

10.4.1 New Construction.

(1) Elements such as ramps, elevators or other vertical circulation devices, ticketing areas, security checkpoints, or passenger waiting areas shall be placed to minimize the distance which wheelchair users and other persons who cannot negotiate steps may have to travel compared to the general public.

(2) The circulation path, including an accessible entrance and an accessible route, for persons with disabilities shall, to the maximum extent practicable, coincide with the circulation path for the general public. Where the circulation path is different, directional signage complying with 4.30.1, 4.30.2, 4.30.3 and 4.30.5 shall be provided which indicates the location of the nearest accessible entrance and its accessible route.

(3) Ticketing areas shall permit persons with disabilities to obtain a ticket and check baggage and shall comply with 7.2.

(4) Where public pay telephones are provided, and at least one is at an interior location, a public text telephone shall be provided in compliance with 4.31.9. Additionally, if four or more public pay telephones are located in any of the following locations, at least one public text telephone shall also be provided in that location:

(a) a main terminal outside the security areas;
(b) a concourse within the security areas; or
(c) a baggage claim area in a terminal.

Compliance with this section constitutes compliance with section 4.1.3(17)(c).

(5) Baggage check-in and retrieval systems shall be on an accessible route complying with 4.3, and shall have space immediately adjacent complying with 4.2.4. If unattended security barriers are provided, at least one gate shall comply with 4.13. Gates which must be pushed open by wheelchair or mobility aid users shall have a smooth continuous surface extending from 2 inches above the floor to 27 inches above the floor.

(6) Terminal information systems which broadcast information to the general public through a public address system shall provide a means to provide the same or equivalent information to persons with a hearing loss or who are deaf. Such methods may include, but are not limited to, visual paging systems using video monitors and computer technology. For persons with certain types of hearing loss such methods may include, but are not limited to, an assistive listening system complying with 4.33.7.

(7) Where clocks are provided for use by the general public the clock face shall be uncluttered so that its elements are clearly visible. Hands, numerals, and/or digits shall contrast with their background either light-on-dark or dark-on-light. Where clocks are mounted overhead, numerals and/or digits shall comply with 4.30.3. Clocks shall be placed in uniform locations throughout the facility to the maximum extent practicable.

(8) Security Systems. [Reserved]

10.5 Boat and Ferry Docks.
[Reserved]

71

2684 **Federal Register** / Vol. 59, No. 11 / Tuesday, January 18, 1994 / Rules and Regulations

A5.0 Restaurants and Cafeterias

A4.33.6 Placement of Listening Systems. A distance of 50 ft (15 m) allows a person to distinguish performers' facial expressions.

A4.33.7 Types of Listening Systems. *An assistive listening system appropriate for an assembly area for a group of persons or where the specific individuals are not known in advance, such as a playhouse, lecture hall or movie theater, may be different from the system appropriate for a particular individual provided as an auxiliary aid or as part of a reasonable accommodation. The appropriate device for an individual is the type that individual can use, whereas the appropriate system for an assembly area will necessarily be geared toward the "average" or aggregate needs of various individuals.* A listening system that can be used from any seat in a seating area is the most flexible way to meet this specification. Earphone jacks with variable volume controls can benefit only people who have slight hearing loss and do not help people who use hearing aids. At the present time, *magnetic induction* loops are the most feasible type of listening system for people who use hearing aids *equipped with "T-coils,"* but people without hearing aids or those with hearing aids not equipped with inductive pick-ups cannot use them *without special receivers.* Radio frequency systems can be extremely effective and inexpensive. People without hearing aids can use them, but people with hearing aids need a special receiver to use them as they are presently designed. If hearing aids had a jack to allow a by-pass of microphones, then radio frequency systems would be suitable for people with and without hearing aids. Some listening systems may be subject to interference from other equipment and feedback from hearing aids of people who are using the systems. Such interference can be controlled by careful engineering design that anticipates feedback sources in the surrounding area.

Table A2, reprinted from a National Institute of Disability and Rehabilitation Research "Rehab Brief," shows some of the advantages and disadvantages of different types of assistive listening systems. In addition, the Architectural and Transportation Barriers Compliance Board (Access Board) has published a pamphlet on Assistive Listening Systems which lists demonstration centers across the country where technical assistance can be obtained in selecting and installing appropriate systems. The state of

New York has also adopted a detailed technical specification which may be useful.

A5.0 Restaurants and Cafeterias.

A5.1 General. *Dining counters (where there is no service) are typically found in small carry-out restaurants, bakeries, or coffee shops and may only be a narrow eating surface attached to a wall. This section requires that where such a dining counter is provided, a portion of the counter shall be at the required accessible height.*

A7.0 Business and Mercantile.

A7.2(3) Assistive Listening Devices. *At all sales and service counters, teller windows, box offices, and information kiosks where a physical barrier separates service personnel and customers, it is recommended that at least one permanently installed assistive listening device complying with 4.33 be provided at each location or series. Where assistive listening devices are installed, signage should be provided identifying those stations which are so equipped.*

A7.3 Check-out Aisles. *Section 7.2 refers to counters without aisles; section 7.3 concerns check-out aisles. A counter without an aisle (7.2) can be approached from more than one direction such as in a convenience store. In order to use a check-out aisle (7.3), customers must enter a defined area (an aisle) at a particular point, pay for goods, and exit at a particular point.*

A10.3 Fixed Facilities and Stations.

A10.3.1(7) Route Signs. *One means of making control buttons on fare vending machines usable by persons with vision impairments is to raise them above the surrounding surface. Those activated by a mechanical motion are likely to be more detectable. If farecard vending, collection, and adjustment devices are designed to accommodate farecards having one tactually distinctive corner, then a person who has a vision impairment will insert the card with greater ease. Token collection devices that are designed to accommodate tokens which are perforated can allow a person to distinguish more readily between tokens and common coins. Thoughtful placement of accessible gates and fare vending machines in relation to inaccessible devices will make their use and detection easier for all persons with disabilities.*

A17

[FR Doc. 94–744 Filed 1–14–94; 8:45 am]

BILLING CODE 4410–01–C

Appendix B

SURVEY OF STATE LAWS

The following chart (from the ADA Compliance Guide, 1990, Thompson Publishing Group, Washington, DC) is a survey of state non-discrimination laws in the areas of employment, housing, places of public accommodation, education, and accessibility. These laws parallel the protections at the federal level extended under the Americans with Disabilities Act, the Rehabilitation Act, and the Architectural Barriers Act.

The following citations reference who is protected under the state law (e.g., physically handicapped people); where there is special coverage (e.g., public employment only), it is so noted.

Citations to "White Cane" laws are included. These are statutes that traditionally provide criminal sanctions for discrimination against blind people, but now also extend in many cases to other disabled people.

In certain states there are generic anti-discrimination laws related to employment or housing that may or may not cover disabled people. These laws are commonly referred to as *fair housing, fair employment*, or *civil rights* laws. Where such laws protect disabled people, it is so noted.

In the accessibility area, application of the law to public and private buildings is noted. Also noted are the current architectural standards in use. For standards, the following abbreviations are used: American National Standards Institute, Inc. (ANSI); Uniform Federal Accessibility Standards (UFAS); Architectural and Transportation Barriers Compliance Board (ATBCB); and Building Operators Code Annotated (BOCA).

Where there is a blank space next to a category, it means the absence of a civil rights law in this area protecting disabled people. It could also mean that an existing civil rights law in the area does not extend protection to disabled people.

(NOTE: In all of these areas, the laws and regulations are dynamic and subject to change. A citation, therefore, should be checked with legal counsel before relying on it. Also, laws covering state-funded programs, such as Education of the Handicapped Act programs, are not noted.)

	Employment	Public Accommodations	Housing	Education	Accessibility
Alabama	Public employment only. Physically handicapped. Ala. Code 21-7-1.	White Cane Law only. Ala. Code 21-7-3.	Physically handicapped. Ala. Code 21-7-9.		Buildings used by the public or constructed with government funds. ANSI A117.1-1961/71. See also state code. Ala. Code 21-4-1.
Alaska	Physically and mentally handicapped. Alaska Stat. 18.80.220. Physically and mentally handicapped. Publicly funded employment. Alaska Stat. 18.47.010.	Publicly funded facilities. Physically and mentally handicapped. Alaska Stat. 18.80.200. Prohibits discrimination in publicly funded programs and activities. White Cane Law. Alaska Stat. 18.06.020.	Publicly funded housing. Alaska Stat. 47.80.010, supra.	Publicly funded education. Alaska Stat. 47.80.010, supra.	State owned buildings. Public buildings ANSI A117.1-1980. See also state code, Alaska Stat 35.10.015.

Figure B.1

	Employment	Public Accommodations	Housing	Education	Accessibility
Arizona	Physically handicapped. Ariz. Rev. Stat. 41-1463.	White Cane Law. Ariz. Stat. 24-411.			Public and private facilities. Coverage of alterations expanding after January 1987. ANSI A117.1-1980. See also state code, Ariz. Rev. Stat. 34-401.
Arkansas	Public employment. Physically handicapped. Ark. Stat. Ann. 82-2901.	White Cane Law. Ark. Stat. Ann. 82-2902.	White Cane Law. Ark. Stat. Ann. 82-2905.		Publicly funded buildings. ATBCB-1981. See also state code, Ark. Stat. Ann. 14-627.
California	Physically handicapped. Also protects persons on the basis of medical condition. Cal. Code Government Sec. 12940.	Physically handicapped. Cal. Civil Code 51-54.3.	Within definition of public accommodation, Cal. Civil Code 51-54.3, supra.	Private (physically handicapped, blind, deaf) within Cal. Civil Code 51-54.3. State-funded post secondary Cal.-Ed. Sec. 67310. Community Colleges. Cal.-Ed. Secs. 72011, 78440.	Public and private facilities. See Cal. Code Government Sec. 4450.
Colorado	Physically and mentally handicapped (state employment). 4CCR 801-1. Physically handicapped. Col. Rev. Stat. 24-34-402. White Cane Law. Col. Rev. Stat. 24-34-801. Mentally handicapped as of July 1, 1992.	Physically handicapped. Col. Rev. Stat. 24-34-602. White Cane Law. Col. Rev. Stat. 24-34-801. Mentally handicapped as of July 1, 1992.	Physically handicapped. Col. Rev. Stat. 24-34-502. Mentally handicapped as of July 1, 1992.	Within definition of place of public accommodations. Col. Rev. Stat. 24-34-602. Mentally handicapped as of July 1, 1992.	Public and private facilities. Col. Rev. Stat. 9-5-101.
Connecticut	Physically and mentally handicapped and mentally retarded. Conn. Gen. Stat. Ann. 46a-60.	Physically handicapped and mentally retarded. Conn. Gen. Stat. Ann. 46a-64.	Physically handicapped and mentally retarded. Within definition of place of public accommodation. Conn. Gen. Stat. Ann. 46a-64.	Physically handicapped and mentally retarded. Conn. Gen. Stat. 46a-75.	Public and private facilities. ANSI A117.1 as revised. See also state code, Conn. Gen. Stat. 29-269 to 29-274. Conn. Gen. Stat. 29-270 repealed 1988: posting of accessibility symbols.
Delaware	Physically and mentally handicapped. Del. Code 19-724.	White Cane Law. Del. Code 9-2903.	Physically and mentally handicapped. Del. Code 6-4601.		State owned, leased, altered public buildings. ANSI A117.1-1980. See also state code, Del. Code 29-73.
District of Columbia	Physically and mentally handicapped. D.C. Code 1-2512. White Cane Law. D.C. Code 6-1504.	Physically and mentally handicapped. D.C. Code 1-2519. White Cane Law. D.C. Code 6-1501.	Physically and mentally handicapped. D.C. Code 1-2515. White Cane Law. D.C. Code 6-1505.	Physically and mentally handicapped. D.C. Code 1-2520.	Public and private facilities. See D.C. Code 6-1703.
Florida	Physically handicapped, mental retardation and developmental disability. Fla. Stat. Ann. 760.22. White Cane Law. Fla. Stat. Ann. 413.08.	White Cane Law. Fla. Stat. Ann. 413.08.	Physically handicapped. Fla. Stat. Ann. 760.23. White Cane Law. Fla. Stat. Ann. 413.08.	"Handicapped person." Fla. Stat. Ann. 228.2001.	Facilities state owned or built on its behalf used by the public. ANSI A117.1-1980. See also state code, Fla. Stat. Ann. 255.21.

Figure B.2

	Employment	Public Accommodations	Housing	Education	Accessibility
Georgia	Physically and mentally handicapped. Ga. Code Ann. 45-19-22. Ga. Code Ann. 34-6A-1.	White Cane Law. Ga. Code Ann. 30-4-1. Ga. Code 8-3-202.	White Cane Law. Ga. Code Ann. 30-4-2.		Public and private facilities. ANSI A117.1-1986. See also state code, Ga. Code Ann. 30-3-2.
Hawaii	Physically and mentally handicapped. Haw. Rev. Stat. Tit. 21, Ch. 378.	White Cane Law. Haw. Rev. Stat. 347-13.	Physically handicapped. Haw. Rev. Stat. 515-1, et seq.		Public facilities. Latest ANSI-A117.1. See also state code, Haw. Rev. Stat. Title 9, Sec. 103.50.
Idaho	Physically and mentally handicapped. Idaho Code 67-5909.	White Cane Law. Idaho Code 18-5812. Idaho Code 67-5909.	Idaho Code 67-5909.	Idaho Code 67-5909.	Public and private facilities. ANSI A-117.1, as amended. See also state code, Idaho Code Title 39, Sec. 3201.
Illinois	Physically and mentally handicapped. Ill. Code 68-2-102. Ill. Const. Art. I, Sec. 19.	Physically and mentally handicapped. Ill. Code 68-5-102. White Cane Law. Ill. Code 23-3363.	Physically and mentally handicapped. Ill. Code 68-3-102. Ill. Const. Art. I, Sec. 19.	Ill. Code 111-1208.	Public and private facilities. See also state code, Ill. Code 111 1/2, Sec. 3711 (relies heavily on ANSI A117.1-1980).
Indiana	Physically and mentally handicapped. Ind. Code Ann. 22-9-3-1.	Physically and mentally handicapped. Ind. Code Ann. 22-9-3-1. White Cane Law. Ind. Code Ann. 16-7-5-2. Right of guide dog extended to "physically handicapped" 16-7-5-2.	Physically and mentally handicapped. Ind. Code Ann. 22-9-3-1.	Physically and mentally handicapped. Ind. Code Ann. 22-9-3-1.	Public and private facilities. Ind. Code Ann. 22-11-1-17.
Iowa	Physically and mentally handicapped. AIDS. Iowa Code 601A.6. White Cane Law. Iowa Code 601D.2.	Physically and mentally handicapped. AIDS. Iowa Code 601A.7. White Cane Law. Iowa Code 601D.4, 601D.11.	Physically and mentally handicapped. AIDS. Iowa Code 601A.8.	Physically and mentally handicapped. AIDS. Iowa Code 601A.9.	Public and private facilities. ANSI A117.1-1980. See also state code, Iowa Code 104A.
Kansas	Physically handicapped. Kans. Stat. 44-1009.	Physically handicapped. Kans. Stat. 44-1009. White Cane Law. Kans. Stat. 39-1101.	Kans. Stat. 44-1016.	Physically handicapped. Public institutions. Kans. Stat. 44-1009.	Public and private facilities. ANSI A117.1-1980. See also state code, Kans. Stat. Ch.13, Sec. 58-1301.
Kentucky	Physically handicapped. Kent. Rev. Stat. 207.130. Affirmative Action Plan, Kent. Rev. Stats. Ch. 18A.	Kent. Rev. Stat. 344.120. White Cane Law. Kent. Rev. Stat. 258.500.	Physically handicapped. Kent. Rev. Stat. 207.180.		Public and private facilities. ANSI A117.1-1980. See also state code, Kent. Rev. Stat. 198.50.
Louisiana	Physically or mentally handicapped. 46 La. Rev. Stat. 2254.	White Cane Law. 46 La. Rev. Stat. Secs. 1952, 1954.	Physically and mentally handicapped. 46 La. Rev. Stat. 2254. White Cane Law. 46 La. Rev. Stat. Sec. 1953.	Physically and mentally handicapped. 46 La. Rev. Stat. Sec. 1954.	Public and private facilities. ANSI 1977 (sic. 1980). See also state code, 40 La. Rev. Stat. 1731.
Maine	Physically and mentally handicapped. 5 Maine Rev. Stat. et seq. 4551.	Physically and mentally handicapped. 5 Maine Rev. Stat. 4551 et seq. White Cane Law. 17 Maine Rev. Stat. 1311. et seq. 5 Maine Rev. Stat. 4593 designated parking.	Physically and mentally handicapped. 5 Maine Rev. Stat. 4551 et seq. White Cane Law. 17 Maine Rev. Stat. 1311 et seq.	Physically and mentally handicapped. 5 Maine Rev. Stat. 1311 et. seq.	Publicly owned or funded facilities, limited private. ANSI A117.1-1980. See also state code, 25 Maine Rev. Stat. 2701.

Figure B.3

	Employment	Public Accommodations	Housing	Education	Accessibility
Maryland	Physically and mentally handicapped. Ann. Code Md. Art. 49B, Sec. 3. White Cane Law. Ann. Code Md. Art. 30, Sec. 33.	Physically and mentally handicapped. Ann. Code Md. Art. 49B, Sec. 8. White Cane Law. Ann. Code Md. Art. 30, Sec. 33.	Physically and mentally handicapped. Ann. Code Md. Art. 49B, Sec. 20. White Cane Law. Ann. Code Md. Art. 30, Sec. 33.	Physically handicapped. Ann. Code Md. Art. 6, Sec. 105.	Public and private facilities. ANSI A117.1-1980. See also state code, Md. Ann. Code Art. 41, Sec. 257JK.
*Massachusetts	Physically and mentally handicapped. Ann. Laws Mass. 151B, Sec. 4.	Physically handicapped. Ann. Laws Mass. 272, Secs. 98, 98A. White Cane Law. Ann. Laws Mass. Sec. 92A. Ann. Laws Mass. 151A Sec. 5.	Physically and mentally handicapped. Ann. Laws Mass. 151, Sec.4.	Blind and deaf. Ann. Laws Mass. 151B, Sec. 6.	Public and private facilities. Ann. Laws Mass. 22, Sec. 13A, 143, Sec. 3W.
Michigan	Physically and mentally handicapped. Mich. Rev. Stat. 37.1202.	Physically and mentally handicapped. Mich. Rev. Stat. 37.1302. White Cane Law. Mich. Rev. Stat. 750.502c.	Physically and mentally handicapped. Mich. Rev. Stat. 37.1502. White Cane Law. Mich. Rev. Stat. 750.502c.	Physically and mentally handicapped. Mich. Rev. Stat. 37.1402. White Cane Law. Mich. Rev. Stat. 750.502c.	Public and private facilities. ANSI A117.1-1961/71. See also state code, Mich. Rev. Stat. 125.1351.
Minnesota	Physically and mentally handicapped. Minn. Stat. Ann. 363.03.	Physically and mentally handicapped. Minn. Stat. Ann. 363.03. White Cane Law. Minn. Stat. Ann. 256.02.	Physically and mentally handicapped. Minn. Stat. Ann. 363.03. White Cane Law. Minn. Stat. Ann. 256.02.	Physically and mentally handicapped. Minn. Stat. Ann. 363.03.	Public and private facilities. ANSI A117.1-1961/71. See also state code, Minn. Stat. Ann. 471.465.
Mississippi	Physically handicapped. State employment only. Miss. Code 25-9-149. White Cane Law. Miss. Code 43-6-15.	White Cane Law. Miss. Code 43-6-5.	White Cane Law. Miss. Code 43-6-3 ("public facilities").		Publicly owned or funded facilities. ANSI A117.1-1980. UFAS. See also state code, Miss. Code 43-6-101.
Missouri	Physically and mentally handicapped. AIDS. Mo. Ann. Stat. Sec. 213.055. Mo. Ann. Stat. Sec. 191-665.	Physically and mentally handicapped. AIDS. Mo. Ann. Stat. Sec. 213.065. White Cane Law. Mo. Ann. Stat. Sec. 209.150. Mo. Ann. Stat. Sec. 191-665.	Physically and mentally handicapped. AIDS. Mo. Ann. Stat. Sec. 213.040-050. Mo. Ann. Stat. Sec. 191-665. White Cane Law. Mo. Ann. Stat. 209.190.	Visual, hearing and physical handicaps, within definition of public accommodations. Mo. Ann. Stat. 213.065. See also Mo. Ann. Stat. 191.665.	Publicly owned or funded. ANSI A117.1-1961/71. See also state code, Mo. Ann. Stat. Sec. 8.610.
Montana	Physically and mentally handicapped. Mont. Code Ann. 49-2-303. White Cane Law. Mont. Code Ann. 49-4-202.	Physically and mentally handicapped. Mont. Code Ann. 49-2-304. White Cane Law. Mont. Code Ann. 49-4-211.	Physically and mentally handicapped. Mont. Code Ann. 49-2-305. White Cane Law. Mont. Code Ann. 49-4-212.	Physically and mentally handicapped. Mont. Code Ann. 49-2-307.	Public and private facilities. UFAS. See also state code, Mont. Code Ann. 50-60-201.
Nebraska	Physically and mentally handicapped. 48 Neb. Rev. Stat. 1101.	White Cane Law. 20 Neb. Rev. Stat. 129.	White Cane Law. 20 Neb. Rev. Stat. 105. 29 Neb. Rev. Stat. 131.	79 Neb. Rev. Stat. 3001.	Public and private facilities. ANSI A117.1-1961/71. See also state code, 72 Neb. Rev. Stat. 1101.
Nevada	Physically handicapped. Nev. Rev. Stat. 613.330.	White Cane Law. Nev. Rev. Stat. 651.070.	People who use guide or helping dogs. Nev. Rev. Stat. 118.105. Nev. Rev. Stat. 118.100.	Within definition of place of public accommodation in White Cane Law. Nev. Rev. Stat. 651.050.	Publicly owned or funded facilities. ATBCB-1982, ANSI.1961. See also state code, Nev. Rev. Stat. 338.180.
New Hampshire	Physically and mentally handicapped. N.H. Rev. Stat. Ann. 354-A.	Physically and mentally handicappped. N.H. Rev. Stat. Ann. 354-A. White Cane Law. N.H. Rev. Stat. Ann. 167-C:2, 167-D.	Physically and mentally handicapped. N.H. Rev. Stat. Ann. 354-A.	Physically and mentally handicapped. N.H. Rev. Stat. Ann. 354-A.	Public facilities. N.H. Rev. Stat. Ann. 155:8-a, 275-C:10.

* Massachusetts constitutional amendment Art. 114 prohibits discrimination against handicapped people in a program or activity within the commonwealth.

Figure B.4

	Employment	Public Accommodations	Housing	Education	Accessibility
New Jersey	Physically and mentally handicapped. N.J. Rev. Stat. 10:5. White Cane Law. N.J. Rev. Stat. 10:5:29.	Physically and mentally handicapped. N.J. Rev. Stat. 10:5. White Cane Law. N.J. Rev. Stat. 10:5:29.	Physically and mentally handicapped. N.J. Rev. Stat. 10:5. White Cane Law. N.J. Rev. Stat. 10:5:29.	Physically and mentally handicapped. Within definition of place of public accommodation. N.J. Rev. Stat. 10:5.	Public and private facilities. ANSI A117.1-1980. UFAS. ATBCB-1982. See also state code, N.J. Rev. Stat. 52:32:6 (amended 1987).
New Mexico	Physically and mentally handicapped. N.M. Stat. Ann. 28-1-7.	Physically and mentally handicapped. N.M. Stat. Ann. 28-1-7. White Cane Law. N.M. Stat. Ann. 28-7-3.	Physically and mentally handicapped. N.M. Stat. Ann. 28-1-7.		Publicly owned facilities. ANSI A117.1-1980. See also state code, N.M. Rev. Stat. 60-13-44.
New York	Physically and mentally handicapped. Exec. Law. Sec. 296. White Cane Law. Civil Rights Law Sec. 47-a.	Physically and mentally handicapped. Exec. Law. Sec. 296. White Cane Law. Civil Rights Law Sec. 47.	Physical. Mental. Exec. Law. Sec. 296. White Cane Law. Civil Rights Law Sec. 47.	Physically and mentally handicapped. Exec. Law. Sec. 296. White Cane Law. Civil Rights Law Sec. 47.	Public and private facilities. ANSI A117.1-1980. New York Public Buildings Law Sec. 50. Transportation Law Sec. 15b.
North Carolina	Physically and mentally handicapped. N.C. Gen. Stat. 168A-5, 143-422.2.	Physically and mentally handicapped. N.C. Gen. Stat. 168A-6.	Physically and mentally handicapped. (Within public accommodations.) N.C. Gen. Stat. 168A-6. N.C. Gen. Stat. 41A-1.	Physically and mentally handicapped. N.C. Gen. Stat. 168A-7.	Public and private facilities. ANSI A117.1-1961/71. See also state code, N.C. Gen. Stat. 143-138.
North Dakota	Physically and mentally handicapped. N.D. Century Code 14-02.4.	Physically and mentally handicapped. N.D. Century Code 14-02.4. White Cane Law. N.D. Century Code 25-13-02.	Physically and mentally handicapped. N.D. Century Code 14-02.4.	Physically and mentally handicapped. N.D. Century Code 14-02.4.	Publicly owned facilities. ANSI A117.1-1961/71. See also state code, N.D. Century Code 23-13-12 and 13.
Ohio	Physically and mentally handicapped. Ohio Rev. Code Sec. 4112.	Physically and mentally handicapped. Ohio Rev. Code Sec. 4112. White Cane Law. Ohio Rev. Code Sec. 955.43.	Physically and mentally handicapped. Ohio Rev. Code Sec. 4112.	Physically and mentally handicapped. Postsecondary education. Ohio Rev. Code Sec. 4112.	Public and private facilities. ANSI A117.1-1980 and BOCA. See also state code, Ohio Rev. Code Sec. 3781.111.
Oklahoma	Physically and mentally handicapped. Ok. Stat. Ann. Title 25, Sec. 1301.	Physically and mentally handicapped. Ok. Stat. Ann. Title 25, Sec.1402. White Cane Law. Ok. Stat. Ann. Title 7, Sec. 19.	Physically and mentally handicapped. Ok. Stat. Ann. Title 25, Sec. 1451.	Within definition of places of public accommodation. Ok. Stat. Ann. Title 25, Sec. 1402.	Publicly owned and funded buildings. BOCA. See also state code, Ok. Stat. Ann. Title 61, Sec. 11.
Oregon	Physically and mentally handicapped. Or. Rev. Stat. 659.400	Physically and mentally handicapped. Or. Rev. Stat. 659.425. White Cane Law. Or. Rev. Stat. 346.610.	Physically and mentally handicapped. Or. Rev. Stat. 659.430. White Cane Law. Or. Rev. Stat. 346.630.	Physically and mentally handicapped. Or. Rev. Stat. 659.150.	Public and private facilities. ANSI A117.1-1980. See also state code, Or. Rev. Stat. 447.210.
Pennsylvania	Physically and mentally handicapped. 43 Penn. Stat. Ann. Sec. 955.	Physically and mentally handicapped. 43 Penn. Stat. Ann. Sec. 955.	Physically and mentally handicapped. 43 Penn. Stat. Ann. Sec. 955.	Within definition of public accommodation. 43 Penn. Stat. Ann. Sec. 955.	Public and private facilities. ANSI A117.1-1980. See also state code, 71 Penn. Stat. Ann. Sec. 1455.

Figure B.5

	Employment	Public Accommodations	Housing	Education	Accessibility
Rhode Island	Physically and mentally handicapped. Gen. Laws. R.I. 28-5-7. State funded or regulated. Gen. Laws R.I. Secs. 28-5.1-1 et seq., 42-87-1 et seq. Also White Cane Law. Gen. Law R.I. 40-9-1.	White Cane Law. Gen. Law R.I. 40-9-1. See also Gen. Law. R.I. 42-87-1 prohibiting discrimination against any qualified physically handicapped person in any program, activity, or service regulated or funded by the state.	Physically and mentally handicapped. Gen. Laws. R.I. 34-37-1. See also Gen. Law. R.I. 28-5.1-1 and 42-87-1, supra.	See Gen. Laws. R.I. 42-87-1 and 28-5.1-1.	Public and private facilities. ANSI-1980. See also state code, Gen. Laws. R.I. 23-27.3-100.15, 37-8-15. Penalty, Gen. Laws R.I. 40-9.1-3.
South Carolina	Physically and mentally handicapped. S.C. Code 43-33-530. See also S.C. Code 43-33-210 on testing for persons unable to use written or visual material.	Physically and mentally handicapped. S.C. Code 43-33-530. White Cane Law. S.C. Code 43-33-20, 43-33-30 and 43-33-70. (Definition broadened to "handicapped person".)	Physically and mentally handicapped. S.C.Code 43-33-530. See also S.C. Code 43-33-70.	Physically and mentally handicapped. S.C. Code 43-33-530.	Public buildings, including publicly or federally funded. Latest ANSI and Southern Building Code. See also S.C. Code 10-5-210.
South Dakota	Physically and mentally handicapped. S.D.C.L.A. 20-13-10.	Physically and mentally handicapped. S.D.C.L.A. 20-13-23. White Cane Law. S.D.C.L.A. 20-13-23.1. Physically and mentally handicapped. S.D.C.L.A. 20-13-20.	Physically and mentally handicapped. S.D.C.L.A. 20-13-20.	Physically and mentally handicapped. S.D.C.L.A. 20-13-22.	Publicly owned or funded facilities. ANSI A117.1-1980. See also state code, S.D.C.L.A. 5-14-13 and S.D.C.L.A. 9-46-1 (wheelchair curb ramps—most current ANSI).
Tennessee	Physically and mentally handicapped. Tenn. Code Ann. 8-50-103.	Tenn. Code Ann. 4-21-501. White Cane Law. Tenn. Code Ann. 62-7-112.	Tenn. Code Ann. 4-21-601. Physically handicapped. Tenn. Code Ann. 66-7-104.	White Cane Law. Tenn. Code Ann. 62-7-112 (public institutions).	Public facilities. North Carolina Illustrated Handbook. Tenn. Code Ann. 68-18-201.
Texas	Physically and mentally handicapped and mentally retarded. Tex. Code Ann. Human Resources 121.003. T.C.S. Vol.16a, Title 92, Art. 5547-300. Texas Human Rights Comm. Sec. 1.01.	Physically handicapped. Tex. Code Ann. Human Resources 121.003.	Physically handicapped Tex. Code Ann. Human Resources 121.003.	Physically handicapped (within definition of public facilities). Tex. Code Ann. Human Resources 121.003.	Public and private facilities. ANSI A117.1-1980. See also state code, Tex. Rev. Stat. Art. 601B, Art. 7, Sec. 7.01.
Utah	Physically and mentally handicapped. Utah Code Ann. 34-35-1.	White Cane Law. Utah Code Ann. 26-30-1.	White Cane Law. Utah Code Ann. 26-30-1 and 26-30-2.		Publicly owned facilities. Utah Code Ann. 26-29-1.
Vermont	Physically and mentally handicapped. 21 Vt. Stat. Ann. 494 et seq.	Physically and mentally handicapped. 13 Vt. Stat. Ann. Ch. 139.	Physically and mentally handicapped. 9 Vt. Stat. Ann. Ch. 139.	Physically and mentally handicapped. 9 Vt. Stat. Ann. Ch. 139 (within definition of public accommodations).	Public and private facilities. ANSI A117.1-1980. See also state code, 18 Vt. Stat. Ann. 1321.
Virginia	Physically and mentally handicapped. Va. Code 51.01-41. Va. Code 2.1-715.	Physically and mentally handicapped. Va. Code 51.01-44. Va. Code 2.1-715.	Physically and mentally handicapped. Va. Code 51.01-45.	Physically and mentally handicapped. Va. Code 51.01-42. Va. Code 2.1-715.	State owned facilities. Limited private. ANSI A117.1-1980. See also state code, Va. Code 2.1-514, 15.1-381.

Figure B.6

Appendix B

	Employment	Public Accommodations	Housing	Education	Accessibility
Washington	Physically and mentally handicapped. Rev. Code Wash. 49.60.180, 49.60.172. White Cane Law. Public Employment. Rev. Code Wash. 70.84.080.	Physically and mentally handicapped. Rev. Code Wash. 49.600.215. White Cane Law. Rev. Code Wash. 70.84.010.	Physically and mentally handicapped. Rev. Code Wash. 49.060.010.	Within definition of public accommodation. Rev. Code Wash. 49.060.040 and 49.060.215.	Public and private facilities. ANSI A117.1. See also state code, Rev. Code Wash. 70.92.100.
West Virginia	Physically and mentally handicapped. W. Va. Code 5-11-9.	Physically and mentally handicapped. W. Va. Code 5-11-9. White Cane Law. W. Va. Code 5-15-4.	Physically and mentally handicapped. W. Va. Code 5-11-9.	Physically and mentally handicapped (within definition of public accommodation). W. Va. Code 5-11-9.	Public owned or used facilities. ANSI A117.1-1961/71. See also state code, W. Va. Code 18-10F-1.
Wisconsin	Physically and mentally handicapped. Wis. Stat. Ann. 111.321.	Physically handicapped and developmentally disabled. Wis. Stat. Ann. 942.04. White Cane Law. Wis. Stat. Ann. 174.056.	Physically and mentally handicapped. Wis. Stat. Ann. 101.22.	Physically handicapped or developmentally disabled in postsecondary or vocational education. Wis. Stat. Ann. 101.223.	Public and private facilities. Most current ANSI. See also state code, Wis. Stat. Ann. 101.13.
Wyoming	Physically and mentally handicapped. Wy. Stat. Ann. 27-9-101.	Wy. Stat. Ann. 6-9-101. White Cane Law. Wy. Stat. Ann. 42-1-126.			State buildings. ANSI A117.1-1961/71. See also state code, Wy. Stat. Ann. 35-13-101.

Figure B.7

Appendix C

THE ARCHITECTURAL BARRIERS ACT (ABA)

The Architectural Barriers Act was adopted in 1968 and requires federal and federally funded buildings/facilities to be readily accessible to, and usable by, handicapped persons in accordance with standards that are to be prescribed. ABA covers buildings designed, altered, or constructed by, or for, the United States. It also includes buildings leased to the U.S. after January 1, 1977, renewals of old leases, buildings financed with federal grants or loans if the building is subject to design and construction standards, as well as the buildings and facilities of the Washington, D.C. Metro Transit System. The law does not apply to leased buildings unless they were leased after design/construction in accordance with federal plans and specifications. The ABA law was redesigned in 1976 to include more leased buildings in the coverage.

"Public" buildings that may employ handicapped persons must be accessible. Under the ABA, "building" includes: recreational, medical, educational, and other structures above and beyond office facilities of the federal government. Non-disabled military structures and private residences do not apply.

Under the ABA, as originally enacted, three agencies issue access standards: The Department of Housing and Urban Development with respect to residential structures, the Department of Defense with respect to military facilities, and the General Services Administration with respect to all other facilities and buildings. The agencies issued standards approximately one year after the law was adopted. A 1976 amendment to the ABA authorizes the United States Postal Service to issue standards for its buildings and facilities. The head of each agency issuing a standard is authorized to waive or modify that access standard on a case-by-case basis when it is clearly necessary.

In issuing accessibility standards, the federal agencies all predicated their work on the original 1961 ANSI standard. Until 1984 the standards varied among the four agencies. With respect to pre-1985 projects, it is important to be alert to the particular standard in effect at the time the contract was awarded so as to be sure what exactly was required.

In 1984, the four agencies issuing standards under the ABA issued the "federal" standard, the Uniform Federal Accessibility Standard (UFAS), which is based on Minimum Guidelines and Requirements for Accessible Design that had been developed by the U.S. Architectural Barriers Compliance Board (ATBCB). ATBCB was established by Section 502 of the Rehabilitation Act to ensure compliance with the standards issued under the ABA. UFAS is intended to bring consistency and uniformity to federal and federally funded design and construction.

The ABA is enforceable in many ways. The agency issuing the funding grant/contract can and should always take appropriate actions to ensure that access requirements, like other mandates, are met. The ATBCB is a separate administrative agency within the federal government that can initiate legal proceedings resulting in funds being cut off or corrective action being taken. The ATBCB proceedings are informal, with due process hearings before an Administrative Law judge, and appeals going to the court.

It is also possible to go to court directly. Cases have been successful in enjoining the use of facilities that were accessible to nondisabled persons, but not in compliance with access mandates for persons with disabilities. The inclusion of operational accessibility features has been judicially compelled. Facilities open to the public and where persons with disabilities may be employed (which are leased by the government – including the U.S. Postal Service) must be accessible when those facilities open, not when and if the facility is subsequently altered. Planning for access is not adequate to comply with the law.

The ABA is not a mandate to go back into older buildings and renovate to make them barrier-free. The underlying philosophy is that when work is done on a building, it must be accessible and usable in accordance with the standards that have been issued. Under the limited approach of the ABA, new buildings are accessible when they are designed and constructed.

The largest difference between the ABA and The Rehabilitation Act is that it pertains to buildings which predate the mandate of the laws. Under the ABA, an older (pre-1969) building which is not leased now or which is not altered, is not required to be accessible. Under the Rehab Act, programs within such a structure, including employment opportunities, must be accessible. The practical result is that at least parts of older buildings have to be renovated and made accessible. The Rehab Act is similar to ADA, in that under the public accommodations provisions (Title III) and state and local government activities and programs (Title II), older (as well as new) structures must be accessible and usable.

Appendix D

DEFINITIONS OF DISABLING CONDITIONS

Amyotrophic Lateral Sclerosis (ALS) or Lou Gehrig's Disease
A motor neuron disease of the anterior horn cells in the spinal cord that progressively weakens the skeletal muscles and strikes 1 in 50,000 people a year. Persons who are afflicted exhibit twitching, spasms, rigidity and muscle stiffness, and eventually lose the ability to walk, talk and breathe while mental faculties remain intact. Some patients afflicted with ALS can live productive lives for up to 20 years after diagnosis. The causes and specific treatments remain elusive.

Apoplexy, Stroke, Cerebrovascular Accident
Sudden mishap to the blood supply to the brain. Blood vessels rupture and bleed into the brain causing oxygen deprivation to brain cells or death of brain cells. In severe strokes, there can be marked loss of memory or alertness, persistent unsteadiness on the feet, disturbing changes in emotional behavior, and paralysis or limited movement on one or both sides of the body, including difficulty with speech.

Arthritis
Inflammation of the joints that causes pain, swelling, stiffness and deformity in one or more joints. Moving of the joints is very painful. Warning signs include: early morning stiffness, redness/warmth in one or more joints, recurring joint pain along with unexplained weight loss/fever/weakness, and the inability to move joint normally.

Cerebral Palsy
This disease can begin in infancy. It is due to damage to one or more of three areas of the brain. It generally interfaces with the nerves controlling the muscles. The disease causes poor speech, loss of motor skills, spastic paralysis with stiffness and muscle impairment, tremors and involuntary movement, and poor circulation.

Disk and Back Problems
Strain or slipping of disks in the back can cause severe and disabling pain. Pain is worse when coughing, sneezing, or straining the back. The problem can be caused by muscle strain/disorder, pressure on a nerve, injury, aging, improper posture, movement, exercise, overexertion, stress, disalignment, or as a symptom of some other disabling condition.

Multiple Sclerosis
This is the most common disease of the nervous system. Hardened patches due to inflammation are scattered at random throughout the brain and spinal

cord, interfering with the nerves in these areas. It can be extremely disabling for periods of time. Symptoms include tremors of the limbs, weakness, interference of fine motor control, unsteadiness and/or stiffness in walking, and an inability to maintain balance, as well as difficulties in vision (e.g., seeing double or loss of parts of the field of vision). Some paralysis may also occur.

Muscular Dystrophy
This disease mainly strikes children. The muscles are weakened and shriveled away by the disease. This disease affects all of the important muscles including the trunk of the body, causing almost complete incapacitation.

Parkinsonism
This is a disease of the brain which is characterized by stiffness of muscles and tremors. It begins with mild tremors to the hands and nodding of the head. As the disease progresses, facial muscles may become stiff and tremors may involve the whole body. The back may become bent.

Polio
A virus that affects the nervous system by attacking cells that control nerves in the muscles. It may destroy or weaken muscles causing paralysis.

Spinal Cord Injury
The majority of spinal cord injuries are caused by automobile or sports-related accidents. Victims of spinal cord injuries are usually 30 years old or younger, and most are men. Spinal cord injuries cause the communication network between the brain and parts of the body to break down. The level at which the spinal cord has been damaged determines the type and severity of the disability. Spinal cord injuries may result in either quadriplegia or paraplegia and may be complete or incomplete in terms of movement and sensation retained by the injured person.

Stroke
See Apoplexy

Tetraplegia
A condition caused by trauma to the spinal cord, either from an accident or as a result of congenital/degenerative diseases. The higher the level of injury to the cord, the greater the motor/sensory loss. Injuries above vertebra C5-6 will usually result in tetraplegia, with subsequent loss of arm/finger movement.

Appendix E

OCCUPATIONAL INJURIES

Carpal Tunnel Syndrome
CTS is often caused by repeated wrist flexion. The median nerve "tunnel" in the wrist is composed of bone, ligament and tendons. If one or all of these becomes inflamed due to repetitive trauma, the walls of the tunnel press on the median nerve, resulting in pain, discomfort, swelling, numbness, tingling, and loss of sensitivity. Persons afflicted may be unable to grasp/hold items, and frequently drop things. If cause is uncorrected, these persons may very well become permanently disabled and unable to earn a living in a job that involves use of their hands.

Hand-Arm Vibration Syndrome
HAVS is a disease caused by using vibrating tools or equipment. Symptoms include: pain and/or numbness and blanching of fingers (Raynaud's Phenomenon), as well as loss of finger dexterity. If the disease is allowed to progress, it can mean loss of hand function or necrosis (death of tissue) of the fingers.

Heat Exhaustion
May be caused by extreme heat in the workplace. The skin becomes pale and clammy, pulse is rapid and strong, and there may even be a loss of consciousness. Persons should be removed from the heat source area immediately and taken to cool off in a cooler, shaded area. Fluid replacement may also be necessary if the person has been exposed for an extended length of time.

Pain
Pain is a subjective experience with two complementary aspects: one is a localized sensation in a particular body part; the other is an unpleasant quality of varying severity commonly associated with behaviors directed at relieving or terminating the experience. It is the experience of pain that affects functioning, including the ability to work. An average of 20% of injured workers, still experiencing pain, never return to work.

Space Invader's Wrist
Named after the popular electronic game and resulting from repetitive motion, it can produce up to 75 different symptoms. Some of these include: stiffness, headaches, numbness, localized swelling, limited movement, spasms, and changes in posture.

Tendonitis
This includes such conditions as "Tennis Elbow" and "Golfers' Elbow."

Tennis elbow usually results from such actions as driving screws for a full shift with an inward twist of the forearm. Golfers' elbow is similar, but comes from an outward twist of the forearm. Muscle-tendon junctions and muscle tissue become inflamed. It is one of the most common degenerating joint diseases in industries.

The Ten Leading Work-Related Diseases and Injuries (according to NIOSH, the National Institute for Occupational Safety and Health) are:

- Occupational Lung Diseases
- Musculoskeletal Injuries
- Occupational Cancers
- Severe Occupational Traumatic Injuries
- Occupational Cardiovascular Diseases
- Disorders of Reproduction
- Neurotoxic Disorders
- Noise-Induced Hearing Loss
- Dermatological Conditions
- Psychological Disorders

Appendix F

ENFORCEMENT PROVISIONS (ADA)

	Responsible Agency	Enforcement Based on	Type of Actions Allowed	Penalties for Non-compliance
Title I (Employment)	EEOC & DOJ	Title VII of Civil Rights Act of 1964	• Complaints filed with EEOC • Private suits • DOJ may bring suit	• Injunction relief/back wages • Attorneys' fees and litigation costs
Title II (State and local governments)	DOJ & D.O.T. individual agencies	Section 504 and 505 of Rehabilitation Act	• Complaints filed with individual funding agencies • Private suits • DOJ may bring suit	• Termination or suspension of federal funds • Monetary damages • Attorneys' fees and litigation costs
Title III (Public accommodations in private sector)	DOJ	Section 204(a) of the Civil Rights Act of 1964	• Department of Justice may bring suit • Private suits	• Permanent or temporary injunctions • Restraining orders • Preventive relief • Litigation costs • Civil penalties: $50,000 for 1st violation; $100,000 for subsequent violations
Title IV (Telecommunications relay services)	FCC	Communications Act of 1934	• Complaints filed with FCC • Certified state commissions	Revocation of certification

Figure F.1

Appendix G

STATISTICS

Figures for disabilities in the U.S. vary widely, from *30 million to 50 million people.* The number of persons who have more than one disability has been estimated at *35 million.*

- **11.7 Million Physically Disabled People include:**
  - Wheelchair users
  - People who use crutches, canes or walkers
  - Mobility-impaired older people, etc.
- **2.4 Million Deaf People**
- **11 Million Hearing-Impaired People**
- **1.8 Million Blind People**
- **8.2 Million Visually Impaired People**
- **6.8 Million Mentally Disabled People**
- **1.7 Million Homebound People include:**
  - People with chronic health disorders
  - People with wasting diseases like multiple sclerosis
- **2.1 Million Institutionalized People include:**
  - People with mental disturbances
  - People with mental retardation
  - People with terminal illness

Department of Health and Human Services, 1981

- 17 million persons of work force age suffer from some form of physical impairment which limits or precludes their vocational opportunities.

United Cerebral Palsy, New York, NY: *FACTS AND FIGURES,* **1986**

- Incidence: 570,000 adults and children; 5,000 to 7,000 born with CP each year, 1,200 to 1,500 acquire before 5 years.

National Health Interview Survey, 1980-1981 Census

- In 1980-1981, the employment rate was 50% for the 3,676,000 people who suffer from orthopedic impairments of the lower extremities or parts of their lower extremities; 719,609 were in wheelchairs.

Population Survey United States Census Labor Force Statistics, 1985

- In 1985, disabled males were 6,137,000 of the population, with only 44.8% employed and 37% receiving benefits.

Social Security Bulletin, **1982**

- 2,772,000 working age individuals were receiving Old Age Survivors and Disability Insurance benefits. The average benefit was $412.34 per month, with the government paying out 1.2 billion per month.

US Census and Disability Adults, 1986

- Labor force participation among working age disabled persons has fallen 17.8% between 1980 and 1985.

Office of Technology Assistance, Dr. Barbara Boardman, *Senate Report* 100-438, July 1988

- Costs to the federal, state and private disability programs are estimated to be 100 million to 1 billion dollars from the unemployment of disabled individuals who could be employed.

Director of the Governor's Initiative on Technology for People with Disabilities, Minnesota, Rachel Wobschall

- Costs to companies for devices and modifications can be expensive, but are cheaper than the cost of long term disability payments.

Appendix H

ADA FACILITIES COMPLIANCE FLOW CHART

Appendix H

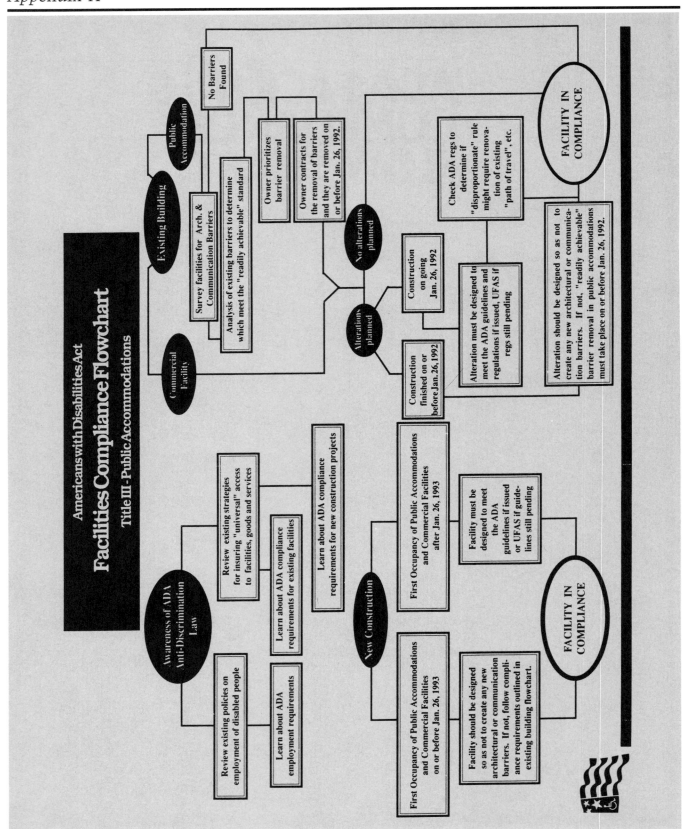

Figure H.1

Appendix I

TAX CREDITS

Vocational Rehabilitation: The Rehabilitation Act of 1973

The Vocational Rehabilitation Program has a 71-year history of assisting people with disabilities to prepare for and enter the competitive work force. This is a federal-state program. The Rehabilitation Act of 1973, as amended, authorizes annual funding to state vocational rehabilitation (VR) agencies in order that they can achieve the goals of the program. An on-the-job training program (OJT) can be set-up by VR with an employer for an individual client of vocational rehabilitation. VR can share in the payment of wages for the employee for a limited time on a negotiated schedule. The position must be permanent, full-time, and pay above minimum wage.

The vocational rehabilitation staff can act as a recruiter and consultant for employers. They can conduct job analysis, and provide rehabilitation engineering services for architectural barrier removal and work site modifications. Also, they can conduct awareness training for a company's management and supervisory personnel. For more information, contact your local vocational rehabilitation office.

Job Training Partnership Act

The Job Training Partnership Act (JTPA) was established by Public Law 97-300 in 1982. It replaced the Comprehensive Employment and Training Act (CETA, P.L. 93-203).

The goal of this act is to train and place individuals who are "economically disadvantaged" in the labor market. This is a joint venture between the public and private sector. The administration of this program is carried out by the governor's office in each state.

JTPA can set up on-the-job training (OJT) at a work site and reimburse an employer for 50% of the first 6 months of wages for each employee who is eligible for this program. Disabled adults (22 years or older) and youths (16-21 years old) are economically disadvantaged if they meet the criteria and definitions set by the federal, state, or local welfare system.

There are 28 services that can be provided, including: job recruiting; counseling in basic work skills; on-the-job training; programs to develop work habits; assistance with the transition from education to work; services to those placed in unsubsidized jobs; and a customized training/retraining program. The agreement with the employer is that the trainee is to be hired with the intent of a permanent, full-time position. For more information, contact your private industry council, the chamber of commerce, city, county or state government, or the local committees on employment of people with disabilities.

The Disabled Access Credit
(Section 44 of the Internal Revenue Code)

P.L. 101-508, The Omnibus Budget Reconciliation Act of 1990, (OBRA '90) contains a new tax incentive to encourage small businesses to comply with the Americans with Disabilities Act (ADA).

The Disabled Access Credit (DAC) is found in Section 11611 of OBRA '90, which establishes Section 44 of the Internal Revenue Code of 1986.

The credit became effective on the date of enactment of the law, November 5, 1990, and applies to expenditures paid or incurred after that date. It is included as part of the General Business Credit and is subject to the rules of the current law which limit the amount of General Business Credit that can be used for any taxable year.

DAC can be carried forward up to 15 years and back for three years, but not back to a taxable year prior to the date of enactment.

In general, all members of a controlled group of corporations will be treated as one person for purpose of credit eligibility, and the dollar limitation among the members of any group will be apportioned by regulation.

In the case of a partnership, the expenditure limitation requirements will apply to the partnership and to each partner. Similar rules will apply to S corporations and their shareholders.

"Eligible access expenditures" are defined as "amounts paid or incurred by an eligible small business for the purpose of enabling small businesses to comply with applicable requirements" of ADA.

All expenditures must be "reasonable" and must meet the standards promulgated by the Internal Revenue Service with the concurrence of the Architectural and Transportation Barriers Compliance Board. Expenses incurred for new construction are not eligible. For the purposes of DAC, disability is defined exactly as in the ADA.

An eligible small business under Section 44 may deduct the difference between the disabled access credit claimed and the disabled access expenditures incurred, up to $15,000, under Section 190, provided such expenditures are eligible for the Section 190 deduction.

For additional information on the Disabled Access Credit, contact a local Internal Revenue Service office.

Tax Credits for Barrier Removal

As part of the Omnibus Budget Reconciliation Act of 1990 (OBRA '90), Congress created a new tax credit to assist certain small businesses in complying with the ADA. During the debate over the act, small business groups sought expanded tax credits as a fair exchange for not being exempted from the public accommodations provisions.

OBRA '90 gives small business owners an annual tax credit to cover expenses incurred from making their facilities and programs accessible to disabled people. Eligible businesses may claim a tax credit equal to 50 percent of the "access expenditures," between $250 and $10,250, incurred to comply with the ADA. Only businesses earning less than $1 million during the taxable year and employing 30 or fewer full-time workers are eligible for the credit.

Specifically, the law allows a business to recover one half the costs of:

- removing architectural, communication, physical or transportation barriers that make a business inaccessible;
- providing qualified interpreters or other effective methods to make aural materials available to hearing-impaired people;
- providing qualified readers, taped texts or other methods to make visual materials available to visually impaired people;
- acquiring or modifying equipment and devices for disabled individuals and
- providing "other similar services, modifications, materials or equipment."

The access credit is limited to the taxable year, and unused portions from one year cannot be carried over to the next. It does not apply to costs incurred from new construction.

Existing Tax Deduction Reduced

To make the small business tax credit "revenue neutral," OBRA '90 reduced from $35,000 to $15,000 an existing tax reduction which all businesses can take to cover the costs of removing architectural barriers from their facilities (Internal Revenue Code 190). This includes changes made to buildings, equipment, walkways, roads and parking lots, and also applies to businesses that make their public transportation vehicles accessible to disabled riders.

For an expense to be deductible, it must meet standards established by the Internal Revenue Service. In general, the expense must be incurred for removing barriers that:

- pose a substantial barrier to disabled people;
- affect at least one major class of disabled people (such as blind, deaf, or wheelchair-using people); and
- are removed without creating new barriers.

In addition, for the expense to be deductible, the removal of barriers must conform to detailed qualification standards to ensure accessibility.

Deductions must be claimed in the year that alterations are made and cannot be claimed for new construction or complete renovation.

Design Guidelines Qualifying for the Tax Advantages of Section 190

Section 190 of the Internal Revenue Code provides a $35,000 tax incentive to businesses to make their facilities and vehicles accessible to handicapped and elderly persons. In general, a taxpayer may elect to treat qualified architectural and transportation barrier removal expenses, which are paid or incurred during each taxable year, as expenses which are not chargeable to a capital account. Such expenditures are to be fully deductible up to a maximum of $35,000 for each taxable year. The maximum $35,000 deduction for a taxpayer applies to individual taxpayers, partnerships and affiliated groups of corporations filing a consolidated return. In the case of a partnership, the selection must be made by the partnership.

Qualified Expenses

Qualified expenses include only those expenses specifically attributable to the removal of existing barriers such as steps, narrow doors, or inaccessible parking spaces, toilet facilities, or transportation vehicles. To meet the test as a "qualified architectural or transportation barrier removal expense," modifications made to facilities or public transportation vehicles must meet the requirements of standards established under Section 190 of the Internal Revenue Code. Expenses incurred in the construction or comprehensive renovation of a facility or vehicle or the normal replacement of depreciable property are not included. However, construction of certain facilities, such as a ramp, qualify if the ramp resulted in the elimination of a barrier (i.e., steps) to mobility-impaired persons.

A Cautionary Note About State Requirements

Persons seeking to use the Section 190 tax deduction for the removal of architectural barriers should check with their local building department to ensure compliance with all local building regulations including local and state standards for access renovations. In some circumstances, state and local requirements may differ. Taxpayers should be cautioned that, in order to qualify for the $35,000 deduction, renovations must meet the minimum requirements set out in Section 190 of the Internal Revenue Code. Taxpayers may, however, comply with state requirements which are *more* stringent or provide a greater level of accessibility and still claim the deduction.

An exact copy of regulations contained in Section 190 can be obtained from your local IRS office, or you may contact:

> Office of the Chief Council
> Legislation and Regulations Division
> Internal Revenue Service, Room 4320
> 1111 Constitution Avenue, N.W.
> Washington, D.C. 20224
> (202) 566-4473 or (202) 566-3553

The Targeted Jobs Tax Credit (Section 51 of the Internal Revenue Code)

The Targeted Jobs Tax Credit (TJTC) was originally established in 1977. It was re-authorized through June 30, 1992, by P.L. 102-227, the Tax Extension Act of 1991.

TJTC offers employers a credit against their tax liability if they hire individuals from nine targeted groups, which include persons with disabilities. The credit applies only to employees hired by a business or a trade, and is not available to employers of maids, chauffeurs, or other household employees. The credit is equal to 40% of the first year wages up to $6,000 per employee, for a maximum credit of $2,444 per employee for the first year of employment.

Employers of disadvantaged summer youth are eligible for a credit of 40% of wages up to $3,000, for a maximum credit of $1,200. Individuals must be employed by the employer at least 90 days (14 days for summer youth), or have completed at least 120 hours (20 hours for summer youth). Employers' deductions for wages must be reduced by the amount of credit.

Individuals with disabilities can contact their local State-Federal Vocational Rehabilitation office to receive a voucher. This is presented to the employer who completes a small portion, and then mails it to the nearest local Employment Service Office. That agency will send back to the employer a certificate which validates the tax credit, and which the employer uses when filing Federal tax forms.

For additional information on TJTC, contact the local State-Federal Vocational Rehabilitation Agency of the local Employment Service Office.

Appendix J

REFERENCE PUBLICATIONS

ADA Compliance Guide, August 1990, Thompson Publishing Group, Washington, DC.

ADA Compliance Guidebook: A Checklist for Your Building, September 1991, Building Owners and Managers Associaton International, Washington, DC.

ADA Searchware (computerized version of the law with search, cross-indexing and clipboard functions), 1992, AIA Press, Washington, DC.

American National Standards Institute 1992 Catalog, New York, NY.

Better Homes and Gardens, April 1992, "Health" section, Amy Roffman New and Norman Brown, Meredith Publishing, Des Moines, IA.

Business Interiors, November/December 1990, Group C Communications, Red Bank, NJ.

Career Development Guide October 1991, CRS Recruitment Publications, Santa Ana, CA.

Carpal Tunnel Syndrome, Selected References, March 1991, U.S. Dept. of Health and Human Services, Public Health Service, Centers for Disease Control, National Institute for Occupational Safety and Health, Cincinnati, OH.

Commonwealth of Massachusetts, Division of Capital Planning & Operations Office of Lease Management – Request for Proposals (RFP), March 19, 1991, Ref. # 910280.1.

Cost Engineering, March 1992, Volume 34, No. 3, "The Effect of the ADA on the Construction Industry," Gregory Hurley, The American Association of Cost Engineers, Morgantown, WV.

Dateline: CDC, September 1988, Volume 21, No. 7, Center for Disease Control.

Design for Aging: An Architect's Guide, 1985, The American Institute of Architects, The AIA Press, Washington, DC.

Design for Dignity: Studies in Accessibility, William L. Lebovich, 1993, John Wiley & Sons, Inc.

Disability Rights Guide, 1991, Charles D. Goldman, Esq., Media Publishing, Lincoln, NB.

Exterior Home Improvement Costs, 1994, R.S. Means Company, Inc., Kingston, MA.

Health Care Architecture, edited by Lynn Nesmith, 1994, AIA Press, Washington, DC.

Interior Home Improvement Costs, 1994, R.S. Means Company, Inc., Kingston, MA.

IFMA News, March 1992, Codes and Regulations Report, ISSN 0747-6221, Houston, TX.

Independent Living, March 1992, Equal Opportunity Publications, Inc., Greenlawn, NY.

Making Your Home Accessible, April 1988, Paralyzed Veterans Administration, Washington, DC.

Manager's Guide to Workplace Ergonomics, Deborah J. Moore, 1991, Business & Legal Reports, Inc., Madison, CT.

Means ADA Compliance Pricing Guide, 1994, R.S. Means Company, Inc., Kingston, MA.

Pain and Disability, Institute of Medicine, 1987, National Academy Press, Washington, DC.

President's Committee on Employment of People with Disabilities. "Tax Incentive," The Disabled Access Credit Report, Washington, DC.

Rehab Management, The Journal of Therapy and Rehabilitation, June/July 1991, Allied Health Care Publications, Los Angeles, CA.

Spinal Network, 1987 – 1989, Sam Maddox (publisher and author), Boulder, CO.

Standardizing Colors for Computer Screens, Proceedings for the Human Factors Society – 32nd Meeting, 1988, Wanda Smith, Palo Alto, CA.

Technology for Independent Living Sourcebook, 1984, Association for the Advancement of Rehabilitation Technology, Alexandra Enders, O.T.R., Editor, Washington, DC.

The Americans with Disabilities Act, U.S. Department of Justice, Washington, DC, Civil Rights Division/Coordination and Review Section pamphlet, GPO: 1990-272-170.

The Americans with Disabilities Act/Questions and Answers, U.S. Equal Employment Opportunity Commission, U.S. Department of Justice/Civil Rights Division, Washington, DC, July 1991.

Today's Facility Manager, March/April 1992, "Signage Update," Group C Communications, Red Bank, NJ.

Appendix K

ADA TELEPHONE INFORMATION SERVICES

U.S. Department of Justice
Civil Rights Division
Disability Rights Section

ADA TELEPHONE INFORMATION SERVICES

This list contains the telephone numbers of federal agencies and other organizations that provide information about the **Americans with Disabilities Act (ADA)** and informal guidance in understanding and complying with the ADA. These agencies and organizations are not, and should not be viewed as, sources for obtaining legal advice or legal opinions about your rights or responsibilities under the ADA.

<u>Department of Justice</u> offers technical assistance to the public concerning title II and title III of the ADA.

ADA documents and questions	800-514-0301 (voice)	800-514-0383 (TDD)
Within Washington, D.C.	202-514-0301 (voice)	202-514-0383 (TDD)
Electronic bulletin board	202-514-6193	

<u>Equal Employment Opportunity Commission</u> offers technical assistance concerning title I of the ADA.

ADA documents	800-669-3362 (voice)	800-800-3302 (TDD)
ADA questions	800-669-4000 (voice)	800-669-6820 (TDD)

<u>U.S. Department of Transportation</u> offers technical assistance concerning the public transportation provisions of title II and title III of the ADA.

ADA documents and general questions	202-366-1656 (voice)	202-366-4567 (TDD)
ADA legal questions	202-366-1936 (voice)	202-366-0748 (TDD)
Complaints and enforcement	202-366-2285 (voice)	202-366-0153 (TDD)
Electronic bulletin board	202-366-3764	
National Easter Seal Society "Project Action"	202-347-3066 (voice)	202-347-7385 (TDD)
"Rural Transportation Assistance Program"	800-527-8279 (voice & TDD)	

<u>Federal Communications Commission</u> offers technical assistance concerning title IV of the ADA.

ADA documents and general questions	202-418-0190 (voice)	202-418-2555 (TDD)
ADA legal questions	202-634-1808 (voice)	202-632-0484 (TDD)
Complaints and enforcement	202-632-7553 (voice)	202-632-0485 (TDD)

<u>U.S. Architectural and Transportation Barriers Compliance Board</u>, or "<u>Access Board</u>," offers technical assistance on the ADA Accessibility Guidelines.

ADA documents and questions	800-872-2253 (voice)	800-993-2822 (TDD)
Within Washington, D.C.	202-272-5434 (voice)	202-272-5449 (TDD)
Electronic bulletin board	202-272-5448	

<u>National Institute on Disability and Rehabilitation Research</u> has funded centers throughout the country to provide technical assistance concerning title I, title II, and title III of the ADA.

ADA technical assistance nationwide	800-949-4232 (voice & TDD)

President's Committee on Employment of People with Disabilities provides information on all titles of the ADA and funds the Job Accommodation Network (JAN), which provides information on the ADA and reasonable accommodation in the workplace.

ADA information	202-376-6200 (voice) 202-376-6205 (TDD)
Job Accommodation Network	800-526-7234 (voice & TDD)
	800-232-9675 (voice & TDD)

Disability Rights Education and Defense Fund provides technical assistance on all titles of the ADA.

ADA technical assistance	800-466-4232 (voice & TDD)

The Foundation on Employment and Disability provides assistance in Spanish, Korean, Cambodian, Vietnamese, Mandarin and Cantonese Chinese, Tagalog, Hindi, Arabic, Armenian, Russian, and Dine.

ADA specialized technical assistance	800-232-4955 (voice) 800-232-4957 (TDD)

OTHER FEDERAL LAWS

The U.S. Congress has established tax credits and deductions that may assist businesses in complying with the ADA. The Internal Revenue Service can provide information about these tax code provisions.

Tax code information	800-829-1040 (voice) 800-829-4059 (TDD)
To order Publication 907	800-829-3676 (voice) 800-829-4059 (TDD)
Within Washington, D.C.	202-622-3110 (voice) TDD: use relay service

U.S. Department of Housing and Urban Development provides technical assistance concerning the accessibility standards that apply to **residential facilities** under the Fair Housing Act Amendments.

Fair Housing Act Amendments	800-795-7915 (voice) 800-927-9275 (TDD)

U.S. Department of Transportation provides technical assistance concerning the accessibility standards that apply to **air transportation** under the Air Carrier Access Act (ACAA).

ACAA technical assistance	202-366-4859 (voice) TDD: use relay service
ACAA complaints and enforcement	202-267-5794 (voice) 202-267-9730 (TDD)

Federal Communications Commission provides technical assistance concerning the accessibility standards that apply to **telephones** under the Hearing Aid Compatibility Act.

Hearing Aid Compatibility Act	202-634-1808 (voice) 202-632-0484 (TDD)

U.S. Department of Labor, Office of Federal Contract Compliance Programs provides technical assistance concerning the accessibility standards that apply to **federal contractors**.

Section 503 of the Rehabilitation Act	202-219-9428 (voice) 800-326-2577 (TDD)

3/95

Appendix L

COMMUNICATIONS GUIDELINES

Now That We've Met, What Do I Say?

Outdated or Offensive	Reason	Currently Accepted
"The" anything, e.g., *the* handicapped. *the* disabled, *the* blind.	Views people in terms of their disability; groups people into one undifferentiated category; condescending.	People with disabilities. Deaf people. Blind people.
Deaf and dumb, dumb, deaf-mute.	Implies mental incapacitation.	Deaf. Hearing-impaired. Speech-impaired.
Confined to a wheelchair; wheelchair-bound.	Wheelchairs don't confine; they make people mobile.	Wheelchair-user. Uses a wheelchair.
Cripple, crippled.	From Old English: *to creep* implies inferiority Dehumanizing.	Physical disability.
Handicapped.	Disabilities don't handicap; attitudes and architecture handicap.	Physical disability.
Deformed, freak, vegetable.	Connotes repulsiveness, oddness. Dehumanizing.	Multiple disabilities, severe disabilities.
Crazy, insane, psycho, maniac.	Stigmatizing.	Behavior disorder. Emotional disability.

Outdated or Offensive	Reason	Currently Accepted
Retarded, retardate, slow, simple, moron, idiot, mongoloid(ism).	Stigmatizing.	People with mental retardation. Developmentally delayed. Has Down's Syndrome.

General Guidelines

1. See the person who has a disability as a person, not as a disability.
2. Do not "talk down" to disabled people. Avoid responding to a person's disabilities out of "gratefulness" for not having a disability yourself.
3. Speak directly to the person who has a disability, not to a companion or an interpreter.
4. Treat adults as adults. Do not use first names unless that familiarity is extended to everyone present.
5. Be considerate. It might take extra time for the person with a disability to say or do things.
6. Relax. Don't worry about using common expressions like "see you later," or "I've got to be running along" when talking to persons with physical or visual disabilities.

Communicating with Persons Who Use Wheelchairs or Crutches

1. Don't lean or hang on a person's wheelchair. It is part of that person's body space.
2. Sit, squat, or kneel if conversation continues for more than a few minutes. Don't be a "pain in the neck."
3. Ask a wheelchair occupant if he or she wants to be pushed *before* you do so.
4. Allow a person who uses a wheelchair or crutches to keep them within reach. Many wheelchair users can transfer to chairs, car seats, etc. Some wheelchair users can walk with crutches part of the time.
5. Consider distance, weather conditions, and surfaces such as stairs, curbs, or inclines when giving directions.

Recommended Books, Films, and Videos

The following materials are available through many local public libraries.

"Who Are the DeBolts?" (16mm film)
Academy Award-winning documentary about the DeBolt family and their nineteen children, all but five of whom have multiple disabilities.

Move Over, Wheelchairs Coming Through! by Ronald Roy (Nonfiction)
Takes a brief look into the lives of seven young people who use wheelchairs. Includes photographs, index, and bibliography of related reading. For ages 8-13. Published in 1985 by Clarion. No longer in print.

Communicating with Persons Who Have Vision Loss

1. Introduce yourself and any others who may be with you. Use a normal tone of voice.
2. Use the person's name when starting conversation so they know you are speaking to them. Let the person know when you are ending a conversation or moving away.

3. Ask the person if he or she wants help. When giving assistance, allow the person to take your arm, which helps you to guide. Warn the person of any steps or changes in level. Use specifics, such as *left* and *right*.

4. Offer seating by placing the person's hand on the back or arm of the seat.

5. Don't pet a guide dog. Remember to walk on the side of the person away from the dog.

Recommended Books, Films and Videos
The following materials are available through local public libraries.

"Finding My Way" (Videocassette)
Produced for WGBH-TV, Boston. Focuses on a boy who is blind, but learning to become independent in his neighborhood and school. For juvenile and young adult viewers.

The Miracle Worker by William Gibson (Play)
A play in three acts based on the life of the young Helen Keller and her teacher, Anne Sullivan.

Annerton Pit by Peter Dickinson (Fiction)
The author has created a ghost story and psychological thriller through the senses of Jake, a boy who is blind. For young adult readers.

Communicating with Persons Who Have Hearing Loss

1. Get the person's attention. Wave your hand, tap the person's shoulder, or bang on the table, if necessary.

2. Speak clearly and slowly. Don't shout or exaggerate lip movements. Keep sentences short.

3. Be flexible in your language. If the person has difficulty understanding you, rephrase your statement using simpler words. Don't keep repeating. If difficulty persists, write it down.

4. Provide a clear view of your face and keep the light source on it. Keep hands, food, etc. away from your mouth when talking.

5. Be a lively speaker. Use facial expressions that match your tone of voice, and use gestures and body movements to aid communication.

Recommended Books, Films, and Videos
The following materials are available through local public libraries.

"Across the Silence Barrier" (16mm film)
Explores the world of deaf people. Part of the NOVA series.

Deaf Like Me by Thomas Spradley and James Spradley (Nonfiction)
True story about a family's struggle to raise their deaf daughter.

The Hunchback of Notre Dame by Victor Hugo (Fiction)
Classic story of a man whose multiple disabilities, not the least of which is his deafness, make him a target for inhumane treatment.

A Button in Her Ear by Ada Litchfield
(Fiction) Illustrated, unsentimental story about a girl who needs a hearing aid. For ages 6-8.

Communicating with Persons Who Have Speech Difficulties

1. Give your complete attention to the person who has difficulty speaking.

2. Be patient. Don't correct and don't speak for the person. Allow extra time. Give help when needed.

3. Maintain an encouraging manner.

4. Ask questions that require short answers or a nod or shake of the head, when necessary.

5. If you have difficulty understanding, don't pretend. Repeat as much as you understand. The person's reaction will clue you in.

Recommended Books, Films, and Videos

The following materials are available through local public libraries and or video rental stores.

"My Left Foot" (Videocassette)
Autobiographical story about Christy Brown, Irish painter and writer, who was born with cerebral palsy. Brown emerges as a wholly realized person. Won Academy Awards in 1990 for Best Actor and Best Supporting Actress.

The Painted Bird by Jerzy Kosinski (Fiction)
Confronted with extreme irrationality and brutality, a six-year-old boy in German-occupied Poland during World War II elects to become mute.

The Night of the Bozos by Jan Slepian (Fiction)
Story about a young man who stutters and his thirteen-year-old nephew who is reclusive. Together they leave their self-imposed isolation for the possibilities of relationships in the real world. For young adult readers.

Communicating With Persons Who Have Mental Retardation

1. Speak slowly and distinctly. *Show* might be more effective than *tell*.

2. Tell the person what to do, *not* what not to do.

3. Help the person feel comfortable. Maintain nonthreatening voice and facial expressions.

4. Treat the adult person who has mental retardation as an adult.

5. Base exceptions to rules on reason, not pity.

Recommended Books, Films, and Videos

The following materials are available through local public libraries.

"Clockworks" (16mm film)
Short story about a boy with Down's syndrome. All the actors are amateurs; the boy who plays the lead actually has Down's syndrome.

The Alfred Summer by Jan Slepian (Fiction)
The setting is Brooklyn in the 1930s. The major characters, who have various physical and emotional disabilities, learn and grow within realistic expectations. For young adult readers.

Note: Guidelines in Appendix L are based on recommendations from the Easter Seals Society.

Appendix M

ADA MODIFICATIONS COST DATA

The cost data in this appendix has been divided into 16 Divisions according to the MASTERFORMAT system as developed by the Construction Specifications Institute. Items presented include material and installation costs, as well as estimated man-hours for installation, where applicable. Prices are 1993 national averages, and are based on union labor rates. The following is a detailed explanation of a sample unit price entry.

Description
The definition of each item; sub-items and additional sizes are indented beneath some line items. The first line or two after the main item (in boldface) may contain descriptive information that pertains to all items beneath this boldface listing.

Unit
The abbreviated designation indicates the unit of measure (e.g., "each" or "s.f.") upon which the price and installation time are based.

Man-hours
The estimated time required to install one unit of work.

Material Cost
This figure represents the "bare" cost of material, that is with no overhead and profit allowances. *Note: Costs shown reflect national average prices for January 1993. No sales taxes are included.*

Total Cost
This figure includes the price of materials (without sales tax), labor and equipment, including the installing contractor's overhead expenses and profit. *Note the minimum quantities used in pricing these items. Costs for smaller, fewer, or specialized installations may be higher.*

Refer to the end of each "Factor" chapter (Part IV) for lists of related items and costs. See Appendix M for a list of compliance product manufacturers with addresses and available 800 numbers.

Note: Complete listings of general construction costs can be found in Means Repair and Remodeling Cost Data, Means Building Construction Cost Data, Means Facilities Cost Data, and other Means specialized cost books.

DESCRIPTION	UNIT	MAN-HOURS	COST MAT.	COST TOTAL

Division 1: General Requirements

DESCRIPTION	UNIT	MAN-HOURS	COST MAT.	COST TOTAL
TESTING				
Air quality survey with air sampling and testing	Day	1.000		$630.00

Division 2: Site Work

DESCRIPTION	UNIT	MAN-HOURS	COST MAT.	COST TOTAL
PAVEMENT MARKING				
Handicap parking stall	Ea.	0.168	$2.15	$8.79
Handicap symbol, 1 to 3	Ea.	0.500	$3.00	$42.00
4 and over	Ea.	0.333	$2.75	$26.00
Minimum labor / equipment charge	Job	3.000		$120.00
CURB RAMP				
Retro-fit, 6" high sidewalk, including cutting and demolition of				
existing sidewalk, and installation of new reinforced concrete ramp	Ea.	12.000	$69.89	$958.00
3" high sidewalk	Ea.	10.000	$46.59	$847.00
Bituminous ramp at curb, no cutting	Ea.	4.000	$25.00	$210.00

Division 3: Concrete

DESCRIPTION	UNIT	MAN-HOURS	COST MAT.	COST TOTAL
CONCRETE ACCESS RAMP				
4' wide, 35' long, 30" rise, including excavation, crushed stone base,				
forms, reinforcing, gravel fill, finishing, backfill, fabricate				
sleeves for pipe rails, and steel railing	Ea.	88.222	$2,730.00	$9,883.00
4' wide, 70' long, 60" rise, with one landing or turnabout	Ea.	140.500	$5,670.00	$19,047.00

Division 5: Metals

DESCRIPTION	UNIT	MAN-HOURS	COST MAT.	COST TOTAL
RAILING, PIPE				
Aluminum, 2 rail, 1-1/4" diam., satin finish	L.F.	0.200	$10.25	$22.50
Clear anodized	L.F.	0.200	$12.75	$25.00
Dark anodized	L.F.	0.200	$14.40	$27.00
1-1/2" diameter, satin finish	L.F.	0.200	$12.35	$25.00
Clear anodized	L.F.	0.200	$13.75	$26.50
Dark anodized	L.F.	0.200	$15.30	$28.00
Aluminum, 3 rail, 1-1/4" diam., satin finish	L.F.	0.234	$15.80	$30.50
Clear anodized	L.F.	0.234	$19.75	$34.50
Dark anodized	L.F.	0.234	$22.00	$37.00
1-1/2" diameter, satin finish	L.F.	0.234	$19.20	$34.00
Clear anodized	L.F.	0.234	$21.50	$36.50
Dark anodized	L.F.	0.234	$23.50	$39.00
Steel, 2 rail, primed, 1-1/4" diameter	L.F.	0.200	$7.65	$19.60
1-1/2" diameter	L.F.	0.200	$8.40	$20.50
Galvanized, 1-1/4" diameter	L.F.	0.200	$10.60	$23.00
1-1/2" diameter	L.F.	0.200	$11.85	$24.00
Steel, 3 rail, primed, 1-1/4" diameter	L.F.	0.234	$11.35	$25.50
1-1/2" diameter	L.F.	0.234	$12.10	$26.50

DESCRIPTION	UNIT	MAN-HOURS	COST MAT.	TOTAL
Galvanized, 1-1/4" diameter	L.F.	0.234	$15.95	$30.50
1-1/2" diameter	L.F.	0.234	$17.30	$32.00
Minimum labor / equipment charge	Job	8.000		$360.00
Wall rail, alum. pipe, 1-1/4" diam., satin finish	L.F.	0.150	$5.90	$14.60
Clear anodized	L.F.	0.150	$7.20	$16.00
Dark anodized	L.F.	0.150	$8.70	$17.65
1-1/2" diameter, satin finish	L.F.	0.150	$6.50	$15.25
Clear anodized	L.F.	0.150	$8.20	$17.10
Dark anodized	L.F.	0.150	$10.15	$19.25
Steel pipe, 1-1/4" diameter, primed	L.F.	0.150	$4.50	$13.05
Galvanized	L.F.	0.150	$6.50	$15.25
1-1/2" diameter, primed	L.F.	0.150	$4.75	$13.30
Galvanized	L.F.	0.150	$6.75	$15.55
Stainless steel pipe, 1-1/2" diam., #4 finish	L.F.	0.299	$19.95	$38.00
High polish	L.F.	0.299	$40.00	$60.00
Mirror polish	L.F.	0.299	$48.00	$69.50
Minimum labor / equipment charge	Job	8.000		$360.00
STEEL ACCESS RAMP				
4' wide, 35' long, 30" rise, including excavation, crushed stone base,				
metal decking, structural steel, anchor bolts, forms, concrete slab,				
backfill, steel pipe railings	Ea.	72.000	$3,253.00	$8,060.00

Division 6: Wood & Plastics

DESCRIPTION	UNIT	MAN-HOURS	COST MAT.	TOTAL
WOOD ACCESS RAMP				
5' wide, 35' long, 30" rise, including excavation of post holes,				
concrete post footings, 4" x 4" posts, 2" x 10" joists, 2" x 6"				
decking, steel pipe railing	Ea.	55.000	$935.00	$4,176.50
4' wide, 70' long, 60" rise, with one landing or turnabout	Ea.	102.000	$2,010.00	$8,671.00

Division 7: Thermal and Moisture Protection

DESCRIPTION	UNIT	MAN-HOURS	COST MAT.	TOTAL
SKYLIGHT				
Plastic roof domes, flush or curb mounted,				
curb not included, "L" frames, 30" x 18"	Ea.	12.000	$176.00	$716.00
26" x 46"	Ea.	16.000	$330.00	$1,050.00
38" x 54"	Ea.	16.000	$671.00	$1,391.00
26" x 68"	Ea.	16.000	$577.00	$1,297.00
Ventilating insulated plexiglass dome with				
curb mounting, 36" x 36"	Ea.	16.000	$398.00	$1,143.00
52" x 52"	Ea.	16.500	$830.00	$1,575.00
28" x 52"	Ea.	16.000	$447.00	$1,192.00
36" x 52"	Ea.	16.000	$575.00	$1,320.00
For electric opening system, add	Ea.		$498.00	$657.36

Division 8: Doors and Windows

DESCRIPTION	UNIT	MAN-HOURS	COST MAT.	COST TOTAL
WIDEN EXISTING DOOR OPENING FOR 36" METAL DOOR				
Exterior, masonry veneer wall	Ea.	20.000	$583.00	$2,179.00
Interior, gypsum board on metal studs	Ea.	10.000	$470.00	$1,093.00
Gypsum board on CMU	Ea.	14.000	$480.00	$1,110.00
COMMERCIAL STEEL DOORS				
Flush, full panel, including steel frame and butts				
Hollow core, 1-3/8" thick, 20 ga., 3'-0" x 6'-8"	Ea.	1.941	$269.50	$352.00
Half glass, 20 ga., 3'-0" x 6'-8"	Ea.	1.941	$320.38	$403.25
Hollow core, 1-3/4" thick, full panel, 20 ga., 3'-0" x 6'-8"	Ea.	1.941	$282.98	$366.25
Insulated, 1-3/4" thick, full panel, 18 ga., 3'-0" x 6'-8"	Ea.	2.067	$329.18	$417.25
Half glass, 18 ga., 3'-0" x 6'-8"	Ea.	2.000	$380.88	$464.25
Minimum labor / equipment charge	Job	4.000		$180.00
WOOD DOOR, ARCHITECTURAL				
Flush, 5 ply particle core, including frame and butts, lauan face				
3'-0" x 6'-8"	Ea.	2.003	$161.00	$252.25
Birch face, 3'-0" x 6'-8"	Ea.	2.003	$156.00	$247.50
Oak face, 3'-0" x 6'-8"	Ea.	2.003	$187.00	$283.00
Minimum labor / equipment charge	Job	4.000		$180.00
SOUND RETARDENT DOORS				
Acoustical, including framed seals, 3' x 7', wood, 27 STC rating	Ea.	10.667	$510.00	$1,025.00
LOCKSET				
Standard duty, cylindrical, with sectional trim				
Lever handle, non-keyed, passage	Ea.	0.667	$98.50	$138.00
Privacy	Ea.	0.667	$105.00	$145.50
Keyed	Ea.	0.800	$128.50	$177.00
Residential, interior door, lever handle, minimum	Ea.	0.500	$20.00	$44.50
Maximum	Ea.	1.000	$53.00	$103.00
Exterior, minimum	Ea.	0.571	$29.00	$58.00
Maximum	Ea.	1.000	$150.00	$210.00
For tactile handles add	Ea.			$21.00
Minimum labor / equipment charge	Job	2.500		$112.50
MORTISE LOCKSET				
Commercial, wrought knobs & full escutcheon trim				
Passage, lever handle, minimum	Ea.	0.889	$147.00	$202.00
Maximum	Ea.	1.000	$250.00	$320.00
Privacy, lever handle, minimum	Ea.	0.889	$163.00	$220.00
Maximum	Ea.	1.000	$265.00	$336.50
Keyed, lever handle, minimum	Ea.	1.000	$189.00	$253.00
Maximum	Ea.	1.143	$307.00	$389.00
For tactile handles add	Ea.			$21.00
Non-touch electronic key reader	Ea.	2.667	$799.00	$998.00
Adapted lever handle, bolt-on	Ea.	0.125	$25.00	$33.00
Minimum labor / equipment charge	Job	2.500		$112.50
WINDOWS				
Casement, including accessible handles				
Vinyl-clad, premium, insulating glass, 2'-0" x 3'-0"	Ea.	5.200	$228.00	$550.00
2'-0" x 4'-0"	Ea.	5.700	$250.00	$604.00
2'-0" x 6'-0"	Ea.	6.500	$324.00	$740.00
Solid vinyl, premium, insulating glass, 2'-0" x 3'-0"	Ea.	5.200	$235.70	$560.00
2'-0" x 5'-0"	Ea.	6.500	$283.25	$686.00
SPECIAL HINGES				
Swing clear hinges, full mortise, average frequency, steel base 4.5" high	Pr.		$72.00	$79.00
AUTOMATIC OPENERS				
Swing doors, single, motion-activated	Ea.	20.000	$2,000.00	$3,000.00
Handicap opener, button-operated	Ea.	2.000	$1,025.00	$1,200.00

Division 9: Finishes

DESCRIPTION	UNIT	MAN-HOURS	COST MAT.	COST TOTAL
ACOUSTICAL CEILINGS				
Suspended ceilings, complete, including standard suspension system				
mineral fiber, cement binder, T bar susp., 2' x 2' x 3/4" board	S.F.	0.023	$1.33	$2.37
2' x 4' x 3/4" board	S.F.	0.021	$1.18	$2.12
Minimum labor / equipment charge	Job	4.000		$180.00
RESILIENT TILE FLOORING				
Rubber tile, raised, radial or square, minimum	S.F.	0.020	$4.55	$5.80
Maximum	S.F.	0.020	$5.40	$6.75
Minimum labor / equipment charge	Job	4.000		$180.00
CARPET				
Commercial grades, direct cement				
Nylon, level loop, 26 oz., light to medium traffic	S.Y.	0.140	$12.95	$19.70
32 oz., medium traffic	S.Y.	0.140	$15.10	$22.00
40 oz., medium to heavy traffic	S.Y.	0.140	$19.10	$26.50
Olefin, 26 oz., medium traffic	S.Y.	0.140	$7.10	$13.25
32 oz., medium to heavy traffic	S.Y.	0.140	$9.80	$16.20
42 oz., heavy traffic	S.Y.	0.140	$14.45	$22.50
Wool, 40 oz., medium traffic, level loop	S.Y.	0.140	$24.50	$32.50
50 oz., medium to heavy traffic, level loop	S.Y.	0.140	$33.50	$42.50
Minimum labor / equipment charge	Job	4.000		$180.00
PAINTING				
Walls and ceilings, including protection of adjacent items not painted				
Concrete, dry wall or plaster, oil base, primer or sealer coat				
Smooth finish, brushwork	S.F.	0.006	$0.04	$0.27
Roller	S.F.	0.004	$0.04	$0.19
Sand finish, brushwork	S.F.	0.007	$0.07	$0.34
Roller	S.F.	0.005	$0.07	$0.25
Spray	S.F.	0.003	$0.05	$0.17
Paint 2 coats, smooth finish, brushwork	S.F.	0.012	$0.08	$0.53
Roller	S.F.	0.007	$0.07	$0.33
Spray	S.F.	0.005	$0.08	$0.26
Less than 600 S.F., roller	S.F.	0.011	$0.11	$0.47
Sand finish, brushwork	S.F.	0.013	$0.11	$0.61
Roller	S.F.	0.008	$0.10	$0.40
Spray	S.F.	0.005	$0.09	$0.27
Minimum labor / equipment charge	Job	2.500		$112.50

Division 10: Specialties

DESCRIPTION	UNIT	MAN-HOURS	COST MAT.	COST TOTAL
PARTITIONS, TOILET				
Cubicles, handicap unit incl. 52" grab bars, ceiling-hung, marble	Ea.	9.000	$1,272.00	$1,714.00
Painted metal	Ea.	5.000	$522.00	$739.00
Plastic laminate on particle board	Ea.	5.000	$652.00	$884.00
Porcelain enamel	Ea.	5.000	$887.00	$1,139.00
Stainless steel	Ea.	5.000	$1,032.00	$1,314.00
Floor & ceiling anchored, marble	Ea.	7.400	$1,372.00	$1,789.00
Painted metal	Ea.	4.200	$527.00	$719.00
Plastic laminate on particle board	Ea.	4.200	$657.00	$859.00
Porcelain enamel	Ea.	4.200	$907.00	$1,134.00
Stainless steel	Ea.	4.200	$1,172.00	$1,414.00
Floor-mounted, marble	Ea.	6.333	$882.00	$1,189.00

DESCRIPTION	UNIT	MAN-HOURS	COST MAT.	COST TOTAL
Painted metal	Ea.	3.286	$492.00	$634.00
Plastic laminate on particle board	Ea.	3.286	$622.00	$779.00
Porcelain enamel	Ea.	3.286	$887.00	$1,069.00
Stainless steel	Ea.	3.286	$1,142.00	$1,364.00
Floor-mounted, headrail braced, marble	Ea.	6.333	$997.00	$1,314.00
Painted metal	Ea.	3.667	$502.00	$664.00
Plastic laminate on particle board	Ea.	3.667	$617.00	$789.00
Porcelain enamel	Ea.	3.667	$897.00	$1,100.00
Stainless steel	Ea.	3.667	$1,152.00	$1,364.00
Wall-hung partitions, painted metal	Ea.	3.286	$577.00	$729.00
Porcelain enamel	Ea.	3.286	$902.00	$1,089.00
Stainless steel	Ea.	3.286	$1,137.00	$1,339.00
Minimum labor / equipment charge	Job	5.000		$225.00
CORNER GUARDS				
Steel angle w/anchors, 1" x 1" x 1/4", 1.5#/L.F.	L.F.	0.100	$3.15	$9.05
2" x 2" x 1/4" angles, 3.2#/L.F.	L.F.	0.107	$5.20	$11.65
3" x 3" x 5/16" angles, 6.1#/L.F.	L.F.	0.116	$6.10	$13.20
4" x 4" x 5/16" angles, 8.2#/L.F.	L.F.	0.133	$7.90	$16.15
For angles drilled and anchored to masonry, add	L.F.		15%	
Drilled and anchored to concrete, add	L.F.		20%	
For galvanized angles, add	L.F.		35%	
For stainless steel angles, add	L.F.		100%	
Minimum labor / equipment charge	Job	2.500		$112.50
FIRE EXTINGUISHERS				
C02, portable with swivel horn, 5 lb.	Ea.		$96.00	$106.00
With hose and "H" horn, 10 lb.	Ea.		$145.00	$160.00
15 lb.	Ea.		$167.00	$184.00
20 lb.	Ea.		$202.00	$222.00
Dry chemical, pressurized	Ea.			
Standard type, portable, painted, 2-1/2 lb.	Ea.		$21.00	$23.00
5 lb.	Ea.		$38.00	$42.00
10 lb.	Ea.		$50.00	$55.00
20 lb.	Ea.		$80.00	$88.00
ABC all purpose type, portable, 2-1/2 lb.	Ea.		$21.00	$23.00
5 lb.	Ea.		$37.00	$40.50
9-1/2 lb.	Ea.		$58.00	$64.00
20 lb.	Ea.		$80.00	$88.00
Pressurized water, 2-1/2 gallon, stainless steel	Ea.		$71.00	$78.00
With anti-freeze	Ea.		$100.00	$110.00
CANOPIES	Ea.			
Canvas awning, half round, 4' wide, 20' long	Ea.	14.000	$1,450.00	$2,080.00
40' long	Ea.	28.000	$2,900.00	$4,160.00
For clear plastic side curtains add	L.F.	0.125	$27.50	$33.10
BATHROOM ACCESSORIES				
Grab bar, straight, 1-1/4" diameter, stainless steel, 18" long	Ea.	0.333	$25.00	$41.50
24" long	Ea.	0.348	$28.00	$45.50
30" long	Ea.	0.364	$36.00	$54.50
36" long	Ea.	0.400	$39.50	$60.00
40" long	Ea.	0.420	$47.50	$67.25
1-1/2" diameter, 24" long	Ea.	0.348	$29.00	$46.50
36" long	Ea.	0.400	$36.00	$56.00
Tub bar, 1-1/4" diameter, 24" x 36"	Ea.	0.571	$74.50	$106.00
Plus vertical arm	Ea.	0.667	$65.00	$99.50
End tub bar, 1" diameter, 90 degree angle, 16" x 32"	Ea.	0.667	$53.00	$86.50
Minimum labor / equipment charge	Job	2.500		$112.50
Tilt mirror, stainless steel frame, 16" x 30"	Ea.	0.400	$79.50	$97.50
Adjustable tilt	Ea.	0.400	$57.00	$75.00

DESCRIPTION	UNIT	MAN-HOURS	COST MAT.	COST TOTAL
Minimum labor / equipment charge	Job	2.500		$112.50
Shower seat, retractable, steel tube frame, wooden seat	Ea.	1.000	$402.00	$487.00
Minimum labor / equipment charge	Job	2.500		$112.50
MIRRORS				
Hallway corner mirror, acrylic, full dome, 18" diameter	Ea.			$69.37
36" diameter	Ea.			$170.21
Half dome, 18" diameter	Ea.			$40.95
36" diameter	Ea.			$98.70
Minimum labor / equipment charge	Job	2.000		$90.00
PARTITIONS, PORTABLE				
Divider panels, free standing, fiber core, fabric face, straight				
3'-0" long, 4'-0" high	L.F.	0.160	$95.00	$112.00
5'-0" high	L.F.	0.178	$101.00	$118.00
6'-0" high	L.F.	0.213	$120.00	$141.00
5'-0" long, 4'-0" high	L.F.	0.091	$71.00	$82.00
5'-0" high	L.F.	0.107	$75.00	$87.00
6'-0" high	L.F.	0.128	$84.00	$98.00
6'-0" long, 5'-0" high	L.F.	0.099	$72.00	$83.00
3'-0" curved, 5'-0" high	L.F.	0.178	$128.00	$148.00
6'-0" high	L.F.	0.213	$140.00	$163.00
Economical panels, fabric face, 4'-0" long, 5'-0" high	L.F.	0.121	$74.00	$86.50
6'-0" high	L.F.	0.143	$84.00	$98.50
5'-0" long, 5'-0" high	L.F.	0.107	$68.00	$79.50
6'-0" high	L.F.	0.128	$76.00	$89.00
3'-0" curved, 5'-0" high	L.F.	0.178	$113.00	$131.00
6'-0" high	L.F.	0.213	$127.00	$149.00
Acoustical panels, 60 to 90 NRC, 3'-0" long, 5'-0" high	L.F.	0.178	$115.00	$134.00
6'-0" high	L.F.	0.213	$140.00	$163.00
5'-0" long, 5'-0" high	L.F.	0.107	$90.00	$103.00
6'-0" high	L.F.	0.128	$101.00	$116.00
6'-0" long, 5'-0" high	L.F.	0.099	$95.50	$109.00
6'-0" high	L.F.	0.116	$114.00	$130.00
Economy acoustical panels, 40 NRC, 4'-0" long, 5'-0" high	L.F.	0.121	$53.00	$63.50
6'-0" high ı	L.F.	0.143	$62.50	$75.00
5'-0" long, 6'-0" high	L.F.	0.128	$56.50	$67.50
6'-0" long, 5'-0" high	L.F.	0.099	$56.50	$67.50
Minimum labor / equipment charge	Job	6.000		$270.00
SIGNAGE				
ADA-recommended pictograms (8" x 9"), minimum	Ea.			$28.30
Maximum	Ea.			$32.34
Aluminum access parking signs (12" x 18")	Ea.			$26.25
10' high upright on 2" post in concrete	Ea.	2.500	$35.00	$147.50
Elevator braille plates, minimum	Ea.			$5.78
Maximum	Ea.			$15.02
English/ Spanish symbol signs (3" x 9"), minimum	Ea.			$6.93
Maximum	Ea.			$10.40
English/ Spanish symbol signs (9" x 6"), minimum	Ea.			$10.40
Maximum	Ea.			$14.44
Engraved signs for indoors (6" x 6"), minimum	Ea.			$17.33
Maximum	Ea.			$34.65
Entrance door decals (4" x 4"), minimum	Ea.			$4.04
Maximum	Ea.			$23.10
Hi-Mark tactile material	Ea.			$4.62
Plastic braille & tactile nameplates (10" x 2"), minimum	Ea.			$17.90
Maximum	Ea.			$21.89

Division 12: Furnishings

DESCRIPTION	UNIT	MAN-HOURS	COST MAT.	COST TOTAL
BLINDS, INTERIOR				
Horizontal, 5/8" aluminum slats, custom, minimum	S.F.	0.014	$2.60	$3.49
Maximum	S.F.	0.018	$7.38	$8.93
1" aluminum slats, custom, minimum	S.F.	0.014	$2.28	$3.08
Maximum	S.F.	0.018	$6.65	$8.05
2" aluminum slats, custom, minimum	S.F.	0.014	$3.37	$4.28
Maximum	S.F.	0.018	$5.60	$6.90
Stock, minimum	S.F.	0.014	$2.19	$2.98
Maximum	S.F.	0.018	$4.39	$5.60
2" steel slats, stock, minimum	S.F.	0.014	$1.12	$1.80
Maximum	S.F.	0.018	$3.37	$4.47
Custom, minimum	S.F.	0.014	$1.12	$1.80
Maximum	S.F.	0.020	$5.60	$7.00
Minimum labor / equipment charge	Job	1.000		$35.00
FLOOR MATS				
Anti-fatigue mat, 1/2" thick, 2' x 3'	Ea.			$41.52
3' x 5'	Ea.			$103.84
3' x 12'	Ea.			$221.00
FURNITURE FOR PHYSICALLY CHALLENGED				
Chair, moble with L-shaped arm	Ea.			$600.00
power lift, with 6" lift	Ea.			$1,800.00
with 12" lift	Ea.			$2,200.00
Desk, non-electric, student	Ea.			$800.00
Computer	Ea.			$1,485.00
Desk, power lift, with 6" variable lift	Ea.			$1,800.00
12" - 18" variable lift	Ea.			$3,600.00
Student school model	Ea.			$1,200.00
File, pedestal-mounted, 360 degree revolving	Ea.			$600.00
fold down, wheelchair accessible	Ea.			$800.00
Kitchen unit, with three pedestal lifts, unaccessorized	Ea.			$3,885.00
With cook top and sink	Ea.			$5,355.00
4 tier work surface	Ea.			$4,515.00
Industrial facilities, rectangle platform, minimum	Ea.			$3,045.00
Maximum	Ea.			$4,095.00
L-shaped work surface, minimum	Ea.			$3,045.00
Maximum	Ea.			$4,095.00
Wall-mount work surface	Ea.			$3,045.00
Rectangular work surface, minimum	Ea.			$3,045.00
Maximum	Ea.			$4,095.00
Shelving fully adapted / adjustable, minimum	Ea.			$109.20
Maximum	Ea.			$309.75
Standard bookcase	Ea.			$624.75
PORTABLE WHEELCHAIR RAMPS				
Expanded metal, non-skid, folding, 26" x 60"	Ea.			$379.50
26" x 120"	Ea.			$669.50
Curb model, non-folding, 26" x 30"	Ea.			$142.00
26" x 42"	Ea.			$165.00
Rollup type, non-skid track, 30" x 36"	Ea.			$159.95
Aluminum Track type, folding, 7" x 60"	Pr.			$278.00
7" x 90"	Pr.			$335.00

Division 14: Conveying Systems

DESCRIPTION	UNIT	MAN-HOURS	COST MAT.	COST TOTAL
ELEVATOR MODIFICATIONS				
Relocate control panel to 54" maximum height	Ea.	8.000	$1,800.00	$2,325.00
Add audible or visual signals in cab	Ea.	6.000	$150.00	$398.00
Add braille and raised lettering at entrance jamb /stop	Ea.			$95.00
ELEVATORS				
Passenger, 2 story, holeless hydraulic, 2000 lb. capacity	Ea.	320.000	$15,200.00	$31,000.00
2500 lb.	Ea.	320.000	$18,000.00	$34,100.00
3 story, 2000 lb., hydraulic	Ea.	320.000	$29,631.00	$43,967.00
2500 lb.	Ea.	320.000	$30,051.00	$44,387.00
4 story, 2000 lb.	Ea.	360.000	$35,091.00	$51,219.00
2500 lb.	Ea.	360.000	$35,511.00	$51,639.00
STAIR CLIMBER				
Chair lift, single seat, up to 16' stairway length	Ea.	8.000	$2,800.00	$3,440.00
Add per foot over 16'	L.F.		$25.00	$27.50
WHEELCHAIR LIFT				
Wheelchair lift, inclined, residential	Ea.	16.000	$7,425.60	$8,872.50
add per LF over 18' stairway length	L.F.		$81.39	$89.53
add per inch over 40" wide stairway	In.		$36.56	$40.22
Commercial, 15' straight run	Ea.	16.000	$8,006.25	$9,502.50
15' with 1 turnback, on inside core	Ea.	32.000	$9,650.25	$11,865.00
15' with 1 turnback, on outside core	Ea.	48.048	$10,815.00	$13,965.00
Vertical, 42" lifting height	Ea.	12.003	$7,600.00	$8,900.00
72" lifting height	Ea.	16.000	$8,400.00	$9,960.00
144" lifting height	Ea.	20.000	$13,400.00	$15,640.00
Add for emergency stop and alarm	Ea.		$340.00	$374.00
Add for 90 degree exit / entry	Ea.		$250.00	$275.00

Division 15: Mechanical

DESCRIPTION	UNIT	MAN-HOURS	COST MAT.	COST TOTAL
FAUCETS / FITTINGS				
Automatic flush valve with sensor and operator for urinals or w.c., battery operated	Ea.	0.500	$378.00	$440.00
Kitchen faucet, handicap, 4" wrist blade handles	Ea.	0.800	$112.00	$148.00
with spray spout	Ea.	0.800	$137.00	$173.00
Lavatory faucet, handicap, 4" wrist blade handles, with pop-up	Ea.	0.800	$118.00	$163.00
slant back, gooseneck spout, strainer drain	Ea.	0.800	$144.00	$192.00
with spray spout	Ea.	0.800	$152.00	$200.00
Automatic sensor and operator, with faucet head, thermal	Ea.	1.300	$616.00	$674.00
cold water only	Ea	1.300	$473.00	$579.00
Medical faucet, gooseneck spout, wrist blade handles, grid drain	Ea.	0.800	$160.00	$209.00
Handicap, 6" elbow handles, 10 1/2" spout	Ea.	0.571	$200.00	$244.00
14-1/2" spout	Ea.	0.571	$210.00	$255.00
Minimum labor / equipment charge	Job	2.500		$112.50
LAVATORY				
With trim, white, wall hung				
Vitreous china, 27" x 20", wheelchair type	Ea.	2.286	$214.00	$325.00
Rough-in, supply, waste and vent for above lavatories	Ea.	9.639	$127.00	$555.00
SHOWERS				
Handicap, acrylic, grab bars, hand held shower head,				
Transfer unit, 41" W x 36-3/4" D x 84" H, folding seat	Ea.	6.667	$1,700.00	$2,170.00
Molded seat	Ea.	6.667	$1,260.00	$1,690.00
Roll-in unit, 64" W x 36-3/4" D x 84" H, no seat	Ea.	8.000	$1,520.00	$2,030.00
Folding seat	Ea.	8.000	$1,950.00	$2,500.00

DESCRIPTION	UNIT	MAN-HOURS	COST MAT.	COST TOTAL
Tub/Shower unit, 60" W x 32" D x 84" H, no seat	Ea.	8.000	$1,600.00	$2,120.00
Drop-in removable seat	Ea.	8.000	$2,040.00	$2,600.00
Rough-in, supply, waste and vent for above showers	Ea.	7.805	$75.00	$410.00
Mixing valve, built-in	Ea.	1.333	$90.50	$161.00
TOILET SEATS				
Clamp-on raised, for handicap use	Ea.		$95.00	$114.50
URINALS				
Wall hung, vitreous china, handicap type	Ea.	5.333	$380.00	$630.00
Rough-in, supply, waste and vent for urinal	Ea.	5.654	$81.50	$325.00
WASH CENTER				
Prefabricated, stainless steel, semi-recessed lavatory, storage				
cabinet, mirror, light & switch, electric outlet, towel				
dispenser, waste receptacle & trim				
Foot water valve, cup & soap dispenser, 16" W x 54-3/4" H	Ea.	2.000	$1,050.00	$1,225.00
Handicap, wrist blade handles, 17" W x 66-1/2" H	Ea.	2.000	$1,275.00	$1,567.00
20" W x 67-3/8" H	Ea.	2.000	$1,300.00	$1,595.00
Push button metering & thermostatic mixing valves				
Handicap 17" W x 27-1/2" H	Ea.	2.000	$900.00	$1,075.00
Rough-in, supply, waste and vent	Ea.	7.619	$58.50	$380.00
WATER CLOSET				
Floor-mounted, with 18" high bowl	Ea.	3.019	$282.00	$435.00
Rough-in, supply, waste and vent for water closet	Ea.	5.246	$106.00	$385.00
WATER COOLER				
Wall-mounted, non-recessed, wheelchair type, 8 GPH	Ea.	4.000	$995.00	$1,275.00
Rough-in, supply, waste and vent for water cooler	Ea.	3.620	$46.50	$218.00

Division 16: Electrical

DESCRIPTION	UNIT	MAN-HOURS	COST MAT.	COST TOTAL
DETECTION SYSTEMS				
Smoke detector, light and horn	Ea.	1.509	$100.00	$165.00
Annunciator, light and horn	Ea.	1.509	$200.00	$265.00
Minimum labor / equipment charge	Job	2.500		$112.50
ELECTRIC HEATING				
Snow melting for paved surface, embedded mat heaters & controls	S.F.	0.062	$5.65	$8.95
FULL SPECTRUM LIGHTING				
4' fluorescent tube	Ea.		$13.95	$16.00
Minimum labor / equipment charge	Job	1.500		$68.00
SWITCHES				
Motion-activated light switch, minimum	Ea.	0.533	$50.00	$78.00
Maximum	Ea.	0.533	$96.00	$130.00
Minimum labor / equipment charge	Job	1.500		$68.00

Miscellaneous Support Materials

DESCRIPTION	UNIT	MAN-HOURS	COST MAT.	COST TOTAL
AIR QUALITY				
Air purifiers, minimum	Ea.			$346.50
Maximum	Ea.			$606.38
Electronic voice / light-controlled environmental systems, minimum	Ea.			$577.50
Maximum	Ea.			$2,310.00
Enlarged dial thermostats	Ea.			$60.00
Heavy duty micro air cleaners	Ea.			$612.00

DESCRIPTION	UNIT	MAN-HOURS	COST	
			MAT.	TOTAL
Individual electrostatic air filters (for central air systems)	Ea.			$179.00
Individual room heat accelerators, minimum	Ea.			$32.00
Maximum	Ea.			$155.93
Table-top air cleaners, minimum	Ea.			$36.96
Maximum	Ea.			$98.18
COMMUNICATION SUPPORT				
Artificial voice simulators (larynx)	Ea.			$265.65
Braille, bookmaker	Ea.			$2,887.50
Labeler	Ea.			$42.74
Notetaker (typewriter), minimum	Ea.			$1,039.50
Maximum	Ea.			$1,501.50
Translating computer system	Ea.			$2,310.00
Communication, board creators, minimum	Ea.			$91.25
Maximum	Ea.			$577.50
Stickers (color)	Ea.			$28.88
Computer, screen magnifier, minimum	Ea.			$91.25
Maximum	Ea.			$340.73
Large print system	Ea.			$2,650.73
Lap top, talking, minimum	Ea.			$4,158.00
Maximum	Ea.			$11,550.00
Software, speech communication, minimum	Ea.			$462.00
Maximum	Ea.			$687.23
Lamp telephone alerter	Ea.			$46.20
Large print dictionary	Ea.			$33.50
Maps, tactile	Ea.			$26.57
Network captioning for televised programs, per month	Ea.			$86.63
Speech synthesizer, minimum	Ea.			$2,310.00
Maximum	Ea.			$13,860.00
Telephone, amplifying handset, minimum	Ea.			$40.43
Maximum	Ea.			$92.40
Lamp alerter	Ea.			$46.20
Voice-activated, minimum	Ea.			$219.45
Maximum	Ea.			$265.65
TDD, memory printer	Ea.			$693.00
Unit, minimum	Ea.			$265.65
Maximum	Ea.			$346.50
Voice mail services / systems	Ea.			$924.00
Wireless hearing assistance system, minimum	Ea.			$393.75
Maximum	Ea.			$2,310.00
NOISE CONTROL				
Computer sound shields, minimum	Ea.			86.625
Maximum	Ea.			144.375
Easy listening cassette tapes (for public address systems), minimum	Ea.			6.3525
Maximum	Ea.			11.55
Sound absorption pads, for typewriters	Ea.			11.55
Sound absorption products				
Acoustical windows & doors, minimum	S.F.			$103.95
Maximum	S.F.			$202.13
Enclosures, curtain type	S.F.			$13.86
Full metal type	S.F.			$23.10
Foams, faced	S.F.			$4.62
Unfaced	S.F.			$3.47
Panels, fabric-covered	S.F.			$8.09
Perforated metal	S.F.			$13.86
White noise generator	Ea.			472.5
OFFICE COMFORT / ASSISTANCE				
Adapted computer keyboard (wand), minimum	Ea.			$1,386.00
Maximum	Ea.			$1,848.00

DESCRIPTION	UNIT	MAN-HOURS	COST MAT.	COST TOTAL
Adjustable book / copy stands, minimum	Ea.			$17.33
Maximum	Ea.			$43.89
Anti-fatigue insoles, minimum	Ea.			$33.50
Maximum	Ea.			$144.38
Automated Office, robotic system	Ea.			$3,118.50
Braille software, minimum	Ea.			$75.08
Maximum	Ea.			$635.25
Break-away back support, minimum	Ea.			$75.08
Maximum	Ea.			$173.25
Folding reachers / grabbers	Ea.			$26.57
Footrest, minimum	Ea.			$18.74
Maximum	Ea.			$65.26
Low-vision wall clock	Ea.			$34.65
Lumbar (back) supports, minimum	Ea.			$16.17
Maximum	Ea.			$34.65
Magnetic padlock	Ea.			$5.78
Manual wheelchair power unit	Ea.			$404.25
Multi-purpose braille timers, minimum	Ea.			$21.95
Maximum	Ea.			$28.88
Robotic worksite attendant, minimum	Ea.			$11,550.00
Maximum	Ea.			$115,500.00
Spinal supports, minimum	Ea.			$17.33
Maximum	Ea.			$32.34
Talking calculators	Ea.			$28.88
Voice-activated computer components	Ea.			$462.00
Wrist supports (for computers), minimum	Ea.			$16.17
Maximum	Ea.			$46.20
SAFETY DEVICES				$0.00
Anti-skid stair tape, minimum	Roll			$9.82
Maximum	Roll			$75.08
Chime-Com	Ea.			$57.75
Emergency transportation wheelchair, minimum	Ea.			$912.45
Maximum	Ea.			$1,004.85
Lighted signal device for cars (engages for approaching emergency vehicles), minimum	Ea.			$375.38
Maximum	Ea.			$693.00
Video sentry, minimum	Ea.			$2,743.13
Maximum	Ea.			$4,620.00
VISION SUPPORT				
Computer screen filters, minimum	Ea.			$33.50
Maximum	Ea.			$202.13
Copyholders, with auxiliary lighting, minimum	Ea.			$23.10
Maximum	Ea.			$69.30
Glare-decreasing neutral color desk blotters	Ea.			$6.93
High-intensity magnifier lamp, minimum	Ea.			$34.65
Maximum	Ea.			$86.63
Task lighting, minimum	Ea.			$11.55
Maximum	Ea.			$207.90

GLOSSARY

GLOSSARY
OF TERMS

ABA
The Architectural Barriers Act of 1968, P.L. 90-480 as amended.

Accessible
Anything that is approachable, functional and can be used by people with disabilities, independently, safely and with dignity.

Affirmative action
A commitment to positive action to accomplish the purposes of a program. It may involve goals or timetables and specifically outlined steps that will be pursued to ensure that objectives are attained. The ADA does not mandate affirmative action for disabled people. Rather, the ADA requires that covered entities ensure *nondiscrimination*. In the context of civil rights for disabled people, affirmative action must be taken under Section 503 of the Rehabilitation Act, which requires affirmative steps and positive outreach by federal contractors in employment considerations.

American National Standards Institute (ANSI)
A private organization which develops consensus industry specifications in building design and construction and other fields. ANSI A117.1, originally issued in 1961 and revised every five years (most recently in 1986), is a key technical basis for the federal government's accessibility standards.

Architectural Barriers Act (ABA) of 1968
As amended, 42 U.S.C. 4151 et. seq., requires that certain buildings and facilities owned, occupied (leased) or financed by the federal government be designed, constructed or altered so as to be accessible to and usable by physically disabled people.

ANSI
See American National Standards Institute.

Architectural and Transportation Barriers Compliance Board (A&TBCB)
A federal agency established by Section 502 of the Rehabilitation Act as a regulatory and investigative body, particularly to ensure compliance with accessibility standards developed under the Architectural Barriers Act. Under the ADA, this agency sets minimum guidelines to ensure that places of public accommodation and transportation facilities are accessible.

Barrier-free environment
Containing no obstacles to accessibility and usability by disabled people. The

ADA, which emphasizes the concept of accessibility, mandates a barrier-free environment in new construction of public accommodations.

CFR (Codes of the Federal Registry)
Published as part of amendments or extensions to acts and federal statutes.

Department of Justice
The federal agency responsible for enforcing the public accommodations section (Title III) of the ADA, as well as overseeing state and local government compliance under Title II of the law. The department also coordinates government-wide enforcement of the regulations, implementing Section 504 of the Rehabilitation Act.

Department of Transportation
The agency that enforces nondiscrimination in public and private transportation (Titles II and III of ADA). This includes access to public bus, train and paratransit service, as well as privately operated bus and shuttle transportation. ADA does not cover air transportation, which is subject to the Air Carrier Access Act.

Environmental Protection Agency (EPA)
Established to protect the quality and quantity of lands that are deemed dedicated to the public citizens of the nation, to include the United States, districts, commonwealths, and trust territories of the continent of North America, including its air and water systems (inland and oceanic) for the public good.

Equal Employment Opportunity Commission
The U.S. agency that enforces the nondiscrimination requirements in Title I (employment) of the ADA.

Equal Opportunity
The elimination of unfair and unnecessary discrimination. Equal opportunity for qualified disabled people is an objective of the ADA. This goal translates into the achievement of accessibility, the provision of benefits, services and aids that are equally effective for disabled and nondisabled people, and programs and activities that are otherwise free from discrimination based on disability.

Ergonomics
The science that seeks to adapt work or working conditions to suit the worker.

Federal Communications Commission (FCC)
The Federal agency that regulates and oversees public and commercial communication services.

Individual with a disability
Any person who:
1. has a physical or mental impairment that substantially limits one or more life activities (e.g., caring for oneself, performing manual tasks, walking, seeing, hearing, speaking, breathing, learning and working);
2. has a record of such impairment (has a history of, or has been misclassified as having, a mental or physical impairment that substantially limits one or more major life activity); or
3. is regarded as having such an impairment.

Injunctive relief
A remedy based on the issuance of an injunction to remove an obstacle to accessibility.

National Fire Protection Association (NFPA)
A non-profit organization dedicated to providing information and training, as well as establishing national standards for fire prevention.

National Institute of Occupational Safety and Health (NIOSH)
A federal agency that performs research in areas of occupational safety and health under the Department of Health and Human Services.

Nondiscrimination
A policy mandated by the ADA that conveys the following: No otherwise qualified disabled individual can, solely by reason of his or her disability, be subjected to discrimination. Covered entities are required under the ADA to ensure nondiscrimination by providing accessibility, equal opportunity, and full participation in employment and public facilities and services.

Occupational injury
Injury that occurs as a result of job routines, equipment or environment failures under these conditions: repetitiveness, posture, force, mechanical stresses or temperature.

Occupational Safety and Health Act of 1970 (OSHA)
The Act which specifies the regulations to reduce occupational injuries and illnesses in the work place. The focus of the act is on safety and health efforts by employers in an effort to reduce high risk injuries in industry and in the private sector "for every working man and woman in the nation."

Paratransit
Door-to-door or demand-responsive transportation (usually accessible van or small buses) for people who are unable to use conventional or mainstream public transportation. Paratransit service is usually provided by a public transit agency, but can be contracted out to a private company.

Physically challenged
Person with physical disabilities.

Physical or mental impairment
1. Any physiological disorder or condition, cosmetic disfigurement, or anatomical loss affecting one or more of the following body systems: neurological, musculoskeletal, special sense organs, respiratory, speech organs, cardiovascular, reproductive, digestive, genitourinary, hemic and lymphatic, skin, and endocrine; or
2. any mental or physical disorder, such as mental illness, and specific learning disabilities.

The term "physical or mental impairment" includes, but is not limited to, such diseases and conditions as orthopedic, visual, speech, and hearing impairments, cerebral palsy, epilepsy, muscular dystrophy, multiple sclerosis, cancer, heart disease, diabetes, mental retardation, emotional illness, past drug addiction and alcoholism.

Public Accommodations
Title III of the ADA mandates that privately owned places of public accommodation be accessible to people with disabilities. The act contains a specific list of businesses and other facilities open to the public that are covered by the act. This includes, but is not limited to, hotels and places of lodging; restaurants, movies, theaters, stadiums and places of exhibition and entertainment; auditoriums, convention centers and other places of public gathering; food stores, shopping centers or other sales or retail establishments; service establishments such as lawyers' and doctors' offices, hospitals, and

insurance offices; public transportation stations; places of public display or galleries; places of recreation including parks and zoos; private schools; and social service centers.

Qualified individual with a disability
With respect to employment, a disabled person who, with or without reasonable accommodation, can perform the essential functions of the job in question; and with respect to public services, an individual who, with or without reasonable modifications to rules, policies or practices, the removal of architectural, communication or transportation barriers, or the provision of auxiliary aids and services, meets the essential eligibility requirements for the receipt of services or participation in the program or activity.

Readily Achievable
Under Title III of the ADA (relating to public accommodations), this term means easily accomplishable and able to be carried out without much difficulty or expense. Factors to be considered include, but are not limited to, the nature and cost of the action; overall financial resources of the covered entity and facility or facilities involved; the number of people employed at such facility; and the type of operation(s) of the covered entity, including the composition, structure and functions of the workplace of the covered entity. Note the factors here are similar to those under "undue hardship," as applied to employment decisions under Title I of the ADA.

Reasonable Accommodation
The principle by which employment and public accommodations are made accessible to qualified disabled people. Employers are required under the ADA to make certain adjustments to accommodate known physical and mental limitations of otherwise qualified disabled applicants and employees, unless it can be demonstrated that a particular adjustment or alteration (an "accommodation") would be unreasonable or impose an undue hardship on the owner/employer. For example, an employer might be required to rearrange office furniture to allow for passage of a wheelchair, relocate some offices or classrooms to a ground floor or other accessible location, or relieve a deaf secretary of telephone responsibilities.

Rehabilitation Act of 1973
Prohibits federal agencies and their grantees and contractors from discriminating against people based on disability in employment, programs and activities. Title V of the Rehabilitation Act, 29 U.S.C. et. seq., is the legislative forerunner of the ADA in developing the concepts of a "qualified individual with a disability" and "reasonable accommodation."

Section 502
Section 502 of the Rehabilitation Act of 1973 established the Architectural and Transportation Barriers Compliance Board (A&TBCB) to ensure enforcement of the Architectural Barriers Act of 1968 and accessibility standards for federally owned, occupied, or leased buildings or facilities.

Section 503
Section 503 of the Rehabilitation Act of 1973, administered by the U.S. Department of Labor's Office of Federal Contract Compliance Programs, applies to all federal contractors and subcontractors with contracts of $2,500 or more. It mandates affirmative action to employ and advance in employment qualified disabled people. In addition, it requires all recipients with 50 or more employees and one or more federal contracts of $50,000 or more to prepare and maintain affirmative action programs.

Section 504
Section 504 of the Rehabilitation Act of 1973 prohibits discrimination against qualified individuals with disabilities in federally funded programs and activities. The Justice Department's Civil Rights Division is responsible for ensuring compliance with the provisions of Section 504.

TDD (Telecommunications Device for the Deaf)
A machine that uses graphic communication and the transmission of coded signals through a wire or radio communication system. Sometimes also referred to as TTY (teletypewriter).

Telecommunications Relay System
Telephone transmission service that enables an individual with a hearing or speech impairment to communicate by wire or radio with a hearing individual in a manner that is functionally equivalent to the ability of someone who does not have a hearing or speech impairment.

Undue Burden
The point at which an employer is no longer required to make accommodations in employment under Title I of the ADA, since the action involved would require significant difficulty or expense. Considerations are the same as those used to determine whether an accommodation is "readily achievable." These include, but are not limited to, the nature and cost involved in the accommodation, overall financial resources of the facility or facilities involved, number of people employed at the facility, the type of operation(s) of the employer, including the composition, structure and functions of the work force.

Uniform Federal Accessibility Standards (UFAS)
The standards the federal government uses to meet accessibility requirements for the design, construction, and alteration of buildings under Section 504.

INDEX

INDEX

Notes

Notes

596

Notes

Notes

Notes

Notes